So many of the books I see are crammed with "filler" to increase the size of the book. Not yours.

George Reeves
Novell CNA/CNE

I just wanted to say that your book…is a piece of art! It is put together such that the simplest of minds can figure out the whole mess!

Tony Scarola
System Administrator
TDS Incorporated

Your book has proved to be an invaluable asset in my new job. No other book covered backup procedure and the need to create a user account for the Schedule service as well as did your book. It is this kind of attention to detail that sets your book apart from the others.

Andrew Nicholson
Certified Novell Engineer

I purchased your book *Mastering Windows NT Server 3.51,* and I found it very enlightening. I have read it probably three times now during my installation, as well as some other NT Server publications…and yours is by far…the "Ultimate" NT Server manual.

Doug Kramer
Network Administrator
MICARD Services

I think your book maintains a useful balance between overview and detail. It allows a beginner (me) to pick up the info they need to get started. Later, it allows an intermediate user (me several months later) to go in and pick up details that they might not have needed before…

Adam Rodman
Screenwriter

Mastering Windows NT Server 4

Mastering™ Windows NT® Server 4

Mark Minasi
Christa Anderson
Elizabeth Creegan

Third Edition

NETWORK PRESS

SYBEX

San Francisco • Paris • Düsseldorf • Soest

Associate Publisher: Gary Masters
Acquisitions Manager: Kristine Plachy
Acquisitions Editor: John Read
Developmental Editor: Neil Edde
Editor: Peter Weverka
Project Editor: Lee Ann Pickrell
Technical Editor: Howard Crawford
Book Designer and Book Design Director: Catalin Dulfu
Graphic Illustrators: Patrick Dintino, Inbar Berman
Desktop Publisher: Susan Glinert Stevens
Desktop Publisher Liaison: Scott McDonald
Production Coordinator: Anton Reut
Indexer: Matthew Spence
Cover Designer: Archer Design
Cover Photographer: Doug Plummer

Library of Congress Card Number: 96-69286
ISBN: 0-7821-1920-4

Manufactured in the United States of America

10 9 8 7 6 5 4 3 2

This book is dedicated to my management team at TechTeach International. Without Donna Cook, our marketing director, Patrick Campbell, our chief instructor, and Cynthia "Ceen" Dowell, our business manager, I'd never have gotten the time to write this book—or many others. Donna, Pat, and Ceen, you're the best I've ever worked with!

ACKNOWLEDGMENTS

I wish I could truthfully say that I wrote this book. It didn't work that way, however. Very few books get written by just one person.

First of all, I want to thank Elizabeth "Maeve" Creegan and Christa Anderson, the two other names you see on the spine. When we first put together the book that covered NT 3.1, Maeve and Christa were both research assistants in my employ, and I envisioned them merely doing some of the spadework needed to get the book underway. I became very busy, however, so I asked them to try their hands at writing some of the chapters. They both performed many times better than I imagined possible and wrote some very good stuff indeed. They weren't involved in the massive rewrite that version 4 required, but a fair amount of their writing is still on these pages. Christa's work is still evident in Chapters 4, 8, and a bit in 16, and Maeve's appears in Chapter 11 as well as Chapter 15 and the Appendix. That said, however, the buck stops with me (Mark), so errors or oversights are my fault.

Second, I must thank our "silent" co-authors, Kris Ashton, Patrick Campbell, and Eric Christiansen. Kris knows about a million times more about Macs than I do and wrote Chapter 10. Pat updated Chapter 13, which covers Novell, to include the latest software. Eric did the write-up on the kernel debuggers that now fills out the chapter on disaster recovery. By now you're wondering what I *did* write. Well, I had to do this acknowledgments page without help...

The folks at Sybex are always a pleasure to work with. Without the vision of people like Gary Masters, Rodnay Zaks, and the late, lamented Rudy Langer, these books wouldn't exist. Peter Weverka edited both our first edition and this most recent edition, and Lee Ann Pickrell joined us this time. Many thanks to both. I would also like to thank desktop publisher Susan Glinert Stevens, production coordinator Anton Reut, and graphic illustrators Patrick Dintino and Inbar Berman.

My research assistants Holliday Ridge and Eric Christiansen suffered the tireless drudgery of actually *reading* this stuff and converting it into a format that Sybex could work with. Their comments and suggestions were always invaluable.

Thanks also to the folks at Microsoft for the betas—and for a high-quality product worth writing about!

CONTENTS AT A GLANCE

Introduction   *xxxvii*

| PART I | **Getting Acquainted** | **1** |

   1   NT Server Overview   3

   2   Microsoft Enterprise Concepts   29

| PART II | **Setting Up NT Server** | **91** |

   3   Installing NT and NT Server   93

   4   RAID for Speedier, Safer Disks   173

   5   Understanding the Registry Database   229

| PART III | **NT Server Administration** | **249** |

   6   Managing and Creating User Accounts   251

   7   Creating and Managing Directory Shares   315

   8   Managing Printing Services with NT Server   369

   9   Connecting PCs to NT Networks   413

   10   Making the Mac Connection   441

   11   Managing Servers and Domain Controllers   475

PART IV Managing NT Server in an Enterprise Network 543

12 Cross-Domain Management in NT Networks 545

13 Novell NetWare in an NT Server Environment 589

14 TCP/IP on Windows NT 633

15 Tuning and Monitoring Your NT Server Network 811

16 Troubleshooting and Disaster Recovery 875

17 Using Dial-Up Networking 979

PART V Appendix 1035

A NET-ing Results: Using the Command Prompt 1037

Index 1091

TABLE OF CONTENTS

Introduction   *xxxvii*

PART I **Getting Acquainted**   **1**

1 NT Server Overview   **3**

NT Server Capabilities   4
Architecture Independence   5
Multiple Processor Support   7
Multithreaded Multitasking   8
Massive Memory Space   10
Centralized User Profiles   11
Enhanced Metafile Printing   12
Enterprise Networking Features   13
Internet and TCP/IP Compatibility   13
Event and Account Logging   13
Remote Access Services   14
Domain and Workgroup-Based Administration Features   15
Fault Tolerance and RAID Support   16
Reasonable Price for Server and Client Software   17
NDIS Protocol Support   18
Protocol Compatibility with Forebears   19
Netware Support   19
NetBEUI, DLC, and TCP/IP Options   20
Macintosh Connectivity   21
What's New in Version 4?   21
New GUI   21
Little Change in Administration Tools   22

Internet Information Server   22
New Communications Protocol Support   23
Network Administration Tools   23
RIP Routing and DNS Server Support   24
Network Monitor   24
Beyond Version 4: What You Can Expect   25

2   Microsoft Enterprise Concepts   29

Setting the Stage: A Primitive Microsoft Network   30
Assigning Network Names   32
Sharing File Directories on the Network   33
Accessing a Shared Directory over the Network   34
Introducing UNCs   35
Sharing a Printer on the Network   36
Problems with the Primitive Network   37
Who's Out There: Browsers and Workgroups   38
Solving the Directory Service Problem   38
Microsoft's Answer: Browse Services   41
When Browse Lists Get Too Large:
    Workgroups to the Rescue   43
How Do I Join a Workgroup?   47
How Do I View a Browse List?   48
Security in a Workgroup   48
Domains: Centralized Security   55
Multiple Servers Means Multiple User Accounts   55
Multiple User Accounts Means Multiple Logins   56
Domains: One Account, One Password, Many Servers   58
Network Citizens: Users and Machines   63
Users in a Microsoft Enterprise Network   63
User Rights and Permissions   64
Groups   64
User Characteristics   65

Machine Types: Servers, Messengers, Receivers,
and Redirectors   66
Machine Characteristics   67
Inter-Domain Security: Trust Relationships   68
Network Software: Drivers, Protocols, and Redirectors   71
Understanding Network Software Parts   72
A Simple Network Problem   75
The Bottom Layer: The Board Driver   77
The Top Layer: Network Services   78
The Middle Layer: Network Protocols   81
Network Binding Interfaces   85
Network Application Interfaces (APIs)   86

PART II Setting Up NT Server   **91**

3 Installing NT and NT Server   **93**

Preparing the Hardware   94
Getting Ready to Install   95
Testing Memory   100
Testing Disks   101
Preparing the Data   103
Backing Up to Another Machine   103
Temporarily Installing the Tape to Another Machine   103
Setting Up the Server for FAT, Restore, and Convert   105
How Do I Convert a FAT Volume to an NTFS Volume?   105
Making Backups If You're Converting
from LAN Manager   106
Setting Up the LAN Card   106
A Word about PCI Systems   114
Answer These Questions Before Running NT Setup   115
What Kind of Server Will This Be?   116
What Will This Be Named?   118
How Will This Server Be Licensed?   118

Starting the NT Install Program   121
  Installing from the Setup Floppies   121
  Installing with WINNT and WINNT32   122
Running the NT Install Program   123
  Starting with the Floppies   123
  Welcome to Setup   124
  Scanning for SCSI Adapters   124
  Upgrade or Fresh Install?   125
  What Do You Have and Where Does It Go?   125
  Choosing an NT Partition   127
  Which Directory Do I Put It On?   130
  Entering Graphical Setup   130
  Who Are You?   131
  The Per-Connection or Per-Seat Licensing Option?   131
  Choosing a Computer Name   132
  Domain Controller or Server   132
  Creating the Emergency Repair Disk   133
  Selecting Components   134
  Beginning Network Setup   134
  Setting Up Network Cards   135
  Domain/Workgroup Followup   137
  Video Test Screen   139
After the Installation, What Next?   139
Migrating Windows Applications   141
  Not Every Windows Program Will Run   141
  Moving the Fonts   141
  Getting Your Apps Back   143
  How Do I Get My Old Windows Fonts Back?   144
Choosing and Installing an Uninterruptible Power Supply   144
  The Problem with Electrical Outlets   145
  Power Conditioners for Protecting Data   146
  Backup Power Supplies   146
  Interfacing the UPS/SPS   150
  Testing the UPS Service   155

Installing Tape Drivers 155
How Do I Send a Broadcast Message to the Entire Network? 156
How Do I Install an NT Server Tape Driver? 159
The License Manager 159
Common Installation Problems 162
How Do I Fix the System After It Can't Find NTLDR? 164
Where Do I Load ANSI.SYS? 164
Must My RISC Computer Be FAT-Based? 165
Re-Installing NT Server 165
Creating an NT Boot Disk 169
How Do I Create a Generic NT Boot Floppy? 170

4 RAID for Speedier, Safer Disks 173

Disk Administrator Terminology 175
SLED 175
RAID 176
Free Space 176
Physical Drives versus Logical Partitions 176
Partitions 177
Logical Drive 178
Volume Set 179
Mirror Set 180
Stripe Set 180
Before Using the Disk Administrator... 181
Keeping It All Together with SLED 182
Using Logical Drives to Divide Up Information 183
Converting the Extended Partition to a Logical Drive 184
Formatting the New Drive 186
How Do I Create a Logical Drive? 188
Use the Most Recent Drivers! 188
Deleting a Logical Drive 189
How Do I Delete a Logical Drive? 189
Using Space Efficiently 190
Cautions about Volume Sets 191

Creating a Volume Set	192
Formatting the Volume Set	194
Deleting a Volume Set	194
Enlarging a Volume Set	194
How Do I Create a Volume Set?	*195*
How Do I Delete a Volume Set?	*196*
How Do I Extend a Volume Set?	*197*
Nonparity Disk Striping to Increase Throughput	198
Creating a Stripe Set	199
How Do I Create a Stripe Set without Parity?	*200*
Deleting a Stripe Set	201
How Do I Delete a Stripe Set?	*203*
Protecting Your Data	204
Disk Mirroring	204
Establishing a Mirror Set	205
How Do I Set Up a Mirror Set?	*205*
Breaking a Mirror Set	206
How Do I Break a Mirror Set?	*207*
Recovering Data from a Mirror Set	208
How Do I Repair a Broken Mirror Set?	*209*
Mirroring Considerations	210
Disk Striping, the Slow But Steady Method	210
How Disk Striping Works	211
Updating the Parity Information	212
Establishing a Stripe Set with Parity	213
How Do I Create a Stripe Set with Parity	*216*
Retrieving Data from a Failed Stripe Set	217
How Do I Regenerate a Failed Stripe Set?	*219*
Deleting a Stripe Set	219
How Do I Delete a Stripe Set?	*220*
Things to Remember about Disk Striping with Parity	220
Working with NTFS	221
NTFS Naming Conventions	221

File Forking and Extended Attributes 223
Long Names on Floppies 224
Final Thoughts about Drives and NT Server 224
Hardware or Software RAID? 224
Double-Check for Viruses 225
Leave a FAT Partition 226

5   Understanding the Registry Database **229**

What Is the Registry? 230
Registry Terminology 231
Subtrees 232
Registry Keys 233
Key Naming Conventions 234
Value Entries, Names, Values, and Data Types 234
Working with the Registry: An Example 237
How Do You Find Registry Keys? 239
Even More Cautions about Editing the Registry 240
Where the Registry Lives: Hives 242
A Look at the Hive Files 242
Fault Tolerance in the Registry 243
Remote Registry Modification 245
Backing Up and Restoring a Registry 246

PART III   NT Server Administration **249**

6   Managing and Creating User Accounts **251**

Introducing the User Manager for Domains 252
User Manager for Domains versus User Manager 253
User Accounts Sit on the PDC 253
User Manager for Domains Functions 254
A Look around the User Manager for Domains 255
Security Identifiers 259
Prebuilt Accounts: Administrator and Guest 260

Creating a New User Account 261
 Assigning Groups 263
 Permissible Logon Hours 264
 Controlling Where Users Can Log On 268
 Account Duration and Type 269
 How Do I Create a User Account in a Domain? 271
Managing User Accounts 271
 Copying Accounts 272
 Managing Properties for More Than One Account 273
 How Do I Make Sure That a Selected List of Users
  *Are **Not** Members of a Particular Group in a Domain?* 276
 Deleting User Accounts 276
Managing Groups 277
 Creating and Deleting Groups 277
 Examining the Predefined Groups 280
Managing Security Policies 286
 Password Characteristics 286
 User Rights and Object Permissions 288
 Security Event Auditing 293
 Summary: Managing User Accounts 295
The System Policy Editors 296
 Installing the System Policy Editor (Windows 95 Users) 298
 Building a Policy 298
 Other Things System Policy Editor Can Control 303
 Defeating a Policy 304
 Keeping Users from Defeating Policies 305
 What If You Want CONFIG.POL Somewhere Else? 307
 Using Templates 308

7   Creating and Managing Directory Shares   315

Creating a Shared Directory 317
 Handling Share Names 318
 Hiding Shares 320

Using the Comment Field 320

Restricting Access to Shares 321

Sharing Directories on Remote Servers 322

Share-Level Permissions and Access Control Lists 325

Everyone Includes, Well, Everyone 326

Share-Level Access Types 327

Adding to the ACL 329

File and Directory Permissions 331

File and Directory Permission Types 332

File and Directory Permissions
versus Share Permissions 334

Home Directories: An Application of File
and Directory Permissions 336

Controlling File and Directory Permissions
from the Command Line 343

Default Directory Permissions
for NT Server Directories 344

Monitoring Access to Files and Directories 347

File Ownership in NT 350

The Definition of "Ownership" 351

Experimenting with Ownership 352

Taking Ownership 354

Controlling the Rest of the Profiles Dialog Box 356

NT User Profiles 357

Logon Batch Scripts 359

Controlling the Home Directory Setting 364

8 Managing Printing Services with NT Server 369

NT-Specific Print Sharing Features 371

Who Can Be a Print Server? 372

Adding a Printer 373

Adding a Second Printer for the Same Print Device 378

How Do I Set Up a Printer the First Time for Network Use? 379

Customizing a Printer's Setup 379

Using the Printer Properties Dialog Box 379

Setting the Printer Timeout Number 382

*How Do I Set Up More Than One Printer
  under the Same Name?* 382

How Do I Print Directly to Ports? 383

How Do I Set Printer Timeouts? 383

Connecting to a Shared Printer 384

Printing from MS-DOS 384

Printing from Windows and Windows for Workgroups 385

Printing from OS/2 388

Printing from Windows NT 388

How Do I Connect a Workstation to a Shared Printer? 391

Controlling and Monitoring Access to the Printer 391

Setting Printer Permissions 392

How Do I Set Printer Permissions? 395

Hiding a Printer 395

How Do I Hide a Shared Printer? 396

Setting Print Job Priorities 396

How Do I Set User Print Priorities? 396

Setting Printing Hours 397

Receiving Status Messages 398

How Do I Set Different Printing Hours for Different Groups? 399

Logging and Auditing Printer Usage 399

How Do I Set Up Event Auditing for the Printer? 402

Separator Pages for Sorting Documents 402

Creating a Separator Page 403

How Do I Create a Separator Page? 404

Choosing a Separator Page 405

Solving Common Shared Printing Problems 406

Connection Problems 406

Basic Troubleshooting Tips 408

Keeping Track of Printing Errors 409

9 Connecting PCs to NT Networks   413

Connecting a DOS Workstation to NT   414
  To Use or Not to Use the Network Client Administrator   415
  The Microsoft Network Client 3 for MS-DOS   416
  Connecting to Directories and Print Shares   421
Attaching Windows Workstations to NT Networks   423
  Doing the Network Setup Work   424
  Setting and Changing Domain Passwords   427
  Attaching to Network Resources   430
Attaching Windows 95 Workstations to NT Networks   432
  Configuring the Workstation   432
  Attaching to the Network   435

10 Making the Mac Connection   441

The Features and Benefits of Services for Macintosh   442
Mac Connection in a Nutshell   443
Preparing the Server to Support Your Mac   444
  The Physical Connection   444
  Preparing the NT Server Hard Disk   445
Getting Services for Macintosh Up and Running   445
  Installing Services for Macintosh   446
  Setting Attributes for Mac-Accessible Volumes   452
  Setting Up Microsoft Authentication   453
  Creating Mac-Accessible Volumes   455
Setting Up the Mac for NT Connection   457
  First Time Logon   457
  Next Time Logon   461
Services for Macintosh Printer Support   462
  Avoiding "LaserPrep Wars"   463
  Installing Services for Macintosh Printing   463
Transferring Data between Macs and PCs with NT Server   465
  Forks, Forks Everywhere—and Nothing to Eat   466
  Those Pesky File Names   466

To Which Application Does the Data File Belong?   467
About File Filters and Translations   470
Using Cross-Platform Applications   471
The Downside (and You Knew There'd Be One)   472

11   Managing Servers and Domain Controllers   475

Server Manager's Capabilities   476
Server Manager Functions   476
Not Everyone Is Allowed to Use Server Manager   477
Gathering Cumulative Server Data   478
Who's Who in the Domain   478
Server Properties   480
Hiding a Server from the Browser   481
User Sessions   482
How Do I Disconnect Users from the Server?   *483*
Controlling Automatic Disconnection   484
Available Shares   484
Managing Shared Directories in Server Manager   486
Active Resources   488
Sending Alerts to a Workstation   489
Sending Messages to Users   491
Adding Computers to a Domain   492
Managing Services   497
Scheduling Events   501
Setting Up a Scheduled Event   502
Using WinAT to Schedule Events   503
Directory Replication   504
How Do I Set Up a Prescheduled Job at the Local Server?   *505*
Machines Replicate, Not Users   505
Uses for Directory Replication   506
Who Can Import? Who Can Export?   506
Setting Up the Directory Replicator Service   508
Configuring the Export Server   511
Configuring the Import Computers   515

How Often Does the System Replicate?   516

Summary: Creating an Import/Export Pair   517

Summary: Setting Up Your PDC to Replicate
Login Scripts to the BDCs   523

Changing the Logon Script Path   524

How Do I Set the Logon Script Path for a Server?   525

Troubleshooting Directory Replication   525

Managing Domain Controllers   526

Promoting a Primary Domain Controller
with Server Manager   527

Synchronization: Keeping a Uniform Security Database   528

Controlling Synchronization   529

What Happens When a PDC Fails?   531

How Many BDCs Do You Need?   535

Estimating the Size of the SAM   539

PART IV   **Managing NT Server in an Enterprise Network**   **543**

12   **Cross-Domain Management in NT Networks**   **545**

Multi-Domain Management Tasks   547

Getting Acquainted: Trust Relationships   548

What Is a Trust Relationship?   548

Avoiding Trust Relationships: A Note   552

Establishing Trust Relationships   553

Terminating a Trust Relationship   557

Extending File Permissions across Domains   558

Reprise: Everyone Means, Well, Everyone   558

How Do I Get One Domain to Trust Another?   559

Adding a User from a Foreign Domain
to Share Permissions   560

Cross-Domain Groups: Local and Global Groups   564

Adding Users from One Domain
to Another Domain's Domain Users Group   564

Local Groups and Global Groups in NT Domains 565

Using Global Groups across Domains 575

Granting User Rights and Printer Permissions
across Domains 577

Logging on from Foreign Domains 577

Planning Your Enterprise: Single- versus
Multiple-Domain Networks 579

The Fewer Domains, the Better 580

Domains Might Mirror Organizational Structures 580

Domains Might Follow Geographic Boundaries 581

You Might Have Too Many Accounts for One Domain 581

Enterprise Designs: Single- and Multiple-Domain Models 584

Single-Domain Enterprise Model 584

Complete Trust Model 584

Master Domain Model 585

Multiple Master Domain Enterprise Model 587

13   Novell NetWare in an NT Server Environment   589

How NT and NetWare Interact 590

Netware Client Software for NT 592

Using NWLINK without the Gateway Service 592

Running NetWare and NT Server in Parallel 593

Configuring NT to Run in Parallel 595

Microsoft Gateway Service 597

Installing the NetWare Gateway 598

Creating the User 599

The Gateway Service Setup, Part 2 600

Testing the Gateway 604

Security for Novell Volumes: The Bad News 604

Providing Print Gateway Services 606

How Do I Share a Novell Printer with an NT Network? 608

Novell Commands Available from NT 609

Potential Problems with the Gateway Service 610

Migrating Users from Novell to NT   610
    Using the Migration Tool for NetWare   611
    File and Print Services for NetWare   616
    Directory Service Manager for NetWare   623
    One Final Note…   630

14   TCP/IP on Windows NT   **633**

A Brief History of TCP/IP   634
    Origins of TCP/IP: From the ARPANET to the Internet   636
    Goals of TCP/IP's Design   639
The Internet Protocol (IP)   641
    A Simple Internet   642
    Subnets and Routers   643
    IP Addresses and Ethernet Addresses   643
    IP Routers   646
    Routing in More Detail   647
A, B, and C Networks, CIDR Blocks, and Subnetting   649
    A, B, and C-Class Networks   650
    You Can't Use All of the Numbers   652
    Subnet Masks   654
    Subnetting a C-Class Network   657
    Classless Internetwork Domain Routing (CIDR)   659
    What IP Doesn't Do: Error Checking   662
TCP (Transmission Control Protocol)   663
Sockets and the WinSock Interface   666
    How Sockets Work   667
    WinSock Sockets   668
Internet Host Names   669
    Simple Naming Systems (hosts)   670
    Domain Naming System (DNS)   671
    E-Mail Names: A Note   673
Getting onto an Internet   675
    Dumb Terminal Connection   676

SLIP/PPP Serial Connection 677
LAN Connection 678
Terminal Connections versus Other Connections 678
Setting Up TCP/IP on NT with Fixed IP Addresses 680
Installing TCP/IP Software with Static IP Addresses 681
Testing Your TCP/IP Installation 689
How Do I Make Sure That TCP/IP Is Set Up Properly? 690
Setting Up Routing on NT and Windows Machines 691
An Example Multi-Router Internet 692
Adding Entries to Routing Tables: Route Add 693
Understanding the Default Routes 695
Adding the "Default Gateway" 698
All Routers Must Know All Subnets 701
Using RIP to Simplify Workstation Management 703
Using an NT Machine as a LAN/LAN Router 703
How Do I Build an IP Router with NT? 705
Using an NT Server Machine as an Internet Gateway 707
The Overview 707
The Obstacles 708
Login Options 709
Obtaining an IP Address from Your ISP 711
The Recipe 712
Interior and Exterior Routing Protocols 718
Installing TCP/IP with DHCP 719
Simplifying TCP/IP Administration: BOOTP 719
DHCP: BOOTP Plus 721
Installing and Configuring DHCP Servers 721
DHCP Scopes 723
DHCP on the Client Side 728
DHCP in Detail 728
Getting an IP Address from DHCP: The Nuts and Bolts 731
DHCP Is a "Pull" Protocol, Not a "Push" Protocol 737
Designing Multi-DHCP Networks 739

Backing Up a DHCP Database 740
Restoring a DHCP Database 742
DHCP's Downside 743
Installing TCP/IP with WINS 743
Names in NT 744
Name Resolution before WINS 753
How WINS Works 755
Installing WINS 757
Restoring a WINS Database 760
WINS Proxy Agents 761
DNS in the NT World 763
DNS Pros and Cons 764
Getting the Microsoft DNS Program 766
The Setup Files 767
The BOOT File 768
The DNS Name Resolver File 770
The Reverse Name Resolution Files 772
Using the Graphical DNS Manager and Service 774
Name Resolution Sequence under WinSock 779
Review: WinSock versus NBT 779
Examining Network Traces 779
Controlling WINS versus DNS Order in WinSock 783
Name Resolution Sequence under NetBIOS 784
What If DNS and WINS Conflict? 787
Using Telnet for Remote Login 788
Seeing What's Out There: Using Archie 789
Non-Standardization Problems 792
Why Use Telnet? 793
Using FTP for File Transfer 795
FTP Organization 795
File Navigation 797
An Example of Navigation: Go Get Alice 798
Transferring a File 802

E-Mail on TCP/IP	806
How E-Mail Works	807
E-Mail Security Concerns	808
A Brief Summary to a Very Long Chapter	808

15   Tuning and Monitoring Your NT Server Network   **811**

Using the Performance Monitor	812
Charting with the Performance Monitor	813
Tracking CPU Hogs with a Histogram	816
Building Alerts with the Performance Monitor	818
Logging Data for Statistical Reports	819
Exporting Logged Data to CSV Files	820
Tuning Your System: The Big Four	822
Solving Disk Bottlenecks	824
Tuning Network Boards and Drivers	827
Watching the CPU	830
Monitoring Memory	832
Tuning Multitasking	838
A Tuning Summary	839
Growth Counters	841
Understanding and Troubleshooting Browsers	841
Electing a Master Browser	842
Preventing Computers from Being Browser Masters	846
Browse Masters on a TCP/IP Network	848
Refreshing a Browse List	849
Browsing with LAN Manager	849
Why Isn't My Resource on the Browse List?	849
How Do I Enable LAN Manager to Understand Broadcasts?	850
Why Is My Browser So Slow?	853
Hiding a Server from the Browser	854
Monitoring the Network with the Event Viewer	854
Reading Log Information	857
Interpreting Event Details for Log Entries	861

Changing the Size and Overwrite Options
for an Event Log   867
Archiving Event Logs   868

16   Troubleshooting and Disaster Recovery   875

Defeating Disasters: An Overview   876
Network Physical Security   877
Preventing Environmental Problems   877
Preventing Theft and Tampering   879
How Much Protection Is Too Much?   884
Backup Strategies   884
Performing Backups   885
The Backup Information Dialog Box   886
Performing Automatic Backups   889
How Do I Back Up Data?   890
Special Backup Operations   895
How Do I Back Up a Removable Drive?   899
Protecting Backups   901
Restoring Files   902
Special Restoration Operations   908
How Do I Restore Data from Backups?   909
Restoring a Configuration   910
Backing up the Registry (and the SAM)   914
Planning for Disaster Recovery   916
Creating a Disaster Recovery Plan   917
Implementing Disaster Recovery   917
Making Sure the Plan Works   918
Diagnosing Server Boot Failures   920
Before the Boot: The Hardware Must Work   920
Step One: NTLDR   922
Step Two: NTDETECT   923
Step Three: NTOSKRNL   924

Debugging Windows NT 4   927
  Debugging Terminology   927
  Finding Kernel STOP Errors   929
  Memory Dump Files   929
  How Do I Create a Memory Dump File?   *930*
  Kernel Debuggers   934
  Setting Up Your Machine for Kernel Debugging   934
  Setting Up the Symbol Tree on the Host Computer   939
  Setting Up the Debugger on the Host Computer   942
  Starting the Debugger   943
  Debugger Commands   946
  Examining Crash Dumps with DUMPEXAM   958
  The Bottom Line: What They're Good For   960
The Windows NT Diagnostics Tool   961
  Remote Diagnostic Viewing   961
  How Do I Find the Diagnostics Information
    of a Remote Workstation or Server?   *962*
  Viewing Diagnostic Information   963
  Printing the Results   975
  How Do I Print a Report of a Single Tab Section
    of the Diagnostics File?   *976*

17 Using Dial-Up Networking   979

An Overview of Dial-Up Networking   981
Sample Applications   983
  Remote Dial-In to Company NT Servers   983
  Remote Dial-In to Non-NT Servers   983
  Dial-Up Networking as an Internet Gateway   984
  Dial-Up Networking as an Internet Service Provider   984
  Dial-Up Networking as a LAN/WAN Gateway   984
  Virtual Private Networking with PPTP   985
Connection Types   985
  Modem Support   985

ISDN Support 987

Direct Serial Connection 990

Dial-Up Networking Server Installation 992

Installing the Dial-Up Networking Module 992

Installing a Modem for Dial-Up Networking 992

Controlling Dial-Up Networking
Client/Server Behavior 994

Choosing Protocols for Dial-Up Networking 996

Controlling Login Security 998

Using Dial-Up Networking Administrator 999

Allowing Users from Other Domains
to Log In to a Dial-Up Networking Server 1002

Setup Considerations When Using ISDN 1003

Setup Considerations for X.25 1005

Connecting to Dial-Up Networking Servers from Clients 1006

Connecting from an NT Machine 1007

Connecting from a Windows 95 Client 1016

Connecting from a Windows for Workgroups Station 1022

Connecting from Other Operating Systems 1023

How Do I Connect a Non-NT Workstation to a DUN server? 1023

Connecting to a Netware Server 1024

Keeping Dial-In Intruders off the Network 1024

Modem Security 1024

Enabling and Disabling Bindings 1026

Troubleshooting DUN 1026

If the Connection Has Never Worked Before 1026

If the Connection Has Worked Before 1027

Checking the Audit Records 1027

How Do I Create Device.LOG? 1032

Running Applications Remotely 1033

PART V Appendix **1035**

A **NET-ing Results: Using the Command Prompt** **1037**

What You Can Do with the NET Commands 1038

Getting Help 1039

NET HELP: Getting Help from the Command Prompt 1040

How Do I Get Help from the Command Prompt? *1042*

NET HELPMSG: Decoding Error, Warning, and Alert Messages 1042

How Do I Decipher the Help Message Numbers? *1043*

Manipulating User Accounts 1043

NET USER: Creating User Accounts 1044

How Do I Set Up a User Account from the Command Prompt? *1048*

NET ACCOUNTS: Making Adjustments to the Entire User Database 1048

How Do I Make Changes to the Entire User Account Database? *1051*

NET GROUP: Changing Global Group Membership 1051

How Do I Change Global Group Settings? *1053*

NET LOCALGROUP: Changing Local Group Membership 1053

How Do I Change Local Group Settings? *1055*

Computer and Session Information 1055

NET COMPUTER: Adding or Deleting Computers from a Domain 1056

How Do I Change the Domain That a Computer Is In? *1056*

NET CONFIG: Learning about and Changing Configurations 1057

NET SESSION: Accessing Connection Information 1060

How Do I Forcibly Break a Connection between Computers? *1062*

NET STATISTICS: Getting a Report on a Computer 1062

What's Out There? Connecting to Networked Devices 1064

NET VIEW: Seeing the Resources Being Shared 1065

How Do I View the Available Resources on the Network?   *1066*

NET USE: Connecting to Other Drives
and Printer Ports   1067

How Do I Connect to a Shared Resource?   *1069*

NET SHARE: Creating and Deleting
Shared Resources   1070

How Do I Share a Device with the Network?   *1072*

NET FILE: Finding Out What's Open
and Who's Using It   1072

NET PRINT: Controlling Print Jobs   1073

How Do I Control a Print Job from the Command Prompt?   *1074*

Using Network Services   1074

NET START: Starting a Service   1075

How Do I Start a Network Service?   *1075*

NET PAUSE and NET CONTINUE:
Halting a Service Temporarily   1082

NET STOP: Stopping a Service   1083

How Do I Stop, Pause, and Continue a Service?   *1083*

Sending Messages   1083

NET NAME: Adding or Deleting a Messaging Name   1084

How Do I Forward My Messages to Another Machine?   *1085*

NET SEND: Sending Messages   1085

How Do I Send Messages?   *1088*

Getting Synched: Viewing and Setting the Time   1088

NET TIME: Coordinating Server
and Workstation Clocks   1088

How Do I Synchronize a Workstation's Time with the Server's?   *1090*

Why Use the Command Prompt?   1090

Index   *1091*

INTRODUCTION

Did you *plan* to become a network administrator? I sure didn't. Very few of us answered the childhood question, "What do you want to be when you grow up?" by saying, "A network administrator." Nevertheless, there are plenty of network administrators. (The money's good, right?) For me, running a network was kind of a "sink or swim" exercise, but I initially managed to keep my head above water, and now administering a network is actually a lot of fun.

And it *ought* to be some fun. NT Server version 3.51 and 4 (this book will help you with *either* version) is a terrific but not flawless network operating system. I find it enjoyable to work with even when I struggle with it in the wee hours of the morning. ("It's *my* data, you stupid operating system—give it to me, you scurrilous software!") NT was surprisingly robust and well-designed from its first incarnation. However, I'm told that an F-18 fighter jet is well-designed too, but I wouldn't want to fly one of *those* without guidance from someone who has flown them before—hence this book. There are a number of books about NT Server, but the one you are holding in your hands has been for the past three years the best-selling book on NT. How is this book different from the rest?

When NT first arrived, I looked around for a book about running a LAN with NT. Amazingly, there was only one: John Ruley's (still a good book and a worthy competitor). Virtually every publisher had put out a book about NT Workstation, but most had skipped NT Server altogether! The best I could do was find a few books that claimed to cover both Workstation and Server. In reality, these books were Workstation books with a few bones tossed to us Server folks. Server-centric books are scarce to this day, and most of *them* are basically old Workstation books with some Server advice thrown in. Books like that are certainly large and impressive, but finding answers in them is something of a treasure hunt. I didn't need a huge book. I just needed a *how-to* manual on NT networking. And not only did I have to run a network, I had to teach classes on NT networking, so I started assembling notes on NT networking as I learned. The result: this book.

Along the way, I noticed a few things that hindered my NT education. I'd stumble across a dialog box that solved a particular problem and think, "Why did it take me so long to find this?" Those of us who worked on this book agreed to the following rule: If we got stuck trying to get a task done and needed more than 30 seconds to figure out how to do it, we would cover the problem and give its solution in a "How Do I..." section of the book. In each "How Do I..." in this book, you will find click-by-click instructions for solving a particular problem.

Another problem I ran up against was the poor quality of Microsoft documentation. My intention isn't to beat up on Microsoft, and in fact there is, in some areas of the documentation, a completeness that I find truly amazing. But Microsoft's documentation tends to be organized along the lines of "We have a program called the User Manager, and here's what all of its menu items do," when what I *needed* was "How do I create and maintain user accounts?" or "How do I build a login script?" The documentation is often silent on some very basic questions, such as these:

- How should I organize the shares on a basic file server?

- How can I build some fault-tolerance into my DHCP (Dynamic Host Configuration Protocol) servers?

- What steps do I go through to get DOS clients on my NT network?

- How do I troubleshoot a "no domain controller was available" error?

Nearly everyone comes up against these questions early when setting up an NT network, but the answers to these questions are not mentioned in the Microsoft documentation. Normally, that's not a terrible thing (hey, nobody's perfect), but in the case of NT, Microsoft charges $195 to answer questions about NT Server! (For questions about NT Workstation, you get *one* free call—kind of like when you get arrested, I suppose.)

This book's intent is to introduce you to NT and NT's way of doing things, show you how to set up NT so it gives you minimum trouble, teach you how to use the built-in tools to administer the network, and show you how to move from there to building and running big networks. With this book, you can plan, configure, install, run, and repair networks that include NT Server. And, again, because many of you won't stampede to NT version 4, we cover 3.51 as well.

But that's not all I intended for this book. Networks in the late 90s don't just need simple file server capabilities; more and more networks require client-server capabilities, and NT Server actually rivals Novell NetWare in that department. Furthermore, NT Server is fairly cheap compared to Novell NetWare, which makes it even more attractive as a simple file server.

Still, most companies don't throw away their existing NetWare networks, which means that today's networks often have more than one kind of server software. There are often Novell file servers, NT Server database servers, perhaps a UNIX NFS system, and of course let's not forget the connections to the old mainframes. Additionally, everyone's jumping on the Internet bandwagon. This multi-network world is great for users, but it's a real headache for network managers, who not only have to support all the different network operating systems, but also have to support their interaction. Too many networking books, however, are written on the assumption that the reader has one and only one kind of network. Throughout the planning of *this* book, however, I assumed that only the lucky few have networks composed solely of NT Server servers. (Those of you in that category should count your blessings.)

I'll show you what's in this book in a moment, but first, a little NT history lesson…

A Brief History of NT

Even in the early 1980s, Bill Gates knew that networking was a key to owning the computer business. So, on April 15, 1985, Microsoft released its first networking product, a tool called MS-NET, and its companion operating system, DOS 3.10. Most people knew about the new DOS and were puzzled at its apparent lack of new features. What it contained, however, were architectural changes to DOS that made it a bit friendlier to the idea of networks.

Now, Microsoft wasn't big enough at that time to create much hoopla about a new network operating system, so they let others sell it. It sold mainly in the guise of the IBM PC Network Support Program; IBM viewed it as little more than some software to go along with their PC Network LAN boards and, later, their Token Ring cards. The server software was DOS-based, offered minimal security, and, to be honest, performed terribly. But the software had two main effects on the market.

First, the fact that IBM sold a LAN product legitimized the whole industry. IBM made it possible for others to make a living selling network products. And that led to the second effect: the growth of Novell. Once the idea of a LAN was legitimized, most companies responded by going out and getting the LAN operating system that offered the best bang for the buck. That was an easy decision: NetWare. In the early days of networking, Novell established itself as the performance leader. You could effectively serve about twice as many workstations with Novell NetWare as you could with any of the MS-NET products. So Novell prospered.

As time went on, however, Microsoft got better at building network products. 3Com, wanting to offer a product that was compatible with the IBM PC Network software, licensed MS-NET and resold it as their "3+" software. 3Com knew quite a bit about networking, however, and recognized the limitations of MS-NET. So 3Com reworked MS-NET to improve its performance, a fact that didn't escape Microsoft's attention.

From 1985 to 1988, Microsoft worked on their second generation of networking software. The software was based on their OS/2 version 1 operating system. (Remember, Microsoft was the main driving force behind OS/2 from 1985 through early 1990. Steve Ballmer, Microsoft's number two guy, promised publicly in 1988 that Microsoft would "go the distance with OS/2." Hey, the world changes and you've got to change with it, right?) Seeing the good work that 3Com did with MS-NET, Microsoft worked as a partner with 3Com to build the next generation of LAN software. Called Microsoft LAN Manager, this network server software was built atop the more powerful OS/2 operating system. As with the earlier MS-NET, Microsoft's intention was never to directly market LAN Manager. Instead, they envisioned IBM, 3Com, Compaq, and others selling it.

IBM did indeed sell LAN Manager (they still do in the guise of OS/2 LAN Server). 3Com sold LAN Manager for years as 3+Open, but found little profit in it and got out of the software business to the chagrin of the businesses who'd invested in the 3+Open software. In late 1990, Compaq announced that they would not sell LAN Manager, because it was too complex a product for their dealers to explain, sell, and support. Microsoft decided then that if LAN Manager was to be sold, they'd have to do the selling, so they announced on the very same day as the Compaq withdrawal that they would begin selling LAN Manager directly.

LAN Manager in its 1.0 incarnation still wasn't half the product that Novell NetWare was, but it was getting there. LAN Manager 2 greatly closed the gap, and in fact, on some benchmarks LAN Manager outpaced Novell NetWare. Additionally, LAN Manager included administrative and security features that brought it even closer to Novell NetWare in the minds of many network managers. Slowly, LAN Manager gained about a 20-percent share of the network market.

When Microsoft designed LAN Manager, however, they designed it for the 286 chip (more accurately, I should say again that LAN Manager was built atop OS/2 1.x, and OS/2 1.x was built for the 286 chip). LAN Manager's inherent 286 nature hampered its performance and sales. In contrast, Novell designed their premier products (NetWare 3 and 4) to use the full capabilities of the 386 and later processors. Microsoft's breakup with IBM delayed the release of a 386-based product and, in a sense, Microsoft never released the 386-based product.

Instead of continuing to climb the ladder of Intel processor capabilities, Microsoft decided to build a processor-independent operating system that would sit in roughly the same market position as UNIX. It could then be implemented for the 386 and later chips, certainly, but it also could run well on other processors, such as the PowerPC, Alpha, and MIPS chips. Microsoft called this new operating system NT, for *new technology*. Not only would NT serve as a workstation operating system, it would also arrive in a network server version to be called *LAN Manager NT*. No products ever shipped with that name, but the wallpaper that NT Server displays when no one is logged onto it is called LAN-MANNT.BMP to this day.

In August of 1993, Microsoft released LAN Manager NT with the name *NT Advanced Server*. In a shameless marketing move, they referred to it as version 3.1 in order to match the version numbers of the Windows desktop products. This first version of NT Advanced Server performed quite well. Network planners took a closer look at the new networking product; however, it was memory-hungry, it lacked Novell connectivity, and it had only the most basic TCP/IP connectivity.

September of 1994 brought a new version and a new name: Microsoft Windows NT Server version 3.5. Version 3.5 was mainly a "polish" of 3.1; it was less memory-hungry, included Novell and TCP/IP connectivity right in the box, and included Windows for Workgroups versions of the administrative tools so network administrators could work from a Workgroup machine rather than an NT machine. Where many vendors would spend 13 months adding silly bells and whistles, NT 3.5 showed that the Microsoft folks had spent most of their time fine-tuning the operating system, trimming its memory requirements, and speeding it up a bit.

After another 13 months came NT version 3.51, in October of 1995, which brought mainly support for PCMCIA cards (a real boon for us traveling instructor types), file compression, and a raft of bug fixes.

NT version 4, 1996's edition of NT, has a new face and a bunch of new features, but no really radical networking changes. If you are a network administrator under NT version 3.51, you'll find 4 a snap to learn. The *big* changes will come with the version of NT called *Cairo*, which will probably appear in late 1997 or early 1998.

What's in This Book

If you're reading this, then you made it past that huge table of contents. Here's the 25-cent tour of what's inside this book.

The book starts in Part I with an overview of NT's strengths, as well as a look at the features new to version 4. Then I take you through an extremely important chapter (Chapter 2, "Microsoft Enterprise Concepts,"), where I introduce you to the overall Microsoft approach to networking, so you understand what a workgroup and a domain are, among other things.

In Part II, we roll up our sleeves and install NT Server. I show you the step-by-step method that works best for me and produces the least problems in the long run. Following that, you'll want to set up your disk drives for maximum performance and fault-tolerance, and Chapter 4 shows you how to do that. Part II finishes off with a chapter on the NT Registry, the place where NT keeps all of its internal configuration information. All network administrators end up twiddling the Registry, and this chapter shows you how.

Part III shows you how to run an NT network—it's the "administration" unit, so to speak. Chapter 6 shows you how to create user accounts. Working with passwords, groups, profiles, logon hours, auditing—it's all there. Following that is a complementary chapter on creating file shares on an NT network. You learn the differences between share-level permissions and file and directory permissions, how file ownership works, and how to create home directories. Chapters 6 and 7 conclude with an explanation of how to write top-quality logon scripts. Chapter 8 follows that with a discussion of sharing printers. Chapters 9 and 10 show you how to attach client PCs (Chapter 9) and Macintoshes (Chapter 10) to an NT network. You see how to put the client software on the machine, how to attach it to a domain, and how to log in, change passwords, browse the network, and attach to shares.

In Chapter 11, you see how to manage multiple servers without having to run around the office (or the world, if your firm has multiple locations). You see how to create directory replication, something that *looks* scary but isn't bad when someone takes you through it step-by-step. In this chapter, I also explain the nuts and bolts of how to design a domain. How many users should you have in the domain? How many backup domain controllers do you need? It's all there.

In Part IV, we'll talk about managing NT Server in an enterprise network. Chapter 12 shows you how to run an "enterprise" network, a network of some size and perhaps with more than one network architecture all under one roof. In Chapter 12, you see how to design and manage multi-domain networks. Chapter 13 covers Novell integration. NT networks with NetWare servers will adopt one of the "three D's"—détente, deception, or dismissal. Put more simply, you either continue to run two networks in parallel (détente), run some software to fool your system into thinking that the NT servers are NetWare servers or vice versa (deception), or look for advice on how to smoothly move from NetWare to NT (dismissal).

You can't spell *Internet* without *NT,* so that's the topic of the largest chapter in this book, Chapter 14. If, like others, your firm has been swept up in the tide of Internet fever, you may be a bit confused about IP addresses, CIDR blocks, subnet masks, and static routing. That's covered in the first part of the chapter, a tutorial on the Internet's TCP/IP protocol. Then we move along to an in-depth discussion of implementing TCP/IP on your NT network, including the Dynamic Host Configuration Protocol (DHCP) and the Windows Internet Naming Service (WINS). There's also a big section on name resolution, where you learn about both WINS and the Domain Naming Service (DNS), what they do, how they're similar, and how they're different.

Chapter 15 discusses tuning and monitoring an NT network. It is an essential guide to the Performance Monitor. I show you a few counters that you can monitor to keep track of your network's health. But if the network *does* take ill, you can turn to Chapter 16 to see how to recover from disaster. Ever wondered how to read an NT "blue screen?" It's there. And Chapter 17 wraps things up with an explanation of Dial-Up Networking, the technology formerly known as Remote Access Services.

Last but not least, the appendix shows you how to use the command prompt to "NET results."

Conventions Used in This Book

In this book, things can be quite complex, so I've followed some conventions to make them clearer and easier to understand.

*x*86 versus RISC

The term *x86*, which is used in this book and in similar books, refers to any machine that uses a processor in the Intel line, including the 8086, 8088, 80188, 80186, 80286, 80386DX, 80386SL, 80386SX, 80486DX, 80486SX, 80486SL, 80486DX2, Intel DX4, the Pentium, and Pentium Pro processors.

When I am referring to client machines, I could be referring to any of these processors. When I am referring to an NT Server or NT workstation system, then it must be one of the 386, 486, Pentium, or Pentium Pro families of chips.

RISC is short for, as you probably know, Reduced Instruction Set Chip. As I write this, NT is available for the MIPS R4000 RISC processor in both the workstation and server mode, and for the DEC Alpha and the IBM/Motorola/Apple Power PC chip.

All RISC systems must follow a standard called the Advanced RISC Computer (ARC) standard. For that reason, I generically refer to these three RISC families all as "RISC," even though internally they are quite different. That's the good thing about NT; as an architecture-independent operating system, it masks hardware differences.

Our Assumption: The System Is on the C: Drive

If you're running NT Server on an *x86*-based machine, I've assumed that you've installed your operating system in c:\winnt. That would mean that you have a C:\winnt\system directory, which I'll refer to as the *system* directory, and a C:\winnt\system32 directory, which I'll refer to as the *system32* directory. (Actually, things don't get all that different if the system is on another drive.)

The Text Icons

As you read through the text, you'll see icons and sidebars used in different ways. I include them to point out items of particular interest.

Tips, Notes, and Warnings

Tips, Notes, and Warnings are "aside" information. Often I enclose information I stumbled on when researching NT in Notes, Tips, and Warnings.

NOTE This is a Note. Notes offer definitions, advice, and the like.

TIP This is a Tip. Tips tell you shortcuts and highlight information that is well worth knowing well.

WARNING This is a Warning. When you see one of these, prick up your ears.

"How Do I" Sidebars

NT's big. I mean, really big. As such, quite a number of procedures aren't hard to do or even hard to learn, but they do take time. As I mentioned earlier, I decided when writing this book that any step-by-step procedure that took me more than 30 seconds to figure out would take you more than 30 seconds, too, and those procedures have been pulled out of the text and put in sidebars for easy reference.

How Do I Read a Sidebar?

 This is a sidebar. All sidebars begin with the words "How Do I" and the icon shown here. You will find a complete list of "How Do I" sidebars (along with the numbers of the pages where they are found) on the last page and inside back cover of this book.

Enterprise Networking

ENTERPRISE NETWORKING

Much of what NT makes sense for, and one of my main objectives in writing this book, is enterprise networking. An *enterprise network* is one that is built with heterogeneous pieces. Issues that are specific to connecting NT networks to other NT networks, connecting NT networks to wide area networks (WANs), and connecting NT networks to other local area networks are marked by the Enterprise Networking icon you see here. (Originally, we were going to use a little picture of *Star Trek's* NCC 1701D starship, but you'd be *amazed* how closely Paramount protects its copyrights...)

NT Server

As I mentioned earlier, I set out originally to write a book for people who would mainly work with NT Server, rather than NT. There were books aimed at NT users in general, but no books aimed at NT Server users, at least not until I finished writing this one. But I found to my surprise that most of the power of NT Server was shared by the basic NT workstation product, so this book is of value to users of the NT workstation product after all. For that reason, I attempted to make clear which parts of the text were only relevant to NT Server with the icon you see here.

I'm as Close as Your (E-) Mailbox

NT is an enormous system. I've worked with it as long as anyone has, but I don't know it all, not by a long shot. Got a tip that you'd like me to share with the rest of the world? Send it to me, and I'll acknowledge your help in the next edition of this book. Got a question that I didn't answer? Mail it to me, and I'll do my best to get an answer. Found a (*gasp!*) error? You can find me at mark@mmco.com. When I'm out of the country (which is two months a year), I don't pick up my e-mail, so if I don't get back to you immediately, don't be offended, because I'll respond as soon as I can. (And please don't send me mail with receipts; our mail server automatically deletes them. Hey, it's kind of rude, you know what I mean?)

One of the things I've learned after working with NT for three years is I'm always learning new things, but I've only been able to tell you about them when we update the book once a year. Now Sybex is giving me a new way to share that information with you as I learn about it. As I update the book, the updates will appear on Sybex's Web site. These updates will appear in the next edition of the book, but to see them sooner, point your Web browser to www.sybex.com. (Don't expect anything new until October, however.)

Thanks for reading, and I hope you find this book to be the ultimate NT Server guide!

PART I

Getting
Acquainted

■ **CHAPTER 1** • NT Server Overview

■ **CHAPTER 2** • Microsoft Enterprise Concepts

CHAPTER
ONE

NT Server Overview

Pretty much all of the big companies and government offices were already networked by mid-1993, back when the first version of NT arrived. Since network administrators—and most people in general—aren't fond of change, the product must have been good (or especially well marketed) to have been brought to market *that* late and to have still succeeded.

One analysis says that by end of the decade, 60 percent of the desktop servers in the world will be running NT. A statistic from early 1996 claims that one half of World Wide Web servers are running NT. I personally have been amazed at how quickly some of my large Fortune 500 clients have just wiped NetWare off their servers' hard disks and replaced it with NT Server.

If you're a NetWare, VINES, or LAN Server administrator and you've looked around and said to yourself, "What's going *on*?" or you've decided to finally take the plunge and learn a major network operating system, then you'll want an overview of NT's strengths.

In many ways, NT Server is a big departure from previous PC-based server products. Those currently managing a LAN Server, Novell NetWare, or LAN Manager LAN will have to understand the ways that NT Server departs from its LAN Manager past in order to get the most from NT Server.

NT Server Capabilities

Whether it is to be used as a workstation operating system or a server operating system, the NT operating system itself has some quite attractive features. Let's take a look at some of the features that make NT Server stand out from the competition.

Architecture Independence

Most operating systems are designed from first conception with a particular target processor in mind. Operating system designers get caught up in things like the following:

Word size   How many bits does the CPU work with on each operation? CPUs once handled only 8 bits at a time, then 16-bit processors appeared, 32-bit processors appeared, and now there are 64-bit and even 128-bit processors.

Page size   What's the size of the "quantum" of memory that a processor works with? On an Intel Pentium Pro, it's impossible for the processor to allocate less than 4K of RAM to any given application. For example, if an application wants 2K, then it gets 4K, and if it wants 5K, then it gets 8K. This is called the *page size* of the processor. On a DEC Alpha CPU, the page size is 8K, so the smallest memory allocation is 8K. That means that whether an application wants 2K or 5K, it gets 8K on an Alpha. While this seems like a small thing, it's just the kind of minutiae that operating system designers get caught up in. They embed that 4K or 8K value throughout the operating system code, making the prospect of porting the operating system's code to another processor sound impossible. NT avoided that problem, as you'll see.

Big-endian or little-endian   How are bytes organized in memory? Here is another example of the kind of minutiae that can make an operating system end up very, very processor-dependent. RAM in most desktop computers is organized in 8-bit groups called bytes. (I *knew* you knew that, but I defined it just in case someone out there doesn't.) But most modern CPUs store data in 32-bit groups. You can write 32 bits as four bytes. Reading those four bytes left to right, let's call them byte one, two, three, and four. Now, here's the question: When the processor stores that one word—that four bytes—in what order should it store it in memory? Some store the leftmost byte first and move to the right, so the order in which the bytes appear is one, two, three, and four. Other processors store the bytes in reverse order: four, three, two, one. The first approach is called a *little-endian* storage approach; the second is called *big-endian*.

Tons of other things are processor-specific, but those are three good examples. What I want you to understand is the trap that operating system designers can fall into; a trap of building their operating systems to be very specific to a particular processor. The powerful-but-gimmicky features of a processor become integral parts of operating systems, while essential features that the processor doesn't support go by the wayside. For example, look at the pervasive 16-bit nature of many Intel-based operating systems, a nature directly attributable to the 8088 and 80286 processors. The first member of the Intel processor family that PC compatibles were built around, the 8086, first appeared in 1977. Eight years went by before a 32-bit Intel *x*86 processor appeared (*x*86 refers to the family of PC-compatible processors: the 8086, 8088, 80188, 80186, 80286, 80386, 80486 and Pentium chips). Even though that 32-bit processor has been available since 1985, it took nearly ten years for 32-bit operating systems to appear.

When Microsoft designed NT, it initially did *not* specifically implement it on an *x*86 chip. Microsoft wanted to build something that was independent of any processor's architecture. They were aware that Microsoft programmers knew the *x*86 architecture intimately and that the intimate knowledge would inevitably work its way into the design of NT. So, to combat that problem, Microsoft first implemented NT on a RISC chip, the MIPS R4000. Since then, NT has been ported to the *x*86 series (the 80486, Pentium, and Pentium Pro chips), the PowerPC CPUs, and the Alpha chips.

The parts of NT that are machine-specific are all segregated into a relatively small piece of NT (compared to the total size of the operating system). This small piece is made up of the Hardware Abstraction Layer (HAL), the kernel, and the network and device drivers. Implementing

NT on a new processor type, therefore, mainly involves just writing a new HAL, processor, and network subsystem.

What does this mean to a network manager? Well, many LANs have used Intel *x*86-based servers for years. As the needs of the LANs grew, so (fortunately) did the power of the *x*86 family of Intel processor chips. These chips steadily grew faster and more powerful. When the average network had about fifteen users, 286-based servers were around. When people started putting a hundred users on a server, 486s could be purchased.

Unfortunately, however, *x*86 processors since 1991 haven't really grown in power as quickly as they did previously. RISC machines that are reasonably priced and that offer pretty high-speed processing have begun to appear. That's why the architecture-independent nature of NT Server is so attractive. The next time you need a bigger server, you needn't buy a PC-compatible machine, with all that PC-compatibility baggage weighing the machine down. Instead, you can buy a simple, fast, streamlined machine designed simply to act as a LAN server and potentially provide decent service to hundreds of users.

Multiple Processor Support

I just said that CPUs weren't getting faster quite as quickly as they once did. There's more than one way to make a faster computer, however: you can use a faster processor *or* you can just use *more* processors.

Compaq's Systempro was the first well-known PC-compatible computer to include multiple processors; its modern equivalent would be the Compaq Proliants. Nowadays, *everybody* offers a two-Pentium or two-Pentium Pro system, even the "Jeff and Akbar's House of Clones" guys. That's true for the RISC world as well. Where multiprocessor machines once cost over $100,000, you can now put together a pretty decent multiprocessor PC for about $10,000.

NT in its basic form was designed to support up to 32 processors in a PC. NT Server can also split up its tasks among 32 processors. For some reason, however, Microsoft chose to cripple the basic versions of NT workstation and NT Server, shipping Hardware Abstraction Layers (HALs) that only support 2 and 4 processors, respectively. If you want to use more than 2 processors on an NT workstation or 4 processors on an NT Server, then you'll have to bug your hardware vendor for an improved HAL that supports more than those numbers of processors. (All you need is a HAL—no new kernel, drivers, or network subsystem is necessary to use multiple processors.) In any case, servers can have up to 32 processors in them, with the right HAL.

Among multiprocessing systems, a computer is said to be a *symmetric* or *asymmetric* multiprocessor. An asymmetric multiprocessor has more than one processor, but each processor has a different, specifically defined job. The early Systempros were asymmetric systems. A symmetric multiprocessing system, in contrast, has processors that can take over for one another without skipping a beat. Each processor has complete access to all hardware, bus, and memory actions. NT and NT Server must have symmetric processor systems in order to use multiprocessor capabilities.

Multithreaded Multitasking

Whether you have just one processor or more than one processor in your system, NT supports multitasking. The multitasking is true multitasking in that it is preemptive, time-sliced, priority-driven multitasking. (All that is explained in Chapter 15, on server tuning.)

Multitasking usually means that a single computer can run several different programs. Each program, however, usually is only single-tasking within itself. Consider, for example, how a word processor is built. It picks up keystrokes, then it does something with them, and then it goes on to the next keystroke. Apply that to a *graphical* word processor, and you can see that problems can result.

Suppose you press the Page Down key, so the word processor retrieves a page of text either from memory buffers or from the disk and then displays the text. That can take a bit of time, particularly if the page contains a few graphics, each of which must be retrieved and rendered in a fashion consonant with the abilities of the particular graphics board that you're using. But now suppose you're on page 30 and you want to move to page 33. You just press Page Down three times, and the three Page Down keystrokes go into the keyboard buffer of the word-processing program. Now, because the word-processing program is single-threaded—that is, because it does just one thing at a time, and in a particular order—it will see the first Page Down key, and it will then retrieve and render the entire page 31. Only after it's through doing that does it look again in the keyboard buffer, see another Page Down, and goes through the whole process again for page 32 and then for page 33.

One way to avoid this kind of time-wasting "tunnel vision" is to build the word processor as a group of smaller programs, all of which run simultaneously. There could be a kind of "boss" program that reads the keystrokes, calling the "render the page" routine. That program could interrupt the "render the page" routine when a new keystroke comes in, keeping it from wasting time displaying pages that would be over-written on the screen immediately.

NT lets developers create such a program, called a *multithreaded* program. Each of the small independent subprograms is called a *thread*, hence the term multithreaded. Whether the developers actually *use* that capability is quite another story; some major NT applications are multithreaded, and some aren't. On a single-processor system, being single-threaded isn't terrible. On a multiprocessor system, being single-threaded is a crime—it wastes that extra processor, because each thread can live on one and only one processor at a time. A single processor can handle multiple threads, of course; but a single thread can't span multiple processors.

How can you find out if your application is multithreaded? Run it on a multiprocessor NT system and give it something pretty time-consuming to do, then run the Performance Monitor and monitor how much of each CPU is taken up by the application. If one processor is 99-percent utilized and the other one is 11-percent utilized, then it's pretty clear that the application is single-threaded. Again, see Chapter 15 for more on the Performance Monitor and on tuning.

Multithreading is essential for server-based programs like database servers, which must be able to respond to multiple requests for information from many client sources.

Massive Memory Space

NT programs don't have to worry about running up against some kind of 640K or 16K barrier. The NT architecture can support RAM of up to 4096MB (four *gigabytes*). (Now, where did I put those one gig SIMMs...?)

I should mention, by the way, that it's not a good idea to put more than 16MB on an ISA (Industry Standard Architecture) bus machine. If your servers are to have more than 16MB, get a PC based on the Micro Channel Architecture (MCA), Extended Industry Standard Architecture (EISA), or Peripheral Component Interconnect (PCI) bus. Or you could get a RISC machine, where there is no 16MB boundary.

Now, that last paragraph generated a lot of reader letters in previous editions, so let's elaborate on it. Machines with old ISA buses (and most modern PCs still come with ISA bus slots in combination with PCI bus slots) have a problem because the ISA bus can only address 16MB of memory. Virtually all NT Server machines have at least that much memory, and usually more, which presents a problem to the ISA bus. The bus "overhears" all addressing references, no matter if they're intended for a piece of hardware in an ISA slot, for a PCI slot, or are on the system motherboard. As the ISA bus can only work with 16MB of memory addressing space, any references to memory above 16MB just "wrap around," so that accessing a memory location like 17MB looks like accessing address 17-1 or 1MB to the ISA bus. If there were a memory board in an ISA slot with address 1MB, then the ISA bus would mistakenly send the message to that board.

Now, normally that's not a big problem, as people don't usually put memory in ISA slots. But some boards that might end up in ISA slots have a small amount of memory in them, and some ISA boards access memory directly in the form of something called *bus mastering*. If you had a bus master board in an ISA slot, it could conceivably lose or damage data because of the confusion about memory addresses. Now, motherboard designers know that, so they placed extra circuitry to check for these problems and to avert them. But using that circuitry slows down PCs a bit, with the result that many PCs actually run slower with more than 16MB of RAM than they do with less memory. It's another argument for buying RISC-based servers, I guess.

Centralized User Profiles

Each Windows or DOS program seems to need its own configuration file or files, leading to a disk littered with a lot of files with the extensions INI, CNF, and the like. NT centralizes program initialization information with a database of program setup information called *the Registry* and part of that database, a user-specific part, is called a *user profile*. NT even allows you to store an NT workstation's profile on a server, making it possible to centrally control the equivalent of CONFIG.SYS and AUTOEXEC.BAT (and Windows.INI) files for a workstation from a central server. Heaven for support folks.

If your work takes you from workstation to workstation, then you may feel a bit like a Bedouin, with no home but the great wide world itself. Nomadic computing means that when you log on to a new workstation, you have to spend time arranging the look of that workstation to your particular tastes. (And, of course, the person who *usually* uses the workstation may not appreciate your "improvements.")

NT improves upon that with the notion of a *profile*. A user profile contains information like

- Background colors

- Wallpaper

- Screen saver preferences

- Program manager groups

- Persistent network connections

Under NT, you can create a profile *for an NT workstation* (this is no good for a regular Windows or Windows 95 workstation) and then you can tell NT to cause that profile to follow you around. Windows 95 has profiles as well, but unfortunately Windows NT and 95 profiles are incompatible, so you end up with at least one of each.

As a support person, you'll like the fact that you can use a profile to restrict the kinds of things a user can do. You can even make a profile mandatory, moving us one step closer to central control of desktop PCs. The only catch? Again, NT profiles are different from Windows 95 profiles, so the profiles you set up for your NT clients won't work for 95 clients, and vice versa.

Enhanced Metafile Printing

If you have both NT workstations and servers, then you'll find a really neat approach to network printing. When you print to a network server, the entire print job goes out to the *server* to print, leaving the workstation with little to do in the printing process. That means that the workstation is available much more quickly after you tell it to print something. Additionally, print drivers sit only on the server, so when a new print driver comes out, you needn't put it on every workstation—just the servers. A terrific feature if you're using NT workstations.

Enterprise Networking Features

ENTERPRISE NETWORKING

On top of NT Server's basic operating system features, however, is a wide array of networking capabilities, many of particular value to builders of multi-operating system *enterprise* networks. Enterprise networks are those networks built of large numbers of machines and servers. Enterprise networks have some special needs; here's how NT meets those needs.

Internet and TCP/IP Compatibility

Whether your company intends to get onto the Internet or not, most networks speak the language of the Internet, a protocol called Transmission Control Protocol/Internet Protocol (TCP/IP). Many companies build TCP/IP-based networks and never connect them to the Internet for security reasons. Such networks are called *private IP networks*, or, more recently, *intranets*. In any case, TCP/IP is the way to go for many networks. NT supports most of the protocols of the Internet, so it's possible to build your own enterprise intranet based on Windows NT.

Event and Account Logging

When I got started in the computer business, I worked on a mainframe-based system. Like all users on that system, I had an account that kept track of a balance of "pseudomoney." Whenever I "logged on to" my mainframe, the account would be debited a bit for every minute that I was on, a bit more for each byte of shared disk storage that I used, and some more for each program run on that mainframe.

The other mainframe users and I used to call these accounts "funny money" because after running a program, you'd get a printout detailing the charges that you engendered by running the program; so much for each page printed, so much for the disk space used, and so on. Although it would have a dollar total, no money changed hands. The whole purpose of "funny money" accounts was to impress upon the mainframe's users that the mainframe was a limited resource and shared computer resources should not be wasted.

LANs are getting to be more and more like mainframes. They serve hundreds of users in many companies, they're a shared resource, and they cost a lot of money to keep up and running. Eventually, companies will assign "funny money" accounts to LAN users as a means of keeping track of who is putting the greatest strain on the system. While this may sound a trifle authoritarian, it's not. Users depend on LANs more and more, and if just a few users make it difficult for others to get *their* jobs done, then there must be a way for network administrators to figure out who's killing the network.

That's what event logging and auditing is all about. Under NT Server, you can keep track of who prints on what printer at what time, who uses what files at what time and for how long, and who's logged onto which server. NT Server provides a great deal of power for keeping track of what's happening on your network.

Remote Access Services

There's always been a need for information workers to be able to take their work home. Once, workers brought a briefcase stuffed with papers home. Then mainframe users dragged home a thermal paper terminal called the "Silent 700." More recently, people with PCs at home dialed up to the company LAN via a program like Carbon Copy or PC Anywhere, or perhaps via a more expensive solution like the Khiva NetModem. It's not just office workers who need remote access, either; members of roving sales forces may only physically touch their home bases once a month or so, but they need to exchange data with that home base.

NT Server has a remote access capability built right into it. The remote access software shipped with NT is the *server* end of the software; the client end—the piece that goes on the workstation—is included in the NT workstation software and Windows version 3.11 and later. Microsoft also offers remote access client software for DOS and earlier versions of Windows; those files can be found in the \CLIENTS\RAS directory of the installation CD-ROM disk.

Also included in RAS are two powerful TCP/IP protocols: Point to Point Tunneling Protocol (PPTP) and Multilink PPP. The first allows you to use the entire Internet as a "router," so to speak, to communicate with your office network. Multilink PPP lets you take several slower-speed communication links and blend them into just one link. For example, you could have three phone lines that each have 28.8Kbps modems. All connect to the same Internet service provider, and those connections would together look like one single connection running at 86.4Kbps.

Domain and Workgroup-Based Administration Features

NT Server includes programs that make it simple to control security on a number of servers.

If your company has just one server, then these features won't be very attractive. But if your firm has a number of servers, then you'll soon find that administering groups of servers can be a real pain in the neck. For example, suppose you want to add a user to the Finance department. There are four servers in Finance. That means you've got to log on to each one individually and create the same user account on each one; ditto if you have to delete a user account. With the domain management capabilities of NT Server, you can make those changes to a whole group of servers with just a few mouse-clicks.

As NT Server is a modern LAN operating system, it goes without saying that you can assign security access rights all the way down to the user and file level; you can say that user X can only read file Y, but user Z can read and write file Y. You can also set files to an "execute-only" privilege level, making it possible for someone to run a program on the server, but *im*possible to copy the program from the server.

About the only thing that you can't do with the security features of NT Server is to link them to security programs in the mainframe world, like ACF/2 and RACF, unfortunately.

Fault Tolerance and RAID Support

 Part of security involves keeping people from data that they're not supposed to have access to, but an equally big part of security's functions includes keeping safe the data that people have entrusted to the network. To that end, NT Server incorporates a number of features that support fault tolerance:

- The database of domain security information resides on a single server called the *domain controller*, but other servers can act as backup domain controllers in the domain, ready to step in as domain controller whenever the primary goes off-line.

- NT Server supports multiple network cards in a server, so a network card failure doesn't necessarily bring down a server.

- *Directory replication* makes it possible to designate a directory on a particular server and then create a backup server whose job it is to match, on a minute-by-minute basis, the contents of that directory. That makes sure that essential things like logon scripts are available from several sources, making logons quicker.

- *Hot fixes* are a feature on any NT Server whose disk has been formatted under the NTFS file system. NTFS constantly monitors the disk areas that it is using, and if it finds that one has become damaged, then it takes the bad area out of service and moves the data on that area to another, safer area automatically.

- RAID (Redundant Array of Inexpensive Drives) is a six-level method for combining several disk drives into what appears to the system to be a single disk drive. RAID improves upon a single-drive answer in that it offers better speed and data redundancy.

- Level 0, or *disk striping*, improves speed only. It creates what appears to be one disk out of several separate physical disk drives. Areas that appear to be a cylinder or a track on a logical disk drive are actually spread across two or more physical disk drives. The benefit is realized when accessing data; when reading a block of data, the read operation can actually become several simultaneous separate disk reads of several physical disks.

- Level 1 is a straightforward *disk mirroring* system. You get two disk drives and tell NT to make one a mirror image of the other. It's fast and fault-tolerant.

- Levels 2, 3, and 4 are not supported by NT Server.

- Level 5 is very much like level 1, in that data is striped across several separate physical drives. It differs, however, in that it adds redundant information called "parity" that allows damaged data to be reconstructed.

The different levels of RAID do not get better as they rise in numbers; they're just different options. The interesting part about NT's RAID support, however, is that it happens in *software*, not hardware. You needn't buy a specialized RAID box to get the benefits of RAID— all you have to do is just buy a bunch of SCSI drives and use the NT Disk Administrator program to RAID-ize them. (You need not use SCSI drives, but they are easier to connect. SCSI drives also support sector remapping, which is another fault-tolerant feature that other drives may not support.)

Reasonable Price for Server and Client Software

Pricing server products is a difficult thing. On the one hand, network server software equals mainframe operating systems in complexity, so software vendors want to realize the same kind of return that they would from mainframe software. That's not possible, however, because no one would pay mainframe software prices for software running on a server with eight workstations. But a *hundred* workstations...?

Server software must be reasonably priced for small LANs. But the very same software runs on large LANs, so how does a LAN software vendor justify charging more money for the very same software, based solely on the number of people using it? Nevertheless, major vendors *do* charge more for server software, depending on the number of users; NetWare can cost from hundreds of dollars to tens of thousands of dollars, depending on the number of users on a server.

NT is priced in two parts. Basically, you buy the server for $700 and you buy a "client license" for each user at $40 apiece. Those are, of course, list prices, so your mileage will vary, but basically you can estimate how much it will cost you to set up an NT Server network by taking the number of servers you'll need and multiplying by $700, and then taking the number of people who will access the network and multiplying by $40.

There are some specific "gotchas" that you have to know about, but they're covered in Chapter 3, on setting up NT Server.

NDIS Protocol Support

Getting network boards to work with network operating systems has never been a simple thing. Even more difficult has been supporting multiple protocols on a single network card, and most unpleasant of all has been getting multiple protocols to work on multiple network cards.

Novell attacks this problem with its Open Data-Link Interface (ODI) standard. Microsoft's answer is the Network Driver Interface Specification (NDIS). Each has its own pluses and minuses, but NDIS 3 and later has a terrific feature in its ability to load client software in extended memory, which is quite a plus for those running memory-hungry DOS software.

One of NT's problems over its brief lifetime has been getting decent driver support. Buy a high-performance Ethernet card and there will certainly be a Novell NetWare driver in the box for that card. But there may or may not be an NT driver. Microsoft wants this problem to go away forever, and their plan for doing that is to integrate the driver model for Windows 97 (no, that's not a misprint) and Windows NT. The widespread nature of Windows 95 means that it will be easy to find a Windows 95 driver for a given board, and that, no doubt, will be true for Windows 97 as well. But fully integrated drivers (for display boards, SCSI host adapters, tape drives, and the like) aren't scheduled to appear until the late 1997 or 1998 edition of NT, code-named "Cairo." (Of course, Cairo was *originally* supposed to appear in 1995, so don't hold your breath…)

Protocol Compatibility with Forebears

Obviously, NT Server communicates with its forebears. In particular, LAN Manager 2.2 servers can act as members of NT Server's domains and can assist in some but not all domain control functions.

NetWare Support

Knowing that much of its audience needs to be able to interface with existing Novell NetWare servers, NT Server contains some capabilities to communicate with Novell products. The connectivity isn't perfect, however. You can't unify the domain administration for your Novell NetWare network with the administration for NT Server.

NT includes the network protocol used in NetWare networks, a protocol called IPX/SPX; NT calls it NWLink. NWLink is actually the default network protocol that the NT setup program suggests when you install NT.

With NT's Client and Gateway Services for NetWare, you can extend Novell services to parts of your network that don't even run Novell software. That's a sneaky way to bend Novell's maximum number of users on each server, but it's a little *too* good: NT makes it tough to carry over Novell security to NT users. (In any case, you can learn all about it in Chapter 12.) And two new tools, File and Print Services for NetWare and Directory Services Manager for NetWare, allow you to smooth the path from NetWare to NT.

NetBEUI, DLC, and TCP/IP Options

Over the years, a number of network/transport/session protocols have become significant in the networking industry. There is a great variety of these protocols for two reasons. First, some are just products of large computer companies that want to build their own proprietary protocols and give themselves a competitive advantage. Second, different protocols are built to serve different needs.

NetBEUI was originally built by IBM to quickly zip data around small LANs. It's a really "quick and dirty" protocol in that it's not easy to move NetBEUI data over wide area networks (WANs). You'll hear people beat up on NetBEUI for its simplicity, but make no mistake: for a single-segment network, it is *the* fastest transport protocol available.

TCP/IP is a kind of *de facto* standard for building networks composed of many different vendors' products. TCP/IP has until recently not been very popular in the role of LAN protocol, but it *can* serve quite well in that role, and recent improvements to TCP/IP have made it even more attractive on LANs. It is possible to replace NetBEUI with TCP/IP in NT Server, and in fact for a network of any size, I highly recommend it.

DLC (Data Link Control), also known as IEEE 802.2, is not a complete protocol, so it can't serve in the role of LAN or WAN protocol. But DLC can provide connectivity to many mainframe gateway products and to some printers that attach directly to the network, such as any Hewlett-Packard LaserJet with a JetDirect print server (network interface) card.

Macintosh Connectivity

Getting Macs and PCs to communicate has always been a bit of a headache. But NT Server makes it very simple. I connected a Mac to my NT Server within 15 minutes, and it worked the first time.

Under NT Server, you need only create a directory on your server, designate it as a Mac-accessible volume, and start up the Mac Server subsystem.

NT Server has all the ingredients necessary to make it successful as an enterprise network server in many organizations. In the next chapter, we'll look at the network concepts that you have to understand in order to work in the Microsoft networking world.

What's New in Version 4?

Everything you've read about so far has existed in NT since version 3.1. Microsoft has spent a fair amount of money selling version 4, although most of the marketing money has gone into selling NT Workstation 4. What's new in NT Server 4?

Some of the big news in NT is built into NT Server 4 and comes right in the box. Other news appears in the form of new and separate products, only some of which I cover in this book.

New GUI

A new GUI is the "big news" in NT Server 4, although truthfully it's not that important for network administrators; after all, who cares what user interface is on the server? Having said that, however, it's worth noting that adding the Windows 95 user interface to NT Server 4 will make it just a bit easier to teach new network administrators how to do their jobs, because many of those people will have already worked with Windows 95.

Little Change in Administration Tools

Besides the change in the user interface, veteran users of NT Server will see (thankfully!) very little change in the basic tools that they've come to know and love. The User Manager for Domains, the Print Manager, the Server Manager, Performance Monitor, NT Backup, DHCP Manager, WINS Manager, and the User Profile Editor are basically unchanged—and that's good. Someone already using NT Server version 3.51 will find the transition to version 4 simple.

Internet Information Server

The latest fad sweeping corporate America is the "home page," a marketing presentation of some kind on the World Wide Web. You ain't nobody unless your company has a Web page. (Ours is at www.mmco .com.) Setting up your own Web page, however, requires a connection to the Internet and a computer of some type running a Web server.

Web server programs used to cost a fair amount of money, and one company, Netscape, has Wall Street believing that it will make tons of money selling them. Now, Microsoft is *scared* of Netscape (Microsoft Executive Vice President Steve Ballmer said recently that Microsoft wants to "crush" Netscape) so Microsoft is giving away a Web server, which they call their Internet Information Server. Included in that is an improved FTP server (an FTP server was always included with NT, but this one has a few more bells and whistles) and a Gopher server.

You can learn more about the Internet Information Server in Chapter 14, on TCP/IP.

New Communications Protocol Support

As mentioned earlier, version 4 has the multilink PPP and PPTP protocols, both new to NT. The Remote Access Server (RAS) now has "autodial" capabilities whereby you can tell your computer that you are linked to another computer over a phone line. That's not new; RAS has been around all along. What *is* new is that now you can create all sorts of connections to other computers via RAS, and the computer will act as if those virtual connections actually exist, even though it hasn't dialed up the connection yet. Then, when you try to actually use one of those connections, the system automatically dials the other computer to enable the connections.

NT 4 also includes the Telephony Application Program Interface (TAPI), a very nice feature that unified communications programming under Windows 95 and will no doubt benefit NT as well. You see, in older operating systems, each communication program had to load its own modem-specific drivers; if you ran four different communications programs on your computer, you ended up telling four different programs what kind of modem you had, which was cumbersome. Under NT 4, you'll be able to buy communications applications that are "TAPI-enabled," meaning that they'll interrogate your system for modem information rather than interrogating *you*.

Network Administration Tools

Windows 95 had a powerful administrative tool in the form of the System Policy Editor (SPE). The SPE didn't work in NT, until NT 4. With the SPE, you can control a particular user's machine so completely that it's possible to say that a given user can only run Word and Excel on her machine. For the control freaks out there, this is a blessing. For the rest of us, it's a new tool to master.

RIP Routing and DNS Server Support

With every release of NT, Microsoft makes it clearer and clearer that their network direction is TCP/IP and the Internet. Up to now, most of the computers running the Internet were UNIX machines, mainly because most of the Internet tools are available for free on UNIX. But that's a part of the world that Microsoft wants to own, so each new version of NT includes some new essential Internet tool. In addition to the Web server, NT Server 4 includes a Domain Name Service (DNS) server and support for the Routing Internet Protocol (RIP) standard. If you've never heard of them, trust me, they're pretty essential—and, again, you can learn more about them in Chapter 14.

The DNS server in version 4 comes with a graphical front-end and helpful wizards that you can use to quickly set up a DNS server.

Network Monitor

In the years that I've worked with PC networks (since 1985), one of the most desirable, sought-after, and *expensive* tools for network trouble-shooting has always been the network sniffer. Put simply, a *sniffer* turns your network cable figuratively into a "piece of glass," meaning that you can see everything that goes on in it. A full-blown network sniffer records every piece of data that goes back and forth on the net-work—a troubleshooter's dream and a security officer's nightmare. At one point, one network sniffer product was going for $18,000.

Microsoft has shipped a sniffer application called the Network Mon-itor as part of the Server Management System (SMS) for the past few years, but SMS is expensive and it really should have been part of NT Server from the start. In NT Server version 4, Microsoft fixes that by including a slightly dumbed-down version of the Network Monitor in NT Server.

Why "dumbed-down?" Because the full-blown version of Network Monitor tracks and records all data going on the network, and the ver-sion shipping with Server Management System still does that. The version of Network Monitor that ships with NT Server, in contrast, will only record network frames that either originate with or are destined for the particular server on which it is running. So, if you want to use Network Monitor to examine traffic from your server to machine X, and from machine X to your server, then you'll love the version that ships with NT Server; on the other hand, if you want use Network Monitor to examine traffic moving between machine X and machine Y, then you can't do that from your server (assuming that your server is neither machine X nor Y). Still, it's a neat tool, and you can learn more about it in Chapter 15, "Tuning and Monitoring NT Server."

Beyond Version 4: What You Can Expect

Microsoft isn't done with NT, not by a long shot. The year 1998 will probably see the release of another version of NT named "Cairo" with the following features:

- Cairo will include Plug and Play, thankfully.

- Part of every network is something called "name resolution," which converts friendly English-like names like MarksPC to low-level network addresses like 199.34.57.66. Most of the world uses something called the Domain Naming Service (DNS), but Microsoft for its own reasons uses a home-grown name resolver called the Windows Internet Naming Service. With Cairo, Microsoft surrenders and moves over to DNS.

- While you can currently build a complete top-to-bottom Internet using only NT, a few pieces aren't as filled out as would be nice. For example, there is no way to use NT machines to connect two geographically separated networks with modems or ISDN or the like, unless you connect the two networks and *leave* them connected. With Cairo, you'll be able to tell those two NT "router" machines to only connect with each other when necessary, allowing potential communications savings.

- Under Cairo, it will be possible to gather together groups of files from different hard disks, directories, and even different machines, but to put them all together to look like one unified drive or directory. This new system, called the "Object File System," will be a cornerstone of Cairo.

I hope that by now I've sparked some interest in learning how to use NT Server in networks great and small. Before going any further, however, we have to get some very important basic networking concepts out of the way—and I don't mean the "Ethernet versus token ring" stuff, I mean learning the particular terms that Microsoft uses when discussing networking. We do that in Chapter 2.

CHAPTER

TWO

Microsoft Enterprise Concepts

The first thing you've got to understand when you want to become an expert in any network is how the networking company *thinks*. Just as would-be Novell administrators must learn how the Novell Directory Services system works, or beginner Banyan administrators must learn what StreetTalk is, so also must new Microsoft network administrators learn all of the Microsoft networking lingo. It's something that you have to do even if you're an expert at some other network already, because every company that writes networking software has a different networking paradigm. (And you know what they say about paradigms—shift happens.) For example, Novell's networks have always been strongly oriented toward workstation/server architecture. In contrast, Microsoft's networks grew out of a peer-to-peer network approach, and they still have a bit of that flavor today.

So that's the goal of this chapter, to learn the basic concepts that you need in order to plan and manage a Microsoft network. I'll start out by building the simplest network possible. From there I'll be able to clarify why certain basic things about Microsoft networks are as they are. If you're already comfortable with concepts like Universal Naming Convention names, domains, workgroups, browse lists, and how NetBEUI is different from NetBIOS, then skip along to the next chapter. If not, stay with me a few pages, and in no time you'll become fluent in "speaking Microsoft."

Setting the Stage: A Primitive Microsoft Network

Basically, all networks allow you to share files and printers, and most of them nowadays let you build and use client-server systems as well.

Another thing that all networks have in common is that they soon get large and hard to manage if they're successful. How their creators choose to solve management problems is mainly what makes different brands of network software different, so let's start out with a simple circa 1985 Microsoft network, kind of a Mesozoic network. (I suppose on a network like that, you'd "Jurassic Park" the drive heads ... sorry, couldn't resist.)

Back in April of 1985, Microsoft shipped their first networking product, a tool called MS-NET. You couldn't buy MS-NET directly from Microsoft under that name, because Microsoft only sold it through other vendors, most prominently IBM. IBM sold it as the "IBM PC Network Program." Basically, it was just a bunch of programs that you'd load on a DOS PC to allow the PC to share its files with other PCs. It's still sold today, although in a considerably more jazzed-up form, as Artisoft's LANtastic package. Imagine an office with just two PCs, as you see in Figure 2.1.

Now, in our simple office, Jennifer's got more storage capacity on her machine than Joe does on his, but Joe's got the office laser printer attached to *his* PC. (It's there because he's bigger than she, and, as he could carry it to his desk, he got it, rapscallion that he is.) Each PC has

FIGURE 2.1

A simple
Microsoft network

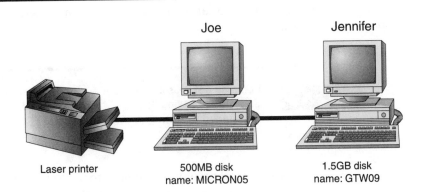

Joe   Jennifer

Laser printer   500MB disk
name: MICRON05   1.5GB disk
name: GTW09

an inventory control number, like MICRON05 or GTW09; that will be important soon.

Both Jennifer and Joe work on the office accounting system, so they need to share the accounting files—either that or they have to pass floppies around. Since Jennifer's got more disk space, they put the accounting files on her machine. So, the network problems that they have to solve are to

- Share Joe's printer with Jennifer, and

- Share Jennifer's disk with Joe.

Let's see how they solve their problem with a simplified Microsoft network. With this network, Jennifer just puts her hard disk on the network so that Joe can use it, and Joe puts his printer on the network so that Jennifer can use it.

Assigning Network Names

The first step in setting up a Microsoft network is to name the PCs, both servers and workstations. Then, you have to give a name to each user—Joe and Jennifer work fine for this network. We may as well name the PCs with their inventory numbers, so Jennifer's machine is named GTW09 and Joe's machine is named MICRON05. This leads me to a tip…

TIP PCs may get reassigned, so it's a bad idea to name machines after their users. Calling Joe's PC "JOESPC" could cause confusion if it's reassigned to someone else later.

In Microsoft networking there are machine names, user names, share names, and passwords—and they all have different rules about how long they can be and whether case matters or not.

NOTE Each PC's machine name can be no longer than 15 characters. Upper- and lowercase do not matter. You can have blanks in a machine's name, but I wouldn't recommend it because blanks will crash some setup programs.

Sharing File Directories on the Network

The first network task Jennifer and Joe set themselves to is getting Jennifer's hard disk onto the network so Joe can get to it. The two basic steps are (1) Jennifer must tell the network software on her computer that it's okay to offer her disk to the world in general, and (2) Joe must tell the network software on his computer that it should go out and exploit Jennifer's newly offered network resource.

Now, despite her obviously giving nature, Jennifer doesn't want Joe to get access to *everything* on the network, just some files that they share in her directory of accounting data, a directory called C:\ACCNTING. She wants to tell the network software, "Take the \ACCNTING subdirectory on my C: drive and offer it to anyone who wants it. Call it ACCT.'"

Understanding Share Names

ACCT is then called, in Microsoft enterprise networking terminology, the *share name* of the C:\ACCNTING directory on Jennifer's machine. It's the name that others will use to access the directory over the network. Jennifer *could* have called it ACCNTING, just like the directory name, but I gave it a different name just to underscore that it's not necessary to give a directory share the same name as its directory name. And since a share name is a new kind of name in Microsoft networking, let's take a second and mention the rules for creating share names.

So let's see, machine names can be 15 characters long and share names can be up to 12 characters long...

> **NOTE** Share names must be 12 characters or less. Case does not matter. You can use blanks, but it's not recommended.

Offering the Share on the Network

In a simple Microsoft network, the command that Jennifer would issue (after loading the network software, of course) would be

```
net share acct=c:\accnting
```

Now the network software running in Jennifer's machine (GTW09) knows that if anyone asks for a shared named ACCT, it should go ahead and share it.

> **NOTE** That particular "net share" command works with certain types of Microsoft network products (NT server and workstation, Windows for Workgroups, the Workgroups Add-On for MS-DOS, and LAN Manager) but not with all (Windows 95, for example). Be prepared for the fact that network commands in all Microsoft networking products are *similar,* but not always exactly the same.

Accessing a Shared Directory over the Network

Now Joe wants to use ACCT. Joe is, of course, running DOS, and DOS is pretty dumb when it comes to networks. DOS thinks that all data is stored on devices with names like A:, B:, C:, and so on. Now, the network software running on Joe's machine is built with the understanding that it's running on the network-challenged DOS, and so it fools DOS into letting Joe use network shares by giving network shares names like hard disks—names like D:, E:, and the like.

Joe then says to the networking software on his PC, "Attach me to the ACCT share on Jennifer's machine." Joe doesn't know whether ACCT is all of Jennifer's drive or just part of it. Joe's networking software then says something like, "You're now attached to ACCT on Jennifer's machine. It will appear to you as local drive D:."

The actual command that Joe would issue would look like this:

```
net use d: \\gtw09\acct
```

All those backslashes need some explaining, as they're very important. Better read on.

Introducing UNCs

Notice the \\GTW09\ACCT term; it's called a *universal naming convention* name, or a *UNC name*. You'll use UNCs again and again in NT networking, so let's pick that term apart. Also pay attention to this NET USE command; even though it's been around for a long time, it is still extremely useful even in modern Microsoft networking. It is one command-line networking command that you'll find in all Microsoft networking products (as far as I know).

First, the two backslashes are a warning that the name following is a *machine* name, and the backslash after that refers to the *share name* ACCT, rather than the directory name. Because Jennifer's machine, which owns the share, is named GTW09, and the share is named ACCT, the UNC for that share is \\GTW09\ACCT. Upper- and lowercase don't matter when you're working with UNCs, by the way.

Again, Joe doesn't really *have* a D: on his machine; he's just got network software that takes read and write requests for a mythical (logical) "drive D:" and reformulates those requests into network communication to Jennifer's machine.

Sharing a Printer on the Network

Joe now has access to Jennifer's disk and can clog it up with whatever garbage he likes. (Oddly enough, in Microsoft networking there is no notion of "disk quotas," the limitations on how much a user can dump into a share. There's no way for Jennifer to say, "Joe can use this share, but he can't put more than 10 megabytes of files in it." This weakness extends even to the most recent version of NT Server.) In return, however, Joe promised Jennifer that he'd let her use his printer over the network. So he must tell the network software on his PC to share the printer. Back in the MS-NET days, the command looked like

```
net share joeshp=LPT1:
```

This says, "Share the printer attached to LPT1:, giving it the share name of JOESHP.

> **NOTE** ○ I said a couple of lines ago, "Back in the MS-NET days..." because that syntax doesn't work with NT, so don't try it. It seems to only work in Windows for Workgroups, LAN Manager, and the Workgroups Add-on for MS-DOS. As I said before, the NET commands vary from Microsoft product to Microsoft product.

Jennifer then tells her networking software to attach JOESHP, on Joe's machine, to her LPT1: port, with the command

```
net use lpt1: \\micron05\joeshp
```

Picking that command apart, Jennifer has told her PC to look on a machine named MICRON05 for a share called JOESHP and to attach it to her LPT1:. From now on, whenever Jennifer tells an application program to print to a LaserJet on LPT1:, the network software will intercept the printed output and direct it over the network to Joe's machine. The networking software on Joe's machine will then print the information on Joe's printer.

By the way, remember when I said not to use blanks in names? Here's an example why. If Joe's machine were named Micron no. 5, Jennifer would have to put the UNC in quotes, like this:

```
net use lptl: "\\micron no. 5\joeshp"
```

And it's more than just an annoyance; several Microsoft setup utilities don't work properly when you ask them to set up over a network from a machine with a blank in its name.

Problems with the Primitive Network

Now, this is a nice network so far, as long as it never gets much bigger. But if it *does* get bigger, then there can be problems like these three:

- How did we know that Joe's LaserJet was called JOESHP, or that Jennifer's drive was called ACCT?

- What if Jennifer wants Joe to have access to *some* of the files in the shared directory, but not *all* of them?

- Once the network gets bigger—as other people want to join it— it will have to communicate with other networks. As different networks use different "languages," or, more correctly, *protocols*, how can our one network manage multiple kinds of networks with their multiple languages/protocols?

In short, the problem posed by the first question was solved by a Microsoft notion called a workgroup, the second problem is solved by another Microsoft notion called a domain, and the third problem is solved with Microsoft's layered structure of networking software. Those three topics will take up the rest of the chapter.

Who's Out There: Browsers and Workgroups

Years ago, I actually used an IBM PC Network program on a network like Jennifer and Joe's. As you saw with Joe and Jennifer, you hooked up to a drive on a server by saying to the PC Network program, for example, "Attach me to drive E: on the machine named AVOCADO." Nice and simple, but it had a major flaw: How did you find out in the first place that the server was named AVOCADO and that the drive that it was offering was called E:? The answer is, *you just had to know the name of the resource before you could use that resource.* There was no "scan the network to find out what's available" feature to the network. (An IBM guy once explained to me that this was "a security feature." Now, why didn't *I* think of that?)

I wanted a kind of "net scan" command, something that would shout to the other systems, "Hey! Whaddya got?" As it turns out, that's not very simple. The whole process of offering services on a network is part of what's known generically as *name services,* or *directory services,* and they're not easy to offer.

Solving the Directory Service Problem

How would you make a workstation know about every service on the network? There are several approaches.

Static Service Lists

The simplest approach would be to put a file with some kind of services database on every workstation, a kind of "yellow pages" of system capabilities. For example, you might have an ASCII file on every PC that says, "There is a file server on machine BIGPC with a shared disk called BIG-DISK, and the computer named PSRV has a shared printer called HP5SI."

This has the advantage of being very fast and very simple to understand. To add a new resource, just modify the service list file.

It has the *disadvantage*, however, of being static. Any changes to the system, and some poor fool (that would be *you*, the network administrator) has to go around to all the workstations and update the file. If there were two hundred workstations on your network, then you'd have to actually travel to all two hundred and copy that static service list file to each workstation's hard disk. Even worse, this method wouldn't take into account the services that were temporarily unavailable, such as a downed server.

This method sounds too primitive to use, but it's not completely useless. In NetWare 3.*x*, you identify yourself to your desired server via information in NET.CFG. That's a hard-wired server name, and would require a fair amount of editing on every workstation if you wanted to rename an important server—which is why, I suppose, you don't rename servers often in a NetWare world, and it's probably why Novell handles it differently in NetWare 4.

Periodic Advertising

Another approach is an occasional broadcast. Every 30 to 60 seconds (depending on how the network administrator sets it up), each resource on NetWare 3.11 tells the rest of the network about itself by shouting, "I'm here!" Novell calls this the Service Advertising Protocol (SAP). This is another very good idea and it works great in many cases.

It's not the perfect answer, however. Its problem is that broadcasts can clog up a network if that network has a fair number of servers, all advertising. (Imagine if every store in the U.S. were to remind you that it exists *every minute or so*—you'd spend so much time responding to advertising that you'd get nothing else done, and your mailbox would be full.) Periodic advertising works on small to medium-size LANs, but on larger networks it is unworkable due to the sheer number of broadcasts flooding the net.

Furthermore, those advertisements probably wouldn't be able to travel around an enterprise network due to *routers*. Most networks of any size are divided up into *segments*, and the segments are connected with devices called routers. In general, routers carry messages from one segment to another, when necessary; they're smart enough to avoid retransmitting messages unnecessarily. That's good because it means that routers cut down on network congestion.

The problem that routers pose to periodic advertisements is that routers do not in general retransmit broadcasts; a SAP broadcast in one segment generally isn't heard on any other segment. I say "generally" because you can configure most routers to retransmit broadcasts, but you usually don't want to do that because it defeats the congestion-reducing aspect of routers. Anyway, the result of periodic advertising on most networks would be that a server's advertisements would only be visible to workstations within its local segment.

Larger networks, then, need some other method of spreading the news about services.

Name Servers

ENTERPRISE
NETWORKING

Yet another approach, and the one used by most enterprise network products, is to assign the task of keeping track of network services to one or more computers called *name servers*. Servers identify themselves to these name servers, and the name servers keep a list of the servers that they know of as well as the shares offered by each of those servers. Each segment gets its own name server, and the name servers know of one another and compare notes about what's available. Because the name servers talk to one another in one-to-one directed communications rather than broadcasts, routers are no longer an obstacle to making an entire large network aware of a given server's services.

A machine that's acting as a name server usually isn't dedicated to that task; usually it's also a file server. Particular machines become name servers when a network administrator installs name server software on them. Setting up name servers is a bit more work for a network administrator, which is about the only downside of a name server.

Microsoft's Answer: Browse Services

Microsoft decided (perhaps rightly) that name servers were hard to set up, but that something like a name server was essential, so Microsoft networking uses a kind of name server system where you, the network administrator, don't have to do *anything*; the name servers set themselves up automatically.

Microsoft doesn't have a "name service" per se; the Microsoft name for name services is "browse services." What most of the network world would call name servers Microsoft calls *browse masters* or *master browsers*. A search of the April 1996 TechNet CD shows 53 occurrences of "master browser" and 41 occurrences of "browse master," so I guess either name is correct. What's different about the Microsoft browse servers concept is that no one computer is fixed as the browse master. Instead, when your computer logs on to your network, it finds a browse master by broadcasting a request for a browse master and saying, "Are there any browse masters out there?" The first browse master to hear the workstation (there can be multiple browse masters, as you'll see) responds to the workstation by saying, "Just direct all your name service requests to me."

When a server starts up, it does the same thing. It broadcasts, "Are there any browse masters out there?," and when it finds one, it says to it, "I am a server with the following shares. Please add me to your list of servers." The list of servers that a browse master maintains is called the *browse list*, not surprisingly.

By now, you may be wondering, "How come I've never seen one of these browse lists?" You have. If you ever work with earlier versions of NT or with Windows for Workgroups, then you saw Figure 2.2 when you opened up the File Manager and clicked Disk/Connect Network Drive.

FIGURE 2.2

Sample browse list from
Windows for Workgroups
or Windows NT version 3.x

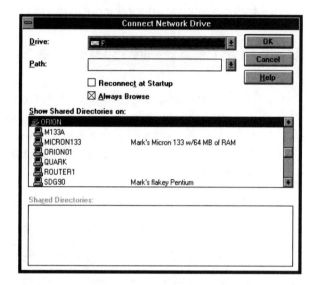

From Windows 95 or Windows NT 4, you can see a browse list by opening up the Network Neighborhood folder, as in Figure 2.3.

From DOS, you can see a browse list by typing

`net view or net view` *machinename*

You see a screen like the one in Figure 2.4.

FIGURE 2.3

Sample browse list
from Windows NT 4 or
Windows 95

FIGURE 2.4

Sample browse list
from DOS

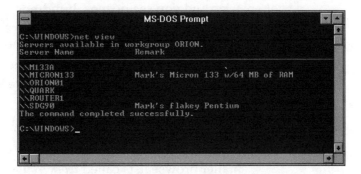

Each figure shows you the list of servers available: M133A, Orion01, Router1, and SDG90. Other servers—Micron133 and Quark—appear only in some of the browse lists because a few minutes passed between taking the screen shots, and a few "test" servers went up or down in those few minutes. In all three cases, the workstations that these screens were taken from got their browse lists from a local browse master.

You can drill down further into these browse lists as well. In Windows 95 or Windows NT 4, you can double-click on any one of those servers and see the list of shares that the servers offer; that, too, is information from the browse list. In Windows for Workgroups or Windows NT 3.x, you'd just click once on a server, and the list of its shares would appear in the bottom pane of the dialog box. From DOS, you'd get the list of servers by typing **net view**, as you've already seen, and then you get the list of shares for any given server by typing **net view ** *servername*, where *servername* is the name of the server you want to see the shares of.

When Browse Lists Get Too Large: Workgroups to the Rescue

As I've described them so far, browse lists seem pretty convenient. But in the little test network that I used for the previous screen shots, you saw only a few servers. Hell, *everything* works fine on *small* networks.

Now let's talk about *your* network. Sit down at a corporate network of any size and you see dozens, hundreds, or *thousands* of servers. Scrolling down through a 500-server browse list would be a bit time-consuming—to say nothing of how much work the browse master would have to do to keep it up to date! The problem to solve is, then, managing the size of the browse list. There are two ways to do that:

- Reduce the number of servers in your enterprise, and

- Divide up the enterprise-wide browse list into a number of smaller browse lists called *workgroups*.

Disable Peer-to-Peer Sharing on Workstations

The first answer is actually a bit off the main topic, but let me digress for a moment and talk about it before returning to the main item, workgroups. When I say "reduce the number of servers," I'm talking about an unfortunate side-effect of running Windows for Workgroups, Windows 95, and Windows NT workstations—they all have the capability to become peer-to-peer servers. The browse masters don't distinguish between industrial-strength servers running NT Server and low-octane peer-to-peer servers, so you could end up with a browse list that's *supposed* to only list your servers, but *actually* lists all of your servers and workstations. In general, I think peer-to-peer networking is a bad idea. If a piece of data is important enough to be used by two employees, then it's a company asset that should be backed up regularly and so should go on a managed file server, not a desktop machine that's probably backed up once a decade. My recommendation is this: disable the peer-to-peer sharing option on your Windows for Workgroups, Windows 95, and Windows NT workstations. Not only will your network have less traffic—every workstation will no longer have delusions of serverdom, so they won't be chattering at the browse master all of the time—but not loading the server part of the workstation's operating system saves RAM on the workstation.

Divide the Browse List Up into Workgroups to Keep it Manageable

The other approach to keeping a browse list to a manageable size is to subdivide it in some way. That's a reasonable thing to suggest if you realize that, no matter how large an organization *seems* to be, it's usually composed of lots of smaller groups, such as Manufacturing, Sales, Marketing, Accounting, Finance, Personnel, Senior Management, and so on. Each of those groups can be called "workgroups" and you can pretty much chop up your enterprise into workgroups in any way you like (but a rule of thumb says that a workgroup should be a group of people for whom 95 percent of the data generated by that group stays within that group).

From a more network-technical point of view, the minimum definition of a workgroup is just *a group of workstations that share a browse list*. (That's my definition, not Microsoft's.) The idea is that when someone in Accounting opens up her browse list, you want her to see just the Accounting servers, not the Manufacturing servers, as she's got no use for the Manufacturing servers. (Besides, there's a good chance that she doesn't have permission to access the Manufacturing servers anyway— but I'll get to workgroups and security in a little bit.)

> **NOTE** Workgroup names are like machine names, and can be up to 15 characters long.

So, to review what we've seen so far:

- Network browse lists allow a user at a workstation to see all of the servers on the network, and from there to see all of the shares on a given server.

- Browse lists can get fairly long, so you can partition your entire network into *workgroups*, which are just groups of people that share a browse list.

- When you request a browse list, you don't get the entire list of servers in your enterprise network, you only get the list of servers within your workgroup.

- Each workgroup has one or more servers that act as gatherers of browse information. They're called browse masters or master browsers, and they're picked automatically.

- Machines that are only workstations and don't act as servers even in a peer-to-peer capacity do not appear on browse lists.

As the question of what machines go on a browse list and what machines don't is important to the length of a browse list, let me list the kinds of machines that can act as servers in a Microsoft enterprise network:

- Windows 3.x (with the Workgroup Add-On for MS-DOS clients)

- DOS (with Workgroup Add-On for MS-DOS clients)

- Windows for Workgroups

- Windows 95

- NT workstation

- NT Server

As it's an unusual product, let me just explain that the Workgroup Add-On for MS-DOS is a separate Microsoft product that lets you use a DOS machine as a peer-to-peer server. Again, I recommend that you disable file and print sharing on all of these machines except, of course, for the machines dedicated to the task of being servers, all of which are probably running NT Server.

And once you're in a workgroup, you'll no doubt want to see your browse list; "How do I View a Browse List" tells you the specifics.

How Do I Join a Workgroup?

Generally, all you need to do is to just tell the networking software on your workstations and servers that they're members of a given workgroup. There isn't any "security" in being part of a workgroup—you pretty much just declare yourself a member and you are a member. (As a matter of fact, if you misspell the name of the workgroup, you end up accidentally founding a whole new workgroup all by yourself, which I'm sure was not your intention!)

Specifically, you designate which workgroup you're a member of in one of the following ways:

- **From a DOS or Windows for Workgroups workstation** In the [network] section of the SYSTEM.INI file you'll find a WORK-GROUP= parameter. (You'll have a SYSTEM.INI even if you're just running DOS because the network client software creates one.) You can also set the workgroup from the MS-DOS Network Client Setup program, or in the Windows for Workgroups's Network applet of the Control Panel.

- **From Windows 95** Open the Control Panel and double-click on the Networks Icon. In the property sheet that you see, click the Identification tab. You see the place to fill in the workgroup name.

- **On Windows NT 3.*x*** Open the Control Panel and double-click the Networks applet. You'll see a button labeled Domain or Workgroup. (NT has a kind of confusing way of blurring workgroups and domains, which I'll make clearer later in this chapter.) Click that button, and you can change the workgroup you're a member of. Again, NT complicates choosing a workgroup somewhat, so read the rest of this chapter if you want to change an NT workgroup.

- **On Windows NT 4** Open the Control Panel and double-click on the Network applet. Like Windows 95, Windows NT 4 has a property sheet with an Identification tab. Click on Change to change the workgroup. Again, with NT you may see no references to workgroups at all; instead you see references to domains. Read on to understand the differences.

How Do I View a Browse List?

 Microsoft has built different browse programs into its different network client software.

- **From DOS**   Type **net view**. That shows you the list of servers. You can view the shares on a given server by typing **net view \\\\server-name.** To see the browse list for a workgroup other than your own, type **net view /workgroup:***workgroupname*.

- **From Windows for Workgroups** *or* **Windows NT 3.***x*   Open up the File Manager, click Drive and then Connect Network Drive. You'll see a window with two panes. The browse list for your workgroup and a list of the other workgroups on the network appears as the list of possible servers in the top pane and, when you click on a server, that server's shares appear in the bottom pane. To see the browse list for a workgroup other than your own, double-click on the name of the workgroup in the top pane.

- **From Windows 95 or Windows NT 4**   Open up the Network Neighborhood folder. You'll see the servers in your workgroup represented as PC icons in a folder. Double-click on one of the servers, and a folder will open up showing you the shares. To see the browse list for a workgroup other than your own, double-click on the Entire Network icon and you'll see a list of workgroups. On Windows NT 4, you click on "Entire Network" and then Microsoft Network, and then you'll get a list of the other workgroups.

Security in a Workgroup

When it comes to security and workgroups, I'm tempted to shorten this entire section down to a few words: "There isn't any." But it's a bit more complex than that....

I made a passing reference to security a few paragraphs back when I suggested that not only would an Accounting user not want to see the servers in Manufacturing, but also that The Powers That Be in the Manufacturing network might not *want* the Accounting user to see the servers in Manufacturing. Security is important—it's essential—in every network, even Jennifer and Joe's network. For example, suppose after a while Joe finds that he doesn't want everyone in the world using his laser printer. He has discovered that every time someone prints a document on his machine, his computer slows down as a result because, after all, the very act of being a print server takes up a fair amount of Joe's CPU time. He wants *some* people to be able to get the printer, but not *most* people. What should he do? There are two possible answers in a workgroup:

- He could hide his laser printer, sharing it but keeping it off the browse list.

- He could put a password on his laser printer.

Hiding Shares in Microsoft Networks

Joe can share his printer but hide it from the browse list by putting a dollar sign ($) at the end of its name. For example, if in sharing his printer he didn't name it "joeshp," but rather "joeshp$," then *the printer share would not show up on the browse list*. Someone could still get to it, but she'd have to know the name of the printer, as she couldn't get it off the browse list if she forgot. Other than that, you attach to a hidden share in the usual way—Jennifer would now type **net use lpt1: \\micron05\joeshp$** rather than **net use lpt1: \\micron05\joeshp**, as she did before.

> **NOTE**
>
> Here's an example of why knowing the command-line versions of the networking commands (rather than only knowing how to get to the network via the graphical user interface) is essential—the "net use" command is one way to attach to a hidden share from Windows 95 or NT Workstation 4 machine. (Other ways are via Disk/Connect to Network Drive in NT 3.*x* or Tools/Map to Network Drive in the Explorer under NT 4.)

Password-Protecting Shares in Microsoft Networks

Clearly, hiding a share and trying to keep the existence of joeshp$ a secret is not exactly great security, but it's a sort of minimum way to keep other people off your printer or directory share. The other way to secure a share is by putting a password on it. Exactly *how* you do that depends on what kind of server you're using. Some Microsoft networking systems let you create user-specific passwords, and others only offer you the ability to put a single share on a password, which is then the password for *all* users.

Let's first look at the server products that only let you put a single password on a share. (This includes the Workgroup Add-on for MS-DOS, Windows for Workgroups, and, optionally, Windows 95.) The problem with putting a single password on a share is that it's the *same* password for *all* of the share's users. (Remember that "share" generically means "shared printer" or "shared disk directory.") If you wanted to exclude one current user, you could only do it by first changing the password, then finding every one of the other printer's users and telling them the password.

How NT Improves upon Workgroup Security

Now let's see how NT handles security in a workgroup. When you set up a Windows NT computer, the setup program asks you if you want to use workgroup-level security or "domain"-level security. I'll discuss domain-level security later in this chapter and setting up in the next chapter, but for the moment let's look at how NT brings its own twist to the *workgroup* security that you've met so far.

As you've already read, you can still hide a share under NT by suffixing a dollar sign on the end of its name; that's no different from any other Microsoft networking product. What *is* different about workgroup security under NT is that NT lets you separate security information *by user*, rather than only letting you set a single password on a share for all of that share's users. This is one way in which NT is fundamentally different from Windows for Workgroups and Windows 95. On DOS, Windows, and Windows 95, those earlier operating systems don't maintain separate user accounts.

For example, suppose you've got a small network, so small that you've decided to use a Windows 95 machine as your "server" (can't you just see the sneer when I write that?). Suppose in a fit of originality you call it SERVER and create a disk share called DISKSHARE. You then have a bunch of workstations running DOS with some network software added to it, like Windows for Workgroups or Windows 95. You hire a new employee named Gertrude who sits down at a workstation, starts up the network software, and does a **net use e: \\server\diskshare**, which of course attaches her to the Windows 95 machine that acts as the "server." SERVER asks her for DISKSHARE's password, which is (for example) "swordfish," and since Gertrude and the rest of the office know that the password is "swordfish," she types in **swordfish** and she's in.

Notice that you never had to "introduce" a user named Gertrude to the server. Anyone who knows the password "swordfish" can attach to the server. *That's* where NT is different, even with a workgroup. Now suppose we re-run the above scenario, but this time, instead of using a Windows 95 machine as the server, let's use an NT Workstation machine with workgroup-level security.

You create the shares as before, but you do not put passwords on the shares. Instead, you must first use a program called the User Manager to create a user account for each person who will access the shares on this server. Then, you go to the shares and explicitly name the people who can access which shares. Now if you want to access an NT machine on a workgroup, you must have been properly introduced—so Gertrude isn't going *anywhere* until you (1) create a Gertrude account on the NT Workstation machine and (2) add Gertrude to the list of approved users for DISKSHARE. Gertrude then must use her name and password to get onto the NT machine, even if she's communicating with the server from a DOS or Windows workstation.

NOTE
Now that I've introduced user names, I should tell you that user names can be up to 20 characters long. According to Microsoft, passwords can in theory be up to 128 characters long, but the program that you use to create user accounts—the User Manager, which you'll meet in a later chapter—only lets you type in 14 characters. To summarize: machine names and workgroup names can be up to 15 characters long, share names up to 12 characters long, user names up to 20 characters long, and passwords up to 14 characters long. Bizarre, eh?

All this talk of user accounts and user-specific abilities sounds a bit more strict, doesn't it? That's how NT is "Security" is its middle name, so to speak. It also sounds like there's not much more you could want in terms of security, right? Well, not exactly, which is why understanding domains is fundamental to understanding how to build a good NT-based network. And while I've been keeping you waiting about domains for a while now, I've got to cover *one* more thing before we get to domains.

Keeping One Workgroup from Peeking into Another's Shares

Before moving on to domains, let's cover an important aspect of NT networking that many people consider a real security breach, but that you can't do anything about. It applies to *all* Microsoft enterprise networks, whether built with workgroups or domains.

Let's return to our accountant who normally only sees the ACCOUNTING browse list. There is another workgroup on the same enterprise network called MANUFACTURING, and let's suppose that the manager of the MANUFACTURING workgroup doesn't want those accountants seeing *anything* about manufacturing's network. Now, supposing our accountant is bored one day, and wants to see if she can peek into some manufacturing files. To do that, she has to do the following:

1. Find out the workgroup name of the manufacturing department.

2. Find out the names of the servers in that workgroup.

3. Retrieve a list of shares on those servers.

4. Actually access one of the shares.

How hard is it to do that? The first two steps are pretty easy; the last two can be a bit more difficult. Retrieving the names of the workgroups on your network is easy, as the browse lists show you not only your workgroup, but also the names of the other workgroups. Remember, the name servers (browse masters) all talk to one another. The only browse program that I know of that does not show other workgroups is the one built into the DOS redirector; the "net view" command only shows you your workgroup, and I haven't been able to figure out how to make it show me the names of the other workgroups.

Second, once she knows that the name of the other workgroup is MANUFACTURING, then all she has to do is to ask for its browse list. In the graphical browse lists that are part of NT, Windows for Workgroups, and Windows 95, it's just a matter of clicking. On DOS, again, if she figured out a way to get the workgroup name and typed **net view /workgroup:**workgroupname, she would get the list of servers in that workgroup.

> **NOTE**
>
> Note one deficiency of browse lists: there's no easy way to find out which of the "servers" that you see are truly servers, and which are just workstations that have the ability to do peer-to-peer networking.

Now that she's got the list of servers, she drills down to the share list for each server. Ah, but here our intruder may run into some trouble. Double-click on an NT machine (workstation or server) and the NT machine will say to the intruder's workstation, "Who wants to know what shares I've got?" The intruder's workstation then automatically and invisibly replies with the user's name and password. The NT machine then checks that against the list of names and passwords that it knows. If there's a match, then she gets the browse list. If not, then she either gets a message like "System error 5 has occurred; access is denied" or simply "Access is denied," or she gets a dialog box that says something like (I'm being vague because every operating system handles it differently) "Incorrect password or unknown username," with the chance to type in a new user name and password.

Here is the question, then. We have an unrecognized individual who requests that the browse list show her the list of shares on a server. Does she get the list? The extremely specific, 100-percent complete answer is pretty lengthy, but the basic conditions are

- If the server is a Windows for Workgroups machine, it always gives out the list of its shares to anyone.

- If the server is a Windows 95 machine that employs share-level password authentication for its shares, then it always gives out the share list.

- If the server is a Windows 95 machine that employs user-level password authentication, then it only gives out its share list if the server that it gets its user names from recognizes the user.

- If the server is a Windows NT machine and its Guest account is enabled, then it always gives out its share list.

- If the server is a Windows NT machine and you're logged into your workstation with a user name and password that match a known user name and password on the Windows NT machine, even if you're currently a member of a different workgroup (or domain), then you get the share list.

Finally, if the intruder from Accounting tries to actually access a share, she will only be successful if she's got the permissions to access that share.

To review the facts about browsing and security:

- Anyone who's physically attached to your network can find out the names of your workgroups (and domains, actually).

- Anyone who's physically attached to your network can retrieve the list of servers on any workgroup.

- Someone who's physically attached to your network may or may not be able to see the list of shares on a given server. Basically, Windows for Workgroups and Windows 95 "servers" give out their share list to anyone, but Windows NT machines must know you before they do that.

I know I had to be a bit fuzzy on some of this, but it will make more sense when we get to domains, the next topic in this chapter.

Domains: Centralized Security

You've already seen that you could set up a network with an NT Server machine and a workgroup. You'd just install NT Server on a computer, declare it a member of workgroup XYZ, and create a user account for each user. Then you'd create directory and printer shares on that server, and designate which users can access what shares. So far, so good. What do domains do for us, then?

Well, not a heck of a lot … until you want to add another server.

Multiple Servers Means Multiple User Accounts

You see, you've got to build each user on each NT server or workstation in a workgroup. (Remember that there's no such thing as a user account for DOS, Windows for Workgroups, or Windows 95.) Just to make this clear, suppose you had users named John, Mary, Sue, Paul, and Ignatz in your workgroup, two NT Servers named S1 and S2, and an NT Workstation named W1. (There's DOS, Windows for Workgroups, and Windows 95 workstations here also, but they don't matter for this example, as they don't maintain user accounts on each mainframe.) Suppose also that there are shares on S1, S2, and W1 that everyone will need to get to. To set up *this* network, there are a few more steps:

1. Install NT Server on S1 and S2, and NT Workstation on W1. Make sure they all describe themselves as being members of workgroup XYZ.

2. In the process of installing S1, S2, and W1, you have to create an Administrator account which, as you'd expect, has powers and abilities far beyond those of normal users. Each Administrator account is only an Administrator account recognized at its particular computer, so you'll end up with three distinct accounts, one on each machine. That also means that you may have chosen to give them all different passwords, so you need to somehow keep track of those three passwords.

3. Go to S1, log on as Administrator using the Administrator password for S1, and create users John, Mary, Sue, Paul, and Ignatz.

4. Go to S2, log on as S2's Administrator using the Administrator password for S2, and create users John, Mary, Sue, Paul, and Ignatz—and, of course, *these* user accounts are totally separate and distinct from the ones you just created on S1, so you could end up with different passwords.

5. Go to W2, log on as W1's Administrator using the Administrator password for W1, and create users John, Mary, Sue, Paul, and Ignatz—and, of course, *these* user accounts are totally separate and distinct from the ones you just created on S1 and S2, so you could end up with different passwords.

Multiple User Accounts Means Multiple Logins

Now suppose John fires up his Windows 95 workstation first thing in the morning and grabs his e-mail, which is sitting on S2. When he first tries to attach to the directory that holds the e-mail, S2 stops and says, "Should I let this guy get to my directory?" It then asks John for a user name and password. He complies, and all is well. Then, a little later, John needs something from S1. This is the first time today that S1 has seen John, and so S1 challenges him for a user name and password. John's an organized kind of guy, so he's got the user name and password that he uses for S1 right at his fingertips. He'll have to do the same thing if ever he tries to get data from W1—he'll need another user name and password.

Local Password Files

Microsoft network client software simplifies this process a bit with files called *password lists*. They're distinguished by the extension PWL. Every time you type in a user name and/or password at the request of a server, your local workstation software remembers it for you, and stores it in this PWL file. Then, all you have to do is identify yourself to your workstation once in the morning, and from there the workstation software automatically responds to any user name or password challenges that a server makes. But PWL files don't follow you around the network, so you have to repeat the process every time you log on to a new workstation. In addition, some people don't like the idea of having all of their passwords stored on their local hard disk, even if they *are* encrypted. Worse yet, in the mid-90s, some Windows 95 users figured out how to crack PWL files, so many companies forbid their use.

One Answer: Multiple User Accounts, One Password

For security's sake, then, it's best to tell your workstation software not to create PWL files, which means we're back to typing in a slew of passwords and user names each and every day. Is there an easier way? Well, yes, kind of. If the network administrator sets it up so that John has the same user name and password on all three servers, then the first time each day that John types in his name and password, that information is cached by his workstation and, the next time he tries to connect to a server, the workstation offers that user name and password to that second (or third or whatever) server. If all of the servers that John uses all see him as a user named "John" with password "hassenpfeffer," then he need only log on to one server explicitly, and all subsequent logons that day will be automatic.

This *kind of* works, but it surely means that password-changing day will be a busy one for John—and for every other user, for that matter. And that's just with three servers; this scheme would be unworkable with more than that.

Let's see, now… So far, with just three servers and five users, you could have up to 18 different passwords, and each user must remember at least three passwords.

The main problem here seems to be that every server insists on handling its own security. Why not designate one server to handle all of the user validations? We've met print servers, file servers, and name servers. Why not a *security* server? That's the whole idea of a domain. A domain is basically a "super workgroup," a workgroup with centralized control of security. Figure 2.5 shows a simple workgroup, for comparison's sake.

Just to keep things simple, I've diagrammed a workgroup with several servers, each of which some imaginary user uses the password "swordfish," "fred," or "secret" to access. You or your workstation must remember a whole bunch of passwords.

Domains: One Account, One Password, Many Servers

In a domain, in contrast, you need only remember one password—the password for your domain account, as you see in Figure 2.6.

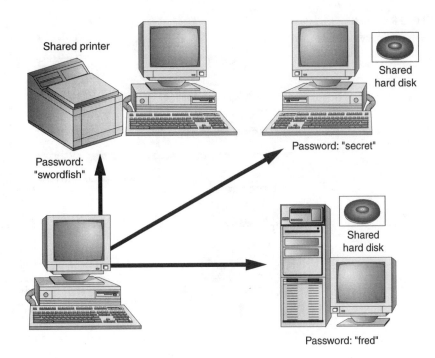

FIGURE 2.5

Workgroup security relationships

Shared printer

Shared hard disk

Password: "secret"

Password: "swordfish"

Shared hard disk

Password: "fred"

Domains Need Domain Controllers

Domains are groups of NT machines—DOS, Windows for Workgroups, and Windows 95 machines can't join a domain—that delegate all of their security tasks to one or more machines called *domain controllers*. One machine is called the *primary domain controller*. It maintains a central database of users, passwords, and things that those users are allowed to do. Other machines are called *backup domain controllers* and basically all they do is share the work of verifying user authentication requests. With workgroups, you didn't need any central machine; one computer merely declaring itself a member of workgroup XYZ was sufficient to bring workgroup XYZ into being. But you can't have a domain until you've got a computer designated as the primary domain controller for that domain.

FIGURE 2.6

Domain security
relationships

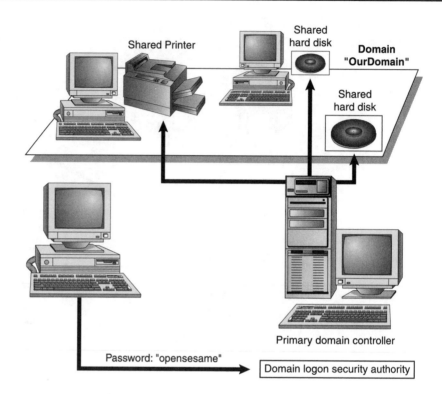

Domain Controllers Keep a Security Database

The primary domain controller holds the Security Access Manager (SAM) database. The program that reads the database is called in some Microsoft documents the "domain logon security authority." The NT servers and workstations that have chosen to join a domain look to the domain controllers to verify access. For example, suppose W1 has joined a domain in which S1 is the primary domain controller. Now, when John tries to access a share named FILES on W1, W1 says to S1, "Can John have access to this share?" S1 first checks if John is a valid user, asking John for a user name and a password. Assuming that John gives S1 a valid name and password, S1 then looks at the SAM entries for John. There is an entry for every share on every machine that has joined S1's domain. S1 looks up the share FILES on machine W1 in the SAM (and the SAM resides physically *on* the primary domain controller, which is S1 in this case) and sees that John is allowed to access FILES. S1 tells that to W1, and W1 gives John access to the files.

A Simple Domain Setup

Let's compare how to set up domain XYZ to the earlier description of how to set up workgroup XYZ:

1. When you install the NT Server machines, choose one to be a domain controller. Only NT Server machines can be domain controllers, and you have to make an NT Server machine a domain controller when you first install the NT Server software (you can't make a machine a domain controller later on without completely reinstalling the NT Server software). Suppose you choose to make S1 the domain controller. Because the first domain controller in every domain is by definition the primary domain controller, S1 is the domain controller. The primary domain controller designates the name of the domain, and that's where you'd say that the name of the domain is XYZ.

> **NOTE**
> You *can* choose to make each NT Server a domain controller. If you do that, you have to designate the second domain controller a backup domain controller because only one machine per domain can be a primary domain controller.

2. S1 will still be a file and print server, as it was before; the duty of the domain controller probably won't eat up too much CPU time. S2 and W1 get installed as before, *except* that they will get a chance to *either* join a workgroup *or* a domain. They should opt to join the domain named XYZ.

3. Domains automatically offer all of the browsing services that workgroups offer, so the dumber workstations—the DOS, Windows for Workgroups, and Windows 95 workstations—should all declare that they are members of the *workgroup* XYZ. Why workgroup rather than domain? Because these operating systems aren't built to exploit the centralized security features of a domain. The only real benefit that they get from joining "workgroup" XYZ is that they will be able to use the browse lists generated by the servers in both domain XYZ and workgroup XYZ; the NT servers will show up on their browse lists.

4. On S1, create user accounts for John, Mary, Sue, Paul, and Ignatz. This is the only time you'll have to create user accounts for them.

Then suppose Mary starts up her workstation, a Windows for Workgroups machine. At some point in the day she ends up doing something that attracts the attention of S1, the primary domain controller. That something could be either trying to access a share on S1, S2, or W1, or trying to explicitly log on to the XYZ domain. *Note* that merely requesting the browse list for workgroup XYZ will not attract the domain's attention, nor will asking for the share list of one of the non-NT machines (unless it's a 95 machine using user-level security access). Trying to retrieve the share list of S1, S2, or W1—one of the machines that are members of the domain—will also count as "attracting the domain's attention." Mary will have to be recognized by the domain before she'll get that share list. "Recognized by the domain" means, again, either that she should have explicitly logged onto the domain by now, or, if she hasn't, then the domain will probably ask her for a password. ("Probably" because the exact behavior depends on which operating system her workstation is using. Some just reject the request, others display a dialog box that requests a password.)

A domain, then, is just a collection of NT machines that share a "security server," or primary domain controller. The PDC keeps the database of users and user permissions, and any NT machine that has joined the domain may avail itself of the PDC's database of user permissions. If a large number of servers are on a network, then a network administrator may "deputize" some or all of those servers to be *backup domain controllers* (BDCs), machines that can respond to authentication requests. The PDC replicates its user database to the BDCs at a particular interval (five minutes by default, but you can change it.)

What complicates a domain a bit is that it also acts as a workgroup. In my XYZ example, remember that only the NT machines could join the XYZ domain and share in the centralized security services, but *any* machine could join the XYZ *workgroup*, which automatically includes the XYZ domain members in itself.

The notion of a domain is the foundation upon which Microsoft enterprise networks are built. You'll learn more details about domain management in Chapters 10 and 11, on the Server Manager program and on multi-domain management.

Network Citizens: Users and Machines

I've discussed the first and second problems that I posed—how we keep track of available network resources automatically and how we manage security—and I'll get to the third question in a few pages. First, however, let me digress a bit about the things that make up a Microsoft enterprise network, *users* and *machines*.

Users in a Microsoft Enterprise Network

A user is just a person who uses the network. Each user has a *user account*, a small database record of information about that user. At minimum, a user account includes information like this:

- User name

- User password

- Use restrictions or, more formally, user *permissions* and *rights*

The actual meaning of "user account" here is a bit nebulous if your network consists only of simple workgroups; "user account" is a more important piece of information for a user in a domain.

The user account is part of a file called SAM (Security Account Manager) in your primary domain controller's SYSTEM32\CONFIG directory. That file is part of the *Registry*, which you'll learn more about in Chapter 5. Basically the Registry is a central database of information about the network system itself, its applications, and its users.

User Rights and Permissions

Every network has its own terminology that it uses to describe how it protects its data from its users. In the NT Server world, we talk of rights and permissions.

A *right* is the ability to do a particular thing, like back up data on the file server—a security risk, as whoever is doing the backups could also abscond with them—or log on to the server, whether via the network (not much of a security risk) or locally at the server (a much greater risk). Rights are the difference between administrators and users.

A *permission* is simply a grant of access to a printer, a directory, a file, or some other network resource. There are different levels of access—read-only, execute-only, read/write, and so on—and they can be applied on a file-by-file, user-by-user basis.

Groups

Of course, setting specific permissions for specific users can be tedious and time-consuming. That's why NT Server offers *groups*. Groups let you assign common rights and permissions to collections of users.

Examples of groups of users include:

- Administrators, which have a lot of control over the network

- Users, which have areas over which they have a lot of control, but no control over the administration of the network

- "Enterprise" administrators (Domain Admins), administrators with control over several domains

Those are by no means the only possible groups—they're just examples. For example, suppose you had a single server shared by two departments, the biology researchers and the chemical researchers. Each user has her own area. Meanwhile, the biology researchers have a common area that they want other biologists to be able to access, but that they don't want anyone else to be able to get to. The chemical researchers, likewise, have a common area of their own that they want to keep biologists from getting into.

Instead of just making all of the researchers "users," you can create a group called Biology and another called Chemistry. You'd start off by copying the user rights and permissions from the generic Users group into the two new groups, then you could give the Biology group access to the shared biology area, and *deny* them access to the shared chemistry area. The Chemistry group, similarly, could be granted access to their area and denied access to the biology area.

User Characteristics

We'll mainly be concerned in this book with the *networking* implications of NT, but it's worthwhile taking a quick look at how NT handles users who physically log on to an NT workstation or NT Server.

If you use Windows, then you're accustomed to being able to set your machine's colors, wallpaper, video drivers, and the like. With NT workstations in a domain, however, the notion of "my machine" fades a bit, as the security information on you is, you recall, kept on a central repository.

Settings on NT machines are either user-specific or machine-specific. The user-specific settings include:

- Colors

- Wallpaper

- Mouse settings

- Cursors

- Personal groups

- Persistent network connections

User names are one of the most important characteristics that the network keeps track of for a user. A user name can be up to 20 characters long. Passwords can actually be 128 characters long, sort of. According to Microsoft Knowledge Base Article Q109927, an NT password can be up to 128 characters long, but the User Manager only accepts passwords of up to 14 characters.

Machine Types: Servers, Messengers, Receivers, and Redirectors

In the Microsoft networking world, a server or a workstation can exhibit four kinds of capabilities: redirector, receiver, messenger, or server. These capabilities can appear in combinations. Following is a discussion of each of these network roles.

Redirector   The redirector capability allows software running on your workstation to intercept (redirect) requests for data from network drive letters and printer ports and convert them into network I/O requests. You need a unique user name and machine on the network. A machine running redirector software can request data from a server—that is, it can *initiate* a communication with a server. However, it cannot receive or act upon a *request* from a server. A server can't, so to speak, tap a redirector on the shoulder and hand it a message. You might say that a redirector can talk, but it can't listen.

Receiver   The receiver has redirector capabilities, but can also receive messages forwarded from a computer set up as a messenger. It's an old and basically obsolete type of network citizen, but you see a reference to it now and then.

Messenger   The messenger module sends and receives messages from administrators or from the Alerter service. Messages like print job notification or imminent server shutdown are examples of messages that require the messenger service. While it sounds a bit circular-defining, the main value of supporting the messenger service is that you can then receive SMB messenger-type blocks from other networked machines. Messenger service is supported via broadcast datagrams. Messenger service uses your user name and your workstation name in the NetBIOS name table, with a hex 03 appended to the end of each name. Messenger service will also support forwarding messages from one workstation to another. In that case, the name has a hex 05 appended to its NetBIOS name and that name type is called a *type 5 name*.

Server   Server refers to service that allows a device to accept requests from another computer's redirector. It supports remote procedure calls (RPCs), file and print sharing, and named pipes.

Machine Characteristics

You saw earlier that some characteristics of an NT machine are user-specific, and some are machine-specific. The machine-specific characteristics include the following:

- Initial logon bitmap
- Shared groups
- Network settings, including persistent connections

- Drivers, including video, sound, tape, SCSI, network card, and mouse drivers

- The "services" settings in the Control Panel

- The "system" settings in the Control Panel

- Printer settings

Again, machine names can be up to 15 characters in length. Before going on, let's summarize legal lengths of names and passwords.

Name/Password	Length
User names	Up to 20 characters
Passwords	Up to 128 characters in theory, but 14 characters in practice
Share names	Up to 12 characters
Machine names	Up to 15 characters

Inter-Domain Security: Trust Relationships

The users in a domain control how they share information via the user rights and permissions of that domain. Again, that information is maintained for that domain by the primary domain controller and its backup domain controllers in the domain security database.

But suppose you need information in *another* domain? How do you access the resources of that domain?

Inter-Domain Relationships without Trusts

Well, obviously, one way to get to another domain's resources is to become a user on that domain. Figure 2.7 shows an example of that.

FIGURE 2.7

Becoming a
user on
another domain

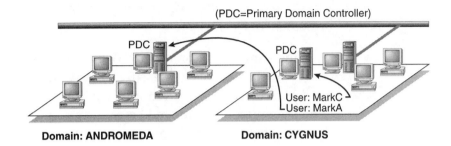

(PDC=Primary Domain Controller)

Domain: ANDROMEDA   **Domain: CYGNUS**

In the figure, you see two domains, one named Andromeda and the other named Cygnus. Both domains are on the same Ethernet. In fact, from the Ethernet's point of view, there aren't two domains here, just one big Ethernet segment with a whole bunch of machines on it. The question of which domain a particular workstation is in is a *software* question, not a hardware question.

What all that means is that there's no reason at all why my workstation can't be a part of two different domains and use two different identities. In the figure, my user ID is MarkC for the Cygnus network, and MarkA for the Andromeda network. What this really means is that there is an entry in the Cygnus security database recognizing someone named MarkC with certain rights and permissions, and there's an entry in the Andromeda database recognizing someone named MarkA with certain rights and permissions.

More specifically, suppose I log on as MarkC. Now, Cygnus knows MarkC, but Andromeda does not. That means that Andromeda's primary domain controller wouldn't log MarkC on to the Andromeda domain at all, but the Cygnus primary domain controller would accept MarkC's logon.

This underscores an important point: when you log on to a Microsoft enterprise network, you've got to specify which domain you're logging on to. You specify that with your startup parameters. Once I log on as MarkC, I cannot access the resources of Andromeda, but I *can* access the resources of Cygnus.

In the same way, I can use my MarkA account to access resources in Andromeda, but not Cygnus. (By the way, the choice of names MarkA and MarkC are purely arbitrary; I could have had user names Orca and Delphinus for all it would matter. I just picked MarkA and MarkC to make it easier to remember what each user name did.)

What's wrong with this scenario? Two things. First, it involves administration headaches. If there are five domains in your company, then consider what you'd have to do in order to maintain accounts on the five domains. You'd have to physically travel all over the company to each domain, log on to a workstation on that domain as an administrator, and make whatever changes were required—and you'd have to do it for each domain, *every time* you needed to change a password, user right, or the like. This would, as you'd imagine, get old quickly.

The second problem is that you can't simultaneously access resources from more than one domain. Each account, like MarkA or MarkC, could only access one domain's resources, so to get to the resources of Andromeda while in domain Cygnus, you would have to log off the MarkC account and log back in on the MarkA account. Again, no fun for someone trying to run a network.

One way around this would be for Mark to have an account on Cygnus and one on Andromeda, both named "Mark" with an identical password. But managing *that* is no joy, either, as it means password-changing day gets a bit cumbersome.

Trust Relationships

It would be really convenient to be able to essentially be a part of more than one domain. You can accomplish that with *trust relationships*.

One domain can choose to "trust" another in that it allows users from the trusted domain to access resources in the trusting domain. If

Andromeda trusts Cygnus, then Cygnus users can access Andromeda resources, as you see in Figure 2.8.

With a trust relationship, the only account that I need is the MarkC account. Because Andromeda trusts Cygnus, the primary domain controller for Andromeda extends the normal user rights and permissions to any "visitor" that has been vouched for by the primary domain controller for Cygnus (i.e., any normal user on the Cygnus domain).

Notice in this example that Cygnus members can access the Andromeda resources, *but the reverse is not true.* If I were a member of the *Andromeda* domain, I would only be able to access Andromeda resources. Just because Andromeda trusts Cygnus, that does not imply that Cygnus trusts Andromeda. Each trust relationship is a one-way relationship. That's not to say that you *couldn't* also build a Cygnus-to-Andromeda trust link, but it would require an extra, explicit step.

FIGURE 2.8
A trust relationship

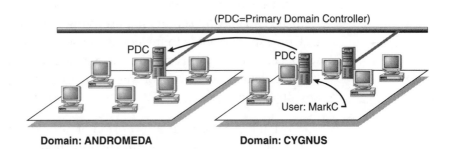

Domain: ANDROMEDA   **Domain: CYGNUS**

Network Software: Drivers, Protocols, and Redirectors

The last "basic" that you really have to master in order to be comfortable with NT networking is Microsoft enterprise network software components.

Understanding Network Software Parts

Not too many years ago, one company would assemble an entire soup-to-nuts package of networking software. Not only would you buy the network boards and cables from them, but you'd also get a single large piece of software that served as one-stop shopping for everything that the network accomplished.

Why Are There Different Parts to Networking Software?

As it turns out, that was a major problem. Why? Well, it's probably best illustrated with an example. Suppose that there is a networking company named Ajax Network Solutions. Ajax sells a hardware/software network solution. Suppose also that it's pretty popular and that Ajax is the market leader with 50 percent of the network market. They're falling prey to that killer of market leaders, complacency. (Note: in the text that follows, you may *think* that I'm parodying a network vendor; I'm not. A lack of responsiveness to the needs of users is something that all network vendors are guilty of, some to a greater degree than others. So no, I'm not picking on Novell, or Microsoft, or Banyan, or IBM, or DEC, or any other company.)

Way back in the Cretaceous period of networking, say around 1987, Ajax realized that people wanted to hook their PCs together and share files. Ajax also figured that people would only run DOS, since it didn't look like OS/2 was going anywhere and NT was just an idea that Dave Cutler was still mulling around. So the Ajax guys ("guys" because this is 1987, recall, when the only female in the business was Esther Dysan) got the Acme Ethernet Board Company to sell tons of Ethernet cards to Ajax for a good price, and then Ajax put its name on the boards. Once they had boards, the Ajax folks wrote a DOS TSR that was about 60K in size. It installed on a DOS system as a device driver, and only worked with the Ajax network cards. But hey, it worked, and you could share files and printers over a network among DOS workstations. Pretty cool, the industry thought, and started buying the stuff.

Almost a year goes by, and Ajax has taken the PC world by storm. Everybody's buying their networking kits. Everybody loves the Ajax package. Soon, however, computer experts are noting that the Ajax network cards cost $200 apiece, and that another firm, 2Com, makes pretty good Ethernet cards for a mere $180. Ajax claims, however, that the 2Com cards are not Ajax cards, haven't been tested for compatibility, and, worst of all, the Ajax software can't control the 2Com cards, so while the Ajax management regrets that their boards cost $200, the true reason for the higher price is that quality costs money, and the Ajax boards guarantee quality. Everyone buys this explanation, as Ajax are the *wunderkinden* of the industry and have the trust of their customers.

Shortly thereafter, however, someone notices the similarities between Ethernet cards sold by the Acme Ethernet Board Company and Ajax. Noticing also that the boards are $170 and that they work fine with the Ajax software, Ajax finds sales of their Ethernet cards quickly declining. Pretty soon, they don't sell many Ethernet cards, and so they really don't care *whose* Ethernet cards you buy, just as long as you keep buying Ajax software. The problem with supporting other Ethernet cards, however, is that the piece of the network software that communicates with the network board must be modified a bit for each new brand of network card. For every single board that Ajax supports, they must modify their network software. Clearly that's no fun, and will mean a larger network program as well, but the customers are demanding support for more boards. Ajax finds out what network card models are the 20 or so most popular on the market. About a year later, they release separate versions of their network software that supports those boards.

By the time they've done that, however, more network boards have come out that are cheaper and faster. Ajax is still behind the 8-ball. But that's nothing compared to the fact that people are now demanding support of mainframe protocols like SNA and DECnet. So Ajax returns to the drawing board. Now, they're smart people, and putting SNA and DECnet support into their software isn't that hard. It does, however, make their software significantly bigger, and their DOS TSR is now up to 160K. Most people don't care about the mainframe protocols and complain about the new bloated TSR, so Ajax is forced to offer separate versions of their software categorized by the boards supported and the protocols included.

By 1993, there are too many new network cards to keep track of, and Ajax is falling hopelessly behind. They can't realistically support thousands of versions of their software, so they've got to triage all but the most popular boards. About 30 percent of the users are now demanding new network services like e-mail, and 40 percent want to connect their networks to the Internet, which means a new network protocol and a bunch of new network services. The marketing directory calculates that if they support 40 network cards, six protocols, and 15 different network services—the bare minimum they must have in order to survive, surveys show—Ajax will have to support 40 times 6 times 15, or 3600, different versions of their network software! Further, Ajax was spending more and more of its time just treading water, while its competition just sailed by it. By 1996, Ajax was a minor player in the network market, and in 1997 a competitor bought it and closed it.

What went wrong?

Put simply, too many things that are part of the job of "networking" to think that they can all be lumped together into one piece of software. Things change for pricing reasons (new, better, cheaper network cards) and reasons of technological advancement (the Internet, new protocols). The best answer is a flexible, modular answer.

Now, in actual fact, networking people knew that way back in the early 80s when sat down to create a standard that would act both as a model for networks and as a kind of "reference" network that companies could implement. It was called the Open Systems Interconnection (OSI) model, and it was developed by the International Standards Organization (ISO). Thus, it was called the *ISO OSI 7-layer model.* It's also one of those really terrific examples of the evil that a committee can do with a good idea, as I have yet to meet someone who thinks it's a great idea. When people try to explain networks, they often use the OSI model, but I find it to be of limited value. Instead, it seems that most network products use a kind of *three*-layer model, which I'll present here.

A Simple Network Problem

I'll underscore the functions of a network with a simple example involving a fairly dumb workstation (not surprisingly, it will run DOS) and a dedicated file server. It could be an NT Server, but it could just as easily be a NetWare server, a VINES server, or a LAN Server machine.

Looking at networks from a high-level point of view, LANs have this basic job: let the applications programs (WordPerfect, Lotus 1-2-3, Quicken, or whatever) on the workstations utilize the network hardware to get at data on the network. Figure 2.9 shows this.

Put in concrete terms, there a number of things that this network must accomplish. First, on the workstation side, the workstation is

FIGURE 2.9

How applications exploit network hardware to access data

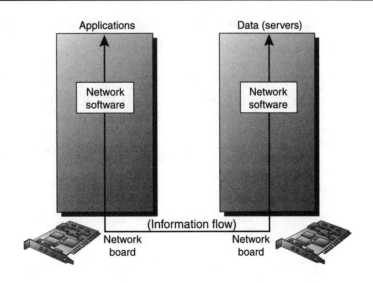

running DOS, which, as I've already observed, is network-dumb. The workstation needs to get to a file called LETTER.DOC, which is in a directory named DOCUMENT, which is sitting on a server called SERVER01 in a share called BIGSHARE. In one sense all the workstation has to say is, "Go get me \\server01\bigshare\document \letter.doc." The problem is that, among other things, DOS and most DOS programs know nothing of UNCs. So the first problem to solve is the DOS and DOS application ignorance of networks. Other kinds of compatibility problems that the network must face include the following:

File name length Most servers allow long file names, not all client operating systems do. For example, most DOS and Windows applications still can't handle file names longer than eight characters.

Multiple networks Your network may need to talk to more than one kind of server, and perhaps may need to have a wide area network portion that communicates with a mainframe network, the Internet, or some other value-added network service.

Differing hardware As described in the Ajax example, new network boards appear all the time, and the network must be able to support them quickly.

Third-party solution providers If Ajax had had a well-documented way for third parties to add network applications, then it could have relied on the hundreds of independent software vendors to offer an e-mail package, rather than derailing itself from the process of making its central networking package fast, bug-free, and secure.

My simple three-layer network consists of three layers and two interfaces:

- The bottom layer is the *board driver*, which controls the network board.

- The middle layer is the *transport protocol*, the rules of communication in the network.

- The top layer is the *network service* itself, like the e-mail package or a network fax application.

- In between the board driver and the transport protocol is the *network binding interface*, which assures that a board driver written by one vendor will communicate with a transport protocol written by another vendor.

- In between the transport protocol and the network services layer is the *network application program interface*, which is a published, standard, well-defined interface that network applications can sit atop, making it possible for someone to write a network application that isn't specific to a particular network.

The Bottom Layer: The Board Driver

For the application to use data, messages go across network boards and through the network software that runs in both the client and the server machine. The first, and easiest, piece of software to understand is the network board driver, as you see in Figure 2.10.

Drivers decouple the network board from the network operating system. For example, suppose you have a token ring-based network. When you first create your network, you may start off by buying boards from IBM, but you don't want to be locked into IBM or any other vendor for that matter. And you wonder whether or not a competitor's token ring boards, like the Madge or 3Com token ring boards, will continue to work with your NT Server-based network. For that matter, token-ring cards offer another reason why separate drivers makes sense. If your networking software were tied to a network board, then there would probably only be support for Ethernet cards, as they're more popular than token-ring cards. But separating the specifics of the network card into a modular driver eliminates that problem.

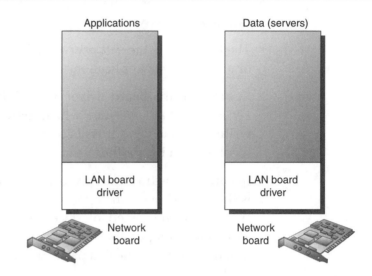

FIGURE 2.10

A network
board driver

Looking specifically at NT, we can see that NT needs an ability to incorporate any kind of network card into its networking system, whether that card is an Ethernet, token ring, ARCnet, FDDI (Fiber Digital Distributed Interface), or other board, and it's got to be able to incorporate boards from virtually *any* vendor.

The board driver must know things like which IRQ a LAN board is set for and which I/O address it uses. And for some boards, it must know which RAM base address it uses.

The Top Layer: Network Services

I'll jump to the top because in general it's easier for people to understand network services than to understand protocols, since we *use* network services.

A *network service* is any application that leverages the network to provide some capability. For example, in my company we use a network fax application that, as you'd guess, lets us share a fax machine over the network. It is just a simple program that we load on each workstation. The effect of that program is, however, that when you want to print a document at your workstation and you choose from a list of printers, a new printer called "network fax" appears. You print to that "printer" and the network fax application invisibly converts that command into a command to grab the document, shoots it across the network to the fax server, and tells the fax server to dial somewhere and fax the document.

E-mail is another example. E-mail wouldn't exist if it weren't for networks. You type a message to Sally and click Send, and it's sent. The e-mail program, an example of a network service, takes the message and sends it to a machine on your network that acts as the "post office" for your network's e-mail system.

But the most common network application is one that most people aren't even aware exists. It goes by several names, "shell," "redirector," and "client" being the most common. A redirector fools applications into thinking that the application gets data from a local drive, rather than from the network.

For example, let's return to the dumb DOS workstation in my example, and let's run ancient WordPerfect 5.1 on it. Now consider the case of WordPerfect reading a document from a network drive. From WordPerfect's point of view, there *is* no network. Instead, it knows that one or more disk drives are available, with names consisting of a letter and a colon, as in A:, B:, C:, and so on. WordPerfect 5.1 was not built to accommodate storage devices that don't have names like A: or D:. Therefore, a layer of software must be placed just below WordPerfect, a layer of software whose job it is to present a letter-and-colon face to WordPerfect when supplying data stored on the network. WordPerfect thinks that it is addressing local drives, but its requests for information from drives with names like D: must be *redirected* to network requests, like "Get the data from directory WPFILES on the server named SEYMOUR." The redirector software does that, as you see in Figure 2.11.

But the redirector doesn't do all of the work, just as the e-mail package or the network fax application doesn't do all of the work. Most network

FIGURE 2.11

Using the redirector
software

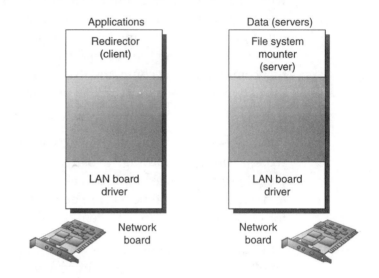

Applications

Redirector
(client)

LAN board
driver

Network
board

Data (servers)

File system
mounter
(server)

LAN board
driver

Network
board

services are part of a two-part team; one part of the team is called the
server application, and that part goes on the server. The other part is
called the *client* application, and it sits on a user's workstation.

The redirector is only half of a client-server team of software. The
redirector is the piece that goes on the client or workstation, and the *file
system mounter* is the piece that goes on the server. There are several
file system mounters in the network world—the best-known are Novell's
NetWare File System, UNIX's Network File System (NFS), and Microsoft's file system mounter, which they usually just call the "server." The
redirector on the client and the file system mounter on the server must
match for the client to use the server's resources.

In the Internet world, servers may run an "NFS server"; workstations
must run "NFS client" software. In the Novell world, servers run a program called NFS.NLM to support the Novell File System mounter, and
workstations run a client program called NET3, NET4, NETX, or the like
in order to communicate with the Novell server. Banyan users run a
program called REDIRALL to access shared volumes on their servers.

The Internet also provides me with a number of other network applications as examples. Web browsers and servers, FTP client and server programs, and Telnet clients and servers are examples of applications that only exist because of a network. Your firm may well be using client-server applications that they designed themselves.

The Middle Layer: Network Protocols

Third in the trio of network software components is the network protocol. In general, a *protocol* is just a set of rules that have been standardized for the sake of compatibility. For example, when I call you on the phone, we've got a protocol that says, "When you hear the phone ring and you pick it up, then *you* should talk first, not me." There's no good reason for why it happens this way—it's just the common agreement in our culture as to how to conduct a phone communication.

I left this middle piece for last, as it's the most abstract of the three network software components. You might think of it this way: the board driver keeps the LAN board happy, the redirector keeps the applications happy, and the *transport protocol* glues the two of them together by establishing the rules of the road for network communications. You can see the result of adding the transport protocol to our network software system in Figure 2.12.

Just as we couldn't use the phone without some agreements about how to use it, NT needs a common communication language so that all of the machines on an NT network can talk to one another without confusion. NT also needs to be able to speak the networking languages used by *other* kinds of networks, so it needs to be something of a polyglot. Networking protocols—"protocol" is a somewhat more accurate term than "language" here—differ widely because they were each originally designed to do different things, and because network protocols were never designed toward being compatible with other kinds of networks.

FIGURE 2.12

Adding the transport protocol to the network software system

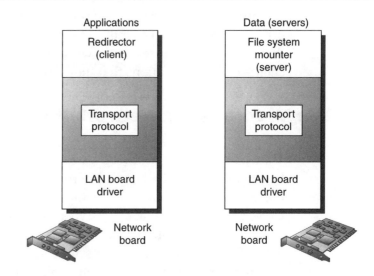

There are a number of transport protocols, unfortunately. Every vendor has its own favorite protocol. On the following pages is a quick overview of the ones you'll run across.

NetBIOS/NetBEUI

Back when IBM first started marketing its PC Network, it needed a basic network protocol stack. IBM had no intention of building large networks, just small workgroups of a few dozen computers or fewer.

Out of that need grew the Network Basic Input/Output System (Net-BIOS). NetBIOS is just 18 commands that can create, maintain, and use connections between PCs on a network. IBM soon extended NetBIOS with the NetBIOS Extended User Interface (NetBEUI), which was basically a refined set of NetBIOS commands. Over time, however, the names NetBEUI and NetBIOS have taken on different meanings.

- NetBEUI refers to the actual transport protocol; it has been implemented in many different ways by different vendors, to the point where it's in some ways the fastest transport protocol around for small networks.

- NetBIOS refers to the actual set of programming commands that the system can use to manipulate the network. The technical term for it is an Application Program Interface (API).

NetBEUI is the closest thing to a "native" protocol for NT. Unless you tell your system to use another protocol, NetBEUI is one of the protocols that the NT Setup program installs by default (IPX/SPX is the other). NetBEUI should be your protocol of choice for small networks, however, as it's the fastest one around.

TCP/IP (Transmission Control Protocol/ Internet Protocol)

The famous "infobahn," the information superhighway, is built atop a protocol created by the U.S. government over the years—a protocol stack called the *TCP suite.* The TCP suite is a very efficient, easy-to-extend protocol whose main strength has been in *wide* area networking, gluing together dissimilar networks and bringing together similar networks that are separated by distance and low-speed connections. It's one of the best-supported, well-designed internetworking protocols around today.

ENTERPRISE
NETWORKING

Traditionally, however, microcomputer networks haven't used TCP/IP as a *local* area network protocol. But that's not true any more. In fact, if you're building an NT network of any size, I strongly recommend building it on TCP/IP; that's why the TCP/IP chapter is the largest in the book.

DLC (Data Link Control)

Data Link Control is related to an international standard protocol called IEEE 802.2. You'll see it used for two main reasons.

First, many token ring shops use DLC to allow their PC workstations to talk to mainframe gateways. If you use token ring and your CONFIG.SYS contains three device drivers whose names start with DXM, then you're using DLC drivers. Not all gateways require DLC, but many do.

The second common use is to communicate with network printers. The most common example is if you've got a laser printer on the network that is attached *directly* to the network via a JetDirect print server (network interface) card, then you can use DLC to control that printer.

IPX/SPX (Internetwork Packet Exchange/ Sequenced Packet Exchange)

The most popular local area network type in the world is Novell Net-Ware. When the Novell folks were building NetWare, they decided to build their own protocol, rather than use an existing protocol. (It's actually based on a Xerox protocol called Xerox Networking Services, or XNS.)

IPX/SPX support came late to NT, but it's here in NT 4 as part of the NetWare Compatible Services.

Multiple Transport Stacks

It should be obvious by now that, first of all, there is no single best network protocol, and second, you may want to run all four of the protocols described here. You can.

One of the values of the NT networking model is that it supports *multiple* transport protocols, as you see in Figure 2.13. In the figure, you can see that the client machine has four transport protocols loaded, and the server has one protocol loaded. This could happen if the client machine connected to more than one server. For example, the IPX stack might talk to a Novell server, the DLC stack might allow the workstation to talk to a mainframe gateway, and the TCP/IP stack might talk to an Internet mail router.

FIGURE 2.13

Running multiple
transport protocols

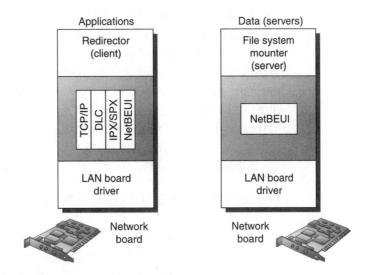

Network Binding Interfaces

But to make all of this *work*, we need a way to attach the network boards to the transport stacks—to *bind* the network transport layer to the LAN board's driver. (The definition of "binding" is to create a software connection between, to essentially "marry," a network card driver and a network transport protocol.) That leads to the need for a very important standard interface: the interface between a LAN board driver and a transport stack. There are two competitors for the title of "world standard binding interface," Microsoft's NDIS and Novell's ODI.

Network Driver Interface Specification (NDIS)

Microsoft's standard defines the interface between a network card driver and a protocol stack with an interface called the Network Driver Interface Specification (NDIS).

NDIS-compliant drivers are easy to find for most network boards, so availability is a strong plus for NDIS. Furthermore, there are NDIS-compatible versions of the NetBEUI, TCP/IP, DLC, and SPX/IPX protocol stacks. NDIS 3.0 drivers are particularly attractive in the DOS/Windows world because they load up in extended memory, away from the precious lower 640K. NDIS 3.1 drivers added support for "hot plug and play," which unfortunately NT still doesn't support. NDIS 4.*x* drivers will appear with the next versions of NT and Windows and will let Microsoft unify the drivers for NT and Windows, which will be a great thing for us NT users. *Everyone* supports Windows, right?

Open Data-link Interface (ODI)

Novell's answer to the binding problem is a different standard, one named the Open Data-Link Interface (ODI). ODI drivers do not, unfortunately, load high, but they are the easiest drivers to obtain. If a board has any drivers at all, they will be DOS ODI drivers.

Packet drivers

Some PC-based UNIX implementations use TCP/IP but don't write their own drivers. These usually rely upon a driver called "packet drivers" and are sometimes called the "Clarkson drivers" after Clarkson Tech, where they were invented.

Network Application Interfaces (APIs)

As you've already read, most applications are unaware of the network or networks that they use. But some, like e-mail or groupware programs, must be cognizant of the network, and exist only *because* of the network. They need to be able to "plug in" and communicate with other programs running on other machines in the network.

Programmers build network-aware programs to be tailored to sets of commands that a network offers to applications programs. Those sets of commands are called APIs, or application program interfaces.

Think of an API as being somewhat like the dashboard of a car. Your car's dashboard is the interface that you see, and you learn to use it in order to operate the car. You actually have no idea while you're driving what's under your car's hood—you just push down the accelerator and the car goes faster.

A dashboard consists of just a few "primitive" commands: brake the car, accelerate the car, shift the car's transmission, and so on. There is no command "back the car out of the driveway," and yet you can still back a car out of a driveway by just assembling a number of the primitive commands into the actual action of backing a car out of a driveway. Once you learn how to drive one car, you can instantly use another. In other words, you are "designed for the car dashboard API." In the same way, if you buy a network fax application that was designed for a network API named NetBIOS, you should be able to run that network fax application on any network at all, so long as the network supports the NetBIOS API.

In contrast, consider how private pilots learn to fly. They have two pedals on the floor of their plane, but the left pedal turns them left and the right pedal turns them right. Taking someone who can fly a plane and plunking him down in a car without any other training wouldn't work too well. In the same way, if an application is built for *one* network API, then it won't work on another. But if you built a car with an airplane's "dashboard," airplane pilots could drive the car without any trouble. For example, NetBIOS is an API that first appeared on Microsoft networks, but Novell included it in their network. As a result, many applications designed for Microsoft networks work fine on a Novell network.

You'll probably come across three APIs in the NT enterprise world:

NetBIOS A simple set of 18 commands implemented on an NT network. It is Microsoft's "native" network API.

TCP/IP Sockets   The preferred API for working over the Internet. Sockets are commonly implemented on PCs—and on NT—under a standard called WinSock. If you bought Netscape Navigator and you want to run it, then your network must offer the WinSock network API. Now, NT only implements WinSock on its TCP/IP protocol, not on IPX or NetBEUI. Consequently, if you loaded Navigator on an NT (or a Windows 3.1 or DOS or Windows 95) workstation that didn't have TCP/IP loaded, then it couldn't work.

Novell Sockets   Novell's API.

Getting comfortable with NT networking requires learning a new language, but it's not an impossible language to learn. In this chapter, you've gotten the background that you need to "speak NT." Next, you'll see how to *install* NT.

PART II

Setting Up
NT Server

CHAPTER 3 • Installing NT and NT Server

CHAPTER 4 • RAID for Speedier, Safer Disks

CHAPTER 5 • Understanding the Registry Database

CHAPTER
THREE

Installing NT and NT Server

Installing NT Server is simple…*if* you do your homework beforehand. This chapter provides a step-by-step plan for getting a server up and running. It is also of value if you are installing NT on a workstation.

In this chapter, I'll discuss

- Getting ready to install
- The options for installing
- The confusing parts of the installation program

Preparing the Hardware

Despite the fact that NT is a big, complex operating system, you have a pretty good chance of getting it installed right the first time *if* you first make sure that you're free of hardware problems. If not, NT can be kind of picky—but that's a good thing, at least in contrast to DOS. Under DOS, you can have some pretty glaring hardware problems, but DOS runs nonetheless. The reason why DOS works—or *appears* to work—on a machine with major hardware problems is simple: DOS isn't really an operating system. It doesn't monitor the hardware, so it never really gets a chance to notice a hardware failure or conflict. DOS basically leaves the problems of hardware control to device drivers and applications programs. When a hardware problem arises, it arises while an application program is running, and it is the *DOS application program* that must detect, diagnose, and recover from the hardware failure. Or at least that's the ideal situation.

The reality is, of course, that most DOS programs just crash when hardware problems happen. I just implied that DOS program designers should plan for these problems and attempt to avert them in their code, but the fact of the matter is that the DOS application designers shouldn't *have* to worry about this kind of thing—the operating system should.

Under DOS, a memory failure usually doesn't show up until you actually try to *use* that memory. Disk failures cause the "Abort, Retry, Fail?" error message, with no real recovery. Interrupt conflicts become mysterious freeze-ups.

You can't afford any of that kind of behavior on your NT server (or workstation, for that matter). For that reason, my strong advice to you is to *test your hardware thoroughly before installing NT*.

Having said that, I've got to admit that it's pretty hard to build any kind of hardware diagnostic program under NT, because a hardware diagnostic must be able to directly access the hardware in order to test it, and one of NT's stated design goals is to make it *impossible* for an application to get to the hardware. Furthermore, most diagnostics require that they be the only thing running in the system, and NT is built out of literally dozens of mini-programs called "threads."

For that reason, I recommend that you run your system through a gamut of specialized DOS-based diagnostics before proceeding with the NT installation. I'll discuss them in more detail a bit later in this chapter.

Getting Ready to Install

First of all, make sure that you have the right hardware for an NT installation. Check the latest Windows NT Hardware Compatibility List for any hardware you are thinking of buying (you can find it at http://www.microsoft.com/ntserver/hcl/hclintro.htm, among other places). If it's not on the list, check with the manufacturer to be sure it will work with Windows NT. You see, a piece of hardware may well be NT-compatible but not be on the HCL. Microsoft manages the

HCL, and they charge hardware vendors tens of thousands of dollars to test hardware before Microsoft will put that hardware on the HCL. On the one hand, this seems like a pretty good deal for us, the consumers because somebody big tests compatibility. But on the other hand, the fact that Microsoft controls the HCL, which is the "hardware certification" program, as well as the MSCE certification program, the "expert certification" program, means that Microsoft has a kind of scary incentive to keep turning out upgrades whether we need them or not. Personally, I'd rather see an independent group like ACM or DPMA put in charge of certification because there would be less of a "fox guarding the hen house" air to it. In any case, here are a few things to consider when choosing hardware.

CPU   In the Intel *x*86 world, you need a 486-class processor or better; 486 is recommended. If you're going to run on a MIPS or Alpha, make sure that you have the right software for *your* system; NT 3.1 shipped the MIPS and Intel versions in the same box, but later versions don't include Alpha code, for example. Version 4 ships with MIPS, Intel, PowerPC, and Alpha versions.

RAM   I strongly recommend not running NT with less than 16MB of RAM. Oddly enough, NT Server seems to need less memory to do *its* job than does the workstation product; my NT Server system has only 16MB and performs superbly for our network, but the workstation product seems sluggish until you put 24MB of RAM on it. If you intend to load SQL Server on an NT Server, then you'd best have about 32MB of RAM. Unfortunately, the general rule with NT is "the more memory, the better."

NT Server needs more RAM if you ask it to do more things. If you're going to load RAS or TCP/IP, you need more memory. NT Server also needs more memory if it will serve more people. Chapter 15, "Tuning and Monitoring Your NT Server Network," has more information on this.

Video   You need at least a VGA video board in order to load NT Server. (This surprised me when I first loaded it, because I was used to being able to put low-quality video on a server; after all, nobody's going to use it as a workstation, so who cares what kind of video it has?) It's chic to buy the fastest turbo-charged PCI video accelerator board for systems nowadays, but there's no point to doing that for an NT Server installation; a cheap VGA board is fine and, indeed, is *recommended*.

With NT 4 came a change in NT architecture, a change intended to speed up the performance of NT Workstation. The change did, indeed, make NT Workstation faster—but at the price (in my opinion) of reduced system robustness. It's a long story, but the basics of it are this: parts of NT are housed in one of two places, either the *kernel mode* or the *user mode*.

Kernel mode programs can, in general, run faster than user mode programs, but they do it at the price of reduced security. When a kernel mode module in NT crashes, it's likely to take the entire operating system with it. One of the things that has made NT so stable is the fact that it stores relatively few things in kernel mode (well, relatively few things compared to *other* operating systems). The video drivers and printer drivers are two examples of modules that lived in user mode under NT 3.*x*. That means that if you were to install a particularly buggy printer driver under NT 3.51, then the worst that would happen would be that you couldn't print—everything else would work fine.

Under NT 4, however, print and video drivers are moved into kernel mode. Again, that speeds up video performance noticeably; run the 3-D Pinball game from Windows 95's Plus Pack on NT Workstation 3.51 and its performance is glacial. Run it on NT 4, however, and it flies. Most definitely, this is an improvement....

If you run video games on your servers, that is.

This architecture shift was clearly done to make NT Workstation more competitive. I can't say I like it much, however. If you've been in the PC business for any time, you know what a pain it can be to procure up to date, properly debugged video drivers. Owners of ATI or Diamond video cards jokingly refer to themselves as the "driver of the week club." Since its introduction in 1993, NT has distinguished itself from other PC operating systems in that it is slow, expensive, and doesn't boast much native software—but it's stable. Rock solid. Microsoft's move of the video and print drivers into kernel mode threatens that, in my opinion at least. Which brings me back to my recommendation: *use the VGA driver on servers.* You're not doing anything fancy on the server, and the NT VGA driver is one of the best, most bug-free pieces of software that Microsoft offers. It was written by Michael Abrash, probably the guy on the planet who understands the VGA better than anyone. It runs in kernel mode, so a crash in the VGA driver can kill your system, but the chances of that happening are considerably reduced if you stay with Mike's driver.

If you're running an NT *workstation*, in contrast, by all means invest in better video. The Matrox-based boards are probably the best way to go, and by the time you read this there should be a good set of drivers for them.

As video accelerators go, the S3-based systems are definitely not the fastest boards around. As I've said, you could look to an ATI or Matrox video system, but, on the other hand, think twice before straying from S3-based systems. S3 boards are the ones that will always get the most solid, debugged drivers among the video accelerator bunch, and they likely get the *earliest* drivers when beta versions of new software arrive. The S3 systems also tend to be cheaper than the other accelerators. Be careful with Diamond systems; some use S3 chips, but some are based on the "ARK" chip set, and as I write this there are no NT drivers for this chip set, which would mean spending a lot of money for a board that just runs the VGA driver. Please don't write to me and ask me what board to buy. I get a lot of that kind of mail, and I really can't help you there. Just be sure to follow a simple rule: if it's not on the Hardware Compatibility List, don't buy it.

CD-ROM You definitely want a CD-ROM for the server, if you're loading NT Server. As you'll read later in this book, you can't get to a number of pieces of software in the NT package from the floppies because they're only on the CD-ROM. Additionally, one NT floppy installation will convince you that CD-ROM installations are the way to go.

What about CD-ROMs on workstations? I'd still think about getting at least a cheap quad-spin CD-ROM. Software has gotten so huge that even *games* are shipping on CD-ROMs. Terrific, inexpensive databases are available on CD-ROM; for example, you can buy 12 months' worth of *PC Magazine* on CD-ROM for about $20! Think of the time saved with just one literature search, and the CD-ROM drive starts to look like a bargain. NT troubleshooters will want to subscribe to Microsoft's TechNet service, a complete set of all Microsoft literature on supporting their applications and environments. There's a fantastic trove of goodies there, but you can't get to them if you don't have a CD-ROM.

If you decide to buy a CD-ROM, I recommend a SCSI-based CD rather than one of the EIDE-based CD-ROMs. NT has always supported SCSI better than IDE or EIDE. The older CD-ROMs that are attached to a proprietary interface card are generally not supported by NT, and I've never gotten one of those CD-ROMs that attach via the parallel port to work on an NT install.

A last, somewhat esoteric but important point about CD-ROMs under NT: not only must they be SCSI-based, they must also support the newer SCSI-II interface, since NT requires that a feature called *SCSI parity* be enabled in order for the installation to go well.

Tape Drive   It is essential that any enterprise server have a tape backup unit. I use a 4mm DAT tape, a Sony SCSI-II compatible drive, and it suits the backup job just fine. The tape subsystem should be SCSI-based.

Hard Disk   If you want to support large drive sizes *and* low-level device multitasking, then you'd do well to choose some kind of SCSI-based hard disk. NT supports SCSI host adapters very well, so you can choose from a large number of adapters. (It would be a good idea to consult the Hardware Compatibility List, available from Microsoft, before buying a SCSI host adapter.)

- Any machine that is running NT Server should have some kind of advanced 32-bit bus, preferably PCI that supports bus mastering. (VESA slots that lack bus mastering are not all that good an idea.) It is a good idea to stay with a big name SCSI vendor, like Adaptec. Their 2940 adapter is probably the most popular SCSI host adapter among NT users, and its 32-bit EISA cousin the 2742T is a mite pricey—about $300—but quite a performer, and serves as two SCSI controllers on a single board. I strongly recommend that you avoid the somewhat cheaper Ultrastor controllers. My experience with Ultrastor has been that they're slow to deliver drivers, difficult to get in touch with for technical support, and tend to completely abandon any controller that isn't their latest and greatest.

- One of my Micron servers shipped with the BusLogic FlashPoint host adapter. It's powerful, but the drivers for it are always a bit hard to find. I hope that will change eventually.

- Another reason to buy SCSI-based storage systems is fault tolerance: disk mirroring and RAID pretty much *require* SCSI disk subsystems in order to work. You can create a mirrored set of non-SCSI drives, but the drives may not have sector-remapping capability (which is an important part of any fault-tolerance scheme), so I would not recommend it.

Mice and Serial Ports This is pretty straightforward, but one word of advice: get PS/2 type or InPort mice. You need a port for your mouse, a serial port to which attach to your Uninterruptible Power Supply (UPS), and a serial port for a modem to support the Remote Access Services (RAS). If the mouse is a serial mouse, the system requires three serial ports, which gets problematic because you can't really have more than two serial ports on most PC-compatible systems.

Once you have the hardware together, you have to test it.

Testing Memory

An awful lot of people think that the short ten-second memory test that their systems go through every time the system is turned on actually *does* something. (Now, if you believed *that*, you probably think that those buttons next to the "Don't Walk" signs on the street corners actually do something.) The quick power-on RAM test is just a quick "Are you there?" kind of memory inventory.

The problem with this approach is that many memory errors are not absolute errors that essentially "sit still" and let you find them. Some memory errors appear because of addressing logic problems: change a bit at address X, and bits change at address Y. Others occur because the memory modules have a trifle different access speed from other memory modules in the system. A third group of errors can appear from differences in electrical characteristics between memories on a motherboard and memories on a high-speed expansion card.

In any case, thorough memory testing is a step that shouldn't be skipped. To that end, here are a few suggestions:

- Use either Checkit from Touchstone software, or QAPlus from DiagSoft. They're the only two programs I've ever looked at that can find those pesky odd errors.

- Run these tests in their "slow" mode. By default, they run a quick test, but you don't want a quick test—you want all of the tests, like "walking bit," "checkerboard," "address line," and whatever your package supports.

- Run the tests from DOS, and do *not* load a memory manager before you do.

- If you're using an ARC (Advanced RISC Computer) machine, ask your vendor for a recommendation on a stringent memory tester.

Don't be surprised if a memory test takes up to eight hours; that's possible on a 32MB system.

Testing Disks

You'll find that NT relies heavily upon *paging* data out to disk. *Paging* is a process wherein disk space is used as a stand-in for memory space. Whenever data is paged from RAM to disk, the operating system assumes that the data will remain safe and sound out on the disk. When NT reloads the data from disk to RAM, it doesn't even check to see that the data is undamaged. Therefore, you need a 100-percent reliable disk to support NT.

As with memory, disks often show problems only under certain circumstances. It would be nice if you could just write out a simple bit of data like the word *testing* all over the disk, then go back and read the disk to be sure that the word *testing* was still on it, but a test like that would only find the grossest of disk errors. DOS's SCANDISK is a tester of this variety, useful only in the most disk-damaged situations.

Instead, you need a *pattern tester* for your disk drive. There is one that I can recommend: SpinRite 3.1 from Gibson Research. SpinRite is a high-quality disk tester.

Now, there are two disadvantages to disk testing: the time involved, and the fact that all the good ones are DOS-based. It can literally take *days* to do a thorough test on a disk. Running SpinRite on a 1700MB disk took *three days,* but when it was done, SpinRite had found some errors on the disk that hadn't been found by the manufacturer, the low-level format program, or the DOS FORMAT program. SpinRite is a bit of a pain, however, in that it can only test partitions up to .5GB in size, forcing you to chop your disk up into small pieces, test the pieces, and then repartition it.

The DOS heritage of these programs means that the only disk system that they recognize is the FAT file system, *arrgh!* That implies that when you get a new server, you should put DOS on it temporarily, format its disk to a FAT format, install NT Server, and convert the FAT format to NTFS format.

Here's a case where those of you installing an NT workstation system will have it better, as you'll probably stay with the FAT file system for an NT workstation.

You may be scowling right now because of the work that I'm setting out for you; *don't.* Believe me, I've seen a number of client network problems boil down to flaky memory or flaky disks. You really only need to test RAM once, when you first install it. Disks really should be tested once a year.

Preparing the Data

If this is a brand-new server, there's really nothing to do in the way of backup.

If you're converting your server from another operating system to NT Server, then you first have to protect the data on your server's disk. Here are a few strategies.

Backing Up to Another Machine

If you have another computer around with enough mass storage to hold your server's data, you could run some kind of peer-to-peer LAN (like Windows for Workgroups), share that machine's drive, and then just copy the whole drive over with an XCOPY /S command. Then, once NT Server is up, you can connect the NT Server machine easily to the Windows for Workgroups machine, and XCOPY back.

Temporarily Installing the Tape to Another Machine

Suppose you're currently using a lower-level, FAT-based server system like LANtastic or Windows for Workgroups, and you're going to change over to NT Server. You run a DOS-based tape backup program, put the tape drive away, and install NT Server. In the process, you format your server to the New Technology File System (NTFS). Then try to restore the data to the server.

And that's when the problem becomes evident.

You see, just about every backup program saves data in a different way. Say you have some program—let's call it SB, for Simple Backup—that shipped with the tape drive. It's a DOS-based program, so it ran fine when you were backing up the disk, but *now it won't run under NT*. Why? Two reasons. First, it probably directly controls the tape drive, and NT absolutely forbids DOS programs (or NT applications programs, for that matter) to directly manipulate hardware; try to run the program, and it would crash. Second, the tape restore program *might* work by directly writing data to the disk, and that would not only be intercepted by NT, it would fail even if NT didn't stop the restore program—after all, this disk is now formatted in NTFS, not FAT.

Or perhaps you could buy a piece of big-name software like Backup Exec or ArcServe for Novell (presuming you're moving the server from Novell to NT). Can you back it up with the Novell version and then restore with the NT version? In my experience, you can't do it. I guess the security models of NetWare and NT are too different to allow a simple crossover.

What about going at it the other way? Just boot the server from a DOS floppy and run the restore program. That'll work, won't it? Unfortunately, no, it won't work. Remember, the disk is now formatted under NTFS, so a DOS program couldn't recognize the C drive anyway.

Well, NT comes with a tape backup program. Won't it read my DOS backups? No. Emphatically, *no*. The NT backup program uses its own Microsoft Backup Format to write tapes, a format that, so far as I know, is unique in the industry. (Question: "How many Microsoft programmers does it take to change a light bulb?" Answer: "None; they just declare darkness a Microsoft standard.")

So what's the answer? One approach is to just take the tape drive out of the server, install it in another computer, use Windows for Workgroups or something like it to share the hard disk of the soon-to-be NT Server machine, and then do the backup over the peer-to-peer network onto the tape. Then set up the server, reconnect it to the Windows for Workgroups machine, and restore from the Windows for Workgroups machine. Cumbersome, but it'll work.

Setting Up the Server for FAT, Restore, and Convert

This last approach takes a bit more time, but it is simpler, and truthfully it's the one that I've used. The best way to restore your backups may be to restore your backups to a FAT volume and then convert the volume to NTFS. Read the "How Do I" sidebar to find out how.

How Do I Convert a FAT Volume to an NTFS Volume?

 To convert a FAT volume to an NTFS volume:

1. Do the backup under DOS, a FAT-based backup.

2. Install NT Server, but don't reformat the disk to NTFS.

3. Reboot under DOS, from a floppy.

4. Run the tape restore program and restore the files.

5. Boot the server, and run the FAT-to-NTFS conversion program CONVERT.EXE to make the server's disk NTFS (CONVERT *drive:* /FS:NTFS).

After you've done the conversion, run NTBACKUP *immediately* and get a first backup of the new disk format.

One of the morals of the story: backups look different on different operating systems. I found that out a few years ago when using a portable Bernoulli box.

My Bernoulli box was a 90MB cartridge storage device (they have them in 150MB and larger now, but the one I worked with was a 90) whose most interesting feature was that it could be hooked up to a parallel port via a converter built by the Iomega people, makers of the Bernoulli box. The Bernoulli box really uses a SCSI interface, but the Iomega parallel port converter faked the box out into thinking that the parallel port was a SCSI port.

Anyway, you could do backups easily, if not quickly, via the parallel port with the Bernoulli Box. A few of my systems, however, already have SCSI ports built right into them, so I tried hooking the Bernoulli right into the SCSI port. It worked, but not with the Iomega software; I ended up using a generic SCSI removable cartridge hard disk formatting software. I was able to back up, and back up much more quickly than via the parallel port, but the resulting cartridges couldn't be read when the Bernoulli was attached via the parallel port. So be careful when backing up!

Making Backups If You're Converting from LAN Manager

One more thought: Microsoft distributed SyTOS, a tape backup program, with its LAN Manager 2.2 product. The version of SyTOS that came with LAN Manager won't run under NT, but the NTBACKUP program *can* read SyTOS-formatted tapes, *if you get the LAN Manager upgrade version of NT Server, that is*. Even better, the Upgrade is less than half the list price of NT Server.

Further, the LAN Manager Upgrade package has a utility to convert from the HPFS and HPFS386 formats used by LAN Manager to NTFS *in situ*, so you may never need those backups at all.

Setting Up the LAN Card

Next, get your network card set up properly. If you're just installing the network card now, be careful that the things you do right now don't get you in trouble later. Now is the time to be sure that

- Your system doesn't have any interrupt (IRQ) or input/output (I/O) address conflicts.

- You've written down any settings that you've made to the system.

- The card works in a stand-alone mode.

The first step is to find acceptable interrupts and input/output addresses.

Setting an Interrupt

Interrupts are how your LAN card tells the CPU that the CPU must pay attention to the LAN card, *now!* Why does the LAN card have the right to bug the CPU like that? Well, mainly because the LAN card has only a limited amount of buffer space, and if the CPU doesn't come get this data quickly, then *more* data will come into the LAN card, knocking the current data right out of the LAN card's buffers and off to data heaven.

Your system can support up to 16 different devices interrupting your CPU. Each one of those interrupts is more properly called a "hardware interrupt" or an "IRQ (interrupt request) level." In general, you can only have one hardware device on a given IRQ level. I say "in general" because it is *possible* to share IRQs on a machine with a Micro Channel, EISA, or PCI bus architecture. EISAs and PCIs, however, usually coexist with older, ISA bus slots, making interrupt sharing impractical in most cases.

You can see common IRQ settings in Table 3.1.

Part of setting up a LAN board involves setting an IRQ level. You set a board's IRQ either by moving a switch or jumper on the card, in the case of older cards, or by running a setup program, in the case of most modern LAN boards. For example, in the case of the Intel EtherExpress LAN boards, you run a program called SoftSet, which is shipped with the EtherExpress board. It examines your system and attempts to find a good IRQ address (and I/O address, for that matter) for your system. It then suggests these settings, and you can either accept them or reject them. If you reject the settings, then you can directly enter the ones that you desire.

TABLE 3.1   Common IRQ Settings

IRQ Level	Common Usage	Comments
0	Timer	Hard-wired on motherboard; impossible to change.
1	Keyboard	Hard-wired on motherboard; impossible to change.
2	Cascade from IRQ 9	May or may not be available, depending on how the motherboard is designed; best to avoid if possible; some old VGAs may use this for "autoswitching"; disable the feature, if present.
3	COM2 or COM4	
4	COM1 or COM3	
5	LPT2	Most of us don't use a second parallel port, and so can use this for something else. It is safe to use this if you have a "virtual" LPT2, as in the case of a network connection.
6	Floppy disk controller	
7	LPT1	
8	Real-time clock	Hard-wired on motherboard; impossible to change.
9	Cascade to IRQ 2	Wired directly to IRQ 2, so this does not exist as a separate interrupt. Sometimes when you set a board to IRQ 2, you have to tell the software that you set it to IRQ 9 to make it work.
10	unused	
11	unused	
12	PS/2, InPort mouse	
13	Math coprocessor	Used to signal detected errors in coprocessor.
14	Hard disk controller	
15	unused	

These software setup programs are a great improvement over the LAN boards of just a few years ago, which required interminable DIP switch flipping and jumper-setting. The process that I described for the Intel board is similar to what I've seen on the SMC Elite cards, the GVC NE2000-based boards, and the 3Com 3C509 cards.

But let's get down to work. Which interrupt is the right one to choose?

A lot of people buy themselves grief by putting their network cards on IRQ 2. Don't do it. IRQ 2 was available back on the 8-bit PC/XT type designs, but it serves a valuable role in modern PCs.

The PC/XT systems had a single interrupt controller, an Intel 8259 chip. The 8259 could support up to eight interrupt channels, and the original PC/XT systems hardwired channels 0 and 1 to the system timer (a clock circuit that goes "tick" every 18.2 microseconds) and the 8042 keyboard controller.

The system was wired with those interrupts because IBM wanted to make sure that the keyboard and the timer had high priorities. You see, with an 8259, when two interrupts occur at the same time, the one with the lower number gets priority.

Interrupts 3 and 4 went to COM2 and COM1, respectively; the idea was that COM2 would support a modem and COM1 would support a printer, and so the modem would have slightly higher priority.

TIP   To this day, it's usually a good idea to use COM2 for higher-speed communications.

Interrupts 5, 6, and 7 were assigned to the hard disk controller, the floppy disk controller, and the parallel port.

In 1984, the first 16-bit PC compatible system was released—the IBM AT. The proliferation of add-in devices on the market made it clear that eight interrupt levels just weren't enough. So IBM decided to add another 8259. The problem was that just slapping the extra 8259 onto the motherboard might present some backward compatibility problems, so IBM decided to kind of slip the extra 8259 in "via the back door," as you can see in Figure 3.1.

The way IBM did it was to take the new IRQs 8 through 15 and route them through IRQ 9, then connect IRQ 9 to IRQ 2. Result: whenever IRQ 8 through 15 is triggered, IRQ 9 goes off, which makes IRQ 2 look like *it* went off. The PC's BIOS then knows that whenever IRQ 2 appears, that *really* means to check the second 8259 to find out which IRQ *really* triggered. By the way, they also freed up IRQ 5; it's no longer needed by your AT or later hard disk controller.

FIGURE 3.1

Extra 8259 on the
IBM AT

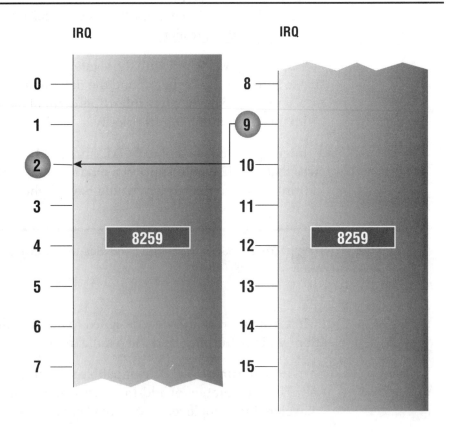

These IRQ changes imply a few things:

- Don't use IRQ 2, as it's already got a job: it's the gateway to IRQs 8-15.

- If you *do* use IRQ 2, then you may have to tell the NT software that your network card is set to IRQ 9. IRQ 9 and IRQ 2 are electronically equal under this system, because they're tied together.

- Because interrupts 8-15 slide into the architecture via IRQ 2, they essentially "inherit" IRQ 2's priority level. That means that IRQs 8-15 are of higher priority than IRQs 3-7.

- Don't use IRQ 9, because it has a cascade responsibility.

- Safe IRQs are 5, 10, 11, and 15; avoid the others. You probably need these IRQs for the following hardware:

  - Sound card: if it's an 8-bit card, then your only option is IRQ 5 for the sound card

  - LAN board, as we've already discussed

  - SCSI host adapter (although an Adaptec 2742 can actually forgo interrupts, needing only a DMA channel)

TIP

Whatever you set your boards to, *write it down!* You'll need the information later. I tape an envelope to the side of my computers. Each time I install a board (or modify an existing board), I get a new piece of paper and write down all the configuration information on the board. For example, I might write, "Intel EtherExpress 16 card installed 10 July 1994 by Mark Minasi; no EPROM on board; shared memory disabled; IRQ 10 used; I/O address 310 set."

Setting an I/O Address

IRQs are a mite scarce, so they're the things that you worry about most of the time. But LAN boards also require that you set their *input/output address*, or I/O address (it's sometimes called the "port address").

I/O addresses are generally three digit numbers, and for LAN cards they're typically a range starting at either 300 hex or 310 hex.

A LAN board's input/output address is the electrical "location" of the LAN board from the CPU's point of view. When the CPU wants to send data to a LAN card, it doesn't issue an instruction that says, "Send this data to the EtherExpress board," because the computer's hardware has no idea what an EtherExpress board *is*. Instead, every device—keyboard, video adapter, parallel port, whatever—gets a numerical address between 0 and 1023 called its *input/output address*. The value is usually expressed in hex, so it ends up being the range 000-3FF in hex. (A discussion of hexadecimal is beyond the scope of this book, but many other sources cover hex.) Just as the postal deliverer would be confused if there were two houses at 25 Main Street, a PC system can't function properly if there is more than one device at a given I/O address. Hence, part of your installation job is to ensure that you don't set the LAN card to the same I/O address as some other board.

In general, I/O addresses won't give you too much trouble, but once in a while... On one of my systems, I had a video accelerator that used I/O addresses around 300 hex. My newly installed board, which also was set to 300 hex, didn't work. My clue to the problem was that the video display showed some very odd colors when first booting up. I checked the video accelerator's settings, and *voilà!* the problem became apparent. I then changed the Ethernet card's address and the problem went away.

In any case, the I/O address is another thing that you have to be sure to write down in that envelope attached to your computer. For those of you working for larger companies, an envelope taped to the side of a computer isn't a practical answer, of course, but why not build a small database of PC information? Keep it on your system and key it to an ID number that you can affix to a PC either by engraving it on the side of the case or with hard-to-remove stickers.

Stand-Alone Card Tests

Now that the card is installed, it's a good idea to test the card and the LAN cable before going any further. The four kinds of tests that you do on most networks include:

- An on-board diagnostic
- A local loopback test
- A "network live" loopback test
- A sender/responder test

These three tests are usually encapsulated in a diagnostics diskette that you get with the LAN board. The first is a simple test of the circuitry on the board. Many of the modern boards have a "reset and check out" feature on their chips, so this program just wakes that feature up. If the chips check out okay, then this step is successfully completed.

That first test can be a useful check of whether or not you've set the IRQ to a conflicting level, or perhaps placed any on-board RAM overlapping other RAM.

The second test is one wherein you put a loopback connector (exactly what a loopback connector *is* varies with LAN variety) on your network board. The loopback connector causes any outgoing transmissions from the LAN board to be "looped back" to the LAN board. The loopback test then sends some data out from the LAN card and listens for the same data to be received by the LAN card. If that data *isn't* received by the LAN card, then there's something wrong with the transmitter or the receiver logic of the network card.

Notice that for the first two tests, you haven't even connected your system to the network yet. In the third test, you do the loopback test again, but this time while connected to the network. The board should pass again.

The final test involves two computers, a sender and a responder. The responder's job is to echo back anything that it receives. For example, if Paul's machine is the responder and Jeff's is the sender, then any messages that Jeff's machine sends to Paul's machine should cause Paul's machine to send the same message back to Jeff's machine.

To make a computer a responder (and any computer can be a responder; you needn't use a server) you have to run a program that makes it into a responder. But that's where the problem arises. The responder software is packaged on the same disk as the diagnostic software that comes with the network board and, unfortunately, the responder software usually only runs on network boards made by the company that wrote the diagnostic software. So, for example, if you have an Ethernet that is a mixture of 3Com, SMC, and Intel LAN boards, and you want to test a computer with a new 3Com Ethernet board, you have to search for another computer that has a 3Com board so that you can run the responder software on that computer.

Once you're certain that the hardware is all installed, you're ready to start installing NT or NT Server.

A Word about PCI Systems

More and more servers are Pentium or Pentium Pro-based systems built around the Intel chip sets. These computers usually have a few PCI slots and a few ISA slots.

Their power is terrific, but they have one major problem: hardware configuration. You see, PCI systems are pretty much all designed with a single assumption in mind, that they will run a plug-and-play operating system like Windows 95. But, unfortunately, NT *isn't* a plug-and-play operating system, making setting up PCI systems a bit tougher.

The problem arises when you try to set the resources—IRQs, DMAs, I/O addresses, and the like—on a PCI board. Most of them don't have jumpers or DIP switches, nor do they have software setup programs. How, then, does a PCI network card figure out which IRQ to use? Well, it depends on the manufacturer of the computer. The only people who really know how to design a PCI-based system correctly is Compaq (which is why they're so expensive); there's a neat built-in configuration program that lets you set up a PCI board as if it were an EISA or MCA board. For most vendors, however, it works like this: a board in the first PCI slot gets IRQ 9, the second PCI slot gets IRQ 10, and so on. Of course, this can be a real problem if you already have an ISA board in your system that uses one of those IRQs. There's no way for the PCI board to know that the conflict exists. How, then, to set up a PCI/ISA hybrid system?

Two possibilities come to mind. First, buy PCI systems without any ISA boards, if possible; the PCI components will keep from conflicting with one another. Second, try installing all of the PCI boards and find out what resources they are using. Then, once you know what DMA channels, memory addresses, and IRQs are being used by the PCI cards, install the ISA boards with those already-taken resources in mind. Essentially, I'm telling you to install the PCI cards and let them settle down, then set up the ISA cards to tiptoe around them. A sad approach, yes, but probably the best one we've got until Cairo, when NT is supposed to be plug-and-play compliant.

Answer These Questions Before Running NT Setup

One last thing before you start the Setup program: figure out what this computer will do in the network and make sure you have the answers to the questions that Setup will ask. You already have some hardware information written down:

- What kind of network card you have

- What IRQ and I/O addresses it is set to

- What kind of disk adapter you have

- How you want to partition the drive

- Optionally, make and configuration information for a sound card

But consider these next questions before you start running Setup.

What Kind of Server Will This Be?

An NT Server machine can assume one of three roles in the network:

- A primary domain controller in a brand-new domain

- A backup domain controller in an existing domain

- An ordinary file and/or application server

This decision is important because *once you've made it, you can't change it*—at least not without doing a completely fresh installation.

Only install an NT Server machine as a primary domain controller if you are creating a new domain. Since no machines around are members of this domain, by definition—you don't have a domain without a primary domain controller—there are no security considerations. But in the process of creating the primary domain controller, NT will also create an account that is the Administrator account for the entire domain, so you have to pay attention there. NT will prompt you for an administrative password if you create a new domain (that is, if you install a primary domain controller). You can make up any password that you want, but *please* be sure to write it down! If you don't, then you have to start all over again because you can't retrieve a forgotten password, and, without the domain administrator's password, you can't even log on to the primary domain controller that you just installed.

If you're going to install a backup domain controller, an existing primary domain controller must already be set up, and the machine that you're installing must be on the network with that machine. Setup will reject an attempt to install a backup domain controller if it can't see the primary domain controller. In that case, you will again be asked for an administrative password, but this time you're not making one up; rather, you must supply the name and password of an existing domain administrator account. Don't install backup domain controllers willy-nilly throughout your network. In fact, Microsoft reckons that you only need one backup domain controller per 2000 users. You can read more about domain design in Chapters 11 and 12.

If you opt to just install an NT Server machine with no domain respon-sibilities, then you will be asked again to think up a new password for an administrative account on the server that you are installing, but it's an administrative account solely for that server, not for the entire domain. You will also be asked if you want to join a workgroup or a domain. This is a little misleading.

Every domain contains a workgroup. Remember that a number of types of machines can join a workgroup but not a domain. For example, suppose I create domain US out of two NT machines and two Windows for Workgroups machines. The NT machines can join the domain; the Windows for Workgroups machines cannot. But the two NT machines automatically constitute a *workgroup* named US as well, and the Windows for Workgroups machines can join that workgroup.

What does the following question mean: "Do you want to join a domain or a workgroup?" If you join the workgroup, you see all of the servers on the workgroup, but you can't make use of the central user account's database on the domain controllers. Everyone who wants to access data on your workgroup server must have a personal account on that server, independent of their account on the domain. In contrast, joining the domain means that you essentially don't have to bother cre-ating user accounts on the server, because the server just uses the user accounts on the domain controllers' SAM database.

If you want to join a domain or workgroup, make sure you know how it's spelled. To join a domain, you need the name and password of a domain user account that has administrative privileges. You can't just join a domain all by yourself; an administrator must approve it. Alternatively, an administrator can create a *machine account* beforehand using the Server Manager (see Chapter 11).

What Will This Be Named?

Before running the installation program, think about what to name the server. As I said in a previous chapter, don't name it after people. Use a name that will be of value to you in supporting the network, like an inventory number or the like. Similarly, you'll be prompted for a name, organization name, and product ID number. Make sure in particular that you can lay your hands on the ID number.

And if your network runs on the TCP/IP protocol, then you may have to gather this information for your new installation:

- IP address
- Subnet mask
- Default gateway(s)
- DNS server(s)
- WINS server(s)
- LMHOSTS file
- Domain name

All of this is explained in Chapter 14, on TCP/IP.

How Will This Server Be Licensed?

Like all software vendors, Microsoft has a real problem trying to figure out how to price its products. Economic theory says that, in a correctly competitive market, a price will (in the short term) drift toward the short-run marginal cost of the product. In other words, if the software industry were properly competitive, NT Server would cost what Microsoft paid to produce the floppies, CD, box, and manual—probably a wholesale price of about $20, with normal profit margins included.

Of course, that isn't how Microsoft prices its server product because, first of all, the server market is *not* properly competitive, not by a long shot, and second, the software business is one in which much of the costs are invested up front, on programmers and computing equipment. And that's the problem.

You see, we consumers of Microsoft products are allowed to know so little about how Microsoft (a publicly traded company, remember) runs its development efforts that we have no idea whether $700 for NT Server is a bargain or a boondoggle. And, judging from how Microsoft changes its pricing structure, they have no idea either.

The latest approach, which has existed all the way back to version 3.51, goes something like this. First, as you know, you must buy the NT Server software itself; it lists for $700 when last I checked. But you don't have the right to use that software unless you (or anyone else who wants to use it) own a *client license*. A client license is just a piece of paper—no ID codes, no passwords, just the "honor" system—saying that Microsoft allows you to use the software. Client licenses list for $40.

Let's stop and be clear about what a client license is. Again, it's just a piece of paper. It doesn't give you the right to put NT Server on any machine you like; you paid the $700 for the right to put NT Server on *one* machine. But if 100 users want to access that server, you have to buy a client access license for each one of them. Then, on top of that, you *still* must buy them all copies of Windows 95, NT Workstation, Windows for Workgroups, or the like. Ignoring the client operating system costs, the network software costs $700 plus 100 licenses at $40 apiece, or $4700.

But now suppose you put that server on the Internet and put a Web page on it. Some random surfer checks out your Web page, which technically means you have 101 people on your network. Microsoft wants you to buy a license for that surfer as well. Or suppose you buy another PC and put NT Server on it. Must you buy 100 more licenses to access that second server? Maybe yes, maybe no. Suppose you only allow one person on your Web site at a time, but 100 people visit per day. There's never more than one on the network at a time, but 100 different people connect to your network. Do you need one license or 100?

Microsoft allows you to make a choice about how to use those $40 client licenses. They call the options *per seat* and *per server*. For each server, you must decide whether to treat client licenses as per seat or per server.

"Per server" is also known as a *concurrent* license. Buying a license for a per-server machine means that one person can access that server at a time. For example, if you had 100 employees that worked in two shifts, 50 in the day and 50 at night, then you'd never have more than 50 people on the network at any time, so you could install the server as "per server" and buy 50 licenses. If you bought another server, you would need another 50 licenses, and so on for each new server.

"Per seat" is not oriented to the number of network connections, as is per server, but instead to the number of enterprise network users. If you set up your servers as per-seat servers, then all you need to do is buy one license for each user. That license allows that user to access any and all servers on your network. If your enterprise has 100 servers in it, one client license gives one user the right to access all of the servers in the enterprise. In the case of the company with the one server and two employee shifts, you'd have to buy 100 licenses, however, as the per-seat arrangement requires you to buy one license for each user.

Think about it for a bit, and you'll see that for anyone with two servers or more, per seat is the way to go. But there is one exception: servers attached to the Internet. If 1000 different people just happen to stop by once and never return to your FTP site, you certainly don't want to have to buy 1000 client licenses, right? The answer there is per server. In general, that's the rule that I use: for most servers, set up licensing as per seat. For Internet service servers (Web, Gopher, FTP), use per server.

Armed with hardware, software, and network knowledge, we're ready to start installing NT Server.

Starting the NT Install Program

Briefly, there are two ways to kick off the NT installation program, both of which have their pros and cons:

- Put the NT Server CD-ROM into your drive, take the three setup floppies out of the NT box, insert the NT Setup diskette into drive A:, and reboot.

- Run the WINNT or WINNT32 program from the I386 directory on the CD-ROM.

Both techniques are discussed below.

Installing from the Setup Floppies

Look in the NT box, and you see floppies labeled "Windows NT setup boot disk," "NT disk 2," and "NT disk 3." These floppies don't contain all of NT; they contain enough software to kick off the installation process so that the NT installation CD can take over.

This is the preferred method in many cases. But it won't work if you have a CD-ROM that is accessible from DOS but not from NT, like the CD-ROMs on the old Creative Labs Multimedia kits. The NT Setup program just can't recognize the CD-ROM and stops working. That's when WINNT or WINNT32 is useful.

Installing with WINNT and WINNT32

In the case of Intel users, all the files that you need to install NT are in the folder on the CD named I386. You can install NT just as long as you can get access of some kind to this directory—over the network, on the hard disk, or even from a CD-ROM that can only be accessed by DOS.

There's no real trick to this. Just make sure that all of I386—including its subdirectories—are on a CD, hard disk directory, or network drive. Log on to that I386 directory and either type WINNT if you're upgrading from DOS or Windows, or WINNT32 if you're upgrading from a previous version of NT. If you're using Windows 95, I recommend that you reboot Windows 95 in "safe mode command prompt" and use WINNT because WINNT32 seems not to work under Windows 95.

WINNT and WINNT32 have a couple of disadvantages. First, they require you to format three floppies before you start it up. You can often avoid that by using the /b option (WINNT/b or WINNT32/b), which skips the floppies. You need the floppies, however, if you either want to specify a nonstandard disk controller driver or you want to do an NT repair from WINNT.

> **NOTE** You can't do an NT repair on a computer without a CD-ROM drive. You can do WINNT or WINNT32 installs, but the repair process fails if NT can't find a CD-ROM drive.

The second disadvantage is time. Before taking you to the initial setup screens that you would see if you were installing from the three floppies and the CD-ROM, you have to sit through about 45 minutes of file copying. You can shorten that a bit by using WINNT32 and choosing to make the setup floppies, but uncheck the Create local source option in the dialog box that appears.

Running the NT Install Program

Next, you start the Setup program. My examples assume that you're installing from the CD-ROM. Floppy installations are nearly the same but are more tedious.

Starting with the Floppies

Pop the "Setup Boot Disk" into drive A: and reboot. NT then runs NTDETECT.COM, which figures out what kind of hardware you have on your system. You see a message that says, "Windows NT Setup/Setup is inspecting your computer's hardware configuration."

Next, you see the following on a blue screen with white letters:

```
Windows NT Setup
```

And on the bottom of the screen:

```
Setup is loading files (Windows NT Executive)…
```

NT next loads the Hardware Abstraction Layer, after which you are prompted to insert Setup Disk number 2 and press Enter. You see some messages on the bottom of the screen about what's loading, including

- "NT config data"
- Fonts
- Locale-specific data
- Windows NT setup
- PCMCIA support
- SCSI port driver

- Video driver

- Floppy disk driver

- Keyboard driver

- FAT file system

Setup then turns the screen to 50-line mode. It announces how much system memory you have in megabytes and says that the NT kernel as well as a "build number" is loading. For example, NT version 3.51 was build 1057.

Welcome to Setup

The screen shifts back to normal mode and the "Welcome to setup" message appears. It offers these choices:

- To learn more, press F1

- To set up Windows NT now, press Enter

- To repair a damaged installation, press R

- To quit, press F3

Press Enter, insert Setup Disk #3, and press Enter again. Setup goes into device detection.

Scanning for SCSI Adapters

Setup auto-detects any SCSI adapters in your system. Your adapter should be auto-detected properly (I've installed systems with four different SCSI adapters, and they all installed correctly). If the adapter wasn't recognized, you have a chance to punch it in directly, or if it's not on NT's built-in list of adapters, you can tell NT to use a device support disk.

If your adapter is on the NT compatibility list and wasn't recognized, I recommend *not* hand-configuring the SCSI adapter by pressing S. Instead, I recommend that you exit Setup (press F3) and go back and recheck that the SCSI adapter is installed correctly. In the SCSI host adapter scanning process, you have to insert the third (and final, if you're doing a CD-ROM installation) diskette. If you *do* have to insert a manufacturer's extra driver, you have to swap disk 3 and the driver disk a couple of times before going any further; just follow the prompts.

Upgrade or Fresh Install?

Next, you often see this message:

```
Setup has found Windows NT on your hard disk in the directory
shown below. To upgrade, press Enter. To cancel upgrade and
install a fresh copy of Windows NT, press N.
```

This is an important choice. If you choose to upgrade an existing copy of NT rather than do a fresh install, you will preserve all of your user accounts—the data in your SAM—as well as all directory share information that existed before this upgrade. If you are upgrading a primary domain controller, you probably want to upgrade. If you want to clean out old user accounts and start all over, a fresh install is probably the right choice.

What Do You Have and Where Does It Go?

NT Setup then tells you what it thinks you have in terms of

- Basic PC type
- Video system
- Keyboard
- Country layout for keyboard
- Mouse

The list is usually correct, except for the video. The NT Setup program seems to set just about every video board to basic VGA, and there's a good reason for it. The NT designers reasoned that if you choose a super VGA type, you may choose wrong, and if you choose wrong, the system won't be bootable and you will have to re-install from the ground up. In contrast, VGA drivers work on just about any video board around. They may not exploit the full resolution or color depth of most boards, but they *do* work. So, once the system is up and running with the VGA drivers, you can install the super VGA drivers. If, after installing the new drivers, your system doesn't work, you can always load the "last known good" configuration, as you'll see in Chapter 16.

Actually, even if you *do* mess up when picking a video type, NT resolves the problem by including an option on the Operating System Picker called NT 4 [VGA mode]. No matter how badly you've bollixed up the video, you can always reboot and choose the VGA option. Then, once you've booted, you can adjust your video driver to something more appropriate.

When you're satisfied that the list matches your configuration, highlight "The above list matches my computer," and press Enter.

At this point, if you're installing the NT workstation operating system and you intend to coexist with DOS, or if you're installing an NT Server on top of an existing DOS machine, you may see a message that tells you that you are using the Delete Sentry or Delete Tracking features of Undelete under DOS. NT does not recognize that feature (it doesn't have either Delete Sentry or Delete Tracking), and so NT may end up reporting different amounts of free space than DOS does.

In English, this means that NT may think that you don't have as much free space on your disk as DOS reported before you got started. Unless you're going to reformat the partition, this may make it impossible for NT to install on your system. If that's the case, reboot under DOS, disable the Delete Sentry system, and destroy the \SENTRY directory. (This defeats the Delete Sentry feature, but that may be necessary in order to get NT to load.)

Choosing an NT Partition

Next, NT Setup shows you the partitions on your system and asks which one you want to install NT on. You can delete partitions with this option, but, as always, be aware that you're permanently destroying data if you do that. (You *did* back up before you started doing this, didn't you?)

TIP

> If you're converting a server from Novell NetWare, you must delete the existing NetWare partition before proceeding. Again, that will destroy data on your partition, so don't do it unless you've backed up to a backup format that can be restored under NT, as discussed earlier in this chapter.

Picking Your Drive

Select the partition that you want to install NT on and press Enter. You next choose how you want to format the partition, if you want to format it at all. Your choices are

- Wipe the disk, formatting to a FAT system
- Wipe the disk, formatting to an NTFS system
- Convert an existing FAT system to NTFS
- Leave current file system and data alone
- Convert an existing HPFS/HPFS386 system to NTFS (LAN Manager upgrade of NT Server only)

FAT or NTFS Disk Partitioning Options?

Of the FAT or NTFS disk partitioning options, which should you use?

On an NT server, you should use NTFS partitions on the data drives unless you have a very good reason not to. But let's look at the details.

The File Allocation Table file system has only one advantage, but it's a compelling one: it's the file system that DOS uses. If you're moving from a FAT-based workstation (which is likely) or a FAT-based server (which is unlikely), you may want to be able to boot from a DOS floppy and read the hard disk. That's possible if you leave the disk in a FAT format. Moving to NTFS makes it impossible to boot from a DOS floppy and still be able to read the hard disk (a security feature of NTFS). That's why I like to keep a 200–500 MB bootable FAT partition on my servers; it makes working on a nonbooting server easier, since I can use my DOS-based data recovery tools. Again, however, the drives that contain the data shared on the network are always NTFS on my servers.

The main features that NTFS offers include:

- Directories that are automatically sorted.

- Support of upper- and lowercase letters in names.

- Support of Unicode in file names.

- Allows permissions to be set on directories and files.

- Multiple "forks" in files—subfiles that essentially "branch off" from a file (the closest analogy would be to the data fork and resource fork in the Macintosh file system).

- Faster access to large (over .5MB) sequential access files.

- Faster access to all random access files.

- File and directory names up to 254 characters.

- Long names are automatically converted to the 8+3 naming convention when accessed by a DOS workstation.

- Macintosh compatibility (you cannot share volumes with Mac clients on an NT network unless the host disk partition has been formatted to NTFS).

- NTFS uses the disk space more sparingly than does FAT. Under FAT, the minimum size that a file *actually* uses on a disk is 2048 bytes, and as disk partitions get larger, that minimum size also gets larger: on the 1700MB disk I use on my server, that minimum size would be *32768* bytes! Under NTFS, that same hard disk—and any hard disk, in fact—supports files so that no file actually takes more than 512 bytes of space.

I'll discuss all of this in more detail later in Chapter 4, but as I've said earlier, it's just plain crazy to use NT Server with any disk format other than NTFS. Without NTFS, you lose most of the security options, a good bit of performance, and some of the disk space currently wasted by the FAT file system for its clusters. The FAT and HPFS conversion routines both have worked without a hitch for me, so long as enough free space is on the hard disk (make sure there's about 118MB free before proceeding).

For an NT workstation, you may want to stay with the FAT file system so that you can dual-boot to DOS, because DOS can't read or write a disk partition formatted to the NTFS format.

CHKDSK in Disguise

NT Setup runs a special version of CHKDSK to make sure that the file system is clean. This test is *not* a disk media test like the old Novell COMPSURF, so—as I've said earlier in this chapter—the onus is on you to make sure that you have a reliable disk before beginning the installation process. This CHKDSK-like program runs if you're not formatting the partition. If you're formatting, you see a message to that effect, and the Setup program will format the hard disk. Then, unbelievably, Setup will run the CHKDSK program on your just-formatted disk (*grrr...*).

Which Directory Do I Put It On?

Choose the directory that you'll install the NT files to. The recommended directory, \winnt, is fine. Next you see the message, "Setup will now examine your hard disk(s) for corruption." Press Enter to run CHKDSK.

When CHKDSK is done NT Setup copies a bunch of files, just enough to boot the system, to your hard disk. If you're installing from floppies, you get a minor workout. These files are mainly just enough to get the graphical portion of Setup running, although a number of help files get installed in the process, including help files for things that aren't necessary until the system's up and running (Mail, Schedule+, and so on).

Even with a quad-spin CD-ROM, this takes about ten minutes, so be patient until you get a message like the following:

```
This portion of Setup has completed successfully.
If there is a floppy disk inserted in drive A:, remove it.
Press ENTER to restart your computer.
When your computer restarts, Setup will continue.
```

Pop out the Installation disk and reboot the computer. It then boots a kind of mini-NT into a graphical Setup program.

> **TIP**
> If you told the Setup program to use NTFS, you'll be confused when Setup reboots. A message says "Check in file system on C:... the type of the file system is FAT." Don't worry about it; you won't see NT say that you have an NTFS volume until you're done with the installation.

Entering Graphical Setup

As the system reboots, you first see NTDETECT's announcement; NTDETECT runs every time you boot NT. You then get a black screen with white letters that tell you to press the spacebar now to return to the "Last Known Good" menu. That's really not relevant here, as you don't yet *have* a Last Known Good menu. (Why you don't is explained in "Common Installation Problems" at the end of this chapter.) Then the screen turns blue because the NT kernel has loaded, and the graphical portion loads.

The first thing you see is the End User Licensing Agreement, kind of a "Microsoft loyalty oath." You're required to click Yes, because if you don't you can't go further. Once you've done that, NT builds the Setup Wizard.

Then you choose the type of installation: Typical, Portable, Compact, or Custom.

Who Are You?

As with many products these days, you personalize your copy of NT or NT Server by entering your name and company name. Enter those and click the Continue button; you are asked to verify what you entered and click Continue again. (Be sure to put the correct product number in your server. If you must make one up or leave it blank, remember that your server won't be able to communicate with any other NT Server machine with the same product number.)

The Per-Connection or Per-Seat Licensing Option?

Next, your licensing choices appear. In the dialog box, you are presented with two licensing options; per connection and per seat. As I've explained, the implications of these two choices are:

Per seat   Per-*seat* licensing means that you need a license for every workstation that will ever log onto the domain. Per seat is the kind of licensing that first appeared back in NT 3.5. Per-seat licensing has a few advantages. First, it's easy to understand; you count the number of people that log onto the domain and you have the number of licenses that you need. Second, you don't have to worry about the number of servers in the domain. Whether you have one server in the domain or six, per seat licensing requires that you have one license for each workstation that logs into the domain.

Per server   Per-*server* licensing means that you need a license for every simultaneous NT Server connection. If user Ignatz logs onto server RAMSES, that uses up one license. If she then logs onto server ISIS to get to the printer (without leaving her user directory on RAMSES), that uses up another license. If Ignatz connects to six servers, she uses up six licenses.

Think about your needs before choosing a licensing method. You get one shot at changing the licensing style from per server to per seat (by using the Licensing icon in the Control Panel). After that, or if you originally specified per-seat licensing, you have to re-install to legally change it.

NOTE   Oh, and if you *do* choose per-seat licensing, be sure to specify at least one client license, or the file server and print server services will refuse to start up.

Choosing a Computer Name

NT next prompts you for a computer name. Recall that it cannot exceed 15 characters in length, and while you can use blank spaces, it's best to avoid them.

Domain Controller or Server

Recall from the last chapter that an NT domain differs from a workgroup in that a domain has a master security database, and that security database is used to approve or reject requests for data or other resources on the network. In a simple NT network, all of the burden of security verification is shouldered by an NT Server machine acting as the primary domain controller. The workload of verifying requests can be shared, however, among a number of NT servers by making them backup domain controllers.

NT Server machines do not *have* to be domain controllers, however; they can simply act as servers. The Setup dialog box labeled "Windows NT Server Security Role" lets you choose which part this server will play in your domain—primary domain controller (which implies a new domain), backup domain controller (which implies an existing domain), or server.

The first NT server that you install in a domain *must* be a primary domain controller. The second should be a backup domain controller, because it's just about impossible to re-install a primary domain controller, if you need to, without a backup domain controller to stand in for the primary while you're re-installing the primary. Designate other servers as just "Server."

You can't change a machine's status from server to domain controller without re-installing NT Server.

You are prompted to create an administrative password if you're installing a primary domain controller or a server. Again, if it's a primary domain controller, then you are creating an administrative account for the entire domain. If it's for a server, then that administrative account only controls that one server.

Creating the Emergency Repair Disk

I have mentioned the important emergency repair disk before; this is where you create it. This part of the installation asks if you want to create one. Later on, Setup will prompt you to create it. Just put a floppy that you don't mind zapping into the A: drive and Setup will format it and create an emergency repair disk. This isn't a *bootable* disk. The emergency repair disk is just a disk that contains the data necessary to reconstruct a configuration if your NT system is no longer able to boot.

The formatting part of the program seems to run the drive pretty hard. You may find that the format process gets a bit noisy after about 75 percent, but don't worry about it. If the floppy is bad, you get a chance to insert a different floppy.

Selecting Components

Here you get the list of things you can add to your system, like Microsoft Exchange. Choose whichever pieces are appropriate for your installation. Then NT will move to Phase 2, Network Setup.

Beginning Network Setup

NT then asks

```
Windows NT needs to know how this computer should participate in
a network.
```

The options are

- Do not connect this computer to a network at this time
- This computer will participate on a network
  - Wired to the network
  - Remote access to the network

If it's to be a domain controller, you must be on the network. Therefore, choose "This computer will participate in a network/Wired to the network."

Next, choose if you would like to install Microsoft Internet Server (for Windows NT Server OS only).

Setting Up Network Cards

Next, you have to set up your network card. One of NT's really nifty features is an "auto-detect" system that is right most of the time. You see a dialog box labeled "Network Adapter Card Detection." Click Continue and, the vast majority of the time, NT figures out which network card you have without any trouble.

On the other hand, if Setup can't detect your network, card, or, in rare instances, if it locks up when it tries to detect your network card, then rerun Setup, choose "Do Not Detect," and directly choose the network card. If the driver for the card isn't on the NT setup disks, you're probably out of luck. There is not a huge market for NT LAN card drivers, so you probably won't find them on the driver disk that came with your LAN card (that may change with time, however). As I suggested a few pages back, it's a good idea to buy one of the top twenty or so LAN cards, since it's easy to find drivers for those cards. And if you want to be pretty *sure* that your NT drivers are good, consider this: much of Microsoft uses the Intel EtherExpress 16 LAN boards. Guess which drivers are likely to be the most stable under NT?

Once Setup has detected your LAN card, click Continue to set up the card. One thing that Setup is *not* good at is figuring out things like which IRQ, I/O address, and RAM addresses your card uses, but that isn't a problem if you took my advice earlier in this chapter and documented those things. Enter those values and click Continue. NT moves on to the main installation process.

Next, you select the protocols that you use on the server. NetBEUI is *de rigeur*, and IPX/SPX is checked by default. Don't install IPX/SPX unless you need it for Novell.

Then Setup prompts you to see if you want to install services. The ones it installs by default are

- RPC Configuration
- NetBIOS interface

- Workstation

- Server

Optionally, you can also install

- Microsoft Internet Information Server 2.0

- DHCP Relay Agent

- Gateway (And Client) Services for NetWare

- Microsoft DHCP Server

- Microsoft DNS Server

- Microsoft TCP/IP Printing

- Network Monitor Agent

- Network Monitor Tools and Agent

- Remote Access Service

- Remoteboot Service

- RIP for Internet Protocol

- RIP for NwLink IPX/SPX compatible transport

- RPC support for Banyan

- SAP Agent

- Services for Macintosh

- Simple TCP/IP Services

- SNMP Service

- Windows Internet Name Service

You will meet most of those services in this book.

If you chose the TCP/IP protocol, you are prompted to see if you want to use the DHCP protocol to assign TCP/IP addresses. For many systems, you say yes; but read Chapter 14 for the details of TCP/IP setup.

NT now installs the networking components you selected.

Domain/Workgroup Followup

Next, NT asks more questions about the security role that your computer plays. I don't like the arrangement of these dialog boxes because they really should follow the earlier question about whether the machine is to be a primary domain controller, backup domain controller, or server.

If you're just installing an NT Server machine in an existing domain, you see a dialog box called Domain/Workgroup Settings. You have the choice of joining an existing workgroup or becoming a member of an existing domain.

Remember that NT is massively security-conscious. As a result, not just any NT workstation or server can be part of an NT domain; instead, it has to be *granted* access to the domain by the Primary Domain Controller. That happens one of two ways:

- An administrator of the domain creates a machine account with the Server Manager (covered in Chapter 11) before installing the new server.

- The Setup program gives an administrator the option to create a machine account right here in the "Domain/Workgroup Settings" dialog box.

This can be a bit confusing (at least, it threw *me* when I first started working with NT), so let's look at what's going on in more detail. Most kinds of workstations can just jump right onto an NT domain without any kind of prior notice. For example, DOS, Windows, OS/2, and Windows for Workgroups machines can just "appear" on an NT domain without the permission of the NT Primary Domain Controller, *except* for the fact that whoever is logging on to the NT domain must be a user with a valid network account created by the User Manager for Domains (see Chapter 6).

In contrast, an NT domain won't even *talk* to an NT workstation or server to whom it has not been "properly introduced." Now, in general, you introduce a machine to a domain by first logging onto the domain as an administrator, then running the Server Manager. In the Server Manager, you can tell the domain to expect to hear from a new machine called, say, Ignatz. Then, when you're installing your next NT machine—workstation or server—you just name that machine Ignatz. The domain says, "Oh, *you're* Ignatz! We've been expecting you!" and all is well.

The problem with that approach, of course, is that nine times out of ten you end up forgetting to run the Server Manager before installing NT, which forces you to abort an NT installation in midstream or to run around looking for an already-working NT machine from which to run the Server Manager. For that reason, Microsoft decided to make your life easier and just put a tiny piece of the Server Manager in the Setup program. If you are installing NT *and* if you are an administrator (which you must verify by entering the user name for your administrative account and password), you can create the machine account right then and there in the Setup program.

In the Create Computer Account in Domain part of the dialog box, you're prompted for a User Name and a Password. It kind of looks like you're being prompted to create a new user in this dialog box, but you're not; this is the user name and password of your administrative account, the administrative account that you use to create the new *machine* account on the NT domain.

Once that's all plugged in, click OK.

If you are upgrading a machine, your domain controller may become confused about why a machine that it already knows is all of a sudden a different operating system version. If that happens, you may have to rebuild your machine's account, and you need to know a trick to do that. Wait until the server is set up and running, then go to Network in the Control Panel and choose Identification. Click Change Name and you get the chance to change from a domain to a workgroup. Change to a workgroup of any name. Then close the Control Panel. It prompts you to reboot, but you needn't do that. Reopen Network in the Control Panel and again choose Identification and press Change. Now choose to join your old domain, but also check the box labeled "Create Computer Account in [fill in blank] domain." Punch in the name and password of a domain administrator, and your domain will build a new machine account for your server.

Video Test Screen

Finally, NT offers to test your video driver. Go ahead and set up whatever color depth and resolution you like, but recall that I advise you to use the VGA driver on server machines.

NT then finishes up and tells you to reboot.

Now, it may have to go through another boot or two if you are converting from FAT to HPFS, but by then you have finished getting the basic operating system on your server.

After the Installation, What Next?

But you're not done yet, not by a good bit. Network installations vary from location to location, but at this point some tasks usually remain. The following list describes those tasks. If an item is followed by a chapter subject, then you can read about it there; otherwise, I'll cover it in the remainder of this chapter.

- Finish setting up Windows apps on a workstation

- Create users (Chapter 6)

- Set the policy for the Guest account (Chapter 6)

- Make whatever modifications are necessary to user rights (Chapter 6)

- Install, interface, and configure a UPS

- Install optional modules, like Mac support, TCP/IP, DLC, or Remote Access Services (Chapters 10, 14 and 17, respectively)

- Tuning (Chapter 15)

- Install fault-tolerant features (Chapter 4)

- Create a directory structure and share it (Chapter 7)

- Install tape drivers

- Set up scheduled events (Chapter 11)

- Install extra printer drivers (Chapter 8)

- Share printers (Chapter 8)

- Set default printer (Chapter 8)

- Establish links to and from trusted domains (Chapter 12)

While I'd like to cover every detail of a complete installation in this chapter, I felt that some of the larger issues should stay in their own chapters. In the next few sections, we'll take a look at some of the simpler setups you'll do to move your server install further along.

Migrating Windows Applications

For some reason, even though Setup promises to migrate your Windows applications over to your NT setup, it doesn't do it—and version 4 is particularly bad at it. That means that you have to sort of lead it by the nose. This part of the chapter explains how.

Not Every Windows Program Will Run

Understand right off that not every Windows program will run. In particular, say goodbye to your programs like

- Undelete

- Many DOS-based fax programs

- System utility

Those will, in general, not work under NT.

Moving the Fonts

Even though the Event Log shows that the Registry was updated with font information, NT seems unaware of your old Windows fonts. Fixing that is a snap.

1. Open the Control Panel.

2. Open the Fonts applet. You see a dialog box like the one in Figure 3.2.

3. Choose File/Install New Font, as shown in the figure. Now you see a dialog box like the one in Figure 3.3.

FIGURE 3.2

Fonts dialog box

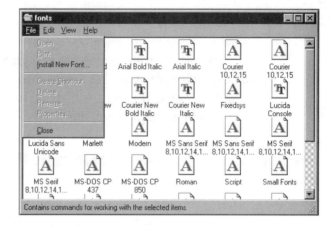

FIGURE 3.3

Adding fonts

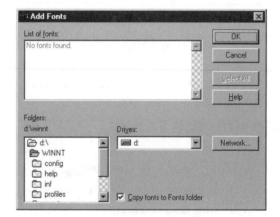

4. Uncheck the Copy fonts to Fonts folder check box at the bottom of the dialog box. No sense in having two copies of a font on your already-overworked hard disk.

5. Click the C:\windows\system directory. After a minute or two of disk activity, your fonts appear.

6. Select them all (just click on the top one, then scroll down to the bottom font, press the Shift key, and click the bottom item), or click the Select All button and click OK. You soon see a dialog box like the one in Figure 3.4.

FIGURE 3.4

Control Panel asking about an already-recognized font

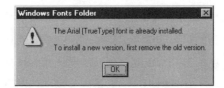

The dialog box is just telling you that you asked for a font that is already recognized by the system. That's okay.

7. Click OK and keep going. You see a bunch of these dialog boxes, but just keep clicking OK until you're done.

8. After the last "Remove this font and re-install" dialog box, just click Close on the Fonts dialog box, and close up the Control Panel. Your fonts are now restored.

In short, read the "How Do I" sidebar for a quick summation.

Getting Your Apps Back

For some reason, migrated Windows apps don't get migrated properly. The result: you probably experience problems getting your Windows apps to run on an NT workstation. My suggestions for fixing this are

- Make sure that the application's directories are on the right path.

- You may have to copy the application's INI files to the C:\winnt directory, or whatever directory you've put NT in.

- In many cases, you simply have to re-install the application.

How Do I Get My Old Windows Fonts Back?

To get your old Windows fonts back:

1. Open the Control Panel.

2. Open the Fonts applet and Choose File/Install New Font.

3. Uncheck the Copy fonts to Fonts folder check box and select the C:\windows\system directory.

4. After a minute or two of disk activity, you see your fonts appear. Select them all (just click on the top one, then scroll down to the bottom font, press the Shift key, and click the bottom item) or click the Select All button and click OK. You see dialog boxes that tell you that a copy of this font is already on the system, but just click OK and keep going.

After the last "Remove this font and re-install" dialog box, click Close on the Fonts dialog box, and close up the Control Panel. Your fonts are now restored.

Believe me, re-installing seems to be the best method. I know, it's bad news, but there doesn't seem any way around it. Funny thing: install OS/2 2.*x* on a system and it effortlessly moves your Windows applications over to its desktop. Odd that IBM can do with *its* operating system what Microsoft can't do with *its own*.

Choosing and Installing an Uninterruptible Power Supply

One of the most important parts of server security is *power* security. Once backup power supplies were tremendously expensive, but that's not true any more. You can buy a cheap, basic *standby power supply* (SPS) for around $200. Better yet, that cheap SPS can alert NT as to when the power's going down. But let's take a moment and look at what kinds of power protection devices you should invest in.

The Problem with Electrical Outlets

Power coming in from outlets is of a high quality, but it's not reliable enough to trust your server to it. For example, on my sites (two commercially zoned buildings), we experience about three or four outages per year. They're not *long* outages—usually just a minute or two—but that's quite enough to shut down the servers and sometimes damage data.

Power problems come in three main types:

Surges and spikes   Transient noise appearing on the power line that can permanently damage electronic components.

Voltage variation   The power coming out of the wall is supposed to be 120 volts in North America, 240 volts in the UK and Ireland, and 220 throughout continental Europe. (EC members will note how delicately I sidestepped the "Is the UK part of Europe?" question.) Usually too *little* voltage is the problem, but sometimes you get too much voltage. In any case, neither is desirable.

Outages   Whether they last for a second or a day, a power outage crashes servers, which can spell disaster for application servers.

You've heard of surge protectors, and perhaps some of you *use* them.

But I recommend avoiding them because they are really only rated to catch one surge. After that, they're not reliable. (Honest, it's true—surprising, though, isn't it?) Worse yet, there's no way to find out if that surge has *already happened*! Furthermore, surge protectors are of no value whatsoever in low voltage or outage situations.

What, then, is the best answer for power protection? Some combination of a *power conditioner* and a battery-backed power supply.

Power Conditioners for Protecting Data

Between a surge protector and a backup power supply is a device called a *power conditioner*. A power conditioner does all the things that a surge protector does—it filters and isolates line noise—and it does more besides. Rather than relying on the non-reusable components found in surge protectors, a power conditioner uses the inductance of its transformer to filter out line noise. Additionally, most power conditioners boost low voltage so that machines can continue to work through brownouts.

Which power conditioner is right for you? The one that I use is Tripplite's LC1800. I've seen it in mail-order ads for as little as $200, and I've used mine for many years.

The LC1800 even shows incoming voltage via some LEDs on its front panel. *Do not* plug your laser printer into a power conditioner, as most power conditioners are only rated for a few amps; laser printers, in contrast, draw up to 15 amps. If you *do* want to use a power conditioner for a laser printer, make sure that the power conditioner is one of the more expensive models that provide sufficient amperage to keep the laser going.

Backup Power Supplies

In addition to protection from short power irregularities, you may need backup power. I have lived in a number of places in the northeastern U.S. where summer lightning storms kill the power for just a second—enough to erase memory and make the digital clocks blink. Total loss of power can only be remedied with battery-based systems. Such systems are in the $200 to $1200 range and up. There are two types of backup power systems, *standby power supplies* (SPSes) and *uninterruptible power supplies* (UPSes). Figure 3.5 illustrates the differences between them.

FIGURE 3.5

How UPSes and SPSes work

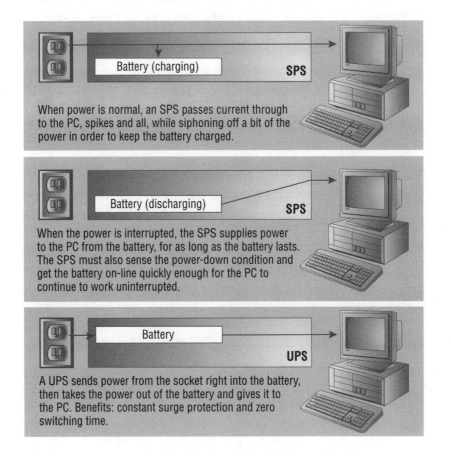

Battery (charging) · SPS

When power is normal, an SPS passes current through to the PC, spikes and all, while siphoning off a bit of the power in order to keep the battery charged.

Battery (discharging) · SPS

When the power is interrupted, the SPS supplies power to the PC from the battery, for as long as the battery lasts. The SPS must also sense the power-down condition and get the battery on-line quickly enough for the PC to continue to work uninterrupted.

Battery · UPS

A UPS sends power from the socket right into the battery, then takes the power out of the battery and gives it to the PC. Benefits: constant surge protection and zero switching time.

Standby Power Supplies SPSes charge their batteries while watching the current level. If the power drops, the SPS activates itself and supplies power until its batteries run down.

The key difference between a good SPS and a not-so-good SPS appears when the power goes out. When that happens, the SPS must quickly figure out that power's going down and must start supplying power from the battery just as quickly. A fast power switch must occur here, and it's important to find out what that switching time *is* for whatever model SPS you are thinking of buying. The speed is rated in milliseconds (ms); 4ms or under is fine. Eight ms—the speed of some SPSes—is, in my experience, not fast enough.

Uninterruptible Power Supplies   UPSes, the other kind of battery backup device, is a superior design, but you pay for that superiority. A UPS constantly runs power from the line current to a battery, then from the battery to the PC. This is superior to an SPS because no switching time is involved. Also, surges affect the battery charging mechanism, not the computer. A UPS also serves in the role of a surge suppressor and a voltage regulator.

A UPS or SPS must convert DC current from a battery to AC for the computer. AC is supposed to look like a sine wave, but cheaper UPS and SPS models produce square waves. The difference between the two is shown in Figure 3.6. Square waves are bad because they include high frequency harmonics which can appear as EMI or RFI to the computer. Also, some peripherals (printers in particular) can't handle square wave AC. So, when examining UPSes, ask whether they use

FIGURE 3.6
USP AC wave forms

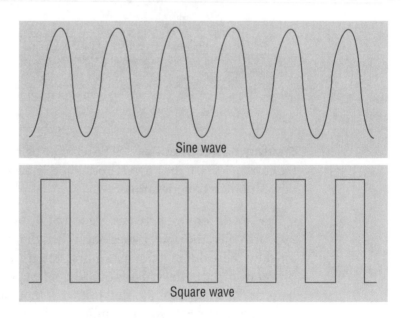

square wave or sine wave. Some produce a pseudo-sine wave. It has the "stairstep" look of a square wave, but fewer harmonic problems.

Ordinarily, the purpose of a UPS is to allow enough time to save whatever you're doing and shut down gracefully. If you are in an area where the power may disappear for hours and may do so regularly, look for a UPS to which you can attach external batteries so that you can run the PC for longer periods.

Remember that a sine-wave UPS is the only way to really eliminate most power problems. The reason *everyone* doesn't have one is cost.

A decent compromise can be found in a fast (4ms) square-wave SPS. I know I said square waves are bad for your peripherals, but how often will the SPS actually do anything? Not very often. Remember that an SPS only supplies power when the line voltage drops out, which isn't a common occurrence. The brief minute or two each month of square-wave power that your peripherals end up getting won't kill them. And you save a pile over a UPS by using an SPS.

On the other hand, a UPS is *always* online, and so must produce sine-wave output. But UPSes have the benefit of providing surge protection by breaking down and reassembling the power, and SPSes *do not* provide this protection. You must still worry about surge protection when you buy an SPS, but not if you buy a UPS. So make the choice that your budget allows.

Whether you buy an SPS or UPS, be sure to look for a backup power supply with a serial port. *Serial port*? Yes, a serial port. NT and NT Server can monitor a signal from a serial-port-equipped UPS/SPS. When power fails, the operating system is informed by the backup power supply of that occurrence, and the operating system does a graceful shutdown in the battery time remaining. Table 3.2 summarizes what we've seen about power problems and solutions.

Notice that a combination of a power conditioner and an SPS would provide all the power protection that you need. Recognizing that, a firm called American Power Conversion has made a device that combines an

TABLE 3.2   Power Problems and Solutions

Protection Method	Remedies Surges?	Remedies Low Voltage?	Remedies Outages?
Power Conditioner	yes	yes	no
SPS	no	no	yes
UPS	yes	yes	yes

SPS with a power conditioner. Called their Smart-UPS (okay, so even *they* don't understand the difference between a UPS and an SPS), they offer 400-watt models (the mail-order price is about $350) on up to 1800-watt models. I use Smart-UPS 400s in my office and have had very good luck with them. (Of course, they have the serial port connection.)

Interfacing the UPS/SPS

NT in both its server and workstation configuration is designed to be able to control and act on information from a UPS/SPS. NT expects two kinds of signals *from* the UPS/SPS ("power failed" and "battery low"), and can give one signal *back* to the UPS/SPS ("remote UPS shutdown").

Power failed   This signal goes from the UPS/SPS to the NT machine. When this signal is activated by the UPS/SPS, it means that input power has failed and that the NT machine is now running on battery power.

Battery low   Some UPS/SPS systems can only signal that the power has failed, leaving NT to guess how much battery life is left on the UPS/SPS. Others can signal that about two minutes of battery life is left. If you have such a UPS/SPS, then NT can recognize the "battery low" signal.

Remote UPS shutdown   If your power backup device is an SPS rather than a UPS, it may sometimes be desirable to temporarily disable the battery. NT does this if it senses extremely erratic signals from the "power failed" or "battery about to fail" signal. If that happens,

NT instructs the SPS to shut down its "inverter," a part of the SPS circuitry, so that all the SPS does is charge the battery and provide power from the mains. This is a signal *from the PC* to the SPS.

If you have a UPS/SPS with a serial port, you should get a cable built for that UPS/SPS from its manufacturer. The manufacturer can also probably guide you in how to set the UPS service settings.

TIP

If your UPS/SPS manufacturer does not sell a cable for interfacing with NT Server, buy the cable for Microsoft LAN Manager. The interfacing is the same, except that the third parameter is not referred to as "remote UPS shutdown" in LAN Manager documentation, but rather as "Inverter shutdown."

Configuring a UPS

To configure your UPS, get the correctly wired cable from the UPS/SPS manufacturer and hook it up to a serial port on the server and to the back of the UPS/SPS. Then, in NT, start up the Control Panel and choose UPS. You see a screen like the one in Figure 3.7.

FIGURE 3.7

Configuring the UPS

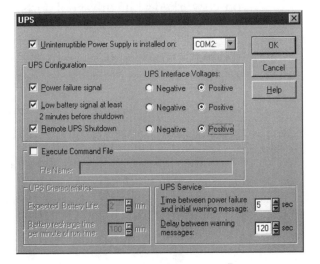

This is a setup screen for an SPS that supports all three features. Notice that, next to Power failure signal, Low battery..., and Remote UPS Shutdown options, there are radio buttons called Negative and Positive. These radio buttons refer to the kind of signal from the UPS/SPS. No real standard exists for using a serial port to interface a UPS/SPS with a PC, and there are 25 different control lines on a serial port. Furthermore, each one of those 25 lines can either display negative voltages or positive voltages. The purpose of these radio buttons is to inform NT of what a signal means. You see, on one UPS, a negative signal might mean, "We're losin' power, Captain! Better evacuate while we still can!" *or* it might mean, "All is well." Where do you get this information? Well, the best source is, again, the manufacturer. Failing that, however, you can just try the combinations until the system works. Or you can do what I ended up doing: working with a breakout box.

Breakout Boxes

Interpreting serial port signals involves a bit of experience with a data communications test device called a *breakout box*. If you don't know what they are or how to use them, I'm afraid that explaining that is a bit beyond the scope of this book. There are, however, many good sources on the subject, including a book by me called *The Complete PC Upgrade and Maintenance Guide* (Sybex). This discussion assumes that you've worked a bit with serial ports, but even if you're not an expert, you may find it useful anyway.

Serial ports have either a 9-pin or 25-pin connector. Every UPS/SPS system that I've ever worked on used the 9-pin, so I'll assume that we're working on one of those. Most breakout boxes are equipped with 25-pin connectors, so get one of the 25-to-9 converters and plug the breakout box into the port on the back of the UPS.

Turn the UPS on. On the breakout box, you see LEDs up to 25 different signal lines (depending on how well-designed the breakout box is), but you should notice the ones labeled as follows:

- CD or DCD (carrier detect)
- CTS (clear to send)

- DSR (data set ready)

- DTR (data terminal ready)

- RTS (request to send)

- RX (receive data)

- TX (send data)

NT expects three signals on these lines:

- Power failed must appear to the PC on its CTS line.

- Low battery must appear to the PC on its DCD line.

- Remote UPS shutdown signals are provided from the PC on its DTR line.

Breakout boxes display the status of a serial port's 25 lines with LEDs. Some breakout boxes' LEDs glow whether the line is positive or negative; those breakout boxes aren't of any help to you. The LEDs on better-designed breakout boxes glow either red or green depending on whether the line is positive or negative; that's the kind of breakout box that you want.

With the breakout box connected, unplug the UPS/SPS. You see one of the LEDs change color. That line is the Power Failed line; it should connect to the CTS line on the PC serial interface. Leave the UPS/SPS unplugged until it runs out of power. A bit before the batteries run down all the way, you see another one of the LEDs change color. That's the Low Battery connection; that line should connect with the DCD line on the PC serial interface. You may not see any LED change color before the UPS/SPS fails. If so, that means that your UPS/SPS does not support the Low Battery signal. There really is no reliable way to detect which line to use for the Remote UPS shutdown.

Before you start playing around with a UPS and a breakout box, however, let me stress that this is a time-consuming project, inasmuch as your hard work won't really pay off until you take the information that you've gained and construct a cable to connect your PC and your UPS/SPS.

What Does the UPS Service Do When Power Fails?

When the Power Failure signal is asserted to the PC, the NT machine sends a broadcast to all users like the one in Figure 3.8.

Your workstation only gets this message if you've enabled the Messenger service or run the WinPopup program or an equivalent. This message gets rebroadcast every x seconds, where x is set in the UPS dialog box that you saw a page or two back. You can also specify a delay between the power failure signal and the first message, although I'm not sure why you would want to do this. After all, the sooner people know that there was a power failure at the server, the sooner they can save their work to another drive or shut down their application. At this point, however, the Server service is paused and new users cannot attach to the server.

If power is restored before the batteries fail, the UPS service sends out an "all clear" message like the one in Figure 3.9.

Two fields are relevant if your UPS/SPS does not support the Battery Low signal:

- Battery recharge time
- Expected battery life

FIGURE 3.8

NT broadcast concerning power failure

154

FIGURE 3.9

NT's power restoration
message

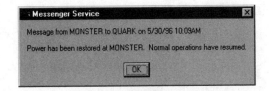

Both of these fields are basically "guesses" of how much time is left
before the system fails. Use the manufacturer's suggested values, but
be darn sure to test them, which brings me to...

Testing the UPS Service

Whether you have a UPS/SPS that supports Low Battery or not, you
should do a scheduled test of the UPS/SPS. How do you do it? Simple.
First, be sure to run the test after hours. Second, send a network broadcast to everyone warning them that the server is going down because
of a planned power outage, and that they should log off *immediately*!

The "How Do I" sidebar explains how to notify everyone of the
imminent server shutdown.

Setting up the UPS is a bit of a pain, but once it is done, write down
what you did so that you can redo it quickly if you ever re-install.

Installing Tape Drivers

Most servers have a backup device of some kind, usually a tape drive,
but it is smarter to use a SCSI tape drive because that is supported by
the most backup software.

While the beauty of SCSI is supposed to be that it is "plug-and-play,"
you still need a driver for your tape drive. Therefore, it wouldn't be a

How Do I Send a Broadcast Message to the Entire Network?

 To send a broadcast message to an entire network:

1. Start the Server Manager.
2. Click on the primary domain controller.
3. From the menu, select Computer/Send Message.
4. Fill in the message and click OK.

Make sure that you're on a workstation, either Windows with WinPopup, or an NT workstation. Then go to the UPS/SPS and pull out its power plug. Let it run until the server loses power altogether.

Then check the following:

- Did your workstation get a message about the power failure?
- Did you get a message every two minutes, or however far apart you set the messages?
- Did you get a final "The UPS service is about to perform final shutdown" message?
- How long was the server able to run with the UPS?

If necessary, go back and adjust the UPS service software if you don't have a Low Battery support or if your guesses were wrong about how much time you had on the battery.

bad idea to look at the current Hardware Compatibility List that Microsoft publishes before purchasing a tape drive (there is a copy in the NT Server box, but it's also on CompuServe, TechNet, and a number of other sources).

I use a Tandberg model 4100 and have had very good luck with it. The product is packaged by Colorado Memory Systems as a "Power-Tape." As with many tape drives, however, Colorado falsifies the tape's capacity by claiming that it is a 2GB tape drive when actually it is a 1.2GB tape drive. However, with the data-compression software included with the tape, you can store 2GB of data. I say that it's falsification for these reasons:

- Not all data *can* be compressed.

- The compression and backup software that gives this "2GB" tape its supposed 2GB capacity is *DOS* software that doesn't run under NT or OS/2.

It's a good idea to look closely when buying a tape drive, as this blatant lying about tape capacities seems to be business as usual in the tape business. For example, every single tape on the market that advertises itself as a 250MB tape drive is actually a 120MB drive that assumes a 2-to-1 compression ratio. I mean, optimism has its *place*, but... And even worse, the NT Backup program doesn't compress.

You install the tape drive just as you would any SCSI device. When you power up your system, your SCSI BIOS will probably list the SCSI devices that it finds on the SCSI bus. The tape drive should show up. Now, if the tape drive *doesn't* appear on the list, you've probably installed the tape drive incorrectly. Go back and get the physical installation straightened out before going any further.

Then, once the drive is recognized on the SCSI bus, you have to install an NT driver for it. Here's how to do it:

1. Open Control Panel, then double-click on Tape Devices.

2. Click on the Drivers tab and you see a dialog box like the one in Figure 3.10.

Don't panic when you don't see your tape drive in the box; that's normal.

3. Click Add and you see a dialog box like the one in Figure 3.11.

FIGURE 3.10

Tape Devices setup
dialog box

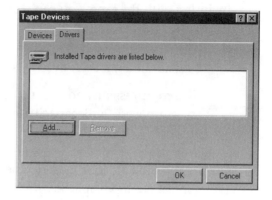

FIGURE 3.11

Select Tape Driver
dialog box

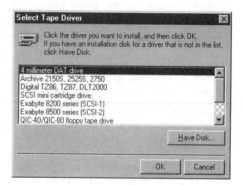

4. Browse through the model numbers to see if you can find a tape drive that matches yours. If you can't find an exact match, try something close to it. Again, using my Tandberg as an example, when I turn my system on I see the following report from my SCSI BIOS:

```
SCSI ID #0 - FUJITSU M2652S-512  -Drive C: (80h)

SCSI ID #1 - MAXTOR 7290-SCSI   -Drive D: (81h)

SCSI ID #2 - TANDBERG TDC 4100

SCSI ID #3 - MAXTOR 7290-SCSI   -Drive 82h

SCSI ID #5 - NEC  CD-ROM DRIVE:841
```

I see from my device number 2 that I've got a Tandberg 4100, which unfortunately does not match any option. The closest option is the Tandberg 3660, 3820, 4120, 4220 option. I tried that option for my 4100 and it worked. Later, Microsoft agreed in a Knowledge Base article that the 4100 would work with the other Tandberg drivers.

Once you have the driver set up, you have to restart your server. After restart, you can use the NTBACKUP program.

The "How Do I" sidebar gives a brief rundown on installing an NT Server tape driver.

How Do I Install an NT SERVER Tape Driver?

 To install an NT Server tape driver:

1. Start NT Setup.
2. Click on Options, and then Add/Remove Tape Devices.
3. Don't panic when you don't see your tape drive in the box; that's normal. For some reason, Microsoft did not include auto-detect on tape drives. You're pretty much on your own here. Click Add.
4. Browse through the model numbers to see if you can find a tape drive that matches yours. If you can't find an exact match, try something close to it.

Once the driver is set up, you have to restart your server. After you restart, you can use the NTBACKUP program.

The License Manager

Okay, you've installed all of these clients and they're merrily accessing the servers in your domain. Ah, but have you *licensed* all those users?

If so, how have you organized it so that you can keep track of new and outdated users?

Licensing can be a pain to administer, and the bigger the network the harder it becomes. To help you do it, NT Server comes with a tool called the License Manager. This tool can monitor licensing not just on the local machine but on NT Servers in other domains with which the domain you're starting from has a trust relationship. With the License Manager, you can monitor the entire network without trotting from server to server.

When you install NT Server, its icon automatically goes into the Administrative Tools group. Click it and you see a dialog box like the one in Figure 3.12.

Microsoft went to a lot of work to create some very good help files for the License Manager, so there's not much to be said that the help files don't say already. Just to review, however, following are the basics of the License Manager and how you can use it to inventory software licenses. This isn't all there is to this tool, but these essentials will get you started.

FIGURE 3.12

Opening screen of
License Manager

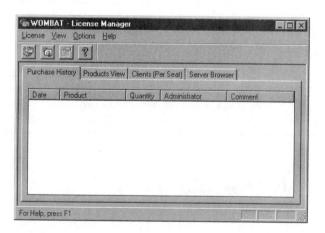

Purchase History

Click on the Purchase History tab and you see a record of all the software licenses that you've purchased and entered into this database. (If you don't enter them, this database can't help you—it only knows what you tell it.) You also enter new per-seat licenses and change the domain to administer here.

Products View

From the Products View tab, you can view product information either for the entire network or a selected domain. Select the Per Seat or Per Server mode as needed to get information about

- Which products are licensed properly (and which are not)

- Which products are at their license limit

From here, you can also add and delete per-seat licenses or view the properties of a particular license.

Clients (Per Seat)

Click on the Clients (Per Seat) tab to access information about clients who have accessed a particular product (such as NTS) throughout the domain or entire network. From here, you can see the number of licenses already used, those still available, and the dates on which all the licenses were last accessed.

Server Browser

From the Server Browser tab, you can access other domains to see their licensing information, add and delete per-server client licenses for servers and products, and add new per-seat licenses for the entire enterprise.

Common Installation Problems

Most installations of NT Server (or NT workstation, for that matter) are pretty trouble-free. But here's a look at some of the more common problems and questions that *do* arise.

Lockups on Install   NT ties to the hardware on your system with a program called, appropriately, NTDETECT.COM. Sometimes NTDETECT gets confused, however, and all you're left with is a message that NTDETECT version 1 is running—forever. What to do? You can troubleshoot hardware detection with a "debug" version of NTDETECT.COM.

Located in the \SUPPORT directory of NT CD-ROM disc, the file is called NTDETECT.CHK. Just DISKCOPY the NT Setup installation disk (the one you boot from to start off NT installation), erase the original NTDETECT.COM from the copied disk, and replace it with NTDETECT.CHK. (Rename NTDETECT.CHK to NTDETECT.COM, of course.) You then get a blow-by-blow description of what NTDE-TECT sees as it examines your hardware.

Incorrect Hardware   If you can't get *anywhere*, did you make sure that you have "regulation" NT hardware? Check back in this chapter to ensure that you have the right hardware and that it's configured correctly. Use the debugging version of NTDETECT.COM to find out where Setup is hanging up. Remember that interrupt conflicts that never gave you trouble under DOS stick out like a sore thumb under NT!

Image Can't Be Relocated, No Fixup Information   NT requires that 600K of memory be free in the low 1MB of RAM space. While most computers have 640K of conventional memory, a few either have only 500K of conventional memory, or—in the case of some high-performance server computers like the Compaq System Pro XL—have no conventional memory at all. Now, if you *do* have an XL, you can run its EISA configuration program and set the memory on the motherboard from "linear" to "640K Compaq compatible." That will solve the problem on that machine.

How Do I Remote Boot NT?   Most PC operating systems support remote boot. NT, however, does not, at least not now.

"Boot couldn't find NTLDR. Please insert another disk."   One of the essential files to boot NT, a file that you can't hope to start up without, is the NT loader program NTLDR. It *must* appear in the root directory, and that's where you can get in trouble.

You see, on hard disks formatted with the FAT file system, you are limited to 512 files in the root directory. That's an unusual number of files to see in a root, but some people do have that many files in their root.

It's particularly easy to accumulate files in the root if you've had disk problems and you ran CHDKSK/F under DOS or OS/2 before installing NT. The result is potentially hundreds of files with names like FILE0000.CHK. Having 512 of them means that you can't put any more files on your root, including NTLDR.

You see this problem crop up if your system is unable to perform the reboot that happens about one third of the way through the installation process.

The fix is simple: clean out some files from your root directory and do the installation again. If you don't want to do the whole installation, read the "How Do I" sidebar.

TIP   If you're expanding NTLDR from floppies, it is called NTLDR.$ on floppy disk 2.

How Do I Fix the System After It Can't Find NTLDR?

To fix a system after it can't find NTLDR:

1. Boot the system with a DOS bootable floppy (assuming you have a DOS partition). If you have an NTFS partition instead, use the Emergency Repair Boot disk mentioned in "How Do I Create A Generic Boot Floppy?")

2. Eliminate unnecessary files in the root directory.

3. In the \i386 directory of the NT setup CD-ROM (or disk 2 of the setup floppies—*not* the CD-ROM Installation disk), you see NTLDR._. It is the compressed version of NTLDR. (I understand why Microsoft compressed the files on the *floppies*; but why the CD-ROM version? There's plenty of space on that CD-ROM disk.)

4. Expand the file onto your root directory by using the EXPAND program from MS-DOS 6.0, Windows 3.1, or Windows for Workgroups. For example, if the NTLDR._ file were on the CD-ROM and the CD-ROM is drive D:, then the command would look like this:

```
expand d:\i386\ntldr._ c:\ntldr.
```

You should be able to continue with Setup now.

Where Do I Load ANSI.SYS?

Problem: I've got DOS programs that require ANSI.SYS, but I can't get them to run under NT.

There is a file in your SYSTEM32 directory called CONFIG.NT that tells NT how to run DOS sessions. Add this line to CONFIG.NT:

```
device=c:\winnt\system32\ansi.sys
```

Alternatively, you can say

```
device=%systemroot%\system32\ansi.sys
```

Then start up a command-line session by starting the COMMAND .COM that comes with DOS 5.0 (gotta search around for that one...).

While it *is* a pain having to find a copy of DOS 5.0's COMMAND .COM, it *is* pretty neat that you can change this CONFIG.NT file and see its effects without having to reboot.

Must My RISC Computer Be FAT-Based?

The FAT file system has its problems, but it's your *only option* if you're using a RISC-based system, at least for your boot partition.

The answer is to create a small FAT partition that contains your boot files, and format most of the hard disk as NTFS, so that you can keep the data files secure on the NTFS partition. Microsoft claims that you can actually make this boot partition only about 1MB in size, and the only files that *must* be on that partition are HAL.DLL and OSLOADER.EXE.

Another problem that some RISC machines (MIPS machines, in this case) may show is that the MIPS machines must have an R4000 chip that is version 2 or later.

Re-Installing NT Server

Once you get NT Server up and running, you probably never have to re-install it. But, if you *do*...

Recall that an NT domain keeps track of the particular machines in the domain that run NT or NT Server as part of the security that is so integral to the design of NT. A side-effect of this security is that you can't simply re-install NT on a workstation, server, or domain controller, and expect it to work. NT reasons something like this: "Well, you *say* that you're a machine named PSERVER01, and I know a machine named PSERVER01, but how do I know that *you're* that computer?"

NT internally creates passwords that you never see. These passwords are used by the primary domain controller to verify that a machine is, indeed, who it says it is. As a result, if you re-install NT or NT Server on a machine that's already running NT or NT Server and you give the machine the same name that it was previously using, you get a message that looks like this: "No domain controller was available to validate your logon."

That means that there is a *very* specific way to re-install NT or NT Server on a computer. It's just three steps:

1. Shut down the computer that you're going to re-install NT or NT Server on.

2. Log on to your domain as an administrator, run the Server Manager, and delete the to be re-installed computer from the domain.

3. Re-install NT on the computer, specifying that you are not *upgrading* but rather are *replacing* the NT software on the machine. During the re-installation process, you are given the chance to create a new machine account on the domain. Take that opportunity and you'll be back up and running.

Don't ignore this! In the course of writing this book, I re-installed NT Server a number of times. I thought that I understood how the system worked fairly well—but I *didn't* understand the re-installation procedure. Worse yet, I only had one domain controller on my network for quite some time. That's why it surprised me when the following happened.

One of my networks had been based on Windows for Workgroups prior to using NT Server. As I was previously using Windows for Workgroups, I didn't have a domain, I had a workgroup—a workgroup somewhat facetiously named "us." In my other office, we had a workgroup named "NextGeneration." When I first installed NT Server, I frankly expected to spend several days on it. After all, I've installed a pile of networks. I've installed IBM PC LAN, LAN Manager 1.*x* and 2.*x*, Novell 2.15, 3.11, LANtastic, PC-Office, PC-Net, and a number of others (if you've never heard of some of those, don't worry about it because no one else has either). And when I installed networks, I learned the hard way that you have to set aside a day or two *at least* the first time that you install a server.

That's why installing NT Server the first time was such a pleasure. The whole installation took me about two hours, including all the ancillary stuff. Of course, to do it I just converted my workgroup "us" to a new domain named "us."

By the next time I installed NT Server—*re*-installed it on that same server machine—we had an ISDN bridge in place between the LANs in the two buildings. Since the workgroup in the other building ("Next-Generation") would interact with our workgroup, "us" seemed like a silly name. Casting around for domain names, I picked a constellation name, figuring that many constellations are easy to spell (well, okay, except for Sagittarius, Cassiopeia, and Ophiuchi). The idea was, if necessary, to name machines in the domain after stars in the constellation.

So this time I installed NT Server with a new domain name, Orion (a nice, easy-to-spell name). Knowing that all the workstations would run into trouble because they were set up to log onto a domain named "us," I went to all the workstations in the office and reset their logon domain to "Orion." I was able to do this because, as you probably surmised, I did the work after hours, just as *you* probably have to do just about *all* the work on *your* server after hours.

The *next* time I re-installed NT Server, however, I was merely re-installing the primary domain controller for Orion, so when I installed the server software (after hours, again), I just typed in "Orion" as the domain name. I didn't go to the workstations and make any changes, as it didn't seem that I'd changed anything.

Hoo boy. *Big* mistake.

The DOS and Windows for Workgroups workstations were quite happy, logging on and emitting no complaints. But two things were quite wrong:

- The NT workstations all complained that "a domain controller could not be found." They refused to let me get to any server resources.

- The domains that we previously trusted, and that trusted us, wouldn't talk to us any more.

After a little thought, the answer dawned on me: *I had created a completely new domain.* A new domain named "Orion," to be sure, but a new domain nonetheless. I mean, suppose you're a foreign domain that trusts another domain named Orion? Some domain named Orion says, "Here I am," but the foreign domain's got to ask itself, "Yeah, this guy *says* he's Orion, but how do I know?"

NT uses not merely *names* like Orion to identify objects, but also internal security ID numbers (or SIDs, as Microsoft calls them). When you re-install a primary domain controller, you create new security IDs, even if you use an old name.

Each domain needs a primary domain controller. Primary domain controllers *must* be computers running NT Server. But in my domain—as in many domains in the real world—there is only one NT Server, so when you take the server down and re-install it, you kind of create a vacuum. When the server's running again, it says, "I'm the primary domain controller of Orion," and the NT machines on the network say, "Okay, but you're not the primary domain controller of the Orion that *we* know."

What's the answer? Two possibilities:

- If you only have one NT Server in your domain, then do the following. First, make sure you have an Emergency Repair Disk for that machine. Re-install NT Server on the computer—a fresh installation—and then run Setup again with the intention of doing a "repair." The repair routine will prompt you for an Emergency

Repair Disk. Give it the original one, and the repair routine will restore the old Registry with the old Security IDs. Then your PDC is back in business.

- That first answer sounds like a bit of work, and it is. A better answer requires that you have a backup domain controller in your domain. Just promote the backup domain controller to primary domain controller, demote the one that you're going to re-install, then re-install the machine as a backup domain controller, and promote it to primary domain controller, which will in passing demote the other domain controller.

Creating an NT Boot Disk

Those of you who've had to support DOS in the past (and those who haven't, spare us the condescending grins, okay?) know that an essential support tool is the boot floppy.

A boot floppy is just a floppy diskette that contains a minimum operating system. You used it to get a faulty system started. Is it possible, then, to create a boot disk for NT Server? Not completely. NT Server is so large that there isn't a prayer of getting it running simply from a floppy.

Sometimes, however, an important boot file can get lost and keep NT from booting. For example, I recently added two SCSI hard drives to my server. Either some sort of power glitch occurred, or NT doesn't like you adding drives, or…. I'm not sure what caused it, but when I turned the system on and tried to boot, I got this message:

```
error 08: error opening NTDETECT.COM
```

Now, NTDETECT.COM is the first program that NT loads, and this error message indicated that NT couldn't load it, so the server would not boot. As it turned out, the only file damaged on the server was NTDETECT.COM, so it would have been nice to have a floppy around that contained NTDETECT.COM to get the server started in the boot process. After that, the hard disk could take over.

One good answer—and the one that I eventually used—was the Emergency Repair Floppy. But each Emergency Boot Floppy is specific to a particular NT machine, and this bootable NT floppy is generic.

Given that bit of information, the "How Do I" sidebar explains how to create a generic NT boot floppy.

How Do I Create a Generic NT Boot Floppy?

To create a generic NT boot floppy:

1. Format a floppy under either NT File Manager or from a command line under NT. *Do not use a DOS-formatted floppy, or this won't work.* A DOS-formatted floppy looks for the DOS boot files IO.SYS and MSDOS.SYS; an NT-formatted floppy looks for the NT boot file NTLDR. (From File Manager, just click Disk, and then Format Disk.)

2. You're going to copy a bunch of files from the root directory of your server to the floppy in the A: drive. The files are hidden, however, so you have to tell the File Manager to show you hidden files. To do that, click View, then By File Type, and then check the Show Hidden/System Files box.

3. Looking in your server's root directory, copy the following files from the server's root to the floppy disk:

   • NTLDR

   • NTDETECT.COM

   • BOOT.INI

   • NTBOOTDD.SYS (if your server boots from a SCSI hard disk; if not, you probably don't have this file in the root and you don't need to copy it)

When you are finished, you have a floppy that can essentially "jump start" your system.

As John Ruley at *Windows* magazine has pointed out, this doesn't constitute a complete NT boot disk—but it's enough to get NT running in some situations.

Setting up NT Server right is essential if you want a trouble-free network from the beginning. And you can take another step toward keeping your network trouble-free by setting up fault-tolerant disk systems, which just happens to be the subject of the next chapter.

CHAPTER

FOUR

RAID FOR SPEEDIER, SAFER DISKS

Disk
Administrator

Disks on servers are different from disks on workstations.

Server disks must be faster, more reliable, and larger than their workstation-based cousins. How do you achieve those goals of speed, reliability, and size? Well, there's always the *simple* answer: spend more money for a drive with more of those three characteristics. But the past few years have yielded another solution: a group of mediocre drives can band together and, acting in concert, can provide speed, capacity, and high fault tolerance. The process of doing that is called *redundant array of inexpensive drives* (RAID). Until recently, putting a RAID on your server required buying an expensive RAID system (the *drives* are inexpensive, but the entire RAID subsystem *isn't*, unfortunately). However, NT changes that with the Disk Administrator. With the Disk Administrator, you can take a bunch of hard disks and "roll your own" RAID system.

The Disk Administrator offers a lot of options, and this chapter explains what your organization and protection options are and how you can use the Disk Administrator to best arrange your data for your particular situation.

While you'll set up the initial disk partitioning when you install NT Server, you can use the Disk Administrator (it is found in the Administrative Tools program group) to make changes to your disk setup after you've installed NT. With the Disk Administrator, you can

- Create and delete partitions on a hard disk and make logical drives.

- Get status information concerning these items:

  - The disk partition sizes

  - The amount of free space left on a disk for making partitions

  - Volume labels, their drive-letter assignment, file system type, and size

- Alter drive letter assignments.

- Create, delete, and repair mirror sets.

- Create and delete stripe sets and regenerate missing or failed members of stripe sets with parity.

Don't recognize some of these terms? Hang on, they're defined in the section below.

Disk Administrator Terminology

Before we get into the discussion of how you can use the Disk Administrator to arrange and protect your data, you need to know some of the terms that we'll be tossing around. These terms will be explained further in due course, but this section introduces them.

SLED

An acronym for *single large expensive drive*, SLED is a way of arranging your data on one very large, very (I hope) reliable drive. SLED is currently the most popular method of arranging data for two reasons.

- It's simple. You only have to buy one disk and store your data on it.

- Dedicated RAID hardware has been expensive in the past.

RAID

"Apply a shot of RAID, and all those nasty data problems will be gone!" No, it's not really a household product. RAID, which stands for redundant array of inexpensive drives, is a method of protecting your data by combining smaller, less expensive drives in such a way that your data redundancy and therefore security (fault tolerance) is increased. There are six kinds of RAID implementation, each of which works in a different way and has different applications. NT Server can handle levels 0, 1, and 5. We'll talk about exactly what those levels are later in this chapter.

Free Space

This sounds like an obvious term. "Free space on a disk is just space that's free, right?" It's not. *Free space* is space on the disk that is *not part of a partition.* That means that it's not committed to be a simple logical drive, a volume set, mirror set, or stripe set. You can convert free space to anything else. In the Disk Administrator, it is indicated with diagonal striping.

Notice here that free space refers to *uncommitted* space, space that is not part of any drive letter. Free space does not refer to unused areas within established drives.

Physical Drives versus Logical Partitions

Physical drives are not usually important in the Disk Administrator, but getting the difference between physical drives and logical drives or partitions clear is worthwhile. A *physical drive* is that contraption of plastic and metal that you inserted in your server's case or have stacked up next to it. Numbers such as 0, 1, 2, 3... that you cannot change are assigned to physical drives. You cannot change the size of a physical drive. In order to use it, you must do a *low-level* format or a *physical* format, two synony-mous terms for a software preparation that all hard drives must undergo before an operating system can use them. There is no way in NT to do that, because formatting is usually handled by directly executing a pro-gram on the disk drive controller. Consult the documentation on your disk controller to see how to do a low-level format on your drive. The size to which it is low-level formatted is the size that it will always be.

Note, by the way, that if you're putting a number of hard disks on a PC, the PC may only recognize two of those drives when it boots up. Don't worry about that; what you're seeing is a limitation of the DOS-based BIOS on the SCSI host adapter. Once you've booted NT, it will be able to see however many drives you've attached to your system. Similarly, DOS and BIOS have a lot of trouble seeing more than 1GB on a hard disk, so you may be told by the installation program that you've only got 1GB on your hard disk, even if you have a larger disk. The installation program is misinformed because it's still relying on your PC's BIOS, which can't usually see more than 1GB. Once NT is up and running, however, it will see all of your hard disk.

In contrast to a physical drive, a *logical partition* is a volume set, logical drive, primary partition, or anything else in the Disk Administrator that is assigned a drive *letter*. You can change drive letter assignments and adjust the sizes of logical partitions, as they have no physical presence. A logical partition can be part or all of a physical drive, or even (in the case of volume sets, mirror sets, and stripe sets) extend across more than one physical drive.

Partitions

A *partition* is a portion of a hard disk that is set up to act like a separate physical hard disk, rather like splitting a single physical hard disk into several logical drives. Partitions are referred to as either *primary* or *extended* partitions.

Primary Partitions

A primary partition is a portion of a physical hard disk that has been marked as bootable by an operating system (like Windows NT). Primary partitions cannot be broken down into sub-partitions, and there can only be up to four partitions per disk. You might, for example, partition your hard disk so that one primary partition is running Windows NT and another part is running OS/2. In the Disk Administrator, a primary partition is indicated with a dark purple stripe across the top. The exact colors you see vary depending on your video card's capabilities. The legend at the bottom of the screen tells you the status of your drives. They also can be changed by the user according to the user's preference.

Extended Partitions

An extended partition, on the other hand, is created from free space on the disk. Extended partitions can be broken down into smaller logical drives. You can only have one extended partition per hard disk, but you don't have to have a primary partition to have an extended one. In the Disk Administrator display, an extended partition is striped and labeled just like free space. The only way that you can tell a free space area from an extended partition is by clicking on the area. In the status bar below the color legend, you'll see a description of exactly what the area that you selected is.

Once you've established an extended partition, you can convert it to a logical drive.

Logical Drive

A *logical drive* is a partition on one disk that behaves as an entity unto itself. You can divide an extended partition into as many logical drives as you like, with only two limitations:

- NT Server only supports 24 fixed-disk drive letters (25 if you don't have a second floppy drive).

- There is a minimum size for each logical partition. This shouldn't be much of a limitation, however, because the minimum size is 2MB. That's not much bigger than a floppy disk's capacity.

> **NOTE** The logical drive that the NT operating system itself is installed on cannot be larger than 2GB. Data can go on logical drives of any size.

Logical drives are indicated in the Disk Manger display with a royal blue stripe. (I'm sorry this book's not in color and I can't show stripe colors. You'll have to take my word for it.)

Volume Set

A *volume set* is a drive or portion of a drive that has been combined with space on another physical drive to make one large volume. You can assign a drive letter to a volume set and format it like a logical drive, but a volume set can extend across two or more physical disks, while a logical drive is restricted to one physical disk.

Why use a volume set rather than a logical drive? The ability to extend across more than one disk is the answer. Since volume sets are not limited to one physical disk, you can make a quite large volume set out of a bunch of tiny little pieces of free space (defined below). Therefore, you can use your disk space as efficiently as possible. It's much easier to figure out how to fit 30MB of data into a 35MB volume set than it is to fit it into two 10MB logical drives and one 15MB logical drive. What if you need to resize a volume set? You can make a volume set larger by *extending* it if more free space becomes available, but you cannot make it smaller unless you delete it and create a new one.

That's worth repeating: you can enlarge a volume set without damaging the data on it, but you cannot *reduce* a volume set without destroying it and rebuilding it altogether.

Volume sets do not protect your data; they only give you more efficient use of your available drive space. If something happens to one of the hard disks used in a volume set, that volume set is dead. Since the more hard disks you have, the more likely it is that one will fail at any given time, be sure to back up volume sets regularly.

In the Disk Administrator display, a volume set is indicated with a yellow stripe across the top of the area in it.

Mirror Set

Disk mirroring helps protect your data by storing a copy of all your data on an identically sized area of free space on another disk. The original and the copy together are called a *mirror set*. If anything happens to your original data, you still have an identical copy on the other half of the mirror set. Mirror sets are not very space-efficient because every piece of data that you record has an identical twin on the other half of the mirror set. You need exactly twice as much storage space as you have data. The Disk Administrator displays mirror sets with a magenta stripe across the top.

Stripe Set

For data protection, or to decrease your disks' read time, you can select areas of free space on your disks (three or more if you want parity, two or more if not) and combine them into a *stripe set*. Data stored in a stripe set is written in chunks of a certain size, called *stripes*. A stripe set is assigned a drive letter and, once it has been formatted, behaves as a drive.

Once the stripe set is established, every time you write to the drive letter that represents the set, your data is written in stripes across all the members of the stripe set. In other words, not all your data ends up in one place. Even if there's room for an entire file in one of the areas in the set, the data won't all be written there. If you've established a stripe set *with parity*, then parity information is written to the disks along with the data. Parity information is always stored separately from the data to which it corresponds. That way, if something happens to the disk with the original data, the parity information will still be all right and the data can be reconstructed from the parity information. Obviously, a stripe set without parity cannot be reconstructed if the disk with the original data on it fails, since the data only exists in one place in the stripe set.

The Hazards of Striping without Parity

And there's the rub: since the stripe set, although spread out over a number of disks, acts as one drive, all the parts of the stripe set must be working for any of the data to be accessible. If one member of a stripe set without parity information becomes inaccessible for whatever reason, all the data in the stripe set is lost.

You can see, therefore, how striping without parity actually increases your failure risk. While it's true that the more disks you have, the less likely it is that *all* of them will fail at the same time, the flip side of this is that the more disks you have, the more likely it is that *one* of them will fail at any given time. In a situation in which one disk failure brings down the entire system, having more disks actually increases your vulnerability to hardware failures. As with volume sets, you must back up nonparity stripe sets regularly.

With or without parity, all stripe sets are shown in light green in the Disk Administrator. You can tell what kind of stripe set a particular one is by clicking on it and looking at the status bar below the color legend.

Before Using the Disk Administrator...

The Disk Administrator is very easy to use and can be fun to play around with. (When experimenting with it for this chapter, my assistant Christa spent a couple of hours creating and deleting logical partitions and cackling, "The power is mine, all mine!") This is fine, as long as you keep a couple of things in mind:

- You can make any change you like in the Disk Administrator, adding, adjusting, or deleting partitions, and the changes will not take effect until you save them.

- Once you *do* save them, the changes will take effect as soon as you shut down the system and restart.

- If you save a change, the system will want to shut down and reboot when you exit the Disk Administrator. If you're not in a position where you can reboot, press Ctrl+Esc to switch to the Program Manager.

- If you add a new physical disk to your system, it should automatically show up in the Disk Administrator after you reboot. If it doesn't, then something is wrong with the installation.

- Deleting a partition of any kind will destroy any data saved there.

- If you intend to experiment with a partition or drive on which you have data, back it up before doing anything else.

Keeping It All Together with SLED

Even if it's partitioned into smaller logical drives, most of us use a single large expensive disk (SLED) as the arrangement for our data storage. Why SLED? Essentially, SLED is so popular because it's easy. You buy a large disk from a trusted manufacturer, slap it in, save your data there, perform regular backups, and you're good to go. Using SLED is like buying all your stock in one giant company with an excellent track record. It's dependable, but if it goes, you're sunk—time to haul out the backups. (Pity that you can't haul out the backup *money* when it comes to stock losses.)

Using Logical Drives to Divide Up Information

Even if you rely on the SLED model for your data storage, you may want to divide that single large physical drive into smaller logical ones. You could, for example, keep all the accounting information on logical drive C, the engineering information on logical drive D, the personnel information on logical drive E, and so on.

Creating an Extended Partition

To create a logical drive, you must first take free space and convert it to an extended partition. Open the Disk Administrator, so that you see the screen in Figure 4.1.

Notice that my example screen shows three drives on my server. Drive 1 is taken up almost entirely with a large FAT partition where I

FIGURE 4.1

Disk Administrator window

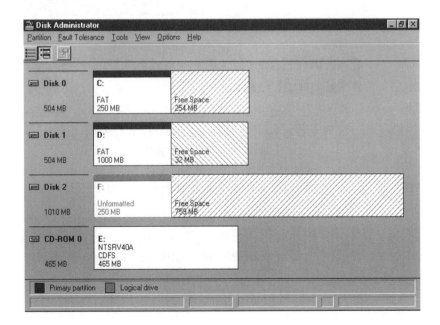

put my data. Drives 0 and 2 have 254MB and 759MB, respectively, of free space that I will use for my examples. Click on the free space, and then choose Create Extended Partition from the Partition drop-down menu. When you have done so, you'll see a dialog box like the one in Figure 4.2. It asks how big you want to make the extended partition.

Select the size that you want (you don't have to use up all the free space available) and click OK.

FIGURE 4.2

The Create Extended
Partition dialog box

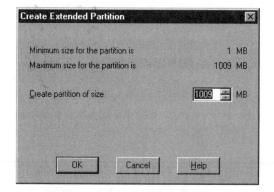

Converting the Extended Partition to a Logical Drive

Once you've created the extended partition, you're ready to create a logical drive. To do so, click on the area of the extended partition to select it, and then select Create from the Partition drop-down menu. You see a dialog box that looks like Figure 4.3.

Type in the size of the logical drive that you want to create, or press Enter to select the default option and take all the available space. Once you've pressed OK, your logical drive is set up.

FIGURE 4.3

The Create Logical Drive
dialog box

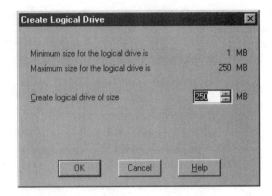

When you exit from the Disk Administrator, you see a dialog box like Figure 4.4. Click Yes to save. Disk Administrator confirms that it made the changes with the dialog box shown in Figure 4.5.

When you quit the Disk Administrator, you see a dialog box like the one in Figure 4.6. It advises you that the changes you have made

FIGURE 4.4

Confirm configuration
changes dialog box

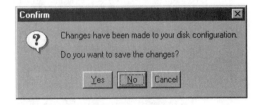

FIGURE 4.5

A dialog box confirming
your configuration

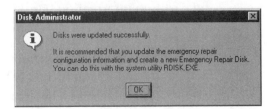

FIGURE 4.6

The dialog box asking you to restart your computer

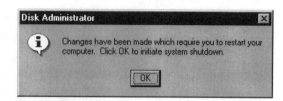

require restarting your computer. Click OK and the system will shut down and restart automatically.

 If you don't want to shut down now, you can press Ctrl+Esc to switch to the Program Manager. However, the changes have still been made, and, once you shut down and restart the system, the repartitioning will take effect.

Formatting the New Drive

Before you can store data on the new drive, you've got to format it. In previous versions of NTS, you could only format disks from the command prompt—kind of silly for a graphical operating system. With version 4 comes the My Computer and Explorer folders. Open either folder and right-click the logical drive. You'll see an available option to format a drive.

To format, you must first create a partition or logical drive; you can't format free space. Click on the partition to be formatted to select it, and then choose Commit Changes Now from the Partition menu. When the partition information has been stored, keep the partition highlighted and choose Format from the Tools menu.

In the Format dialog box, choose the file system that you want to use on the partition. If you format NTFS, you can even change the cluster size—but don't do that. The default works fine for most uses. For best security, make all of your partitions NTFS. The only exception to this is that it may be a good idea to keep the boot partition FAT, so you can boot from a DOS system floppy if necessary; and any partitions that you need to be available if you boot from DOS must use the FAT system as well. (DOS doesn't recognize NTFS partitions.) Please note: that's "if you boot from DOS." DOS machines connected to the server can access data in an NTFS partition without any problem.

If you're formatting a partition or logical drive, you can check Quick Format to tell NT Server not to scan the disk for bad sectors. If the section you're formatting is a fault-tolerant volume such as a mirror set or stripe set with parity, then this is not an option.

Click OK to start the format. A dialog box will appear and ask you to confirm the format; click OK again and the format operation will begin. A dialog box will show you the process of the format. Be warned: although the dialog box has a Cancel button, canceling the format won't necessarily restore the partition to its original condition.

If you're addicted to the command prompt, you can still use it to format disks. To do so, open an MS-DOS prompt and type

```
format driveletter: /fs:filesystem
```

where *driveletter* is, of course, the drive letter of the logical drive, and *filesystem* is either FAT or NTFS. (You could format drives in HPFS in version 3.1, but not in any version since then.) For example, to format a newly created drive E: as NTFS, you would type **format e: /fs:ntfs**.

If you open Windows Explorer and try to access the new drive letter before you format it, you get a nastygram like the one in Figure 4.7.

FIGURE 4.7

An "Is Not Accessible" error message

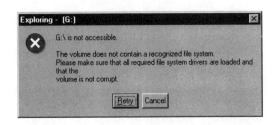

How Do I Create a Logical Drive?

 Take the following steps to create a logical drive:

1. Open the Disk Administrator and select an area of free space.

2. From the Partition menu, select Create Extended and choose the size of the extended partition that you want to make.

3. Having selected the extended partition that you just made, select Create from the Partition menu and choose the size of the logical drive that you want to make.

4. You see the new logical drive in royal blue. Open the Partition menu and choose Commit Changes Now for the changes to take effect.

5. Format the drive to NTFS, HPFS, or FAT by using the Format option on the Tools menu.

You can now use the logical drive letter as you would any other.

Use the Most Recent Drivers!

If you experience strange problems with the Disk Administrator, make sure that you've got the most recent drivers. For example, if your NT Server has an EIDE (Enhanced Integrated Drive Electronics) drive controller for which you're using the DOS drivers, you may notice problems with the Disk Administrator. First of all, when you open the Disk Administrator and then exit, the system demands that you reboot even if you didn't do anything. Second, the EIDE hard disk won't hold a partition no matter what you try. What's going on?

It appears that the two sides of the problem have their root in the same difficulty: the EIDE disk won't hold a partition, so every time you run the Disk Administrator, it perceives changes whether you personally made them or not. There is a happy end to the story, however. When we called the EIDE controller manufacturer and had them send us the NT drivers, the problems went away. Other Disk Administrator problems may also be caused by obsolete driver software.

Deleting a Logical Drive

Deleting a logical drive will destroy all the data on it, so back up before you do anything drastic. The next "How Do I" sidebar explains how to delete a logical drive.

How Do I Delete a Logical Drive?

To delete a logical drive:

1. Select the drive in the Disk Administrator and choose Delete from the Partition drop-down menu.

2. A message like this one appears:

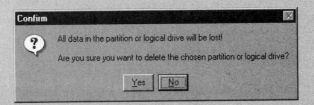

3. Yes is the default. Once you've confirmed, the logical partition will be deleted and will become an empty extended partition. If you want to convert the extended partition to free space, you must delete it as well.

When you exit the Disk Administrator, you are prompted to confirm your changes. Once you've confirmed, click OK to restart the system or press Ctrl+Esc to go to the Program Manager.

Using Space Efficiently

Even if you're a SLED aficionado, you may one day be faced with space restrictions that force you to get another drive. In that event, you'll want to use the space on that new drive as efficiently as possible.

Volume Sets to Get the Most Out of Existing Disks

How can you use disk space efficiently? Well, keeping the drives separate from each other clearly isn't the way. Unused space is more efficient if combined because, even if you have a total of 40MB of unused data space on the two drives, you can't fit one 35MB chunk of data in it if 25MB of unused space is on one disk and 15MB is on the other. If you want to get as much data squeezed onto your disks as possible, therefore, you can combine the two (or more) disks into a volume set, as seen in Figure 4.8.

FIGURE 4.8

How a volume set works

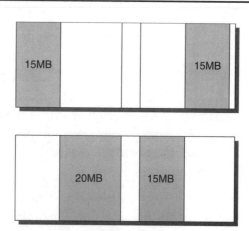

In this figure, 65MB of free space is available, but no more than 20MB of this space is contiguous. To get the most efficient use of this space, you could combine it together in a volume set, so all of the data is considered in one large chunk. Once this free space has been made into a volume set, you could store a 65MB chunk of data in it, even though the largest contiguous space is only 20MB in size.

Cautions about Volume Sets

Don't forget that volume sets have one big drawback: They span more than one physical disk and are dependent on all of those disks to function. If one disk turns belly-up and dies, the rest of your volume set is inaccessible. If you try to read or write to a dead volume set, you get several messages like the ones in Figure 4.9 and Figure 4.10

Here's a case where the user interface folks were out to lunch. At this point it would have been easier and clearer to just put up a dialog box that said, "One of your drives isn't working. You can no longer access data on drive X." This is just another reason why frequent backups are essential.

TIP

If you accidentally switch off an externally mounted drive that's part of a volume set and get messages like those in Figures 4.9 and 4.10 when you try to write to or read from that drive, just reboot. The volume set will recover without any problems.

FIGURE 4.9

System Process—Lost Delayed-Write Data message box

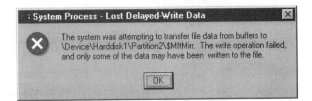

FIGURE 4.10

Another System Process—Lost Delayed-Write Data message

Creating a Volume Set

To create a volume set, back up any data on your disks, make sure that there is free space on them, and follow these steps:

1. Open the Disk Administrator in the Administrative Tools program group.

2. Select one or more areas of free space on your hard disk(s) by clicking on the first one and then Ctrl+clicking on the others to select them all at once—just like selecting more than one file at a time in Windows Explorer. This is demonstrated in Figure 4.11

3. Go to the Partition menu and choose Create Volume Set.When you've done this, you'll see a dialog box that displays the minimum and maximum sizes for the volume set, as in Figure 4.12.

FIGURE 4.11

Selecting free space on a hard drive

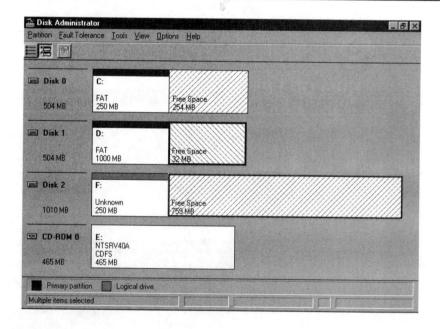

FIGURE 4.12

The Create Volume
Set dialog box

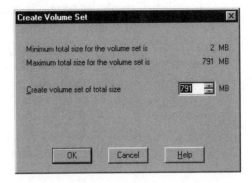

4. In the box, type the size of the volume set that you want to create. Obviously, the size must be somewhere between the minimum and the maximum sizes available, here, 2MB and 759MB, respectively. When you've got the proper size entered, click OK. You'll return to the Disk Administrator display and see the members of the volume set in yellow. In Figure 4.13, drive G: is the volume set.

Figure 4.13 shows a volume set on two disks that already have primary partitions. If there is still free space left on the disks, it could be

FIGURE 4.13

The Volume Set
dialog box

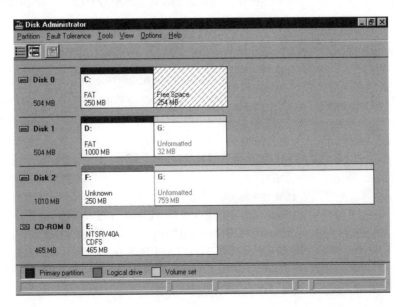

used for something else. When creating a volume set, you don't have to use all the available space. If you select a size smaller than the maximum, the Disk Administrator divides the size you choose roughly equally across all the partitions that you selected to be part of the volume set, so that all the partitions in the volume set are approximately the same size (so far as possible).

When you exit the Disk Administrator, you are prompted to save your changes and shut down the system, as discussed in earlier sections. Shut down, restart, and the volume set will be created.

Formatting the Volume Set

After you've restarted the system, format the disk either from the Tools menu or from the command line with the following command:

```
format x: /fs:filesystem
```

where *x* is the appropriate drive letter and *filesystem* is the type of file system (NTFS or FAT) to which you want to format that drive. Formatting may take a while, depending on the size of the set you've created.

Read the "How Do I" sidebar to review how to create a volume set.

Deleting a Volume Set

Ultimately, you may want to reorganize the data on your disks, or you might start having problems with one of your disks and need to replace it. If one of these situations is the case, you need to delete the volume set.

Enlarging a Volume Set

If it turns out that your volume set is smaller than you need it to be, it's not necessary to delete it and re-create it from scratch. Instead, you can *extend* it by adding areas of free space to its volume. The instructions in the "How Do I Extend a Volume Set?" sidebar also apply to extending existing primary partitions to make their area bigger. (Once

How Do I Create a Volume Set?

To create a volume set, do the following:

1. Open the Disk Administrator and select all the areas of free space that you want to be in the set.

2. From the Partition menu, choose Create Volume Set.

3. Choose the size of the set that you want and click OK. You can choose any size as long as it is within the maximum and minimum parameters.

4. Exit the Disk Administrator. You'll are prompted to reboot the system.

When you return to the Disk Administrator, the new volume set appears in yellow. It has a drive letter but won't yet be formatted.

5. To finish, you have to format the new logical drive, using either the command prompt or the Format command on the Tools menu. To format from the command prompt, open a DOS window and type

```
format driveletter: /fs:filesystem
```

where *driveletter* is, of course, the drive letter of the logical drive, and *filesystem* is either FAT, HPFS, or NTFS. For example, to format a newly created drive E: as NTFS, type

```
format e: /fs:ntfs
```

TIP

Deleting the volume set will permanently delete all the information that was in it, so back up any data in the set before deleting it. The next "How Do I" sidebar explains how to delete a volume set.

you extend them, however, they show up in the Disk Administrator color-coded as volume sets.)

You cannot use the instructions in the "How Do I" sidebar to make volume sets *smaller*. To do that, you must delete the volume set and create it again.

How Do I Delete a Volume Set?

To delete a volume set:

1. Go to the Disk Administrator.

2. Click on the volume set that you want to delete to select it. It will become outlined in black.

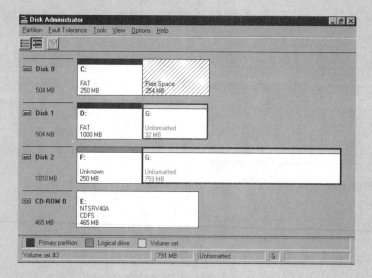

3. From the Partition menu, select Delete.

A message box like the one following tells you that all data in the set will be lost. The message box asks you to confirm the action before continuing.

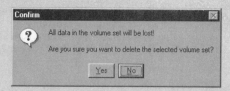

4. Click Yes to continue.

Once the set is deleted, the area used in the volume set reverts to free space.

How Do I Extend a Volume Set?

To extend a volume set:

1. From the Disk Administrator, select an existing volume set or primary partition that has been formatted (one that is not part of a mirror set or stripe set) and one or more areas of free space. The volume set *must* have been previously formatted to extend it.

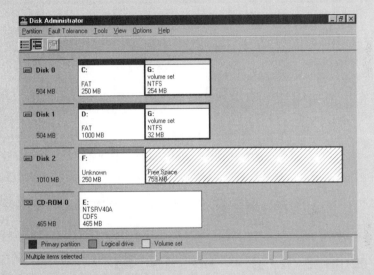

2. Go to the Partition menu and select Extend Volume Set. As you did when you created the volume set, you see a dialog box showing the minimum and maximum sizes for the volume set:

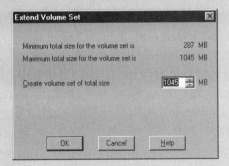

How Do I Extend a Volume Set? (Cont.)

3. Enter the size of the volume set that you want and click OK.

The volume set is now the larger size that you specified, and all the area in it will have the same drive letter. The free space that you added is automatically formatted to the same file system as the rest of the volume set.

These three limitations apply to extending volume sets:

- Again, you cannot use this procedure to make a volume set smaller. To do that, you need to delete the volume set and create a new one.

- You cannot extend the volume set for the partition with the system files on it. The Disk Administrator will not let you add free space to this partition.

- You cannot combine two volume sets, nor add a logical drive to a volume set.

Nonparity Disk Striping to Increase Throughput

Another way to get more bang for your disk-buying buck is with disk striping without parity, also known as RAID level 0. When you create a stripe set from free space on your disks, each member of the stripe set is divided into stripes. Then, when you write data to the stripe set, the data is distributed over the stripes. A file could have its beginning recorded onto stripe 1 of member 1, more data recorded onto stripe 2 of member 2, and the rest on stripe 3 of member 3, for example. If you're saving data to a stripe set, a file is never stored on only one member, even if there is room on that member for the entire file. Conceptually, striping looks something Figure 4.14.

If you take free space on your disks and combine it into one stripe set with its own drive letter, the seek-and-write time to that drive will be improved, since the system can read and write to more than one disk at a time. To do striping without parity information included, you need a minimum of two disks and a maximum of 32.

FIGURE 4.14

Stripe set without parity

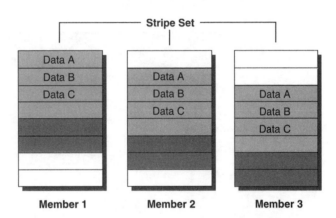

Different data files are represented here with different shades of gray. As you can see, an entire data file is never all put onto one member of the striped set. This improves read time, since, if Data A is called for, the disk controllers on all three members of the set can read the data. With a SLED data arrangement, only one of the members could read the data.

Creating a Stripe Set

Creating a stripe set without parity is quite simple. Just follow the steps in the "How Do I" sidebar.

How Do I Create a Stripe Set without Parity?

To create a stripe set without parity:

1. In the Disk Administrator, select two or more areas of free space on 2 to 32 hard disks (without parity, you need a minimum of only 2 disks, not 3). To do this, click on the free space on the hard disk and then Ctrl+click on the others as though you were selecting more than one file in Windows Explorer.

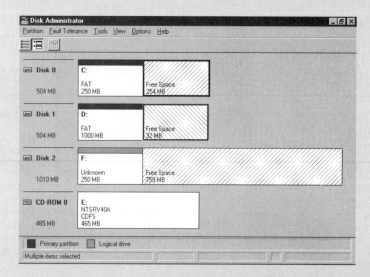

2. From the Partition drop-down menu, choose Create Stripe Set. You see a dialog box that displays the minimum and maximum stripe sizes:

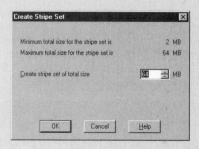

How Do I Create a Stripe Set without Parity? (Cont.)

3. Choose the size stripe you want, and click OK.

The Disk Administrator will now divide the total size of the stripe you selected equally among the available disks, and then assign a single drive letter to this set. If you selected a size that could not be divided equally among the number of disks involved in the stripe set, the Disk Administrator rounds to the nearest number. When you exit, the system reboots to implement the change, unless you press Ctrl+Esc.

The stripe set is now created but not formatted, as you can see from this picture:

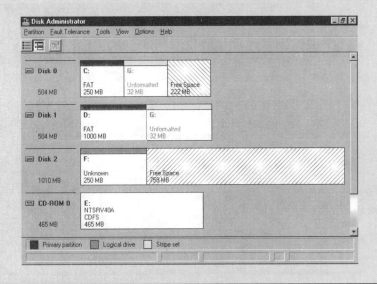

Deleting a Stripe Set

If anything happens to any member disk of your nonparity stripe set, all the data in the set is lost. Not only can't you get the data back (except through backups), but the disks that are part of the stripe set

How Do I Create a Stripe Set without Parity? (Cont.)

To format the stripe set, either choose Format on the Tools menu or open a command prompt and type

```
format driveletter: /fs:filesystem
```

where *driveletter* is, of course, the drive letter of the logical drive, and *filesystem* is either FAT or NTFS. For example, to format a newly created drive E: as NTFS, you would type

```
format e: /fs:ntfs
```

When you're done, the stripe set will show up like this:

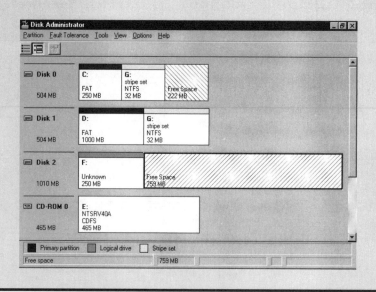

are unusable until you delete the stripe set and establish a new one. If the disk is dead, you have to delete the stripe set and start over. How to do that is explained in the sidebar.

How Do I Delete a Stripe Set?

To delete a stripe set:

1. In the Disk Administrator, select the stripe that you want to delete, as you see in the next graphic.

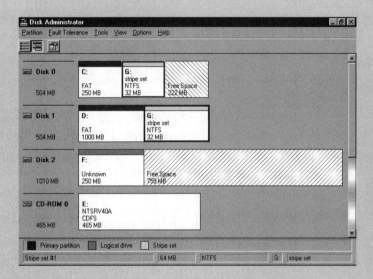

2. From the Partition drop-down menu, select Delete.

You see a message advising you that this action deletes all the data. The box asks you to confirm that you want to delete:

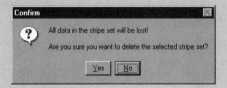

3. Click on the Yes button in this message box.

Protecting Your Data

Using your disk space efficiently and improving data throughput are important, but they don't do anything to protect your data's integrity. If you want to do that, NT Server offers you two methods: disk mirroring and disk striping.

Disk Mirroring

If you have more than one disk, you can *mirror* a partition on one disk onto free space on another. By doing so, you keep an exact copy of one partition on another disk. Once you have established this relationship between the two disk areas, called a *mirror set* (mirror sets are explained earlier in this chapter), every time that you write data to disk a duplicate of that data is written to the free space on the other half of the mirror set. Disk mirroring is equivalent to RAID level 1.

How well does disk mirroring perform? Data must be written to both drives in the mirror set, but it suffers no performance lag because each disk can do its own writing. In addition, mirrored drives are fast when it comes to reads, as data can be pulled from both halves of the mirror set at once.

Mirroring and Duplexing

If you've ever heard or read anything about disk mirroring, you've probably also heard a term called disk *duplexing*. Disk duplexing is much the same as disk mirroring, except that duplexing generally refers to mirroring information on disks that each have their own disk controller, so that the data is not vulnerable to controller failures. When NT Server talks about disk mirroring, it is referring to both duplexing and mirroring, as Figure 4.15 demonstrates.

FIGURE 4.15

Disk mirroring versus
disk duplexing

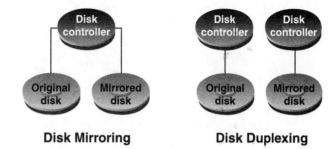

Disk Mirroring   **Disk Duplexing**

Establishing a Mirror Set

You can mirror a drive's data without affecting that drive's accessibility while you do it. See the sidebar to find out how.

How Do I Set Up a Mirror Set?

To set up a mirror set:

1. Click on the partition that you want to maintain a copy of (such as the primary partition).

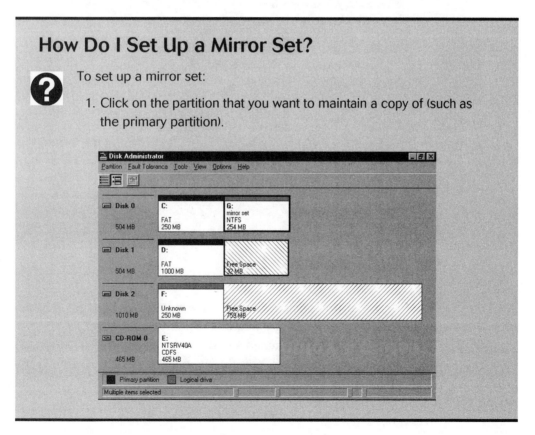

How Do I Set Up a Mirror Set? (Cont.)

2. By pressing Ctrl and clicking at the same time, choose the free space on another disk that you want to make the other half of the set.

This area must be the same size or greater as the partition or drive that you are mirroring. If you select an area of free space that is too small, the system will complain, "The free space you have chosen is not large enough to mirror the partition you have chosen."

3. From the Fault Tolerance drop-down menu, select Establish Mirror.

Once you've done this, you have established the mirror set. The Disk Administrator now establishes an equal-sized partition in the free space to be the mirror. It also assigns the drive letter to the mirror set. Now, whenever you save a file to that drive letter, two copies of the file will really be saved.

4. Format the new logical drive. You do that either with the Format command in the Tools menu or by opening a command prompt and typing

```
format driveletter: /fs:filesystem
```

5. Where *driveletter* is, of course, the drive letter of the logical drive, and *filesystem* is either FAT or NTFS. For example, to format a newly created drive E: as NTFS, you would type

```
format e: /fs:ntfs
```

Breaking a Mirror Set

If something unrecoverable—like hardware damage—happens to half of the mirror set, you need to break the mirror set to get to the good data that you've backed up. It will be pretty apparent when something's gone wrong. You'll see a message like the one in Figure 4.16 when you try to write to the mirrored drives if one of the disks isn't

FIGURE 4.16

System Process
message box

working. Kind of looks more like a fortune cookie fortune than a system message, doesn't it? You can still use the drive, but the benefits of mirroring will be suspended.

How Do I Break a Mirror Set?

To break a mirror set:

1. Open the Disk Administrator and select the mirror set that you want to break. When you open the Disk Administrator, you see a message like this that tells you something is different:

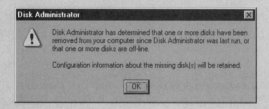

2. From the Fault Tolerance menu, select Break Mirror. You then see a message like this one:

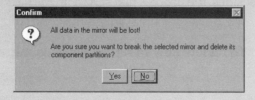

How Do I Break a Mirror Set? (Cont)

3. Click on Yes to break the mirror set.

Breaking a mirror set does not affect the information inside it. Still, as always before doing anything drastic with the drive that holds your data, it's a good idea to back up first.

If you break a mirror set when nothing's wrong with it, each half becomes a primary partition with its own drive letter. The original partition keeps its original drive letter, while the backup partition gets the next available one.

Recovering Data from a Mirror Set

Once you've broken the mirror set so that you can get to the good data, the good half of the mirror set is assigned the drive letter that belonged to the now-defunct mirror set. The half that crashed is now called an *orphan* and is, in effect, set aside by the fault-tolerance driver so that no one will attempt to write to that part of the disk. When you reboot, the dead disk disappears, as in Figure 4.17.

At this point, you take the good half of the old mirror set and establish a new relationship with another partition, as was discussed earlier in "Establishing a Mirror Set." When you restart the computer, the data from the good partition is copied to its new partner. While the regeneration process is going on, the type on the new half of the mirror set shows in red, but it doesn't take long to regenerate mirrored material. Besides, the process takes place in the background anyway, so you don't have to wait for it to finish to use the computer.

To review how to repair a broken mirror set, read the sidebar.

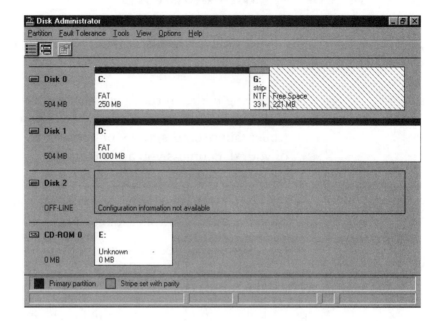

FIGURE 4.17

Recovering data from
a mirror set

How Do I Repair a Broken Mirror Set?

To repair a broken mirror set:

1. Open the Disk Administrator and select the good half of the mirror set and an area of free space the same size or larger than the area to be mirrored.

2. Choose Establish Mirror from the Fault Tolerance menu.

The new mirror set will be displayed in magenta.

Mirroring Considerations

As you're deciding whether or not to protect your data by mirroring it, keep these things in mind:

- Mirroring to drives run from the same drive controller does not protect your data from drive controller failure. If any kind of controller failure occurs, you won't be able to get to the backup copy of your data unless you are mirroring to a disk run from a separate controller.

- For higher disk-read performance and greater fault tolerance, use a separate disk controller for each half of a mirror set.

- Disk mirroring effectively cuts your available disk space in half. Don't forget that as you figure out how much drive space you've got on the server.

- Disk mirroring has a low initial cost, since you must purchase only one extra drive to achieve fault tolerance, but a higher long-term cost due to the amount of room your redundant information takes up.

- Disk mirroring will slow down writes, as the data must be written in two places every time, but will speed up reads, as the I/O controller has two places to read information from. For (like the network you're using NT Server for), it gets the best performance of all the RAID levels.

Disk Striping, the Slow But Steady Method

In addition to disk mirroring, NT Server gives you the option of using level 5 RAID, also known as *disk striping with parity*. Disk striping with parity differs from regular disk striping in the following ways:

- Although data lost from a stripe set without parity is unrecoverable, data from a parity stripe set can usually be recovered. ("Usually" because if someone puts a bullet through every one of your disks, all the parity information in the world won't help you.) If more than one disk of the 2 to 32 hard disk drives fails, you will not be able to recover your data.

- Regular disk striping improves data read and write speeds. Striping with parity slows down writes but improves access speed.

How Disk Striping Works

Every time you write data to disk, the data is written across all the striped disks in the array, just as it is with regular disk striping (RAID level 0). In addition, however, parity information for your data is also written to disk, always on a separate disk from the one where the data it corresponds to is written. That way, if anything happens to one of the disks in the array, the data on that disk can be reconstructed from the parity information on the other disks.

Level 5 RAID differs from level 4, which also uses parity information to protect data, in that the parity information in level 5 RAID is distributed across all the disks in the array. In level 4, a specific disk is dedicated to parity information. This makes RAID level 5 faster than 4, as it can perform more than one write operation at a time. This is shown in Figure 4.18.

If you think about it, writing parity information every time that you save a document could turn into quite a space-and-time waster. Take, for example, the document I'm creating for this book. If I've protected my data with level 5 RAID, and parity information is stored to disk every time that this file is saved, does that mean that there is parity information for every incarnation of this document from the time I

FIGURE 4.18

Disk striping with
parity information

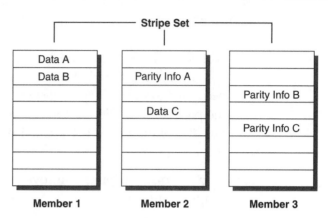

As you can see, no single member of the stripe set keeps all the original data or all the parity information. Instead the data and parity information are distributed throughout the stripe set, so if one member disk fails, the information can be reconstructed from the other members of the stripe set.

began writing? If so, how can all the parity information and data fit on the disks?

The answer is, of course, that it doesn't, and this is what produces the performance degradation that's unavoidable in striped disk writes. Every time a document is saved to disk, its parity information must be updated to reflect its current status; otherwise, you would have to keep backup parity information for every version of the document that you ever saved.

Updating the Parity Information

There are two ways to update the parity information. First, since the parity information is the XOR (exclusive OR) of the date, the system could recalculate the XOR each time data is written to disk. This would require accessing each disk in the stripe set, however, because the data is distributed across the disks in the array, and that takes time.

What is an *XOR?* On a very *simplistic* level, the XOR, or *exclusive OR arithmetic,* is a function that takes two one-bit inputs and produces a single-bit output. The result is 1 if the two inputs are different, or 0 if the two inputs are the same. More specifically:

0 XOR 0 = 0

1 XOR 0 = 1

0 XOR 1 = 1

1 XOR 1 = 0

When you're XORing two numbers with more than one bit, just match the bits up and XOR them individually. For example, 1101010 XOR 0101000 equals 1000010. The result you get from this function is the parity information, from which the original data can be recalculated.

A more efficient way of recalculating the parity information, and the one that NT Server uses, is to read the old data to be overwritten and XOR it with the new data to determine the differences. This process produces a *bit mask* that has a 1 in the position of every bit that has been changed. This bit mask can then be XORed with the old parity information to see where *its* differences lie, and from this the new parity information can be calculated. This seems convoluted, but this second process only requires two reads and two XOR computations, rather than one of each for every drive in the array.

Establishing a Stripe Set with Parity

To create a stripe set with parity, follow these steps:

1. In the Disk Administrator, select three or more areas of free space on from 3 to 32 hard disks (the exact number is determined by your hardware configuration; NT Server can handle up to 32 separate physical disks but your hardware setup may not be able to). To select the free space areas, click on the free space on the first hard disk and then Ctrl+click on the others in the same way that you select more than one file in Explorer.

As you can see in Figure 4.19, the areas of free space that you select don't have to be equal in size because the Disk Administrator distributes available space evenly and adjusts the size of the stripe set as necessary.

2. From the Fault Tolerance menu, choose Create Stripe Set With Parity. You see a dialog box like the one in Figure 4.20 that displays the minimum and maximum sizes for the stripe set with parity.

3. Choose the size stripe you want and click OK.

The Disk Administrator will now equally divide the total size of the stripe you selected among the available disks. Then it will assign a single drive letter to this set, as you see in Figure 4.21. In this case, the stripe set has been assigned letter G.

FIGURE 4.19

Choosing free space for a stripe set with parity

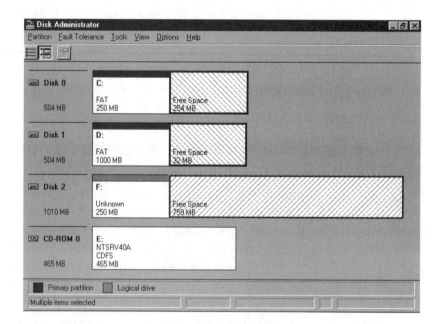

FIGURE 4.20

The Create Stripe Set With Parity dialog box

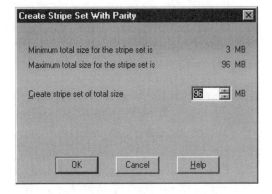

If you selected a size that could not be divided equally among the number of disks involved in the stripe set, the Disk Administrator rounds down the size to the nearest number evenly divisible by the number of disks in the stripe set.

FIGURE 4.21

The Disk Administrator after creating a stripe set with parity

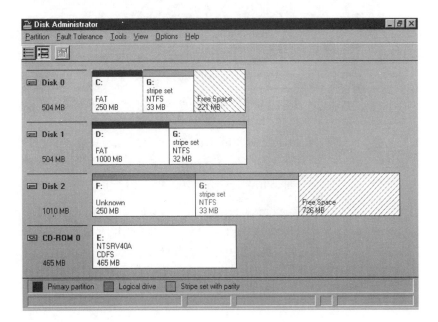

After you've created the stripe set and try to exit the Disk Administrator, you see the usual dialog box that tells you the changes that you have made require you to restart your system. Click OK to begin shutdown.

When you restart, rebooting takes a little longer than normal. When you reach the blue screen that tells you what file system each of the drives on your system is using, the system informs you that it cannot determine the file system type of the stripe set's drive letter—not that it is RAW, as you've seen before, but that it can't determine it. This may look worrisome, but it's just due to the fact that the system has to initialize the stripe set. Wait for the drive activity on the stripe set drives to subside, and then format the new partition. If you don't format first, you get an error message like the one in Figure 4.22, but once you have formatted, everything should be ready to go.

To recap, the next sidebar explains how to stripe with parity.

How Do I Create a Stripe Set with Parity

 To create a stripe set with parity:

1. Open the Disk Administrator and select areas of free space on at least three physical disks.

2. Pull down the Fault Tolerance menu and select Create Stripe Set With Parity.

3. Fill in the size that you want the stripe set to be and click OK.

The system will reboot upon your confirmation, and the stripe set will be initialized. As always, you've got to format it from the command line before you can use the drive.

FIGURE 4.22

Error Selecting Drive
message box

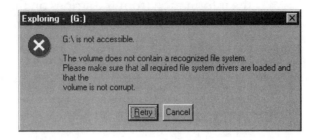

Retrieving Data from a Failed Stripe Set

If an unrecoverable error to part of a striped set with parity occurs, you can regenerate the information stored there from the parity information stored on the rest of the set. You can even do this if one of the member disks has been low-level formatted.

How do you know when something's wrong? If you attempt to write to a stripe set and see an error message like the one in Figure 4.23, it's a bad sign.

To recover the data, put a new disk in place and reboot so the system can see the new disk. Next, go to the Disk Administrator and select the stripe set that you want to fix and a new piece of free space that is at least equal in size to the other members of the set. Choose Regenerate from the Fault Tolerance menu, quit the Disk Administrator, and restart the computer.

FIGURE 4.23

Error message while
writing a stripe set

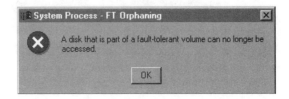

When you restart the computer, the fault-tolerance driver collects the information from the stripes on the other member disks and then re-creates it onto the new member of the stripe set. If you open the Disk Administrator while it is doing this, you'll see that the text on the part being regenerated is displayed in red. Although the regeneration process may take a while, you can still use the server. You don't need to keep the Disk Administrator open because the restoration process works in the background and you can access the information in the stripe set.

Once the stripe set is fixed, you need to reassign it a new drive letter and restart the computer. The failed portion of the original stripe set is set aside as unusable and is called an *orphan*. In the Disk Administrator, the failed disk looks like Figure 4.24.

FIGURE 4.24

Failed disk in the
Disk Administrator

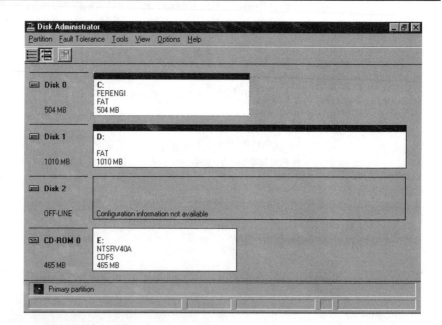

TIP

When you're regenerating an NTFS stripe set with parity, make sure that you have a new disk in the system. When a disk goes bad and you're trying to regenerate its data onto a new one, NT Server does not gray out the Regenerate option even if you don't have a new disk in yet to put the data on. Instead, it tells you that the stripe set with that number has been recovered, but when you reboot and check the Disk Administrator, you see that the stripe set is still listed as "Recoverable."

The next sidebar reviews how to regenerate a failed stripe set.

How Do I Regenerate a Failed Stripe Set?

To regenerate a failed stripe set:

1. Put a new disk in place and reboot the system.
2. After you've logged on, go to the Disk Administrator and select both the stripe set that you need to fix and an area of free space at least equal in size to the other members of the set.
3. Choose Regenerate from the Fault Tolerance menu.

The system shuts down and the regeneration process takes place in the background after it restarts. The regeneration process doesn't affect your ability to use the computer or access the information being regenerated.

Deleting a Stripe Set

Deleting a stripe set is quite simple. It is explained in the next "How Do I" sidebar.

How Do I Delete a Stripe Set?

To delete a stripe set:

1. In the Disk Administrator, select the stripe that you want to delete.

2. From the Partition drop-down menu, select Delete. You see a message that advises you that this action will delete all the data and asks you to confirm that you want to do this.

3. Click on the Yes button in this dialog box.

Don't forget that deleting a stripe set destroys the data in it—even the parity information.

Things to Remember about Disk Striping with Parity

Keep these things in mind when it comes to disk striping with parity:

- When you first set up the stripe set and reboot, the rebooting process takes longer than normal because the system must initialize the stripe set before it can be used.

- Striping with parity has a greater initial cost than disk mirroring does (it requires a minimum of three disks, rather than two). Nevertheless, it allows you to get more use out of your disk space.

- Although you can access the information in a stripe set even after one of the members has failed, you should regenerate the set as quickly as possible. NT Server striping cannot cope with more than one error in the set, so you're sunk if anything happens to the unregenerated stripe set.

- Striping with parity places greater demands on your system than disk mirroring, so you may get better performance from your system if you add 2MB of RAM to the system minimum of 16MB.

- If you have fewer than three physical hard disks on your server, you cannot make stripe sets with parity. The option in the Fault Tolerance menu will be grayed out.

Working with NTFS

NTFS is the filing system especially designed for use with Windows NT and NT Server. It is significantly different from the FAT system that you're used to if you've been working with DOS:

- NTFS supports filenames up to 256 characters long (including spaces and periods), with multiple extensions; FAT supports 8-character filenames with 3-character extensions.

- NTFS is designed for system security (i.e., setting file permissions); FAT is not. (You can, however, restrict access to directories even when using FAT.) To learn how file permissions work, see Chapter 8.

- NTFS preserves upper- and lowercase filenames (although it does not distinguish between upper- and lowercase when searching for filenames); of course, FAT does not.

- FAT is not equipped to deal with the stripe sets, volume sets, and mirror sets, so any of these partitions will be invisible to anyone trying to read them from DOS.

- NTFS keeps a log of activities, in order to be able to restore the disk after a power failure or other interruption.

In short, Table 4.1 gives you an at-a-glance comparison of NTFS and FAT.

NTFS Naming Conventions

NTFS file names can be up to 256 characters long with the extension, including spaces and separating periods. You can use any upper- or

TABLE 4.1   Comparing NTFS and FAT

	NTFS	FAT
File name length	256 characters	8+3 characters
File attributes	Extended	Limited
Associated operating system	NT *and* NT Server	DOS
Organization	Tree structure	Centrally located menu
Multidisk drives?	Yes	No
Software RAID support?	Yes	No

lowercase character in an NTFS filename except the following characters, which have special significance to NT:

? " / \ < > * | :

Even though NTFS supports long filenames, it maintains its compatibility with DOS by automatically generating a conventional FAT filename for every file. The process doesn't work in reverse, however, so don't save a file when working with an application that doesn't support long filenames. If you do, the application that doesn't like long names will save the file to the FAT name and erase all memory of the NTFS filename. The data won't be erased, however; only the descriptive filename is affected.

When converting a long filename to the FAT format, NT Server does the following:

- Removes spaces

- Removes periods, all except the last one that is followed by a character—this period is assumed to herald the beginning of the file extension

- Removes any characters not allowed in DOS names and converts them to underscores

- Converts the name to six characters, with a tilde (~) and a number attached to the end

- Truncates the extension to three characters

Given how NT Server converts NTFS filenames to FAT conventions, you may want to keep that in mind when using long filenames, so that your filenames make sense in both FAT and NTFS. For example, you could name a file PRSNLLET-Personal letters file.SAM, so that the shortened name would be PRSNLLET.SAM.

File Forking and Extended Attributes

Two of the things that make NTFS extra easy to work with are its ability to use file forking and extended attributes.

The term *file forking* has been used primarily in the Mac world, so don't be surprised if it sounds unfamiliar. Essentially, file forking is an association, so that if one file gets opened, another one associated with the first gets opened too. AmiPro, a Windows word processor, saves files with a SAM extension. Due to file association, if you open a SAM file from the File Manager, a copy of the AmiPro program opens to support it. Under true file forking, each AmiPro document would contain a small program that would tell NT to start up AmiPro. That would allow an AmiPro document to have *any* extension, instead of requiring the SAM extension.

Like file forking, *extended attributes* is a concept that sounds much trickier than it is. If you're familiar with DOS, you're familiar with file attributes. You can attach an attribute to a file to say that it's been modified since the last backup, that it should be read-only, or that it should be a hidden or system file. You do this by setting the *archive bit* on the file to whatever you like.

FAT's attributes are limited, however. You can say that a file should be read-only, but you can't identify it as the last CONFIG.SYS that you got to work properly on your machine. NTFS, on the other hand, allows you to tack extended attributes onto filenames to get a more complete description of what a file is for. Essentially, in combination with its ability to handle 256-character filenames, NTFS's extended attributes give your system a somewhat more Mac-like feel. You're no longer dependent on FAT's 8+3 naming conventions or limited attributes.

Long Names on Floppies

NT's support of NFTS sort of slops over into floppies. You can't format a floppy to NTFS format. If you try, you get an error message that says, "Cannot lock current drive." However, you *can* create files with long names on a floppy.

NT keeps two names for floppy files, the long name that you originally assigned and a truncated 8+3 name. DOS sees the shorter 8+3 name, however, making it possible for you to work with files that have long names under NT but short names under DOS.

Final Thoughts about Drives and NT Server

Let's wrap up with a few pieces of advice concerning hardware or software RAID, viruses, and FAT partitions.

Hardware or Software RAID?

You've seen here that you can hang a bunch of drives on your computer and that you can weave them into RAID sets and mirror sets. That all sounds good from a fault-tolerance point of view, since the probability that you'll actually lose any of your data is considerably reduced. Consider what you'll do when drive damage does occur, though.

You've got a mission-critical system up and running and one of the four drives in a stripe set with parity goes to its maker. Your next move is to bring the server down, replace the bad drive with a new good one, and then reintegrate that new one into the stripe set in order to recover the data.

Sounds good, until you really think about it. First of all, you've got to bring down this mission-critical server for several *hours* while you take out the old drive, install a new drive, and put the stripe set back together. In contrast, you could buy a *hardware* RAID system, a box containing several drives that act as one and that look to the NT system as just one drive. An external RAID box costs a bit more, but a hardware-based RAID system can rebuild itself faster than can NT's software. And, best of all, most hardware-based RAID systems allow you to "hot-swap" the bad drive—that is, to replace the bad drive without bringing down the server. So if your application is *truly* mission-critical, think about investing in RAID hardware. Of course, if you can't afford it, NT's solution isn't bad either.

Double-Check for Viruses

Around my company, we occasionally come across a computer that just won't take NT. You try to install it, and you get past the text part just fine. Then the NT install program reboots…and you get nothing but blue screens.

There are two likely causes for this. The first is that you've got a disk adapter whose NT driver is buggy. I've seen it on no-name SCSI and EIDE host adapters. But a surprising number of times, the cause is a boot sector virus like Form, Stoned, Anti-EXE, Anti-CMOS, NYB, Michelangelo, Stealth-B, or Joshi. So before you try to install NT (or *any* operating system, for that matter), turn the computer off, cold-boot it with a write-protected DOS floppy containing an up-to-date virus checker, and scan the computer's disks. Even if they're all formatted as NTFS, the virus checker can still scan the boot record, which is operating system-independent and is the home of the aforementioned viruses. In one case, we had a computer with a virus that wouldn't go away until we discovered that there was also a virus on the bootable floppy that we had to run in order to set up the EISA boards in our machine (*Arghh...*).

Leave a FAT Partition

Some people get positively antsy about the very *notion* that you should put anything but an NTFS partition on your server. I disagree.

You'll probably end up reinstalling NT a time or two on your system. And it's easiest to do that if the contents of the NT setup directory—I386 for most people—are right there on a local hard disk, rather than a CD-ROM. So make sure you've got about 100MB of FAT partition on your system and I386 on that.

CHAPTER

FIVE

Understanding the
Registry Database

Is there anybody out there who had to support Windows 3.1? Okay, then here's a quiz: Where did Windows keep its color settings? Let's see, it could be SYSTEM.INI or WIN.INI. But wait, that kind of stuff is set by the Control Panel, and there's a CONTROL.INI. Or maybe it's in AUTOEXEC.BAT?

NT tries to improve upon this configuration mess with something called the *Registry*. (Microsoft always capitalizes it—"the Registry"—so I will, too, but it always seems a bit overdone, don't you think?) The Registry is terrific in that it's one big database that contains all of the NT configuration information. Everything's there, from color settings to users' passwords. (In case you're wondering, you can't directly access the part with the passwords.) Even better, the Registry uses a fault-tolerant approach to writing data to ensure that the Registry remains intact even if there's a power failure in the middle of a Registry update.

So you've just *got* to like NT's Registry. Except, of course, for the *annoying* parts about the Registry, including its cryptic organization and excessively complex structure. But read on and see what you think.

What Is the Registry?

The Registry is a hierarchical database of settings, much like INI files, that describe your user account, the hardware of the server machine, and your applications. Knowing how to work with the Registry is an important key to being able to tune and control NT servers and NT workstations. It is *not*, by the way, the same as the Registry that is part of Windows 95, although it is similar. For example, Windows 95 experts will know that you can do a multitude of very powerful things under Windows 95 by "exporting" a Registry to an external file, modifying that file, and re-importing it to a Windows 95 Registry. You can't do anything like that here.

Now, editing the Registry is likely the part that you *won't* like about NT. The Registry is not documented in the pile of manuals that came with NT Server, but many Microsoft help files and bug-fix reports refer to it. You're just supposed to *understand* phrases like this one:

> "You can...force a computer to be a Browse Master by opening HKEY_LOCAL_MACHINE\SYSTEM\Current-ControlSet\Services\Browser\Parameters, and creating an IsDomainMasterBrowser value, defining it as type REG_SZ, and specifying the text TRUE for the value of the string."

Quotes like those are a major reason for this chapter. You will come across phrases like that in Microsoft literature, magazine articles, and even parts of this book. Much of that information contains useful advice that will make you a better network administrator if you understand how to carry it out. My goal for this chapter, then, is to give you a feel for the Registry, how to edit it, and when to leave it alone.

Registry Terminology

What did that stuff with all the backslashes mean? To get a first insight, let's look at the Registry. You can see it by running the program REGEDT32.EXE (it's in the C:\winnt35\SYSTEM32 directory) or by accessing it through WINMSD.EXE (click File and Run and a list of programs to run appears, one of which is "Registry Editor [Please use caution]"). Run it and click on the HKEY_LOCAL_MACHINE window. You'll see a screen like the one in Figure 5.1.

The terms to know in order to understand the Registry are subtree, key, value, data type, and hive.

FIGURE 5.1

Registry Editor dialog box

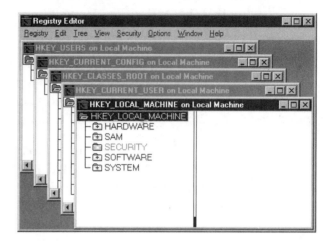

> **WARNING**
> It's easy to accidentally blast important data with the Registry Editor, so it might be a good idea at this point to put the Editor in *read-only* mode by clicking on Options, then on Read Only Mode. You can always reverse the read-only state whenever necessary in the same way. It is truly simple to render a server completely unusable with a few unthinking Registry edits, so be careful, please.

Subtrees

If you ever supported Windows 3.1, you know that there were two essential INI files, WIN.INI and SYSTEM.INI. Roughly speaking, WIN.INI contained settings specific to a user and SYSTEM.INI contained settings specific to the machine. NT's Registry is divided up as well.

The Registry stores all information about a computer and its users by dividing them up into five subtrees:

Subtree	Description
HKEY_LOCAL_MACHINE	Contains information about the hardware currently installed in the machine and about programs and systems running on the machine. You do most of your work in this subtree.

Subtree	Description
HKEY_CLASSES_ROOT	Holds the file associations, information that tells the system "whenever the user double-clicks on a file with the extension BMP in the File Manager, start up PBRUSH.EXE to view this file." It also contains the OLE registration database, the old REG.DAT from Windows 3.x. This is actually a redundant subtree, as all its information is found in the HKEY_LOCAL_MACHINE subtree.
HKEY_USER	Contains two user profiles, a DEFAULT profile used for someone logging in who hasn't logged in before, and a profile with a name like S-228372162..., which is the profile of a user already known to the system. The long number starting with the *S* is the Security ID of the user.
HKEY_CURRENT_USER	Contains the user profile for the person currently logged on to the NT Server machine.
HKEY_CURRENT_CONFIG	Contains configuration information for the particular hardware configuration you booted up with.

Sometimes there is conflicting information in these subtrees. For example, data in HKEY_CURRENT_USER may include some of the same parameters as HKEY_LOCAL_MACHINE; in that case, HKEY_CURRENT_USER takes precedence.

Registry Keys

In Figure 5.1, you saw the Registry Editor display five cascaded windows, one for each subtree. HKEY_LOCAL_MACHINE was on top; you can see the other four subtrees' windows too. HKEY_CURRENT_USER's window has a right and left pane to it. The pane on the left looks kind of like a screen from the Explorer or the old Windows 3.1 File Manager.

In the File Manager, those folders represented subdirectories. Here, however, they separate information into sections, kind of in the same way that old Windows INI files had sections whose names were surrounded by square brackets, names like [386enh], [network], [boot], and the like. Referring back to the HKEY_LOCAL_MACHINE picture a page or two back, let's compare this to an INI file. If this were an INI file, the name of its sections would be [hardware], [sam], [security], [software], and [system]. Each of those folders or sections are actually called *keys* in the Registry.

But here's where the analogy to INI files fails: you can have keys within keys, called *subkeys* (and sub-subkeys, and sub-sub-subkeys, and so on). I've opened the SYSTEM key. It contains subkeys named Clone, ControlSet001, ControlSet002, CurrentControlSet, Select, and Setup, and CurrentControlSet is further sub-keyed into Control and Services.

Notice, by the way, that key called CurrentControlSet. It's very important. Almost every time you modify your system's configuration, you do it with a subkey within the CurrentControlSet subkey.

Key Naming Conventions

The tree of keys gets pretty big as you drill down through the many layers. CurrentControlSet, for example, has dozens of subkeys, each of which can have subkeys. Identifying a given subkey is important, so Microsoft has adopted a naming convention that looks just like directory trees. CurrentControlSet's fully specified name would be, then, HKEY_LOCAL_MACHINE\SYSTEM\CurrentControlSet. In this book, however, I'll just call it CurrentControlSet to keep key names from getting too long to fit on a single line.

Value Entries, Names, Values, and Data Types

If I drill down through CurrentControlSet, I find subkey Services, and within Services, there are many subkeys. In Figure 5.2, you can see some of the subkeys of CurrentControlSet\Services.

One of those keys, Browser, contains subkeys named Linkage, Parameters, and Security. Once we get to Parameters, however, you can see that it's the end of the line—no subkeys from there. Just to

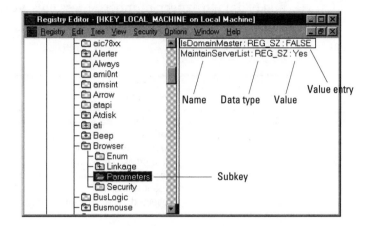

FIGURE 5.2

Subkeys of Current-
ControlSet\Services

quickly review Registry navigation, the key that we're looking at now is in HKEY_LOCAL_MACHINE\SYSTEM\ CurrentControlSet\ Services\Browser\Parameters.

In the right-hand pane, you see two lines:

```
IsDomainMasterBrowser : REG_SZ : False
MaintainServerList : REG_SZ : Yes
```

This is how the registry says what would be, in the old INI-type files, something like this:

```
IsDomainMasterBrowser=Yes
MaintainServerList=Yes
```

Each line like IsDomainMasterBrowser:REG_SZ:False is called a *value entry*. The three parts are called *name*, *data type*, and *value*, respectively. In this example, IsDomainMasterBrowser is the *name*, REG_SZ is the *data type*, and False is the *value*.

Microsoft notes that each value entry cannot exceed about 1MB in size. It's hard to imagine one that size, but it's worth mentioning.

What is that REG_SZ stuff? It's an identifier to the Registry of what *kind* of data to expect: numbers, messages, yes/no values, and the like. There are five data types in the Registry Editor (although others could be defined later):

Data Type	Description
REG_BINARY	Raw binary data. Data of this type usually doesn't make sense when you look at it with the Registry Editor. Binary data shows up in hardware setup information. If there is an alternative way to enter this data other than via the Registry Editor—and I'll discuss that in a page or two—then do it that way. Editing binary data can get you in trouble if you don't know what you're doing. The data is usually represented in hex for simplicity's sake.
REG_DWORD	Another binary data type, but it is 4 bytes long.
REG_EXPAND_SZ	A character string of variable size. It's often information understandable by humans, like path statements or messages. It is "expandable" in that it may contain information that will change at run time, like %username%—a system batch variable that will be of different sizes for different people's names.
REG_MULTI_SZ	Another string type, but it allows you to enter a number of parameters on this one value entry. The parameters are separated by binary zeroes (nulls).
REG_SZ	A simple string.

Those who first met a Registry with Windows 95 will notice a few differences here. Windows 95 has six subtrees, but only three data types—"string," which is like REG_SZ, REG_MULTI_SZ and REG_EXPAND_SZ; "dword," which is like REG_DWORD; and "binary," which is like REG_BINARY.

And if you're wondering how on earth you'll figure out what data type to assign to a new Registry value, don't worry about it; if you read somewhere to use a particular new value entry, you'll be told what data type to use.

Working with the Registry: An Example

Now, I know you want to get in there and try it out despite the warnings, so here's an innocuous example. Remember it's only innocuous if you *follow* the example to the letter; otherwise, it will soon be time to get out your installation disks.

That's not just boilerplate. Don't get mad at *me* if you blow up your server because you didn't pay attention. Actually, you *may* be able to avoid a reinstallation if the thing that you modified was in the Current-ControlSet key; NT knows that you often mess around in there, and so it keeps a spare. In that case, you can reboot the server and wait for the message that says, "Press spacebar now to restore Last Known Good menu." That's NT-ese for "press the spacebar and I'll restore the last control set that booted well for you." Again, that doesn't restore the entire Registry, however; it just restores the control set. Fortunately, the current control set is a *lot* of the Registry.

In any case, let's try something out, something relatively harmless. Let's change the name of the company that you gave NT when you installed it. For example, my firm changed its name back in 1995 from Mark Minasi and Company to TechTeach International, but all of the Help/About dialog boxes still say that I work for Mark Minasi and Company. Fortunately, the Registry Editor lets me change company names without re-installing:

1. Open the Registry Editor. From the Start menu, choose Run.

2. In the command line, type **REGEDT32** and press Enter.

3. Click Window and choose HKEY_Local_Machine. Maximize that window and you see a screen somewhat like the one in Figure 5.3.

4. We're going to modify the value entry in HKEY_LOCAL_ MACHINE\Software\Microsoft\Windows NT\CurrentVersion. Double-click on the Software key, then double-click the Microsoft key, then double-click the Windows NT key, and finally double-click the CurrentVersion key. You see a screen like the one in Figure 5.4.

On the left pane, you still see the Registry structure. On the right, you see the value entries in the RegisteredOrganization subkey.

FIGURE 5.3

Registry Editor – HKEY _LOCAL_MACHINE on Local Machine dialog box

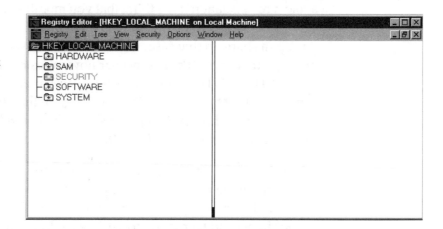

FIGURE 5.4

CurrentVersion— RegisteredOrganization

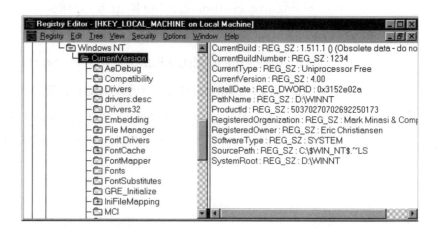

5. Double-click on RegisteredOrganization, and you see a screen like the one in Figure 5.5.

6. Highlight the old value and replace it with TechTeach International. Click OK, and close up the Registry Editor.

Now click Help and About for any program—even the Registry Editor will do—and you'll see that your organization is now TechTeach International.

> **NOTE**
> Click all you like, you will not find a Save button or an Undo button. When you edit the Registry, it's immediate and it's forever. So, once again, be *careful* when you mess with the Registry.

FIGURE 5.5
The String Editor dialog box

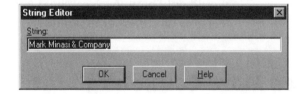

How Do You Find Registry Keys?

How did I know to go to HKEY_LOCAL_MACHINE\Software\Microsoft\Windows NT\CurrentVersion in order to change my organization name? I found it by poking around the Registry.

If you have the *Windows NT Resource Kit* from Microsoft—and if you don't, then *get it!*—you'll find 150 pages detailing each and every key. (That, by the way, is why there isn't a complete key guide in this book. First of all, there wasn't anything that I could add to what's in the *Resource Kit;* second, Microsoft has already published the Kit; and third, 150 pages directly lifted from someone else's publication is a pretty serious copyright violation. I don't think it's possible to "paraphrase" 150 pages of reference material.) Additionally, the Registry keys are documented in an online help file. Unfortunately, some keys aren't documented anywhere except in bits and pieces on Microsoft TechNet or the like, and I'll mention *those* in this book.

If you do *not* have the *Resource Kit,* you can download the Registry key help file from the WINNT forum on CompuServe. There are also some tools that make it easier to search for things in the Registry.

In my opinion, the Registry Editor has a glaring weakness: no effective search routine. Suppose you knew that there was something called "RegisteredOrganization" but you had no idea where it lives in the Registry? You'd be out of luck. Regedit includes a View/Find Key, but it only searches the names of *keys*, not value entries. As RegisteredOrganization is a value name within the key CurrentVersion, I would only be able to search if I knew that the key's name was CurrentVersion, which isn't very likely.

Even More Cautions about Editing the Registry

If you're just learning about the Registry, you're probably eager to wade right in and modify a value entry. Before you do, however, let me just talk a bit about using caution when you manipulate the Registry. (I know I've mentioned it before, but it's important, so I'm mentioning it again.)

The vast majority of Registry items correspond to some setting in the Control Panel, Server Manager, User Manager for Domains, or the like. For example, you just saw where we could change the RegisteredOrganization directly via the Registry Editor. I only picked that example, however, because it was fairly illustrative and simple to understand. In general, *don't use the Registry to modify a value that can be modified otherwise.*

For example, suppose I choose to set a background color on my screen to medium gray. That color is represented as a triplet of numbers: 128 128 128. How did I know what those color values meant? Because they're the same as Windows 3.*x* color values. Color values in Windows are expressed as number triplets. Each number is an integer between 0 and 255. If I input a value greater than 255, the Registry Editor would neither know nor care that I was punching in an illegal color value. Now, in the case of colors, that probably wouldn't crash the system. In the case of *other* items, however, the system could easily be rendered unusable. For example, I'm running NT Server on a system with just a single 486 processor, so the Registry reflects that, noting in one of the Hardware keys that NT is running a "uniprocessor" mode. Altering that to a multiprocessor mode wouldn't be a very good idea.

Why, then, am I bothering to tell you about the Registry Editor? Three reasons.

First, there are settings—important ones—that can only be altered via the Registry Editor, so there's no getting around the fact that an NT expert has to be proficient in the Editor.

Second, you can use the Registry Editor to change system value entries on *remote* computers. To use a very simple example: I'm at location A and I want to change the background color on the server at location B, and to do that I have to physically travel to location B in order to run the Control Panel on the NT machine at that location. Instead of doing that, however, I can just start up the Registry Editor, choose Registry/Select Computer, and edit the Registry of the remote computer. (This assumes that you are running NT Server and you have the security access to change the registry of the remote computer—that is, you're a member of the Administrators group on that computer.)

Third, a program comes with the *Resource Kit* called REGINI.EXE that allows you to write scripts to modify Registries. Such a tool is quite powerful; in theory, you could write a REGINI script to completely reconfigure an NT setup. Again, however, before you start messing with that program, *please* be sure that you have become proficient with the Registry. I've explained the various kinds of mischief that you can cause working by hand with the Registry Editor. Imagine what kinds of *automated* disasters you could start at 66 MHz with a bad REGINI script!

Where the Registry Lives: Hives

The Registry is mostly contained in a set of files called the *hives*. ("Mostly" because some of it is built automatically every time you boot up your system. For example, devices on a SCSI chain aren't known until you boot.) Hives are binary files, so there's no way to look at them without a special editor of some kind, like the Registry Editor. Hives are, however, an easy way to load or back up a sizable part of the Registry.

Most, although not all, of the Registry is stored in hive files. They're not hidden, system, or read-only, but are always open, so you're kind of limited in what you can do with them.

A Look at the Hive Files

The hive files are in the \WINNT\SYSTEM32\CONFIG directory. You can see the hive files that correspond to parts of the subtree listed in Table 5.1.

Table 5.1 needs a few notes to clarify it. First, about the HKEY_CLASSES_ROOT subtree: it is copied from HKEY_LOCAL_MACHINE\SOFTWARE\Classes at boot time. The file exists for use by 16-bit Windows applications. While you're logged onto NT, however, the two keys are linked; if you make a change to one, then the change is reflected in the other.

TABLE 5.1   Hive Files

Subtree/Key	File Name
HKEY_LOCAL_MACHINE\SAM	SAM (primary) and SAM.LOG (backup)
HKEY_LOCAL_MACHINE\SECURITY	SECURITY (primary) and SECURITY.LOG (backup)
HKEY_LOCAL_MACHINE\ SOFTWARE	SOFTWARE (primary) and SOFTWARE.LOG (backup)
HKEY_LOCAL_MACHINE\SYSTEM	SYSTEM (primary) and SYSTEM.ALT (backup)
HKEY_USERS\DEFAULT	DEFAULT (primary) and DEFAULT.LOG (backup)
HKEY_USERS\Security ID	*xxxxxnnn*, *xxxxnnn*.LOG
HKEY_CURRENT_USER	USE###, or ADMIN###(primary), USER###.LOG, ADMIN###.LOG(backups); ###=system ID for user
HKEY_CLASSES_ROOT	(Created from current control set at boot time)

The user profiles now live in \winnt\profiles*username*, where each user gets a directory named *username*. For example, I've got a user account named "mark," so there's a directory named d:\winnt\ profiles\mark on my computer. If I look in it, I find the files ntuser.dat and ntuser.dat.log.

One question remains about the user profiles, however. Why do all the files have a paired file with the extension LOG? Read on.

Fault Tolerance in the Registry

Notice that every hive file has another file with the same name but the extension LOG. That's really useful, because NT Server and NT workstations for that matter use it to protect the Registry during updates.

Whenever a hive file is to be changed, the change is first written into its LOG file. The LOG file isn't actually a backup file; it's more a journal of changes to the primary file. Once the description of the change to the hive file is complete, the journal file is written to disk. When I say "written to disk," I *mean* written to disk. Often, a disk write ends up hanging around in the disk cache for a while, but this write is "flushed" to disk. Then the system makes the changes to the hive file based on the information in the journal file. If the system crashes during the hive write operation, there is enough information in the journal file to "roll back" the hive to its previous position.

The exception to this procedure comes with the SYSTEM hive. The SYSTEM hive is really important because it contains the Current-ControlSet. For that reason, the backup file for SYSTEM, SYSTEM.ALT, is a complete backup of SYSTEM. If one file is damaged, the system can use the other to boot.

Notice that HKEY_LOCAL_MACHINE\HARDWARE does not have a hive. That's because the key is rebuilt each time you boot, so that NT can adapt itself to changes in computer hardware. The program NTDETECT.COM, which runs at boot time, gathers the information that NT needs to create HKEY_LOCAL_MACHINE\HARDWARE.

Confused about where all the keys come from? You'll find a recap in Table 5.2. It's similar to the table a few pages back, but it's more specific about how the keys are built at boot time.

TABLE 5.2   Construction of Keys at Boot Time

Key	How Constructed at Boot Time
HKEY_LOCAL_MACHINE:	
HARDWARE	NTDETECT.COM
SAM	SAM hive file
SECURITY	SECURITY hive file
SOFTWARE	SOFTWARE hive file
SYSTEM	SYSTEM hive file
HKEY_CLASSES_ROOT	SYSTEM hive file, Classes subkey

TABLE 5.2   Construction of Keys at Boot Time (Continued)

Key	How Constructed at Boot Time
HKEY_USERS_DEFAULT	DEFAULT hive file
HKEY_USERS\Sxxx	username000 hive file
HKEY_CURRENT_USER	username000 hive file

Remote Registry Modification

You can modify another computer's Registry, perhaps to repair it or to do some simple kind of remote maintenance, by loading that computer's hive. You do that with the Registry Editor by using the Load Hive or Unload Hive commands.

You can only load or unload the hives for HKEY_USERS and HKEY_LOCAL_MACHINE. The Load Hive option only appears if you've selected one of those two subtrees. Unload Hive is only available if you've selected a subkey of one of those two subtrees.

Why, specifically, would you load a hive or a remote registry?

First of all, you might load a hive in order to get to a user's profile. Suppose a user has set up all of the colors as black on black and made understanding the screen impossible. You could load the hive that corresponds to that user, modify it, and then unload it.

Second, you can use the remote feature to view basically *anything* on a remote system. Suppose you want to do something as simple as changing screen colors. You'd do that on a local system by running the Control Panel, but the Control Panel won't work for remote systems. Answer: Load the Registry remotely.

You could load and save hive files to a floppy disk, walk the floppy over to a malfunctioning machine, and load the hive onto the machine's hard disk, potentially repairing a system problem. This isn't possible if you're using NTFS, unless you have multiple copies of NT on your system, something most of us don't have. But if you've got an NT workstation running a FAT file system, then you can always boot from DOS, replace the hive files under DOS, and then reboot under NT.

When you boot under NT, you see the reference to a "known good menu." That's because NT keeps track not only of the current control set, but also the *previous* control set. That way, if you mess up your system, you can always roll back to the previous configuration. Those control sets are kept in the same key as the CurrentControlSet. Within HKEY_LOCAL_MACHINE\SYSTEM\Select\Current, \Default, \Failed, and \LastKnownGood are numbers indicating which of the two kept control sets are failed, current, good, and the like.

Backing Up and Restoring a Registry

By now, it should be pretty clear that the Registry is an important piece of information and should be protected. It protects itself pretty well with its LOG files, but how can you back it up?

Unfortunately, the fact that Registry hive files are always open makes it tough to back up the Registry, since most backup utilities are stymied by open files. The NTBackup program that comes with NT works well, but it only backs up to tape. Nevertheless, if you use NTBackup—and it's pretty good, particularly for its price—then you should tell it to back up your Registry every night.

Outside of NTBackup are a couple of other protection possibilities. A program named RDISK creates emergency repair disks (you can learn about it in Chapter 16, on failure recovery). And the *Resource Kit* includes two useful utilities: the REGBACK.EXE program allows you to back up a registry file; the REGREST.EXE restores it.

PART III

NT Server
Administration

■ **CHAPTER 6** • Managing and Creating User Accounts

■ **CHAPTER 7** • Creating and Managing Directory Shares

■ **CHAPTER 8** • Managing Printing Services with NT Server

■ **CHAPTER 9** • Connecting PCs to NT Networks

■ **CHAPTER 10** • Making the Mac Connection

■ **CHAPTER 11** • Managing Servers and Domain Controllers

CHAPTER

SIX

6

Managing and Creating
User Accounts

User Manager
for Domains

I have introduced NT Server and some of its components. Now let's tackle the job of actually being an NT Server administrator. As an administrator, you have to

- Create accounts for network users and define what those users can do

- Create shared areas on server disks and define who can access those shares

- Create shared printers and define access to them

- Set up desktop computers to connect with the servers

Those are the goals of the next few chapters. The first goal, setting up user accounts, is the primary object of this chapter. The tool you use to set up user accounts is called the User Manager for Domains.

Introducing the User Manager for Domains

In Windows NT Server, the User Manager for Domains is the primary administrative tool for managing user accounts, groups, and security policies for domains and computers on the network. User Manager for Domains only runs on NT Server machines, and even then by default only on domain controllers. Run User Manager on another machine, such as a regular old NT Workstation or an NT Server that is not a domain controller, and you get a cut-down version called simply the User Manager rather than the User Manager for Domains. You *can* run User Manager for Domains on those machines (heck, there are even versions for Windows for Workgroups and Windows 95), but you've got to load them from the NT CD-ROM in the \CLIENTS\SRVTOOLS directory.

User Manager for Domains versus User Manager

What does it mean to be the User Manager *for Domains*? Well, recall from Chapter 2 that NT machines of all stripes flatly refuse to share data with anyone that they don't recognize; in a simple nondomain network, every single server would have to be introduced to every single user. NT workstations create and manage user accounts with a program called simply User Manager. The job of the User Manager on machine XYZ is to create user accounts that are only relevant and useful on machine XYZ. If a user on machine ABC wanted to get access to data on machine XYZ, the owner of machine XYZ would have to create an account for the ABC owner on the XYZ machine with the User Manager on machine XYZ.

That would lead to a situation wherein a company with 20 servers (and therefore 20 copies of User Manager running) and 100 users would have to keep track of 2000 accounts, making for an administrative nightmare. To simplify things, NT provides for a kind of "account sharing" called a *domain*. One NT machine, the Primary Domain Controller (PDC), holds a shared database of all users known to the machines that have all agreed to constitute a domain. That way, if user John needs access to all 20 servers in the domain, then all you've got to do is to build a single domain-wide account for John—and build a domain-wide account with the User Manager for *Domains*.

User Accounts Sit on the PDC

User accounts contain information like the user name, the password, and a description. All of that data sits in a file called SAM in the primary domain controller's \winnt\system32\config directory. SAM, which is short for Security Access Manager, lives in the PDC's Registry, in an area that's grayed out if you try to peek into it.

> **NOTE**
>
> Backing up the Registry of your PDC is an important part of disaster prevention, as it contains all of your user accounts. If you ever have to rebuild a PDC from scratch, then you can restore your user accounts by restoring the Registry.

Whenever you run the User Manager for Domains, you're directly manipulating that part of the Registry on the PDC. No matter what machine you run the User Manager for Domains from, your changes get stored in the PDC's Registry.

User Manager for Domains Functions

User Manager for Domains provides the network administrator with the means to

- Create, modify, and delete user accounts in the domain
- Define a user's desktop environment and network connections
- Assign logon scripts to user accounts
- Manage groups and group membership within the accounts in a domain
- Manage trust relationships between different domains in the network
- Manage a domain's security policies

If you are logged on as an administrator and you start up the User Manager for Domains, all of its features are available to you. If you log on as a member of the Account Operators group, you won't be able to use some of the User Manager for Domain's capabilities; you can manage most user accounts, but you cannot implement any of the security policies. If you log on as a mere mortal—"user," I believe, is the common term—you can only look at user names with the User Manager for Domains; the User Manager for Domains won't let you make any changes to those accounts. Which reminds me...

> **NOTE** Most changes that you make to a user's account will not show up until the next time she logs on. That means, if she is in the middle of a network session, any changes you've made won't take effect until she logs off and then back on.

A Look around the User Manager for Domains

When you open User Manager for Domains, you see a screen like Figure 6.1. In that screen, you can see a list of all of the accounts in the domain, followed by a list of the groups defined in the domain. The user and group information displayed initially is that for the domain where your user account is located (your home domain), and the name of the domain appears in the title bar; in this case, it's ORION.

FIGURE 6.1

User Manager for Domains

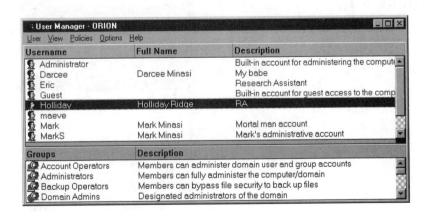

To view users and groups from other trusted domains (trust relationships are discussed in detail in Chapter 12), use the Select Domain command under the User menu. In the resulting dialog box, seen in Figure 6.2, select or type in the name of the domain whose accounts you wish to view.

You can also use this command to view the accounts on individual computers that maintain their own security databases (that is, workstations running Windows NT). To do this, type in the computer name preceded by two backslashes (*computername*) in place of the domain name. At that point, the User Manager for Domains looks more like the regular old User Manager that comes with NT Workstation. Oh, by the way, if the computer that you choose is a domain controller, the domain information is displayed instead. If you want to, you can open multiple instances of User Manager for Domains, each with a different domain's data.

If the domain or computer you choose happens to communicate with your computer through a connection that has relatively low transmission rates, select Low Speed Connection on the Options menu (or in the Select Domain dialog box). This option disables the producing and displaying of lists of user accounts and groups in the User Manager for

FIGURE 6.2

Select Domain dialog box

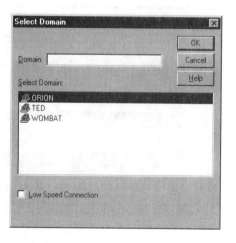

Domains window (which can take a long time across a low-speed link). Although the option is disabled, you can still create or manage user accounts and local groups by using these commands: New User, New Local Group, Copy, Delete, Rename, or Properties. Under the Low Speed Connection option, global groups can't be created or copied, but global group membership can still be managed, somewhat indirectly, by managing the group memberships of individual users. Global and local groups are explained in detail in Chapter 12.

Lists of users and groups can be sorted by either username or by full name with the options on the View menu. Bear in mind that View menu commands are unavailable if the low-speed connection is selected. Any changes made to any account or group while in User Manager for Domains are automatically updated in the view. Other changes, such as an administrator adding an account in your domain from a different, trusted domain, are updated at fixed intervals. If necessary, use the Refresh command to get the latest information for the domain.

To view and manage the properties of a displayed user account or group, simply double-click on the name of the account or group (alternately, you can select the entry and then choose Properties on the User menu). You see the User Properties dialog box in Figure 6.3.

I'll explain what the Groups, Hours, Logon To, and Account buttons do in this chapter. The Profile button is easier to understand once you've learned how to create file shares, so I'll wait to tackle the Profile button in the next chapter.

Sometimes you want to make a change to several user accounts at the same time—to change logon hours, for example. All you have to do in that case is choose a number of users (Ctrl+click on the ones you want to work with) and then choose Users/Properties.

In NT Server, a user account contains information such as the user name, password, group membership, and rights and privileges the user has for accessing resources on the network. These details are explained in Table 6.1.

FIGURE 6.3

User Properties
dialog box

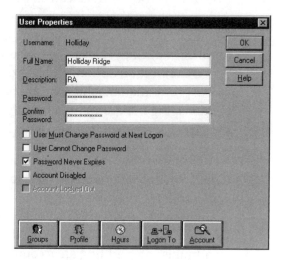

TABLE 6.1   Information in a User Account

Part of User Account	Description
Account type	The particular type of user account; i.e., a local or global account.
Expiration date	A future date when the user account automatically becomes disabled.
Full name	The user's full name.
Home directory	A directory on the server that is private to the user; the user controls access to this directory.
Logon hours	The hours during which the user is allowed to log on to and access network services.
Logon script	A batch or executable file that runs automatically when the user logs on.
Logon workstations	The computer names of the NT workstations that the user is allowed to work from (by default, the user can work from any workstation).
Password	The user's secret password for logging on to his or her account.

TABLE 6.1   Information in a User Account (Continued)

Part of User Account	Description
Profile	A file containing a record of the user's Desktop environment (program groups, network connections, screen colors, and settings that determine what aspects of the environment the user can change) on NT workstations.
Username	A unique name the user types when logging on. One suggestion is to use a combination of first and last names, such as JaneD for Jane Doherty.

Security Identifiers

User accounts, when first created, are automatically assigned a *security identifier* (SID). A SID is a unique number that identifies an account in the NT Server security system. SIDs are never reused; when an account is deleted, its SID is deleted with it. SIDs look like

S-1-5-D1-D2-D3-RID

where *S-1-5* is just a standard prefix (well, if you *must* know, the 1 is a version number, which hasn't changed since NT 3.1; the 5 means that the SID was assigned by NT; and D1, D2, and D3 are just 32-bit numbers that are specific to a domain). Once you create a domain, D1 through D3 are set, and all SIDs in that domain henceforth have the same three values. The *RID* stands for Relative ID. The RID is the unique part of any given SID.

Each new account always has a unique RID number, even if the user name and other information is the same as an old account. This way, the new account will not have any of the previous rights and permissions of the old account, and security is preserved. (I know, you're wondering, "What if I run out of RIDs?" Well, there are 4 billion of them, so you're not likely to run out. If you *did* end up running so many people through your system that you ran out, would the system start reusing RIDs? I have no idea.)

Prebuilt Accounts: Administrator and Guest

If you're creating a new domain, you'll notice that two accounts called Administrator and Guest are built already. The Administrator account is, as you've guessed, an account with complete power over a domain. You can't delete it, but you can rename it. (For security's sake, it's not a bad idea.) You assigned the password for the domain's Administrator account when you installed NT Server on the machine that became the Primary Domain Controller for the domain. Don't lose that password, as there's no way to get it back! (Well, you can always rebuild the domain from scratch with the installation diskettes, but it's no fun.)

The other account is the Guest account. "Guest" means "anyone that the domain doesn't recognize." By default, this account is disabled, and it should *stay* that way. If you've ever worked with a different network, like a UNIX or NetWare network, then you're probably familiar with the idea of a guest account—*but NT's works differently, so pay attention!* With most other operating systems, you can get access to the operating system by logging on with the user name "Guest" and a blank password. That Guest account is usually pretty restricted in the things it can do. That's true with NT, as well, although remember that the Everyone group includes the guests.

Here's the part that *isn't* like other operating systems. Suppose someone tries to log on to an NT network that has the Guest account enabled. She logs on as melanie_wilson with the password "happy." Now, suppose further that this domain doesn't *have* a melanie_wilson account, so it rejects her logon. On a DOS, Windows for Workgroups, or Windows 95 workstation, Melanie can still do work, because none of those operating systems require you to log on to a domain in order to get access to the local workstation. On an NT workstation, she might log on to an account on the local machine. Now she's working at a computer and tries to access a domain resource. And guess what?

She gets in.

Even though an explicit domain login requires that you use a user-name of "Guest," you needn't explicitly log on to a domain to use guest privileges. If your network is attached to my network and your Guest account is enabled, then I can browse through your network and attach to resources that the Guest can access. I needn't log on as "Guest"; the mere fact that there *is* an enabled Guest account pretty much says to NT, "Leave the back door open, okay?" So be careful when enabling the Guest account.

Creating a New User Account

Creating new user accounts in NT Server is fairly easy. Under the User menu, choose the New User option. You'll see the dialog box shown in Figure 6.4.

To begin, type in a unique user name in the Username box (as suggested in Table 6.1, one option is a combination of the user's first and last names). The user name can have up to 20 characters, either upper- or lowercase, and can't include the following characters:

    " / \ [ ] ; : | = , + * ? < >

FIGURE 6.4

The New User dialog box

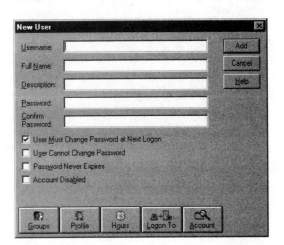

Blanks are okay, but I'd avoid them, as they make it necessary to surround user names with quotes when executing commands.

In the Full Name and Description boxes, type in the user's full name and a short description of the user or of the user account. Both of these entries are optional, but recommended. Establish a standard for entering full names (last name first, for example), because the viewing options in User Manager for Domains allow you to sort user accounts by the user's full name instead of the user name.

Next, type a password in both the Password and Confirm Password boxes. Passwords are case-sensitive, and their attributes are determined under the Account Policy, which I'll cover a bit later in the section about managing security. After you've entered and confirmed a password, select or clear the check boxes that determine whether or not the user can or must change the password at the next logon. If you don't want anyone using the new account just yet, check the Account Disabled box. All of the options in this series of check boxes are described in Table 6.2.

TABLE 6.2   Password and Account Options for Creating a New User Account

Option	Default	Description
Change Password at Next Logon?	Yes	Forces the user to change the password the next time that he or she logs on; this value is set to No afterwards.
User Cannot Change Password	No	If yes, prevents the user from changing the account's password. This is useful for shared accounts.
Password Never Expires	No	If yes, the user account ignores the password expiration policy, and the password for the account never expires. This is useful for accounts that represent services (such as the Replicator account) and accounts for which you want a permanent password (such as the Guest account).
Account Disabled	No	If yes, the account is disabled and no one can log on to it until it is enabled (it is not, however, removed from the database). This is useful for accounts that are used as templates.

At the bottom of the New User dialog box are five buttons: Groups, Profile, Hours, Logon To, and Account. With these buttons, you define the properties of the user account. You'll learn about them in detail in the next sections, save for Profile, which I cover in the next chapter.

Assigning Groups

Selecting the Groups button allows you to specify which groups the new user account will have membership in. NT Server has a number of useful predefined groups, and I'll explain them in more detail a bit later in this chapter in "Managing Groups." (For a more complete description of groups—in particular, local groups versus global groups—look at Chapter 12, on multi-domain planning and management.) Group membership is shown in the Group Memberships dialog box, seen in Figure 6.5.

You can click on the Groups button to open this dialog box. The dialog box displays which groups the user is or isn't a member of. Note the icons next to the group names:

- An icon representing a white woman and a black man in front of a globe indicates a global group.

- A computer terminal behind the two faces indicates a local group.

FIGURE 6.5

Group Memberships dialog box

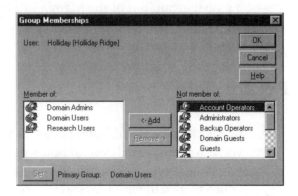

I can't help but observe that the icon for single user accounts is neither white nor black, but *gray*. Perhaps these users are dead? Could this be a George Romero operating system—the User Manager of the Living Dead? (Sorry, couldn't resist.)

Again, sorry to appear to be ducking the explanations of global and local groups, but the whole discussion of global and local groups is completely incomprehensible until you understand how to manage multiple domains under NT; hence locals and globals are covered in Chapter 12. To quickly summarize the differences, however, global groups are groups that can be made accessible to the entire network, while local groups are local to the domain in which they are defined.

To give new group memberships to the user account, select those groups from the Not Member of box, then choose the Add button or drag the group icon(s) to the Member of box. To remove membership in any group from the user account, select the desired groups from the Member of box and click on the Remove button or drag the icon(s) to the Not member of box.

User accounts must be a member of at least one group, referred to as the *primary group*, which is used when the user logs on to NT Services for Macintosh or runs POSIX applications. Primary groups must be global groups, and you can't remove a user from that user's primary group. To remove a user from that user's primary group, you have to first move the user to a different primary group. To do this, select a global group out of the Member of box, then click the Set button beneath the Member of frame. When you're finished configuring the group membership, click OK.

Permissible Logon Hours

By selecting the Hours button in the New User dialog box (see Figure 6.4), you can specify the days and hours during which a particular user can access the network. Similarly, choosing the Logon To button lets you limit which workstations a user can log on from. Push the Hours button from the Properties dialog box of any user or group of users, and you see a dialog box like Figure 6.6.

By default, a user can connect to the network all hours of all days of the week. If for some reason you don't want a user to get access to the network all hours of the day, you can restrict logon hours with this dialog box.

To administer the hours during which the user account is allowed to access the network, select the hours by dragging the cursor over a particular block of hours. Conversely, you can select all the hours of a certain day by clicking on that day's button, or you can choose certain hours across all seven days by clicking the button on top of an hour's column. Then click either the Allow or Disallow button to grant or deny access to the network at those selected hours. Filled boxes indicate the hours when the user is authorized to connect to the network; empty ones indicate the time when access is denied. When done, click OK.

As its title implies, you must understand that this dialog box controls *logon* hours. Suppose you've restricted someone so that she can only log on between 9 A.M. and 5 P.M., and she tries to log on at 8:59.

FIGURE 6.6

The Logon Hours
dialog box

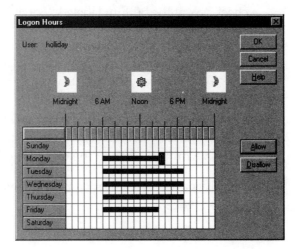

She won't get on, and will see a message something like this (on an NT workstation):

```
Your account has time restrictions that prevent you from logging
on at this time. Please try again later.
```

Or, if she's at a Windows 95 workstation, she'll see:

```
You are not allowed to log on at this time.
```

From a DOS workstation, the message is a bit more garrulous:

```
Error 2241: You do not have the necessary access rights to log
on at this time. To change access rights, contact your network
administrator about changing the logon hours listed in your
account.
```

Of course, if our imaginary user tries to log on a few minutes later, after 9 A.M., she gets in without a hitch. But what happens toward the *end* of the logon hours? What happens, for example, when 5:01 P.M. rolls around? Does the system dump her off?

No, not by default. A bit later in this chapter, you'll see a dialog box labeled Account Policy. (If you want to look ahead to it, turn to Figure 6.18 or go to the User Manager for Domains and click Policies/Account.) Account Policy is a big dialog box, and it would be easy to miss one small check box at the bottom labeled "Forcibly disconnect remote users from server when logon hours expire."

That's not a very clear statement in the Account Policies dialog box, is it? To me at least, a "remote user" is someone who's dialing into the network; but to NT, it just means anyone who's accessing the server via the network, rather than sitting right down at the server itself. By default, the box isn't checked. If you check it, the user gets this message five minutes before the end of the logon hours:

```
Your logon time at [domain name] ends at [end time]. Please clean
up and log off.
```

Three minutes after that, the message gets a bit more nasty:

```
WARNING: You have until [end time] to log off. If you have not
logged off at this time, your session will be disconnected, and
any open files or devices you have open may lose data.
```

Finally, at the appointed hour, you're history:

```
Your logon time at [domain name] has ended.
```

To get those messages, you must be running a message receiver like Winpopup (for Windows for Workgroups or Windows 95) or the Alerter service on a Windows NT workstation. You get logged off even if you're not running a message receiver.

Once a user has been booted off, whatever network resources she was using just seem to vanish. Looking at a network drive named F:, for example, will likely generate this error message or one like it: "No files found on directory F:." Trying to browse in a domain server may lead to an error message like this: "[*servername*] is not accessible. You are not allowed to log on at this time."

Remember that changes to a user's account don't take effect until the next time he logs on, so changing someone's logon hours today probably won't have any effect until tomorrow.

This talk of enforced logoff hours leads to a common question: "How can I boot everyone off the server at 2 A.M. so that the scheduled backup can occur?" That's simple. Just write a batch file with these commands:

```
Net pause server
Net send * The server is going down in 5 minutes for maintenance.
Sleep 300
Net stop server
```

The pause command keeps anyone new from logging on. The send command sends a message to everyone running the messenger service and a network pop-up. The sleep command tells NT to just wait for 300 seconds (five minutes). SLEEP.EXE isn't shipped with NT, but it *is* on the CD-ROM that comes with the NT *Resource Kit*, and I highly recommend installing the SLEEP program. The stop command shuts down the server, disconnecting everyone.

Controlling Where Users Can Log On

When you select the Logon To button in the New User dialog box (see Figure 6.4), you get the Logon Workstations dialog box shown in Figure 6.7. This dialog box allows you to restrict which workstations the user can log on from. Now, I know you're wondering, "Why does the button say 'Logon To' when it means 'Logon From?" As to that question, all I can do is quote a Microsoft employee: "Well, yes, it should be 'logon from,' but…well…a programmer built the dialog box, you know what I mean?" (For obvious reasons, the Microsoft employee asked to remain anonymous.) As with the logon times, the default is No Restrictions; a user is allowed to log on at any workstation on the network.

If you want to restrict the user's choice of workstations where he or she can log on to the network, select the User May Log On To These Workstations button and type in the computer names (without preceding backslashes) of the allowed workstations. Up to eight workstations can be specified. For example, if the machines that I regularly log on to are called

FIGURE 6.7

Logon Workstations
dialog box

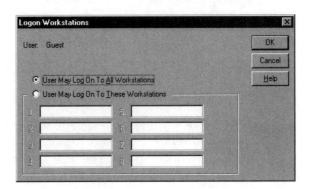

SDG90 and LAPDOG, then I just punch in those names, again with no preceding backslashes.

This feature works for all workstation types.

Account Duration and Type

When creating or managing a user account, you can set the account to expire after a certain time period. If you have a summer intern or other temporary personnel, you don't want them to be able to log on to the network beyond the time that they're authorized. Setting an account to expire will avoid this problem. Click the Account button in the New User dialog box to display the Account Information dialog box shown in Figure 6.8.

An account with an expiration date becomes disabled (not deleted) at the end of the day specified in the Account Expires box. If the user happens to be logged on, the session is not terminated, but no new connections can be made, and once the user logs off, he or she can't log back on.

In addition to setting an account expiration date, you can also set whether the user account in question is a *global account* or *local account* (don't confuse these with global and local *groups*).

FIGURE 6.8

Account Information dialog box

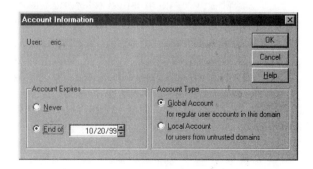

Global accounts, the default setting, are normal user accounts in the user's home domain. These accounts can be used not only in the home domain, but also in any domain that has a trust relationship with the home domain. (More on trust relationships shortly.)

Local user accounts, on the other hand, are accounts provided in a particular domain for a user whose global user account is not in a trusted domain (i.e., an untrusted NT Server domain or a LAN Manager 2.x domain). A local account can't be used to log on interactively at an NT workstation or an NT Server server. Like other accounts, however, a local account can access NT and NT Server computers over the network, can be placed in local and global groups, and can be assigned rights and permissions. If a user from an untrusted domain (either NT Server or LAN Manager 2.x) needs access to other NT Server domains, that user needs to have a local account on each of those other domains, since local accounts from one domain (the user's home domain) can't be used in other trusting domains.

Now, by default, all user accounts are global—you've got to click a radio button, as you can see in the dialog box in Figure 6.8, to make a user account a local account. The main difference between a local account and a global account is that you can never get an external domain to recognize a local account. When would you use a local user account, then? "I wouldn't," replied a Microsoft employee, when I asked. "It really doesn't have much use right now," he continued, implying, I suppose, that it had some meaning once but no longer does.

When you've finished selecting the desired account options, choose Add, choose Close, and then choose OK. Then, choose OK in the New User dialog box to create the new user account with the properties you've just specified. The new account will now appear in the list of users on the current domain shown in the User Manager for Domains window.

How Do I Create a User Account in a Domain?

 Open User Manager for Domains. Under the User menu, select New User. In the New User dialog box, do the following:

1. Type in a user name and the user's full name.

2. Type in a description of the user or account (optional).

3. Type in a password in the Password and Confirm Password boxes. Select the password's characteristics from the options presented. Choose whether or not the account will be disabled.

4. Using the Groups, Profile, Hours, Logon To, and Account buttons, do the following: set the user's group membership; user profile, logon script, and/or home directory; hours that the network will be available to the user; from which workstations the user is allowed to log on; and account characteristics (expiration date and account type).

5. When you're done configuring the account using the options in step 4, choose Add.

Managing User Accounts

Once a user account has been created, you can look at and modify its properties either by double-clicking on that account or by highlighting the account and choosing Properties from the User menu. You'll see the User Properties dialog box, as shown in Figure 6.9.

Anyone logged on as an administrator or as a member of the Account Operators local group (more on groups shortly) can then reconfigure the account's properties, following the same procedure used for creating a new user account.

FIGURE 6.9

FIGURE 6.9

User Properties
dialog box

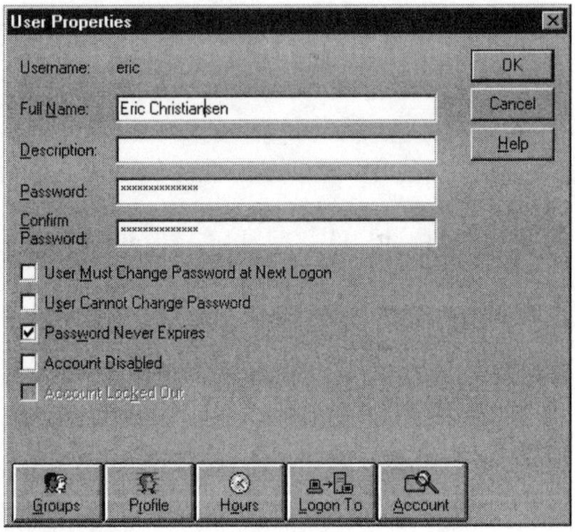

Copying Accounts

Instead of creating each user account on your network individually, you can also copy existing user accounts. The primary advantage of creating user accounts this way is that all of the original user account's properties (including group memberships) are copied over to the new user account, thus speeding up administrative chores. If you have a large network, you might want to create one or more template accounts that contain specific properties shared by groups of users. For greater security, keep the template accounts disabled so that no one can actually log on to them.

To copy an existing user account, select the account from the list of user accounts in the User Manager for Domains window, then choose Copy from the User menu. You see the Copy dialog box shown in Figure 6.10.

The copy retains all of the information from the original, except for the username, full name, and password, which you must provide. Configure the new account, making changes to names and properties as needed, and then choose Add. When done, select Close.

FIGURE 6.10

FIGURE 6.10

Copying an existing
user account

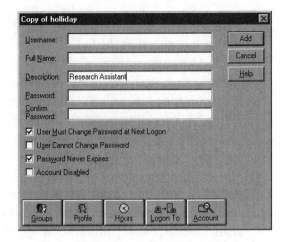

Note that the original user's rights, as defined by the User Rights command under the Policy menu, are not copied from one user account to another. If the newly copied accounts must have certain rights, you must grant them separately. Granting rights to a group and putting accounts in that group is the best way to manage rights for multiple users.

All user accounts, including the built-in ones, can be renamed by choosing the Rename command in the User menu. Renamed accounts retain their original security identifier (SID), and thereby keep all of their original properties, rights, and permissions.

Managing Properties for More Than One Account

You can manage several user account properties for more than one account at once. To do this, first select two or more user accounts. You can select a number of accounts either individually with the mouse from the currently displayed list of users, or (if there are a significant number of user accounts) you can select all members of a particular group within the domain with the Select Users command in the User menu. You see the Select Users dialog box shown in the Figure 6.11.

You'll notice that the Select Users command is actually more of a "Select Group" command; by choosing a group on the domain, you are selecting all of the users who are members of that group. The Select Users option is cumulative; if you first select Administrators and then select Backup Operators, all members who are either in the Administrators group or the Backup Operators group are selected (the Deselect button lets you take groups off of the selected list). Note that when you choose a group using the Select Users command, only members from the local domain are chosen. For example, if you select a local group (which can contain both users from the home domain as well as users from other, trusted domains), any changes that are made won't affect members from the trusted domains.

After you've selected the user accounts, choose Properties from the User menu. Figure 6.12 is the screen you see next.

As with a single user account, you can select any of the buttons at the bottom of the dialog box to make certain modifications to all of the selected accounts.

For example, let's say you want to modify the group membership for the selected user accounts. By choosing the Groups button, you can see the group memberships that each of the selected accounts have in common in the All Are Members Of box. You can see this box in Figure 6.13.

FIGURE 6.11

Users dialog box

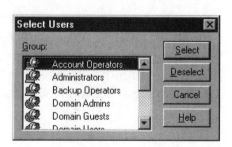

FIGURE 6.12

Modifying the
properties of a group
of user accounts

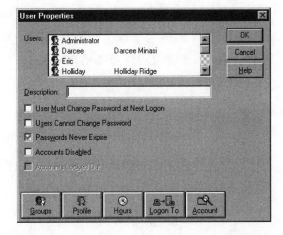

FIGURE 6.13

Modifying the group
membership of
selected users

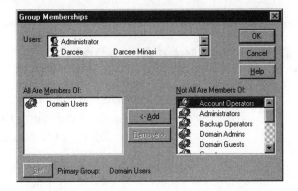

You can then add or remove group membership from the selection of users by highlighting the groups and choosing the Add or Remove button.

How Do I Make Sure That a Selected List of Users Are *Not* Members of a Particular Group in a Domain?

 To make sure, do the following:

1. Select the users in the User Manager for Domains window.

2. From the User menu, choose Properties.

3. In the User Properties dialog box, choose Groups. Add the particular group from the Not All Are Members Of box to the Members Of box.

4. Choose OK to save the change.

5. In the User Properties dialog box, choose Groups again.

6. Select the group in the All Are Members Of box and choose Remove.

Deleting User Accounts

There are three ways to rescind a user's ability to log on to the network with his or her account: by disabling the account, by restricting the access hours, and by deleting the account.

As mentioned earlier, a disabled account continues to exist on the server, but no one can access it. Even so, it (and with it, its properties) can be copied, it appears on lists of user accounts, and it can be restored to enabled status at any time. A deleted account, on the other hand, is completely removed from the system, vanishes from user account lists, and cannot be recovered or restored.

A new user account can be created with the same name and properties as a deleted account, but it will receive a different, unique security identifier (SID). Because internal processes in NT refer to a user account's SID rather than its username, none of the rights or permissions granted to the deleted user account will transfer to any new account that has the same name as the old.

As a measure against inadvertent, hasty, and perhaps regretted deletions of user accounts, you might choose to first disable unused accounts, then periodically remove those disabled accounts. Incidentally, NT Server prevents the deletion of the built-in Administrator and Guest accounts.

To delete one or more user accounts, select the account or accounts from the list in the opening window of User Manager for Domains. Then, under the User menu, choose Delete. Confirmation boxes appear to remind you of your choice and ask if you want to continue. Select OK to proceed.

Managing Groups

In NT Server, a user group is a set of users who have identical network rights. Placing your domain's user accounts in groups not only simplifies general (as well as security) management, but also makes it easier and faster to grant multiple users access to a network resource. Additionally, to give a right or permission to all of the users in a single group, all you have to do is grant that permission or right to the group.

Creating and Deleting Groups

To create a new local group, select New Local Group under the User menu. You see the dialog box shown in Figure 6.14.

Type in the name of the local group you wish to create (in this example, I'm creating a group called Instructors). Include a description of the group, if you want.

Select the Add button to add members to the group. You will see the Add Users and Groups dialog box in Figure 6.15.

FIGURE 6.14

New Local Group
dialog box

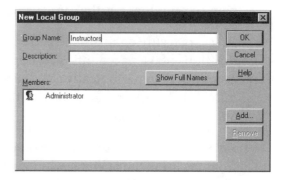

FIGURE 6.15

Adding accounts to the
new local group

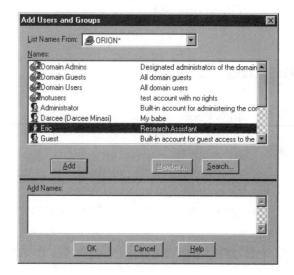

In the Add Users and Groups dialog box, select a name or global group from the desired domain list, and click the Add button to place group in the Add Names list (remember, a local group can contain both users and global groups from trusted domains as well as from the local domain). Alternately, you can type the user names into the Add Names list; make sure you separate the names with a semicolon. When you've collected all of the names in the Add Names list, click OK.

The names you've chosen will appear in the Members box of the New Local Group dialog box. (To see their full names, click the Show Full

Names button.) To remove a name from the list, just highlight it and click on the Remove button. When your new local group's membership is to your satisfaction, click OK. The new group will now appear in the User Manager for Domains list of groups.

Creating a Global Group

Creating a new global group is just as easy. Under the User menu, choose New Global Group. In the New Global Group dialog box, as seen in Figure 6.16, type in a name and description for the new group. In this example, the new global group is called Research Assistants.

A global group can only contain user accounts from the domain where it is created, so the Not Members box will contain only those accounts on the current domain. To give any user on the list group membership, select one of the entries in the Not Members list and click on the Add button. When finished, choose OK; the new global group will be visible in the User Manager for Domains group list.

You can change any user's or group's membership in another group by displaying that group's Properties (in the User Manager for Domains window, either select the group and choose Properties from the User menu, or double-click on that group). The dialog boxes for Group Properties are identical to those for New Groups, and you can add and remove members using the same procedures described above.

FIGURE 6.16

New Global Group
dialog box

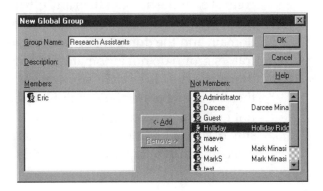

Deleting groups is accomplished by selecting the group in the User Manager for Domains window and choosing Delete (in the User menu). The same cautions about deleting user accounts also apply to deleting groups, since groups also have their own unique security identifiers (SIDs). Before allowing you to delete a group, NT Server prompts you with a reminder message, as in Figure 6.17. Deleting a group removes only that group from NT Server; all user accounts and groups within the deleted group are unaffected.

FIGURE 6.17

Warning message for deleting a group

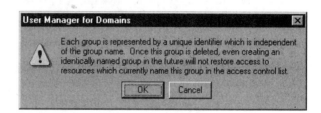

Examining the Predefined Groups

A number of predefined groups, both local and global, are built into NT Server to aid network administration and management. The local groups are described in the following pages.

Administrators   Not surprisingly, Administrators is the most powerful group. Members of the Administrators local group have more control over the domain than any other users, and they are granted all of the rights necessary to manage the overall configuration of the domain and the domain's servers. Incidentally, users in the Administrators group do not automatically have access to every file in the domain. If the file's permissions do not grant access to Administrators, then the members of the Administrator's group cannot access the file. If it becomes necessary, however, an administrator can take ownership of such a file and thus have access to it. If he or she does, the event is recorded in the security log (provided that auditing of files has been activated) and the administrator does not have the ability to give ownership back to the original owner (or to anyone else for that matter).

Within the Administrators group is a built-in Administrator user account that cannot be deleted. By default, the Domain Admins global group is also a member of the Administrators group, but it can be removed.

Given that it's possible for the Administrator account to be disabled, it might be wise to create a backup administrator account to be used in case of emergency.

Server Operators　The Server Operators local group has all of the rights needed to manage the domain's servers. Members of the Server Operations group can create, manage, and delete printer shares at servers; create, manage, and delete network shares at servers; back up and restore files on servers; format a server's fixed disk; lock and unlock servers; and change the system time. In addition, Server Operators can log on to the network from the domain's servers as well as shut down the servers.

Account Operators　Members of the Account Operators local group are allowed to use User Manager for Domains to create user accounts and groups for the domain, and to modify or delete most of the domain's user accounts and groups.

An Account Operator cannot modify or delete the following groups: Administrators, Domain Admins, Account Operators, Backup Operators, Print Operators, and Server Operators. Likewise, members of this group cannot modify or delete user accounts of administrators. They cannot administer the security policies, but they can use the Server Manager to add computers to a domain, log on at servers, and shut down servers.

Print Operators　Members of this group can create, manage, and delete printer shares for an NT Server server. Additionally, they can log on at and shut down servers.

Backup Operators   The Backup Operators local group provides its members the rights necessary to back up directories and files from a server and to restore directories and files to a server. Like the Print Operators, they can also log on at and shut down servers.

Everyone   Everyone is not actually a group, and it doesn't appear in the User Management list, but you can assign rights and permissions to it. Anyone who has a user account in the domain, including all local and remote users, is automatically a member of the Everyone local group. Not only are members of this group allowed to connect over the network to a domain's servers, but they are also granted the advanced right to change directories and travel through a directory tree that they may not have permissions on. Members of the Everyone group also have the right to lock the server, but won't be able to unless they've been granted the right to log on locally at the server.

Users   Members of the group simply called Users have minimal rights at servers running NT Server. They are granted the right to create and manage local groups, but unless they have access to the User Manager for Domains tool (such as by being allowed to log on locally at the server), they can't perform this task. Members of the Users group do possess certain rights at their local NT workstations.

Guests   This is NT Server's built-in local group for occasional or one-time users to log on. Members of this group are granted very limited abilities. Guests have no rights at NT Server servers, but they do possess certain rights at their own individual workstations. The built-in Guest user account is automatically a member of the Guests group.

Replicator   This local group, different from the others, supports directory replication functions. The only member of a domain's Replicator local group should be a single domain user account, which is used to log on to the Replicator services of the domain controller and to the other servers in the domain. User accounts of actual users should *not* be added to this group at all. (Wondering what you'd use the Replicator group for? It's instrumental to directory replication, which is discussed in Chapter 11.)

The Table 6.3 summarizes the user rights (more on user rights in the next section) and special abilities granted to NT Server's predefined local groups.

TABLE 6.3   Rights/Special Abilities Granted to Predefined Local Groups

User Rights	Members Can Also
Group: Administrators	
Log on locally	Create and manage user accounts
Access this computer from the network	Create and manage global groups
Take ownership of files	Assign user rights
Manage auditing and security log	Lock the server
Change the system time	Override the server's lock
Shut down the system	Format the server's hard disk
Force shutdown from a remote system	Create common groups
Back up files and directories	Keep a local profile Share and stop sharing directories Share and stop sharing printers
Group: Server Operators	
Log on locally	Lock the server
Change the system time	Override server's lock
Shut down the system	Format the server's hard disk
Force shutdown from a remote system	Create common groups
Back up files and directories	Keep a local profile
Restore files and directories	Share and stop sharing directories Share and stop sharing printers

TABLE 6.3   Rights/Special Abilities Granted to Predefined Local Groups (Continued)

User Rights	Members Can Also
Group: Account Operators[1]	
Log on locally	Create and manage user accounts, global groups, and local groups
Shut down the system	Keep a local profile

[1] They cannot, however, modify administrator accounts, the Domain Admins global group, or the local group's Administrators, Server Operators, Account Operators, Print Operators, and Backup Operators.

User Rights	Members Can Also
Group: Print Operators	
Log on locally	Keep a local profile
Shut down the system	Share and stop sharing printers

User Rights	Members Can Also
Group: Backup Operators	
Log on locally	Keep a local profile
Shut down the system	
Back up files and directories	
Restore files and directories	

User Rights	Members Can Also
Group: Everyone	
Access this computer from the network	Lock the server[2]

[2] In order to actually do this, the member of the group must have the right to log on locally at the server.

User Rights	Members Can Also
Group: Users	
(none)	Create and manage local groups[3]

[3] In order to actually do this, the user must either have the right to log on locally at the server, or must have access to the User Manager for Domains tool.

User Rights	Members Can Also
Group: Guests	
(none)	(none)

NT Server has only three built-in global groups, Domain Admins, Domain Users, and Domain Guests.

Group	What It Does
Domain Admins	By placing a user account into this global group, you provide administrative-level abilities to that user. Members of Domain Admins can administer the home domain, the workstations of the domain, and any other trusted domains that have added the Domain Admins global group to their own Administrators local group. By default, the built-in Domain Admins global group is a member of both the domain's Administrators local group and the Administrators local groups for every NT workstation in the domain. The built-in Administrator user account for the domain is automatically a member of the Domain Admins global group.
Domain Users	Members of the Domain Users global group have normal user access to, and abilities for, both the domain itself and for any NT workstation in the domain. This group contains all domain user accounts, and is by default a member of the Users local groups for both the domain and for every Windows NT workstation on the domain.
Domain Guests	This group allows guest accounts to access resources across domain boundaries, if they've been allowed that by the domain administrators.

Built-in Special Groups In addition to the built-in local and global groups, a few special groups appear now and again when viewing certain lists of groups:

INTERACTIVE: Anyone using the computer locally

NETWORK: All users connected over the network to a computer

SYSTEM: The operating system

CREATOR OWNER: The creator and/or owner of subdirectories, files, and print jobs

Incidentally, the INTERACTIVE and NETWORK groups combined form the Everyone local group.

Managing Security Policies

The User Manager for Domains is part of a quartet of programs that provide network security options in NT Server. While the Explorer/My Computer team and the Printer Folder control specific access to files, directories, and printers, User Manager for Domains gives the administrator the ability to assign system-wide rights and to determine what the auditing policies of the network will be.

In User Manager for Domains, an administrator can manage the following security policies:

- Account, which controls the characteristics of passwords for all user accounts

- User Rights, which determines which user or group is assigned particular system rights

- Audit, in which the kinds of security events to be logged are defined

- Trust Relationships, which establishes how other domains on the network interact with the local domain

Password Characteristics

Under the Account policy, you can set and adjust the password characteristics for all user accounts in the domain. From the Policies menu, choose Account. You see the Account Policy dialog box in the Figure 6.18.

Make your selections for the following options:

Maximum Password Age   This option sets the time period in which a password can be used before the system requires the user to pick a new one.

FIGURE 6.18

Account Policy
dialog box

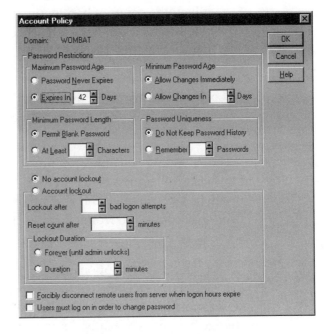

Minimum Password Age   The value set here is the time that a password has to be used before the user is allowed to change it again. If you allow changes to the password to be made immediately, make sure you choose Do Not Keep Password History in the Password Uniqueness box.

Minimum Password Length   This option defines the fewest number of characters that a user's password can contain.

Password Uniqueness   Here you can specify the number of new passwords that must be used before a user can employ an old password. If you choose a value here, you must specify a password age value under Minimum Password Age.

Account lockout   This option prevents anyone from logging on to the account after a certain number of failed attempts:

Lockout after "x" bad logon attempts   This value defines how many times the user can attempt to log on.

Reset count after "x" minutes This setting defines the time in which the count of bad logon attempts will start over. For example, suppose you have a reset count of two minutes and three logon attempts. If you mistype twice, by waiting two minutes after the second attempt, you'll have three tries again.

Lockout Duration This setting determines whether the administrator must unlock the account manually or can let the user try again after a certain period.

The "Forcibly disconnect remote users from server when logon hours expire" option is tied in to the available logon hours you specified when you created the user account. If this option is selected, the user is disconnected from all connections to any of the domain's servers once the logon hours expire.

Not selecting this option enables the user to stay connected once the logon hours expire, but no new connections will be permitted. Checking "User must log on in order to change password" requires the user to change her password after demonstrating that she knew it already.

User Rights and Object Permissions

User access to network resources—files, directories, devices—in NT Server is controlled in two ways: by assigning *rights* to a user that grant or deny access to certain objects (e.g., the ability to log on to a server), and by assigning *permissions* to objects that specify who is allowed to use objects and under what conditions (e.g., granting read access for a directory to a particular user).

Consider the groups Users and Administrators. What makes administrators different from users? Well, administrators can log on right at the server; users can't. Administrators can create users and back up files; users can't. Administrators are different from users in that they have rights that users don't have. The central thing to remember here is that the very thing that separates one group in NT from another mostly has to do with the rights the groups have. You control who gets which rights via the User Manager for Domains.

Rights generally authorize a user to perform certain system tasks. For example, the average user can't just sit down at an NT Server and log on right at the server. The question, "Can I log on locally at a server?" is an example of a right. "Can I back up data and restore data?" "Can I modify printer options on a shared printer?" These are also user rights. User rights can be assigned separately to a single user, but for reasons of security organization it is better to put the user into a group and define which rights are granted to the group. You manage user rights in User Manager for Domains.

Permissions, on the other hand, apply to specific objects such as files, directories, and printers. "Can I change files in the LOTUS directory on the BIGMACHINE server?" is an example of a permission. Permissions are set by the creator or owner of an object. Permissions regulate which users can have access to the object and in what fashion.

TIP

You can only set permissions on particular files on an NTFS volume. Directory and file permissions are administered in My Computer and the Explorer, or from the command line; printer permissions are regulated in the Printers folder.

As a rule, user rights take precedence over object permissions. For example, let's look at a user who is a member of the built-in Backup Operators group. By virtue of his or her membership in that group, the user has the right to back up the servers in the user's domain. This requires the ability to see and read all directories and files on the servers, including those whose creators and owners have specifically denied read permission to members of the Backup Operators group; thus the right to perform backups overrides the permissions set on the files and directories.

There are two types of user rights: regular user rights and advanced user rights. NT Server's built-in groups have certain rights already assigned to them; you can also create new groups and assign a custom set of user rights to those groups. As I've said before, security management is much easier when all user rights are assigned through groups instead of being granted to individual users.

To look at or change the rights granted to a user or group, select the domain where the particular user or group resides (if they are not in the local domain), then choose User Rights from the Policies menu. You see the User Rights Policy dialog box, as shown in Figure 6.19.

Check the arrow box next to the currently displayed user right to see the entire list of regular user rights. By clicking one of the rights, you can see the groups and users who currently have been granted that particular right. In the figure, you can see that the right "Access this computer from network" has been granted to the Administrators and Everyone group.

The regular rights used in NT Server are:

Access this computer from network   Allows a user to connect over the network to a computer.

Add workstations to domain   Makes machines domain members.

FIGURE 6.19
User Rights Policy
dialog box

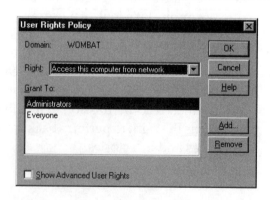

Back up files and directories   Allows a user to back up files and directories. As mentioned earlier, this right supersedes file and directory permissions.

Change the system time   Grants a user the right to set the time for the internal clock of a computer.

Force shutdown from a remote system   Note that, although presented as an option, this right is not currently implemented by NT Server.

Load and unload device drivers   Lets a user add or remove drivers from the system.

Log on locally   Allows a user to log on locally at the server computer itself.

Manage auditing and security log   Gives a user the right to specify what types of events and resource access are to be audited. Also allows viewing and clearing the security log.

Restore files and directories   Allows a user to restore files and directories. This right supersedes file and directory permissions.

Shut down the system   Grants a user the right to shut down Windows NT.

Take ownership of files or other object   Lets a user take ownership of files, directories, and other objects that are owned by other users.

The advanced rights in NT Server are summarized in the Table 6.4. These rights are added to the rights list when you click the Show Advanced User Rights option located at the bottom of the User Rights Policy dialog box.

Most of the advanced rights are useful only to programmers who are writing applications to run on Windows NT, and most are not granted to a group or user. However, two of the advanced rights—Bypass traverse checking and Log on as a service—might be useful to some domain administrators. Bypass traverse checking is granted by default to the Everyone group in NT Server. And notice the Increase object

TABLE 6.4   Advanced User Rights

Advanced User Right	Allows Users To
Act as part of the operating system	Act as a trusted part of the operating system; some sub-systems have this privilege granted to them.
Bypass traverse checking	Traverse a directory tree even if the user has no other rights to access that directory; denies access to users in POSIX applications.
Create a pagefile	Create a pagefile.
Create a token object	Create access tokens. Only the Local Security Authority can have this privilege.
Create permanent shared objects	Create special permanent objects used in NT.
Debug programs	Debug applications.
Generate security audits	Generate audit-log entries.
Increase quotas	Increase object quotas (each object has a quota assigned to it).
Increase scheduling priority	Boost the scheduling priority of a process.
Load and unload device drivers	Load and unload drivers for devices on the network.
Lock pages in memory	Lock pages in memory to prevent them from being paged out into backing store (such as PAGEFILE.SYS).
Log on as a batch job	Log on to the system as a batch queue facility.
Log on as a service	Perform security services (the user that performs replication logs on as a service).
Modify firmware environment values	Modify system environment variables (not user environment variables).
Profile single process	Use Windows NT profiling capabilities to observe a process.
Profile system performance	Use Windows NT profiling capabilities to observe the system.
Receive unsolicited device input	Read unsolicited data from a terminal device.
Replace a process level token	Modify a process's access token.

quotas right. Hey, sounds like it's possible to control how much disk space a user takes up. A "disk quota?" Nope. It's a right that's existed in NT since version 3.1, and one small notation in the documentation says that the quota feature "is not in use yet." Oh well. Maybe in Cairo…

In general, I find that the only user right that I ever end up granting is to log on to the server locally; now and then, a user needs that ability. Additionally, the Internet mail package that I use to route my company's Internet mail requires that I allow users the right to "log on as a batch job."

Security Event Auditing

NT Server maintains three event logs to which entries are added in the background—the System log, the Applications log, and the Security log. You can set up security auditing of a number of events on NT Server in User Manger for Domains to help track user access to various parts of the system. To enable security auditing, pull down the Policies menu and select Audit. You see the dialog box in Figure 6.20.

As you can see, the Audit Policy dialog box gives you the option to activate auditing, followed by a list of the types of security events you can audit. The default setting is Do Not Audit; with this option selected,

FIGURE 6.20

Audit Policy dialog box

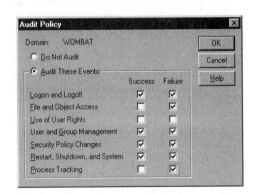

all of the Audit These Events options are grayed out. If you choose to activate auditing, the information about that event is stored as an entry in the computer's Security log. This log, along with the System and Application logs, can then be viewed with the Event Viewer.

Table 6.5 describes the auditing options you can select.

TABLE 6.5   Security Auditing Options

Events to Audit	Description
File and Object Access	Tracks access to a directory or file that has been selected for auditing under File Manager; tracks print jobs sent to printers that have been set for auditing under the Printers folder
Logon and Logoff	Tracks user logons and logoffs, as well as the creating and breaking of connections to servers
Process Tracking	Records detailed tracking information for program activation, some types of handle duplication, indirect object accesses, and process exit
Restart, Shutdown, and System	Tracks when the computer is shut down or restarted; tracks the filling up of the audit log and the discarding of audit entries if the audit log is already full
Security Policy Changes	Tracks changes made to the User Rights, Audit, or Trust Relationship policies
Use of User Rights	Notes when users make use of a user right (except those associated with logons and logoffs)
User and Group Management	Tracks changes in user accounts or groups (creations, changes, deletions); notes if user accounts are renamed, disabled, or enabled; tracks setting or changing passwords

It's important to keep in mind that all of the event logs are limited in size. The default size for each of the logs is 512K, and the default overwrite settings allow events older than seven days to be discarded from the logs as needed. When managing the auditing policy in User Manager for Domains, choose your events to audit carefully. You may find that you get what you ask for, sometimes in great abundance. For example, auditing successful File and Object Accesses can generate a tremendous number of security log entries. A reasonably simple process, such as opening an application, opening a single file within that application, editing and saving that file, and exiting the application, can produce more than 60 log events. A couple of users on a system can generate 200 log entries in less than two minutes. Auditing successful Process Tracking events can produce similar results.

If your network requires you to monitor events that closely, make sure you choose the appropriate log size and overwrite settings. You can change these settings for the Security log (and for the other two logs, for that matter) in the Event Viewer.

Summary: Managing User Accounts

That's not all that the User Manager for Domains can do. I haven't covered trust relationships and local and global groups, but, again, I *will* cover those things in Chapter 12.

Notice that the User Manager does more than just manage users; it is, in some way, the Security Manager for NT—but just a *part* of the Security Manager role. Before leaving the User Manager for Domains, let's review what it does. It lets you

- Create, destroy, and modify network user accounts
- Assign and remove user rights
- Create, destroy, and modify groups
- Control which users go in which groups
- Assign and remove rights to and from groups
- Create and destroy trust relationships

That's a lot of what you need to create and manage user accounts, but you will find another pair of tools useful in that line—the System Policy Editors.

The System Policy Editors

Thus far in this chapter, you've seen how to create user accounts and how to control things like when they can log on. But in many networks, you need even greater control.

That's where the System Policy Editors come in. "Editors" is plural because there are two of them, one for controlling PCs running Windows 95 and one for controlling PCs running Windows NT. The System Policy Editors are (you've got to breathe loudly and slowly in your best Darth Vader voice to do these words justice) tools of immense power for desktop control. However, as this power, once unleashed, can make everyone—including *you*—totally unable to start up their workstations, much less get on the network, consider it (and here you need your Obi-Wan-Kenobi voice) power that should be used for good, and not for evil.

Kidding aside, here is an overview on what the System Policy Editors do:

- There is one for Windows 95 and a different one for Windows NT, as I've already mentioned. The Windows 95 System Policy Editor is on the Windows 95 CD-ROM in the \ADMIN directory, and the Windows NT System Policy Editor is automatically installed on any NT Server machine.

- Both work in the same way: they modify the Registry of a workstation so as to add restrictions to what the Windows Explorer user interface lets you do. Oddly enough, the System Policy Editors do not control any other application directly; but by controlling the user interface, which launches all programs, they can establish enough control to keep users from doing a goodly number of things.

- You needn't go to every workstation and install these restrictions. Windows 95 and Windows NT both know to look in the NET-LOGON share on a domain controller (where the logon scripts are kept) to look for a file, and to use that file to add restrictions to their local Registry. The name of the file, by the way, is CONFIG.POL for the Windows 95 restrictions, and NTCONFIG.POL for the NT restrictions.

- This is very important: once you use a System Policy Editor to restrict a Registry, that change stays on the local Registry. I once created a draconian set of restrictions in an NTCONFIG.POL, restrictions that made someone essentially incapable of doing anything on their NT desktop. I logged on as my administrator account and, sure enough, even that administrator account couldn't do much of anything. I figured, "No problem, I'll just disconnect my PC from the network, reboot, and get back control of my Registry." Not so. My local Registry stayed by its last set of orders: "Don't let that Mark guy do *anything*." About all I could do was to log on to *another* computer under Windows 95, get access to NETLOGON, erase the NTCONFIG.POL, and keep from polluting anyone else's account. I had to destroy my administrative account, by the way, and rebuild it; there didn't seem to be a way to fix it.

- First, it controls how NT Workstation and NT Server machines run. It does not control Windows 95 workstations; to do that, you need a tool called the Windows 95 System Policy Editor. You *can* read about it in *The Expert Guide to Windows 95* (Sybex), but...

Using system policies requires that you have a network and that people log on to the network; a loose association of Windows machines doing peer-to-peer networking can't use system policies. Or, alternatively, you could sit down and use the Windows 95 and Windows NT System Policy Editors to hand-edit each workstation's Registry, but that's not a lot of fun.

Here is an overview of creating and using system policies:

1. If you're using Windows 95, you have to install the System Policy Editor from the Windows 95 CD-ROM; it's in the \ADMIN\APP-TOOLS\POLEDIT directory.

2. Create a policy file with the Policy Editor.

3. If the workstations you want to control are Windows 95 workstations, then save the policy file as CONFIG.POL in your NETLOGON directory on an NT system or in the \SYS\PUBLIC directory on the user's preferred NetWare server. If you're controlling NT machines, use the NT version of the System Policy Editor and save the file as NTCONFIG.POL in the same locations, NETLOGON or \sys\public.

4. Ensure that all your workstations log on to an NT domain or a NetWare preferred server.

And that's it. Now let's take a closer look.

Installing the System Policy Editor (Windows 95 Users)

If you're controlling Windows 95 desktops, first you have to install the editor and some support files. Just open up the Control Panel, choose Add/Remove Programs, and click the Windows Setup tab. Click the Have disk button, and then direct it to the directory that contains the Policy Editor, most likely \ADMIN\APPTOOLS\POLEDIT. You get the option to install both the Policy Editor and something called Group Policies; take them both. The Policy Editor is now in Programs/Accessories/System Tools.

If you're controlling NT machines, you'll find the System Policy Editor in the Administrative Tools group.

Building a Policy

Let's see how to use this tool to start to control how people work with Windows 95 or NT desktops. My example assumes that you have an NT-based network, but it works on Novell in just about the same way.

Start up the Policy Editor. Click File and New Policy. You see a screen like Figure 6.21.

The Policy Editor lets you make either policies that are specific to particular people or blanket policies with the Default User or the Default Computer. It is *very dangerous* to make changes to Default User or Default Computer, because any mistakes that you make apply to everyone *except* for people who have a specific account. Let's instead make our changes to a user called Aaron. You create a set of restrictions for Aaron by clicking Edit, clicking Add User, and then typing in Aaron's name and clicking on the OK button.

Let's set Aaron's wallpaper to Rivets and take away his ability to change it (heh, heh). Wallpaper is a user-specific item, so we'll find it by double-clicking on Aaron. At that point you see a screen like Figure 6.22.

The wallpaper is a Desktop item, so click the Desktop item to open it up. You see Wallpaper as an option, as shown in the dialog box in Figure 6.23.

Notice that I can control Aaron's wallpaper and his color scheme. But notice that the box is gray. In this case, gray options are options that you *can* control but that you're not doing anything with yet. Leave as many things gray as you can because the more system policies that are in effect, the longer it takes your workstation to read and interpret

FIGURE 6.21

Blank user profile file

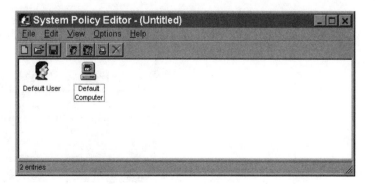

FIGURE 6.22

User properties for
user Aaron

FIGURE 6.23

Controlling Wallpaper
with System Policy Editor

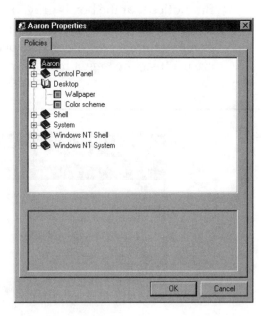

the policy file every time you boot up. If I checked the box twice, that would leave it white and empty. How is a white, empty box different from a gray box? In this case, a white box would say, "Aaron should not have wallpaper." But I want to force Blue Rivets on Aaron, so I check the Wallpaper box. The System Policy Editor screen then looks like Figure 6.24.

Notice that now a pane appears on the window that allows me to type in the location of a particular wallpaper file.

So the next time Aaron logs on, he'll get blue rivets. This may annoy him, but he can always go to the Control Panel and change it. Hmmm… as part of our company's mind control program, we *must* have Blue Rivets on every desktop! No problem: we'll just take away Aaron's ability to *change* his wallpaper. To do *that*, I have to control his Control Panel. Close the Desktop book and open up the Control Panel book, and you see a Display book; open that, and you see a check box for Restrict Display; check it, and you see a screen like Figure 6.25.

FIGURE 6.24

Choosing wallpaper

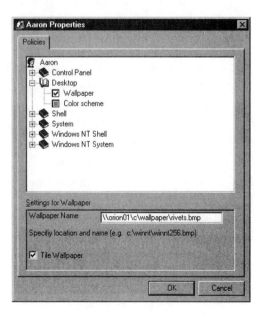

FIGURE 6.25

Restricting the ability to
change wallpaper

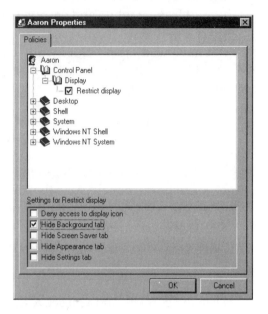

I've also checked Hide Background tab. This has the effect of removing
the tab on the Display applet of the control panel that lets a person control
his or her background wallpaper.

Now all you need to do is to save this to the proper place. (When you
are finished, close Aaron's properties sheet by clicking OK and choosing
to File/Save or File/Save As.) Its name should be NTCONFIG.POL if
you're creating a policy file for NT machines, or CONFIG.POL if you're
creating a policy file for Windows 95 machines. (Remember that you
must use the Windows 95 tool to create Windows 95 policies and the
Windows NT tool to create Windows NT policies.) Where do I put this
file? Well, since I'm running an NT network, I save the file in NET-
LOGON share on my primary domain controller in a directory called
C:\WINNT35\SYSTEM32\REPL\EXPORT. On a NetWare server, I'd
just put it on my users' preferred server's sys\public directory.

Other Things System Policy Editor Can Control

Okay, I promised you *frightening* stuff. Wallpaper hardly sends a chill down one's spine. What kind of dangerous stuff can you do with the System Policy Editor? Most of the really powerful stuff is in a user's set of restrictions, in Shell/Restrictions. For example, suppose you want to control exactly which programs users can run. Users can start up programs in several ways:

- From an icon on the Desktop or by clicking Start/Programs

- By clicking Start/Run

- By opening up the Explorer or My Computer and browsing the drives to find the program file, then double-clicking the program file

- By opening up the Command Prompt and typing in the name of the program

- By browsing the Network Neighborhood to find a computer that has the program, and then starting the program from that computer

Take a look at Figure 6.26. It shows how we can pretty much lock up an NT (or 95, for that matter) desktop.

You can remove the Run command, drives from the My Computer folder, and the entire Network Neighborhood. Under Windows 95, you can remove the Command Prompt from a user's menu; under NT, you can always erase CMD.EXE from the user's local hard disk to make the Command Prompt option no longer exist. You can even open System/Restrictions and restrict which programs will run. You can say to Windows NT or Windows 95, "Only Word for Windows and Freelance are allowed to run on this machine." Obviously, be careful when you do this kind of thing.

FIGURE 6.26

Shell restrictions in the System Policy Editor

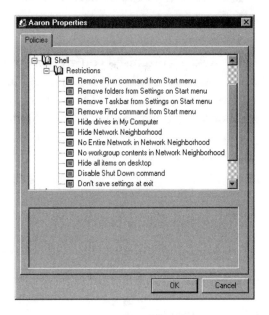

Defeating a Policy

Now suppose I'm a smart but evil user. I want to *change* my wallpaper, dammit! Let my pixels go!

Just remember how policies work: they are Registry entries that restrict the behavior of the Explorer, the GUI on Windows 95 and Windows NT. The restrictions get transmitted from CONFIG.POL or NTCONFIG.POL to the workstation, and you'll see how to undo this. First a workstation boots up, then it attaches to its NETLOGON or mail directory. It then reads the policy file and changes its local Registry accordingly. A user could, of course, disconnect herself from the network and restart her computer, but the restrictions on the Registry remain. How can she undo this control of her system?

Step one is, again, to disconnect from the network. Step two is to run a Registry editing tool and remove the entries. Of course, the Registry

Editor is one such tool, but, oddly enough, so is the System Policy Editor. You can start up the System Policy Editor on your system, and instead of choosing New Policy or Open Policy, you can choose File/Open Registry.

The result is that the screen looks exactly like a policy file—but you're editing your own Registry! Oddly enough, the System Policy Editor is just a Registry editor, but a bit more user-friendly Registry editor. If Aaron had a copy of the System Policy Editor on his Windows NT machine (which is unlikely, since it only comes with NT Server), he could start up the System Policy Editor, click File/Open Registry, and remove all the restrictions from his system. Two notes about that, however:

- You must be an administrator to do this. Changing a policy on Aaron's domain account is tantamount to running the User Manager for Domains, which really only works if you're a domain administrator.

- Again, you have to get access to a System Policy Editor, whether for Windows 95 or Windows NT.

There's a way around this, also with the help of the System Policy Editor. I (the evil user) start up the System Policy Editor. This time, however, I click File/Open Registry. I see a user and a machine, just as before—except *this* time what I'm seeing refers to my machine. I double-click on the User and I see the same categories as before: Control Panel, Desktop, Shell, System, Windows NT Shell, and Windows NT System. I click on Desktop and there's the wallpaper. I change it, and the change takes place immediately; no more rivets!

Keeping Users from Defeating Policies

Okay, you're now thinking, "Gee thanks Mark, I was getting all excited about these system policies, but now you tell me that any user can defeat them with her own copy of the System Policy Editor. *Now* what do I do?" If you're in the System Policy Editor at the moment, take a look at Local User\System\Restrictions. One of the things that you can restrict is called Disable Registry editing tools. Click that one, and the Windows 95 or Windows NT Registry Editors won't run. (The System Policy Editor *will* run, strangely—after all, it's a Registry editing tool—but you can keep it out of the hands of the NT users, as we've seen. What about Windows 95 users? Read on.)

Your next question will no doubt be, "Um, what happens when I...I mean a *friend* of mine...disables the Registry editing tools just for fun, but now can't do anything about it, because it's no longer possible to run REGEDIT or System Policy Editor?"

If it's a Windows NT restriction, then there's only one thing to do:

1. Log on under a different operating system, like DOS or Windows, by using an administrator account. Go to the NETLOGON directory and erase the policy file (CONFIG.POL or NTCONFIG.POL) before any more damage gets done.

2. By now, you've polluted the Registry of any machine that you logged onto. But the damage may be restricted to just your user's profile. Try logging on to the NT machine as a local administrator, and try to erase the profiles of any user accounts that logged on while the overly restrictive policy file was in effect.

3. Go to the home directories of any users who logged on while the overly restrictive policy was in effect and try to delete their profiles.

4. In the end, you may have to just delete and rebuild any user accounts affected by an overly restrictive policy file. If you made changes to machine registry entries (rather than user registry entries, which are more common), then you may have to reinstall the entire NT system from scratch.

If it's Windows 95, you have a few more options:

- If you put the restriction in CONFIG.POL rather than the Registry of a particular machine, and if you applied it to a particular user rather than all users, then you can just log on as someone else, run the System Policy Editor, and then change the setting.

- If you did it for *everyone*, then just log on to the network as a supervisor and take it out of the NETLOGON or \sys\public directory. Use the backups from the day before as a starting point for rebuilding where you were. (CONFIG.POL is not an ASCII file, so it wouldn't be very easy to splice out *just* the no-edit rule.)

- If you did it in the local Registry, then you might try booting up from the Windows 95 Startup Disk and running the simple Registry editor that comes on that disk. Delete the RestrictRun entry from the following key: HKEY_CURRENT_USER\SOFTWARE\ MICROSOFT\WINDOWS\CURRENTVERSION\POLICIES\ EXPLORE key.

What If You Want CONFIG.POL Somewhere Else?

You've already seen where the policies file CONFIG.POL or NT-CONFIG.POL should go. But what if you want to put it somewhere else? You can do that by telling your Registry to find the policy file in another location.

The System Policy Editor is also a Registry editor. From the File menu, choose Open Registry, and you see a subset of Registry entries. Change where your computer gets its policy file from with the following changes:

1. Open up Default Computer.

2. Open up Network, then open System policies update.

3. You see an option called Remote update; choose it. You see the dialog box shown in Figure 6.27.

4. Where you see Update Mode, select Manual. Then, in the field labeled Path for manual update, find the path—the manual says a UNC name is required, but a drive designation seems to work sometimes—and enter the location and name of the policy file. Include the name of the file; it shouldn't be \\server\share; it should be \\server\share\config.pol.

This can be useful for network systems that aren't NetWare- or NT-based.

FIGURE 6.27

Changing the location of CONFIG.POL

Using Templates

Think of the System Policy Editor in this way: insofar as it modifies Registries, it's kind of an alternative Registry Editor. But it's more than that, as you know if you ever *used* REGEDIT. REGEDIT is about as user-unfriendly as programs get. In contrast, the System Policy Editor presents a subset of the Registry in an easier-to-read fashion.

In a sense, that's also what the Control Panel does. So how are the Control Panel and the System Policy Editor different? Well, first of all, the Control Panel only works with Registry settings; it doesn't create constraints (policies). Second, the Control Panel isn't really config-urable, save for the fact that you can remove things from it—you can't add things.

Add things? Yes. Open up the System Policy Editor and you see a number of settings—all controls for parts of the Registry. But *which* parts of the Registry? Ones specified by a file called ADMIN.ADM.

ADMIN.ADM is a *template*, an ASCII file written in a programming language defined in the *Resource Kit.* Summarized, there are several parts to a template:

- A *class* is the subtree, like Local User or Machine.

- A *category* is just a name used to group a number of Registry items. For example, if you wanted to organize your policies so that a small book icon for "color" controlled the colors of a number of disparate keys, then you'd end up taking keys from different parts of the tree. Each category entry creates one of the book icons. You can nest categories.

- *Policy* is the description of the particular value entry that you're going to modify.

- *Keyname* is, as you'd imagine, a Registry key name like Software\ Microsoft\Windows\CurrentVersion\Policies\Explorer\ RestrictRun. It specifies the target of the editor item.

- *Valuename* is the actual name of the value within the specified key.

- *Part* tells the System Policy Editor what kind of interface item to use—a check box, list box, or whatever.

This is perhaps understood best with an example. Here, I've opened the System Policy Editor, double-clicked on User, opened Control Panel and Display, and within that found Restrict Display, which I checked. The dialog box appears as in Figure 6.28.

Here's the fragment of code that handles this:

```
CLASS USER

CATEGORY !!ControlPanel
      CATEGORY !!CPL_Display
            POLICY !!CPL_Display_Restrict
            KEYNAME
Software\Microsoft\Windows\CurrentVersion\Policies\System
                  PART !!CPL_Display_Disable CHECKBOX
                  VALUENAME NoDispCPL
                  END PART

                  PART !!CPL_Display_HideBkgnd CHECKBOX
                  VALUENAME NoDispBackgroundPage
                  END PART
```

FIGURE 6.28

Options for
restricting display

```
                        PART !!CPL_Display_HideScrsav CHECKBOX
                        VALUENAME NoDispScrSavPage
                        END PART

                        PART !!CPL_Display_HideAppearance CHECKBOX
                        VALUENAME NoDispAppearancePage
                        END PART

                        PART !!CPL_Display_HideSettings CHECKBOX
                        VALUENAME NoDispSettingsPage
                        END PART
                END POLICY
        END CATEGORY          ; Display
```

The CLASS USER defines the part of this file that describes the User
icon. Category !!ControlPanel says first, create a book icon, and second,
name it something defined by !!ControlPanel. !!ControlPanel is a string
variable defined later in the file as

```
ControlPanel="Control Panel"
```

The characters "Control Panel" are then displayed next to the book icon.

POLICY !!CPL_DISPLAY_RESTRICT says to display CPL_DISPLAY_
RESTRICT, which I found later in the program to equal Restrict Display
Control Panel. You see that displayed in the top pane, but there are sev-
eral potential ways to restrict the Display Control Panel. As it turns out,
they are all values within the Software\Microsoft\Windows\Current-
Version\Policies\System key.

The triples that appear next look like this:

```
PART !!CPL_Display_Disable CHECKBOX
VALUENAME NoDispCPL
END PART
```

Each one of these triples describes a value that can live within the
key. The string variable is just the label to put in the dialog box, and
CHECKBOX says to just use a check box rather than an edit field, list
box, or whatever. VALUENAME says, "Once you have the value
checked or not checked by the user, then this is the name of the actual
value to stuff in the Registry."

Templates make the System Policies Editor an incredibly flexible tool; you can even use it to control Registry entries created by third-party vendors. The main problem with it is that Microsoft hasn't documented all of *their* Registry entries. (Grumble, grumble—they did it for NT, and that's been tremendously helpful.)

Let's build a sample template for an imaginary Registry entry. Suppose I have a software company named MarkSoft and all of my programs open up with a welcome banner. I could modify that welcome banner by adding a value called WText to Software\MarkSoft\ CurrentVersion\Settings; you put text in there to control the welcome banner. A template file might look like this in its entirety:

```
CLASS USER
CATEGORY !!GenlSettings
      POLICY !!WelcomeBanner
      KEYNAME Software\Marksoft\CurrentVersion\Settings
             PART !!WelcomeText EDITTEXT
             VALUENAME WText
             END PART
      END POLICY
END CATEGORY
[strings]
GenlSettings="General settings"
WelcomeBanner="Welcome banner"
WelcomeText="Text to display in welcome banner"
```

Now open the System Policy Editor, click Options/Template, and tell it to Add your file (save it with the extension ADM so it's easier for the Editor to find it). Click File/Open Registry, then open the User class, and you see a screen like Figure 6.29.

Fill in the text and save it. Restart, and start up the Registry Editor, and you see an entry for MarkSoft, as you see in Figure 6.30.

I won't deny that building your own templates isn't something you do every day. But what's truly exciting (to me, anyway) is that this is a powerful support tool that I can shape to my own needs. Other utility vendors could learn from this.

FIGURE 6.29

Adding an entry to
a template

FIGURE 6.30

New entry displayed
in Registry

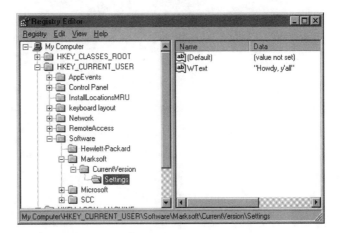

Creating users is useful, yes, but users can't enjoy a network too much
unless there is something on the network for them to access. You'll see
how to do that—how to create directory shares—in the next chapter.

CHAPTER

SEVEN

Creating and Managing Directory Shares

Once you've created some users, you need to give them a reason to use the network. People get three main services from a network: shared directories and files, shared printers, and shared applications. In this chapter, you will see how to handle the first of those services—shared directories and files.

You share files with the My Computer folder, the Explorer, or the command line. In this chapter, I'll focus on using the My Computer folder and the Explorer's graphical user interface (GUI) to share data; the appendix shows you how to do it from a command line with the NET SHARE command. And, if you're an NT 3.51 administrator, you can do all of the same things that version 4 users can do, save that 3.51 doesn't have an Explorer or My Computer; in 3.51, you use File Manager to share directories and control directory and file access over the network.

Sharing data under NT gets a little confusing because NT offers several levels of control over who can access a given set of files. It offers "share-level" permissions, "directory-level" permissions, and "file-level" permissions. You have to understand those levels of control, and we'll cover them in this chapter. Then, once you understand how data shares work, I will backtrack a bit and explain user profiles and home directories, a subject that kind of fits with the previous chapter's discussion of user accounts, but doesn't make sense until you understand the different levels of permissions. Finally, when you're comfortable with home directories, it will make sense to explain file "ownership" and file access auditing.

Creating a Shared Directory

Most servers on networks function as repositories for files and directories that must be accessible to the network's users. Files and directories on a server running NT Server must first be *shared* before network users can access them. Merely setting up a server won't do anything, because the server will just announce itself by saying, "Hi, I'm a server, but I'm not sharing anything."

To share a directory, you must be logged on as a member of the Administrators or Server Operators group. Creating a share is easiest if you're physically logged in at the server itself (that's how I'll describe most of the examples in this chapter), but you can also create new server shares remotely with a program called the Server Manager, as I'll show you a little later.

NT can only share *directories*, not files; it's not possible to pick just one file and say to an NT Server, "Share this on the network as SFILE," or something like that. You have to specify an entire directory when sharing.

> **NOTE**
>
> The Server service must be running on an NT Server before you can share a directory on that server. Of course, it's usually started by default on NT Server machines, but I've seen NT machines occasionally start without the Server service started. I'm not sure why it happens, but it seems that if you install NT on a system with fewer than 16MB of RAM, the Server service does *not* start by default. (Of course, in truth this won't matter, as you really should have at least 16MB on an NT Server, and 32MB is an even better minimum.) If you *do* find that you have to start up the Server service, you can start the Server service by using the Services option in Control Panel. (In Control Panel, click on Services, then on Server, and, finally, click the Start button.) Or you can open up a command line and type net start server.

Open up the Explorer and you'll see what is probably a familiar view of your computer. An Explorer view of NT Server is shown in Figure 7.1.

In the figure, you can see a directory named STUFF in drive C:. (The same thing works with the My Computer folder.) I can share that by right-clicking on the STUFF folder, which produces a drop-down menu like the one in Figure 7.2.

Notice the Sharing option. Click it and you get a Properties dialog box like the one in Figure 7.3. When this dialog box first appears, the Not Shared radio button is selected and everything is grayed out (which would make for a rather dull book illustration). I clicked Shared As to enable the sharing options that are shown in Figure 7.3.

FIGURE 7.1

Explorer view of a NT Server

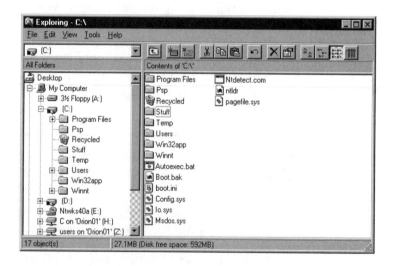

Handling Share Names

You already learned about share names in Chapter 2, but as a reminder, share names can be up to 12 characters long. However, you may not want to use all 12 characters but keep to 8 characters instead, because the DOS redirector doesn't like 12 characters much. (If all of your clients

FIGURE 7.2

Object menu for the
STUFF directory

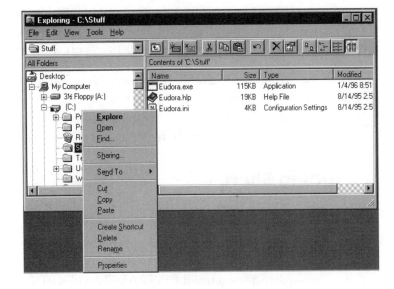

FIGURE 7.3

Sharing tab of the
Properties dialog box

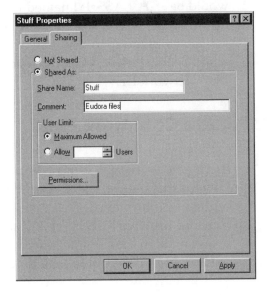

are Windows for Workgroups, Windows 95, or Windows NT, then 12 characters are fine.) You *can* use blanks in a share name, but I strongly suggest that you don't, because you will have to surround the name with quotation marks every time you want to use it.

By default, the share name is the same as the last part of the directory name. For example, if you shared a directory called C:\TRAVEL\ TICKETS\1STCLASS, then the offered share name would be 1STCLASS. You can change a share name, but the default is usually good enough.

Hiding Shares

I mentioned this in Chapter 2, but just in case you've forgotten, you can create a directory share that won't show up on the browse list by ending the share name with a dollar sign ($). For example, if I shared a directory named C:\TRAVEL\TICKETS\1STCLASS on a server, then, as the previous paragraph explains, the suggested share name would be 1STCLASS. If I named it 1STCLASS$ instead, then anyone browsing that server would not see that hidden share. Someone could still attach to the share, but they would have to do it from the command line (net use x: \\server\1stclass$) or from the Explorer (Tools/ Map Network Drive).

Using the Comment Field

In a big network with hundreds of shares, it may not be immediately obvious that OB12A36, for example, is the share that contains the retirement information. That's why the Comment field is useful. When someone browses in a server and sees that server's list of shares, the text you put in the Comment field shows up as well, and the user can read the brief description to find out what the share is all about.

Restricting Access to Shares

Sometimes you want to restrict the number of people who can access a network share. Most likely you'll find the options useful for satisfying the need of some software license. For example, suppose you put a program in a directory and tell people to run the program from that directory. If you only purchased ten concurrent licenses for the software, you could tell NT Server not to allow more than ten people to simultaneously access the directory.

Restricting user access to a share is done with the User Limit spinner box. Just designate the maximum number of users who can simultaneously access the share or choose the Unlimited option. If you try to attach to a share that has exceeded its allowable number of users, you get an error message. The error message that is shown on a client workstation varies from operating system to operating system. For example, from a DOS workstation you see this message:

```
Error 71: This request is not accepted by the network. The server
may have run out of resources necessary to process your request.
Try the request again. If the error persists, contact your net-
work administrator. For more information, type NET HELP 71 at
the command prompt.
```

Windows 95 workstations are more terse:

```
An extended error has occurred
```

Windows for Workgroups workstations also keep it brief and uninformative:

```
This request is not accepted by the network
```

And NT clients are a bit more chatty and descriptive:

```
No more connections can be made to this remote computer at this
time because there are already as many connections as the com-
puter allows.
```

Now, before you start relying on this feature, let me tell you about a problem that I saw in NT Server 3.1 and 3.5: the user maximum seemed not to work. I would create a share, give it a maximum number of users of 1, fire up twenty Windows for Workgroups machines, and watch all twenty get onto the share. My experience with version 4 leads me to believe that NT Server 4 *does* enforce the user maximum, but test it before you build a security system around this feature.

The last button in the Create New Share dialog box is Permissions. It's important, but before I get to it, let me bring up one more topic, sharing directories on remote servers.

Sharing Directories on Remote Servers

If you're not physically logged onto a server, you can't use the Explorer or My Computer to share volumes on that computer. If you want to use Explorer to create a share named BIGFILES on server AJAX, for example, you have to go over to AJAX, sit down, and log on. But if AJAX isn't located nearby—perhaps you can only get to it over a long-distance link (or you're feeling lazy)—then you can still create new shares with another tool, the Server Manager.

Running Server Manager

You'll find the Server Manager in an NT computer's Start menu under Programs, then Administrative Tools—that is, *assuming* that you're sitting at a machine running NT *Server*. If not, you have to install Server Manager from either the NT *Resource Kit* CD-ROM or find it in the CLIENTS\SRVTOOLS directory of the original NT Server CD-ROM. Earlier versions of NT Server included a version of Server Manager that ran atop Windows for Workgroups, but NT Server 4 only includes versions of Server Manager that you can run on Windows 95 and Windows NT. The opening screen looks something like Figure 7.4.

FIGURE 7.4

Server Manager
opening screen

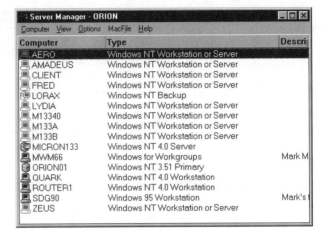

Here, Server Manager shows me the machines that can potentially share data in this workgroup. The gray computers are not currently active, but Server Manager knows of them because it has met them before.

TIP

Once in a while, Server Manager fails to notice an active computer. If you think a computer *ought* to be enabled but it's grayed out, try this trick: type net use *machinename*\IPC$. where *machinename* is the name of the machine that's grayed out. It doesn't always work, but it's one way to sometimes "kick Server Manager in the pants" and wake it up. (In actual fact, what you're waking up is called the Remote Procedure Call Locator, but that's a story for another day.)

Click on a server (click *once*—don't double-click!), and then choose Shared Directories in the Computer menu. You see a dialog like the one in Figure 7.5. The Shared Directories dialog box shows the shares that the server currently offers.

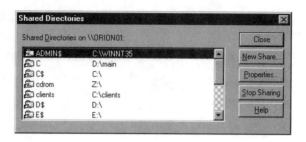

Understanding the Administrative Shares

In Figure 7.5, notice all of the hidden shares: ADMIN$, C$, D$ and E$. Why did I put *those* on this server?

I didn't.

When you run the Server service on an NT Workstation or NT Server machine, NT automatically shares the following:

- Every hard disk partition and CD-ROM drive *at their roots* (that's C$, D$, and E$).

- The directory that the NT programs are in (ADMIN$).

- The directory that contains the logon scripts (NETLOGON$), which is shared if it's a domain controller. Microsoft calls them the "administrative shares."

By now, you must be sweating. "Arghh!" I cried, the first time I realized this. "*Anyone* can just NET USE to get to the root drive of my server! What will I do?" As it turns out, only administrators can gain access to these shares—whew! Oh, and by the way, if you try to unshare these shares, they just get re-created automatically the next time you boot the NT machine.

Creating a New Share on a Remote Machine

Anyway, back to the task at hand. Suppose machine ORION01 is in Milwaukee, and I'm in Dallas. How do I get ORION01 to share a directory named, for example, FACTS? From the Shared Directories dialog box (see Figure 7.5), just click New Share and a dialog box like Figure 7.6 will appear.

The items in this dialog box are pretty self-explanatory. Just type in the name of the new share in the Share Name field, the path (like D:\ FACTS) in the Path field, a comment if you want, and, optionally, the maximum number of users. Notice what is, to me at least, a pretty major flaw in this dialog box: no Browse button.

Once you fill in the share information, the Permissions button is enabled. Which brings me to share-level permissions, my next topic.

FIGURE 7.6

Remotely creating a new share

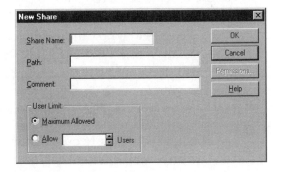

Share-Level Permissions and Access Control Lists

Whether sharing from a local machine (remember, here "local" means the machine you're physically logged on at) or a remote machine, the last button that you have to work with is Permissions. Click it, and you see a dialog box like Figure 7.7.

FIGURE 7.7

Access Through Share
Permissions dialog box

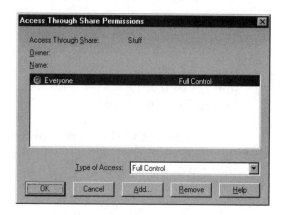

NT uses the word *permissions* to describe the type of access that a particular user has for a particular network resource. For example, if I can read and write files in \\SERVER01\WPFILES, but I can only read files in \\SERVER01\CLIENTSW, then I'd say that my permissions for the first share were "read/write" and my permissions for the second share were "read-only." NT lets you get as specific as you like when it comes to who can do what. For example, although I can only read files in \\SERVER01\CLIENTSW, some other user, perhaps an administrator, could have permissions to both read and write those files. As you do more with NT, you'll see that NT can also assign permissions for printer shares and network applications.

Although there is only one item in the dialog box in Figure 7.7, you can add any number of entries, as you'll see presently. The entire list of permissions for a share is called its Access Control List (ACL).

Everyone Includes, Well, Everyone

The permission list that you see in Figure 7.7 shows a small picture of a globe, the word *Everyone*, and the word *Full Control*. Those permissions—the group Everyone has Full Control—are the default permissions for any share you create in NT. "Everyone" is a group, like the user groups that you learned about in the previous chapter—but it's a special group. "Everyone" means all users on the domain *and* any trusted domains. I know we haven't discussed trust relationships yet, but briefly, a trust relationship is a kind of "treaty" or "trade agreement" between two domains. If you had two domains named RED and BLUE, and RED and BLUE trusted each other, and you created a share that the group Everyone could access, then all of the users in RED and BLUE would be able to access that share. (More on trust relationships in Chapter 12.)

> **WARNING** Be careful what shares you give the group Everyone access to. In my two-domain example, suppose RED is run by very security-conscious people who take the excellent step of disabling the Guest account, and BLUE is run by slobs who keep the Guest account enabled. Since a RED share available to Everyone is available to everyone in the BLUE domain, and since BLUE has the Guest account enabled—in other words, as long as BLUE is essentially open to the whole world—the RED "Everyone" shares are available to the whole world.

Share-Level Access Types

Notice that the Everyone group has access which is "Full Control." There are four levels of share access, as you can see in Table 7.1.

If you look at Table 7.1, you'll probably wonder what the difference is between Change and Full Control. I *will* explain it, but before my explanations make much sense, I have to first explain the concepts of "file and directory permissions," which I'm going to get to in a few pages, and "file ownership," which I'll cover last in this chapter. Put simply, however, the difference between Change and Full Control is that someone with Full Control can change file and directory permissions and the ownership of a file. Oh, by the way, this is only relevant on a share formatted as NTFS, since you've got to have NTFS for it to be possible to set file and directory permissions or file ownership. On

TABLE 7.1   File Attributes

Attribute	Description
Archive	Identifies a file that has been modified since it was last backed up.
Hidden	File does not appear in directory listings from the command prompt; file is hidden from directory lists in File Manager unless Show Hidden/System Files check box (View menu, By File Type) is selected.
Read-only	File can be read, but not written to. Prevents a file from being changed.
System	Identifies a file as a system file. As with hidden files, system files appear in a directory window only if the Show Hidden/System Files check box is selected.

a network volume shared as FAT or HPFS, there is literally no difference between Full Control and Change.

Multiple Groups Accumulate Permissions

It's possible, as you'll see in a page or two, to add a number of other users or groups to this share. You might have one group in your network called Accountants, and another called Managers, and they might have different permission levels. For example, the Accountants might only be able to read the files, and the Managers might have "change" access, which is just NTese for "read and write" access. What about the manager of the Accounting department, who is in both the Managers and the Accountants group? Does he have Read or Change access?

In general, your permissions to a network resource *add up*, so if you have Read access from one group and Change from another group, then you end up with Read *and* Change access. However, because Change access completely *includes* all of the things that you can do with Read access, there's no practical difference between having Read and Change access and having only Change access.

Using "No Access" to Keep the Guests Out

There *is* one exception: No Access. If one of your groups gives you No Access, that trumps all the others. If you're a member of a hundred groups that give you Full Control and a member of just one that gives you No Access, it doesn't matter, because you can't access the share at all.

Where would you use this? Well, one place I've found it useful is in domains that must leave their Guest account enabled. There were more reasons to keep the Guest account enabled back in the NT 3.1 days than there are under NT 4, but there may still be occasions in which you would enable the Guest account. The problem with enabling the Guest account is that the Everyone group, which is normally such a useful and succinct way to grant general network-wide access, becomes useless: granting Everyone access on a network with an enabled Guest account is tantamount to offering access to everybody on the planet.

Ah, but No Access gives us a workaround. Just explicitly add the Domain Guests account, and grant them No Access. Guests are, of course, members of Everyone, and so get Full Control; but they're also Guests, and so get No Access. No Access always wins, so the guests are locked out.

Adding to the ACL

Suppose I want to add a different group to a list of permissions or an access control list (ACL) for the STUFF directory. Click Add and you see a dialog box like the one in Figure 7.8.

You may recognize some of these groups—Domain Admins, Domain Users, Domain Guests, and Everyone. The Notusers group is just something I created while experimenting. INTERACTIVE, NETWORK, and SYSTEM are also built-in groups. And if you're trying this out while sitting at a machine that not only shares files but also acts as a domain controller, you'll see groups named Administrators, Users, and Guests.

Adding a Group to an ACL

Suppose I want to grant Full Control of my STUFF share to Domain Admins. (This is superfluous in this particular example, as the Everyone group already has Full Control and obviously all Domain Admins users

FIGURE 7.8

Adding users or groups to an NT share

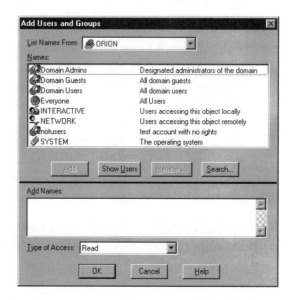

are part of Everyone, but I'm just looking for an example.) From the previous dialog box, click Domain Admins, and the Add button. Then, in the bottom pane of the window, you'll see something like "Domain Admins" and a drop-down list box labeled "Type of Access." By default, the box contains Read, but you can pull it down and choose any one of the four access types.

Adding a Single User to an ACL

Notice that the list only contains the names of groups. What if I want to add one user to a permissions list? I might do that if I didn't trust one particular person and wanted to grant him No Access, or if he were a member of a group with Read access and I wanted to give him Change access.

It's simple to add a user to a permissions list: just click the Show Users button. The top pane of the dialog box then includes the names of particular users. Just click the user's name in the top pane and specify the access level in the bottom pane.

Controlling Permissions from the Command Line

Sometimes in class I get asked about changing ACLs with a command-line command. You may occasionally need to control permissions in a batch file, where it is not so easy to start up the User Manager for Domains and tell the batch file to click its way through the GUI. That's where the Change ACLs or CACLS.EXE program comes in handy. But to use it, you have to be using NTFS, as CACLS doesn't work on share-level permissions; it works on *file and directory* level permissions, which I'll get to very soon.

Changing Permissions on an Existing Share

In my STUFF example so far, I've been modifying permissions on a new share. How do you do it on an existing share?

Well, first of all, you can identify an existing share by opening the Explorer or My Computer folders and examining the folder icons for each directory. Most directory icons look like a manila folder; shared directories look like a folder with a hand below it. Right-click the folder, choose Sharing, and you see the same Properties dialog box as the one I showed you when I first shared STUFF (see Figure 7.3). Again, just click the Permissions button and you can make ACL changes to your heart's content.

File and Directory Permissions

Share-level permissions predate NT and have been around Microsoft networking for years. But NT brought to Microsoft networking a whole new level of security. As you probably know, one of Microsoft's goals in designing NT was to enable you to make the data on your stand-alone workstation as secure from intruders as the data on your network. It's actually possible to set up an NT workstation so that multiple people can share a computer, yet be unable to access each other's data. If Joe and Jane share an NT Workstation machine—perhaps Joe works the day shift and Jane the night shift—then it's possible to create a directory called Joe and make Jane unable to access that data for love or money, and likewise Jane can have a directory that only she can get to. Again, no networking is involved in this scenario—just one computer being shared by two people.

This is a really great feature of NT. In my experience prior to NT with operating systems of all kinds, if you could gain physical access to a computer, you could get to its data. Before NT, the only way to secure data with any confidence was to put the data on a server and put the server behind a locked door.

This ability to attach security information to areas of a disk under NT is called *file and directory permissions*. Notice that NT lets you put file and directory permissions on disk areas even if you've not shared those disk areas. As shared directories are protected by share-level permissions and *all* directories are protected by file and directory permissions, file and directory permissions are, then, an extra layer of "fine-tuned" security for network shares.

There *is* one detail about using file and directory permissions, however, and it is important enough to put in a note.

> **NOTE** You must format a disk volume to NTFS in order to use file and directory permissions.

File and Directory Permission Types

You've already seen that network shares' share-level permissions only come in four types: Read, Change, Full Control, and No Access. File and directory permissions offer more options, as you can see in Table 7.2.

TABLE 7.2   File and Directory Permission Types

Individual Permissions	When Applied to a Directory/File
Change Permissions	*To a directory:* Allows changes to the directory's permissions *To a file:* Allows changes to the file's permissions
Delete	*To a directory:* Allows deletion of the directory *To a file:* Allows deletion of the file
Execute	*To a directory:* Allows display of attributes, permissions, and owner; allows changing to subdirectories *To a file:* Allows running of program files and display of attributes, permissions, and owner (note that it does *not* include Read permissions)
Read	*To a directory:* Allows display of filenames within the directory and their attributes; permissions and owner of the directory *To a file:* Allows display of the file's data, attributes, permissions, and owner
Take Ownership	*To a directory:* Allows changes to the directory's ownership *To a file:* Allows changes to the file's ownership
Write	*To a directory:* Read permissions, plus allows creation of subdirectories and files within the directory, and changes to attributes *To a file:* Read permissions, plus allows changes to the file's data and attributes

Basically, the Change permission in share-level permissions is broken up into three separate permissions under file and directory permissions:

Write   Lets you write files. As a side-effect, it also lets you *overwrite* files, so by saving a new file on top of an old file you can delete it, even if you don't have delete permission.

Execute   Lets you execute a program, usually an EXE. If you do not have Execute permission, you can't run a program, even if you can see it. In actual fact, you wouldn't get much mileage out of giving someone read and write permissions and then not giving them execute permissions, as anyone who *did* want to run the program could just copy the file to a local directory. The copy would end up with the same permissions as everything else in the local directory (which probably includes "execute"), and so that person could then run the copy. What this is useful for is the *opposite* application—give someone execute access but no other access, and she can *run* a program but not copy or modify it. The value of that would be if you had a program on the network that you wanted people to be able to run but not able to steal by downloading it to their local machines and perhaps to floppy disks or ZIP drives.

Delete　This permission is intended to prevent you from deleting a file, but it seems useless. I've had no trouble deleting files that I did not have "delete" permissions for. It *does* seem useful for directories, however. I can't seem to delete directories if I lack "delete" permissions for that directory.

File and Directory Permissions versus Share Permissions

As I've mentioned, one very important thing to understand about file and directory permissions is the fact that they work whether you're networked or not. When you access share-level permissions on the Sharing tab of the Properties dialog box and share or unshare a directory, file and directory permissions show up in a separate tab labeled Security. To see this tab, right-click any file or directory *on an NTFS volume* from the My Computer or Explorer window. You see a window like the one in Figure 7.9.

Recall that even though I shared STUFF, it would have a Security tab whether it was shared or not. Notice the Permissions, Auditing, and Ownership buttons. Click Permissions and you see a dialog box like the one in Figure 7.10.

You may recall that the share-level permissions on STUFF was just Everyone/Full Control. That's quite a bit different from *this* dialog box. Why is that? It's an important question, and understanding the answer will drive home an important point about file and directory permissions.

FIGURE 7.9

Security tab on
STUFF directory

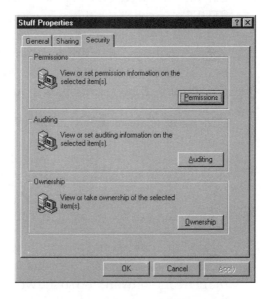

FIGURE 7.10

Directory Permissions
dialog box

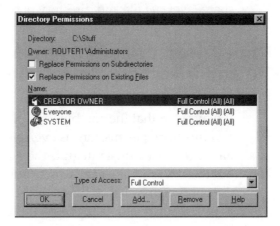

The STUFF folder had file and directory permissions specified on it
before I shared it. Merely sharing it and creating a list of share permissions *does not affect the file and directory permissions at all*. Just to provide
an extreme example, suppose STUFF had file and directory permissions

that only allowed a user named Meredith to access it. Then suppose STUFF was shared with share permissions only allowing share access to another user named Martin. Once I shared STUFF, no change would appear on the file and directory permissions for STUFF. The share-level permissions would think it's okay for Martin to access the file, but the file and directory permissions would only let Meredith in.

In this case, what would happen? Could Martin access STUFF? Could Meredith? Could both or neither access STUFF? The answer is, neither could access STUFF. When Meredith tried to attach to the share, the share-level permissions would keep her out. When Martin tried to attach to the share, the share-level permissions would give him the thumbs-up, but the file system's permissions would nix the connection.

Now, Meredith could physically walk over to the computer that STUFF sits on, log on to it, and access the directory, because she wouldn't tickle the network software and so she wouldn't be denied access. Summarized, here is the basic rule of data access on a network share that's been for-matted as NTFS: to access some data on the network, you must have both share-level *and* file and directory permissions for that data.

Home Directories: An Application of File and Directory Permissions

It may seem that the combination of share-level permissions and file and directory permissions is overkill, but it has its uses. Sure, it would have been nice to just integrate them into one unified set of permissions, but there wasn't any easy way to add file and directory permissions to the old FAT file system. Share-level permissions presented one way to tack security atop a FAT-based file system. Share-level permissions let the network server software check a program's credentials before getting any access to the non-secure FAT file system, but Microsoft wanted to build more fine-tuning into the security, and so file and direc-tory permissions were born.

But back to the question, "Where would you use this stuff?" There's no more perfect application than on a domain controller in the home directories.

The Mechanics of Home Directories

A *home directory* is a directory on the network that is yours and yours alone; no one else can access the data in those directories, save perhaps the administrator. Home directories are often stored on a domain controller, but they needn't be—they only need to be in a share on the network. The home directory is usually the place where users stash personal documents on the network.

The data structure for a home directory is often a root named USERS and subdirectories named after their owners. For example, there would be a USERS\MEREDITH, USERS\MARTIN, USERS\IGNATZ, and so on.

Securing Home Directories with Share-Level Permissions

Suppose you had a thousand users and you needed to create a home directory for each one. How would you do it? Well, one way to do that would be to create the a thousand subdirectories of the USERS directory. (A USERS directory is automatically created when you install NT.) Then, you'd go individually to each directory, share it, and change its permissions so that only its owner could access it.

Now, that's a *lot* of work, but it's possible. It's not a good idea, either, but it's possible. Just imagine—a thousand users would mean a thousand shares, which would mean one heckuva big browse list! Of course, we could always hide those shares, I suppose…but this is turning out to be a major effort.

Securing Home Directories with File and Directory Permissions

There is an easier way, fortunately, one that exploits file and directory permissions:

1. Put the USERS directory on an NTFS volume. Remember that you must be using NTFS, or you will never see the Security tab.

2. Share the USERS directory, giving Full Control to the Everyone group. (Share-level permissions, remember.)

3. For each user, click on that user's directory and choose the Security tab (from the Explorer or My Computer, right-click the directory and choose Properties to see the Security tab).

4. Click Permissions and you see the Directory Permissions dialog box for that directory (see Figure 7.10).

5. Click the Remove button to remove all entries from the dialog box.

6. Click the Add button to add the user. You see a dialog box like the one in Figure 7.11.

7. Click the Show Users button to display the names of individual users.

8. Choose the correct user, click Add, and choose Full Control in the Type of Access: list box.

9. Click OK three times and you'll be back to the NT desktop.

Now you have a share—the USERS share—with user directories in it, like USERS\JOHN, USERS\SUE, USERS\MARY, and the like. Everyone can access the top level of the USERS share, but each user can only get to his or her specific subdirectory.

I know it sounds odd, but think of it this way: Imagine the USERS share is a large hotel and each directory and file is a guest room. Share-level permission for USERS—the fact that the permissions for USER

FIGURE 7.11

Adding users to file and directory permissions

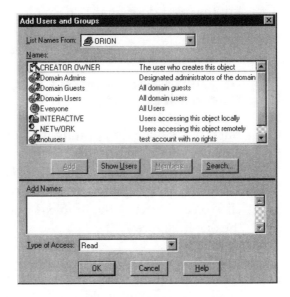

are Full Control for Everyone—just gets you into the lobby. Without a guest room key—file and directory permissions are the guest-room keys in my analogy—someone can't get very far; into the lobby, but no further, save for his or her home directory. One security system guards the front door (the server subsystem and its security) and another security system guards the guest rooms (the NTFS file subsystem and *its* security). You have to get past *both* of them to get to a guest room (your home directory).

Now suppose we return to user Meredith. I give her No Access share-level permissions to the share Users, but Full Control file and directory permissions on her home directory USERS\MEREDITH. She could do anything she wanted to her home directory…if she could get to it.

Essentially, Meredith *has* a guest room key but can't get in the front door. She has no share-level permissions, so she can't attach to the share in the first place. (She'd see a message like "USERS is not accessible. Access is denied.") If she *could* get access to the share, she'd have full control of USERS. The guest room security folks like her fine, but the front-door guard doesn't let her by. The only way for her to access the USERS data is to sit right down at the machine that USERS physically resides on, log on, and access USERS\MEREDITH.

An Even Easier Way to Create Home Directories

But it was some work putting that together, wasn't it? We need an easier way and, fortunately, there is an easier way. It's in the User Manager in the Profiles dialog box (I said in the last chapter that I'd get to it in this chapter). Open the User Manager for Domains, double-click on a user, click the Profiles button, and you see a dialog box like the one in Figure 7.12.

Notice the bottom field in the dialog box. It says, "Connect Z: to \\orion01\users\MarkS." This dialog box is one of the most confusing in all of NT, and this field is no different. If you create a new user or highlight an existing user in the User Manager for Domains, then click Profiles and fill in a location in the To field, NT does several things:

- It remembers that whenever the user MarkS issues a command that involves Mark's home directory, then NT should use the MarkS directory which is in the USERS share on the server ORION01.

FIGURE 7.12

Dialog box controlling user home directories, profiles, and logon scripts

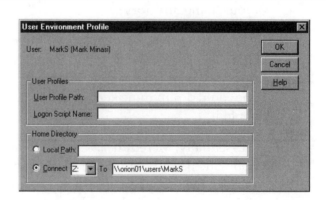

- *If* the directory \\orion01\users\MarkS does not yet exist, then NT creates the directory *and* sets its file and directory permissions so that only MarkS can access it.

- If the directory \\orion01\users\MarkS *does* exist, then NT does nothing to the directory, save to remember that it is MarkS's home directory.

Notice a couple of things here. First, the value in the To field *must* be a universal naming convention (UNC). You cannot fill it with something like C:\USERS\MARKS, because, recall, this is a domain-wide account. If you were allowed to tell NT to put a user's one and only home directory on C:\USERS\MARKS, then NT would have to wonder, "*Which* C:?" There are a lot of machines in the domain, and they all have a C:. That's why you need a UNC.

Second, you're probably going to try this out on your network's domain controller, and it is likely to fail. Microsoft tells you in the NT manual to do something like this: Fill in a UNC in the To field of the "Profile" dialog box to have NT automatically create the home directory. But it ain't so, and it will fail because *NT does not share the USERS directory by default.* As USERS isn't shared, no UNC can refer to USERS, so the attempt fails.

Third (this *still* sounds like a lot of work), how can I get NT to create home directories for dozens of users all in one operation? Follow these steps:

1. In the User Manager for Domains, highlight the users for which you want User Manager for Domains to create home directories. You can select users at random by holding down the Ctrl key and left-clicking on the names for which you want to create home directories.

2. Choose User/Properties. You see a list of the users you selected, and the Groups, Profile, Hours, Logon To, and Account buttons. The User Manager for Domains is functioning just as it always does, except it's simultaneously working on multiple users.

3. Click Profile.

4. Now, in the bottom field where it said "to \\orion01\users\marks" before, you want to put in a kind of "wildcard" value that will work for any user. There is such a thing, the %username% built-in variable. Just fill in the To field with *servername*\USERS\%username%, where *servername* is the name of whatever server holds the home directories. The disk grinds for a moment or two, and in a trice NT has created a pile of home directories.

By the way, if you're wondering what the *other* fields in the Profiles dialog of the User Manager for Domains are good for, hang on for a page or two, because I'll get to them.

Take Note: Administrators Can't Normally Access Home Directories

Suppose you've just created a user directory for someone named James. You've created USERS\JAMES, cleaned out all permissions, and inserted James as the only person with any right to access USERS\JAMES. But you're an administrator, so you can still get in, right?

Try it. Open a command prompt and type **dir c:\users\james**. You'll be told that the directory is empty, even if it isn't. Try to access it from the Explorer or My Computer and you'll be flatly refused entry: "C:\USERS\JAMES is not accessible."

This *really* upsets some administrators, but it's the NT default, and I don't think it's all that bad. I mean, this *is* supposed to be a secure network, right? And besides, an administrator can usually add him- or herself to the ACL for a file or directory—or an administrator can seize control of an object by taking ownership of the object, as I'll describe soon. But before I cover ownership, let me get past a few other issues: changing file and directory permissions from the command line, understanding the default file and directory permissions on a newly installed NT Server, and auditing file access.

Controlling File and Directory Permissions from the Command Line

You've seen that you can control file and directory permissions from the GUI, but sometimes you want to make permission changes from the command line. The tool for that is CACLS. CACLS only works on NTFS volumes, and it doesn't let you change share-level permissions, only file and directory permissions.

Its syntax looks like this:

```
CACLS filename [/T] [/E] [/C] [/G username:permission] [/R user-
name [...]][/P username:permission [...]] [/D username [...]]
```

where each option works as follows:

- If you only specify a filename, you see the current ACL for the file or files (wildcards are acceptable). For example, you might see a response like "letter.txt Everyone: (OI) (CI) F," which means that the Everyone group has Full Control.

- /T says that whatever changes you make to a directory should also be applied to all files in the directory and all subdirectories of that directory.

- /C means to continue on access denied errors. If you make a change to a group of files, there may be files in that group whose ACLs you don't have the right to change. This says to keep on going and do whatever can be done.

- /G *username:permission* grants specified user access rights. Permission can be R (read), C (change), or F (full control). For example, "cacls letter.txt /g MarkS:F" would give Full Control to user MarkS. But note that this will *delete* anyone who currently has access to letter.txt; if, for example, the Everyone group had Full Control before this command, Everyone would no longer have access after this. If that's not what you want—if you want to *add* items to the list of approved users, rather than wipe out the list altogether and start over—then use the /E parameter.

- /E adds the ACL entry to the existing ACLs rather than deleting existing ACLs. In the previous example, "cacls letter.txt /e /g MarkS:F" would have added MarkS to the list of approved users of letter.txt, and Everyone would still be on the list of approved users.

- /R *username* revokes specified user's access rights (only valid with /E).

- /P *username:permission* replaces specified user's access rights. As before, the valid values for *permission* are N (no access), R (read), C (change), and F (full control). Note that this will act like option G in that not only will you change the user's permission, you will also zap any existing users. For example, if letter.txt has MarkS with Full Control and Everyone with Full Control, and you do "cacls letter.txt /P MarkS:C," you'll demote MarkS from Full Control to Change as well as remove Everyone from the list altogether! Note the difference between /G and /P: /G adds a new user to the list and /P just modifies an existing user on a list.

- /D *username* denies specified user access.

You may find this useful when creating large directories and setting their permissions automatically. Along the same lines, the *Resource Kit* includes a program called SCOPY. SCOPY is a large-scale file-copying program very much like XCOPY, but with the added benefit that it not only copies the files, but copies the security information (the ACLs) of the files as well.

Default Directory Permissions for NT Server Directories

Before you leave the topic of permissions, you may find Table 7.3 useful. It is a compilation of all of the default directory permissions of NT Server (and NT) directories. Subdirectories and files created in these directories will inherit the directory permissions unless you set their permissions to something else. Although several of the system directories seem to give the Everyone group Change permission, many of these directories are not accessible over the network unless you are a member of the Administrators or Server Operators groups (see the earlier section on share permissions and administrative shares).

TABLE 7.3   Default Directory Permissions in NT Server

Directory	Groups (Permissions)
\ (root directories of all NTFS volumes)	Administrators (Full Control)
	Server Operators (Change)
	Everyone (Change)
	CREATOR OWNER (Full Control)
\SYSTEM32	Administrators (Full Control)
	Server Operators (Change)
	Everyone (Change)
	CREATOR OWNER (Full Control)
\SYSTEM32\CONFIG	Administrators (Full Control)
	Everyone (List)
	CREATOR OWNER (Full Control)
\system32\drivers	Administrators (Full Control)
	Server Operators (Full Control)
	Everyone (Read)
	CREATOR OWNER (Full Control)
\system32\spool	Administrators (Full Control)
	Server Operators (Full Control)
	Print Operators (Full Control)
	Everyone (Read)
	CREATOR OWNER (Full Control)

TABLE 7.3   Default Directory Permissions in NT Server (Continued)

Directory	Groups (Permissions)
\system32\repl	Administrators (Full Control)
	Server Operators (Full Control)
	Everyone (Read)
	CREATOR OWNER (Full Control)
\system32\repl\import	Administrators (Full Control)
	Server Operators (Change)
	Everyone (Read)
	CREATOR OWNER (Full Control)
	Replicator (Change)
	NETWORK*
\system32\repl\export	Administrators (Full Control)
	Server Operators (Change)
	CREATOR OWNER (Full Control)
	Replicator (Read)
\users	Administrators (Change)
	Account Operators (Change)
	Everyone (List)
\users\default	Everyone (RWX)
	CREATOR OWNER (Full Control)
\win32\app	Administrators (Full Control)
	Server Operators (Full Control)
	Everyone (Read)
	CREATOR OWNER (Full Control)

TABLE 7.3   Default Directory Permissions in NT Server (Continued)

Directory	Groups (Permissions)
\temp	Administrators (Full Control)
	Server Operators (Change)
	Everyone (Change)
	CREATOR OWNER (Full Control)

* No Access, except for Administrators, Server Operators, and Everyone. This is the only case where N1o Access does not override previously granted permissions.

Monitoring Access to Files and Directories

In any network, the administrator needs at times to monitor user activity, not just to assess network performance, but for security reasons. NT Server provides administrators the opportunity to audit events that occur on the network. It maintains three different types of logs in which to record information: the Applications log, the System log, and the Security log, as you've seen if you've ever looked in the Event Viewer.

In order to record, retrieve, and store log entries of events, the administrator must activate auditing on the server. Not surprisingly, file and directory auditing is activated within the Security menu, either the Security menu from the NT 3.*x* File Manager or the Security tab in the Windows Explorer/My Computer in NT 4.

Auditing for File and Object Access

With NT Server, an administrator can specify which groups or users, as well as which actions, should be audited for any particular directory or file. The information is collected and stored in the Security log and can be viewed in the Event Viewer.

For directories and files to be audited, *you must first* set the security audit policy in User Manager for Domains to allow the auditing of file and object access. To do this, open User Manager for Domains and, from the Policies menu, choose Audit. You see the dialog box shown in Figure 7.13.

One of the auditing options available in the list is File and Object Access; make sure you select it. As you can see from the dialog box, you can audit both successful and failed accesses.

Auditing Directory and File Access

After activating file and object access auditing, you have to choose which files and/or directories, as well as which groups or users who might use the files and directories, you specifically want audited.

To do this, highlight the desired directory or file in the Windows Explorer window. Then, from the Security menu, choose Auditing. If you've selected a file for auditing, you see the dialog box in Figure 7.14.

You can choose a specific set of events to audit for each different group or user in the Name list. In this example, everyone's access to the file UPDATE.TXT is subject to auditing; however, only failed attempts to read, write, execute, and delete (as well as a successful deletion of the file) are actually recorded in the Security log. To add users and groups to those

---

FIGURE 7.13

Choosing File and Object Access event auditing in User Manager for Domains

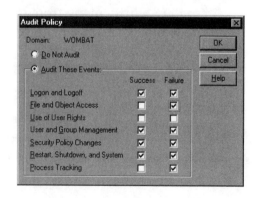

FIGURE 7.14

Setting up file auditing

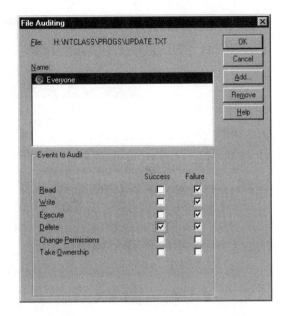

whose access to the file is being audited, click the Add button and specify the new users and groups in the resulting dialog box. Remove a user or group by clicking on it in the current Name list and selecting Remove.

If you are setting up auditing for a directory, there are two additional options to consider, Replace Auditing on Subdirectories and Replace Auditing on Existing Files. Figure 7.15 shows these two options in the Directory Auditing dialog box.

The default replace option is Replace Auditing on Existing Files. When this option is selected, changes made to auditing apply to the directory and the files within that directory only, not to any subdirectories in the directory. To apply auditing changes to the directory and its files as well as existing subdirectories within the directory and their files, check both boxes. Clearing both boxes applies the changes in auditing to the directory only, not to any of the files or subdirectories contained within it. Selecting only Replace Auditing on Subdirectories applies audit changes to the directory and subdirectories only, not to existing files in either.

FIGURE 7.15

Setting up directory
auditing

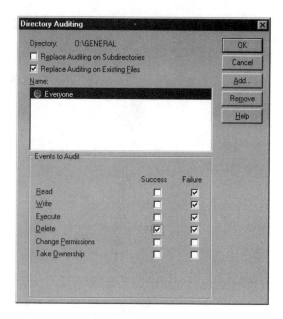

As with file auditing, you can set auditing for each group or user in the list by selecting the name of a group or user in the Names list and specifying which events will be audited for that group or user.

To remove file auditing for a group or user, select that group or user and select Remove. To add groups or users to the audit, use the Add option. When you are satisfied with the auditing options, choose OK. The results appear in the Event Viewer. The Viewer isn't the clearest thing in the world, but it gives you the rough information you need to track a security violation—provided auditing is enabled. On the other hand, auditing costs in terms of CPU time and disk space; if you turn on all file audits, you will fill up your event log in no time at all.

File Ownership in NT

All this talk of file permissions leads to an interesting question (well, interesting to *me*, but then I don't get out much). What happens if I use the GUI or CACLS to remove every entry in the ACLs? No one has access to the file, rendering it sort of useless. *Now* what do we do?

We find the file's owner.

You see, even when an ACL list has been completely cleaned out, there is in fact an extra, invisible entry. A directory or file's "owner" always has full control. Who is the owner of a file? By default, it's the person who created it. It's also possible to take ownership of a file if you have the permission to do so.

The Definition of "Ownership"

Now, having worked with NT since its inception, I don't mind telling you that the whole idea of a directory or file's "owner" seemed a bit confusing until I finally figured out the definition of a file or directory's owner. Here's my definition (and from this point on, let me shorten "file or directory" to "object"): an object's owner is a user who can *always* modify that object's permissions, no matter what entries are in the object's ACL.

Ordinarily, it is only an administrator who can control things like an object's permissions. But you want users to be able to control things in their own area, their own home directory, without having to involve you at every turn. For instance, suppose I have a directory in my home directory that I want to give another user access to. Rather than having to seek out an administrator and ask the administrator to extend access permissions to that other user, I as the owner can change the permissions directly. Ownership is a way for NT to allow you to make users into mini-administrators, rulers of their small fiefdoms.

You can see who owns an object by right-clicking on the object and choosing Properties. You then see a dialog box with several tabs, one of which is Security. Click the Security tab and you see an Ownership button. Click that, and you see who owns the object, as in Figure 7.16.

FIGURE 7.16

Viewing the owner of a
file or directory

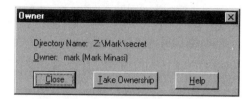

Experimenting with Ownership

If the implications of ownership aren't clear yet, let me walk you through
a little exercise you can do to experiment with ownership. To do this
experiment, you will need:

- An account with administrative powers

- An account with normal user powers

- A PC running NT workstation

- A home directory for the normal user account

Like many administrators, I have two accounts, a Mark account that
has only the powers of normal mortals, and a MarkS account that has
administrative powers (the *S* is for "Supervisor"). You need the NT
workstation machine because it has the versions of Explorer and My
Computer that include the Security tab. (Actually, you can also get
those from Windows 95 if you load the NT Server Tools for Windows 95,
which are on the NT Server CD-ROM in the CLIENTS\SRVTOOL directory.) The home directory should be a regulation home directory with file
and directory permissions set only to the normal user account—"Mark"
in my case—and no one else.

To start off, who owns Mark's, the normal user's, home directory?
Well, an administrator created it, so the Administrators group owns
it. If I look in the USERS directory on my primary domain controller,

where my user home directories are, I will see that indeed Administrators owns the USERS\MARK directory.

So I'm now logged on as Mark, the mere mortal, and am attached to my home directory. I create a file in that home directory. If I check the security settings on the file, I'll see that Mark owns the file. If I create a directory in my home directory, then I'll own that, too. Check the file and directory permissions and you'll see that they've inherited the file and directory permissions of the directory they were created in, and so only Mark has access to them. Now I'll create a directory called SECRET, where I'll store things I don't want anyone else to see.

What I've accomplished so far is to see that when I create a file, I own that file. Now let's see what that does to an imaginary snoopy administrator who wants to poke around my private files.

Assuming the role of that snoopy administrator, I log off and log back on as MarkS, the administrator. It doesn't matter what machine I log on to, because the USERS share has share-level permissions of Everyone/Full Control. I attach to USERS and see that, not surprisingly, there is a directory called MARK, which is the user Mark's home directory. I try to look in \USERS\MARK and I'm denied access because only Mark has access to this directory. Hmmm... What *can* an administrator do? Well, I could just add myself to the list of people with access to Mark's home directory, heh heh... I access the Permissions dialog box, and sure enough, only Mark has access. I add MarkS and I now have access to Mark's directory.

Snooping in Mark's home directory, I see that folder named SECRET. Hey, that sounds interesting; let's take a look. I double-click the SECRET folder and get that snotty "Access denied" message because Mark is the only one with access to that folder. Well, we've gotten past *that* before, right? I just click the button to see the permissions for the Secret folder...and get "Access denied."

Huh?

Well, the SECRET folder is owned by Mark. The only permissions for the SECRET folder are Mark's. The MarkS account is never mentioned in the ACL for SECRET. So MarkS can't get in.

How did MarkS get into \USERS\MARK in the *first* place? After all, MarkS had no permissions for *that*, either. Yet he was able to access and change the permissions for \USERS\MARK.

The answer? MarkS is an administrator. Administrators own \USERS\ MARK because they created it—they create *all* home directories. So, as MarkS was an owner, MarkS can always change the permissions on \USERS\MARK—remember, that's the definition of an owner. But *Mark* created SECRET, not *MarkS*, so Mark is the owner. Moreover, in addition to being the owner, Mark is the only person on the ACL, so MarkS has no access to Mark's home directory.

Sound scary for administrators? Fear not, there's a way to seize control; read on.

Taking Ownership

Look back at Figure 7.16, and you will see a button in the Ownership box labeled Take Ownership. Snoopy MarkS can't force himself onto the ACL for \USERS\MARK, but he *can* become the owner and, once he's the owner, *then* he can add himself to the ACL.

Logged on as MarkS, I attempt to bring up the Ownership dialog box. The system sees that I'm not the owner and that I don't have any access to the object. It shows the dialog box you see in Figure 7.17.

FIGURE 7.17

Attempting to
seize ownership

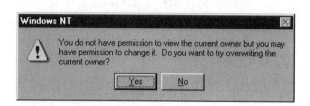

If I click Yes, I will be told that the system couldn't retrieve the ownership information, but other than that the next dialog box looks like the one in Figure 7.16. If I click Take Ownership, then I become the owner. Can I then see what's in SECRET? No, because I'm still not on the ACL. Keep this basic truth in mind: owners of files can't necessarily access those files.

> **NOTE** Owners of files can't necessarily access those files. All owners of files can do is to change the permissions on those files.

Okay then, how do I get to SECRET? Well, since I'm an owner, I can change permissions. So I'll add myself to the ACL and *then* gain access to SECRET.

Now, why was MarkS able to do that? Because of a user right that administrators all have—"Take ownership of files and other objects." By default, administrators have that right. I suppose if you were a more user-oriented than administrator-oriented company, you could remove the Administrators group from that right. If you did that, there would be *no* way for an administrator to poke around a user's area.

Further, a user can always shore up her security just a bit by taking control of her home directory from the administrators. Recall that each user has Full Control of her home directory, and Full Control includes the ability to take ownership of an object.

And if you're concerned about the fact that an administrator can take control at any time—where's the security in that?—then consider that the administrator must *take* ownership in order to add herself to the object's ACL. In doing that, she leaves fingerprints behind. If I log on one day and find that I'm no longer the owner of something that I owned yesterday, then I know that an administrator has been snooping. And if file auditing is in place, then I can even find out who the snoop was.

Let's summarize what we've seen so far about permissions and ownership:

- By default, new files and new subdirectories inherit permissions from the directory in which they are created.

- A user who creates a file or directory is the owner of that file or directory, and the owner can control access to the file or directory by changing the permissions on it (NT machines only).

- When you change the permissions on an existing directory, you can choose whether or not those changes apply to all files and subdirectories within the directory.

- Users and groups can be denied access to a file or directory simply by not granting the user or group any permissions for it. You don't have to assign No Access to every user or group that you want to keep out of a file or directory.

- Permissions are cumulative, except for No Access. No Access overrides all other permissions a user might have by virtue of his or her group membership.

Controlling the Rest of the Profiles Dialog Box

In the last chapter, I promised I'd finish up explaining the rest of the Profiles dialog box in the User Manager for Domains. I couldn't explain all of it then because it doesn't make much sense until you understand all of the file permissions stuff. Just in case you've forgotten, the Profile dialog box in the User Manager for Domain looks like Figure 7.18.

Three user factors are controlled from this dialog box:

- The location of an *NT* user profile, which is only relevant for people who use NT Workstation or NT Server machines as their personal workstations.

FIGURE 7.18

Profile dialog box in User Manager for Domains

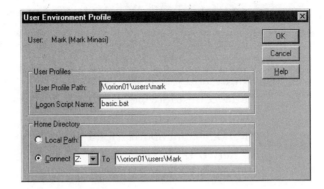

- The name of a logon batch script, which can be useful for someone running a client of virtually any sort save a Macintosh.

- The desired home directory, which is mainly a command that, like the user profile, is only of interest and use to people who use NT machines as workstations, and which has a side-effect that you've already met, of reducing some of the donkey work for the administrator creating home directories.

One of the reasons I left all of this for later, as you can probably see, is the a fair amount of ifs, ands, and buts concerning these features.

NT User Profiles

Once you've been working with a computer for a while, you get it to run just as you like it. From the small things like the desktop colors, to more important features like personalized program groups and persistent network connections, it's nice to have a workstation customized just for you.

But what happens if you share your computer with someone else? You come back after he's been using it, and he's messed with all of your settings. Grumble, grumble. What to do about that? Well, if you're using an NT machine—either Server or Workstation—as your workstation, then that scenario won't happen. NT keeps user-specific information for each user. NT calls this information a *user profile*.

Maintaining user-specific information is terrific, as it means that twenty people sharing a computer all get different desktops, program groups, and persistent network connections. (The twenty people are on the computer one at a time, of course. NT still doesn't come in a "multi-user" version, unless the Citrix people have come out with one.) But what about roving users who move from place to place on the network. Can they carry around the comforts of home easily? Yes, they can by placing their profiles on the network.

By default, NT stores user profiles in \WINNT\PROFILES. For two users named Sam and Julie, NT creates directories called \WINNT\ PROFILES\SAM and WINNT\PROFILES\JULIE. But you can alternatively tell NT to store your profile on a network-accessible volume and to download that profile to whatever machine you log on to at any moment in time. Look back at Figure 7.18 and you'll see that I directed NT to keep the profile for my Mark account in \\ORION01\USERS\ MARK, which you can probably guess is my home directory, not a bad place to stash profiles. (Remember that if you want to set this item for a lot of people at the same time, just use \\servername\USERS\%username% and NT will fill in the names as needed.) If the only thing I store in my home directory is my NT profile, my home directory looks like Figure 7.19.

Application-specific stuff like Application Data and Templates enables NT to keep different settings for a 32-bit application for different people. For example, suppose you shared a copy of Word on a machine with someone else. As Word allows a number of user settings, NT keeps those settings in your profile to keep your users preferences separate from others'. NetHood is the Network Neighborhood, whose main value is to hold persistent network connections. Ntuser.dat holds many of the personal preference settings that I referred to before. ntuser.dat.log is a transaction log file that allows NT to rebuild your profile if the present Ntuser.dat is damaged. If you ever want to freeze a user's profile and keep her from saving any changes to it, just go to her home directory and

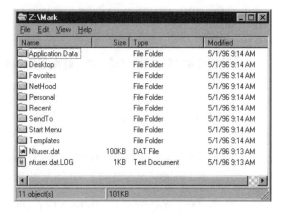

FIGURE 7.19

User profile stored on a home directory

rename ntuser.dat to ntuser.man; from that point on, any changes she makes to her environment won't be saved at the end of her session.

By the way, if you *can't* get to the network, NT always keeps a copy of your profile on your local hard disk just in case. And please remember that these are *NT* profiles; if you use Windows 95, then certainly Windows 95 has user profiles, but NT doesn't keep track of them. If you're using a Windows 95 workstation, all you need do is to use the Microsoft-written client software for NetWare or Microsoft networks and define a home directory for each user. The Microsoft client software will automatically keep the Windows 95 profiles in the user's home directory, where they won't conflict with the existing NT profiles.

Logon Batch Scripts

Most networks have the ability to kick off a set of commands whenever a user attaches to the network; NT's are called *logon scripts*. A logon script is simply a batch file (with the BAT or CMD filename extension) or an executable program (EXE extension). Logon scripts are set to run automatically whenever a user logs on, and the same script can be assigned to one or many user accounts. Unlike user profiles, logon scripts work on computers running on NT, Windows 95,

Windows for Workgroups, and MS-DOS. Logon scripts are used to configure users' working environments by making network connections and starting applications.

Applications of Logon Scripts

Logon scripts aren't as versatile as user profiles, but they are useful in the following situations:

- The network contains users using MS-DOS workstations (user profiles only work on NT workstations).

- You want to manage only part of the users' environments (for example, network connections) without managing or controlling the entire environment.

- You have an NT network using only personal (not mandatory) profiles, and want to create common network connections for multiple users without having to individually modify each profile.

- You have LAN Manager 2.*x* running on your network and you want to keep the logon scripts you made for that system.

Logon scripts are also easier to create and maintain than user profiles; depending on your network situation, they might be the better choice.

Where to Place a Login Script

Whenever a user logs on, the server authenticating the logon looks for the logon script by following the server's logon script path (the default path is WINNT\SYSTEM32\REPL\IMPORT\SCRIPTS). If you place your logon script there, you only have to type in the name of the script itself in the logon script path name box. If the logon script happens to be located in a subdirectory of the logon script path, include that relative path when you type in the name. The entire logon script path can be changed in Server Manager, under Directory Replication. Consult Chapter 11, on server management, for the procedure.

If your domain has more than one NT Server machine (configured as a PDC or BDC), any one of them may authorize a user's logon attempt, so copies of logon scripts for every user in the domain should exist on each of the servers in the domain. Using the Directory Replicator service is the best way to ensure this.

Creating a Logon Script

To create a logon script, simply create a batch file. This file can contain any valid batch commands. For example, you could have a batch file that contains the following two lines:

```
@echo off
net time \\orion01 /set /yes
```

This logon script synchronizes each workstation's clock with that of the primary server in the domain (which, in this case, is the computer \\orion01). As far as I'm concerned, all logon scripts should start with the time synchronization command NET TIME; that way, all of the workstations' times are in sync with the server's. (Of course, before you make everyone fall in line with the server, it would be a good idea to find one of those shareware programs that lets your server dial a time source somewhere and ensure that its time is exactly right. Such a program is in the NT *Resource Kit*.)

Not to belabor the point, but here's another reason to synchronize network time. We had a workstation whose calendar was several months behind; it thought it was March when we were actually in June. Oddly enough, any file saved to the server by that workstation was time-stamped March rather than June! I say "oddly" because when a workstation saves data to a server, it just says to the server, "Time-stamp this with this time and date," and the server blindly obeys. The only possible reason I could imagine for this would be that Microsoft wanted to support people who would have networks that span time zones. But even then, time zones shouldn't be so problematic, because Windows 95 and Windows NT workstations all know what time zone they're in, and some little kludge could certainly have been worked up for the DOS and Windows for Workgroups workstations! (I guess the guy who did the time-stamp is also the one who's responsible for the missing disk quota feature.) If you log on to a Windows NT workstation as a regular user rather than an administrator or power user, you get an error message (error 1340) because you tried to set the time on the workstation, but for some reason regular old users aren't allowed to set time. I just change the user right "Change the system time" and extend it to all users, in particular the Domain Users group in my domain.

By the way, if "net time \\orion01 /set /yes" seems like a lot of typing, you can shorten it. Read the following tip…

TIP

You can tell an NT machine to be the "official" time source of the network by going to the HKEY_LOCAL_MACHINE\System\Current Control Set\Services\LAN MAN SERVER\Parameters. Add a new key TimeSource of the type REG_DWORD and set it to 1. After you reboot the machine, you can enter the command net time /set /yes to have the PC *find* the time source.

Besides the NET TIME command, here's another one you'll find useful:

```
net use h: /home
```

Once you've created home directories for your DOS, Windows for Workgroups, and Windows 95 users, you'll be a bit disappointed at what you see of those directories when you log on…*nothing*! Merely having a defined home directory doesn't do anything for those machines; they still need a NET USE command to attach to the directories. That's the benefit of the /home option: the command above says to your DOS, Windows for Workgroups, or Windows 95 workstation, "Go interrogate the primary domain controller about where my home directory is, then attach me to it as drive H:." (Of course, you needn't use H:.)

Other than those two commands, you can put messages in logon scripts, run antivirus programs, or do a number of other things, depending on your network's needs. But keep your logon scripts short if your network uses Windows and Windows for Workgroups machines. When a Windows 3.*x* user who has been assigned a logon script logs on, the machine starts a virtual DOS session in which to execute the script. The virtual DOS session typically lasts only about 30 seconds and isn't configurable. If the script takes longer than that, it will quit and the user will get a system integrity violation error. This is especially a problem for remote users working over slow links (for example, using RAS or a TCP/IP gateway over async modem lines).

At worst case, you can disable script operation for users with the following procedure:

1. In Control Panel, choose the Network icon.

2. Choose the Networks button.

3. In the Other Networks In Use box, select Microsoft LAN Manager.

4. Choose the Settings option.

5. Clear the Logon to LAN Manager Domain check box.

Using the Logon Script Variables

You can use several wildcards as you write a logon script. They are listed in Table 7.4 (these script variables only work for people with NT workstations).

If you are typing up a logon script for multiple users who, for example, are not all in the same domain, you can type %USERDOMAIN% instead of an actual domain name in a command, and the system will automatically insert the specific user's domain when it executes the logon script.

In addition to the logon scripts, these wildcards can also be used in other situations, such as when specifying application path names in Program Manager, or when assigning user profiles and home directories to a number of users at once. One note about using %USERNAME% to create home directories and user profile filenames: Don't use the wildcard

TABLE 7.4   Logon Script Variables

Parameter	Description
%HOMEDRIVE%	A user's local workstation drive letter connected to the user's home directory
%HOMEPATH%	The full path name of the user's home directory
%HOMESHARE%	The share name containing the user's home directory
%OS%	The operating system of the user's workstation
%PROCESSOR%	The processor type (such as 80486) of the user's workstation
%USERDOMAIN%	The domain containing the user's account
%USERNAME%	The user name of the user

when assigning home directories that are on a FAT volume if at least one of the selected user accounts has a user name longer than 8 (or 8+3) characters. On NTFS volumes, this limit doesn't apply, and you can use the wildcards regardless of name length.

Controlling the Home Directory Setting

The last group in the Profiles dialog (see Figure 7.18) is labeled Home directory, but it includes two seemingly unrelated items offered in the form of radio buttons:

- Local Path

- Connect *driveletter* To

Since this is a set of radio buttons, the choices are mutually exclusive and collectively exhaustive (gosh, I love that phrase). In English, you've got to choose one or t'other. Just what is this all about?

Well, first of all, it is vitally important to understand what the radio buttons mean on DOS, Windows for Workgroups, and Windows 95 workstations. If fact, it's so important that I'm going to put it in a tip.

> **TIP**
>
> Choosing between the two radio buttons in the Home Directory group is almost totally meaningless on DOS, Windows for Workgroups, and Windows 95 workstations. It is only relevant if you use an NT Workstation or NT Server machine as your workstation.

The last group shouldn't be labeled "Home Directory"; it should be labeled "default directory." If you're at a computer running NT and you open a command prompt, what shows up at the command line? C:\>? D:\USERS\IGNATZ? It's controlled by this group in the Profiles field.

Local Path versus Connect...

What the choice between Local Path and Connect really means is, "When a program asks NT for a default directory, do you want that program directed to a network-based personal directory, which will coincidentally act in all other ways like a home directory, or do you want NT to direct the program to a local drive like C:, D:, or the like?"

The consequences of someone's choosing Connect *driveletter* to *UNC* will be that, over time, more and more of her data will end up in her personal directory on some server, rather than her local hard disk. When she installs a new program, it will usually offer to install itself on the personal network area, rather than the local hard disk. In contrast, choosing *local directory* and pointing to some drive letter will mean that things tend to happen on the local hard disk. I'm saying "tend to" because there's nothing keeping that user from overriding the defaults and storing any program or any data anywhere she wants (assuming she has the permissions). Most of us, however, take the defaults and go.

If you *do* choose the Connect radio button, you have to put a UNC into the last field; drive letters won't work. If you want to hard-wire a drive letter in there, select the Local Path option.

Reconciling Home Directories with Non-NT Workstations

Reconciling home directories with non-NT workstations can be tremendously confusing if you chose the Connect option to create a home directory for a DOS user. That's why it's vitally important to understand that the Home Directory group in the Profiles dialog box performs a double duty, and in some ways those duties have nothing to do with each other.

For a DOS, Windows for Workgroups, or Windows 95 workstation, it is convenient to make the domain (that is, the SAM account's user database, which lives on the primary domain controller) aware of a designated home directory for a particular user. It's useful because

- Windows 95 workstations automatically keep Windows 95 user profiles there, provided you are running the right network client software.

- When you execute a "net use *driveletter* /home," your workstation asks the primary domain controller where its home directory is.

That's about all you get in terms of benefits from having a home directory on an NT domain if you're not running an NT machine of some kind as your workstation, but the benefits are significant. NT's home directory function offers only one other benefit and you've already met it—it will create and set permissions for home directories for users automatically. (Remember that if the user's home directory already exists, NT won't change the permissions.)

What is even more confusing is the design of the home directory group. I could enter Connect X: to \\orion01\users\mark, and, assuming that Mark doesn't use an NT machine as his workstation, he sees nothing in the way of a home directory when he boots up. Even more bizarre, when he executes "net use h: /home," he ends up with a home directory mapped to drive *H:* rather than X:! Nowhere does the dialog box say, "When you designate a drive letter in the 'Connect...' field, NT will ignore it." And yet that's exactly what happens, unless you use NT or NT Server machines as workstations. Oh, and one more thing, before I end this chapter...

How Do You Set Disk Quotas in NT?

I've mentioned disk quotas elsewhere in the book, but it's important enough to mention it here as well because someone may flip through the table of contents and look for the answer here. The *question* is, "How can I restrict how much data my users can put in their home directories?" After all, home directories are on a shared volume, and one jerk who uploads his entire 1.3GB of data from his laptop onto his home directory on the server may well fill the disk and make everyone else unable to save data to their home directories. What can we do to prevent that?

Unfortunately, nothing. There is no provision for disk quotas in NT. Supposedly, disk quotas will be included in Cairo, but then Cairo was supposed to ship in September 1995, so I wouldn't hold my breath. A third party makes a utility that is supposed to allow you to impose disk quotas, but they don't supply review copies to journalists, which always kinda makes you wonder...

Well, by now, you have some users, and they have places to put data. But things aren't really true until they're on paper, so we need some printers, and that's where the next chapter comes in.

CHAPTER
EIGHT

Managing Printing Services
with NT Server

Print Manager

Printers are essential in any office where computers are used. I mean, you really don't believe that something is true until you see it on paper, right? (If you don't believe me, wouldn't you feel a little unsure about a notice that you got a raise—delivered via e-mail?) Printers convert all those little electronic bits in your computer into hard copy.

But printers cost money, and, worse yet, they take up space. Laying equipment and toner costs aside, most offices wouldn't have enough office space to give a laser printer to every employee even if they *wanted* to.

Of course, one solution to the printer management and support problem is a network; hence this chapter. In this chapter, you'll learn about

- Creating and fine-tuning network printer queues

- Optimizing the printing process

- Controlling access to the printer

- Troubleshooting printing problems

NT Server uses some special vocabulary when discussing printers:

Network-interface printers   Whereas other printers connect to the network through a print server that is hooked into the network, network-interface printers are directly connected to the cabling without requiring an intermediary. These printing devices have built-in network cards.

Print server   The computer to which the printer is connected and on which the drivers are stored.

Printer   The *logical* printer as perceived by NT Server and NT. As you'll see during this chapter, the ratio of printers to printing devices is not necessarily one to one—you can have one printer and one printing device, one printer and multiple printing devices, or multiple printers and one printing device, or some combination of any of the above. We'll talk about the situations in which you might find each of these arrangements useful.

Printing device   The physical printer, that largish box with the display panel from which you pick up documents.

Queue   This is a group of documents waiting to be printed. In OS/2, the queue is the primary interface between the application and the printing devices, but in NT Server and NT the printer takes its place.

NT-Specific Print Sharing Features

The unique printer sharing features that NT Server has can make the process of connecting to a networked print device easier than it is with other operating systems.

NT Workstations Don't Need Printer Drivers   If you're running an NT workstation with your NT Server, not needing printer drivers is likely one of your favorite features, as it makes the connection process a lot easier. When you're connecting the workstation to a printer on the server, you don't have to specify what kind of printer you want to connect to or tell the system where to find the drivers, as you do when connecting a Windows workstation to a networked printing device. Instead, you need only go to the Printers folder or Add New Printer Wizard (depending on which version of NT you are running, 3.*x* or 4.*x*), look to see what printers are shared on the network, and double-click on the one that you want. Once you've done that, you're connected.

Direct Support of Printers with Network Interfaces   To use a network interface print device (that's one that connects directly to the network, rather than requiring parallel or serial connection to a print server, remember), you need only load the Data Link Control protocol onto the print server. Although network interface print devices can connect directly to the network without an intervening print server, those network interface print devices still work best with a connection to a computer acting in the role of print server because they have only one incoming data path. With only one path, once the printer had received one print job, it would not be able to queue any others until that job was done. More paths mean more efficient use of printing time, as queuing means that you don't have to keep checking to see if the printer's done or worry about someone beating you to the printer.

Network interface printers can be useful because, although they still usually connect to a print server through the network media, they can be physically distant from it because they don't get jobs through the parallel or serial port. The network connection can also speed up the process of downloading documents to the printer, since a network connection is faster than a parallel or serial port. The speed difference isn't great, though, because the printer still has to access the drivers from the print server.

Totally Integrated Printer Support in One Program   The Printers window in Control Panel takes care of all printer maintenance. To connect to, create, fine-tune or manage a printer, you need only open the Printers window.

Who Can Be a Print Server?

Like many networks today, your network's workstations and servers are likely to be pretty heterogeneous when it comes to operating systems. Print servers don't necessarily have to be your main file server, or even NT Server machines, but there are limitations on who can share a printer with the rest of the network.

Machines running the following operating systems can be print servers:

- Windows for Workgroups

- Windows 95

- Windows NT

- Windows NT Server

- LAN Manager

- MS-DOS and Windows 3.1 (when running the MS Workgroup DOS Add On)

Adding a Printer

The process of adding a printer to NT Server 4 has changed significantly from NT 3.51. Although the process is different, the functions have remained similar. With this incarnation of NT, Print Manager is no longer a part of the program. All of the functions previously found in Print Manager are now located in the Printer window.

The Printer window can be found by going to the Control Panel by way of the Start menu. For those of you familiar with NT 3.51 and before, the process of setting up a printer to be shared over the network was called "creating" it. Now you simply go to the Printer window and click on the Add Printer icon. The Printer Wizard walks you through the process of setting up a printer. The properties of the printer, giving permissions for groups to use the computer, and all other functions and settings for printers can be found in the Printer window—more specifically, in the Properties dialog box in the File menu.

To add a printer, double-click on the Add Printer icon in the Printers window. You see the opening dialog box of the Printer Wizard, as shown in Figure 8.1.

FIGURE 8.1

Opening screen of the Add Printer Wizard

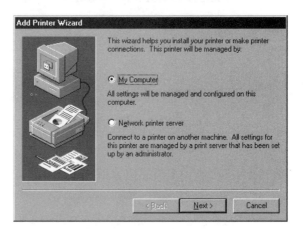

Choose Network printer server to connect your machine to a printer managed by another machine in your domain. Choose My Computer to set up a printer for your server to manage.

You need to set up your own printer (as opposed to connecting to one) if you are

- Physically installing a printer on a computer

- Physically installing a printer that connects directly to the network

- Defining a printer that prints directly to a file (no hard copy)

- Associating multiple printers with diverse properties for the same printing device

Click on My Computer and choose next. The Printer Wizard asks which port the printer is connected to, as shown in Figure 8.2. If you don't see your port listed, click on Add Port to see additional choices.

Click on Next when you are done to get to the next dialog box, which is shown in Figure 8.3. You are asked to tell the Printer Wizard who the manufacturer of the printer is. Click on the manufacturer on the left of the screen. On the right is a list of printers that they make. Choose the

FIGURE 8.2

Choosing a port
for the printer

FIGURE 8.3

Telling the Wizard which
manufacturer and model
your printer is

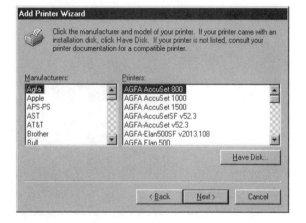

printer. If you wish to use the manufacturer's printer driver, click on
Have Disk and follow the prompts. If you wish to use NT's printer
driver, just click Next. If the driver you selected is already present, the
Wizard asks if you want to replace it, as shown in Figure 8.4.

The Printer Wizard now asks you to name the printer, as you can see
in Figure 8.5. The name can be up to 32 characters, including spaces.
Click Next to continue with the installation.

FIGURE 8.4

Printer driver replacement dialog box

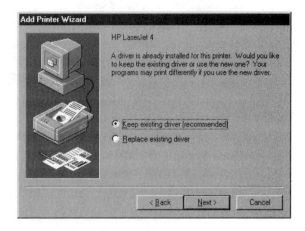

FIGURE 8.5

Entering a name for the printer

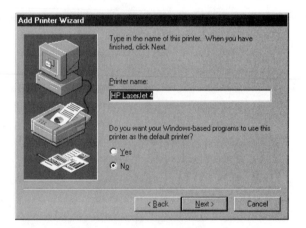

Now you have to say whether the printer is to be shared with others, as shown in Figure 8.6. If you share it, you have to give it a share name. The share name does not have to be the same as the printer name, but it might be easier to manage the printers if your printer names and share names are the same. A share name can be up to 12 characters long, including spaces.

FIGURE 8.6

Sharing the printer

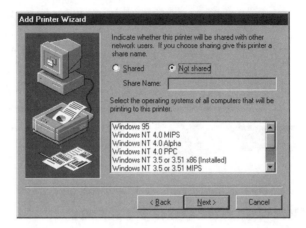

If you want MS-DOS machines to be able to use this printer, you need to make sure that the printer name conforms to DOS's 8+3 naming convention.

You can set the user permissions in the Properties dialog box after you finish adding the printer. However, if you intend to share the printer, tell the Printer Wizard now which operating systems will be used to print from this printer and be sure to have on hand the driver files for each operating system you choose. Printer Wizard will tell you which ones it needs in a dialog box like the one shown in Figure 8.7.

FIGURE 8.7

Telling the Printer Wizard driver files are needed

Click Next when you have finished. You are advised to print out a test page. That is all there is to it—your printer is ready to be used by one and all. Except, of course, that you may not want everyone and her brother to use the printer. That is where the user permissions come in handy. We'll talk about them later in this chapter.

> **TIP**
>
> RISC and *x86* machines use different printer drivers, so you need to install both kinds if you have both kinds of machines on your network.

Adding a Second Printer for the Same Print Device

It's often desirable for you to have two (or more) names for the same print device on the network. Having different people access the same device from different names allows you to assign different printing priorities to different users, assign different hours that the printer is available for printing, make one printer for network use and another for local use, and so forth. Having two or more names allows you to fine-tune the network's access to the printer.

The process of adding a second printer for the same print device is identical to that of adding the first one. Select Add Printer from the Printers window and follow the Printer Wizard's instructions. Make sure to do the following:

1. Select a new name for the printer.

2. Choose the same printer driver for the printer that the other printer on this print device uses, and make sure that all other settings are as they should be. You don't have to share all printers on the network, even if they're attached to the same printing device.

If you shared the new printer with the network, it will now be available for connection.

How Do I Set Up a Printer the First Time for Network Use?

 The first time that you're setting up a printer on the network, you need to add it. To do this, go to the Add Printer option in the Printer window and fill in the appropriate information, including the type of printer, its share name, and whether or not it will be shared with the network.

You can give one physical printer more than one share name and assign each name to a different group, perhaps with different print privileges. Just repeat the creation process, but assign the printer a different name.

Customizing a Printer's Setup

Once you've done the basic work of adding a printer, you can further customize it. You don't have to customize your printer at the same time that you set it up if you don't want to—you can always adjust the settings at a later date with the Properties option on the Printer menu.

Using the Printer Properties Dialog Box

Highlight the printer you want and click on the Properties button in the Printers window. You see a screen that looks like Figure 8.8. From here, you can do many things, including the following:

- List the hours that this printer will print. If you restrict the printing hours, jobs will still spool to the printer during the off-times, but will not print until the hour indicated.

FIGURE 8.8

Printer Properties
opening dialog box

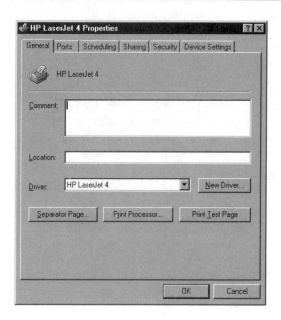

- Choose a separator page file to print before each print job. Separator pages are discussed in detail later in this chapter, under "Separator Pages for Sorting Documents."

- Choose the ports that you want to print to for printer pooling (more on this below).

- Select the print processor.

- Determine the printer's priority, if the printer goes by more than one name on the network. For example, if you have the same printer shared under the name HP4-22 and HP4, and you assign a higher priority to the printer name HP4-22, then print jobs sent to that printer name are printed first. The default priority is 1, which is the lowest priority. You can set the priority from 1 to 99.

Printer Pooling

Just because you send a print job to a particular print name doesn't mean that your print job has to print at one particular printer. To save time for print jobs, you can use the Properties dialog box to pool several *identical* printers into one logical one. If you do this, the first available printer will do the job when you send it to that printer name. This is called *printer pooling*, and it is illustrated in Figure 8.9. Printer pooling will not work unless the pooled printers are physically identical—the same make and model and the same amount of memory.

FIGURE 8.9

Printer pooling

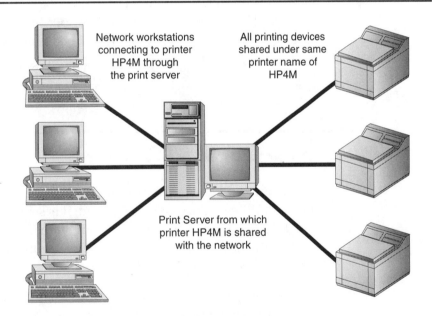

Network workstations connecting to printer HP4M through the print server

All printing devices shared under same printer name of HP4M

Print Server from which printer HP4M is shared with the network

If you have more than one identical printer, you can share them under the same printer name to facilitate speedy printing. This type of sharing is called *printer pooling*. To the network, it will look as though there is only one printer to connect to, but print jobs will automatically go to whatever pooled printer is available first.

TIP

To set up printer pooling, go to the Ports tab in the Printer Properties dialog box and click on the ports where you've plugged in the other printers. If the ports you need aren't on the list, you can add them by clicking on the Add Port button.

How Do I Set Up More Than One Printer under the Same Name?

To have more than one printer handle print jobs sent to the same print name, you must set up printer pooling. To do this, go to the Properties item in the File menu and click on the Ports button. Select the ports that correspond to the ports where you've plugged in the other printers.

On an NT Server machine, you only need one copy of the driver for the type of printer you're pooling, unlike Windows for Workgroups, which requires one copy of the driver for each printer.

Printing Directly to Ports

By default, documents for printing spool to the printer before they are printed. When a document is spooled, it is sent to the print server's hard disk and sent to the printer from there in an effort to save time and let the user get back to what she was doing as soon as possible. This is called *printing in the background.*

If you like, however, you can use the scheduling dialog box to send print jobs directly to the port that a printer is connected to. But if you do this, you won't be able to use your application until the print job is done.

Setting the Printer Timeout Number

If the printer you are setting up is connected to a parallel port, you can specify the time lapse before the print server decides that the printer

How Do I Print Directly to Ports?

 To send print jobs directly to the port to which the printer is connected rather than spooling normally, go to the Properties item in the File menu of the Printers window and click on the Scheduling button.

is not responding and notifies you (as the user) of an error. Setting the Transmission Retry number higher or lower adjusts the amount of time that the Print Server will wait for a printer to prepare itself to accept data.

This setting affects not only the printer that you've selected, but also any other local printers that use the same printer driver. Clicking on the Configure Port button in the Ports tab of the Printer Properties dialog box nets you a small dialog box that looks like Figure 8.10. To adjust the time-out, just click on the arrows on the right side of the box or type in a number by hand. As you can see, the time is measured in seconds.

How Do I Set Printer Timeouts?

 To set the number of seconds between the time that you send a print job to the printer and the time that, if the printer doesn't see the job, it tells you that there is a transmission error, choose the Properties item in the Printer menu, click on Ports tab, choose Configure Port in the dialog box, and type in the number of seconds that you want for the timeout.

FIGURE 8.10

Configure Port dialog box

Connecting to a Shared Printer

How you connect a workstation to a printer that is hooked up to a server running NT Server depends on the operating system that the workstation is using. Windows and Windows for Workgroups machines can connect from the graphical interface, but OS/2 and MS-DOS machines must make connections from the command line. Easiest of all are the Windows NT machines—they don't even require locally loaded printer drivers!

Printing from MS-DOS

All DOS workstations, whether they are running Windows or not, require locally installed printer drivers to share printers on an NT Server network. From a DOS workstation that is not running Windows or Windows for Workgroups, you need to install the MS-DOS printer driver file for the laser printer and make sure that it is accessible to all your applications. Depending on how your disk is set up, you might have to copy the file to all your application directories.

To set up a printing port from MS-DOS, go to the command prompt and type **net use lpt1: ***server******sharename*. For *server* and *sharename*, substitute the name of the print server and the name by which the printer is known on the network. Substitute another port name if LPT1 is already in use.

If you want the connection to be made automatically every time that you log on to the network, add the **/persistent:yes** switch to the end of the command. Just typing **/persistent** won't do anything, but if you leave off the persistency switch altogether, it will default to whatever you selected the last time that you used the NET USE command.

For example, suppose you have an MS-DOS workstation that does not have a locally attached printer on any of its parallel ports. Since some older DOS programs don't really give you the chance to select an output port, you'd like the network printer HP4, which is attached to the server BIGSERVER, to intercept any output for LPT1 and print it on HP4. Suppose also that you want this network printer attached every time that you log on to the network. The command for that would be

```
net use lpt1: \\bigserver\hp4 /persistent:yes
```

TIP

If the print server is using NTFS, workstations may not be able to print from MS-DOS if they only have Read and Execute privileges. The print jobs spool to the print queue, but never print. To resolve this problem, give all users who print from DOS applications or the command prompt full access to the printer.

DOS workstations, whether or not they're running Windows over DOS, use the locally installed printer driver rather than the one stored on the server. Therefore, if you get an updated version of a printer driver, you need to install it at each DOS/Windows workstation individually.

Printing from Windows and Windows for Workgroups

Connecting to an NT Server shared printer from Windows for Workgroups is just like connecting to the same printer on a WfW server. To connect, go first to the Control Panel and select the Printers icon. You see a screen that looks like Figure 8.11. This screen shows you the printer connections that you currently have. To connect an existing printer to a new port, click on the Connect button. You see a screen that looks like Figure 8.12.

If, however, you want to connect to a new printer, you need to click on the Network button in this dialog box. Do so, and you see a screen

FIGURE 8.11

Connecting to an NT
Server printer from
Windows for Workgroups
(screen 1)

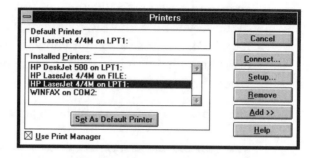

FIGURE 8.12

Connecting to an NT
Server printer from
Windows for Workgroups
(screen 2)

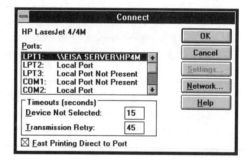

like Figure 8.13. It shows you what printers are available for connection. Click on the printer you want, and when its name appears in the Path box, click OK. You go back to the previous screen, where you can ensure that the printer is connected to the port that you want.

That's how you connect to a networked printer *if* the drivers for that printer are already loaded. If they're not loaded, you need to use the Add button in the first screen (see Figure 8.11) to add the printer driver to the system. Click on the Add button and you see the list of printers shown in Figure 8.14.

Select the printer that you want (for example, the HP LaserJet III), and then click on the Install button. You see a screen like the one in

FIGURE 8.13

Connecting to an NT
Server printer from
Windows for Workgroups
(screen 3)

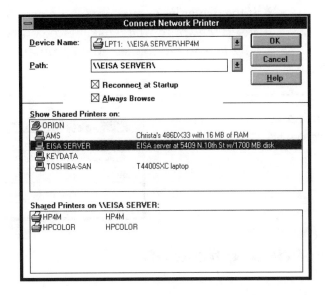

FIGURE 8.14

Adding a printer driver to
the system (step 1)

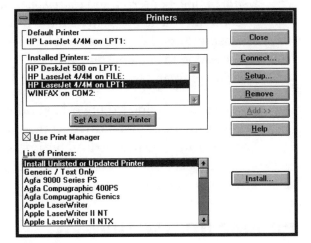

Figure 8.15. You can use the Browse button or type in the proper path if the driver is somewhere on the network; otherwise, you need to insert the appropriate disk. Once you've installed the correct driver, you're ready to connect to the printer.

FIGURE 8.15

Adding a printer driver to the system (step 2)

Printing from OS/2

Connecting to an NT Server printer from OS/2 is much like doing it from DOS. To set up a printing port, go to the command prompt (reached from the System folder) and type **net use lpt1: *server*\ sharename**. For *server* and *sharename*, substitute the name of the print server and the name by which the printer is known on the network. Substitute another port name if LPT1 is already in use. If you want the connection to be persistent, add the **/persistent:yes** switch to the end of the command.

When connecting to networking printers, OS/2, like DOS and Windows uses local printer drivers rather than drivers stored on the print server. Thus, you need to load the printer drivers locally for the printers you connect to, and if you update the drivers, you need to install the new ones at each workstation.

Printing from Windows NT

If you're using Windows NT, connecting to a shared printer is so easy you'll be tempted to believe that you didn't do it right until you try to print and it works. Since NT workstations can access the printer drivers located on the print server, you don't need to load them locally. How this works is illustrated in Figure 8.16.

Therefore, rather than define the proper port, find the drivers, or do anything else, all that you need do is go to the Control Panel, select the Printers icon, and double-click on Add Printer. When you do, you see the first Add Printer Wizard screen shown in Figure 8.17.

When you've reached this screen, choose the Network printer server option button, and then click the Next button. A screen like Figure 8.18 appears. It shows you the available printers that you can connect to. As you can see from the figure, two printers are currently available on this network.

FIGURE 8.16

Locally loaded printer drivers versus centrally loaded printer drivers

Printer drivers stored locally at workstation

Printer drivers stored on server, but inaccessible to non-NT workstations

Windows for Workgroups accessing printer through NT Server print server

No printer drivers stored locally

Printer drivers stored on server, accessed by NT workstations

NT workstation accessing printer through NT Server print server

FIGURE 8.17

First screen in the process of connecting to a shared printer

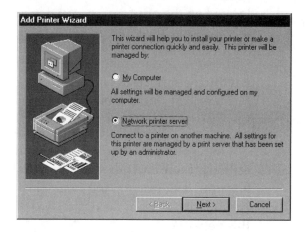

FIGURE 8.18

Display of available printers on the network

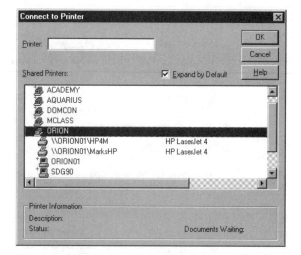

To connect to both HP4M and MarksHP, the printers shown in Figure 8.18, you have to do it one printer at a time. Double-click on HP4M to select it, or click once and then click OK. Once that's done, that's it—you don't have to load drivers or tell the system the kind of printer that you want to connect to. To connect to MarksHP, just repeat the process.

NT workstations use the printer drivers stored on the print server, so if you install a newer version of a driver on the print server, the NT workstations will use it automatically. You don't need to tweak the workstation connection.

How Do I Connect a Workstation to a Shared Printer?

 The process of connecting a workstation to a networked printer varies with the type of operating system that the workstation is using. To connect DOS and OS/2 machines, use the NET USE command from the command prompt. For Windows and Windows for Workgroups, you can use the Printers folder. For Windows NT machines, use the Print Wizard. Printer drivers for each kind of printer must be loaded locally on all kinds of workstations except Windows NT.

Controlling and Monitoring Access to the Printer

Just because you've networked a printer doesn't necessarily mean that you want everyone on its domain to be able to access it. Maybe it's the color printer with the expensive ink that only the graphics people need to use, or you want to reduce the risk of security breaches by limiting the people who can print out company secrets. Either way, you want to control access to the printer just as you would to any other network device.

By default, only Administrators and Power Users have full access to the printer. Only those with full access can pause or resume a printer or set its permissions. Those who just have print access can only administer their own documents.

Setting Printer Permissions

As you'll recall from elsewhere in this book, you secure an NT Server network by setting user rights for what people can *do* on the network, and setting user permissions for what people can *use*. Just as you can with other devices on the network, you can restrict printer use by setting the permissions on it.

To set or change printer permissions, first go to the Printer windows and select the icon for the printer you want. Next, go to the Properties dialog box in the File menu, choose the Security tab, and select Permissions. You see a dialog box that looks like Figure 8.19.

FIGURE 8.19

Printer Permissions
dialog box

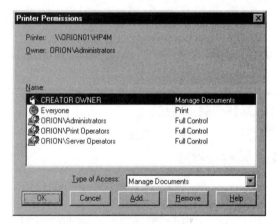

The Printer Permissions dialog box lists the groups for whom some kind of printer access has been set up. From here, you can change the kinds of access that each user group has. The kinds of access are as follows:

Access	What It Means
No Access	No member of that user group can do anything with the printer, including print.
Print	Members of that user group can print documents.

Access	What It Means
Manage Documents	Members can control document settings as well as pause, resume, restart, and delete documents that are lined up for printing.
Full Access	Members can do anything with the printer: print; control document settings; pause, resume, and delete documents and printers; change the printing order of documents; and change printer properties and permissions.

To change a group's type of access, click on the group to highlight it, and then choose the new access type from the Type of Access box in the lower-right corner of the dialog box. Make very sure that you leave one group with Full Access, or you won't be able to change printer permissions in the future.

To add a user group or user to the printer permissions list, click on the Add button. You see a dialog box that looks like Figure 8.20.

FIGURE 8.20

Adding users and groups
to printer permissions list

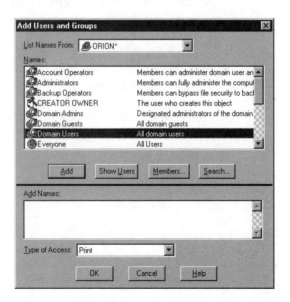

To add a group to the printer permissions list, highlight the kind of permission that you want to give that group, click on the group you want, click Add, and click OK. To add only a particular person to the printer permissions list, you have two options:

- You can select a group that the user belongs to and click on Members. This gives you a list of all the users that belong to the group. Highlight the user that you want.

TIP Clicking on Members to show the members of the Users group does not get you a list of users; use the Show Users button to do that. If you try to see the members of the Domain Users group, you'll only get a message informing you that the composition of that group is identical to that of the Users group.

- Click on the Show Users button and scroll down the user groups list until you see the entry for Users. Below this entry is a list of every user on the system. Double-click on the name, just as you would when selecting a user group.

Once you've selected the group or user, the name should appear in the Add Names box in the bottom half of the screen. When you're done adding groups or users, click OK.

To remove a group or user from the printer permissions list, go to the Printer Permissions dialog box (see Figure 8.19), highlight the name of the user or group, and then click Remove.

TIP

If a user is a member of more than one group with different printer permissions, the system always grants the highest-level permission, so that if Jane is a member of one group with Print privileges and one with Full Access privileges, she always has Full Access privileges. The only time that print permissions are *not* cumulative is when one of the groups that a user belongs to has No Access to the printer. In that case, that permission level overrides all higher levels and the user has no access to the printer, regardless of the access level of other user groups she belongs to.

How Do I Set Printer Permissions?

 To control which groups or individuals have access to a networked printer and the kind of access that they have, go to the Security tab in the Properties dialog box and choose Permissions. Select existing groups and change the kind of printer access that they have, or click on Add and select new groups to configure. To select individual members of a group, click on the Users button to display membership.

For users in more than one group with different printer permissions, permissions are cumulative except for No Access. If any group of which that user is a member is forbidden access to the printer, that overrides all other permissions.

Hiding a Printer

You can conceal the fact that a printer even exists, but still share it with the network for a chosen few to access. To do this, attach a dollar sign ($) to the end of the printer share name. This way, the printer name does not show up on the list of networked printers, but if the user types in the name by hand, she is able to connect to the printer.

How Do I Hide a Shared Printer?

 To share a printer with the network but keep it from showing up when people browse the network for printers, tack a dollar sign to the end of its name. That way, users have to type the printer's name in the printer name box—it doesn't show up on the list of printers shared with the network.

Setting Print Job Priorities

As discussed earlier, you can set printer priorities from the Scheduling tab of the Properties dialog box (see Figure 8.8). This way, if you want to share your printer with the network but don't want everyone else's print jobs crowding out your own, you can give it two names: a name you use that has a high priority, and a name with a low priority that is used by everyone else who connects to the printer. To further hone print priorities for different user groups, you can give the printer three or more different names, each with its own priority attached, and then assign each group that needs access to the printer a name by which to connect. How this works is illustrated in Figure 8.21.

When you're setting the printer priorities in the Scheduling tab of the Properties dialog box, don't forget that higher numbers (up to 99) have a higher priority than lower ones. The default value is 1.

How Do I Set User Print Priorities?

 You can give the print jobs of one person or group priority over another person or group. To do this, create another printer for the same print device. Click on the Scheduling tab in the Properties dialog box, and you see a dialog box in which you can set printer priorities. You can set this number from 1 to 99, with 99 being the highest priority. The default is 1.

FIGURE 8.21

Setting print priorities with different printer names

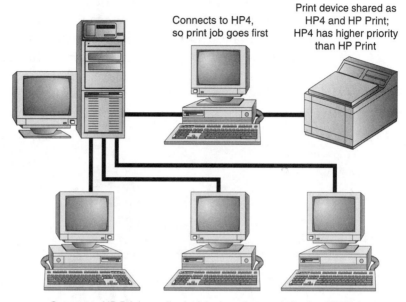

Connects to HP4, so print job goes first

Print device shared as HP4 and HP Print; HP4 has higher priority than HP Print

Connect to HP Print, so all print jobs have lower priority than HP4 jobs

Setting Printing Hours

As discussed in "Using the Printer Properties Dialog Box" earlier in this chapter, you can set the hours during which a printer produces output. To adjust print times, just click on the ↑ or ↓ arrow of the Available From and To boxes, or type in the times that you want the printer to be available. If a print job is sent to a printer during its "off hours," it doesn't disappear but sits there until the printer is authorized to print again.

While you can set user logon hours and printer hours, you can't set printing hours for a particular user or group that are different from those of the others who have access to that printer. For example, you can't restrict users to a particular printer between 9 and 5 if Administrators can access it at any time, unless you adjust the users' logon times and configure their accounts so that the system kicks them off when their time is up. What you *can* do is set up two printer names, one with one time window when it's open for use, and the other with another one. Those who connect to the printer name with the limited hours will only be able to use the printer during those hours. How this works is described in the Figure 8.22.

FIGURE 8.22

Restricting printing hours for a user group

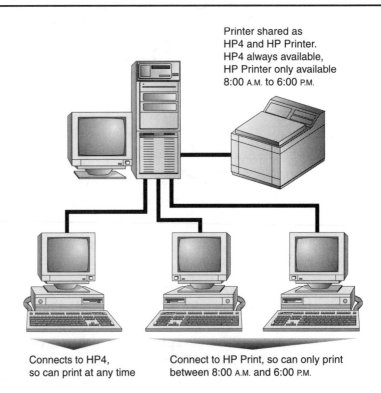

Printer shared as HP4 and HP Printer. HP4 always available, HP Printer only available 8:00 A.M. to 6:00 P.M.

Connects to HP4, so can print at any time

Connect to HP Print, so can only print between 8:00 A.M. and 6:00 P.M.

Receiving Status Messages

One of the auditing functions that you use most often is some kind of messenger service that tells you what's happened to print jobs after you've sent them to the server. Printer status messages can tell you when:

- The print job is done

How Do I Set Different Printing Hours for Different Groups?

 Although you can't make a printer accessible to one group for one set of hours and to another group for a different set, you can still customize printer access hours for different sets of users. Simply add more than one printer (remember, printers are logical entities, distinct from the physical printing devices), set the hours for each printer as you require, and then tell each group what printer to connect to.

- The printer is out of paper or off-line

- The printer is jammed

- A print job has been deleted

Arranging to receive printer status messages is done a little differently, depending on what operating system the workstation in question is using:

NT *and* **NT Server**   Begin the messenger service (it's on by default, so you probably don't have to do anything)

Windows for Workgroups *and* **Windows 95**   Run WINPOPUP.EXE in the Windows directory

DOS *and* **Windows**   Load the messenger service through NET POPUP

NetWare   Begin the CAPTURE program and run the messenger service

Logging and Auditing Printer Usage

In order to keep an eye on a printer's usage, it's a good idea to audit it. To set up auditing, first go to the User Manager and enable file and object access auditing. Once you've done that, you can set up printer auditing for individuals and groups.

To configure printer auditing, go to the Printer Properties dialog box and select the Auditing option in the Security tab. When you do, you see the dialog box in Figure 8.23.

Why are all the auditing options grayed out? Before you can audit printer activity, you have to select a group or user to audit. To do this, click on the Add button. You see a screen like Figure 8.24. To select a group for auditing, double-click on it or click once and then click on Add. When you've selected a user or group, it should show up in the Add Names box in the bottom half of the screen. When you've chosen all the groups that you want to audit, click OK to return to the Printer Auditing screen. It now looks something like Figure 8.25.

FIGURE 8.23

Printer Auditing
opening screen

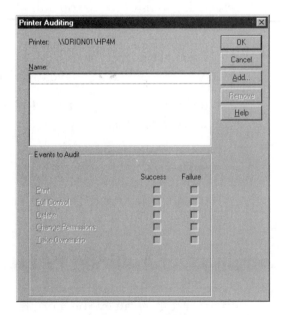

FIGURE 8.24

Add Users and Groups
dialog box for printer
auditing

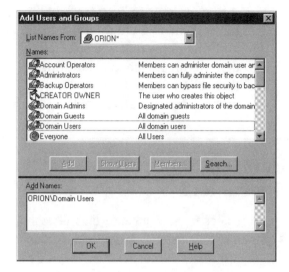

FIGURE 8.25

Auditing screen
with groups chosen
for auditing

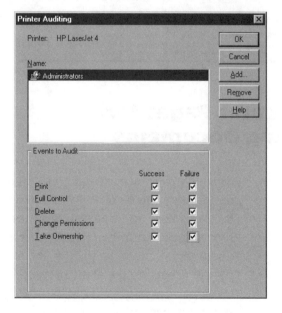

For each group or user that you've chosen to audit, you can select different items to keep track of by checking in the appropriate check boxes. When you highlight a group in the Name box here, you see the auditing items that you selected for that particular user or group. No defaults are attached to auditing a particular group, so you have to set them all by hand. To view the audit information, use the Event Viewer in the Administrative Tools program group.

How Do I Set Up Event Auditing for the Printer?

 To keep track of printer events, go to the Auditing item in the Printer Properties Security tab. By default, no groups are selected for auditing, so you must select a group. Click on the Add button and a list of possible groups to audit appears. Select a group, click on the Add button so that the group name appears in the lower box, and then click OK. Once you've selected a group for auditing, you can choose the events that you wish to audit from the list. For each group that you audit, you can set up a special auditing schedule.

Separator Pages for Sorting Documents

Separator pages are extra pages that are printed before the main document. They can be used to identify the owner of the print job, record the print time and date, print a message to users of the printer, and record the job number. Separator pages are useful mainly for keeping documents sent to the printer separate from each other. If a number of people are using the same networked printer, you probably want to use separator pages to help them keep their documents sorted. Several separator page files are included with NT Server, and you can also create your own by using Notepad.

Creating a Separator Page

To make your own separator page file, begin a new document in Notepad. On the first line, type a single character and then press Enter. This character will now be the *escape character* that tells the system that you're performing a function, not entering text. You should use a character that you don't anticipate needing for anything else, such as a dollar sign ($) or pound sign (#). Here, I've used a dollar sign as the escape character.

Now that you've established your escape code, you can customize your separator page with the following variables:

Variable	What It Does
BS	Prints text in single-width block characters until $U is encountered.
$D	Prints the date the job was printed. The representation of the date is the same as the Date Format in the International section in Control Panel.
$E	Ejects a page from the printer. Use this code to start a new separator page or to end the separator page file. If you get an extra blank separator page when you print, remove this code from your separator page file.
$F*pathname*	Prints the contents of the file specified by path, starting on an empty line. The contents of this file are copied directly to the printer without any processing.
$H*nn*	Sets a printer-specific control sequence, where *nn* is a hexadecimal ASCII code sent directly to the printer. To determine the specific numbers, see your printer manual.
$I	Prints the job number.
$L*xxxx*	Prints all the characters (*xxxx*) following it until another escape code is encountered. You can use this code to enter text exhorting people to not waste paper on unnecessary print jobs, to have a nice day, to save the planet, or do anything else that you like.
$N	Prints the user name of the person that submitted the job.
$*n*	Skips *n* number of lines (from 0 through 9). Skipping 0 lines moves printing to the next line.

Variable	What It Does
$T	Prints the time the job was printed. The representation of the time is the same as the Time Format in the International section in Control Panel.
$U	Turns off block character printing.
$Wnn	Sets the width of the separator page. The default width is 80; the maximum width is 256. Any printable characters beyond this width are truncated.

As an example, consider the following Notepad separator page file:

```
$
$N
$D
$L TEST SEPARATOR. DON'T USE THESE; SAVE THE PLANET.
$T
$E
```

It nets you this output:

```
Mark 4/11/1997 TEST SEPARATOR. DON'T USE THESE; SAVE THE PLANET.
9:21:22 AM
```

Notice that, even though I pressed Enter after each entry, the output is all on one line. This is because I didn't use the $n character to tell the separator page to skip lines between entries.

How Do I Create a Separator Page?

If you don't want to use any of the default separator pages included with NT Server, you can create your own with Notepad. Begin a new document, and, on the first line, type a single character to be the escape character (the system's indicator that the next character is a code). Choose an escape character that you won't need for anything else in the file. On the following lines, use the escape character and the variables described above to make a custom separator page.

Choosing a Separator Page

To specify a particular separator page, choose the General tab in the Properties dialog box and then click the Separator Page button. You see a dialog box that looks like Figure 8.26.

If no separator file is listed, you can select one by typing in the name of the file you want to use or by browsing for the correct file by clicking on the Browse button. Once you've selected a separator file, the page with that information in it prints out before every print job.

To stop using a separator page, just go to the Separator Page dialog box and delete the entry in the text box. There is no <None> setting in a drop-down list as there is in some menus. It's a pity that the separator page selection isn't set up like that, but I suppose it's not because custom separator pages wouldn't necessarily be in the WINNT35\ SYSTEM32 directory where all the defaults are.

When specifying a separator page, you can type a filename (if you're already in the proper path to find the file) or the filename and path (if you're in another path). You must, however, use a file that is *physically* located on the computer that controls the printer for which you're specifying the separator page. Why can't you use any file that's accessible from the network? The answer is that the computer that controls the printer stores separator page information in its registry, and so it needs to have that information available locally. If you tell the printer to use a separator file that is not located on its hard disk or one that is

FIGURE 8.26

Printer Details dialog box

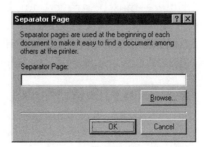

not in the path that you've indicated, you get an error message that says, "Could not set printer: The specified separator file is invalid."

Solving Common Shared Printing Problems

While printing under NT is usually trouble-free, you may run into a few problems. The remainder of this chapter describes some of the most common problems and tells you how to solve them.

Connection Problems

Connection problems appear before you can even use the printer.

Can't Connect to Printer   When connecting to a printer in the Printer Wizard, you may get an error message that says, "Could not connect to the printer: The remote procedure call failed and did not execute." This isn't really your fault. This problem usually occurs after you've set up and then deleted multiple printers, logging off and on in between removes and setups. Essentially, the registry gets confused. If you see this message, click OK in the dialog box with the error message, and then log off and then back on again. When you get back on, you should be able to connect to the printer.

Can't Create Printer   When you go to the Printer icon to remove a printer or create a new one, that option—Create Printer or Remove Printer—may be grayed out, indicating that it's inactive. If you see this, check to make sure that you're logged on as a member of a group with privileges to create or remove printers; only Administrators and Power Users have this privilege.

No Default Printer   If you try to set up a printer from several layers deep in dialog boxes and then select Help while you're still working on the setup, you may get a message that says, "No default printer.

Use Printer Wizard to install and select default printer." You may get this message even though a default printer is already installed. To avoid this bug, set up printers before trying to use Help.

Deleted Port   While it is possible to delete a port in the Printer Properties dialog box, be warned that it's a lot easier to delete a port than it is to retrieve it. If you blow away a port, you need to use the Registry Editor to replace it.

To retrieve a printer port:

1. Start the Registry Editor (REGEDT32.EXE) and go to the following subkey in the HKEY_LOCAL_MACHINE on Local Machine hive:

    ```
    Software\Microsoft\Windows NT\CurrentVersion\Ports
    ```

2. From the Edit menu, choose Add Value.

3. In the Value Name box, type the printer port that you deleted (for example, COM1: or LPT1:). Keep the default value in the Data box (REG_SZ) and click on OK.

4. In the String box, type the appropriate settings that correspond to the port you typed in the Value Name box. For example, you would type 9600,n,8,1 for any COM ports.

Table 8.1 tells you exactly what the values in each section should be for each port. If you're doing this fix, this is a list of the appropriate settings for each port.

TABLE 8.1   Port Settings

Port Name	Data Type	String Value
COM1	REG SZ	9600,n,8,1
COM2	REG SZ	9600,n,8,1
COM3	REG SZ	9600,n,8,1
COM4	REG SZ	9600,n,8,1

TABLE 8.1   Port Settings (Continued)

Port Name	Data Type	String Value
FILE	REG SZ	empty
LPT1	REG SZ	empty
LPT2	REG SZ	empty
LPT3	REG SZ	empty

5. Exit the Registry Editor. Log off and then log back on, and the port should be back.

WARNING   Be *very careful* when using the Registry Editor! It's very possible to completely screw up your NT Server installation with it. In fact, you could screw it up enough that you have to reinstall the operating system to fix the problem.

Basic Troubleshooting Tips

The sections above don't cover every possible printing problem and solution, but are instead meant to give you an idea of what *could* go wrong and how to fix it. If your problem isn't dealt with above, this section should give you an idea of how to attack it.

Software

If your print job isn't coming out quite like you expected it to (or at all), make sure that the printer is set up correctly. Have you specified an existing printer port? What about the printer driver? Did you install the right driver for your printer? If so, you may want to try deleting and re-installing the printer driver. (Remove the printer from the system and re-create it.)

The problem could also be in the application. Can you print to another printer? Can you print to that printer from another application? If it's a DOS application, try copying the driver file to the application's directory and then try to print again.

Hardware

It's perfectly possible for something to go wrong with the printer itself, or the cabling, especially if you can't print from DOS. Once you've checked the printer itself to make sure that it is online, plugged in, and it has paper, check the connection. Will the printer work when attached to another parallel or serial port? You could have a network problem. Try printing the file directly from the print server and see if that works. If nothing else works, try removing extraneous cards from the print server to see if there is a hardware conflict.

Keeping Track of Printing Errors

Being able to choose whether to be notified when someone prints on a remote machine is a new and handy feature of the Print Server Properties dialog box. Those of you familiar with NT 3.51 or before probably remember that you had to go into the Registry in order to turn off the printer notification message, the message that shows up on your server every time someone on a remote machine prints a document. With NT Server 4, it is much easier.

In the Printers window, pull down the File menu, choose Print Server Properties, and click on the Advanced tab. This tab offers several options. A check in the last check box, "Notify when remote documents are printed," gives you the same print notification message you may already be familiar with.

But turning off the notification does not mean compromising security because you can keep a log file to record the status of spooled print jobs. A log file is a combined file for all the printers attached to your print server. Notice in this same dialog box that you can tell the print server to log the following events:

- Error events

- Warning events

- Information events

Just type in a file name and path where it asks for a spool folder. A default file is already listed for you.

You can also tell the server to take a more active role by beeping at you if a spooler event fails. To do that, click the "Beep on errors of remote documents" check box.

Two other tabs appear in the Print Server Properties dialog box. The Ports tab is a recap of the Ports tab in the Printer Properties dialog box, and the Forms tab allows you to define margin sizes. These forms are stored on the print server itself, so all printers can access them.

By now, you've got a server set up, some users, a few shares, and a printer or two. Even though all network administrators know that it's a lot easier to run a network if it doesn't have any users, let's throw caution to the wind and get a few users' PCs hooked up to the network. We do that in the next chapter.

CHAPTER

NINE

Connecting PCs to NT Networks

Once a server is up and running, the next thing you want to do is to set up some workstations to access that server. I'll assume that you already know how to install an Ethernet or token-ring card in your system. What I'm concerned with in this chapter is installing the software to support all of the different workstations that you are likely to find out there: DOS, DOS and Windows 3.*x*, Windows for Workgroups, and Windows 95 workstations.

Setting up workstations is difficult, and you could, in truth, probably figure most of it out yourself—you will find no rocket science in this chapter. What you will find is a walk-through of setting up each kind of workstation. My examples assume that

- I'm attaching to a workgroup and a domain called ORION

- The user's name is MarkM

- The initial password is "hi"

- The workstations will connect with Ethernet

The logical place to start is with DOS.

Connecting a DOS Workstation to NT

DOS is the worst of the bunch to attach to NT, as DOS has no intrinsic knowledge of networking. You must add a few programs to your DOS workstation's AUTOEXEC.BAT and CONFIG.SYS in order to add networking capabilities to DOS.

To Use or Not to Use the Network Client Administrator

NT comes with a program called the Network Client Administrator (NCA) that is *supposed* to make this easier, but I recommend against using it. NCA is intended to simplify the process of getting network code onto a PC, and in some ways it accomplishes that. Basically, you tell the NCA what kind of network card you have, what protocol you want to use, what user name to use, and the like. Then you shove an already-formatted floppy into drive A, and the NCA adds files to the floppy. You then take that single floppy over to the workstation and boot from the floppy. Enough code is on the floppy to get the PC to the NT Server, and from there to kick off a batch file that installs the Microsoft Network Client 3.0 for DOS. Under NT 3.*x*, you could alternatively install Windows for Workgroups from the NT CD-ROM, but that's changed with NT 4, and now you can only install the DOS client software.

Anyway, I recommend against using the Network Client Administrator for several reasons:

- It's not *that* convenient. It's annoying to have a DOS-formatted floppy on hand before the process starts, and there is no reason why Microsoft couldn't have built the NCA to produce DOS-formatted floppies for the convenience of its network administrators.

- While the NCA simplifies the network client setup process, it's not complete by any means. All you tell the NCA is, "I have a 3Com 3C509 card," not, "I have a 3Com 3C509 card set to I/O address 210 and IRQ 11." The NCA requires you to go through the whole process of creating the floppy, after which you have to use the Notepad or something like it to edit a file called PROTOCOL.INI, which is in A:\NET.

- If the NCA includes the drivers for your card, you're in good shape. But if not, then the NCA is of virtually no help. Over the years I have used a number of Ethernet cards from Standard

Microsystems Corporation (SMC), and I've found them to be fast, well-designed cards. But for some reason, Microsoft chose not to include all of them in the NCA's list of known boards. This made installing SMC cards so cumbersome with the NCA that I stopped using the NCA, and not only that, but I don't buy many SMC cards any more, either.

The Microsoft Network Client 3 for MS-DOS

Instead of using the Network Client Administrator, my recommendation is that you create two disks called the Microsoft Network Client 3 Installation Disks 1 and 2. Doing that is simple. You can create these two disks by looking in a directory called CLIENTS on the NT Server CD-ROM. In CLIENTS, there is a directory called MSCLIENT, and under that two directories named DISK1 and DISK2. Just copy all of the DISK1 directory onto one diskette and all of the DISK2 directory onto another diskette—each will fit on a 1.44MB floppy. Label both disks and carry them around with you on network calls.

Installing Microsoft Network Client 3

After you've created the disks, just walk over to the DOS machine, put the first disk into the A: drive, change to that drive, and type **setup**.

Setup will show you the familiar blue screen with white letters that announces you are about to install the Microsoft Network Client 3 for MS-DOS. The first question the screen asks is where to put the network software. C:\NET is the default, and that's as good a place as any. Next, you identify your network card. If you have a card that's not on this list, you will be happy to know that this program is much more forgiving than the Network Client Administrator. You just pick "Network adapter not shown on list." Soon you are prompted for a disk with the network drivers. You received those drivers with the network card.

Now, you are *never* going to find a diskette labeled "Drivers for Microsoft Network Client 3 for MS-DOS." Instead, look for a diskette labeled "NDIS 3.0 driver." Some boards don't call them NDIS 3; they call them "Windows for Workgroups version 3.11 drivers." It's the same in any case.

Next the setup program offers to use more memory for greater speed. Go ahead and experiment with this. I've found that sometimes the Network Client can't load at all with TCP/IP if I give it the extra buffers, so I press C to skip the extra buffers. Then the setup program asks for a user name; fill that in.

After that, the setup program presents you with a sort of overall setup configuration screen labeled "Setup for Microsoft Network Client v3.0 for MS-DOS," with three main sections:

- Change names
- Change setup options
- Change network configuration

You first tackle "Change names." It lets you modify

- The default user name
- The PC's machine name
- The name of the workgroup that the PC will be a member of
- The name of the domain (if any) that the PC's user will log on to

Fill all of these in. I usually give my workgroups and domains the same name, and I recommend that you do also. When you're finished in that section, you get to "Change setup options." It lets you

- Change redir options
- Change startup options

- Change logon validation

- Change net popup key

You don't need to do anything with any of these options except Change logon validation. By default, it doesn't log you on to the domain. Change that option to "logon to domain."

The third and final section of the setup process is called "Change network configuration." It's divided into two parts, network board and network protocols. First you to pick a network board and then you either remove the board, add a new board, or change settings on the board. You almost certainly have to pick "change settings" and set the I/O address and/or the hardware interrupt (IRQ) setting of the network board.

About all you do in the Protocol part is choose a protocol. If it's TCP/IP, then you go through the usual TCP/IP exercise of specifying IP address, subnet masks, and the like, unless you are using DHCP servers, in which case you need only choose "Use DHCP to obtain IP address." If you have no idea what I'm talking about here, hang on until Chapter 14; it will make a lot more sense then.

Once I've set it all the way I like, I choose "The listed options are correct." Network Client Setup then copies some files to my system, modifies AUTOEXEC.BAT and CONFIG.SYS, and prompts me to reboot. I reboot and then log on to the server.

Dealing with Passwords

Suppose I've created a new user account named MarkM with the password "hi." Now, remember, the server requires that I change the password immediately, as this is a new account. Believe it or not, changing my domain password isn't intuitive on the DOS network client. That's unfortunate, because the first contact that any user has with the network is that first logon, which requires the user to figure out how to change a password. So let's see how…

When I reboot the DOS client, I see the system start up and say:

```
Type your user name, or press ENTER if it is MARKM:
```

Since I'm MarkM, I press Enter.

The PC then says:

```
Type your password:
```

Now, believe it or not, the password I am being asked for *isn't* the NT user password "hi" that I just created. Instead, this is a kind of convenience that the Client for Microsoft Networks offers me. You see, you may end up having to use a number of passwords on the network—passwords for things that you may use on the network but aren't covered by the domain. The Client for Microsoft Networks keeps track of all of those passwords for you, so you only need to enter them once. After you've entered them, the Client for Microsoft Networks supplies them automatically.

These passwords are kept in an encrypted file called a *password list file*. You can recognize them because they have the extension PWL. What `Type your password:` really says is, "I want to create a password file, and I'll need a password to lock the password file." A *really* annoying part about this is that the Client for Microsoft Networks requires this password, even if it doesn't keep a password list. For some benighted reason, Microsoft seems to be trying to ensure a level of security by requiring this password *in addition to* the domain password. People have figured out ways to crack the password list files, so I recommend that you don't create one.

In any case, I need something to shut this thing up, so I enter the password **hello** and press Enter. The computer then responds:

```
There is no password-list file for user MARKM.
Do you want to create one? (Y/N) [N]:
```

Only *then* does it ask me for my password to get onto my domain:

```
Please enter your password for the domain ORION:
```

Now, I enter **hi** and get this message:

```
Error 2242: The password of this user has expired.
```

It's almost comical: after all that work, I get the error message that the password has expired.

I said "almost" comical; I do wish Microsoft would make this a bit more logical. They *did* make this first-time logon much easier with later operating systems, as you'll see a bit later in this chapter. In a sense, however, this is actually a *good* message. It tells you that the domain recognized your password, even though it has expired. If you had punched in the wrong password, you would have seen some other error message.

Now you have to change your password so that you can get onto the domain, but it looks like you've got to log on before you can change your password, right? No, actually not; there's a command for that called NET PASSWORD.

Ah, but which password does NET PASSWORD work on, the bogus local password or the domain password? By default, it works on the bogus local password, but there's an option to change the domain password. By specifying the option /domain:, you can change the domain password. You can do it all in one line, like so:

```
net password /domain:orion markm hi hello
```

That's a long line, so let's take it apart. The net password you understand. The /domain:orion says, "The password I'm changing is the password for the orion domain, not my local password list. Markm hi hello is, respectively, my user name, my old password, and my new password."

When I press Enter after I type the command line, I see this useful message:

```
Error 7210: There is no entry for the specified user in the
[Password Lists] section of the SYSTEM.INI file.
```

Yes, it's annoying, but just ignore it. The domain password has been changed just fine. Now I can log on for real, like so (I've included my responses in italics):

```
net logon markm
Type your password: hi
Please enter your password for the domain ORION: hello
The server \\ORION01 successfully logged you on as MARKM.
Your privilege level on this domain is USER.
The command completed successfully.
```

Notice that I had to type the local workstation password first to make the local network software happy, then the domain password. If, by the way, you create a password list, you will never again be prompted for the domain password because your workstation will remember it and fill it in for you automatically.

Connecting to Directories and Print Shares

Now that I'm on the server, there are three basic things to do:

- Browse the network

- Connect to a directory share

- Connect to a print share

Browsing is simple. I just type **NET VIEW** and I see something like this:

```
Servers available in workgroup ORION.
Server Name      Remark
```

```
\\MICRON133
\\ORION01
The command completed successfully.
```

I want to see what's in the ORION01 server, so I can see what shares it has, so I type **NET VIEW \\ORION01**. That produces this:

```
Shared resources at \\ORION01
Sharename    Type        Comment

C         Disk    Main share on ORION01
cdrom     Disk    CD-ROM drive on ORION01
clients   Disk
HP4M      Print   HP LaserJet 4M on LPT1:
NETLOGON  Disk    Logon server share
PUBLIC    Disk    Public directory
USERS     Disk
The command completed successfully.
```

I'm looking for some files on the PUBLIC share, so I connect to that. I attach to it as my E: drive by typing **net use e: \\orion01\public**. Let's pick that command apart, as you'll use it a lot. First, NET USE is the command that says to go find a particular network resource and connect it to a local drive letter. The drive letter I'll use is e:.

If you plan to use drive letters above E:, then you have to add a LAST-DRIVE command to CONFIG.SYS. By default, DOS only sets aside enough space for five drive letters. If you want network drives F:, G:, and H:, add the line LASTDRIVE=H to your CONFIG.SYS. I usually just add the command LASTDRIVE=Z to my CONFIG.SYS files as a matter of course, but if you're running old Novell software, that may not be a good idea. Check with whoever runs the rest of your network before you change the LASTDRIVE statement on all of your computers.

The last part of the command line, \\orion01\public in our case, is the Universal Naming Convention reference to the shared directory. Remember how they're built up? Two backslashes and the server name—that's \\Orion01—and then one backslash and the share name, making \\orion01\public. You can use lowercase or uppercase, it doesn't matter. You get a confirmation that it worked with this message:

```
The command completed successfully.
```

The next time I start up the network client on this system, it will automatically restore this E: drive. If I want to break the connection, I type the following:

```
NET USE E: /delete
```

I can do the same thing to tell my system to use a network printer. As you know, the printer ports on PCs are called LPT1, LPT2, and LPT3. Even though no printer is on this workstation, I'll tell the network software to direct any requests to print to LPT1 to another printer instead, the network printer HP4M. Again, doing that requires a NET USE command:

```
NET USE LPT1: \\ORION01\HP4M
```

The only difference is that I told the network to map to LPT1, not a drive letter, and to use the share HP4M on server ORION01.

You can log off with a net logoff command, and if you ever want to see your current connections, type **net use** all by itself.

Attaching Windows Workstations to NT Networks

Many of you are using one of three kinds of Windows on your workstations: Windows 3.1, Windows for Workgroups 3.11, or Windows 95. If you're using Windows 3.1, you already know how to attach to your NT network. All you have to do is load the Microsoft Network Client and start Windows 3.1 on top of it. If you're using Windows for Workgroups, it's even easier.

Part of the process of installing Workgroups is identifying your network card to the Workgroups setup program and identifying the network card that you're using. Once the Windows for Workgroups setup program is done, you're pretty much connected, except you still have to identify yourself to the domain. I will soon show you how to do that.

Now, if you didn't choose any of the network options when you set up Windows for Workgroups or you have to do some changes to a Windows for Workgroups machine, knowing where all the network setup stuff is can be useful, so let's go through all of it.

Setting up the network portion of Windows for Workgroups happens in two different places, unfortunately. The problem has been fixed in Windows 95 and Windows NT, but fiddling around with network setup in Windows for Workgroups requires doing some work in Network Setup. To find Network Setup, either go to the Main group in the Program Manager, start up Windows Setup, and click Options/Change Network Settings, or go to the Network group and start up the program Network Setup. The rest of the network configuration happens in the Control Panel in the Network applet.

Doing the Network Setup Work

To start out configuring a Windows for Workgroups workstation to access a domain, go to the Network Setup program. Its opening screen looks like Figure 9.1.

FIGURE 9.1

Network Setup screen

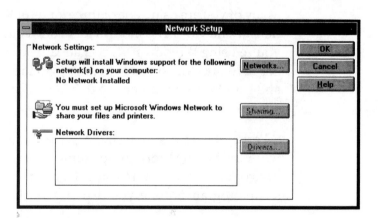

There are three sections to this window. Up top, you choose the redirector or client software that you want your workstation to use. In the middle, you enable or disable the file and print sharing feature of Windows for Workgroups. In the bottom part of the screen, you load network board drivers and protocols, and control settings for board drivers and protocols.

I start off by telling my workstation to load the client for Microsoft networks. To do that, click Networks. You see the dialog box in Figure 9.2.

Click on Install Microsoft Windows Network and click OK. You go back to the Network Setup dialog box. Redirectors are no good without some data, which they get from protocols, which protocols in turn get from boards. To add a board, click the Drivers button. You see the dialog box in Figure 9.3.

Click on the Add Adapter button and choose either a particular adapter or let Windows for Workgroups automatically detect your adapter. If you know what adapter is in your system, I strongly recommend specifying it rather than having Windows for Workgroups automatically detect it. Automatic detection can sometimes crash the system.

FIGURE 9.2

Choosing a network
redirector

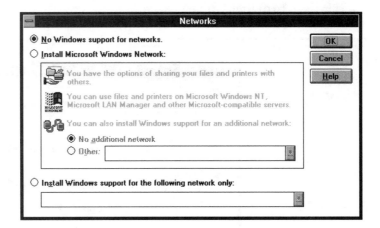

FIGURE 9.3

Adapter and protocol control window

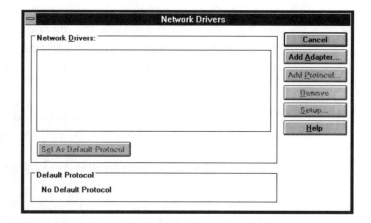

Once you've picked an adapter, your adapter wants you to make hardware settings such as the I/O address, IRQ, memory addresses, whether it's 10baseT or 10base2, and things like that. Fill in the information. When you're done, the dialog box will look something like the one in Figure 9.4.

Notice that it automatically includes the IPX and NetBEUI protocols. Now, in my network I don't make much use of IPX, so I get rid of it by clicking on it and then clicking Remove. It asks if I'm sure, and I confirm that I am.

FIGURE 9.4

The Network Setup dialog with the board filled in

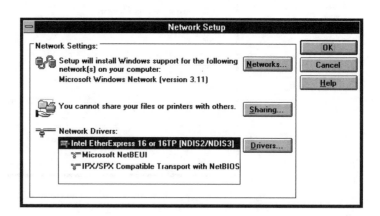

You can choose to make a protocol the "default" protocol, but in the final analysis it doesn't mean anything. One more problem before I go on: my Intel EtherExpress is set to IRQ 5, but the program never gave me the chance to set that. So I click on the Intel EtherExpress line and the Setup button. That lets me alter the IRQ setting. Note that this is specific to network cards; you may or may not have to do this on your system.

Click Close and you're back at the Network Setup screen. As you've seen, there's a button that controls whether the workstation shares its files with other PCs or not. By now, you know that my advice is not to do that. Click OK in the Network Setup screen, and you see the Microsoft Windows Network Names dialog box in Figure 9.5.

The defaults are all wrong, so I fill in the correct values and click OK. The Network Setup program then copies the files and asks to reboot.

FIGURE 9.5

Prompting for network names

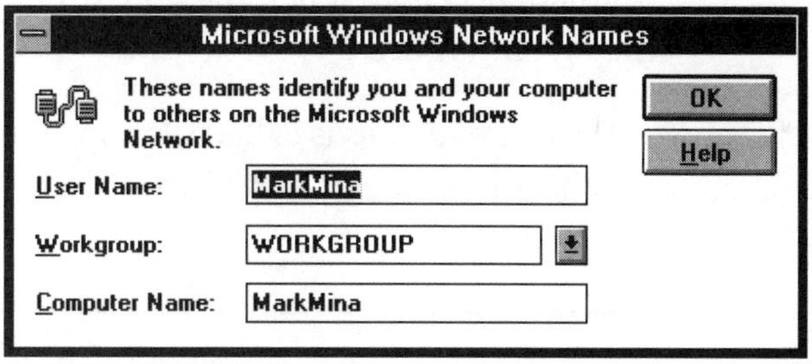

Setting and Changing
Domain Passwords
=================

Do that and type **win** to start up Windows for Workgroups. A dialog box labeled Welcome to Windows for Workgroups prompts you for a name and password. As before, it's not the real domain password, but we'll get to that. You are prompted whether or not to create a password-list file. Again, it's your call whether to do it or not. Just to be different, I let it create a password list file this time around. It will ask you to type in the password again.

TIP

It's a pretty good idea to make your local password the same as your domain password. That's because when you try to access a domain, the domain interrogates your Windows for Workgroups workstation for a password, and, if you haven't yet told Windows for Workgroups your domain password (more on this later), Windows for Workgroups automatically responds with your local password.

You are then logged on to Windows for Workgroups, but not yet to your domain. In the case of my example, the domain isn't yet aware of MarkM. Before trying to access domain resources, I recommend that you set up your Windows for Workgroups workstation to explicitly log on to the domain. To do that, open the Control Panel and double-click the Network applet. It is illustrated in Figure 9.6.

This is an important dialog box. As you can see, you can use it to change the default logon user name or the workgroup. To log on to a domain, however, click the Startup button. You see a dialog box like the one in Figure 9.7.

The center group is called Options for Enterprise Networking. Click the check box labeled Log On to Windows NT or LAN Manager Domain

FIGURE 9.6

Control Panel
Network applet

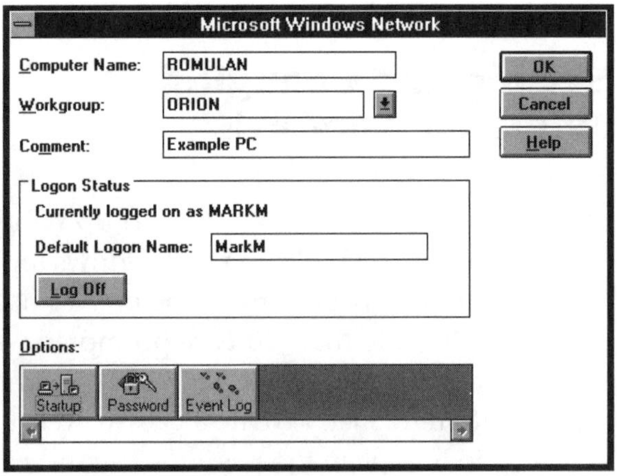

FIGURE 9.7

Startup Settings
dialog box

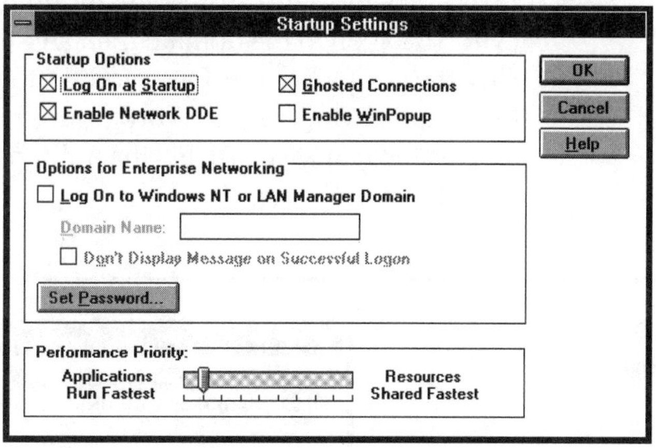

and enter the domain's name. Now, in my case I have to change the password for MarkM, as it's a new account, so I need a way to change my domain's password. I can do that by clicking the Set Password button. I see the dialog box in Figure 9.8.

This dialog box lets me, first of all, inform my Windows for Workgroups workstation what my domain password is so it can automatically supply the password when it logs me on to the domain. This dialog box also gives me a simple vehicle for changing my domain password. When I'm done, I click OK to return to the dialog box labeled Microsoft Windows Network (see Figure 9.6).

FIGURE 9.8

Setting and changing a
domain password from
Windows for Workgroups

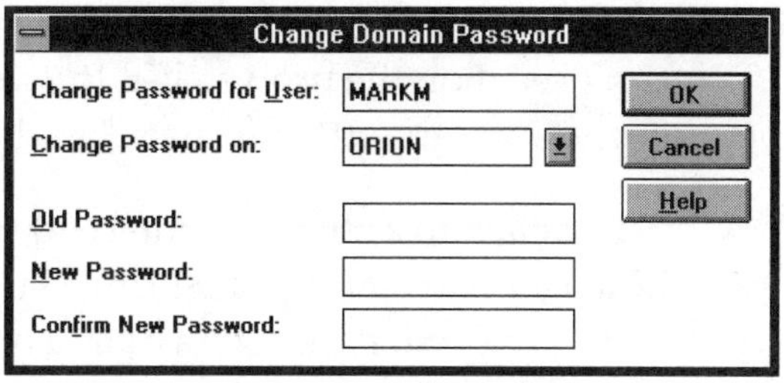

You're pretty much set now, but if you click OK, the system will want to reboot before you can get onto the domain. That's not necessary, however. To log on to the domain then and there without rebooting, just click the Log Off button. Once you've done that, its label changes to Log On; click it. Windows for Workgroups prompts you for your *Windows for Workgroups* password. Fill that in, and then you should get the dialog box shown in Figure 9.9.

FIGURE 9.9

Domain Welcome dialog box

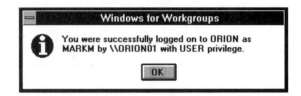

Attaching to Network Resources

Now that you're on the network, you can attach to a network resource. First, what's out there? You can see that by starting up the Windows for Workgroups File Manager and clicking Disk/Connect Network Drive. You see a dialog box like the one in Figure 9.10.

This is the Windows for Workgroups version of a browse list. You can see in the figure that I have three workgroups named ACADEMY, ORION, and TED, and that ORION includes servers named MICRON133 and ORION01 at the moment. If you click on a server, as I have clicked on ORION01, you see the shares available on that server. Click OK and you're connected. If the share is a hidden one, then, of course, you can't see it on the browse list. But you can directly punch in a UNC such as \\server01\myshare$ in the Path field.

To attach to a shared printer, go to the Main group of the Program Manager and start up the Print Manager. Then click Printer/Connect Network Printer. You see a dialog box almost identical to the directory browse list. Choose a networked printer and Print Manager loads the appropriate print driver.

FIGURE 9.10

Windows for Workgroups
directory share browse list

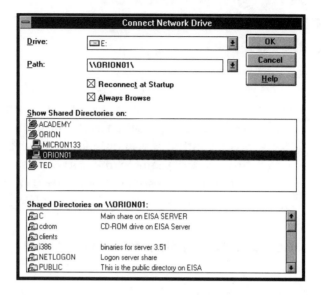

Just to reiterate, you can't change your domain password by clicking Control Panel, then Network, then Password because that changes the local Windows for Workgroups password. I've already explained it, but just as a reminder you can change the domain password by opening the Control Panel, opening Network, clicking Startup, and clicking Set Password (which refers to the domain password).

Before I leave the topic of Windows for Workgroups, let me make a very important point: when Microsoft came out with NT, they improved the networking part of Windows for Workgroups a bit. On the CD-ROM, in the Clients\wfw\Update directory, you see a few files, fewer than ten. If you already have Windows for Workgroups on a computer, then attach it to the NT server and get those files. Copy them to both your Windows and your Windows\System directories, and reboot. Doing so will speed up your networking and at the same time will make your NT connection go a bit more smoothly, because there are some bug fixes in the revised code.

Attaching Windows 95 Workstations to NT Networks

Many of you have moved from Windows 3.*x* or Workgroups to the newer Windows 95. In actual fact, Windows 95 is really just Windows for Workgroups with a pretty face, but finding your way around network controls if you only know Windows for Workgroups can be a little tricky. Again, let me start off by assuming that your workstation knows nothing so far about networking (after all, it's easy enough to get it to that state) and then work from there.

Configuring the Workstation

In Windows 95, click Start, Control Panel, and Networking. You see a screen like the one in Figure 9.11.

FIGURE 9.11

Networking page in Control Panel for Windows 95

As before, this needs a redirector/client, at least one protocol, and at least one board driver. You can add any of those things by clicking the Add button. You then see the dialog box shown in Figure 9.12.

I load a redirector or, as it's more commonly called these days, a *network client.* I click Client and I see the dialog box in Figure 9.13.

Microsoft ships both an NT-compatible and a NetWare-compatible client. To talk to NT networks, I choose the Client for Microsoft Networks and click OK. Now, recall that a client (redirector) sits on top of a protocol, and a protocol sits on top of a board driver. That means that just loading a client without a protocol and board would sort of leave the client software hanging in empty space, so to speak. Therefore, the Control Panel asks also for a board driver, as you see in Figure 9.14.

FIGURE 9.12

Choosing a redirector, protocol, or board type

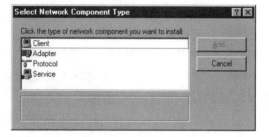

FIGURE 9.13

Picking a Microsoft-written network redirector/client

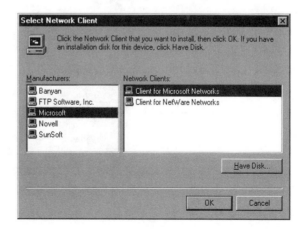

FIGURE 9.14

Prompting for a network
card type

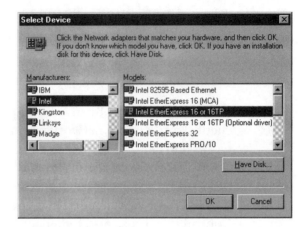

When I choose a board, the Control Panel automatically loads the
NetBEUI and IPX protocols, as did Windows for Workgroups. You
can see that in Figure 9.15.

FIGURE 9.15

New state of the
Network applet of
the Control Panel

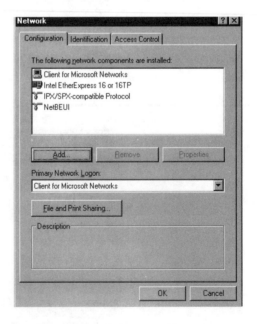

I've already said I don't use IPX, so I highlight it and click Remove; that may or may not make sense for your network. Then I have to double-click on the network card icon to set its I/O address, IRQ, and the like. Again, this will vary from network board to network board. Click the Advanced and Resources tabs to see what you can set for your particular network board, and click Close when you're done.

Attaching to the Network

You then go back to the Network applet. Click the Identification tab to continue. You see a screen similar to the one in Figure 9.16.

In the figure, I've filled in a machine name, a workgroup, and a description. But what about the domain? Where do I specify a domain? Return to the Configuration tab and double-click on the Client for Microsoft Networks. You see a dialog box like the one in Figure 9.17.

FIGURE 9.16

Identification tab of Network applet

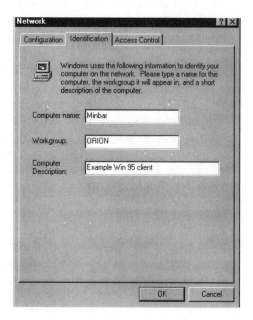

FIGURE 9.17

Setting the
domain settings

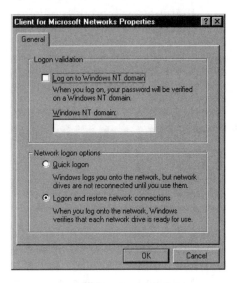

To log onto a domain, just check the box labeled Log on to Windows
NT domain and fill in the domain's name. Click OK to return to the
Network applet and OK again to tell the Control Panel that you're fin-
ished. It will load some files and reboot.

Once your computer has rebooted, you'll see a new login dialog box,
one with three fields: username, password, and domain.

Remember how much trouble it was to change the domain password
the first time around on Windows for Workgroups? Well, in contrast,
you're going to love Windows 95 because it produces a nice dialog box
that tells you that it's recognized your domain password, but that the
password has expired, and would you change it please? It even provides fields in which to type the new password. Much improved!

Once you're in, you can browse your network with the Network
Neighborhood (I imagine calling the folder "browse network" would
have been too complex). Open up Network Neighborhood and you
see a screen similar to Figure 9.18.

FIGURE 9.18

Browsing a network with
Windows 95

Open a server and you can see what it offers. In Figure 9.19, you can
see the shares that ORION01 offers.

Actually, I cheated and clicked View/Details so that you could see the
comments, but that's a basic browse. You can map to a share by right-
clicking on it, choosing Map Network Drive, and clicking OK. In the
same way, you can attach to a shared printer. Look at Figure 9.19 and
you can see that the Network Neighborhood shows not only the directory shares, but the printer shares as well.

To attach to a network printer, click Start, Settings, and Printers. You
see an option to create a new printer. Click on that and you start a
wizard that leads you through the process. First, the wizard asks if
you'll be adding a local or network printer, and you choose network.

FIGURE 9.19

Listing a server's shares

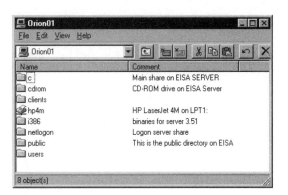

Click Next, and it asks where to find the printer. In response, you can either punch a UNC right in or browse the network. It also asks if you print from DOS programs; what it's really asking is whether or not it should map a printer interface name, like LPT1 or COM2, to the network printer. You have to point it to the drivers (they're on the installation CD-ROM or floppies), after which you are prompted to print a test page. Printing a test page is a good idea, so do it.

And that's about it for setting up an NT Server and DOS, Windows, and Windows 95 clients. Now you can get your *PC*-based workstations onto your NT network. But what about your Macs? That's the topic of the next chapter.

CHAPTER

TEN

Making the Mac Connection

ENTERPRISE NETWORKING

Attaching a Macintosh computer to a PC-based network has never been easier than with NT Server. All the software you need to support Mac clients, called Services for Macintosh, is included right in the box for NT Server. There's nothing else to buy.

The ability to support Macintosh clients is significant, since Apple represents a sizable proportion of corporate networked computers. Users of Mac computers are beginning to demand access to the same shared services that PC users enjoy. In fact, Mac users and PC users often work together on shared projects and *require* access to shared information and resources. Bridging requirements are growing, and until now, Mac to DOS connections have been less than easy.

At the same time, supporting Mac clients is a challenge. Perhaps the biggest challenge lies in working with the filing systems of both Mac and DOS-based computers. The Macintosh file system is significantly different than the DOS file system, and any DOS-based server must be able to accommodate these differences. NT Server uses NTFS to provide what looks to a Mac like native file space, while making the same space available to NT, DOS, Windows, and OS/2 clients.

The Features and Benefits of Services for Macintosh

The following list summarizes some of the other features and benefits of Services for Macintosh.

Feature	Benefit
A file server that is fully compliant with Apple-Share Filing Protocol	Mac users access the NT server in the usual way. They may not know that the server is not a Macintosh computer.

Feature	Benefit
Support of Macintosh file name attributes, such as resource forks and data forks (stored as a single NT file), 32-character file names, icons, and access privileges	Mac users don't have to change their file-names or learn a new file naming convention, although this may be desirable if files are to be shared with PC users.
Native support for AppleTalk protocols	A protocol converter (gateway) is not required.
PostScript emulation for non-PostScript printers	Allows Mac users to access PC printers without converting documents.
Access to LaserWriter printers by Windows, NT, DOS, and OS/2 clients	Allows PC users to access Mac printers without converting documents.
255 simultaneous connections to an NT server, using approximately 15K per session	Relatively low overhead for a large number of potential users.
Support for LocalTalk, Ethernet, Token Ring, and FDDI	Macintosh computers can use any Data Link mechanism to connect to the network.
Extension mapping for PC data files	Enables PC files to be recognized by Mac-based applications, for those apps which are not cross-platform.

Mac Connection in a Nutshell

In this chapter, I'll cover all of the things that you have to do to get Macs to talk to your NT Server. First, you have to get the server ready for Mac support. That means you have to load some NT software that enables NT to create Mac-accessible volumes. Then you create the folders that will hold Mac data.

Next you have to load the NT network software on each Mac work-station. Now, Microsoft could have enclosed a Mac-readable diskette with the drivers to allow a Mac to get onto an NT network, but instead they adopted (in my opinion) a more elegant plan. You see, all Macs have networking capabilities built right into their operating system. That networking capability isn't really compatible with NT, however, because it doesn't enforce the kind of security that NT requires. So NT lets the Mac into the domain solely as a guest who can access one file and one file only—the Macintosh NT client software. Your Mac logs on to the NT Server machine, grabs the NT client software, reboots with the new client drivers, and it is then able to conduct itself as an NT-compatible workstation. Very easy, and very clean. Following are the details.

Preparing the Server to Support Your Mac

All of the software to support Services for Macintosh is included in every box of NT Server, although it is not enabled by default. Before installing the components to support Mac clients, you must prepare the NT server as described below.

The Physical Connection

AppleTalk is Apple's built in networking system. LocalTalk is the physical component of AppleTalk—the port, software driver, and cable used to connect Macs. AppleTalk is not a high-performance network like Ethernet; in fact, it's quite a bit slower, at one-fortieth the speed of the average Ethernet.

Macintosh computers can be connected together via a number of data link mechanisms. LocalTalk is the most inexpensive method since just about everything needed to connect this type of network is included with every Mac computer. If the Macs are connected on a LocalTalk network, a LocalTalk card is needed for the server. A router that knows AppleTalk must exist somewhere on the network; NT Server itself can act as a router, if necessary.

Macintosh computers can also be connected together via Ethernet, Token Ring, or FDDI. In this case, just connect the existing PC network to the Mac network—no additional hardware or routing is needed on the NT server.

Unfortunately, NT Server does not support RAS for Mac clients. Remote or dial-in access is not available.

Preparing the NT Server Hard Disk

Two requirements need to be met before Services for Macintosh can be installed on the server drive:

- Services for Macintosh requires an additional 2MB of space on the server drive.

- Folders for Mac clients must exist on an NTFS partition of the server hard disk or on a CD-ROM drive. You need an NTFS partition to load Services for Macintosh.

Getting Services for Macintosh Up and Running

Installation of Services for Macintosh is straightforward, except for a few diversions along the way. These diversions are not very well documented. After a few false starts, here is what seems to be the best procedure for the installation:

1. Install the Services for Macintosh module. This activates the software required for Mac file sharing, print sharing, and application extension mapping. The installation adds some additional tools to your Control Panel, as well as additional selections to your Server Manager and File Manager menus.

2. Set attributes for all the Mac-accessible volumes that you create on the server. Here you can create a logon message and set security and connection limitations.

3. Prepare the Microsoft UAM Volume for use by Mac clients. This volume is created during the installation and contains software for Mac clients that enables user authentication (a fancy word for encrypted passwords). You can connect Mac users at this point and enable user authentication, or you can continue on with the process and create Mac-accessible volumes, as described here.

4. Create Mac-accessible volumes. These are folders of the NTFS partition to which Mac users have access. Mac users won't have access to any other folders or partitions on the server.

Each step is discussed in this section.

Installing Services for Macintosh

Search through the *Installation Guide* in the NT Server box and you will find a chapter called "Services for Macintosh." Just follow the book for this part of the installation. Here's a recap of the procedure, in case you can't find the book:

1. Open Control Panel, double-click Network, and open the Services tab. You see the Network Settings screen shown in Figure 10.1.

2. Click the Add button. You see a dialog box like the one in Figure 10.2. It says something like "Building Network Service Option List." Scroll down the list until you find Services for Macintosh. Select that and click OK.

3. Enter the path where the NT Server software is located (this is probably the drive that contains the CD that NT Server was originally installed from, or the I386 directory on the hard disk).

FIGURE 10.1

FIGURE 10.1

Network Services
dialog box

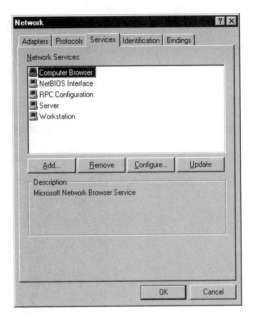

The files to support Mac services are copied to the server drive. Click the Close button and protocol binding will occur. In Figure 10.3, you see the Microsoft AppleTalk Protocol Properties dialog box (now open), where you can set up AppleTalk routing for the network.

FIGURE 10.2

Adding Services
for Macintosh

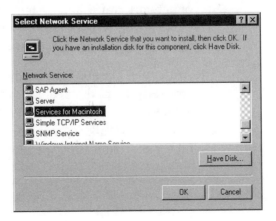

FIGURE 10.3

AppleTalk Protocol
Properties

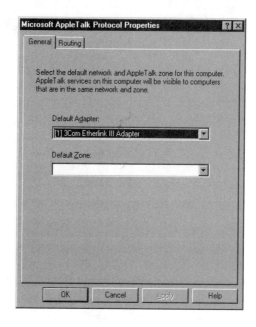

Before you set up routing on the NT Server, there are a few things you should know about routing AppleTalk:

- Using the NT Server as an AppleTalk router enables the entire AppleTalk protocol stack. Many network administrators feel that the AppleTalk protocol is extremely "chatty"; a significant amount of network traffic and system overhead is associated with Apple-Talk. If you are serious about routing AppleTalk traffic, think about using a hardware router and not NT Server.

- An AppleTalk network is divided into *segments*. Each segment, generally a length of cable connected to one of the router's ports (or network adapters, in this case), carries one or more *network IDs*. A LocalTalk segment has a single ID number, whereas an Ethernet, Token Ring, or FDDI segment can each have several network IDs.

- Each network ID supports up to 256 AppleTalk devices. For example, if a length of network cable connects to one NT Server adapter, and that cable has 500 machines connected to it, that segment requires two network IDs (generally configured as a *range* of network IDs for the segment).

- Each network segment can be divided into *zones*. A zone is a logical grouping of machines, generally a group that shares the same purpose. (You might think of an AppleTalk zone as being similar to a Microsoft workgroup.) A LocalTalk segment is a single zone, while Ethernet, Token Ring, and FDDI segments can contain multiple zones. If zones are defined, then each machine on the network, including the NT Server, must be in a default zone.

Let's take an example. Say I have a network with a LocalTalk segment and an Ethernet segment, and I want to use NT Server as a router. The Ethernet segment is connected to a 3Com Etherlink III adapter in the server; I'll configure this adapter for the example.

I want the Ethernet segment to be divided into three logical zones— one for Accounting, one for Graphics, and one for Human Resources. The Ethernet segment has 100 Macintosh devices connected to it.

From the Microsoft AppleTalk Protocol Properties screen, click on the Routing tab. You see a screen similar to Figure 10.4. If an Apple-Talk router already exists on this network segment, network IDs and defined zones are detected and displayed (at which point you probably don't need to configure another router).

Click Enable Routing only if you are using this NT Server as an additional router on the network, and network IDs and zone names already exist. Click both Enable Routing and the Use this router to seed the network check box if you don't have another router.

If you use this router to seed the network, you need to provide a range of network IDs for that segment. I use the range From 10 to 10, which is adequate to support up to 256 devices. (These network

FIGURE 10.4

The Routing tab of the
AppleTalk Routing
Properties dialog box

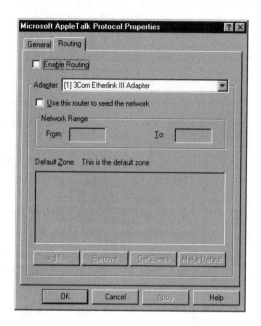

numbers are somewhat arbitrary, although they do correspond to
my overall network numbering plan.) If I had more than 256 devices,
I would create a larger range. A segment of 500 machines, for example,
needs two numbers in the range. I might use the range From 10 to 11, or
the numbers From 100 to 101. The numbers themselves don't matter—
it's the *number of numbers* that is important. Just think of it this way: for
each 256 devices on a segment, you need one number.

Next I add zone names. To add a zone name, click the Add button.
You see a dialog box similar to Figure 10.5.

Enter the zone name and click Add. Add other zone names by using
the same procedure. When all the zone names are added, I'm finished
configuring the router, and the Routing tab looks like Figure 10.6.

FIGURE 10.5

Add Zone dialog box

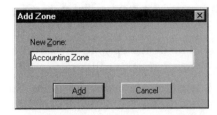

FIGURE 10.6

AppleTalk Routing
completed configuration

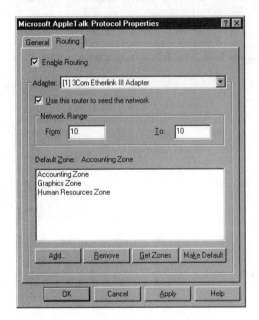

Click OK. The installation is now complete. Click OK in the dialog box that tells you the changes will take effect when you restart Apple-Talk. You will need to reboot the NT server for the changes to take effect, (a dialog box prompts you to reboot). Choose Yes and your machine restarts.

Setting Attributes
for Mac-Accessible Volumes

The next step is to set up access attributes for all of the Macintosh volumes that you'll create. Go to Control Panel (it is open when you restart) and select MacFile. You see the MacFile Properties dialog box, as shown in Figure 10.7. Click on the Attributes button. You see the MacFile Attributes dialog box shown in Figure 10.8.

There's really nothing to change or set in the MacFile Attributes dialog box, unless you want to create a logon message or change the

FIGURE 10.7

MacFile Properties
dialog box

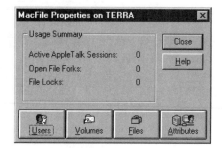

FIGURE 10.8

The MacFile Attributes
dialog box

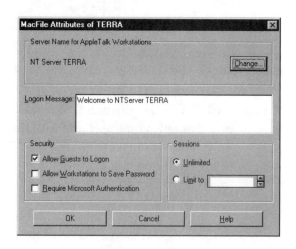

name of the NT server (the name that you use here is the name that appears in the Mac user's Chooser). This does not change the name of the NT server. You will need to reboot the server before Mac clients see the changed name.

At some point, you should come back to this section and check the Require Microsoft Authentication box (it may already be checked on your system—if so, just leave it). This check box enables additional security for Mac clients. Click the OK button when done. Then click the Close button and exit Control Panel.

Setting Up Microsoft Authentication

Any time after restarting the server (this step could be done before the previous step), go to Windows NT Explorer. You see that the Microsoft UAM Volume was added to the NTFS partition, as shown in Figure 10.9. This volume contains the software needed to enable Microsoft Authentication for the Mac clients. Microsoft Authentication enables password encryption for Mac clients. The Mac operating system only supports "clear text" passwords, which can be intercepted by a sniffer device. Clear text passwords violate NT Server's C2 level security.

FIGURE 10.9

The Microsoft UAM volume, now visible in Windows NT Explorer

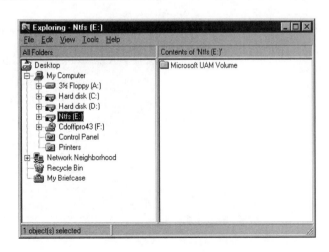

Don't try to get to the volume from the Mac yet. Highlight the volume, select your computer, and go to Server Manager's MacFile menu (it magically appeared when you rebooted with Mac services). On the MacFile menu, highlight the Mac volume, and click the Volume button. You see a dialog box with the volume highlighted, as in Figure 10.10. Click on the button labeled Properties. You see the Properties of dialog box shown in Figure 10.11.

You needn't change this dialog box at all. I bring it to your attention so that you know where to go to control permissions on the volume. (Don't change permissions on *this* volume, as it doesn't contain anything except the Microsoft Authentication software. But other Mac-accessible volumes may require permissions.)

FIGURE 10.10

Configuring the Mac-accessible volume

FIGURE 10.11

Properties of the Mac-Accessible Volume dialog box

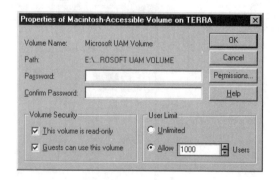

Creating Mac-Accessible Volumes

The final step in the server setup process involves setting up shared folders for Mac clients (called the "Mac-accessible volumes"). This is done in much the same way that shared folders are set up for PC clients. Only permissions are handled differently.

Mac-accessible volumes can be CD-ROMs. Just mark the volume read-only.

First, create a new folder on the NTFS partition. Then, share the folder and follow these steps:

1. From Server Manager, select your computer, select MacFile, Volumes, and select Create Volume.

2. Enter the volume name (usually the name of the folder you created).

3. Enter the full path name for the folder, as seen in the example in Figure 10.12.

4. Set volume security and user limits, if required.

5. Click the Permissions button. You see a screen similar to the one in Figure 10.13.

FIGURE 10.12

Creating a new Mac-accessible volume

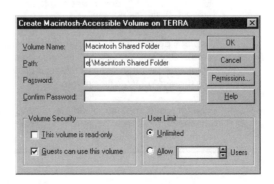

FIGURE 10.13

Directory Permissions
dialog box

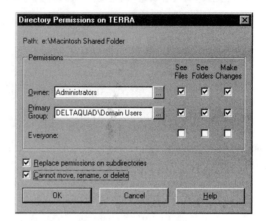

You've probably seen a screen like this before, except the permissions look a little different. Table 10.1 explains what these permissions mean.

TABLE 10.1   Mac versus NT Server Permissions

Mac Permission	NT Server Equivalent
See Files Allows the owner, Primary group, or Everyone to see and open the files that are contained within this folder.	Read
See Folders Allows the owner, Primary group, or Everyone to see and open any folders contained within this folder.	Read
Make Changes Allows the owner, Primary group, or Everyone to add or delete files and folders, and save changes to files in this folder.	Write, Delete
Replace permission on subdirectories Copies the permissions you just set to all folders within this volume or folder. (This is the same as "Make all enclosed folders like this one" on Mac file servers.)	*Same*
Cannot move, rename, or delete Prevents the volume or folder from being moved, renamed, or deleted by Mac users.	*Same*

There's one other main difference between this screen and the others you've seen. With NT Server, permissions for a user or group override those for "Everyone." This is a major difference between NT Server and Macintosh file servers, where permissions for "Everyone" override permissions for an individual or group.

Create additional volumes if you wish, or exit from Server Manager. That's all that needs to be done on the NT server.

Setting Up the Mac for NT Connection

NT Server is an *AFP-compliant* server, which means NT Server directly supports the AppleShare Filing Protocols (AFP) required by Macintosh clients. There's nothing to do from the Mac except log on to the NT server in exactly the same way you logged on to a Macintosh server. NT Server's Mac-accessible volumes and shared printers are directly available through the Apple Chooser. To access them, either click AppleShare for the file server(s) or LaserWriter for the printer(s).

Mac clients that connect to NT require System 6.0.7 or higher. NT Server fully supports System 7.*x* clients. Power Macintosh computers can be clients to an NT server.

No additional software is required for the Mac, although it is advisable to enable Microsoft authentication to maintain NT Server's C2 security. The software for this is included with NT Server and needs to be installed at each Mac workstation.

First Time Logon

Before Mac users log on to an NT server as a registered user, they have to log on as a guest and fetch the software to enable Microsoft Authentication. Here's how that's done:

1. From the Mac's Apple menu, select Chooser.

2. Click AppleShare. A list of available servers appears, as shown in Figure 10.14.

FIGURE 10.14

Selecting the NT server in the Chooser

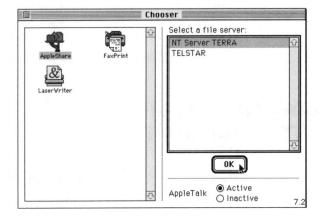

3. From the list, select the NT server, and then click OK.

TIP

Any server that is configured with Services for Macintosh will appear in the Chooser's list of servers, no matter what domain(s) it is in. Mac users don't see domain names or workgroup names—they only see server names.

As shown in Figure 10.15, you get the option to log on as a guest or a registered user.

4. Log on as a guest or a registered user, since it doesn't matter which you log on as the first time, except that a registered user must have an account on the NT server. You might log on as Administrator if the Mac users' accounts haven't been created yet.

Notice that the first time you log on, the Mac doesn't know anything about NT. It looks just like another Macintosh server. Later, when the

FIGURE 10.15

Logging on to
the NT Server

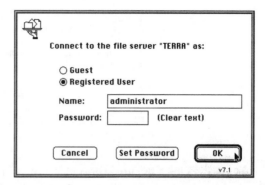

FIGURE 10.15

Logging on to
the NT Server

Microsoft encryption module is installed on the Mac client, this screen
will change.

5. Enter your name and password, and click OK.

6. You see the list of shared volumes, as shown in Figure 10.16. The
first time around you may see only one, the Microsoft UAM
Volume. Click on that, and then click OK.

If a logon message was enabled from MacFile Attributes, you see a
screen similar to the one in Figure 10.17.

FIGURE 10.16

Selecting the volume

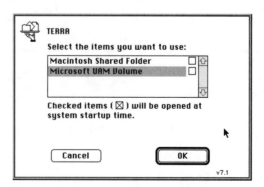

FIGURE 10.17

Logon message
from the NT server

7. Click OK, and then close the Chooser. An icon for Microsoft UAM Volume appears on the Mac desktop, as shown in Figure 10.18.

8. Open the Microsoft UAM Volume. It contains a folder called AppleShare Folder, as seen in Figure 10.19. Drag that folder into your System folder. If this Mac was a client of an earlier version of NT server, there is already an AppleShare Folder in the System Folder. This version of the Microsoft UAM software will overwrite the older version. Don't worry—it's fully backward-compatible with previous versions of NT server. Mac clients can access any NT server on the network, regardless of the version.

FIGURE 10.18

Microsoft UAM icon

FIGURE 10.19

The AppleShare folder

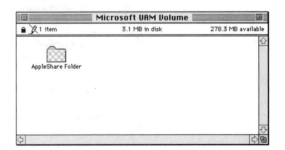

9. Restart the Mac. From now on, when you log on to a server, your password will be encrypted for additional security.

TIP

Before dragging the AppleShare folder into your System Folder, check to see if there is already a folder with that name. If so, take the contents from this folder and drag them into your existing Apple-Share Folder.

Next Time Logon

The next time you log on from the Mac, select the NT server through the Chooser as usual. You get a dialog box asking you to select a logon method, as in Figure 10.20. Choose Microsoft Authentication and click OK.

Then you see a logon screen similar to Figure 10.21, in which you can enter your user name and password. This dialog box looks slightly different from the dialog box that you would see if this were a Mac-based server, because you installed Microsoft authentication support in the previous step.

Click Registered User, enter your user name and password, and click OK. Select from the list of available Mac-accessible volumes. If a

---

FIGURE 10.20

Selecting a logon method

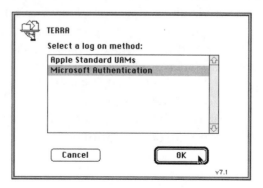

FIGURE 10.21

Logon dialog box after
Microsoft authentication
support is installed

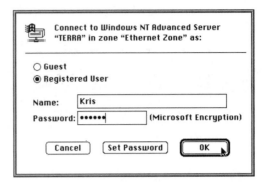

volume name is grayed out, it means that you are already logged on
to that volume or you don't have the correct privileges to access it.

Services for Macintosh Printer Support

Services for Macintosh provides printer support in two different ways:
Mac users can use non-PostScript printers connected to an NT Server
network, and PC users can use Mac printers connected to an Apple-
Talk network.

Mac clients access non-PostScript printers via PostScript emulation.
This emulation is provided as part of Services for Macintosh and is
invisible to Mac users. They don't need to change anything about their
documents or change the way they access the printer. Mac clients
work through the Chooser, as usual.

Mac printers may be made available to PCs by using NT Server's
Print Manager (and the associated print spooler) along with "capturing" the Mac printers. *Capturing* means to create a print spool or
print queue on a print server.

Macintosh printers (we're talking about laser printers here) are usually connected to AppleTalk networks and are network-ready devices. When a Mac user sends a print job to a Mac printer, the Macintosh computer spools the print job to the user's local hard disk and prints it in the background. This often slows response time for the Mac.

Capturing a Mac printer causes a print spool to be created; print jobs are sent to the server and stored in a print queue.

Avoiding "LaserPrep Wars"

LaserPrep is a part of the Mac's built in laser printer driver. The Laser-Prep driver is downloaded to the printer at the beginning of any printer session. If multiple users share the same printer, the first LaserPrep driver is retained in the printer's memory and does not need to be downloaded each time. This saves time when printing.

There are many different versions of LaserPrep, and a network administrator is often faced with the task of making sure that all versions of this driver are the same for every Mac on a network. If all versions are not the same, users complain of slow printing, as the LaserPrep driver is downloaded at the beginning of each print job and the printer resets itself.

By capturing the printer, LaserPrep wars are avoided. NT sends it's own LaserPrep code with each print job—this takes a little time, but not as much as keeping the driver resident in the printer and replacing it each time.

Installing Services
for Macintosh Printing

Installing print services for Mac clients is described in detail in the NT Server documentation, and summarized here for reference.

Start the Print Manager by clicking the Start button, choosing Programs, choosing Accessories, and choosing Print Manager. Then select Printer/Create Printer. You see a dialog box like the one in Figure 10.22.

Type in a name for the printer, select a driver from the available list, and provide a description and location for the printer if you like. If the printer is a networked Macintosh printer, select Other from the Print to menu. If you select Other, you get a dialog box like the one in Figure 10.23. It lists possible print destinations. Select AppleTalk Printing Devices. Click OK. From the Available AppleTalk Printing Devices dialog box, double-click a zone (if zones were created) and then a printing device. Then click OK and click Share This Printer on the Network. The Share Name is shortened if it's too long for DOS system users to see. The Macintosh users will see the name in the Printer Name box. If you like you can fill in the Location box. Click OK. The printer is now available to PC users as usual and appears in Print Manager.

FIGURE 10.22

The Create Printer
dialog box

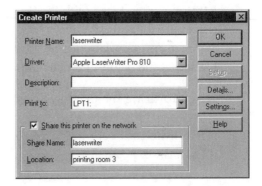

FIGURE 10.23

Print Destinations
dialog box

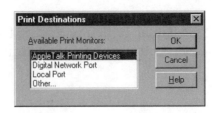

For Mac users, you need to create a user account. Start Control Panel/Services, select Print Server for Macintosh, and click the Startup button. A dialog box like the one in Figure 10.24 appears.

FIGURE 10.24

Print server for
Macintosh services

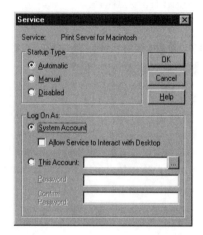

Under the Log On As section, click System Account (the default) to enable all Mac users to access the printer. Click This Account and enter a user name (no groups) to enable only a single Mac user to access the printer. Click OK and then Close to exit Control Panel.

Macs should now have print access. They'll access the printer as usual, through the Chooser.

Transferring Data between Macs and PCs with NT Server

Now that you have the data from the Mac to the NT server, what can you do with it? Well, that depends...

If all you want to do is use the NT server as a place to *store* files, then there's nothing else to do except copy them from the Mac local hard drive to the NT shared volume. But before getting into that, it's good to understand a few things about the Mac file system. Then you can consider the problems of file formats, extensions, filtering, and document translation.

Forks, Forks Everywhere— and Nothing to Eat

Mac files are created as two distinct pieces—a *data fork* and a *resource fork*. The data fork contains the data for the file, while the resource fork contains information needed by the application that created the file, such as fonts, formatting information, and the like. A data file has a big data fork and a small resource fork, while an application program has a large resource fork and a small data fork.

PC-based file systems don't understand forks, since PC files are stored as one distinct entity (albeit that entity may be in fragments on the disk, which is not the same thing). Forks are okay with NT, though. NT stores the data fork and the resource fork together on the server in a single file.

Those Pesky File Names

First, the rules for naming files on DOS, Mac, and NT. Then, let's see what happens to the file names when files are moved around.

File Type	Naming Convention
DOS	8-character file name followed by an optional period and a 3-character extension. DOS file names can't contain spaces and shouldn't contain any special characters. This is the FAT convention.

File Type	Naming Convention
Mac	32 characters, and can include any character on the keyboard with the exception of the colon (:) character. The colon is used to distinguish levels of folders; kind of like a backslash distinguishes levels of directories in DOS or NT.
NT	256 characters, and can include upper- and lowercase characters, spaces, and some special characters. This is the NTFS convention. It is available only to users of Windows NT workstations (and the server, of course).

Now, using those rules, let's see what happens when you move files around:

- A file created using the FAT convention (8+3) displays as created to NTFS users and Mac users.

- A file created using the 32-character Mac limit displays as created to NTFS users. DOS users see the name truncated to 8+3 format. This can have some very unusual (not to mention unwanted) results.

- A file created using the NTFS 256-character limit displays as created to Mac users if it is 32 characters or less. Otherwise, it is truncated to the 8+3 format.

- Mac users should use 8+3 filenames if they are going to *share* the files with DOS users. While this may seem limiting to Mac users, it avoids a lot of confusion down the line.

To Which Application Does the Data File Belong?

The DOS world has something of a convention when it comes to naming files. Many applications attach a particular extension to their data files—SAM to AmiPro documents, WK3 to Lotus 1-2-3 worksheets, DBF to dBASE databases, and so forth. Users can generally change these extensions if they like, although most don't because application programs are written to display data files using their default extensions.

Mac files don't follow these rules; they have their own. Every Mac file that's created is assigned a *type* and *creator* code, which defines which application created it. The type and creator code are embedded in the file's resource fork, and enable the file to be displayed on the Mac desktop with an icon that is unique and recognizable for each application program. This type and creator code enables Mac users to double-click documents to launch their associated applications.

When a Mac file is placed on the NT server, the Mac user loses the ability to determine what type of file it is. Worse yet, any PC file that the Mac user copies to her Mac doesn't have a type and creator code; and the PC file appears as a blank document.

The first problem, determining the type of file, is easy to overcome if Mac users name files using the same conventions that DOS users employ, a three character extension that indicates the file type. The second problem, that of making the Mac understand a PC file type, is overcome by using something called extension mapping.

Extension Mapping

Extension mapping is a process that ensures that users see the correct icon on their computers for a file stored on the computer running Windows NT Server. For example, Macintosh users will see a Macintosh-style icon for a Microsoft Excel file, and Windows users will see the Windows-style icon for the same Microsoft Excel file.

Extension mapping is a good idea in theory, but it doesn't ensure that a data file is compatible with a particular application. The data file may need to be *translated*.

NT Server's Services for Macintosh is already set up for extension mapping when it comes to some of the more popular application programs. A listing of available extension maps can be found in the Services for Macintosh help file. Additional maps can be created using NT Server's File Manager Associations.

To add additional associations, open the File Manager and select MacFile. From the MacFile menu, select Associate. You see a screen similar to Figure 10.25.

FIGURE 10.25

Associate dialog box

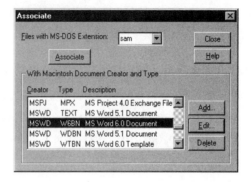

Add the MS-DOS file extension you want to be associated with a Mac application in the appropriate field, and then select from the list the Macintosh application you want to be associated with files containing that extension.

If a Mac application program's name isn't included on the list, you can add it, but you need to know it's creator code and the type codes for the documents it supports. If you don't know this information, you can generally find it in the application program's documentation, or you can get it by calling the manufacturer of the application program.

Let's say you want to add the Mac application Teach Text to the list:

1. Open the File Manager. (From the Start menu, choose Run, and then enter the word **winfile**. There doesn't seem to be any other way to do this.)

2. Select MacFile.

3. From the MacFile menu, select Associate.

4. Click the Add button. You see the screen in Figure 10.26.

FIGURE 10.26

Add Document Type
dialog box

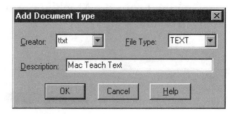

5. Type in the four-letter creator code and the four-character type code for the application you want to add.

6. In the Description field, type in the name of the Mac application program. The name will be added to the list that you used in the previous step.

7. Click OK when you're done.

TIP
Type and Creator codes are four-character codes that are assigned to application programs by Apple. They are not made up by programmers or by users. Be careful when adding type and creator codes. If you don't know an application's codes, check the documentation, call the program's manufacturer, or call Apple.

About File Filters and Translations

Many application programs have built-in *file filters*, the programs that convert one kind of data file to another. Perhaps the best example of this is a program like Microsoft Excel. Excel can read data files created from Lotus 1-2-3 and several other spreadsheet programs and convert them to Excel format. Other programs have optional filters that must be installed. Word processors and graphics programs, for example, often support a number of file formats.

Be careful when using filters. Just because a program has a translator built into it doesn't mean everything translates properly.

If a particular application program doesn't have built-in translators or doesn't include them as options, several third-party programs are available to do the job. Conversions Plus and Mac-In-DOS are two that come to mind. For the Mac, try MacLink Plus, Access PC, or PC Exchange.

Using Cross-Platform Applications

Just about the cleanest way to get applications to understand data files in a shared environment is to use *cross-platform applications*. These applications include both a PC version and a Mac version, and the data files are fully transportable across the two platforms.

Examples of cross-platform applications include:

- cc:Mail
- FileMaker Pro
- First Class Mail
- Lotus 1-2-3
- Microsoft Word, Excel, PowerPoint, and Mail
- PageMaker
- Quark Xpress
- QuickMail
- WordPerfect

Be careful with cross-platform applications. Just because an application is cross-platform doesn't necessarily mean that documents convert entirely correctly. Also, if a document contains embedded graphics (as is the case with PageMaker), the graphics need to be removed from the original, converted separately, and reinserted in the cross-platform document.

Bad Dates

A word of caution about dates: Mac and DOS files are date-stamped differently. At Microsoft, time started on January 1, 1980. At Apple, time began on January 1, 1904. All file dates are internally converted to a Julian dating system, which calls day 1 whatever the first day was for the particular company and numbers each day from there.

The difference in date-stamping methods causes enormous problems when using data files that contain date functions. Suppose you have a spreadsheet with a formula such as (*today*)+30. If this is a Mac file, *today* means something completely different when the file is used by a PC application.

The Downside (and You Knew There'd Be One)

While all of this Mac connectivity stuff sounds good, there are a few limitations to what Mac clients can do in the NT world:

- Dial Up Networking doesn't support AppleTalk, since AppleTalk doesn't send NetBIOS packets.

- MS-Mail is supported, but Mac client support is not provided unless you buy it separately (buy the upgrade kit—Mac clients aren't compatible with Workgroup mail).

- Mac clients do not execute logon scripts and can't take advantage of user profiles.

- Mac clients can't participate in inter-domain trust relationships or see resources from other NT Server domains, unless Services for Macintosh has been enabled in those domains and they are on the *same* network.

CHAPTER

ELEVEN

Managing Servers and Domain Controllers

Server
Manager

In earlier networks, you had to administer servers by physically walking over to a server, sitting down, and working right at it. Modern network operating systems are built with the understanding that you manage multi-server networks and that often you manage networks from many different locations. To help you out in that job, NT includes a number of tools, but the most important is the Server Manager. It is the focus of most of this chapter. But there's another important topic in managing multiple servers—domain controllers. How many domain controllers you need, how to use them in fault-tolerant roles, and how to manage them is covered in the last part of this chapter.

Server Manager's Capabilities

When users successfully connect to the server, they each begin a *session* with that server. Server Manager monitors session activity and keeps track of all resources and which users on the network are accessing those resources. Server Manager displays statistics showing current usage levels on both servers and NT workstations.

Server Manager Functions

With Server Manager, you can view and track

- All users who are currently running sessions on a selected computer

- The resources open during each session

- How long a resource has been open by a user

- How long a session has been idle
- Current information on the number of open file locks, resources, and printers in use

You can also

- Control directory shares on remote servers, removing existing shares or creating new shares
- Add or remove NT machines from the domain
- Shift domain controllers from the role of backup domain controller (BDC) to that of primary domain controller (PDC) and back again
- Send messages to users
- Receive alerts—in other words, messages from the system—at designated computers
- Configure directory replication

You can use the Server Manager to get minute-by-minute server statistics. By familiarizing yourself with the statistics that are generated during normal operation, you will be in a better position to spot abnormal activity. For example, when there's a slowdown in throughput, you might see that a number of users are trying to download data at the same time. Further investigation into share usage might reveal that the problem is concentrated in a particular spot—an overused resource, perhaps.

Not Everyone Is Allowed to Use Server Manager

Server Manager's statistics can only be generated for NT workstations and servers running NT Server or LAN Manager 2.*x*. You can't monitor or modify attributes of a server with Server Manager unless you are a member of either the Administrators or Account Operators group. Members of the Account Operators group can use Server Manager, but only to add computers to a domain.

Gathering Cumulative Server Data

Server Manager displays present usage levels and session information; it does not collect statistics over a period of time. To see a computer's cumulative usage statistics since startup, enter the commands **net statistics server** at the command prompt, or configure the Performance Monitor to collect statistics.

Who's Who in the Domain

As shown in Figure 11.1, the Server Manager window displays a list of all of the computers that are members of the logon domain, plus computers that the Computer Browser service reports as being active in the domain. This list includes NT Servers, NT workstations running the Server service, and LAN Manager 2.*x* servers. Computers running Windows for Workgroups 3.11 and Windows 95 appear in the list, but they can't be remotely administered through Server Manager.

FIGURE 11.1

Server Manager window

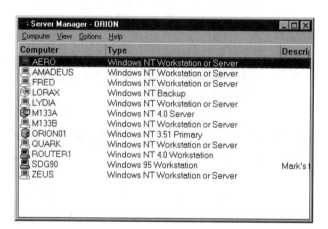

Icons identify the three categories of computers in the Server Manager list:

- *Primary domain controllers*, which maintain the domain's security base and authenticate network logons.

- *Backup domain controllers and NT servers*, NT Server machines that are *not* the primary domain controller. These computers *may* be backup domain controllers, in which case they receive copies of the domain's security base and also authenticate logons, but there's no way to tell from the icon if they're simply servers or servers that also act as backup domain controllers.

- *Workstations*, which are any other listed computer (NT workstations, Windows 95, Windows for Workgroups, DOS machines).

The icons may or may not be dimmed, depending on whether the computer is accessible by the network. If an icon is dimmed on a machine but you know that the machine is active, you can try to force Server Manager to see it by typing

```
net use \\servername\IPC$
```

This may not work if you're using the TCP/IP protocol and WINS (see Chapter 14 for information about TCP/IP and WINS). The icon for a computer is dim, and remains dim, if the computer has been hidden from the browser ("Hiding a Server from the Browser," later in this chapter, explains how to hide a computer from the browser). In other cases, the computer may only "un-dim" if you force it to do something; for example, if you turn on or turn off a service remotely.

Commands in the View menu allow you to filter the list to show all computers or only the servers, workstations, Macintosh computers, or domain members. Press the F5 key to refresh the display.

To administer the servers of a different domain or workgroup, choose the Select Domain command from the Computer menu. If the domain or workgroup happens to communicate with your server over a slow link, make sure you choose the Low Speed Connection option.

Server Properties

The properties of any server on the Server Manager list, whether local or remote (provided that remote administration is supported), can be accessed by using these techniques:

- Selecting the computer on the list and choosing Properties from the Computer menu

- Selecting the computer and hitting Enter

- Double-clicking on the selected computer's name in the list

Once you select the server, you see the Properties dialog box, as in Figure 11.2.

You can also access this dialog box from the Control Panel of the machine for which you want the information. The big value of the Server Manager, however, is that you can access this dialog box for any server on the network, right from your workstation. In contrast, the Control Panel can only show this dialog box for whatever computer you're currently sitting at.

The Usage Summary box displays

- The total number of users who have established sessions—in other words, who have remotely connected to the server

---

FIGURE 11.2

The Properties for dialog box

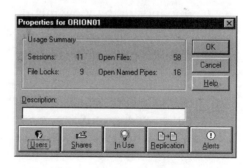

- The total number of shared resources currently open on the server

- The total number of file locks held by open resources on the server

- The total number of named pipes currently open on the server

Beneath the Usage Summary box is a box that contains the server's optional description. If you want to add or change a server's description, just type the new information in the box.

At the bottom of the dialog box are five buttons:

Button	What It Does
Users	Lets you view all users connected to the server, as well as the resources opened by a specific user, and disconnect one or all of the connected users.
Shares	Displays the server's shared resources and those users connected over the network to a selected resource. One or all of the connected users can also be disconnected here.
In Use	Shows the open shared resources on the server and provides the capability to close one or all of the resources.
Replication	Lets you manage directory replication for the server and determine the path for user logon scripts.
Alerts	Allows you to view and manage the list of users and computers that are notified when administrative alerts occur at the server.

Hiding a Server from the Browser

You can't do this with the Server Manager, but it's worth knowing anyway: if you have a workstation or server that is running the Server service and you want to keep it off the browse list for some reason, just modify its Registry.

Look in HKEY_LOCAL_MACHINE\System\CurrentControlSet\Services\LanManServer\Parameters. There should be a value "Hidden" that is, by default, equal to 0; it's of type REG_DWORD.

Set it equal to 1 and reboot, and the server will not appear on the browse list. You can still get to it by using NET USE or NET VIEW command, but you have to know the name in order to see it.

User Sessions

To look at and manage user sessions on the server, click on the Users button in the Properties for dialog box. The resulting User Sessions dialog box, as seen in Figure 11.3, lists all users remotely connected to the server and what resources they are using.

The Connected Users box lists each connected user, the name of the computer the user is on, the number of resources opened by the user, the time since the session was established, the length of time since the user last initiated an action, and whether or not the user is logged on as a guest. Right below the list is a summary of the total number of users remotely connected to the server.

The bottom box displays the resources in use by the currently highlighted user. To view those of a different user, simply click on that user in the Connected Users list. Resources in use are graphically identified by the icons shown in Table 11.1.

FIGURE 11.3

User Sessions on dialog box

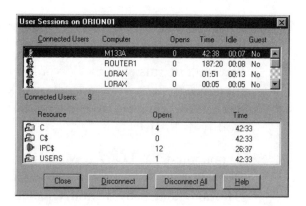

TABLE 11.1   Resource Icons

Icon	What It Is
	A shared directory
	A remote procedure call
	A shared printer
	A communication-device queue (LAN Manager 2.x servers only)
	An unrecognized resource

Next to the icon is the name of the resource, the number of times the selected user opened the resource, the number of times the resource was opened by the selected user, and the time elapsed since the resource was first opened. Incidentally, a connection to a printer sometimes shows up as a connection to a named pipe instead.

How Do I Disconnect Users from the Server?

To disconnect a single user from the server, select the user name from the Connected Users list, then choose the Disconnect button. Selecting the Disconnect All Users disconnects everyone from the server. When administering a remote server, your own user account shows up as a user connected to the IPC$ resource, which will not be disconnected.

This isn't a "hard" disconnect; if a user tries to use something on a disconnected resource, then NT automatically reconnects him or her.

You should inform users before disconnecting them—use Send Message on the Computer menu to relay your intentions to the connected users.

Controlling Automatic Disconnection

On the topic of maintaining connections between servers and users, let me mention a few things that aren't controlled by the Server Manager, but that are important.

NT can monitor how long a user has been using a connection; for example, a connection to a share. If the share has been unused for ten minutes, NT automatically disconnects the user from the share. It's not a very harsh disconnection, despite its sound, because if the user tries to do anything on the share, then NT automatically and invisibly reconnects the user.

Why, then, does NT bother? Well, each user connection takes up server memory, and disconnected users don't take up any memory. That's the good part, but the bad part is that the "invisible" reconnection may take an extra second or two, which can be annoying. You can control these "soft disconnects" with a command, NET CONFIG.

The command net config server /autodisconnect:*value* sets the disconnect period to a value other than ten minutes; the value is in seconds. Using a value of -1 says not to disconnect at all. You can see which of your connections are disconnected by typing **net use** at the command line; under Status, you will either see "OK" or "Disconnected." You can see an example of that in Figure 11.4.

Available Shares

By choosing the Shares button in the Properties for dialog box (see Figure 11.2), you can view the Shared Resources on dialog box, as shown in Figure 11.5. The dialog box lists both the shared resources available on the currently selected server and the users connected to those resources. Shared directories can be managed in either Server

FIGURE 11.4

OK and Disconnected
shares in NET USE

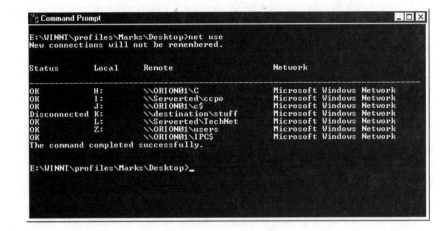

Manager or in File Manager, while shared printers are managed in the
Printers folder.

The top box lists all of the shared resources on the selected computer.
For each share, the share name, the number of uses, and its path are
given. Once again, icons next to the share name show whether the

FIGURE 11.5

Shared Resources on
dialog box

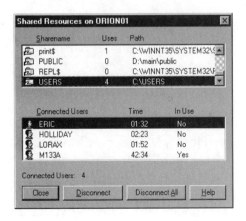

resource is a directory, named pipe, printer, communication-device queue (LAN Manager 2.*x* servers only), or an unrecognized resource (see Table 11.1).

When you click on one of the shared resources in the list, you see a list of the users connected to that resource (and the time elapsed since the connection was made) in the bottom box. For example, in the preceding figure, a user named Eric is connected to the shared directory C:\USERS. Although he has been connected for an hour and a half, the shared directory is currently not in use.

As with User Sessions, you can disconnect one or all users from all shared resources on the server by selecting a user in the Connected Users box and choosing the Disconnect button, or by simply choosing the Disconnect All button. Remember to warn users before disconnecting them from server resources.

Managing Shared Directories in Server Manager

In Server Manager, just as in File Manager, you can

- View shared directories

- Share an unshared directory

- Manage the properties of a shared directory

- Set permissions for a shared directory

- Stop sharing a directory

However, in Server Manager you can create new shares and administer shared directories not only on the local server, but on remote servers in the domain as well.

To view any server's list of shared directories, select the server in the Server Manager window, then choose Shared Directories from the

Computer menu. You see the Shared Directories dialog box, as in Figure 11.6.

The list shows the share names and paths of the shared directories. It includes directories shared by users and administrators, as well as some or all of the following special shares created by the system:

Resource	What It Does
driveletter$	The root directory of a storage device on the server (can be accessed remotely only by members of the Administrators, Server Operators, and Backup Operators groups).
ADMIN$	The resource used by the system during remote administration of a server. It is always the directory where Windows NT is installed.
IPC$	This resource shares the named pipes essential for communication between programs. It is used when a computer is being remotely administered, or when viewing a computer's shared resources.
NETLOGON	The resource used by the Net Logon service for processing domain logon requests; Netlogon is the service that keeps BDCs and PDCs in synchronization, and it only runs on domain controllers.
PRINT$	The resource that supports shared printers.
REPL$	Required for export replication, this resource is created by the system when a server running NT Server is configured as a replication export server.

In general, these system shares should not be removed or modified.

FIGURE 11.6

Shared directories on a selected computer

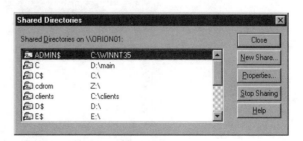

To modify the properties of a shared directory in the list, select the directory and click the Properties button. Share access permissions can be set by choosing the Permissions button in the Share Properties dialog box. To stop sharing one of the directories in the list, select the directory and choose the Stop Sharing button. The directory itself is not removed, but it can no longer be accessed by network users. To share an unshared directory on the server, choose the New Share button and type in the sharename, path, and other properties, including share permissions.

These procedures are covered in Chapter 7. Note that you can modify share permissions on a remote computer with Server Manager, but you can't modify directory or file permissions on a remote computer with Server Manager. For that, you just use File Manager if you're on a 3.*x* machine or the Security tab if you're on a 4.*x* machine. You'll find that the Security menu works just as it always does, assuming that you're logged on as an administrator.

Active Resources

By choosing the In Use button in the Properties for dialog box (see Figure 11.2), you can see how many resources are currently open on the server, as well as a list of those resources, as Figure 11.7 demonstrates. Once again, the resources are graphically distinguished by icons. Table 11.2 tells what the icons mean.

FIGURE 11.7

Open Resources
dialog box

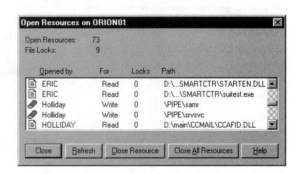

TABLE 11.2   Resource Icons

Icon	What It Is
	A file
	A named pipe (a type of connection between computers)
	A print job in a print spooler
	A communication-device queue (LAN Manager 2.x servers only)
	An unrecognized resource

Following the icon is the name of the user who opened the resource, the permission granted when the resource was opened (read, write, execute, etc.), and the path of the resource. Print jobs are sometimes represented in this list as open named pipes.

Close an open resource by selecting that resource from the list and then clicking the Close Resource button. If you want to close all open resources, hit the Close All Resources button. Make sure you notify the connected users of your intent before you carry it out. To exit, choose Close, then choose OK in the Properties for dialog box.

Sending Alerts to a Workstation

When system errors or important events relating to the server or its resources occur, NT Server generates *alerts*. In Server Manager you can specify which users and computers receive these alerts.

You can alternatively set up a DOS client with the Microsoft Network Client 3.0 for DOS, a slightly more complex operation that you can accomplish with the Network Client Administrator under NT Server.

TIP　In order to generate an alert, a server must be running the Alerter and Messenger services. On computers that must receive alerts, the Messenger service must be up and running. If the destination computer happens to be turned off, the message eventually times out. In practical terms, this means that the workstation must either be running NT, OS/2, Windows for Workgroups, or Windows 95—all four of which ship with Messenger support—or you'll have to load a DOS or Windows-based Messenger driver. The "Workgroup Connection" client software from Microsoft, which will allows a DOS workstation to connect to an NT network, only requires one diskette, and so that's what I usually recommend to carry around for quick-and-dirty network installs. The Workgroup Connection, however, does not include the messenger service, and so no DOS machine set up with the Workgroup Connection would be able to receive alerts.

When you install the Network Client for DOS, you get the option to either "run the Network Client" or "run the Network Client and Load Pop-up." If you load the pop-up, you have the messenger service.

To specify the recipient of administrative alerts:

1. Double-click on the server in the Server Manager window to retrieve its Properties for dialog box.

2. In the Properties for box, choose the Alerts button. You see the Alerts on dialog box, as in Figure 11.8.

FIGURE 11.8

Alerts dialog box

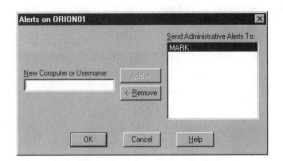

3. To add a user or computer to the list of computers that are receiving alerts, type in the username or computer name in the New Computer or Username box, then choose Add.

4. To remove a user or computer from the list of those set to receive alerts, select the username or computer name in the Send Administrative Alerts To box, then choose Remove.

The Server and Alerter services both need to be restarted in order for the changes to take effect.

Sending Messages to Users

Prior to administering a server, especially if you have to put certain services or resources on hold while working, you can send a message to users currently connected to the server. To send a message:

1. Choose the server from the list in the Server Manager window.

2. From the Computer menu, choose Send Message. You see the Send message dialog box shown in Figure 11.9.

3. Type in the message you want relayed to users.

4. Choose OK.

FIGURE 11.9
Send Message dialog box

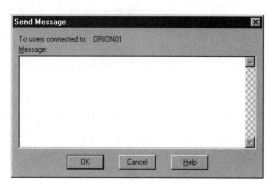

The message is sent to all users currently connected to the selected server, provided that those workstations using NT and NT Server are running the Messenger service and other workstations (such as those running Windows for Workgroups) are using a message utility such as WinPopup.

> **TIP**
>
> If you have an AppleTalk segment on your NT Server network, don't forget to send messages to Macintosh users before taking the server down. From the MacFile menu, choose Send Message.

> **TIP**
>
> To send a message to just one user, open a command window and type net send *name message*, where *name* is the user name or machine name to send the message to, and *message* is the text of the message you're going to send. For example, to say "hello" to a user named Sally, you would type net send Sally hello.

Adding Computers to a Domain

Members of the Administrators, Domain Admins, and Account Operators groups can grant computers membership in a domain (note that it's the *computers*, not their users, that are acknowledged as members of the domain). It makes sense to add an NT machine to a domain because domain members can share access to the common database of user accounts (the Security Access Manager or SAM database), so that the network administrator doesn't have to go out and build an account on every single NT Workstation for every single possible network user.

Adding a computer to a domain is a two-step process. First, the machine account for the computer must be created in the domain. Then, the computer must actually join the domain—a separate step, performed at the computer itself during installation of NT or afterwards in its Control Panel.

Adding Domain Controllers to Domains

You can add a new domain controller to a domain at either of two times:

- During the installation of the NT Server (domain controllers *must* be running NT Server), you're asked if you want to act as a domain controller or a server; choose "domain controller."

- Before installing a new machine, you can tell Server Manager to expect a new domain controller like so:

    1. From the Computer menu, choose Add to Domain. You see the Add Computer to Domain dialog box, as in Figure 11.10.
    2. Under Computer Type, choose the option Windows NT Backup Domain Controller.
    3. Type in the name of the computer (to a maximum of 15 characters), and then choose Add.

This action creates the machine account in the domain's security database for a computer of the specified name. The computer, however, doesn't become a member of the domain until it actively joins it.

Non-Domain Controller Machines (NT Workstations and Servers)

For any other NT machine, domain membership can be granted during the installation of NT on the machine, but only if it's done by

FIGURE 11.10

Add Computer To Domain dialog box

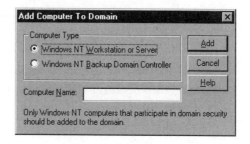

TIP

It is possible in the short period of time between the "pre-creation" of the machine account and when you install NT Server on the machine for someone to masquerade as the intended computer by renaming their computer to that name and joining the domain. If this masquerade computer joins the domain as a server, it gains access to the domain's security database (which is replicated to all domain servers). If you don't want this to happen, don't make any new computer names widely known before the computers actually join the domain, or only use the NT Setup routine to add backup domain controllers to your domain.

an administrator. Once NT has been installed, however, domain membership can be granted in two fashions:

- On the NT workstation itself, by an administrator using the Network option of that workstation's Control Panel.

- Through Server Manager, in which the administrator or account operator adds a machine account for the computer to the domain's security database, then instructs the computer's user to join the domain under that account (using the Network option in Control Panel).

To create a machine account for an NT machine using Server Manager, choose Add to Domain from the Computer menu, select Windows NT Workstation or Server in the Computer Type box, type in the computer name, and choose Add. You can add a number of computers at once. Choose Close when you are finished.

Then, to add the workstation to the domain, log on to that computer. In its Control Panel, choose Network. You see the Network Settings dialog box. Choose the Identification Tab and then select the Change button next to the domain (or workgroup). You see the Domain/Workgroup Settings dialog box, as in Figure 11.11. In the Member of box, select the Domain button and type in the name of the domain that the workstation must join.

FIGURE 11.11

Changing the
domain membership

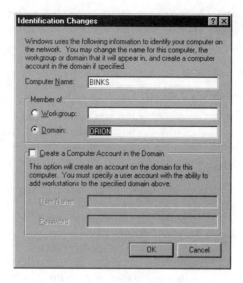

NT machines that are members of a domain don't actually get a copy of the domain's user database and don't help out verifying login requests, but they still get the benefits of the domain's centralized user and groups database.

LAN Manager 2.x Servers

LAN Manager 2.x servers are the only servers outside of NT Servers that can be granted membership in a domain. LAN Manager servers can function as supplementary servers in NT Server domains as long as the domain controller is an NT Server. A LAN Manager server can be designated as a domain controller only in a domain where all of the domain's servers are running LAN Manager 2.x.

As with other NT Servers, LAN Manager servers receive and keep copies of the domain's security database, but they can only validate logon attempts by workstations running Windows for Workgroups or LAN Manager 2.x workstation software (they can't validate logon attempts by NT users).

> **TIP**
>
> When you re-install to an NT server or workstation machine, you end up with a different set of security identifier (SID) numbers than you had before, and that confuses the primary domain controller. As a result, you probably get an error message if you try to log on to the domain with that NT server or workstation. Here's the easiest way around that problem: log on to the NT machine as its local Administrator. (What, you didn't write down the local Administrator's account password when you first installed NT on this machine? Then you're out of luck—time to reinstall from scratch.) Go to the Control Panel, open the Network applet, click Identification, and click the Change button. Select the Workgroup radio button rather than the Domain radio button, click OK, and exit the Control Panel. Then reenter the Control Panel, return to the Identification tab of the Network applet, and click Change again. This time, try to return to your old domain by specifying the Domain radio button and filling in the domain name. Then check the "Create a computer account in the domain" box in the bottom of the dialog box and fill in the name and password of a *domain* administrator. By doing this, you force the NT domain to eliminate the old machine account for this NT machine and create a new one. Log off NT, and you should now be able to log on to the domain from your NT workstation or server. This should never be a problem for a backup domain controller machine. If it *is* a problem for a BDC, then you may have to re-install from scratch.

Because they don't support all of the types of information contained in NT Server accounts, LAN Manager 2.*x* servers don't recognize local groups or trust relationships, and are unable to use the users and global groups that are defined in other NT Server domains. Even so, resources in these domains can be accessed by NT workstation users provided that the user has a second account in the LAN Manager domain, or the LAN Manager domain permits guest logons. All in all, LAN Manager servers should be treated as just servers, not domain controllers under NT.

Managing Services

In addition to providing domain membership and shared resource management capabilities, Server Manager also lets you configure the services available on each of your servers. You can start, stop, pause, continue, and provide startup values to specific services. Each of the services in Server Manager are duplicated under the Services option in Control Panel, but unlike Control Panel (which manages services for the local computer only), Server Manager allows you to manage services for remote servers as well as the local computer.

The default services in NT Server are:

Default Service	What It Does
Alerter	Notifies selected users and computers of administrative alerts that occur on the server. Used by the Server and other services; requires the Messenger service.
Clipbook Server	Supports the Clipbook Viewer application; allows pages to be seen by remote Clipbooks.
Computer Browser	Maintains a current list of computers and furnishes the list to applications when requested; provides the computer lists shown in the main Server Manager window and in the Select Computer and Select Domain dialog boxes.
Directory Replicator	Replicates directories and their contents between computers.
Event Log	Records system, application, and security events in the event logs.
License Logging	Keeps track of used and available licenses.
Messenger	Sends out and receives messages sent by administrators and the Alerter service.
Net Logon	Performs authentications of account logons in NT Server. Keeps the domain's security database synchronized between the domain controller and other servers running NT Server in the domain.
Network DDE	Provides network transport and security for DDE (Dynamic Data Exchange) conversations.

Default Service	What It Does
Network DDE DSDM	The DSDM (DDE Share Database Manager) service manages the shared DDE conversations; it is used by the Network DDE service.
Remote Procedure Call (RPC) Locator	Manages the RPC name service database and allows distributed applications to use the RPC name service.
Remote Procedure Call (RPC) Service	This is the RPC subsystem for Windows NT.
Schedule	Permits the use of the AT command to schedule commands and programs to run on a computer at a specific time and date. For some odd reason, this is not started by default, and so one of the things that you end up doing early on is to set this service to start up automatically.
Server	Provides Remote Procedure Call (RPC) support and allows file, print, and named pipe sharing.
UPS	Manages a UPS (uninterruptible power supply) connected to the server. Should be used in conjunction with Alerter, Messenger, and Event Log services to ensure that events related to the UPS service (such as a power failure) are recorded in the System log and that designated users are notified.
Workstation	Allows network connections and communications.

Additional services appear in the list based on your network configuration. For example, if you installed a Macintosh segment of the network, you may see File Server for Macintosh and Print Server for Macintosh listed as services.

To view and manage the services using Server Manager, select the desired server from the main window, open the Computer menu, and select the Services command. You see the Services on dialog box shown in Figure 11.12. If the entry in the Status column for a particular service is blank, that indicates that the service has been stopped. You should really only manipulate non-automatic services through this dialog box.

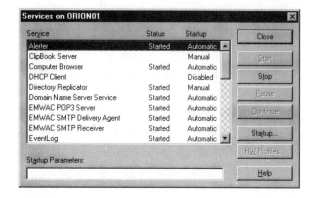

FIGURE 11.12

Services on dialog box

Starting and Stopping Services

You can start, stop, pause, or continue any of the services for a particular computer by following these steps:

1. Select a computer in the Server Manager window.

2. Choose Services from the Computer menu.

3. In the Services on dialog box, select the service in the Services window.

4. Click the Start, Stop, Pause, or Continue button.

If you need to pass startup parameters to a service, simply type them in the Startup Parameters box at the bottom before choosing the Start button.

Stopping the Server service disconnects all remote users. You should follow this procedure for stopping the Server service:

1. Pause the Server service first; users are thus prevented from establishing any new connections.

2. With the Send Message command, tell connected users that they will be disconnected after a specific time period.

3. After the specific time period expires, stop the Server services.

When the Server service is stopped, you can't administer it remotely; you must restart it locally.

Configuring Service Startup

Members of the domain's Administrators local groups can choose whether or not a service is started automatically, manually, or is initially disabled. To do this, select the service in the Services box and choose the Startup button. You see the Schedule Service on dialog box, as in Figure 11.13.

Under Startup Type, you can choose these options:

Automatic   Starts the service each time the system starts

Manual   Allows the service to be started by a user or by a dependent service

Disabled   Prevents the service from being started

TIP   Incidentally, the Server service won't start automatically unless the server has at least 12MB of memory.

FIGURE 11.13

Schedule Service on
dialog box

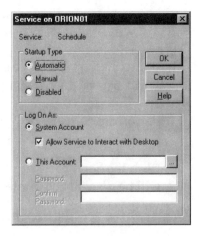

Beneath the Startup Type, you can choose which account the service will log on as. Most services log on using the system account. However, a service such as the Schedule service may need more access than that given by the system account, which only provides Guest access. In such a case, you can create a special user account with the required access for the service to log on as. User accounts that are used to log on as a service must have the Password Never Expires option selected.

For the service to log on using the system account, simply select the System Account button. To specify a different account, choose the This Account button and use the browse button (...) to find and select the user account.

When you've acquired the proper account, type in its password in the Password and Confirm Password boxes. Then choose OK to return to the Services dialog box. When you've finished configuring the services, choose Close.

Scheduling Events

When the Schedule service is activated, you can execute programs or commands on the server (or a remote server) to run at a predetermined time. Scheduling these events uses the network command AT. If you've purchased and installed the NT Server *Resource Kit,* you can also use WinAT, which is a graphical interface for the AT command.

Note that the Schedule service, by default, logs on under the system account, the same account used by most services. Under these circumstances, the AT command can only access those resources that allow Guest access, which may not provide enough access for the desired activity. To gain greater access to network resources when using the AT command, you need to create a special user account, give it the appropriate access (if you're scheduling automatic backups, you might want to put the account in the Backup Operators group), then configure the

Schedule service to log on using that special account. Make sure you select the Password Never Expires option when you create the account.

Setting Up a Scheduled Event

To set up a scheduled event (a "job") using the AT command, open the Command Prompt and type in the command, using the following syntax:

```
at [\\computername] time [/every:date[,...] | /next:date[,...] ]
command
```

where

- *computername* is the computer you are scheduling the event to run on. Leaving it out schedules the event on the local computer.

- The scheduler uses 24-hour time. For 11 A.M., type **11:00**; and for 2:30 P.M., type **14:30**.

- Any legal command, program, or batch file can be used in the *command* field.

- For the /every: and /next: options, you can either type in the days of the week (Sunday, Monday, etc.), or the number corresponding to the day of the month. Don't leave a space between the colon and the date. (You can abbreviate a day of the week in the /every: and /next: options to M, T, W, Th, F, S, or Su.)

For example, to copy a file at 11:00 A.M. of the current day on a computer named Procyon (a one-time event), you would type

```
at \\procyon 11:00 "copy c:\users\ellenh\summary.txt c:\users\
miked"
```

To run a program named CLEANUP.EXE on the local computer at 5:00 P.M. on the 7th, 14th, and 21st of every month, you would type

```
at 17:00 /every:7,14,21 "cleanup"
```

To run a batch file named sayhi.bat on a computer named Rigel at 9:00 A.M. next Thursday, you would type

```
at \\rigel 9:00 /next:Thursday "sayhi"
```

To view any of the jobs currently scheduled at the local computer, type **at**, then press the Enter key (to see the scheduled jobs on another domain server, type **at ***computername***).

Each job is listed with its own ID number. To delete any of the scheduled jobs displayed, type

```
at \\computername [id number] /delete
```

If you wanted to remove a scheduled job (with the ID number 22) from the local computer, the command would be

```
at 22 /delete
```

Using WINAT to Schedule Events

WINAT is simply a graphical interface for the AT command that comes with the NT Server *Resource Kit.* But truthfully, there's no "simply" about it; it's a blessing to work with it instead of the command-line AT command. Opening the WINAT window displays the currently scheduled jobs on the local computer, as shown in Figure 11.14.

You can view the jobs at a remote server by pulling down the File menu and choosing Computer. To add a new scheduled job, select the Add button. You see the Add Command dialog box, as in Figure 11.15.

Type in the desired command in the Command box, and choose the Today, Tomorrow, Every, or Next button. Then, select the days and time the command needs to be run from the Days and Time boxes. When finished, select OK. The new job appears in the list of scheduled jobs in the main window.

If you need to change an existing job, select that job in the main window and click the Change button. You see the Change Command

FIGURE 11.14

The WINAT window

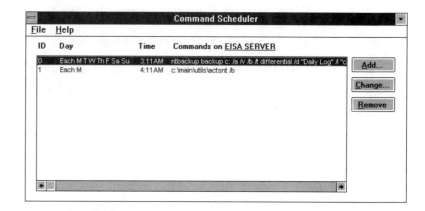

FIGURE 11.15

Add Command
dialog box

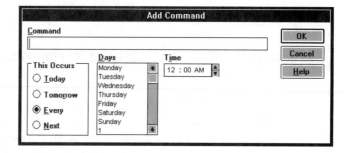

dialog box. Make the necessary changes, then choose OK. To remove
a job on the list, simply highlight it and select Remove.

Directory Replication

Directory replication is exactly what it sounds like: the duplication of a
master set of directories from a server (called an *export server*) to other
NT servers or workstations (called *import computers*). The most common
application for this is to export login scripts from a primary domain

How Do I Set Up a Prescheduled Job at the Local Server?

 In this example, we're going to schedule an incremental backup to take place every morning at 3:00 A.M. Type the following command (in an unbroken line):

```
at 3:00 /every:M,T,W,Th,F "ntbackup backup c: /a /v
/t incremental /d ""Daily backup"""
```

The NTBackup command option /a appends data to the tape; otherwise, you overwrite the tape's previous backups. The /v option verifies the backup, and the /t followed by *incremental* tells NTBackup to only back things up with the archive bit set, and to reset the archive bit once the backup is done. In the label, two sets of quotes are interpreted as a single set of quotes. Truthfully, keeping track of all of those quotes gets to be a pain, and I strongly recommend that you load the WinAT program that comes with the *Resource Kit*; it makes setting up prescheduled jobs much easier.

controller to backup domain controllers; in that case, the PDC is the export server and the BDC the import server.

Now, at the outset, let me warn you that directory replication is a bit more complicated than it ought to be, but stick with me. At the end of this section I have some step-by-step recipes for making directory replication work.

Machines Replicate, Not Users

Just like members of a domain, the exporters and importers are not users, but machines (server ORION01 exports to workstation AMS, not the domain administrator to user Christa.) These duplicate directories are not static copies, but rather remain dynamically linked to the master copy of the directory stored on the export server. If changes or additions are made to that directory, they are automatically reflected in the duplicates on the import computers.

Uses for Directory Replication

Why would you want to duplicate directories? There are two reasons why having constantly updated, identical copies of directories in more than one place can be a good idea. First of all, replicated directories can help you balance workloads. For example, if a number of workstations need to access a certain directory, you can export that directory to another server and direct some of the workstations to access it from there, rather than from the master copy. This way, you avoid bottlenecks at the server.

The *main* application of directory replication, however, is to make sure that all of the backup domain controllers (BDCs) have up-to-date copies of the login batch scripts for all users. That way, when a BDC logs you in instead of the PDC, the BDC can supply the login batch script, and the PDC needn't be burdened with having to always supply login batch scripts.

As a matter of fact, directory replication is almost set up by default to propagate login batch scripts from a PDC to its BDCs, and I'll show you in a bit how to do that.

Who Can Import? Who Can Export?

Potential exporters on an NT Server network are limited; only NT Server machines can export directories to the rest of the network. Importers are less limited, as NT Server, OS/2 LAN Manager, and Windows NT machines can all import directories from the export servers. The only restriction placed on export computers is that the directories or files exported must match the naming conventions of the file system of the volume set to which they are imported. For example, if the volume to which the files are exported is formatted to NTFS, the export directory must be set for NTFS. See Figure 11.16 for a demonstration.

You don't have to name particular computer names when exporting and importing; it's possible to just point to a domain. For example, suppose a machine named WOLF359 says, "I'm exporting to domain LOCALGRP," and the domain LOCALGRP contains machines named ACENTAUR, BCENTAUR, PCENTAUR, SIRIUS, TCETI, EERIDANI, and our exporter, WOLF359. Suppose also that the Directory Replicator service is only active in SIRIUS, TCETI, and WOLF359, and that each of them has specified that it wants to import not from a particular machine but from domain LOCALGRP. The result is that the exported files from WOLF359 appear in the import directories of SIRIUS, TCETI, and WOLF359. Notice that WOLF359 is exporting *to itself* (it can do that, and it's quite useful, as you will learn a bit later).

The only time that you might have problems exporting to a domain is when some of the domain's import computers are located across a WAN (wide area network) bridge from the export server. In that case, when setting up the list of computers to export to from the export server, you should specify the individual importers by name, and

FIGURE 11.16

Exporting either to domain names or to individual import computers

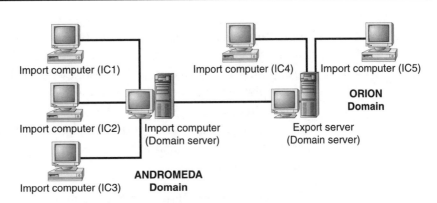

ORION's domain server is the export server in this figure. ORION can export either to domain ANDROMEDA and domain ORION, or to the individuals (IC1, IC2, IC5, etc.), or perhaps to one entire domain and to individuals in the other one.

when importing from another domain across the WAN bridge, specify the name of the export server to import from, rather than the domain name. This is illustrated in Figure 11.17.

FIGURE 11.17

Exporting across a WAN bridge

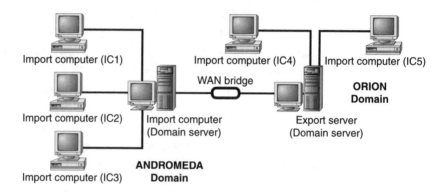

Import computer (IC1)

Import computer (IC2)

Import computer (IC3)

Import computer (Domain server)

ANDROMEDA Domain

WAN bridge

Import computer (IC4)   Import computer (IC5)

ORION Domain

Export server (Domain server)

ORION's domain server is the export server in this figure. Because it is exporting to computers across a WAN bridge, it must refer to all import computers individually by name (even those in its own domain), rather than exporting to the entire domain and letting the domain server distribute the exported directories.

Setting Up the Directory Replicator Service

Before any machine can either send (export) or receive (import) files, its Directory Replicator service must be active. That's very similar to starting any NT service: you can monkey around with it with the Services applet in the Control Panel, but where most services just start up as belonging to the "System," the Directory Replicator service requires you to create a bogus user, give that user some powers, and tell NT that the *bogus user* is starting the Directory Replicator service, rather than the System.

Before you can configure an NT Server computer to be an export server, you need to set up a special user account that is part of the

Backup Operators group. The Directory Replicator service uses this account to log on, so you need to make sure that

- The account's password never expires

- The account is accessible 24 hours per day, seven days per week

- The account is assigned to the Backup Operators group

User accounts are set up under User Manager for Domains (consult Chapter 6 to see how). Don't try to name this account "Replicator"; the system won't let you because there is already a user group by that name. In my examples, I've created a user named REP.

Once you've set up this user account, go back to the Server Manager. You now have to configure the Directory Replicator service to start up automatically and to log on using that separate account for each computer in the domain that will participate in replication. To do this, select the computer in the Server Manager window, and then, from the Computer menu, choose Services. You see the Services on dialog box (see Figure 11.12). Select the Directory Replicator service and then click the Startup button. You see the Directory Replicator Service on dialog box, as shown in Figure 11.18.

FIGURE 11.18

Configuring startup for the Directory Replicator service

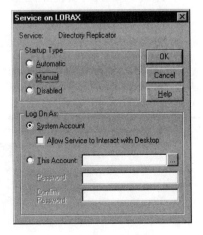

Select the service to begin automatically, select the This Account radio button, and then click the (…) button to select the account that you set up for the Directory Replicator service to use. You see a screen that looks like Figure 11.19.

FIGURE 11.19

Selecting an account for Replicator service to use

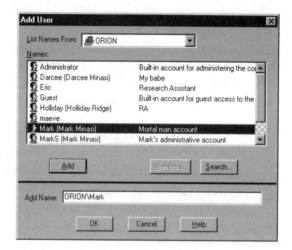

Double-click on the name of the account that you want to use (I called mine REP) and, when the name of the account shows up in the Add Name text box, click OK. You find yourself back in the directory Replicator Service screen, but now it has the name of the account that you want to use.

Type in the password that you assigned to the account and click OK. NT Server shows you a confirmation screen that looks like Figure 11.20. If you like, you can go ahead and manually start the service now, since

FIGURE 11.20

Confirmation of startup configuration

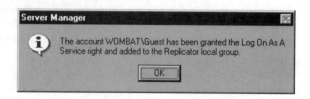

it won't automatically begin until you've logged off and logged back on again.

Configuring the Export Server

Once you've set up the Replicator service properly, you're ready to set up the export server for export. As mentioned before, export servers do the following:

- Contain the master set of directories that will be duplicated during replication

- Maintain the list of computers to which the subdirectories are imported

- Can export to domain names as well as to individual computers in the domain

 Any NT Server computer can become an export server—but *only* NT Server computers can (NT workstations can't be export servers).

Now for the directories to export. When NT Server or NT is installed on a machine, the default export and import paths C:\WINNT\SYSTEM32\REPL\EXPORT and C:\WINNT\SYSTEM32\REPL\IMPORT are automatically created. (If NT or NT Server is installed in a different location than C:\winnt, these default paths are adjusted accordingly.) Any directories created within the export path are automatically exported, and they and their contents are subsequently placed in the default import path.

> **NOTE**
> Note that only directories inside the export directory will be exported! If you put a file in \WINNT\SYSTEM32\REPL\EXPORT, it will not be exported. But a directory under \WINNT\SYSTEM32\REPL\EXPORT *will* be exported, once directory replication is under way.

Unless you've changed your default directories, you will create the directories that you intend to export within C:\WINNT\SYSTEM32\REPL\EXPORT. You don't need to put all the files in the directory yet, since any changes that you make to the directory will be dynamically reflected on the import computers once the replication service is going.

Once you've created your directories, you must configure directory replication so as to tell your system whether it will export, import, or do both. You configure directory replication in Control Panel (if you're seated at the machine you want to configure) or in Server Manager. Server Manager, however, lets you configure directory replication remotely for more than one machine at a time.

To set up replication:

1. Do one of the following:

    • In Control Panel, select the Server option; or

    • In Server Manager, select the computer, then choose Properties from the Computer menu (or simply double-click on the computer in the Server Manager window).

2. Choose Replication from the buttons on the bottom of the window. You see a screen that looks like Figure 11.21.

3. Select the Export Directories radio button and type the name of the path from which you want to export (you can leave it unchanged if you choose to use the default export path).

4. Click on the Add button in the southwest corner of the dialog box, double-click on the domain you want, and select a computer to export to from the list. Your list looks like the one in Figure 11.22.

FIGURE 11.21

Initial screen for
directory replication

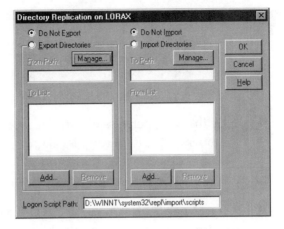

FIGURE 11.22

List of computers to add
to the Export To List

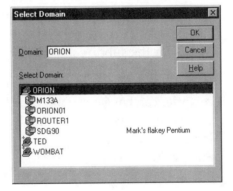

The To List box contains the list of computers that your export directories will be copied to. By default, the list is blank and the local domain automatically receives the exported subdirectories. However, once an entry is made to this list, the local domain is no longer exported to, and must be explicitly added to the list if you want it to receive exported subdirectories.

TIP

If all you want to do is to have your PDC replicate logon scripts to your BDCs, then do *not* enter anything in the To List box. Just tell each of the BDCs to import, tell the PDC to import *and* export, and place your domain's login scripts in \WINNT\SYSTEM32\REPL\EXPORT\SCRIPTS (note the EXPORT, not the usual IMPORT) on the PDC.

By the way, permissions for an export directory grant Full Control to members of the Replicator local group. If you change these permissions, files are copied to the import computers with incorrect permissions and an "access denied" error is written in the event log.

If you need to be more specific as to which subdirectories need to be exported, you can choose the Manage button in the Directory Replication dialog box (see Figure 11.21) to manage locks, stabilization, and subtree replication for the subdirectories exported from the server. You see the Manage Exported Directories dialog box in Figure 11.23. It shows the current locks, stabilization status, and subtree replication status for the subdirectories that are to be exported.

Locks prevent a particular subdirectory from being exported. Subdirectories can have more than one lock applied to them; exportation will occur only if this column contains a zero. If a subdirectory has been locked, the date and time of the oldest lock is displayed in the Locked Since column. To add a lock to a subdirectory, select it from the list and

FIGURE 11.23

Managing the export directories

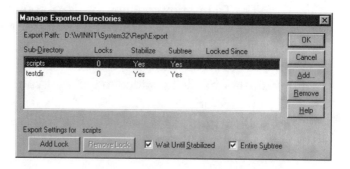

choose the Add Lock button. To take away a lock, choose the Remove Lock button.

If you choose the Stabilize option by selecting the Wait Until Stabilized check box at the bottom, files in the selected export subdirectory will wait two minutes or more after any changes are made before being exported (this helps eliminate partial replication). Otherwise, files are exported immediately. The default is to *not* wait until stabilized.

Selecting the Entire Subtree check box allows all subdirectories and their contents (including additional subdirectories) within the selected subdirectory to be exported. If this option is cleared, only first-level subdirectories are exported. Unless you decide to change it, NT Server exports the entire subtree of the directory.

Configuring the Import Computers

Import computers, you recall, are specific servers and computers in the same or other domains that receive a duplicate set of directories from the export server. They maintain a list of export servers from which subdirectories are imported and can import from domain names as well as from individual export servers. Alternatively, you can choose not to specify any export servers to expect data from, and the import machines will by default collect any files intended for their domain in general.

Both NT Server and NT machines can become import computers, but you have to set them up for the service first, just as you did for the export servers. Likewise, you can configure import servers locally using Control Panel, or you can do so remotely with Server Manager. The procedure is the same, except you choose import options rather than export options in the dialog boxes:

1. Use Administrative powers to create a new user account for the Replication service to use on the import computer, just as you did on the export server.

2. If you're working locally at the workstation, go to the Services icon in the Control Panel and configure the Directory Replicator Service to begin automatically, just as you did on the export server. (If the computer can be remotely administered, you can do this at the server using Server Manager).

3. Using the Server option in the local computer's Control Panel, or by displaying the computer's properties remotely in Server Manager, choose the Replication button and follow the same procedure as for exporting directories, but choose the import directories options instead.

How Often Does the System Replicate?

By default, the export server replicates to its import servers every five minutes. The export server doesn't want to waste bandwidth replicating files that change constantly, however, so a file must have been unchanged for two minutes before the Replicator service propagates it. That "five minute" and "two minute" interval can both be adjusted with Registry entries:

- HKEY_LOCAL_MACHINE\SYSTEM\CurrentControlSet\Services\Replicator\Parameters can contain a value named *Interval* that takes values from 1 to 60 minutes. It is type REG_DWORD, and controls how often to replicate to import servers.

- The same key can hold another value, GuardTime, that says how long a file should be stable before it can be replicated. Again, it's REG_DWORD, value in minutes; it must be one-half of *Interval* or less.

Summary: Creating an Import/Export Pair

You have to worry about an awful lot of things when making an import/export pair work. Here's a step-by-step recipe to make a server named SOURCE replicate to a server named DESTINATION. First, some ingredients (this *is* a recipe, right?):

- You have to be logged on as an administrator to make this work.

- SOURCE must be an NT Server.

- DESTINATION can be any kind of NT machine.

- This works best if Source and Destination are members of the same domain.

To make an import/export pair:

1. With User Manager for Domains, create a user named REP. Give it any password you like, but set "Password never expires," and don't force the user to change the password next time it logs on ("it" because it's not a real human, just a bogus account to make NT happy). Also, don't restrict the logon hours.

2. Click Groups, and add REP to the Backup Operators group. Save the user account, and close User Manager for Domains.

3. Start up Server Manager. Select the SOURCE machine. You see a main Server Manager screen like the one in Figure 11.24.

4. Choose Services on the Computer menu. You see a screen like the one in Figure 11.25.

5. Choose Directory Replicator service and click the Startup button. You see something like Figure 11.26.

6. Under Startup Type, click the Automatic radio button.

7. Under Log On As, click the This Account radio button.

FIGURE 11.24

Initial Server Manager
screen showing SOURCE
and DESTINATION

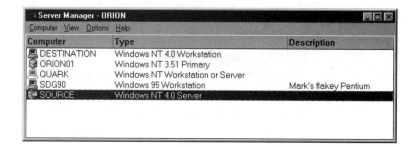

FIGURE 11.25

List of services
on SOURCE

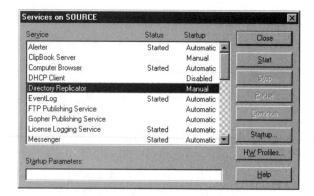

FIGURE 11.26

Controlling startup
of Replicator service
on SOURCE

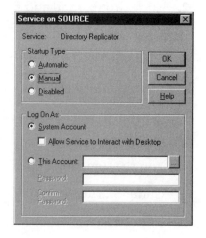

8. Click the ellipsis (…) button and you see a figure like Figure 11.27. This dialog box lists the users of the domain.

9. Choose REP, click Add, and then click OK to return to the previous Service on SOURCE dialog box. REP's name is filled in, as you can see in Figure 11.28.

FIGURE 11.27

Choosing a replicator user account

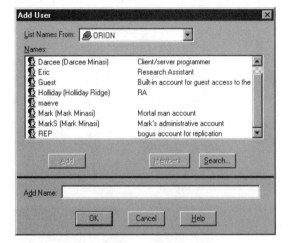

FIGURE 11.28

Service control box after filling in necessary information

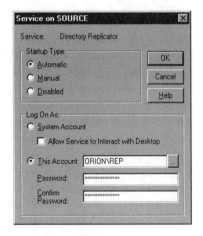

10. You have to prove to NT that you have the right to plunk REP into this dialog box. In other words, you have to prove that you know REP's password. I set it to blank, so I'll just fill in blanks in the Password and Confirm Password boxes and click OK. As this is the first time I've done this, I get the confirming message box shown in Figure 11.29.

11. Click OK to clear that dialog box and you get back to Service on SOURCE dialog box. Notice that it says "Service" and not "Services." Click Close.

12. You are now be back at the main Server Manager screen, with SOURCE still selected. Click Computer, then Properties, and then Replication. You see a dialog box like the one in Figure 11.30.

13. Click the Export Directories radio button. Click Add and choose a computer to export to. First you are asked for a domain; it's

FIGURE 11.29

Confirming that REP is in the Replicator group

FIGURE 11.30

Setting up replication on the export computer SOURCE

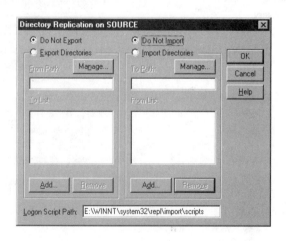

ORION for my example, so I choose that, and then I see a list of machines in ORION. The list is shown in Figure 11.31.

14. Once you've highlighted the target machine, click OK. Notice that the export directory is by default \winnt\system32\repl\ export. You can change that if you want to with the Manage button, but I'm leaving it alone for this example. My target machine is called ORION, so I picked that. Click OK in the Directory replication on Source dialog box to return to the main window of Server Manager. You see a message telling you that the replication service is starting.

15. By now, you should be back in the main window of the Server Manager. Now it's time to set up the receiving import computer, DESTINATION. Choose DESTINATION and click on Computer, then on Services on the menu.

16. You will do the same thing to DESTINATION to make sure that it can receive the files. Click the Directory Replication services, click Startup, choose Automatic in Startup type, put This Account in Log on as, fill in REP's name and password, go to services, tell it to start automatically, fill in the name of REP, punch in REP's password, and click Properties for DESTINATION and Replication.

So far, what you're doing is a complete carbon copy of what you did with SOURCE, so I'll spare you the screen shots. But now take a look

FIGURE 11.31

Choosing a machine to export to

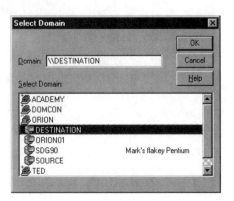

at the directory replication on DESTINATION dialog box shown in Figure 11.32. This is only half the dialog box that SOURCE had. Why? Well, recall that DESTINATION is, for this example at least, an NT Workstation machine. Therefore, it does not have the ability to export.

17. Choose the Import Directories radio button, click Add, and fill in the name of SOURCE. Click OK, and you again see that the system starts up the Directory Replicator service.

18. Put a file into whatever directory you specified for SOURCE to export, and wait five minutes. It should show up in the import directory on DESTINATION; there's no need to reboot.

NOTE Remember that only subdirectories in the \winnt\system32\repl\ export directory will replicate, not files in the export directory itself. To make a file replicate, make sure it's in a subdirectory inside the export directory.

FIGURE 11.32

Directory replication on a non-server machine

Summary: Setting Up Your PDC to Replicate Login Scripts to the BDCs

Here's another summary that shows you specifically how to set up your PDC and BDCs to keep the login scripts on the PDC replicated out to the BDCs. I assume that you want to keep the login scripts in their normal place: \WINNT\SYSTEM32\REPL\IMPORT\SCRIPTS.

1. Set up each PDC and BDC's Directory Replicator service. Follow the steps in the previous section to see how to do this. Again, you have to go through the process for each domain controller.

2. Place the domain's login scripts on the PDC in \WINNT\ SYSTEM32\REPL\EXPORT\SCRIPTS. Make any future changes to this directory, not the \WINNT\SYSTEM32\REPL*IMPORT*\ SCRIPTS directory.

3. Get the Directory Replication control dialog box for the PDC either by double-clicking on the PDC in the Server Manager and then clicking Replication, or by opening up the Control Panel on the PDC, double-clicking on the Server applet, and clicking the Replication button.

4. Click the Export Directories and Import Directories radio buttons. Ensure that there isn't anything in the To List or From List fields. If there is, remove it. Click OK to close the box.

5. For each BDC, open up its Directory Replication control dialog box and click the Import Directories radio button. Again, make sure nothing is in the From List field.

6. Stop and then start the Directory Replication service on the domain controllers and wait at least five minutes. You will find that the batch scripts now sit in the \WINNT\SYSTEM32\REPL\ IMPORT\SCRIPTS directories on the PDC and the BDCs.

Changing the Logon Script Path

At the bottom of the Directory Replication dialog box is an edit field that contains the logon script path. It is shown in Figure 11.33.

Logon scripts are batch files that can be assigned to specific user accounts so that when a user logs on, the script executes. They are assigned as part of a user's profile (see "NT User Profiles" in Chapter 7 for more information). When a user logs on, the system looks for the logon script by combining the script's file name (in the user account data) with the logon script path, which is specified in the Directory Replication on dialog box.

In NT Server, replication is configured so that servers export logon scripts from the directory C:\WINNT35\SYSTEM32\REPL\EXPORT\SCRIPTS and import them to the directory C:\WINNT35\SYSTEM32\REPL\IMPORT\SCRIPTS on the import computer. The path for importing logon scripts must be entered in the Logon Script Path box for the domain controller as well as each server that participates in logon authentication for the domain.

FIGURE 11.33

Directory Replication on dialog box

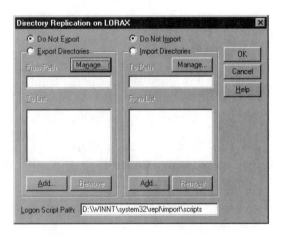

How Do I Set the Logon Script Path for a Server?

 To configure the logon script path for the selected server, type in a local path in the Logon Scripts Path box of the Directory Replication dialog box (the default, C:\WINNT\SYSTEM32\REPL\IMPORT\SCRIPTS, usually suffices). Entries are required in this edit field, so don't enter a blank space.

Troubleshooting Directory Replication

Setting up the replication service properly can be a bit tricky. If you run into problems, these are some things that you might want to check:

- Have you made the replication service's account a member of the Backup Operators group, or given it the rights accorded to that group?

- Has the Directory Replicator service been started on both the import and export computers?

- Are the import and export computers in the same domain? If not, are the username and password the same in both domains? Do the domains trust each other?

- For NTFS partitions, have the permissions for the export directory and its contents been altered? Does the Replicator local group have at least Change privileges to these directories?

- Does an account have a file open (on import or export) all the time? This would appear as a sharing violation in the event log.

- When importing or exporting from an NTFS directory, does either directory have filenames that differ only in case? The export computer may choose one file while the import computer chooses the other; this can set replication out of sync.

- Are some files with extended attributes (EAs) being replicated from an HPFS volume to an NT Server? NT doesn't support EAs that are written in non-contiguous parts of the disk (OS/2 sometimes does).

- Are the clocks of the import and export machines synchronized? If they are too far off, the server cannot export properly to the import computer.

- Did you wait long enough? It make take five minutes before replication kicks off.

If you are using OS/2 LAN Manager, be aware that LAN Manager only allows one set of credentials (i.e., a user name and password) to be used at a time. If someone is logged on locally to one user ID and the Replicator is trying to use another, replication is delayed until that user logs off.

Errors in the replicator service are entered into the applications log. You can view these entries by opening the Event Viewer in the Administrative Tools group and choosing Application from the Log menu. Make sure you check the logs on both the import and export computers.

Finally, make sure you start the Alerter service and configure alerts so that you can receive messages about the success or failure of directory replication in your system.

Managing Domain Controllers

All domains have a primary domain controller (PDC) that keeps a database of users and groups for the entire domain: the SAM (Security Accounts Manager) database I've referred to before. It is part of the Registry on a PDC.

For the sake of fault tolerance, NT allows a network to have more than one domain controller. The first domain controller in a domain must be, by definition, a PDC; subsequently installed domain controllers are all BDCs. All that domain controllers really do is keep track of which users can access what objects (files, directories, printers). The job of domain controller may be low-intensity enough that your domain controllers can serve "double duty" as file servers, name servers, and the like.

While the first PDC is born to the throne, so to speak, it is possible to "promote" a BDC to a PDC and demote the old PDC in the process.

The Server Manager assists with some of these duties. It lets you

- Promote and demote primary domain controllers
- Synchronize backup domain controllers with the primary domain controller

One thing you *can't* do with the Server Manager is create new backup domain controllers. Unfortunately, the only way to make an NT Server machine into a domain controller is to install that machine as a domain controller. You make that decision when you run NT's Setup program, and it's one you can't change without reinstalling from scratch.

I'll cover all of those issues in this section, but I'll also take up more complex questions, to wit: How many domain controllers should I have in my domain? How many users can I have in my domain? How large will the SAM be? How can I fine-tune the communication between PDC and BDCs to minimize unnecessary network traffic?

Promoting a Primary Domain Controller with Server Manager

Let's start off with a simple question: How do I make a BDC into the PDC?

Recall that every domain must have a primary domain controller. The PDC keeps the master copy of the domain's account and security database, which is automatically updated whenever changes are made. Copies of this database are also automatically received by all other servers in the domain. Every five minutes, the other servers query the domain controller, asking if changes in the database have occurred. If any changes were made within those five minutes, the domain controller sends the changes (not the entire database) to the other servers. (That "five minutes" value can be adjusted, as I'll explain shortly.)

You establish which machine is a domain's PDC when you create the domain, and you officially create a domain by installing a PDC for the domain. Other domain controllers are also anointed when you run Setup to create them. Inside Server Manager, though, you can change a domain controller from a PDC to a BDC or vice versa.

To designate one of the domain's BDCs as the PDC, select that computer in the Server Manager window, and choose the Promote to Primary Domain Controller command on the Computer menu. The old PDC will automatically revert to server status unless it's unavailable to the network—for example, if it's turned off. If that is the case, you have to manually demote it (in the Computer menu, the Promote to Primary Domain Controller command changes to the Demote To Backup Domain Controller command). If you don't demote it and the old domain controller returns to service, it won't run the Net Logon service or participate in user logon authentication; but I'll get to that in the section "What Happens When a PDC Fails?" later in this chapter.

Why would you promote a BDC to a PDC, by the way? Probably because you're about to take down the PDC and you want to make sure that the domain continues to run in a smooth, uninterrupted fashion.

Synchronization: Keeping a Uniform Security Database

Server Manager can help out in another place as well: making sure that all the BDCs are in sync with the PDC.

Synchronizing a domain's servers forces the replication of the domain's security database from the PDC to all of the BDCs in the domain. NT Server synchronizes the BDCs automatically, but in the unlikely event that one BDC's copy of the SAM database becomes out of sync with the rest of the domain, you can perform the synchronization manually.

To synchronize the domain account database (the SAM, recall) on a BDC with the SAM on the primary domain controller, select that BDC from the Server Manager list and, on the Computer menu, choose Synchronize with Primary Domain Controller. If you need to synchronize *all* of the BDCs with the PDC in one command, choose the PDC from the Server Manager list. Then, from the Computer menu, choose Synchronize Entire Domain. You see the message in Figure 11.34.

As the message implies, a manual synchronization can take a significant amount of time to complete if the security database is large. (If you're wondering, "*How* large?," stay tuned for the upcoming section "Estimating the Size of the SAM.")

For a LAN Manager 2.*x* server, the Synchronize with Domain Controller command re-establishes the computer account password on both the LAN Manager server and the domain controller.

FIGURE 11.34

The synchronization confirmation message

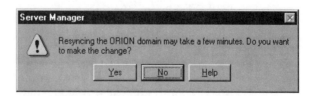

Controlling Synchronization

I mentioned earlier that the PDC replicates its SAM database out to the BDCs every five minutes. That can be adjusted with a number of

parameters in the Registry. All are value entries that go in HKEY_
LOCAL_MACHINE\System\CurrentControlSet\Services\Netlogon\
Parameters.

How Often to Replicate?   First, you can control how often the PDC
replicates to the BDC with the *Pulse* value. It is of type REG_DWORD,
and it is in seconds. The lowest value you can set is 60 (one minute) and
the largest value is 3600 (one hour). You might want to increase the
value from its default of 300 if your BDCs are connected to the PDC via
slower WAN links.

Just Say Hello Now and Then   In general, PDCs don't try to replicate to BDCs if there hasn't been any change since the last update, by the
way. But every once in a while, they go tap the BDCs on the shoulder
just to make sure they're still out there. How often they do that is controlled by a value called *PulseMaximum*, another REG_DWORD, that is
calibrated in seconds. The minimum value is 60 seconds; the maximum
is 86,400 seconds (one day). In general, I wouldn't mess with it.

Tell Me Everything You Know   By default, the PDC doesn't replicate the entire database out to the BDCs; it just sends the changes. But,
if you want (and I can't think of a reason why you would want to), you
can tell the PDC to replicate the whole silly SAM database every time
it replicates by setting a value called *Update* to Yes. The Update value
is of type REG_SZ.

Don't Hog the WAN   Because the replication conversation between
a PDC and a BDC over a WAN link can consume a fair amount of the
bandwidth of that WAN link, Microsoft has included a parameter that
it claims will let you control how the PDC-BDC conversation uses the
WAN link. By default, every transfer of SAM data can be a block of
data up to 128KB. That large a data block would tie up a 64Kbps line
for 16 seconds without overhead and probably 30 seconds *with* overhead, a significant amount of time. You can, instead, tell your BDC to
accept PDC data in smaller chunks with the *ReplicationGovernor* value.

ReplicationGovernor is of type REG_DWORD and it ranges from 0 to 100. The 0 to 100 is a percentage of the basic 128K byte block that NT usually uses in its PDC-BDC conversations. Set it to 50, and you get a transfer block that is 50 percent of 128Kbytes, or 64K bytes. Set it lower, and the DCs will never hog your WAN link for an extended length of time. Set it *too* low, however, and the DCs will spend all day transferring tiny, incomplete pieces of data, and by the time they get done, it will be time to start all over again! Of course, setting this to 0 means that blocks of 0 bytes get used, which means that the BDC *never* gets replicated. This parameter goes on the Registry of the *BDC*, not the PDC.

The Microsoft explanation of this parameter is a little confusing. Microsoft says that it defines "both the size of the data transferred on each call to the PDC and the frequency of those calls." It kind of implies (well, to me anyway) that setting the *ReplicationGovernor* parameter to 50 will halve the size of the replication blocks *and* the frequency with which the BDC/PDC conversation occurs, both of which sound like good methods of reducing WAN traffic. In actual fact, setting the parameter to 50 means that each block *will* be smaller—64K bytes rather than 128K bytes—but, as a result, the *number* of blocks will double, meaning that the PDC and BDC will have to talk more often albeit for shorter times. So, yes, the Microsoft documentation is correct, as this defines both the *size* of the data transferred on each call to the PDC (it gets smaller) and the frequency of these calls (they get *more* frequent).

What Happens When a PDC Fails?

PDCs replicate the SAM database to the BDCs every five minutes. (That value can be changed, as I'll show you later in this section.) The BDCs can authenticate login requests, requests for object access, and the like. Therefore, the BDCs have a complete, up-to-date version of the SAM that they can refer to. What BDCs *can't* do, however, is *change* the SAM. If the PDC is down, then the BDCs can log people on to the domain, but people can't change their passwords. If the PDC is down and an administrator tries to make a change to a user's account, she sees the message in Figure 11.35.

FIGURE 11.35

User Manager cannot save changes to the SAM if the PDC is down.

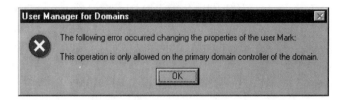

The SAM does not contain share permissions, nor does it contain file and directory permissions for any computer except itself. That means that if the PDC is down, you cannot do the following:

- Change your password

- Change a user's name, account settings, logon hours, or "logon to" list

- Change a user's rights

- Create, destroy, or modify global groups

- Create, destroy, or modify any local groups that are local to the domain

If the PDC is down, you still can do the following:

- Create, destroy, or modify directory shares

- Change, destroy, or modify file and directory permissions

- Access print and directory shares for which you have permission

You can control permissions without a functioning PDC because permissions don't live in the SAM hive; rather, they're in the SECURITY hive, which is machine-specific. (In general, so is the SAM—most machines have their own distinct SAM—but that's not true for BDCs. BDCs don't really have a SAM of their own, just a read-only copy of the SAM on the PDC.)

Anyway, back to the original question: What happens when the PDC dies? Assume that some fool reaches over and disconnects the PDC from the UPS. (You *do* have your domain controllers on UPSes, don't you?) What does that look like?

Well, obviously, any shares on the PDC won't be available any longer, unless by the time you're reading this Microsoft has released the Wolfpack modifications to NT that will allow two PCs to be a "cluster" that acts like one PC. Yes, the services on the PDC won't be available any more. Here is what else will happen:

- Domain logins will still happen, assuming you have at least one BDC—and I *am* assuming that you have at least one BDC.

- Existing sessions will remain in place, but...

- No machine will act as the PDC.

All of the BDCs will have an identical copy of the domain's SAM, but none of them will be able to make any changes to that SAM, as you read a few paragraphs back. Firing up the Server Manager will get an error message that warns you that it couldn't find a primary domain controller, but that it will run anyway. Then, even though it can't find the PDC any more, it still shows up in the Server Manager list, but as a BDC, as you can see in Figure 11.36.

FIGURE 11.36

Server Manager screen with PDC not active

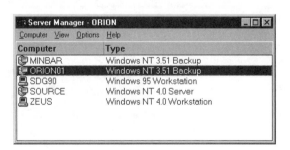

Now, in this actual domain, ORION01 is the PDC, but it is the *downed* PDC. This brings up an important point:

NOTE   When the PDC fails, the BDCs do not automatically become PDCs. BDCs remain BDCs until you promote one of their number to PDC.

So let's anoint a new PDC. I click on the BDC named MINBAR (try it on ORION01, which isn't turned on, and you get, "The network path was not found," as in Figure 11.37).

I click Computer and Promote to Primary Domain Controller. Once I do that, Server Manager looks normal, and MINBAR now has the Borg-like cube icon that indicates that it's a PDC. But suppose I bring ORION01 back now? Well, then Server Manager looks like Figure 11.38.

MINBAR seems now to have gone to "stealth" mode. It is still a cube, so it thinks it is the PDC, but it is a colorless cube. ORION01 also thinks that it is the real deal, so someone has to sort this out. I click on MINBAR and Computer, and I get the menu that you see in Figure 11.39.

FIGURE 11.37

We can't find a PDC, but we'll have a coronation anyway

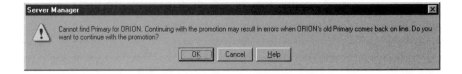

FIGURE 11.38

Gadzooks! The PDC and a pretender!

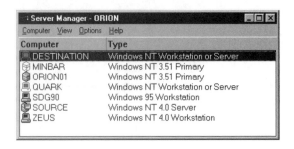

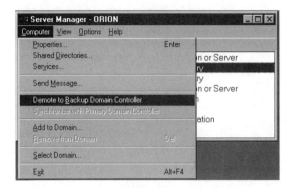

FIGURE 11.39

Server Manager offers to demote the impostor.

When there are two apparent PDCs is the only time you ever see Demote to Backup Domain Controller on the menu.

To summarize: when a PDC fails, the BDCs don't automatically slide into the PDC role. Promote one of them, and when the old PDC returns, it continues to claim that it is the one true PDC, as does the erstwhile BDC. You have to resolve the conflict with the Server Manager and demote one of the upstarts.

How Many BDCs Do You Need?

As you learned in earlier chapters, the primary domain controller can handle logon validations, but it's a good idea to have another domain controller as a backup.

Benefits of BDCs

You want the backup for several reasons:

- A BDC can handle login requests, improving user response time. If there are more DCs around to validate login requests, users can log on quicker first thing in the morning—that's pretty good PR for you network types, right?

- If the primary domain controller goes down, a backup domain controller can be promoted to primary domain controller and the domain will continue to function.

- It is a major pain in the neck to re-install NT Server on the primary domain controller if you have no backup domain controllers, as I explained in Chapter 3.

In a domain with both NT Servers and LAN Manager 2.*x* servers, don't rely solely on LAN Manager servers as your only backups. LAN Manager servers can neither validate logon requests from NT workstations nor be promoted to the domain controller of an NT Server domain.

All right then. I imagine by now you're sold on the idea of BDCs. Suppose you're going to design a domain with a few dozen servers and a few hundred users. How many of those servers should be DCs?

Network Traffic: One BDC Disadvantage

Well, on the plus side, the more BDCs, the quicker logons can be, and, to a much lesser extent, the more reliable the domain is (a disaster would have to kill *all* of the BDCs and the PDC to zap a domain). On the minus side, BDCs are *servers*, which aren't cheap, and they have other things to do.

TIP

If your network is large enough to dedicate a single machine to the role of domain controller (either PDC or BDC), then you can speed up logons by going to that machine's Control Panel/Network applet, clicking on Services, and double-clicking on the Server service to configure it. By default, it will allocate memory to maximize throughput for file sharing. Instead, click the radio button labeled Maximize throughput for network applications. You see, the file server module uses *lots* of RAM, which forces the part of NT that does logins to live in a limited amount of memory. But if you choose to maximize memory for network applications, the login module gets more RAM and can run more quickly—up to three times more quickly by some people's measurements.

Additionally, as I'm going to explain in the upcoming section "Estimating the Size of the SAM," the entire SAM must fit into the physical memory of each of the domain controllers. If your domain's accounts database was, say, 10MB in size, you would have to add 10MB of RAM to each machine that was a domain controller simply because it wanted to be a domain controller; that means making lots of machines into BDCs in addition to their duties as file servers, which is just plain a waste of RAM chips.

Recommended Numbers of BDCs in One Location

Microsoft says they've done studies with big networks and have found that the negatives of BDCs outweigh their positives—that is to say, the network chatter that BDCs cause isn't outweighed by their usefulness as login servers. Their general advice is this:

> **NOTE**   Microsoft's BDC rule of thumb: one BDC for every two thousand users.

That seems a good rule, except for the 8 A.M. problem: everyone wants to log in at the same time—when they come in, around 8 A.M. Microsoft estimates that a PDC built on a 66 MHz 486DX2 with 32MB of RAM can do seven to ten logins per minute. Now suppose our two thousand users all come in and try to log on. At ten logons per minute, with two domain controllers (the PDC and the first BDC), that would be 100 minutes, or right around morning coffee break (9:40 A.M.) before everyone gets logged in!

What can we do about that?

Well, first, we could make the adjustment to the Server service by configuring throughput for network applications rather than file servers. Microsoft says that increases throughput by a factor of up to three, so we'll be generous and say that the login time would decrease to 100/3, or 33 minutes—significantly better, but it still means people are sitting around for a half hour waiting for the logon to finish.

A 133 MHz Pentium can handle many NT operations three times faster than a 486DX2-66 can, so using a Pentium gets it down to 11 minutes, which is much better. And putting more than 32MB of RAM on the DCs would speed things up even more. Which leads me to Minasi's corollary to the Microsoft rule of thumb:

> **NOTE**   One BDC for every two thousand users is fine, as long as they are dedicated machines that don't do anything else, are at least 133 MHz Pentiums, have 64MB of RAM, and are tuned for network applications.

BDCs in Remote Areas

There is another reason to add BDCs: remote locations. Suppose you had a home office in Cincinnati with 1500 users, a branch office in Dayton with 20 users, and an office in Cleveland with 100 users. Suppose that you're connected to the two branch offices via a 64Kbps leased line. Should you put a BDC in Dayton and one in Cleveland?

On the one hand, it's a certainty that at least one server of some kind is in each branch office. Using servers in the central office in Cincinnati would be ludicrous. It would be silly to make over a dozen people wait around for data served up from a 64Kbps line, so it's imperative to have at least one file server locally in each office. And, since there's going to be a file server in each office, why not make it a backup domain controller as well? The benefits would include:

- On days that the leased line was down, people could still log on to the domain, because the local BDC could log them on.

- People's domain logins would be quicker, as the local BDC would log them in, rather than requiring that all of the login verification information be shuttled to and from on the slower 64Kbps WAN link.

But it's not all wine and roses. There's a downside to having a local BDC:

- Remember that the PDC in Cincinnati must replicate the domain SAM to the BDCs in Dayton and Cleveland. In the worst case, that could mean transferring 1.5MB of data (I'll show you how I did that calculation in the next section) over that 64Kbps line. One and a half megabytes over a 64 thousand bits/second line would take a minimum of about three minutes, a fairly long time to take up the WAN link. You *can* tune that with the Registry parameters that I described a few pages back, but 1.5MB is still a lot of data.

- Is it so very bad to do logins over the LAN? A typical domain login transfers about 2Kbytes of data. On a 64Kbps connection, that's only a quarter of a second transfer time. Users may not even notice the difference between logins over the WAN and logins to a local BDC.

The bottom line is this: if you have a large number of user accounts, replication can take a long time, and that can chew up WAN bandwidth. In contrast, if you only have a few users out in the branch offices, the time they waste waiting for logins over the WAN may be negligible. So don't assume that it's always a good idea to put a BDC at every remote location.

Estimating the Size of the SAM

Part of the previous analysis involved estimating how large the SAM was for my mythical Ohio-based company. You need to be able to estimate your SAM for several reasons:

- The entire SAM database must sit in the RAM of your primary domain controller (and backup domain controllers) at all times. If the SAM is too large, your PDC spends too much time paging data into and out of disk.

- The size of the SAM becomes important on replication times and network bandwidth considerations, as you just read.

- You can use this to determine how many domains you should break your network into.

You may be skeptical at this point. How big can a SAM *be*, anyway? Well, it depends, but Table 11.3 shows how to compute the size of the SAM on your domain.

TABLE 11.3   Size of Components in SAM

For Each One of These...	The SAM Grows By...
User account	1024 bytes (1K)
Computer (machine) account	512 bytes (1/2K)
Global group	12 bytes/user + 512 bytes
Local group	36 bytes/user + 512 bytes

Now, suppose you had (just to make the calculation easy) 100 users, 10 machine accounts, five global groups and five local groups. Assume also that every user is in every group. (There are 100 users but only 10 machine accounts because, recall, only NT machines need machine accounts. Windows 3.*x*, Windows 95, and MS-DOS machines don't need machine accounts.) The total size of the SAM would then be

- 102,400 bytes for the user accounts

- 5120 bytes for the machine accounts

- 1200+512, or 1712, bytes per global group, with five groups for a total of 8560 bytes in global groups

- 3600+512, or 4112, bytes per local group, with five groups for a total of 20,560 bytes in local groups

The total is 136,640 bytes.

That's not a very large SAM, and its impact on the design of the domain controllers is minimal because the SAM takes up less than 200K of RAM. Now go back and do the math for a domain with ten thousand users, one thousand machine accounts, and a reasonable number of local and global groups, and it's easy to see that the SAM can grow to megabytes and megabytes in size.

Many wonder how many people can be put in a single domain. The answer is, simply, it depends on how large a SAM you can afford for your PDC (and BDCs) to manage. Microsoft says that a SAM shouldn't exceed 40MB in size, but it's hard to imagine even that. Microsoft itself admits that reading a 40MB SAM increases by 15 minutes the amount of time required to boot a PDC! (Good thing I don't reboot my PDC very often…)

Anyway, the answer to the "How many people can be put in a domain?" question is this: compute how large the SAM would be if you put your whole company on one domain. Figure out roughly how large you think a SAM should be (a matter of some guesswork, of course) and divide the one number by the other. For example, suppose you'd like your SAMs to all be under 10MB in size (a nice, reasonable maximum as far as I'm concerned). You compute that the 22 thousand employees and sundry machines and groups in your firm results in a SAM that is 26MB in size. Divide that by 10, round up, and you see that you need three domains. Or you can go with one very large domain, but you had better be ready to buy some powerful domain controllers— the fastest Alphas money can buy and all the RAM they can stand!

But I see that we're starting to talk about really big, multi-domain networks. It was my intention to start this book out by showing you how to run a small NT network. Once you had those basic tools, I intended to show you how to scale up from there. This is the end of that "basic" section; from here on in, we'll see how to extend NT to an entire enterprise, starting with multiple-domain networks—and that starts in the next chapter.

PART IV

Managing NT Server in an Enterprise Network

■ **CHAPTER 12** • Cross-Domain Management in NT Networks

■ **CHAPTER 13** • Novell NetWare in an NT Server Environment

■ **CHAPTER 14** • TCP/IP on Windows NT

■ **CHAPTER 15** • Tuning and Monitoring Your NT Server Network

■ **CHAPTER 16** • Troubleshooting and Disaster Recovery

■ **CHAPTER 17** • Using Dial-Up Networking

CHAPTER
TWELVE

Cross-Domain Management
in NT Networks

By now, you've learned about the basic administrative tools in the NT Server world:

- The User Manager for Domains lets you manage users, groups, user rights, and trust relationships with other domains.

- Windows Explorer and My Computer (or File Manager, if you're using NT version 3.*x*) let you control user permissions on files and directories.

- The Printers folder lets you control user permissions on printers and printer pools.

- The Server Manager lets you control user permissions on files and directories of other machines in your domain and in other domains, as well as how domain controllers interact.

But so far I've pretty much restricted the discussion to a single-domain network. For many of us, however, that's not how the world is. Instead, any given NT domain is just a part in a larger enterprise network that includes other NT domains, some Novell servers, and perhaps a connection to a TCP/IP-based network like a corporate intranet or perhaps *the* Internet. Those three things—multi-domain NT enterprise networks, coexistence with NetWare, and TCP/IP/ Internet support—are the focus of the next three chapters.

In this chapter, I want to focus on two large issues: how to manage a multiple-domain network as easily as possible, and how to *design* a multi-domain NT network. These are two very different ideas. The first is very "nuts and bolts" and the second more of a "big-picture" concept. I handle them both in this chapter.

Multi-Domain Management Tasks

How is managing a multi-domain network different from running a single-domain network? As I've said, you use the same administrative tools (User Manager, Server Manager, Explorer, and the like), but with a few twists. The particular tasks that you probably perform across domains include (in roughly increasing order of complexity):

- Permitting one domain to communicate with another, a concept called *trust relationships*.

- Permitting one domain's users to physically log on at computers in another domain.

- Permitting one domain's users to access directories and files on machines in another domain.

- Permitting one domain's users to print on printers in another domain.

- Making users of one domain users of another domain as well.

In this chapter, you'll see how to do all of those things. And, in the process, you'll see me spend a hefty amount of this chapter explaining a somewhat thorny concept, *local groups* versus *global groups*.

I find when teaching my classes about NT that cross-domain stuff makes people's heads hurt. ("Now, let's see, domain Personnel trusts domain Finance, but Finance doesn't trust Personnel, so....") In order to make this easier to follow, I've structured much of this chapter around a simple multiple-domain example—my network. My network consists of two domains: WOMBAT, where my researchers and I do most of our work, and TED, the domain that keeps track of where our seminars and consulting work takes place. (In case you're wondering, TED stands for "The Engagements Database," a client-server system that we use to maintain schedules for the company's consultants and teachers.)

Getting Acquainted: Trust Relationships

Because high-quality security was one of the most important design principles of NT Server, communication between domains is tightly controlled. Domains can't even *acknowledge* each other unless they are properly introduced, so to speak. That's done with *trust relationships*.

Furthermore, someone from domain X can't even *sit down* at a machine that is a member of domain Y unless Y trusts X. *That's* how paranoid NT security is: it doesn't even want you working at a workstation unless the workstation is in your domain. (Please note that I'm referring to NT workstations and servers; you don't have to be a member of a given domain to log on to a Windows 95, Windows 3.*x*, or Windows for Workgroups workstation.)

For some reason, trust relationships are controlled with the User Manager for Domains. I guess there's no Domain Security Manager. (Perhaps there should be one.)

What Is a Trust Relationship?

Domains are the basic unit of an NT Server network structure, as you know. But domains by default cannot communicate with one another. It takes a conscious act to make it possible for two domains to communicate. The first step in domain-to-domain communication is to establish a trust relationship.

People get confused when I explain trust relationships in class because they want to know, "When I create a trust relationship, what did I cause to happen? What *is* a trust relationship?" It's important to understand that creating a trust relationship doesn't *do* all that much; it's just the first step in a larger set of actions.

Perhaps it's easier to explain what's going on when there *isn't* a trust relationship. Before TED trusts WOMBAT:

- It is impossible for a TED administrator to extend permissions (for shares, files, directories, or printers) to a WOMBAT user.

- A WOMBAT user can't just sit down at an NT workstation that's a member of TED, even if all the WOMBAT user wants to do is connect to a resource on the WOMBAT domain.

Again, just creating the trust relationship doesn't do much, but from a technical point of view, these are the effects of making TED trust WOMBAT:

- WOMBAT users can sit down and log on to NT workstations— but they won't be able to access TED resources, unless they are given permissions to TED resources by a TED administrator.

- The definition of the "Everyone" group in TED now is "all of the TED users and guests and all of the WOMBAT users and guests."

That's not much, is it? Here's what is important about trusts: trust relationships open the lines of communication between domains, making it possible for administrators in the *trusting* domain to extend permissions and rights to users in the *trusted* domain. In some ways, a trust relationship is like a treaty between two sovereign nations: once the two of them decide to allow trade between their countries, they agree to a treaty between themselves. The treaty doesn't really do anything—no money changes hands (at least, no money's *supposed* to change hands)—but the treaty makes it possible for businesses on either side of the border to do business with one another. Without the treaty, vendor/client relationships can't take place.

Like a treaty between nations, wherein the leader of each nation must initiate the treaty, so must an *administrator* from each domain initiate a trust relationship between two domains. Not surprisingly, you've got to be an administrator to create and maintain trust relationships.

A trust relationship is a link between two domains. It allows one domain (the trust*ing* domain) to recognize all global user accounts and global user groups from another (the trust*ed* domain).

Trust relationships can be one-way or two-way. *A two-way trust relationship* is just a pair of one-way trust relationships, where each domain trusts the other. When established correctly, trust relationships allow each user to have only one user account in the network (defined in the user's home domain), yet have access to network resources in other domains.

For example, Figure 12.1 shows a network containing two domains whose names are TED and WOMBAT.

If TED establishes a trust relationship with WOMBAT, then all user accounts in WOMBAT (the trusted domain) can be used in TED. Now a trust relationship is established, as shown in Figure 12.2.

With the trust relationship established, WOMBAT users can log on at TED's workstations, and user accounts created in WOMBAT can be

FIGURE 12.1

The domains TED and WOMBAT

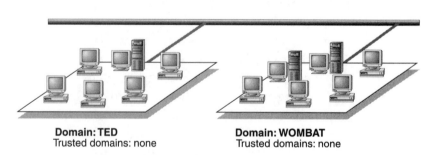

Domain: TED
Trusted domains: none

Domain: WOMBAT
Trusted domains: none

Two independent domains on the network

FIGURE 12.2

A trust relationship
is established.

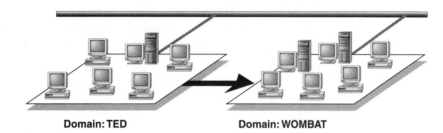

Domain: TED   **Domain: WOMBAT**

Domain TED establishes a trust relationship with WOMBAT.

placed in TED's "local groups" (I *am* going to explain what local groups are, I promise) and be given permissions and rights within the TED domain, even though they don't have accounts there. This does *not* mean that TED users can log on at WOMBAT workstations or use WOMBAT servers or printers. However, since TED trusts WOMBAT, *WOMBAT* gets many benefits, as explained in Figure 12.3.

Unless the WOMBAT domain in turn establishes a trust relationship with TED, accounts in the TED domain can't be used in WOMBAT. In other words, TED may trust WOMBAT, but that doesn't make WOMBAT automatically trust TED.

FIGURE 12.3

The benefits of a
trust relationship

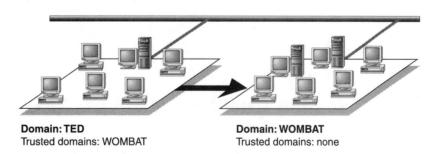

Domain: TED   **Domain: WOMBAT**
Trusted domains: WOMBAT   Trusted domains: none

TED trusts WOMBAT.

ALL WOMBAT users can log on at TED workstations.
WOMBAT user accounts & global groups can be placed in TED local groups.
WOMBAT users can be given rights & permissions in the TED domain.

Trust between different domains is likewise not "transitive" (in the algebraic sense) or transferred. For example, if TED trusts WOMBAT, and WOMBAT trusts a domain named ANDROMEDA, then TED does not automatically trust ANDROMEDA, as shown Figure 12.4. If the TED network administrator wanted to be able to use ANDROMEDA's accounts in the TED domain, she would have to set TED to trust ANDROMEDA.

Bear in mind that trust relationships can only be established between NT Server domains. The Trust Relationships command isn't available when administering LAN Manager 2.*x* domains or NT workstations.

FIGURE 12.4

Trust is not transferred through trusted domains.

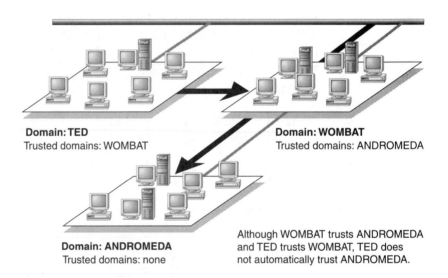

Domain: **TED**
Trusted domains: WOMBAT

Domain: **WOMBAT**
Trusted domains: ANDROMEDA

Domain: **ANDROMEDA**
Trusted domains: none

Although WOMBAT trusts ANDROMEDA and TED trusts WOMBAT, TED does not automatically trust ANDROMEDA.

Avoiding Trust Relationships: A Note

Besides all of this trust relationship stuff, there is another way to get access to resources to multiple domains. It's a bit kludgy and hard to manage, but I'll mention it for the sake of completeness.

If TED and WOMBAT aren't speaking—if they don't have a trust relationship—but I must access both TED and WOMBAT resources, then I can just create a Mark user account on both TED and WOMBAT.

The tricky part (that is, the hard-to-manage part) concerns passwords. In general, to make this work, you have to keep the passwords on the two domain accounts exactly the same. By doing that, I can access both TED and WOMBAT resources. What is actually happening under the hood is that I first log on to WOMBAT, and of course I supply a user name and password to do that. Then, the first time I try to access a TED resource, TED tries to authenticate my Mark user account. The TED PDC asks my workstation for my password, and my workstation just tells the TED PDC the same password that I used for WOMBAT. If the passwords match, I can attach to TED resources. If they *don't* match, then TED asks my workstation to prompt me for a password, and at that time I can type in my TED password if it's different from the WOMBAT password.

Unfortunately, however, not all client software knows how to ask for that TED password. For example, a DOS client doesn't give you the chance to enter the TED password. It just says to TED, "I don't know how to ask for the password," and so the attempted TED access fails. *That's* why the whole thing runs best with identical passwords on all domains for which you are a member. However, identical passwords makes password-changing day a bit more complex.

Establishing Trust Relationships

Establishing a trust relationship with another domain is a two-step process that is performed in two domains. First, your domain must permit a second domain to trust it, and then the second domain must be set to trust your domain. This shouldn't be a surprise; after all (he said with a grin), trust is a two-way street, right?

That sounds a little odd, so let me resay it: if domain CAT wants to trust domain DOG, then domain DOG must *allow* domain CAT to trust it before CAT can trust DOG. And after all that is done, it is only CAT that trusts DOG; DOG doesn't trust CAT at all! Remember, if you want a symmetrical trust relationship—CAT trusts DOG and DOG trusts CAT—then you have to establish two separate trust relationships, one in each direction.

The two steps—DOG allowing CAT to trust it, and CAT actually trusting DOG—can be performed in any order, but if you "permit the trust, then trust," the new trust relationship takes effect immediately. You can reverse the order of the two steps and still establish the trust relationship, but you won't receive confirmation that the trust was established. What's more, the process can be delayed up to fifteen minutes. Let's see how to make TED trust WOMBAT.

Step 1: Permitting the TED Domain to Trust WOMBAT

Permitting TED to trust WOMBAT is done at the WOMBAT workstation. But before we do it, let's look at the domains TED and WOMBAT again. If you want the outside domain TED to trust your domain WOMBAT, you must first *permit* TED to trust WOMBAT. To do this:

1. Log on to the WOMBAT domain as a WOMBAT administrator.

2. Open User Manager for Domains in the WOMBAT domain.

3. From the Policies menu, choose Trust Relationships. You see the Trust Relationships dialog box shown in the Figure 12.5.

The Trust Relationships dialog box shows the domains that WOMBAT is currently permitted to trust, as well as those that are already trusted. In this case, there are none.

4. Select the Add button next to the Trusting Domain box.

5. Type in the name of the domain you want to permit to trust, the TED domain in our sample case.

FIGURE 12.5

Trust Relationships
dialog box

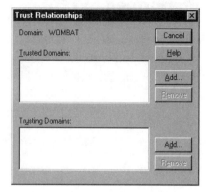

FIGURE 12.5

Trust Relationships
dialog box

6. Type a password in both the Initial Password and Confirm Password boxes, as in Figure 12.6. Passwords are case-sensitive and can be blank. By the way, the password is optional, and is really only relevant in the brief period of time between when WOMBAT permits TED to trust it and when TED actually gets around to trusting WOMBAT.

7. Choose OK. TED, the added domain, now appears in the Trusting Domain section in the Trust Relationships dialog box.

8. Close the Trust Relationships dialog box by double-clicking on the Close button in the top-right corner.

You've basically given one domain (TED) permission to trust your domain (WOMBAT), but the trust relationship isn't complete until the other domain actually takes the action of trusting your domain.

FIGURE 12.6

Add Trusting Domain
dialog box

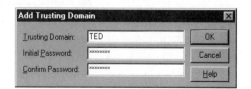

Step 2: Trusting WOMBAT (Performed at TED)

Now that you've permitted TED to trust WOMBAT, you must give the password you entered in the Trust Relationships dialog box to the administrator of the TED domain. He or she should then do the following:

1. Log on to the TED domain as an administrator.

2. Open User Manager for Domains for the TED domain.

3. From the Policies menu, choose Trust Relationships.

4. Select the Add button next to the Trusted Domains list. The Add Trusted Domain dialog box appears, as in Figure 12.7.

5. In the Domain and Password boxes, the TED administrator should type in WOMBAT and the password you provided and choose OK. (If you didn't use a password, then don't put anything in the password field.)

The added domain name, WOMBAT, should now appear in the Trusted Domains list of the Trust Relationships dialog box—TED now trusts WOMBAT.

6. To exit from the Trust Relationships dialog box, double-click the Close button in the upper-right corner.

FIGURE 12.7

The Add Trusted Domain dialog box

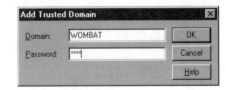

Once a domain is trusted, its users can access the domain that trusts it. Note the following about trust relationships:

- The trusted domain shows up as an option in the logon box on an NT workstation, which means that users from the trusted domain can log on at workstations in the domain that trusts it.

- When you're logged onto an NT machine and you try to browse an untrusted domain, you *can* see the list of servers on that domain. But if you try to view the shares on one of the domain's servers, you are refused. Even if there *is* trust, you've got to have an account on the domain to get the browse list.

- Network connections can be made to shared directories on the trusting domain's servers.

Terminating a Trust Relationship

Just like establishing a trust relationship, terminating a trust relationship is also a two-step process done in two different domains. First, one domain has to stop trusting another domain, then the other domain has to take away the permission of the first domain to trust it.

To stop trusting another domain, open User Manager for Domains and choose Trust Relationships from the Policies menu. Highlight the name of the domain in the Trusted Domains box that will no longer trust your domain, then choose Remove. The explicit message shown in Figure 12.8 appears to remind you about the two-step process. Choose Yes, then close the Trust Relationships dialog box.

Now, still following our "TED trusts WOMBAT" example, the administrator in WOMBAT has to stop permitting the TED domain to trust it. This is done by opening User Manager for Domains in WOMBAT, selecting Trust Relationships under the Policies menu, highlighting TED in the Trusing Domain box, and once again selecting Remove. When finished, close the Trust Relationships dialog box.

FIGURE 12.8

Removing a domain from
the Trusted Domains list

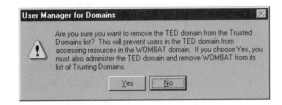

Keep in mind that both of these steps must be performed to properly terminate the trust relationship between domains. Let's summarize this whole process with a "How Do I?"

Extending File Permissions across Domains

Now that the two domains have some trust, let's put it to use. As I told you before, my network includes two domains, WOMBAT and TED. I'm a member of TED, which is to say, I have a user account on TED. How could I get access to files on machines in TED? For example, suppose there's a share on one of the WOMBAT servers named STUFF. How do I get to it?

Reprise: Everyone Means, Well, *Everyone*

Well, first of all, I may *already* have access to STUFF. As you've seen, whenever you create a directory share, it automatically gets the share permissions Everyone/Full Control. (As far as I know, there's no way to change that default set of share permissions.) Unless the WOMBAT administrator customized the share permissions in some way, the Everyone group can get to the share.

How Do I Get One Domain to Trust Another?

Let's say that you have a domain named TRUSTING and you want it to trust the main administrative domain (named TRUSTED) so that its administrator can manage TRUSTING's accounts.

TRUSTED's administrator must complete the following steps:

1. In the User Manager for Domains, open the Policies menu and choose Trust Relationships.
2. Choose the Add button next to the Trusting Domain list.
3. Type **TRUSTING** in the Add box, then type in a password (it can be a blank password). Choose OK.

TRUSTING is now *permitted* to trust TRUSTED, but the trust relationship isn't complete until TRUSTING actually takes the action of trusting TRUSTED. To do this, TRUSTING's administrator must:

1. Open User Manager for Domains in the TRUSTING domain and choose Trust Relationships on the Policies menu.
2. Next to the Trusted Domains box, choose Add.
3. In the Add Trusted Domain box, type in **TRUSTED** and the password provided by TRUSTED's administrator.

This establishes the trust relationship between the two domains—TRUSTING now trusts TRUSTED.

When you trust another domain, you are giving it the potential to control your domain. Users from TRUSTED can log on at TRUSTING's workstations, and TRUSTED's local groups can now contain TRUSTING's global groups.

As long as STUFF is shared to Everyone, my Mark account from TED can get to the STUFF share, because the Everyone group includes all users *from all trusted domains*. Since WOMBAT trusts TED, all TED users are part of WOMBAT's EVERYONE group. (Remember that since TED doesn't trust WOMBAT, the WOMBAT users are *not* part of TED's EVERYONE group. Go ahead, re-read that sentence a couple of times; this trust relationships stuff *does* get confusing.)

Adding a User from a Foreign Domain to Share Permissions

But suppose STUFF has a different set of share-level permissions, perhaps to WOMBAT's group of regular old users, a group called "Domain Users." The reason it has the name Domain Users will get clearer when I explain local groups versus global groups a little later in this chapter.

Basically, a WOMBAT administrator can grant me access via share permissions, just as you saw in Chapter 7, which covered directory shares; there's just an extra step to the process, the step of asking for the list of users and groups not from WOMBAT, but from TED.

Looking at things from the perspective of a WOMBAT administrator, suppose I want to extend file permissions for a share named STUFF to the TED user named Mark. I start off by displaying the permissions dialog box for the STUFF share, as you see in Figure 12.9.

So far, so good—there's nothing here we haven't seen before.

Now, let me see who I can add to this permission list. As you learned before, I just click Add and see a dialog box like the one in Figure 12.10. Notice something that's been in these dialog boxes all along, but that I haven't drawn attention to—the List Names From drop-down list box.

Now, List Names From is an important list box. From now on, whenever you see that, you should have a Pavlovian response (well, I guess

FIGURE 12.9

Access Through Share
Permissions dialog box
for STUFF

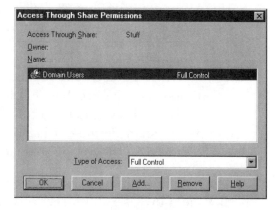

FIGURE 12.10

Adding a user to STUFF's
share list

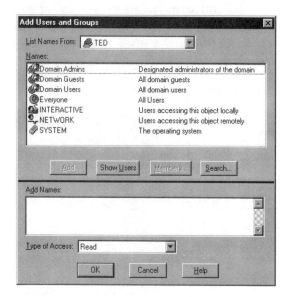

you can skip the salivating part) along the lines of, "Hey, a cross-domain tool!" Not all NT dialog boxes include that list box, so noticing it is important.

Anyway, after I click on the List Names From drop-down list, I see TED as one of my options, so I click that, wait a few seconds, and then see the dialog box shown in Figure 12.11.

This dialog box looks a lot like the previous one, but now we're looking at the TED users as you can see by the presence of a new group called "notusers." Notice that TED, like WOMBAT, has a group called Domain Users. If I wanted to, I could add the TED\Domain Users group to the share permission list for STUFF, and then every user from TED could access the STUFF share in WOMBAT.

But I don't want to do that; I just want to add one TED user, Mark. I click the Show Users button, choose the user Mark, and give him Full Control. Now the permissions dialog box looks like Figure 12.12.

Notice the notation describing the Mark account—TED\Mark. That keeps WOMBAT from becoming confused with a possible account in the *WOMBAT* domain named "Mark."

FIGURE 12.11

Share permissions dialog box after choosing the TED domain

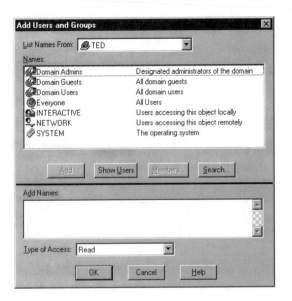

FIGURE 12.12

Adding Mark to
share permissions

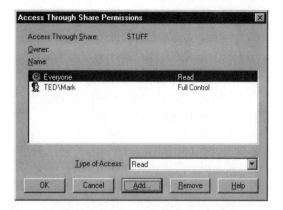

Now, that was a change in the share-level permissions for STUFF. Recall that you can get to that dialog box in one of two ways:

- Physically log on to the server that contains STUFF, open My Computer, open Explorer (or if you're using NT 3.*x*, open File Manager), and bring up the dialog box

- Start up Server Manager, click on the server that holds STUFF, click Computer/Shared Directories, choose Stuff, click Properties, and then click Permissions, just as I discussed in Chapter 7

If the volume in question is an NTFS volume, you may have to worry about file and directory permissions. Use the same procedures to set file and directory permissions across domains that you learned already, except take the extra step of clicking List Names From. Yes, it's in the file and directory permissions dialog box as well. Choose the foreign domain.

Cross-Domain Groups: Local and Global Groups

That was a fair amount of work just to get one user to be able to access one share. What if Mark needed to access a lot of TED things to the point where he needed to access things to the same degree that a normal TED user does?

Unfortunately, there's really no way to accomplish that, at least not simply. The object of this section (and be warned, it's a big one) is basically to explain *why* that's the case, and what you *can* do to extend permissions over domain boundaries.

If you need the short version, however, here it is: if there are ten servers in TED holding 20 shares in total, and if I want Mark from WOMBAT to be able to access all 20 shares, I have to add him to each share, one by one. (In earlier editions of this book, I claimed that there was an easy way to do that, but I'm afraid I was wrong. The method I described only worked if every one of your servers was also a domain controller, which isn't a very good solution.)

Adding Users from One Domain to Another Domain's Domain Users Group

Let's see, though. The name of the "users" group that's prevalent throughout the TED domain is the group called "Domain Users." Can I add the Mark account from WOMBAT to TED's Domain Users group?

To try doing that, a TED administrator would start up the User Manager for Domains and double-click the Domain Users group. That leads to the dialog box shown in Figure 12.13.

FIGURE 12.13

Adding users to TED's
Domain Users group

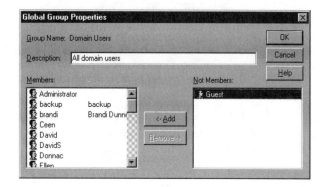

Hmmm… Notice the painful lack of a List Names From drop-down list. No, there's no way to add WOMBAT\Mark to TED\Domain Users. But why not?

The brief but cryptic answer to that question is, "Domain Users is a global group, and global groups cannot contain users from other domains. If Domain Users were a *local* group, then it could contain the WOMBAT\Mark account, but that wouldn't help either, because most servers in the TED domain cannot see a local group." The longer but clearer answer takes up the following bunch of pages.

Now, I *can* make this all make sense, but before I can do this, I have to give you some background on local groups and global groups.

Local Groups and Global Groups in NT Domains

While NT's got some really good, well-thought-out networking features, some of those features *aren't* so stellar, and local and global groups are two such benighted features. You see, the whole matter of local and global groups has as its basis an old and, by now, unfortunately familiar assumption: this feature really makes the most sense if you're using NT *workstations*.

Thus far in this book, we've run across stumbling blocks like this (the "User Profiles" dialog box in the User Manager for Domains is one example) and in general I've been able to say to you, "This is a feature that's really only relevant for people using NT workstations, so if you're using Windows 95 or Windows for Workgroups workstations, don't worry about it."

Local and global groups, however, are quite a different story. Even though they have their roots in networks composed entirely of NT machines, their effects apply to all NT users, and they apply particularly to people trying to design NT domains with workstations of *any* kind.

To explain local and global groups, I need a very simple domain, simpler than WOMBAT or TED. I need a simple network composed only of NT machines, each one a different kind of NT machine:

- A primary domain controller called PDC

- A backup domain controller called BDC

- An NT server that is *not* a domain controller called SERVER (you needn't name machines like this, of course; this is just an example with unoriginal machine names)

- An NT workstation named WS

I'll show you what you must do to make sure that any user can get to any share in this network. I'll start with a simple workgroup and then I'll show you how making these four computers a domain changes things.

Letting a User on One Machine Access a Share on Another without Domains

Suppose these four machines live together in a workgroup (we'll make it a domain later) called MYDOMAIN. I want a user named Jim, who is logged in at WS, to be able to access a share on SERVER. Suppose also that this share is open to the Users group on SERVER. What must I do to get Jim access to SERVER's share?

Recall that NT workstations keep local user accounts—accounts of their own—in their "personal" SAM database in the file \winnt\ system32\config\sam. Those accounts are created with the trimmed-down version of the User Manager that comes with NT workstations. NT Servers that are *not* domain controllers also keep a local SAM.

The WS machine knows Jim because he has a local user account on it, but the SERVER machine doesn't know him. If I want Jim to be able to have any kind of communication with SERVER, I have to build a user account for Jim on the SERVER machine. More specifically, I have to create a SERVER\Jim account that sits in the SERVER\Users group— the normal default user's group for SERVER. Notice that, previously in this chapter, I used NT's notation, so that WOMBAT\Mark meant "the Mark account on the domain WOMBAT." Since you can have local machine accounts on NT workstations and NT servers, the notation holds: SERVER\Jim means "the user account named Jim in the SERVER machine."

Once I've created a user account for Jim on the SERVER machine, Jim sits down at WS and logs in, indicating that he wants to log in as "Jim" on machine "WS." WS then searches its local Users group and finds the WS\Jim account. Assuming Jim remembers his password, WS lets him in. Then, when WS\Jim tries to access a share on SERVER, SERVER says to itself, "Who's this WS\Jim guy? Hey, I know a SERVER\Jim; I wonder if it's the same guy?" SERVER asks the WS workstation for Jim's password. If the password for the Jim account on the WS machine is the same as the password for the Jim account on the SERVER machine, SERVER lets Jim get to the share. But if the passwords are *different*, SERVER asks WS to ask Jim for a password, and Jim punches in the password for his account on the SERVER machine. Jim is not simultaneously logged onto WS and SERVER, with two different accounts; he is logged on with one account and two different passwords.

Then, because SERVER\Jim is a member of SERVER\Users, and SERVER\Users has access to the share on SERVER, Jim can have access. Simple, right? Yeah, sure; that's why there are domains.

Using a Single Domain Account across a Domain

Let's re-examine how domains improve things. Rather than having to go and create a Jim account on each of my four machines (PDC, BDC, SERVER, and WS), I just go to my PDC machine and create a Jim account for the domain—an account MYDOMAIN\Jim. Now, that does *not* go into a group called MYDOMAIN\Users, at least not directly. It goes into a group called MYDOMAIN\Domain Users instead. Why "Domain Users" instead of "Users?" Stay tuned; we have come to the crux of this local versus global discussion.

Here is how domains make things easier for people using NT workstations: to log on to an NT workstation, you must be a member of the Users group of that workstation. As I've said, building a given user on hundreds of workstations would be a pain. Therefore, when an NT workstation (or server, for that matter) joins a domain, the workstation's Users group automatically gets a new member—the Domain Users group of the workstation's new domain. For example, when WS joined MYDOMAIN, the group MYDOMAIN\Domain Users was inserted into the WS\Users group. The net effect is twofold:

- Anyone who is a member of MYDOMAIN can sit down at WS—or any other workstation that has joined MYDOMAIN—and log in.

- Because SERVER has also joined MYDOMAIN, the SERVER\Users group must now contain MYDOMAIN\Domain Users. Since MYDOMAIN\Jim is in MYDOMAIN\Domain Users and MYDOMAIN\Users is in SERVER\Users, Jim can access shares on SERVER that are intended only for people in SERVER's Users group.

Notice something a trifle new to the discussion: NT allowed us to put a *group* into the Users group.

Users versus Domain Users

The "magic" here is that you need only put a new user account in a domain user group. Why? Because NT has placed one group

(MYDOMAIN\Domain Users) into another group (every machine's Users group). Since the domain user group was previously placed in all of the local Users groups, the new user is automatically recognized by all machines in the domain.

But one thing is confusing: Why does NT put the Domain Users group from the domain into the local Users groups of all the domain's servers and workstations? Why not just have a Users group for the domain—MYDOMAIN\Users—and put it into the Users groups of the domain's machines? Why bother with a different group name?

NT's Problem: No Circular Groups

The reason? Laziness on the part of the NT designers. Suppose you could put the Users group from machine A into the Users group for machine B, which in turn puts its Users group into the Users group for machine C. Then, every time machine C's security module needed to verify if someone was in C\Users, it would have to interrogate machine B about *its* users, and machine B in turn would have to interrogate machine A. This might take time.

Worse, what if you then, in a fit of forgetfulness, put the Users group from machine C into the Users group from machine A? You'd have a loop, kind of like a spreadsheet with a circular reference. This sounded like it would complicate NT too much, so the NT designers came up with a rule: "We'll let people put one group into another group, but we won't let them take it any further—no groups inside groups inside groups!"

Local and Global Groups Defined

To prevent "circular groups," the designers of NT created two types of groups, local and global:

- Local groups can contain user accounts, of course, but they also can contain global groups.

- Global groups can contain user accounts, but that's it; they can't contain other groups.

Right about now, most of us start getting confused: "Hey, wait, if it's *global*, how come I can't put anything in it?" I had a lot of trouble remembering what global and local groups do, too, until I realized that I had a problem keeping that information in my brain because the words "global" and "local" mean something to me in English. If it helps, call local groups "group type number 1" and global groups "group type number 2." Group type number 1's can contain group type number 2's, but 1's can't contain 1's, 2's can't contain 2's, and 2's can't contain 1's. Just kind of chant to yourself, "Globals go into locals, globals go into locals, globals go into locals…" In no time, the difference between global and local groups will become second nature.

By creating two types of groups, Microsoft guaranteed that you couldn't go further than putting one group inside another. Put a global group inside of a local group, and you have one level of "nesting" in groups. But you can't go further than that, because you can't put a local group in another group.

Using Local and Globals inside a Domain

Here's how Domain Users relates to Users: the "Users" group that every NT machine has is a local group. The Domain Users group that every domain has is a global group. Since globals go into locals, the domain's Domain Users group can fit nicely into each machine's (local) Users group. Because of the way Domain Users relate to Users, you can't take the Users group from one machine, like WS, and put it into the Users group of SERVER because WS\Users is a local group and SERVER\Users is a local group, and you can't put locals in locals.

Just to be difficult, let's take this a bit further. Could I create a group called Users2 on WS, but make it a *global* group, and then put WS\Users2 into SERVER\Users?

No, I couldn't, for an important reason: only domains can have global groups. Since MYDOMAIN is a domain, it's possible to create MYDOMAIN\Domain Users; it's not possible to create a global group on WS, like WS\Domain Users.

Let's summarize what I've said so far by taking a look at Figure 12.14.

In a well-designed domain, most of the user accounts reside in the domain-wide group Domain Users. In my example, I've created accounts named Jim, Sue, Paul, and Janet (notice that the domain's Administrator account is automatically placed in the domain's Domain Users group). The Administrator account is placed into the local Users groups of each of the NT machines in the domain; that happens automatically when a machine joins the domain. Each computer's database of user and group accounts lives in a file called SAM in the \winnt\system32\config directory of each computer. The domain's SAM lives on the PDC, and any

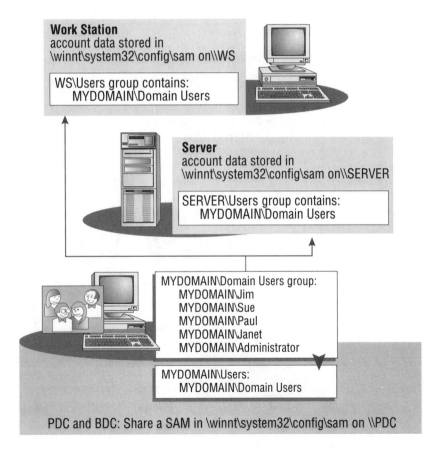

FIGURE 12.14

Local and global user accounts in a domain

Work Station
account data stored in
\winnt\system32\config\sam on\\WS

WS\Users group contains:
    MYDOMAIN\Domain Users

Server
account data stored in
\winnt\system32\config\sam on\\SERVER

SERVER\Users group contains:
    MYDOMAIN\Domain Users

MYDOMAIN\Domain Users group:
    MYDOMAIN\Jim
    MYDOMAIN\Sue
    MYDOMAIN\Paul
    MYDOMAIN\Janet
    MYDOMAIN\Administrator

MYDOMAIN\Users:
    MYDOMAIN\Domain Users

PDC and BDC: Share a SAM in \winnt\system32\config\sam on \\PDC

BDCs really don't *have* SAMs, save for the read-only replicated copy they get from the PDC.

Notice that this implies that domain controller machines don't have local groups of their own—there is no PDC\Users or BDC\Users.

Not only are there global and local users' groups, there are also local and global administrator and guest groups in a default NT setup. It's very important to understand how to use them. With that in mind, take a look at Figure 12.15. It's similar to Figure 12.14, but it now

FIGURE 12.15

Local and global administrator accounts in a domain

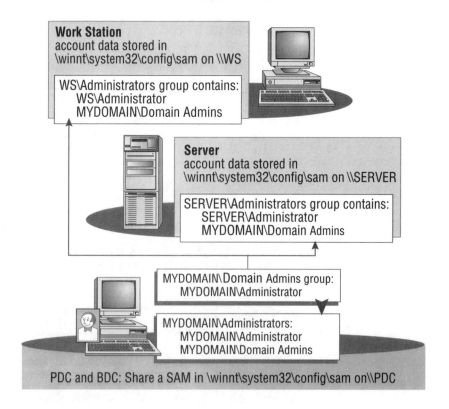

Work Station
account data stored in
\winnt\system32\config\sam on \\WS

WS\Administrators group contains:
    WS\Administrator
    MYDOMAIN\Domain Admins

Server
account data stored in
\winnt\system32\config\sam on \\SERVER

SERVER\Administrators group contains:
    SERVER\Administrator
    MYDOMAIN\Domain Admins

MYDOMAIN\Domain Admins group:
    MYDOMAIN\Administrator

MYDOMAIN\Administrators:
    MYDOMAIN\Administrator
    MYDOMAIN\Domain Admins

PDC and BDC: Share a SAM in \winnt\system32\config\sam on\\PDC shows the relationships of the administrator accounts and administrator groups in a domain.

Let's see why this information is useful. Suppose you went to PDC and created an account for yourself called Super that is supposed to be a domain-wide administrator account. Because you want Super to be an administrator, you put Super in the Administrators group on PDC. What does this accomplish? Do you now have a domain-wide administrator?

Well, you just put Super into the Administrators group on the primary domain controller, right? That must make Super a domain-wide administrator—but it doesn't.

Stop and think for a minute: Is Super now a member of the PDC\ Administrators or MYDOMAIN\Administrators group? It's something of a trick question. As I've already said, domain controller machines don't have local groups, so PDC\Administrators does not exist (and neither does BDC\Administrators).

In contrast, if you want to create an account that controls SERVER (an NT server machine that is *not* a domain controller), you can log on to SERVER by using SERVER's local Administrator account (on the Domain pull-down menu, choose SERVER, not the Domain name). You did remember to make a note of SERVER\Administrator's password when you installed SERVER, didn't you? Start up User Manager on SERVER (remember that, since SERVER isn't a domain controller, the User Manager program isn't User Manager for Domains, and has somewhat less functionality than User Manager for Domains) and add a new user to the Administrators group on SERVER. You can even add a domain account like MYDOMAIN\Super rather than a local SERVER account. Now that you have created an account that controls SERVER, anyone logging on to SERVER who uses the domain user account MYDOMAIN\Super can act as administrator on SERVER.

But, again, domain controllers—PDC and BDC, in my example— are different. There *is* no PDC\Administrators or BDC\Administrators group. Instead, there is a group called MYDOMAIN\Administrators that is shared by PDC and BDC and would be shared by any other domain controllers, if MYDOMAIN had any more. To administer and control the PDC or BDC machines, you must instead be a member of a group called MYDOMAIN\Administrators.

If you don't yet see why I find this a bit jarring, consider this: having a domain-wide global account like Domain Users is useful and makes sense because that Domain Users group is automatically inserted into all of the local Users groups on the domain. In the same way, you'll find another useful global group called Domain Admins that is automatically installed inside the local Administrators group of each NT machine in the domain. But you cannot place the MYDOMAIN\Users group into another machine's Users group, nor can you place the MYDOMAIN\Administrators group into another machine's Administrators group, because that would require placing a local group into a local group, and NT won't let you do that. So, on the one hand we have these local groups named MYDOMAIN\Users and MYDOMAIN\Administrators, but the groups aren't even *visible* to any machines save the domain controllers, which makes them seem less than "domain-ish."

Anyway, the bottom line is this: if you were to create a domain user account called Super that was supposed to be able to act as an administrator on any machine in the domain, then placing that account in the Administrators group would be a mistake. Super would be able to act as an administrator only on domain controllers—PDC and BDC, in my example. The Super account would have been automatically included in the MYDOMAIN\Domain Users group, and so SERVER and WS would recognize the domain account and allow someone to log on to them using the Super account, but SERVER and WS would only extend user-level privileges to Super, not administrative privileges.

"You might be a big guy when you're working the domain controllers," SERVER and WS effectively say, "but you're just a user as far as we're concerned." If you were instead to put Super into the Domain Admins group, *then* the Super account could control all of the machines in the domain, as the MYDOMAIN\Domain Admins group is automatically placed in the local Administrators group of each machine, including the MYDOMAIN\Administrators group itself.

The things to remember, then, are that to create a group that can be seen and exported all over your domain, make it a global group, and place that global group in whatever local groups you require. And, in the particular case of administrators:

- The domain's Administrators group only has administrative powers over domain controller machines.

- The domain's Domain Admins group has administrative powers over *all* machines in the domain.

Using Global Groups across Domains

Having read the lengthy discussion of how you would use local and global groups in a *single* domain, how does that apply across domains? As it turns out, very simply.

Global groups are not only "global" in the sense that they can be placed in a local group of an NT machine; they can also be placed into a local group of any NT machine—workstation, server, or domain controller—in another domain (a *trusted* domain).

Let's use that data to answer the question I posed much earlier, "How do I give WOMBAT users access just like TED users?"

First, recall that many shares on a domain are shared to the group Everyone. The simple action of TED trusting WOMBAT put all of the WOMBAT users into TED's Everyone group. WOMBAT users are thus automatically granted TED-like access to anything shared in the TED domain to Everyone.

Second, if you've had to make restrictions on a share's permissions, you've had to add permitted users or groups one by one. Most commonly, you add the Domain Users group from your domain to the share-level permission list of any share on an NT server or workstation in your domain. It would be great if you could say, "Well, since the TED\ Domain Users group has access to a whole bunch of shares, and I want the WOMBAT folks to get to that too, I'll just put the WOMBAT\Domain Users group into the TED\Domain Users group." But you know you can't do it. So what's the trick? Unfortunately, there isn't one. You just have to go to each share and add the WOMBAT\Domain Users group by hand. But perhaps there's a way to automate the process a trifle…

I'd like to tell you that a command-line utility lets you control share-level permissions, and that you can construct batch files to add a new domain's Domain Users group all in one fell swoop, but there isn't such a utility. But here's an idea. Recall that if a disk share is on a volume formatted as NTFS, then you have to satisfy two levels of security to get in, the original share-level permissions and then the file- and directory-level permissions.

Now, file and directory permissions *do* have a command-line utility called CACLS, which I discussed back in Chapter 7. So you might try this:

1. Make sure all of your disk shares are NTFS.

2. Share them with share-level permission of Full Control to the group Everyone.

3. Do the "real" permissions with file and directory permissions.

This way, it's simple to add a new domain's groups with a batch file using CACLS. Not a great answer, but it will have to do until the release of Cairo.

Granting User Rights and Printer Permissions across Domains

Thus far, I've discussed granting file permissions, which is probably of more concern to you more often than are user rights or even printer permissions.

By now, you've seen that the Add button that appears in many dialog boxes opens up the door, when clicked, to other domains. By using those dialog boxes, you can assign user rights and printer permissions to users from other domains, just as you've seen how to assign file permissions to "alien" users.

Logging on from Foreign Domains

Many companies adopt a model wherein user departments are organized into domains, and the MIS group has its own domain from which all other domains are managed. In that model, the trust relationships look like Figure 12.16.

In that model, all the user departments trust the MIS domain, but the MIS domain doesn't trust any of them. A LAN administrator, who is probably a member of the MIS domain, may find him- or herself at a server in *any* domain, wanting to log on to that server and do some kind of maintenance. How should the accounts be arranged so that this LAN administrator can log on to any server?

Well, logging on to a server requires two things, a recognized account on a trusted domain and the right to log on to a server as a user (ordinary users can't just sit down to the server and start working). As you've seen, it doesn't make sense to give this central administrator an account on

FIGURE 12.16

Special trust
relationship model

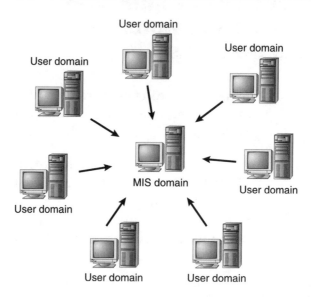

every single domain. Besides, that makes for some cumbersome administrative nightmares.

The LAN administrator in this example can get onto any machine via a two-step process.

First, make sure that the MIS domain's Domain Admins group is in every user department domain's Administrators group. That assures that all MIS administrators are granted Administrator status when they sit down and log on to any domain controller. That also gives the MIS administrators the user right to log on at a server.

Second, be sure to put the MIS Domain Admins group into the Administrators group of all NT servers (and perhaps workstations, as well, depending on whether the workstations will be the MIS people's responsibilities). This way, MIS administrators can get on from anywhere.

Here's an oddity that you may come across. Suppose you were a normal user in the MIS domain, not an administrator. Could you sit down to a Windows for Workgroups machine in a user department's domain and get to your machine? You could, because you can specify from Windows for Workgroups which domain you wish to log on to. Suppose you're at the desk of a member of the Personnel domain, and you go to log on to the MIS domain. You log on okay, but then you notice that the machine that you've logged onto has persistent connections that hook it up to some resources in the Personnel domain. After a moment, it dawns on you: *I shouldn't be able to get to Personnel resources.* And yet you can. What's going on?

The Guest account, that's what's going on. If the Guest account doesn't have a password, and if you haven't restricted its access to domain resources, then someone who logs on whom the domain doesn't recognize gets logged onto the local domain's resources as a guest. This is true even if the user logging on is from a trusted domain. If the Guest account had been disabled, you are prompted for a password before you can go any further, because the Windows for Workgroups machine wants to finish establishing persistent connections.

The thing that separates NT from many other network systems, including earlier Microsoft offerings, is its enterprise-wide structure. By using global groups, by having a good knowledge of cross-domain techniques, you can build a network that is easy to administer, even from miles away.

Planning Your Enterprise: Single- versus Multiple-Domain Networks

It certainly sounds like setting up an enterprise with multiple domains is a lot of work. Why not forgo multiple domains and just create one big domain?

In some cases, that's not a bad answer. Let's spill a little ink and discuss the merits of single- versus multiple-domain networks.

The Fewer Domains, the Better

Domains are the cornerstone of Microsoft's powerful security system in NT, but they were built more with the idea of keeping outsiders out than they were with the idea of making it easy for enterprise network managers to run enterprise networks. Microsoft's own network managers say that keeping Microsoft's domains all linked up with one another is a nightmare.

As a result, you really should minimize the number of domains in your network, at least if keeping your network administration task to a minimum is one of your goals. I'm not saying that last thing facetiously; impregnable security may be your network's number one target, and if that's the case, then by all means separate functional units into domains, fill the moats, and lower the portcullises to be extremely secure.

In the long run, controlling multi-domain networks will get easier, particularly when Microsoft releases Cairo, the next major version of NT, which will probably appear in late 1997 or early 1998. Reportedly, Cairo will introduce "trees of domains" to make it possible to manage a number of domains under a single "tree." It sounds good, but I wouldn't build any important networks based simply on the presumption that (1) there will be a next version of NT, and (2) it will be significantly better than what is out now. As has been true for many computer companies over the years, Microsoft products are usually better *before* they're announced than after they're announced, if you know what I mean...

Domains Might Mirror Organizational Structures

In some cases, you (or your clients) will be happier with multiple domains. It may well be that the Manufacturing division has its own support people and its own networking infrastructure, so it really doesn't want to share much in the way of resources with Sales, which has its own network group. The VP of Manufacturing and the VP of Sales may look the company's IS/IT manager in the eye and say, "Keep your corporate network boys out of our system." In cases like that, the IS/IT department probably serves an advisory or consulting role only, offering recommended server platforms, disaster recovery systems, and the like.

Eventually, however, the various user departments will find places where some synergy should occur, and then they'll ask you to for help in bringing *glasnost* to the network. That's when understanding what you've learned in this chapter will come in handy.

Domains Might Follow Geographic Boundaries

One undeniable fact of life within domains and workgroups is that they do a lot of chattering within themselves. Maintaining the browser means that every server must announce itself every 12 minutes. All session-oriented activity requires that each side of the session say to the other side every now and then, "I'm still here." Such messages are called "keep alive" messages, and they range from one every 30 seconds to one every hour, as you see in Table 12.1.

Notice that some of this chatter goes on twice a minute. All that overhead might take up too much of your WAN connections' bandwidth. If that is the case, it probably makes sense to draw domain boundaries to mirror geographical ones.

You Might Have Too Many Accounts for One Domain

The most compelling reason for building more than one domain is simply that the domains get too large because too many accounts are

TABLE 12.1   Regular Communications on NT Networks

Message Type	Protocol/Transport	Default Interval
PDC-BDC message replication	Any	Every 5 minutes
Master browser to backup browser replication	Any	Every 15 minutes
Server announcement to master browser	Any	1 minute, then 2 minutes, then 4 minutes, then 8 minutes, then 12 minutes, remaining 12 minutes thereafter
NetBIOS keep alive message	TCP/IP	Every 60 minutes
NetBIOS keep alive message	IPX, NetBEUI	Every 30 seconds

in the domain. Recall from the last chapter that a few things, all of them related to the size of the domain's SAM database, limit domain size.

The formula for determining the exact size of a domain was explained in the previous chapter, but to summarize here, a SAM's size is roughly equal to 1Kbytes per user plus ½Kbytes per machine account. As you make domain size calculations, remember that you don't need a machine account for each machine; rather, you only need a machine account for each NT workstation or server that is a member of the domain. Of course, as time goes on, NT workstations will probably be a larger and larger part of your network because, in my opinion at least, it's clear that the NT Workstation will ultimately be the desktop operating system of choice.

The size of the SAM is vital because the entire SAM must remain resident in the memory of your domain controllers at all times ("the SAM lives in the RAM..."). A huge SAM, therefore, could require some serious RAM on your primary and backup domain controllers. If a large company with 200,000 employees wanted to create one large domain, the SAM would be at *least* 200MB in size. It would require at least 200MB of physical RAM on every domain controller—clearly not an acceptable situation in today's hardware market.

Additionally, every domain controller must read and parse the SAM database every time it boots. According to Microsoft, a 40MB SAM adds 15 minutes to bootup time on a PDC built on a 66MHz 486.

The bottom line is this: I can't tell you what to restrict your maximum SAM size to, because I don't know how patient and cheap you are. If you want to buy 33MHz 486 machines with 16MB of RAM for domain controllers, you will find that a hundred users creates a strain on the machine. An Alpha with four processors, a 300MHz clock, and 512MB of RAM could very well be able to handle 10,000 users. Given the speed of modern Intel- and Alpha-based systems, I wouldn't want to exceed about 10MB on a SAM; Microsoft used to agree with me, but in 1996 they revised their recommendation up to 40MB.

To really get the best answer to the question, "How large a SAM should we have?" try loading one of your typical domain controllers up with 1000 user accounts. Then time how long it takes to boot and how long it takes to log on one user. Then create 1000 more accounts and do it again, and then create 1000 more accounts and time bootup and logon a third time. Those three data points will give you a rough idea of how large the SAM can be. Then, once you know the maximum acceptable SAM size, compute the size of a SAM for your whole company by using the formula in the previous chapter. Divide the one by the other, and you get the number of domains.

For example, suppose I've decided that a 5MB SAM is the biggest I want. Suppose also that my firm has 10,000 users and 1000 NT machines. That makes the total SAM size about 10MB + ½MB, or 10.5 MB. (I left the accounts of the calculation for the sake of speed.) Divide 10.5 by 5 and you get a little over 2. If you want to give your domains room to grow, then round up and plan for three domains. If you prefer fewer domains (less management) and don't mind a big loss in network response time, plan for two slightly bulging domains.

Enterprise Designs: Single- and Multiple-Domain Models

Before moving on to the nuts and bolts of multi-domain management, here are some ideas about how to structure your enterprise. There are four basic ways to build an enterprise with NT domains: single domain, master/resource domain, multiple master/resource, and complete trust.

Single-Domain Enterprise Model

For networks with few users that don't need to be logically divided for effective management, one single large domain may suffice. Benefits: Simpler to manage. Drawbacks: Your enterprise may be too big, or links to remote sites may make it ineffective to use a single domain.

Complete Trust Model

Once you've built a bunch of domains, you will probably find that at least one person in any given domain X always needs access to a server in domain Y. Person X hasn't a prayer of getting to a server in domain Y unless Y trusts X, so you're forced to create (and manage) a trust relationship between Y and X. It's extremely likely that at least one person in one domain always needs to get to another given domain, so you end up creating all possible trust relationships.

Benefits: It's certainly flexible for users.

Drawbacks: You've got to be kidding if you think you can keep track of it all. Suppose you have 30 domains. You create a new one. You now have to create 30 trust relationships between the new domain and each existing domain, and 30 trust relationships going in the reverse direction—and each trust relationship requires the cooperation of an administrator from each side of the relationship. And every time you rebuild a domain that's had a disaster, you have 60 *more* things to remember to do.

Master Domain Model

The master domain model came about when Microsoft realized that they couldn't fit all of Microsoft into one domain and when they realized that managing a complete trust enterprise would be an abhorrent task. So they came up with an enterprise model that is built of a single master domain, a domain that contains all of the user accounts for the enterprise, and *resource domains*, domains that only contain machine accounts for servers and NT workstations.

To understand how the enterprise model works, suppose you and I are the network planners for our firm, Ajax Industries, and our firm is located in three places—an office in the U.S., one in Europe, and one in Australia. We could define four domains, which I'll call AJAX, US, EUROPE, and OZ. They work as follows:

- AJAX contains a user account for each Ajax employee. It also contains user groups. It is referred to as the "master" domain.

- US is a domain without any user accounts in it (save for Administrator and Guest, which can't get be removed). It contains the machine accounts for all of the servers in Ajax's U.S. offices. We set up US to *trust* AJAX. Recall that this means that AJAX members—that is, the employees in our firm—can sit down at NT workstations and log on even though the machines are members of the US domain and the employees are members of the AJAX domain. It also means that it is possible to give access to servers in the US domain to AJAX members. As US really only contains network resources—file servers, print servers, applications servers—it is called a *resource domain*.

- Likewise, EUROPE is a resource domain. It does for Ajax's European offices what the US domain does for the American offices. EUROPE trusts AJAX.

- Finally, OZ is another resource domain, for the Australian offices.

Summarized in a few words, you build a master domain-type enterprise as follows.

First, create a domain and put all user accounts into it. That's the master domain.

Then, create domains out in the branch offices called resource domains, and in them place only machine accounts for NT workstations and servers. Your file servers, print servers, and applications servers (SQL Server, SMS) would be in the resource domains.

Next, create trust relationships between the resource domains and the master domain. In my Ajax Industries example, US would trust AJAX, EUROPE would trust AJAX, and OZ would trust AJAX. US, EUROPE, and OZ wouldn't have to trust each other.

In each resource domain's shares, include the Domain Users group from the master domain. For example, if there's a file share in OZ, then include in its permissions AJAX\Domain Users. Of course, you may want to get more specific than simply the entire user community. If that's the case, then create a global group—it must be global!—in the AJAX domain and place *that* in the permission list for the OZ share.

In each server's Administrators group, place the accounts or groups from the master domain that you want to be able to administer that server. For example, if Ajax Industries had decided that it needs a set of company-wide network administrators, then it could put those users into the AJAX\Domain Admins group, and then put the AJAX\ Domain Admins group into the local Administrators group *of every single server in OZ, US, and EUROPE.* (Yes, it's a pain, but it's the only way to do it.)

Just to speed up logins, you might place backup domain controllers from the master domain onto the same networks as the resource domains. As a user from AJAX trying to access a resource in US must be authenticated by a domain controller from AJAX, placing an AJAX controller nearby means faster logins.

Multiple Master Domain Enterprise Model

If the organization is too large to fit all the user accounts into one domain, you end up with the *multiple* master domain model. It works just like the master domain model, except you replace one master domain with a number of master domains. Then you build complete trust among the master domains, and build trust relationships between each of the resource domains and the master domains.

For example, if you had two master domains named M1 and M2, and three resource domains named R1, R2, and R3, you would first create the M1-M2 and M2-M1 trusts; both masters must trust each other. (If you had three master domains, you'd end up with six trust relationships, as four master domains would require 12 trust relationships, and so on; for n master domains, you'd end up with $n(n-1)$ trust relationships.) Then you would create a trust from each resource to each master, like so: R1-M1, R1-M2, R2-M1, R2-M2, R3-M1, and R3-M2. No trusts are necessary between resource domains. None are required from master domains to resource domains, either.

Does this look like a mess? It is. At this writing, I have heard that Microsoft is going to release some kind of command-line tool for creating and managing trust relationships, but it hasn't appeared yet. Of course, the ultimate answer will come in Cairo, when you will be able to build trees of domains.

When you're finished getting your NT domains to talk to each other, it's time to include the NetWare servers. That's the topic of the next chapter.

CHAPTER

THIRTEEN

Novell NetWare
in an NT Server Environment

Novell NetWare commands somewhere between 60 and 70 percent of the PC-based server market, between its three offerings in versions 2.2, 3.12, and 4.*x*. For that reason, many NT networks incorporate some kind of NetWare connectivity. Similarly, many NetWare networks out there find themselves having to deal with NT Server and NT workstations, as networks these days just aren't homogenous.

In this chapter, you'll learn how to integrate NT- and NetWare-based networks, so that you can enjoy the best of both worlds. There are several options for integrating the two networks, but the best one (in my opinion) is the Client and Gateway Services for NetWare that ships with NT Server.

How NT and NetWare Interact

There are three main ways in which NT networks and NetWare networks interact. They are described here.

NT Workstations on Novell NetWare   First, a Novell NetWare network may incorporate NT machines solely as workstations. This is fairly simple, as it requires no work on the server side at all. All you need to do is obtain NT NetWare client software from Novell to accomplish this. Another way to access the Novell servers directly from NT is to use the Client Service for NetWare, which is provided with NT Workstation.

Both versions of this solution are really only relevant to NT *workstations*, however. Users of an NT Server network would not be able to access resources on the Novell network with this solution.

NT Server in a Novell NetWare Network   If your current network is a Novell NetWare-based one, then your workstations all run NetWare client software. If you add an NT Server machine to an existing Novell NetWare network, you have to load *dual* network client software on the workstations. Here are some things to consider with this solution:

- It requires dual network client software, which can be hard to manage and requires more memory.

- It *does* provide for access to both Novell NetWare and NT Server resources, but security and programming interfaces are not integrated.

- Remote access and backup processes could not be shared under this system.

- It involves no special software installation on the *servers*, and so may be attractive to some network administrators. In a sense, it even may be a slightly more reliable solution, as it's the older one.

This second option is, unfortunately, the one that most of use. But many could benefit from the third option, Novell NetWare in an NT Server Network.

Novell NetWare in an NT Server Network   Starting with NT 3.5, a third solution—the Gateway Service—was available. With the Gateway Service, all NetWare resources become NT Server resources. Yes, you read that right: all access to NetWare resources occurs through the NT servers. Aspects of this solution include:

- You need only run one set of network software, the NDIS and Net-BIOS software, on the client in order to access the NetWare servers.

- Backup and remote access services can be integrated.

- Security can be integrated.

- As a side bonus, Novell NetWare server/user limitations can be bypassed.

It's quite an attractive solution, but how does it work? I'll cover that in most of the remainder of the chapter, but first let's take a quick look at Novell's answer.

NetWare Client Software for NT

The NetWare Client for NT (NCNT) software was released by Novell in late June of 1994. It has the following features:

- It replaces the NDIS-based network stack on an NT workstation with and ODI-based stack.

- The Open Data-link Interface (ODI) standard is the Novell analog to NDIS, which is troublesome, because there are likely to be fewer NT-compatible ODI drivers around.

- The NT services that require NDIS get NDIS-like service from ODI via an on-the-fly translation program called ODINSUP.

Overall, it's an answer more appropriate for a few lone NT workstations in a NetWare environment than it is for an NT Server-based environment.

Using NWLINK without the Gateway Service

Using NWLink without the Gateway Service is not really a NetWare connectivity solution, but one thing that ships with NT is NWLink, a transport protocol that is IPX/SPX-compatible. (IPX/SPX stands for internetworking packet exchange/sequenced packet exchange.) NWLink is another STREAMS and TDI-integrated transport protocol, a plug-and-play option like TCP/IP. You could, if you wanted, install it in place of (or in addition to) NetBEUI or TCP/IP as your domain's transport protocol.

Why would you do that? Well, NWLink supports the "sockets" application program interface (API). Since some NetWare-based applications servers, or NetWare Loadable Modules (NLMs), use sockets to communicate with client computers, your NT machines could act as clients in a NetWare-based client/server environment. NWLink is relatively useless all by itself, however, because it does not include a NetWare-compatible redirector. In English, that means that you could not access NetWare file servers or shared printers solely with NWLink.

NWLink mimics Novell's IPX/SPX stack, but many Novell users also load a Novell version of NetBIOS. To maintain compatibility with that NetBIOS, Microsoft also ships NWBLink, a transport stack that runs alongside NWLink and provides NetBIOS support much like that provided by Novell. (Novell's NetBIOS is a bit different from the Microsoft version, as you probably figured out if you ever tried to install something on your Novell network that required NetBIOS.)

If you're installing this product on an Ethernet, you may run up against a common situation that appears under Novell with Ethernets: frame type. In the Ethernet world, you can configure your network to work with either the IEEE 802.3 (CSMA/CD) or IEEE 802.2 (Logical Link Control) frame formats. If you are communicating with a NetWare 2.2 or 3.11 server, the frame format is usually 802.3. NetWare 4.x servers generally use frame type 802.2.

Running NetWare and NT Server in Parallel

The idea here is simple: your office contains both NT servers and a NetWare server or servers. The NT servers talk NetBIOS/NetBEUI and perhaps TCP/IP, and the Novell servers talk IPX/SPX. Getting the two server families (NetWare and NT) to talk to one another is a mite tricky, goes the reasoning, *so don't bother*. Instead, load both IPX/SPX and Net-BIOS/NetBEUI stacks on your workstations.

Many of you have probably already chosen this solution if you're running Windows for Workgroups. Windows for Workgroups ships with an IPX/SPX stack that runs in combination with NetBIOS/NetBEUI and makes it possible to carry on conversations with both servers. Here are some features of the NetWare and NT Server in parallel solution:

- Simplicity, kind of, in that you needn't install any software on the servers. You needn't put NWLink on your NT machines, nor some kind of odd NLM on your NetWare servers.

- Lack of drivers. To date, Windows for Workgroups does not ship with a NetWare redirector. The IPX/SPX protocol is in place, but the redirector is not, so you have to run the redirector that came with Windows for Workgroups version 3.1. Microsoft gives you no warning of this until you're part way through the installation of Windows for Workgroups version 3.11. (Nice touch, boys and girls!) In addition, the combination of 3.11 and the old 3.1 driver is a bit wobbly.

- Lack of drivers II. If you're running NetWare 4.*x* servers, then there's just no way that you can make the old Windows for Workgroups 3.1 NetWare drivers work reliably. You have to download a bunch of drivers from Novell. They seem to work fairly well when it comes to talking to the NetWare servers, but they tend to eliminate some of the benefits of Workgroups. Besides, they cut off your connections to NT Server machines periodically.

- Memory management becomes a problem in that you're loading a *lot* of stuff on the workstation.

- Because you're still running two different server environments, they don't share anything. You have to create separate user accounts on the NT side of the house from the NetWare side. Remote access services aren't shared, so twice as many modems are required. Backup services aren't shared, which means you have to keep track of twice as many tapes.

Windows 95 greatly simplifies matters because Microsoft has written complete protocol stacks and client software for both NT and Novell networks. Use all Microsoft client software and you'll only have to deal with one vendor.

Configuring NT to Run in Parallel

On your NT workstation, running NT Workstation and NetWare in parallel is a straightforward procedure. You will need to enable the Client Service for NetWare:

1. Open My Computer, open Control Panel, and then open the Network Icon.

2. Select the Services property page.

3. Click the Add button. You see the Select Network Service dialog box shown in Figure 13.1.

4. Select the Client Service for NetWare by double-clicking on it.

5. Tell Windows NT Setup the path to the NT 4 files.

6. Click OK.

FIGURE 13.1

Select Network Service
dialog box

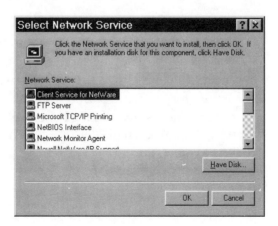

NT copies the appropriate drivers to your system and makes changes to your registry that enable the Client Service for NetWare to load the next time your start your system. Close the Network Dialog box and your bindings will be reconfigured. Once you reboot the system, NT attempts to log on to Novell for the first time. With the client software provided by Microsoft, you can either log on to a Novell 3.*x* Bindery by clicking on the Preferred Server radio button shown in the dialog box in Figure 13.2, or you can log on to a 4.*x* NetWare Directory Service Tree by clicking on the Default Tree and Context radio button. If you are going to log on to an NDS tree, do not provide the parameter codes before each option (i.e., omit the o= and the cn=). Enter the name of the Tree and its context. Figure 13.2 gives an example.

FIGURE 13.2

Select Preferred Server
for NetWare dialog box

On NT Server, the service and the client service are combined when you install the gateway services. All the steps that you took above still apply. The only difference is that you select the Gateway (and Client) Service for NetWare option instead of the Client Service for NetWare option. The last two dialog boxes (see Figures 13.1 and 13.2) are identical, though you have the additional option of configuring the Gateway Service, which is discussed in the next section.

NOTE At the writing of this book, Novell provides a beta copy of their 32-bit drivers for NT on their web site (www.novell.com). The drivers work in 3.51 but crash the system when installed on NT 4. Stay tuned to Novell for updated NT 4 drivers.

Microsoft Gateway Service

The Microsoft Gateway Service could become a good candidate for "the" NT-to-NetWare answer.

In mid-June 1994, Microsoft released the first version of its complete NetWare-to-NT solution. It comes in two parts: the NetWare Client Service and the NetWare Gateway Service. You'll be most interested in the Gateway Service.

The Client Service is a complete NT-based, 32-bit NetWare redirector. It allows you to sit at an NT machine and use all the resources of your NetWare network, just as you've been able to do for years from DOS workstations. The Client Service is just software like TCP/IP or NWLink that you install via the Add Software option on the Control Panel. No changes are required on the NetWare servers except, of course, the NT user must have a valid account. You must load NWLink before the Client Service can function. Fear not, because when you select the Client service, NWLink installs automatically.

Where things get really strange is when you install the Gateway Service, which is only available for NT Server. After you install it, *any workstation that is connected to your NT Server machine can also see the NetWare drives.*

NOTE When you install the Gateway Service, you install the Client Service automatically. You can not load one without the other on the NT Server platform.

Pretty spooky, but the NT Server machine becomes a gateway to the NetWare services. All the NetWare server sees is the one logical connection between NetWare and the NT machine, so actually dozens of people can use a single NetWare connection!

The characteristics of the Gateway Service are:

- It allows shared remote access services.

- It allows shared backup services.

- Accounts become integrated because the NT Server machine is the "front end" to the NetWare network, and so the NT Server machine handles logon validation and permissions as if they were just other resources in the NT domain. However, all of the users that access a NetWare server through the gateway must share identical access rights to Novell server. This situation is ideal for accessing a common post office or public directory that resides on the NetWare server. It would not be a viable option for home directories to be located on the NetWare server, since each user should have explicit and separate security permissions to their own home directory.

- An NT Server machine must serve as the gateway.

- This works on 3.*x* servers and only works with 4.*x* servers that are running bindery emulation; there's no support for NetWare directory services so far.

The Gateway Service answer is the newest one to the "How do I integrate NetWare and NT?" question, and it could be the best one.

Installing the NetWare Gateway

When you install the NetWare Gateway Service, you also install NWLink. As with all NT network software modules, you install the Gateway Service by starting up the Control Panel and clicking on the Networks icon. You see the dialog box shown in Figure 13.3.

FIGURE 13.3

Selecting the
Gateway Service

Select the Services tab, click the Add button, and you see options for other add-ons to NT. Choose Gateway (and Client) Services for NetWare and click Continue. You then have to provide the path where NT can find the setup files (the CD-ROM for most of us), and once again click Continue.

If you have RAS running, you receive the following setup message: "Setup has discovered that you have Remote Access Services installed. Do you want to configure RAS to support NWLink protocol?" If you want to configure remote access for using the IPX protocol, click OK. Click Cancel if you don't want to install the IPX protocol for use with RAS.

Creating the User

As the server boots, move over to a NetWare-attached workstation and run SYSCON, NWADMIN, or its equivalent. You have to get the NetWare servers ready for the NT client by following these steps:

1. Create a user whose name is the same as the user that will log on to the NT machine. In my example, I'm hooking up an NT Server machine to NetWare, so the username that I use to log onto the NT Server machine is "Administrator." Create a *Novell* user named Administrator.

2. Create a NetWare group called NTGATEWAY.

3. Put your user—called Administrator in my example—into that NTGATEWAY group.

4. Set the password of Administrator to the same value as the password of the NT user named "Administrator." (This isn't necessary for the simple Client Services setup, but it will prove essential for the Gateway Services later.)

Now, back to the NT side of the setup.

TIP

If you are going to run the Gateway Service (in contrast to the Client Service), be aware that if you log on to the machine running the Gateway Service, then you may be unable to access the Novell drives unless you supply the gateway name and password. For example, I've been using a user named Administrator for my examples. If I logged onto EISA66, the NT machine that's running the Gateway Service, and used the name "Mark," I would get a password verification the first time that I tried to use the Novell drives locally. All I'd have to do would be to supply the user name "Administrator" and the password for that account.

The Gateway Service Setup, Part 2

When the server comes back up, the client part of the service will attempt to log on to the NetWare server. It will prompt you for a preferred NetWare server if you are logging on to a 3.*x* server or a preferred context, if you are logging on to a 4.*x* server. If you are just going to use the Gateway service, don't pick one yet; choose Cancel for now, and when it asks you if you want to continue, tell it Yes. Start up the Control Panel and you see a new icon labeled GSNW. Click on GSNW, and you see the Gateway Service for NetWare dialog box, as shown in Figure 13.4.

The important areas here are Preferred Server and Default Tree and Context (depending on which version of NetWare you are connecting

FIGURE 13.4

Gateway (and Client)
Service for NetWare
dialog box

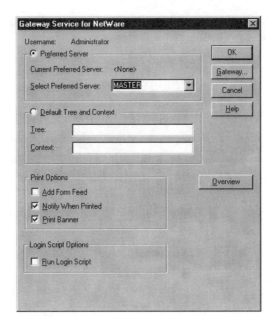

to). Your system should be able to list the available NetWare servers without any trouble. I haven't chosen one yet, but the server that I want to log on to is called Master, so I chose that server. Your server no doubt has a different name.

Note that the dialog box says, "Username: Administrator" at the top. That's the name that the *Novell* network sees. Click OK and close the Control Panel. (You can also do this by starting up the File Manager and then choosing Connect Network Drive.)

To browse the NetWare network, double-click Network Neighborhood, double-click Entire Network, and double-click NetWare or Compatible Network, as in Figure 13.5. NetWare servers and NDS trees become visible.

Notice that there is now a reference to NetWare Network in the Shared Directories box. This and only this NT machine can see the Novell servers;

FIGURE 13.5

Connect Network Drive
dialog box

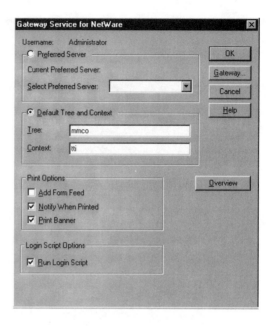

none of the clients of the NT machine can see the Novell resources. This is the *client* part of the NetWare connectivity software. To activate gateway services, go back to the GSNW icon in the Control Panel and click the Gateway button. You see a dialog box like Figure 13.6.

Notice that the buttons in the lower right-hand corner of the dialog box are grayed out. Don't worry, they will be enabled in a minute. Get this going with the following steps:

1. Enable the gateway by checking the Enable Gateway check box.

2. In Gateway Account, enter the username that you've created on your Novell network. In my example it's Ignatz. You could, if you wanted, create a special account just to be the gateway's name.

3. Enter the password. It should be both the NT password and the Novell password.

FIGURE 13.6

Configure Gateway
dialog box

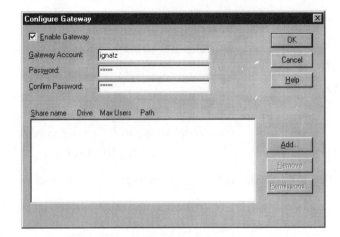

Now you're ready to start making NetWare volumes available for sharing. Now, you're used to using the File Manager to share drives, but you share NetWare volumes right here in the Configure Gateway dialog box. (Not very obvious, but after all this is relatively new software.) The Add button will be enabled by now. Click it and you see a dialog box like the Figure 13.7.

FIGURE 13.7

New Share dialog box

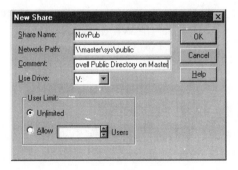

To make NetWare volumes available for sharing:

1. In the Share Name box, enter the share name that you want a workstation to see, as you do with normal NT shared directories.

2. In the Network Path box, enter the name of the Novell volume. Its name should be a UNC-type name, just as you've used so far: *machinename**volumename*. For example, on my network the NetWare 4.*x* server's name is MASTER, and its volume is SYS. The UNC name is, therefore, \\MASTER\SYS.

3. Add a comment if you like, and assign a drive letter to it.

4. Click OK to get out of New Share dialog box.

5. Click OK in the Configure Gateway dialog box.

Testing the Gateway

Now it's time to go see if the gateway works. Just go to any client machine and try to attach to the share name. For example, in the case of my network, I go to a DOS workstation and type

```
net use * \\EISA66\NovPub
```

Notice that EISA66 is the machine name of the NT server, rather than "master," the machine name of the Novell server. If I were connecting from inside Windows for Workgroups, I could, as usual, just use the Network Neighborhood to connect (File/Map Network Drive...).

Security for Novell Volumes: The Bad News

Volumes shared through the gateway are subject to permissions *not* made via My Computer, as you're accustomed to, but rather through the GSNW icon in the Control Panel. The Configure Gateway dialog box includes a button labeled Permissions that you use to control access to the Novell volume.

What this means is that the Gateway Service only provides *share-level* permissions. You can share a particular Novell volume on the NT network, but all Gateway Service users on the NT network will have identical permissions for the data on the Novell volume. If you try to set file or directory permissions with My Computer, you see the following message: "This is an invalid device name."

The downside should be obvious. It's customary to give all users on a network their own "private" directory that only they can access. That's impossible here. The only alternative would be to create different shares and give them different drive letters. For example, you saw how I shared the volume SYS, which was on the server MASTER. Within MASTER\SYS was a subdirectory called MARK. I could add a new share called \\MASTER\SYS\MARK and give only myself access to it. That would give me my own home directory, but that Novell share would get a drive letter on my NT gateway server—and there are only 26 letters in the alphabet.

In case that's not clear, here's an example. Before NT existed, suppose I had a NetWare 3.12 server with fifty users on it. Each of the fifty users had his or her own private "home" directory, and I would have owned a fifty-user license for NetWare 3.12. Could I use the NT/Novell Gateway Service to get around that fifty-user limit?

At first glance, it might seem possible to buy a five-user license for NetWare 3.12, install the NT Gateway Service, and then hook up the fifty users as NT users. They would all then have access to the NetWare volumes via the Gateway. But that wouldn't work, as my NT server probably has four drives already (A through D, including a CD-ROM), so I can only create a maximum of 22 new NetWare shares, drives E through Z. That means that I couldn't serve more than twenty-two users with home drives on the NetWare server.

(In case you're wondering, I'm told that it *is* legal to put those twenty-two users onto Novell via NT because the Novell licenses are not per *user* but per *connection*. Novell sees just one connection, so it's legal. In fact, I imagine that the legality question will boil down to which of the two companies can afford better lawyers.)

The Gateway Service seems to best fit the case wherein I want to share a directory both on the Novell and the NT sides of the house. However, I don't want to have to load IPX/SPX and a NetWare redirector on all of the machines on the NT side just to get to this particular directory on this NetWare volume.

Providing Print Gateway Services

The Gateway Service not only allows NT clients access to NetWare volumes, it also provides access to NetWare print queues. The printer gateway software is activated at the same time as the volume gateway software, but you have to complete one step before the clients can get to the printer: you have to connect your NT Server machine to the Novell printer queues.

Just as you provide access to NetWare drives via a bogus drive on your NT server, so also can you provide access to NetWare print queues by claiming that your NT servers are physically connected to printers that are actually the NetWare printers. That sounds complex, but it's not. Here's how to do it:

1. On the NT Server machine, start up the Add Printer Wizard (My Computer/Printers/Add Printer).

2. Choose Network Printer server, then click the Next button. The Connect to Printer dialog box appears.

3. Click on NetWare Network to open up that network, and you see your NetWare servers. Open them up, and you see the NetWare print queues, as shown in Figure 13.8.

FIGURE 13.8

Connect to Printer
dialog box

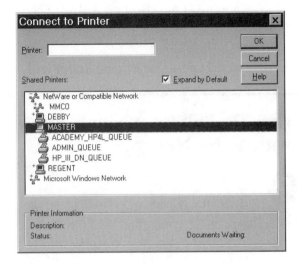

4. Choose a printer. You'll probably get a dialog box that says that a printer driver is not available for the printer you chose. This message just means, "There is no Windows printer driver on that Novell machine." It's not terribly important, as your DOS and Windows clients use their own local drivers anyway.

5. Click OK.

6. You are asked what kind of printer is on the Novell print queue. The driver of the printer you choose will then be grabbed off the NT installation CD-ROM. The Novell printer will then appear on the Print Manager as if it were a locally attached printer. You can view its queue, delete documents, and so on.

Before the rest of your NT network can see the printer, however, you have to share it, just as you always do, by way of the Printer Properties dialog box.

7. Click the Start button, click Settings, and then click Printers.

8. Right-click the printer you want to share and click Properties from the shortcut menu.

9. Click the Sharing tab and then click Shared.

10. Type a share name and it will be available to all NT clients.

How Do I Share a Novell Printer with an NT Network?

To share a Novell printer with an NT network:

1. On the NT Server machine, start up the Print Manager.

2. Choose Printer and then Connect to Printer. The Connect to Printer dialog box appears.

3. Click on the NetWare Network option to open up that network. You see your NetWare servers. Open them up and you see the NetWare print queues.

4. Choose a printer.

5. Even though you probably get a nastygram telling you that there is no Windows printer driver on that Novell machine, it's not terribly important, as your DOS and Windows clients use their own local drivers anyway. Click OK.

6. You are asked what kind of printer is on the Novell print queue, and that printer's driver is then be taken off the NT installation CD-ROM. The Novell printer appears on the Print Manager just as if it were a locally attached printer. You can view its queue, delete documents, and so on.

Before the rest of your NT network can see the printer, you have to share it from the Printer Properties dialog box.

7. From the Print Manager, choose a printer, and then click Printer and Printer Properties. Check the "Share this printer on the network" box.

The printer is now available to all NT clients.

Novell Commands Available from NT

At the NT server, you can open up a command line and run a number of Novell commands, including the ones in Table 13.1.

TABLE 13.1   Novell Commands at NT Command Line

chkvol	help	rconsole	settts
colorpal	listdir	remove	slist
dspace	map	revoke	syscon
flag	ncopy	rights	tlist
flagdir	ndir	security	userlist
fconsole	pconsole	send	volinfo
filer	psc	session	whoami
grant	pstat	setpass	

You can also run NetWare-aware applications (some of them, anyway) with some support programs. Windows-based, NetWare-aware applications may require files NETWARE.386, NWCALLS.DLL, and NWNET-API.DLL. They are in your system32 directory.

Novell supplies a file called NWIPXSPX.DLL that some client-server applications depend upon; Gupta SQLBase and Lotus Notes are two examples. Copy the file to your *systemroot*\SYSTEM32 directory.

Potential Problems with the Gateway Service

The Gateway Service is terrific, but it still has a few wrinkles. Following are problems you may encounter with the Gateway Service:

Slower than NetWare   The gateway overhead of going through NT slows the data transfer process a bit. That's normal, and it's an outgrowth of the "1.0" nature of the Gateway Service. You can monitor the performance of the IPX/SPX module with the Performance Monitor. You'll see new objects called NWLink NetBIOS, NWLink IPX, and NWLink SPX that contain a number of counters. The Bytes/second counter of NWLink IPX gives some idea of the NetWare traffic being generated.

You may be prompted for a password   When the Gateway is first loading, you may get a message from it asking for a NetWare password. This happens if you've set a different NT password than a Novell password. Just use the Novell *setpass* command to change your password so that the two passwords match.

"This is an invalid device name."   Try to share a part of a Novell volume or set its permissions and you get the following message: "This is an invalid device name." That's perfectly normal, and it reflects the fact that you do *not* control shared Novell volumes through the Network Neighborhood. Instead, you use the GSNW icon in the Control Panel.

Migrating Users from Novell to NT

Migration Tool
for NetWare

The fundamental reason why Microsoft offers the Gateway Service is to make it simple for people to gradually move from being primarily Novell-based to being primarily NT-based. Now, suppose you had a Novell-based network and you wanted to become NT-based. What kinds of things would you have to do? Basically, you would have to

- Rebuild all of your Novell users on your NT server

- Move information from the hard disks of the Novell servers to the hard disks of the NT servers

Using the Migration Tool for NetWare

The first concern, rebuilding all of your Novell users on your NT server, isn't a small one. Running a parallel NetWare/NT network means that every time you create a user on the NetWare side of the network, you have to go and duplicate your efforts on the NT side. It would be nice if there were a simple way to essentially "lock together" the NetWare user administration tools and the User Manager for Domains, so that a change in the roster of NT users would be immediately reflected in the roster of NetWare users.

Unfortunately, there isn't a tool like that, at least not yet. (It's a lucrative third-party opportunity for an enterprising software author, however.) Instead, Microsoft includes a tool with NT called the Migration Tool for NetWare. (Its beta name was called "Visine," as in "get the red out." Get it? Yuk. Yuk.) Start up Migration Tool for NetWare by clicking the Start button, Programs, Administrative Tools, Migration Tool for NetWare or by running \WINNT35\SYSTEM32\NWCONV.EXE. You see a dialog box that looks like Figure 13.9.

Now, I'm not going to discuss this very much for an important reason: I think it's a niche product with a fairly limited use. If Microsoft had taken the time to create a product that locks together the user accounts of Novell and NT, it would be exciting and worth explaining in detail. But Migration Tool for NetWare is really only of interest to someone *abandoning* Novell for NT.

FIGURE 13.9

Migration Tool
for NetWare
opening screen

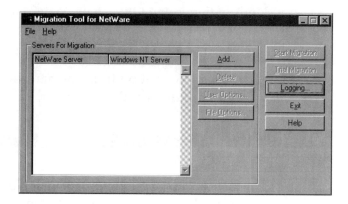

You start off using this program by selecting which servers you'd like to migrate *from* (the Novell ones) and which servers you'd like migrate *to* (the NT servers). Do that by clicking the Add button. You see a dialog box like the one in Figure 13.10.

FIGURE 13.10

Specifying source and
destination servers for
NetWare migration

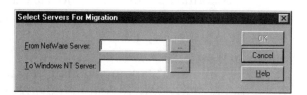

Click the browser buttons (...) to the side of From NetWare Server and To Windows NT Server to choose which server will soon be abandoned and which will soon be flush with users. In my case, I've chosen to migrate users from my NetWare 4.01 server MASTER to my NT server EISA66. The Migration Tool then looks like the Figure 13.11.

Now that the buttons are enabled, you can see what you can do with this tool. Following is an overview of what each of the buttons do.

FIGURE 13.11

Migration Tool after
selecting servers

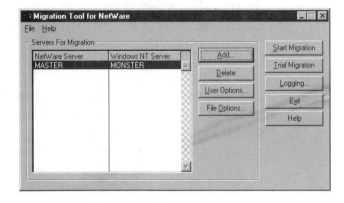

Add, Delete, Exit, and Help Buttons   The Add button is the one that you press to specify which servers you'll be working with. I clicked it to specify MASTER and EISA66. Delete would undo that selection. Exit and Help pretty much do what you expect them to do.

User Options Button   The User Options button controls how the migration will happen. When you select it, you will see the dialog box in Figure 13.12.

You click the Passwords, Usernames, Group Names, or Defaults tab to bring up "index cards." The aim of Passwords is to ask, "What passwords should I assign to the newly created NT users?" My first thought

FIGURE 13.12

User and Group options
dialog box

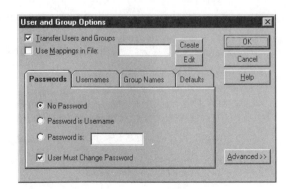

was, "Well, why not keep their old Novell passwords?" But then I realized (I'm a little slow some days) that *there is no way for the Migration Tool to get the passwords; Novell won't give them up*. So you get the options that you see in Figure 13.12—no password at all, a password that matches the user name, or a fixed password.

The Usernames and Group Names tabs are concerned with the question, "What should the Migration Tool do if it finds a Novell user named, say, Jack, and it tries to create an NT user named Jack, but there's *already* a user named Jack?" Your options are as follows:

- To not create a user when there's a conflict, and then either log the problem or ignore it.

- To simply create the new user, thereby overwriting the old user.

- To take the user name and prefix it with some fixed text.

You have the same options for group names.

The Defaults tab controls first how to handle account policies (minimum password lengths and the like) and how to treat Novell users with supervisor privileges. You can opt to automatically put any user with supervisor privileges into the Administrators group.

File Options Button   The Migration Tool can blast a whole server's worth of files from a NetWare server to an NT server, kind of like a monster XCOPY command. The File Options button lets you control which files to copy. When you select this button, you see a dialog box for restricting which files or directories get copied to the NT server.

Logging Button   The Logging button brings up the dialog box that you see in Figure 13.13.

The Popup on errors check box makes the Migration Tool stop and notify you about every single error—*and* warning. I recommend against it. Verbose User/Group Logging is essential, as it produces a record of any problems that arose when converting users from Novell

FIGURE 13.13

Logging dialog box

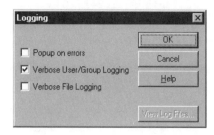

to NT. Verbose File Logging just gives you an exhaustive list of all the files transferred from one server to another.

Trial Migration Button   A server migration is a pretty drastic step, so Microsoft included a "dry run" option, Trial Migration. Click this and you get to see what the results of the migration process will be *before* you commit yourself. This can take *quite* a while, so don't expect immediate results.

The big advantage that I found to a trial migration was that it identified my potential user name and group name conflicts nice and early. I was then able to change the NT names or delete the redundant users, and in so doing prepare for a smoother migration.

Following is an example of the output from the migration process:

```
[ALEX]                     (Added)
Original Account Info:
 Name:
 Account disabled: No
 Account expires: (Never)
 Password expires: (Never)
 Grace Logins: (Unlimited)
 Initial Grace Logins: (Unlimited)
 Minimum Password Length: 0
 # days to Password Expiration: (Never)
 Maximum Number of Connections: (Unlimited)
 Restrictions:
   Anyone who knows password can change it
```

```
    Unique passwords required: No
  Number of login failures: 0
  Max Disk Blocks: (Unlimited)

Login Times:
Midnight        AM          Noon        PM
    12 1 2 3 4 5 6 7 8 9 10 11 12 1 2 3 4 5 6 7 8 9 10 11
    +-----------------------------------------------------------------+
Sun ** ** ** ** ** ** ** ** ** ** ** ** ** ** ** ** ** ** ** ** ** **
Mon ** ** ** ** ** ** ** ** ** ** ** ** ** ** ** ** ** ** ** ** ** **
Tue ** ** ** ** ** ** ** ** ** ** ** ** ** ** ** ** ** ** ** ** ** **
Wed ** ** ** ** ** ** ** ** ** ** ** ** ** ** ** ** ** ** ** ** ** **
Thu ** ** ** ** ** ** ** ** ** ** ** ** ** ** ** ** ** ** ** ** ** **
Fri ** ** ** ** ** ** ** ** ** ** ** ** ** ** ** ** ** ** ** ** ** **
Sat ** ** ** ** ** ** ** ** ** ** ** ** ** ** ** ** ** ** ** ** ** **
```

The bottom line on the Migration Tool is, again, that it can help you if you're abandoning Novell or you want to set up an NT system with users whose NT accounts mirror their Novell accounts. The Migration Tool only creates NT users and groups that mirror the status of the Novell users and groups *at that moment*, and that's the problem with it. What we need is a *dynamic* Migration Tool.

Between the Client Service, the Gateway Service, and the Migration Tool, Microsoft has assembled a nice set of capabilities for those contemplating a dual Novell/NT network. Get to know them and you can simplify your life as a schizophrenic network administrator.

File and Print Services for NetWare

You may be a "Novell-ean" at heart. You may have spent years of your life remembering the correct syntax to get around in the Novell environment. You might know what the slist, userlist, and map command do. And now someone is putting an NT server in your environment and messing up your grand design. If this is a worry for you, then you want to look at File and Print Services for NetWare (FPNW), an add-on utility available from both Microsoft and Novell. FPNW allows the administrator the ease of installation and administration that NT affords, while at the same time giving clients the ability to

- Load a Novell redirector on the client machine
- Access the NT server as if it were a NetWare server

Pre-Installation Notes

In order for the FPNW to function, you need to install the NWLINK IPX/SPX protocol stack on the system that will run the service. The NT server has to appear as a Novell server to your clients. In order to do this, it must run the protocol that NetWare supports.

When you install FPNW, it creates a folder called SYSVOL on your NT server. This folder becomes the "volume" that is advertised to the NetWare environment. You want to put this folder on an NTFS partition in order to be able to secure the data on this "volume" correctly. If you recall, in NT you can only set directory-level and file-level permissions on NTFS partitions. If you forget, NT reminds you during the installation of FPNW with a message box like the one in Figure 13.14.

FIGURE 13.14

Reminder to set
file permissions

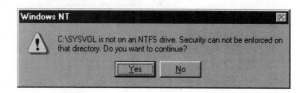

Installing File and Print Services for NetWare

To install FPNW:

1. Open My Computer.

2. Open Control Panel.

3. Double-click on the Network icon.

4. Open Services property page.

5. Click the Add button.

6. Choose File and Print Services for NetWare to install the service. The dialog box in Figure 13.15 appears.

FIGURE 13.15

Install File and Print Services for NetWare dialog box

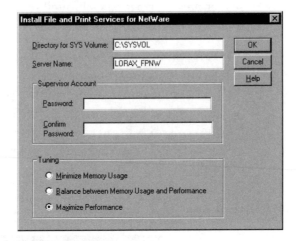

Here is how to fill out this dialog box;

Directory for SYS volume   Enter the path for the folder known as SYSVOL. This folder appears as SYSVOL on the NT server, but will be known as SYS to the NT Server that is masquerading as a Net-Ware server.

Server Name   Enter the name of the server as you wish it to appear to Novell clients.

Supervisor Account   FPNW will create a new user on the NT server known as Supervisor. The Supervisor account automatically has access to the NT server via FPNW. Enter the password for the Supervisor account. This password can be changed at any time.

Tuning Options   Like many network operating systems, NT would like to store a lot of the logon information in the memory of the server. Additionally, NT wants to store software that is needed to run the FPNW service itself on the server. If you opt not to do this, then logon information as well as the FPNW service will be stored on the hard disk, the result being that logons may take longer and the entire service may run more slowly. The tuning options give you a chance to determine how you would like to handle the service. You can choose to store it all in memory for the fastest performance by clicking on the Maximize Performance radio button. Of course, this leaves less memory for the other services on your NT server to use. You could, in contrast, choose to keep all of the information on the hard disk by clicking the Minimize Memory Usage option button. This option takes up no memory on the server, but logons take a little longer. Or you can choose to balance the information between the hard disk and memory by choosing the mid-range solution. To choose the mid-range solution, click the Balance between Memory Usage and Performance option button.

After you finish entering the information click OK and, NT creates a service account. This is the account your NT server logs in as. The name of the user will be FPNW Service Account. You will need to specify a password for this account in the dialog box shown in Figure 13.16. Please take note of the account password.

I hear you asking yourself, "When will this password be relevant?" Look at the services running on your system via Control Panel\Services and look at the Startup option for any of those services. Often there is a password associated with the service when it logs in. If you change the password under services and neglect to change the password for the actual account in user manager (in our case the FPNW Service Account password), the service will not load. After you specify the password for the system account, you have to reboot your system in order for the changes to take effect.

When your system restarts, the FPNW service automatically starts. You are now ready to grant users access to the NT server by using FPNW.

In User Manager, which is shown in Figure 13.17, you will see that three new accounts have been created:

1. FPNW Service Account (user account)

2. Supervisor (user account)

3. Console Operators (group account)

FIGURE 13.16

Creating a password

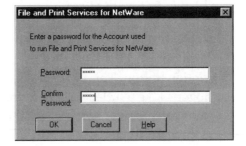

FIGURE 13.17

User Manger dialog box showing the FPNW user account and the Console Operators Group

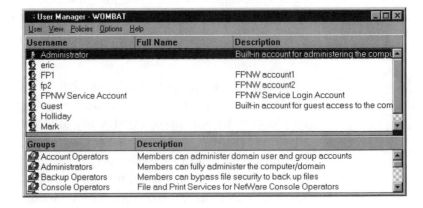

The first two accounts we have already discussed. The Console Operators group is a list of users that can perform administrative functions on the FPNW account both locally and remotely. In essence, this is a list of administrators of the FPNW service.

To grant users access to the NT server via FPNW, you need to edit their user accounts through User Manager. Because the FPNW service is active in the NT server, two new options appear on the New User property page: the Maintain NetWare Compatible Logon check box and the NW Compat button. You can see new options in Figure 13.18. The NW Compat button is grayed out until you check the Main NetWare Compatible Login box.

You can now click on the NW Compat button. When you do, you see the dialog box shown in Figure 13.19. This dialog box is for configuring the user's account to support FPNW.

Notice the NetWare Compatible Password Expired check box. This option informs users when their passwords on NT Server are about to expire. The power of this feature is that users are being notified that their passwords are expiring on NT, even though they are logging on to NT

FIGURE 13.18

New User dialog box

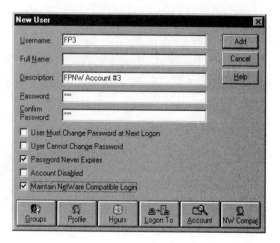

FIGURE 13.19

NetWare Compatible
Properties dialog box

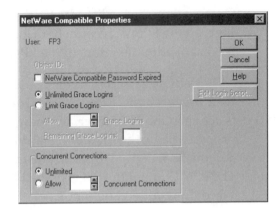

using Novell client software. They can use the Setpass command to
change their password on the NT server just as if it were a Novell server.

FPNW: A Client Machine's Perspective

In order for a client machine to access the NT Server running the
FPNW service, all the client machine has to be running is the normal
Novell redirector software. In Figure 13.20, you can see the server list
you get by using the Novell command SLIST. FPNWSERVER is the
NT server running FPNW.

To log on to the NT server from a client, log on as you normally
would a Novell server. The password that is provided is the password
that was created through User Manager on the NT Server, as shown

FIGURE 13.20

Server list provided
by Novell

in Figure 13.21. The user has access to any resource shared in the SYSVOL folder that the user has permission to use.

FIGURE 13.21

Novell password

Directory Service Manager
for NetWare

One of the biggest headaches with managing a multiple network environment is keeping track of all the user accounts that need to be administered. It is time-consuming to go through the process of adding new users to your environment and remembering all the different locations in which their accounts need to be built. Dealing with users who change their passwords in separate locations is even more time-consuming.

To assist you with this rather daunting administrative task, Microsoft provides the Directory Service Manager for NetWare (DSMN). This service allows you to synchronize your accounts on NetWare bindery with accounts on your NT server. DSMN does require you to load the Gateway Service for NetWare in order to function. If you haven't loaded it, you get the error message shown in Figure 13.22. (Installing the Gateway Service is discussed earlier in this chapter.)

Pre-Installation Notes

DSMN requires that the Gateway service for NetWare be running.

DSMN synchronizes NT accounts with bindery accounts on Net-Ware. As of this writing, it does not support NDS.

FIGURE 13.22

You get an error message if you attempt to install DSMN without having installed GSNW first.

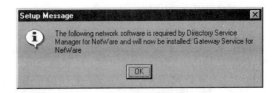

Installing DSMN

To install DSMN:

1. Open My Computer.

2. Open Control Panel.

3. Click on the Network icon.

4. Open the Services Property tab.

5. Click on the Add button.

6. Choose Directory Service Manager for NetWare to install the service. A screen similar to the one in Figure 13.23 appears.

NT will create a new user account called SyncAgentAccount. This is the account that the DSMN service will use to log on to the NT server. You will be prompted to assign a password to this account, just as you were with the FPNW service account. If you change the password for

FIGURE 13.23

Install Directory Service Manager for NetWare dialog box

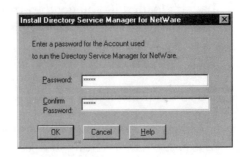

this account, you go into Control Panel/Services and specify the new password in the startup property page of the service.

If you load FPNW ahead of DSMN, the warning message shown in Figure 13.24 appears. It informs you that any user accounts that you enabled with NetWare compatibility will not be transported automatically to the NetWare server. This is not a major concern as long as you are aware of this fact. You will be given an opportunity to transport users to NetWare as you continue the installation process of this service.

The next step in installing DSMN is to specify the NetWare server that you would like to synchronize accounts with. In Figure 13.25, the name of the NetWare server is Debby. A list of NetWare file servers

FIGURE 13.24

DSMN warning message

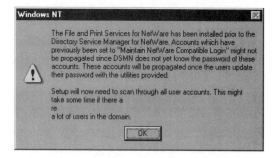

FIGURE 13.25

Select NetWare Server dialog box

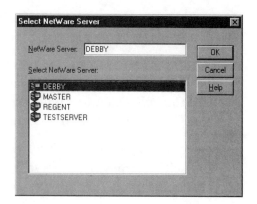

should appear. Simply select the NetWare server with which you would like to synchronize.

After selecting the NetWare server, you need to log on to the server with the supervisor account or with an account with supervisor authority. In Figure 13.26, I am logging in as Supervisor and have provided the password for the supervisor account on the NetWare server Debby.

FIGURE 13.26

Logging on as Supervisor

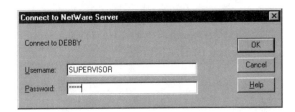

The next dialog box, shown in Figure 13.27, asks you for information about synchronizing your current NT and NetWare accounts. Here are the options in this dialog box:

User Must Change Password   You are beginning the process of moving NetWare Users to NT. In the process, the one item that will not transfer is the password, because NetWare uses a proprietary encryption scheme. You can, however, force users to change their password the first time they log onto NT by selecting this option.

Add Supervisors to Administration Group   By selecting this option, you can make all of the NetWare supervisors NT administrators.

Add File Server Console Operators to Console Operators Group   Along the same lines as the previous option, the NetWare File Console Operators will become part of the NT Console Operators Group that can administrate the server locally.

Synchronize Options   The bottom portion of the screen lets you explicitly state which NetWare accounts you would like to synchronize with NT. Every time one of the users changes a password

FIGURE 13.27

Propagate NetWare
Accounts dialog box

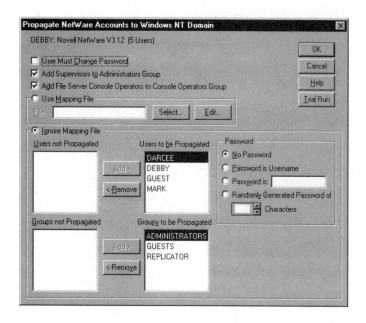

on NT, NT automatically changes the password on NetWare. On the right hand side of the screen you are given an opportunity to specify how you would like to transfer the passwords. I think that the option you choose is less relevant than forcing users to change their passwords the first time they log on to NT. With the DSMN service running, they will change their NT password and their NetWare password simultaneously.

ASCII Text Files for Mapping

Some find the synchronization process easier if they put all of the information in an ASCII text file and have DSMN read that. DSMN refers to this ASCII file as a mapping file, and it is a valid method of specifying the NetWare account that you would like to synchronize.

The format of the file is quite simple. There are three straightforward parameters separated by commas:

Current NetWare UserName, New NT Username, Password.

Listing 13.1 shows an example of a map file.

Listing 13.1: Map File Example

```
;SyncAgentV1.0
;From NetWare Server: DEBBY

[USERS]
;
; Format of each line:
;
; UserName [, New UserName] [, Password]
;   UserName - The user that is to be migrated from the NetWare server.
;   New UserName - The corresponding user name on Windows NT.
;          If this is blank, then the user name remains the same.
;   Password - The password of the user.
;
DARCEE, , DARCEE
DEBBY, , DEBBY
GUEST, , GUEST
MARK, , MARK

[GROUPS]
; Format of each line:
; GroupName
;   GroupName - The group that is to be migrated from the NetWare
       server

ADMINISTRATORS
GUESTS
REPLICATOR
```

After you specify the users to be transferred (called here "propagated"), you need to perform a trial run. The trial run goes through the propagation process without actually creating or synchronizing accounts on NT.

It just checks to see if you will encounter any problem when you perform the actual synchronization.

Listing 13.2 shows an example of a trial run log file.

Listing 13.2: A Trial-Run Log File

```
Directory Service Manager for NetWare: Account Propagation Log File
  From NetWare server: DEBBY
  To Windows NT server: \\TESTSERVER
  Summary:
    4 users were propagated.
    0 users failed to be propagated.
    1 existing Windows NT users' properties were changed.
    3 Windows NT users were added.
    0 users on the NetWare server were renamed.
    0 users were chosen not to be propagated.
    0 users' password were padded to the minimum password length.
    3 groups were propagated.
    0 groups failed to be propagated.
    0 groups added.
    0 groups were chosen not to be propagated.
[USERS]
DARCEE
  Added.
  New Password:
DEBBY
  Added.
  New Password:
GUEST
  Already exists.
  New Password:
MARK
  Added.
  New Password:
[GROUPS]
ADMINISTRATORS
  Already exists.
GUESTS
  Already exists.
REPLICATOR
  Already exists.
```

NT will prompt you to back up the bindery on the NetWare server before conducting the actual propagation, as shown in Figure 13.28. Any time an external process accesses and makes changes to the bindery, there is a risk that the bindery will become corrupt and prevent people from logging onto the NetWare server. The risk is small, but why take the chance?

FIGURE 13.28

Backup warning message

One Final Note...

Before we conclude our discussion on NT and NetWare compatibility, there is one issue that you should be aware of: NT clients accessing the NetWare servers. If you install the Client software for NetWare that comes with NT, you are given the option of processing the NetWare login script. The login scripts usually contain map statements like this following:

```
map z:=den02\sys:public
```

This command makes Z drive the public directory on a NetWare server known as DEN02. This would occur on most DOS client machines, but NT clients only map to the root directory, regardless of the actual map statements. That is to say, if you processed this same statement from an NT client, Z drive would be DEN02\SYS and not the public directory.

The fix for this is straightforward. Instead of using the MAP command, use the MAP ROOT command:

```
Map root z:=den02\sys:public
```

Now the public directory becomes the root directory of Z. If you want to get something from the public directory, simply go to the Z:\—the "root directory" of Z—and you will be in the public directory.

CHAPTER
FOURTEEN

TCP/IP on Windows NT

In the last few years, the term *TCP/IP* has moved from obscurity to a "must-know" concept. TCP/IP has become the *lingua franca* of networks, a network language (*transport protocol* is a more accurate term) like NetBEUI, SNA, IPX/SPX, or X.25, with one very important difference: most of these transport protocols are designed to work well either in a LAN environment *or* in a WAN environment, but not both. In contrast, TCP/IP can fill both needs, and that's one of its greatest strengths, as you'll see in this chapter.

This is a *big* chapter, so here is what to expect. In this chapter, I want to do several things:

- Explain what TCP/IP and the Internet are. You will also learn some of the mechanics of putting together networks to form internets.

- Explore the options you have for setting up IP addresses and computer names: an older method that's a bit more work but is more compatible with other computers doing TCP/IP, and a newer method that incorporates two relatively new protocols called the Dynamic Host Configuration Protocol (DHCP) and the Windows Internet Naming System (WINS). I'll go over how to build an NT-based intranet both ways. I'll also show you how to set up an old standby, DNS (the Domain Naming Service).

- Introduce you to the "big three" of TCP/IP applications—Telnet, FTP, and Internet mail.

When you're done, you'll be at least *dangerous* in TCP/IP administration. As Microsoft says, "On the Internet, no one knows you're running NT."

A Brief History of TCP/IP

Let's start off by asking, "What *is* TCP/IP?" TCP/IP is a collection of software created over the years, much of it with the help of large infusions of government research money. Originally, TCP/IP was intended for the Department of Defense (DoD). You see, DoD tends to buy a *lot* of equipment, and much of that equipment is incompatible with other equipment. For example, back in the late 70s when the work that led to TCP/IP was first begun, it was nearly impossible to get an IBM mainframe to talk to a Burroughs mainframe. That was because the two computers were designed with entirely different *protocols*—something like Figure 14.1.

To get some idea of what the DoD was facing, imagine picking up the phone in the U.S. and calling someone in Spain. You have a perfectly good hardware connection, as the Spanish phone system is compatible with the American phone system. But despite the *hardware* compatibility, you face a *software* incompatibility. The person on the other end of the phone is expecting a different protocol, a different language. It's not that one language is better or worse than the other, but the English speaker cannot understand the Spanish speaker, and vice versa. Rather than force the Spanish speaker to learn English or the English speaker to learn Spanish, we can teach them both a "universal language" such as Esperanto, the "universal language" designed in 1888. If Esperanto were used in my telephone example, neither speaker would use it at home, but they would use it to communicate with each other.

That was how TCP/IP began—as a simple *alternative* communications language. As time went on, however, TCP/IP evolved into a

FIGURE 14.1

Compatible hardware, incompatible protocols

mature, well-understood, robust set of protocols, and many sites adopted it as their *main* communications language.

Origins of TCP/IP: From the ARPANET to the Internet

The original DoD network wouldn't just hook up military sites, although that was an important goal of the first defense internetwork. Much of the basic research in the U.S. was funded by an arm of the Defense Department called the Advanced Research Projects Agency, or ARPA. ARPA gave, and still gives, a lot of money to university researchers to study all kinds of things. ARPA thought it would be useful for these researchers to be able to communicate with one another, as well as with the Pentagon. Figures 14.2 and 14.3 demonstrate networking both before and after ARPANET implementation.

The new network, dubbed ARPANET, was designed and put in place by a private contractor called Bolt, Barenek and Newman. For the first time, it linked university professors both to themselves and to their military and civilian project leaders around the country. Because ARPANET

FIGURE 14.2

Researchers before ARPANET

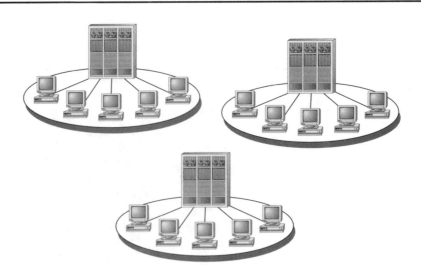

FIGURE 14.3

Researchers after
ARPANET

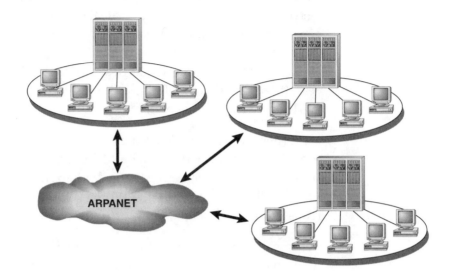

was a network that linked separate private university networks and the separate military networks, it was a "network of networks."

ARPANET ran atop a protocol called the Network Control Protocol (NCP). NCP was later refined into two components, the Internet Protocol (IP) and the Transmission Control Protocol (TCP). The change from NCP to TCP/IP is the technical difference between ARPANET and the Internet. On 1 January 1983, ARPANET packet-switching devices stopped accepting NCP packets and only passed TCP/IP packets, so, in a sense, 1 January 1983 is the "official" birthday of the Internet.

ARPANET became the Internet after a few evolutions. Probably the first major development step occurred in 1974, when Vinton Cerf and Robert Kahn proposed the protocols that would become TCP and IP. (I say "probably" because the Internet didn't grow through a centralized effort, but rather through the largely disconnected efforts of a number of researchers, university professors, and graduate students, most of whom are still alive—and almost *all* of whom have a different perspective on what the "defining" aspects of Internet development were.) Over its more than 20-year history, the Internet and its prede-cessors have gone through several stages of growth and adjustment. Ten years ago, the Internet could only claim a few thousand users. When last I heard, five *million* computers and 100 million users were on the Internet. The Internet appears to double in size about every year. It can't do that indefinitely, but it's certainly a time of change for this huge network of networks.

Internet growth is fueled not by an esoteric interest in seeing how large a network the world can build, but rather by just a few applica-tions that require the Internet to run. Perhaps most important is Internet e-mail, followed closely by the World Wide Web, and then the File Transfer Protocol (FTP)...but more on those later in this chapter.

Originally, the Internet protocols were intended to support connections between mainframe-based networks, which were basically the only ones that existed through most of the 1970s. But the 1980s saw the growth of Unix workstations, microcomputers, and minicomputers. The Berkeley version of Unix was built largely with government money, and the gov-ernment said, "Put the TCP/IP protocol in that thing." There was some resistance at first, but adding IP as a built-in part of Berkeley Unix has helped both Unix and internetworking grow. The IP protocol was used on many of the Unix-based Ethernet networks that appeared in the 1980s and still exist to this day. As a matter of fact, you probably have to learn at least a smidgen of Unix to get around the Internet—but don't let that put you off. In this chapter, I'll teach you all the Unix you need and show you how much of the old Unix stuff can be fulfilled by NT.

In the mid-1980s, the National Science Foundation created five super-computing centers and put them on the Internet. This served two purposes: it made supercomputers available to NSF grantees around the country, and it provided a major "backbone" for the Internet. The National Science Foundation portion of the network, called NSFNET, was for a long time the largest part of the Internet. It is now being super-seded by the National Research and Education Network (NREN). For many years, commercial users were pretty much kept off the Internet, as most of the funding was governmental; you had to be invited to join the Net. But those restrictions have been relaxed and now the majority of Internet traffic is routed over commercially-run lines rather than government-run lines.

People now and then predict that the Internet will fall into decline "once the government privatizes it." That's a lot of wind and little substance. First of all, the Internet is *already* privatized for the most part. As time has passed, the concern about the Internet's death due to a lack of government funds has essentially become moot. As more commercial providers hook up with one another, more traffic goes over completely commercial routes than goes over government routes, at least in the continental U.S.

It's customary to refer to the Internet as the "Information Superhighway." I can understand why people say that; after all, it's a long-haul trucking service for data. But I think of it more as "Information Main Street." The Internet is growing because businesses are using it to get things done and to sell their wares. Much of this book was shipped back and forth on the Internet as it was being written. Heck, that sounds more like Main Street than it does like a highway.

If your company isn't on the Internet now, it will be...and soon. Remember when fax machines became popular in the early 1980s? Overnight people stopped saying, "Do you have a fax?" and just started saying, "What's your fax number?" It's getting so that if you don't have an Internet address, you're just not a person. For example, my Internet mail address is mark@mmco.com.

Goals of TCP/IP's Design

But let's delve into some of the techie aspects of the Internet's main protocols. When DoD started building this set of network protocols, they had a few design goals. Understanding those design goals helps understand why it's worth making the effort to use TCP/IP in the first place. Its intended characteristics include:

- Good failure recovery

- Ability to plug in new subnetworks without disrupting services

- Ability to handle high error rates

- Independence from a particular vendor or type of network

- Very little data overhead

I'm sure no one had any idea how central those design goals would be to the amazing success of TCP/IP both in private internets and in *the* Internet. Let's take a look at those design goals in more detail.

Good Failure Recovery   Remember, this was to be a *defense* network, so it had to work even if portions of the network hardware suddenly and without warning went off-line. That's kind of a nice way of saying the network had to work even if big pieces got nuked.

Can Plug in New Subnetworks "on the Fly"   This second goal is related to the first one. It says that it should be possible to bring entire new networks into an internet—and here, again, *internet* can mean your company's private internet, or *the* Internet—without interrupting existing network service.

Can Handle High Error Rates   The next goal was that an internet should be able to tolerate high or unpredictable error rates, and yet still provide a 100-percent reliable end-to-end service. If you're transferring data from Washington, DC to Portland, Oregon, and the links that you're currently using through Oklahoma get destroyed by a tornado, then any data lost in the storm will be re-sent and rerouted via some other lines.

Host Independence   As I mentioned before, the new network architecture should work with any kind of network, and not be dedicated or tied to any one vendor.

This is essential in the '90s. The days of "we're just an IBM shop" or "we only buy Novell stuff" are gone for many and going fast for others. (Let's hope that it doesn't give way to "we only buy Microsoft software.") Companies must be able to live in a multivendor world.

Very Little Data Overhead　　The last goal was for the network protocols to have as little overhead as possible. To understand this, let's compare TCP/IP to other protocols. While no one knows what protocol will end up being *the* world protocol twenty years from now—if any protocol *ever* gets that much acceptance—one of TCP/IP's rivals is a set of protocols built by the International Standards Organization, or ISO. ISO has some standards that are very similar to the kinds of things that TCP/IP does, standards named X.25 and TP4. But every protocol packages its data with an extra set of bytes, kind of like an envelope. The vast majority of data packets using the IP protocol (and I promise, I *will* explain soon how it is that TCP and IP are actually two very different protocols, and a bit of what those protocols are) have a simple, fixed-size 20-byte header. The maximum size that the header can be is 60 bytes, if all possible options are enabled. The fixed 20 bytes always appears as the first 20 bytes of the packet. In contrast, X.25 uses dozens of possible headers, with no appreciable fixed portion to it. But why should *you* be concerned about overhead bytes? Really for one reason only: performance. Simpler protocols mean faster transmission and packet switching—and we'll take up packet switching a little later.

But enough about the Internet for now. Let's stop and define something that I've been talking about—namely, just what *are* TCP and IP?

Originally, TCP/IP was just a set of programs that could hook up dissimilar computers and transfer information between them. But it grew into a large number of programs that have become collectively known as the *TCP/IP suite*.

The Internet Protocol (IP)

The most basic part of the Internet is the Internet Protocol, or IP. If you want to send data over an internet, then that data must be packaged in an IP packet. That packet is then *routed* from one part of the internet to another.

A Simple Internet

IP is supposed to allow messages to travel from one part of a network to another. How does it do this?

An internet is made of at least two *sub*-nets. The notion of a subnet is built upon the fact that most popular LAN architectures (Ethernet, Token Ring, and ARCNet) are based on something very much like a radio broadcast. Everyone on the same Ethernet segment hears all of the traffic on their segment, just as each device on a given ring in a Token Ring network must examine every message that goes through the network. The trick that makes an Ethernet or a Token Ring work is that while each station *hears* everything, each station knows how to ignore all messages save for the ones intended for it.

You may have never realized it, but that means that in a single Ethernet segment or a single Token Ring ring there is *no routing*. If you've ever sat through one of those interminable explanations of the ISO seven-layer network model, then you know that in network discussions much is made of the "network" layer, which in ISO terms is merely the routing layer. And yet a simple Ethernet or Token Ring never has to route. There are no routing decisions to make; everything is heard by everybody. (Your network adapter filters out any traffic not destined for you, in case you're wondering.)

But now suppose you have *two* separate Ethernets connected to each other, as you see in Figure 14.4.

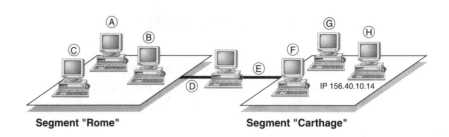

FIGURE 14.4

Multisegment internet

Segment "Rome"   Segment "Carthage"

IP 156.40.10.14

In Figure 14.4, you see two Ethernet segments, named Rome and Carthage. (I was getting tired of the "shipping" and "finance" examples that everyone uses.) There are three computers that reside solely in Rome that I've labeled A, B, and C. Three more computers reside in Carthage, labeled F, G, and H.

Subnets and Routers

Much of internet architecture is built around the observation that PCs A, B, and C can communicate directly with each other, and PCs F, G, and H can communicate directly with each other, but A, B, and C *cannot* communicate with F, G, and H without some help from the machine containing Ethernet cards D and E. That D/E machine will function as a *router*, a machine that allows communication between different network segments. A, B, C, and D could be described as being in each others' "broadcast range," as could E, F, G, and H. What I've just called a broadcast range is called more correctly in internet terminology a *subnet*, which is a collection of machines that can communicate with each other without the need for routing.

For example, F and H can communicate directly without having to ask the router (E, in their case) to forward the message, and so they're on the same subnet. A and C can communicate directly without having to ask the router (D, in their case) to forward the message, and so they're on the same subnet. But if B wanted to talk to G, it would have to first send the message to D, asking "D, please get this to G," so they're not on the same subnet.

IP Addresses and Ethernet Addresses

Before continuing, let's briefly discuss the labels A, B, C, and so on, and how those labels actually are manifested in an internet. Each computer on this net is attached to the net via an Ethernet board, and each Ethernet board on an internet has two addresses: an *IP address* and an *Ethernet address*. (There are, of course, other ways to get onto an internet than via Ethernet, but let's stay with the Ethernet example, as it's the most common one on TCP/IP internets.)

Ethernet Addresses

Each Ethernet board's Ethernet address is a unique 48-bit identification code. If it sounds unlikely that every Ethernet board in the world has a unique address, then consider that 48 bits offers 280,000,000,000,000 possibilities. Ethernet itself only uses about one quarter of those possibilities (two bits are set aside for administrative functions), but that's still a lot of possible addresses. In any case, the important thing to get here is that a board's Ethernet address is predetermined and hard-coded into the board. Ethernet addresses, which are also called Media Access Control (MAC) addresses (it's got nothing to do with Macintoshes) are expressed in twelve hex digits. (*MAC address* is synonymous with *Token Ring address* or *Ethernet address*.) For example, the Ethernet card on the computer I'm working at now has MAC (Ethernet) address 0020AFF8E771 or, as it's sometimes written, 00-20-AF-F8-E7-71. The addresses are centrally administered, and Ethernet chip vendors must purchase blocks of addresses. In the example of my workstation, you know that it's got a 3Com Ethernet card because the Ethernet (MAC) address is 00-20-AF; that prefix is owned by 3Com.

NOTE You can see an NT machine's MAC address in a number of ways. You can type net config workstation or net config server (it's the string of hex in parentheses), or run Windows NT Diagnostics and click Network/Transports.

IP Addresses and Quad Format

In contrast to the 48 bits in a MAC address, an IP address is a 32-bit value. IP addresses are numbers set at a workstation (or server) by a network administrator—they're not a hard-coded hardware kind of address, unlike the Ethernet address. That means that there are four billion distinct Internet addresses.

It's nice that there's room for lots of machines, but having to remember—or having to tell someone else—a 32-bit address is no fun. Imagine having to say to a network support person "just set up the machines on the subnet to use a default router address of 10101110100-101010010101100010111." Hmmm...doesn't sound like much fun—we need a more human-friendly way to express 32-bit numbers. That's where *dotted quad* notation comes from.

For simplicity's sake, IP addresses are usually represented as *w.x.y.z*, where *w*, *x*, *y*, and *z* are all decimal values between 0 and 255. For example, the IP address of the machine that I'm currently writing this at is 199.34.57.53. Each of the four numbers are called *quads*, and, as they're connected by dots, it's called "dotted quad" notation.

Each of the numbers in the dotted quad corresponds to eight bits of an Internet address. (*IP address* and *Internet address* are synonymous.) As the value for eight bits can range from 0 to 255, each value in a dotted quad can be from 0 to 255. For example, to convert an IP address of 11001010000011111010101000000001 into dotted quad format, it would first be broken up into eight-bit groups:

11001010 00001111 10101010 00000001.

And each of those eight-bit numbers would be converted to their decimal equivalent. (If you're not comfortable with binary-to-decimal conversion, don't worry about it: just load the NT calculator, click View, then Scientific, and then press the F8 key to put the Calculator in binary mode. Enter the binary number, press F6, and the number will be converted to decimal for you.) Our number converts as follows:

```
11001010   00001111   10101010   00000001
   202         15         170          1
```

Which results in a dotted quad address of 202.15.170.1.

So, to re-cap: each of these computers has at least one Ethernet card in it, and that Ethernet card has a predefined address. The network administrator of this network has gone around and installed IP software on these PCs, and, in the process, has assigned IP addresses to each of them. (Note, by the way, that the phrase "has assigned IP addresses to each of them" may not be true if you are using the Dynamic Host Configuration Protocol, or DHCP. For the first part of this chapter, however, I'm going to assume that you're not using DHCP and that someone must hand-assign an IP address to each Ethernet card.)

Let me redraw our internet, adding totally arbitrary IP addresses and Ethernet addresses, as shown in Figure 14.5.

FIGURE 14.5

Two-subnet internets with Ethernet and IP addresses

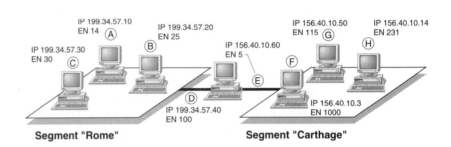

IP Routers

Now let's return to the computer in the middle. It is part of *both* segments. How do I get one computer to be part of two networks? By putting two Ethernet cards in the computer in the middle. (A computer with more than one network card in it is called a *multihomed* computer.) One of the Ethernet cards is on the Rome subnet, and the other is on the Carthage subnet. (By the way, each computer on an internet is called a *host* in TCP-ese.)

Now, each Ethernet card must get a separate IP address, so, as a result, the computer in the middle has *two* IP addresses, D and E. If a message is transmitted in Rome, then adapter D hears it, and E doesn't. Then, if a message is transmitted in Carthage, then adapter E hears it, but D doesn't.

How would we build an internet from these two subnets? How could station A, for example, send a message to station G? Obviously, the only way that message will get from A to G is if the message is received on the Ethernet adapter with address D, and then re-sent out over the Ethernet adapter with address E. Once E re-sends the message, G will hear it, as it is on the same network as E.

In order for this to work, the machine containing boards D and E must be smart enough to perform this function whereby it re-sends data between D and E when necessary. Such a machine is, by definition, an *IP router*. It is possible with Windows NT to use an NT computer—any NT computer, not just an NT Server computer—to act as an IP router, as you'll learn later.

Under IP, the sending station (A, in this case) examines the address of the destination (G, in this case) and realizes that it does not know how to get to G. (I'll explain exactly *how* it knows that in a minute.) Now, if A has to send something to an address that it doesn't understand, then it uses a kind of "catchall" address called the *default router* or, for historical reasons, the *default gateway* address. A's network administrator has already configured A's default router as D, so A sends the message to D. Once D gets the message, it then sees that the message is not destined for itself, but rather for G, and so it resends the message from board E.

Routing in More Detail

Now let's look a little closer at how that message gets from A to G. Each computer, as you've already seen, has one *or more* IP addresses. It's important to understand that there is no relationship whatsoever between an Ethernet card's address and the IP address associated with it: the Ethernet MAC address is hardwired into the card by the card's manufacturer, and the IP addresses are assigned by a network administrator.

But now examine the IP addresses, and you'll see a pattern to them. Rome's addresses all look like 199.34.57.*x*, where *x* is some number, and Carthage's addresses all look like 156.40.10.*x*, where, again, *x* can be any number. The Ethernet addresses follow no rhyme or reason and are grouped by the board's manufacturer. That similarity of addresses within Rome and Carthage will be important in understanding routing.

Now, let's re-examine how the message gets from A to G.

1. The IP software in A first says, "How do I get this message to G—can I just broadcast it, or must it be routed?" The way that it makes that decision is by finding out whether or not G is on the same *subnet* as A is. A subnet is simply a broadcast area. Host A then, is asking, "Is G part of Rome, like me?"

2. Station A determines that it is on a different subnet from station G by examining their addresses. A knows that it has address 199.34.57.10, and it must send its message to 156.40.10.50. A has a simple rule for this: if the destination address looks like 199.34.57.*x*, where, again, *x* can be any value, then the destination is in the same subnet, and so requires no routing. On the other hand, 156.40.10.50 is clearly *not* in the same subnet.

   If, on the other hand, G *had* been on the same subnet, then A would have "shouted" the IP packet straight to G, referring specifically to its IP and Ethernet address.

3. So station A can't directly send its IP packets to G. A then looks for another way. When A's network administrator set up A's IP software, she told A the IP address of A's *default router*. The default router is basically the address that says, "If you can't get directly to somewhere, send it to me, and I'll try to get it there." A's default router is D.

   A then sends an Ethernet frame from itself to D. The Ethernet frame contains this information:

   • Source Ethernet address: 14

   • Destination Ethernet address: 100

   • Source IP address: 199.34.57.10

   • Destination IP address: 156.40.10.50

4. Ethernet card D receives the frame and hands it to the IP software running in its PC. The PC sees that the IP destination address is not *its* IP address, so the PC knows that it must route this IP packet. Examining the subnet, the PC sees that the destination lies on the subnet that Ethernet adapter E is on, so it sends out a frame from Ethernet adapter E, with this information:

- Source Ethernet address: 100
- Destination Ethernet address: 115
- Source IP address: 199.34.57.10
- Destination IP address: 156.40.10.50

5. G then gets the packet. By looking at the Ethernet and IP addresses, G can see that it got this frame from E, but the original message really came from another machine, the 199.34.57.10 machine.

That's a simple example of how IP routes, but its algorithms are powerful enough to serve as the backbone for a network as large as the Internet.

TIP
There are different kinds of routing algorithms in TCP/IP. Windows NT only supports the simplest routing approaches: *static routes* and the Routing Internet Protocol (RIP). NT does not support the more robust protocols, like the Open Shortest Path First (OSPF) or External Gateway Protocol (EGP). You either need third-party software, or a dedicated hardware router to build large, complex internets with NT. But NT can route adequately in a small to medium-sized internet.

A, B, and C Networks, CIDR Blocks, and Subnetting

Before leaving IP routing, let's take a more specific look at subnets and IP addresses.

The whole idea behind the 32-bit IP addresses is to make it relatively simple to segment the task of managing the Internet or, for that matter, *any* internet.

To become part of the Internet, contact the Network Information Center, or NIC; its e-mail address is hostmaster@rs.internic.net, or you can get them at (703) 742-4777 from 7 a.m. through 7 p.m. Eastern time, or point your Web browser to www.internic.net.

A, B, and C-Class Networks

The NIC assigns a company a block of IP addresses according to that company's size. Big companies get A-class networks (there are none left; they've all been given out), medium-sized companies get B-class networks (we're out of those, too), and others get C-class networks (they're still available). Although there are three network classes, there are five kinds of IP addresses, as you'll see in Figure 14.6.

Because it seemed, in the early days of the Internet, that four billion addresses left plenty of space for growth, the original designers were a bit sloppy. They defined three classes of networks of the Internet: large networks, medium-sized networks, and small networks. The creators of the Internet used 8-bit sections of the 32-bit addresses to delineate the difference between different classes of networks.

A-class networks   A large network would have its first eight bits set by the NIC, and the network's internal administrators could set the remaining 24 bits. The left-most eight bits could have values between 0 and 126, allowing for 127 class A networks. Companies like IBM get these, and there are only 127 of these addresses. As only eight bits have been taken, 24 remain; that means that class A networks can contain up to 2 to the 24th power, or 16 million hosts. Examples of A-class nets are BBN (1.0.0.0), General Electric (3.0.0.0), Hewlett-Packard (16.0.0.0), Apple (17), Columbia University (15), Xerox (13), IBM (9), DEC (16), and M.I.T. (18).

FIGURE 14.6

Internet network classes and reserved addresses

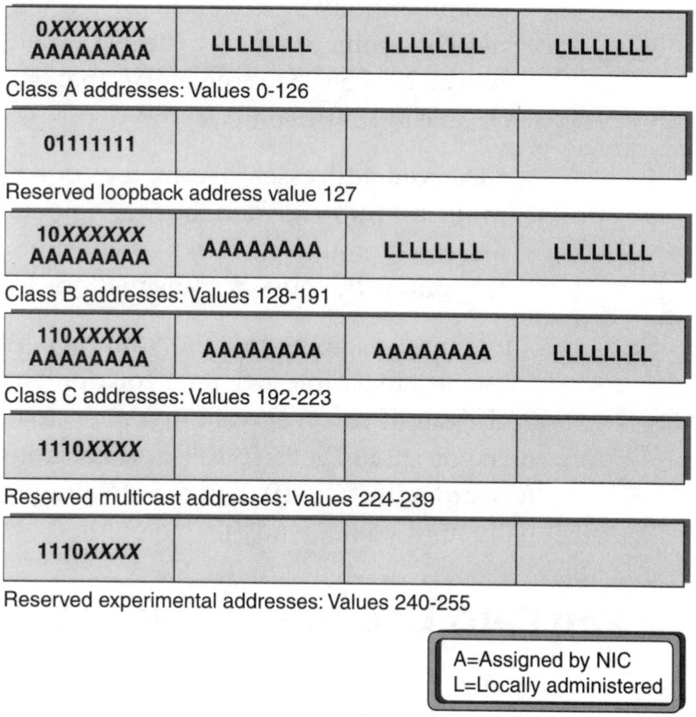

0XXXXXXX AAAAAAAA	LLLLLLLL	LLLLLLLL	LLLLLLLL

Class A addresses: Values 0-126

01111111			

Reserved loopback address value 127

10XXXXXX AAAAAAAA	AAAAAAAA	LLLLLLLL	LLLLLLLL

Class B addresses: Values 128-191

110XXXXX AAAAAAAA	AAAAAAAA	AAAAAAAA	LLLLLLLL

Class C addresses: Values 192-223

1110XXXX			

Reserved multicast addresses: Values 224-239

1110XXXX			

Reserved experimental addresses: Values 240-255

A=Assigned by NIC
L=Locally administered

B-class networks   Medium-sized networks have the left-most 16 bits preassigned to them, leaving 16 bits for local use. Class B addresses always have the values 128 through 191 in their first quad, then a value between 0 and 255 in their second quad. There are then 16,384 possible class B networks. Each of them can have up to 65,535 hosts. Microsoft and Exxon are examples of companies with B-class networks.

C-class networks   Small networks have the left-most 24 bits preassigned to them, leaving only 8 bits for local administration (which is bad, as it means that class C networks can't have more than 254 hosts), but, as the NIC has 24 bits to work with, it can easily give out class C network addresses (which is good). Class C addresses start off with a value between 192 and 223. As the second and third quads can be any value between 0 and 255, that means that there can potentially be 2,097,152 class C networks. (That's what our network, mmco.com, is.) The last C network, when it's assigned, will be 223.255.255.*x*; remember that the owner of that network will be able to control only "*x*."

Reserved addresses   A number of addresses are reserved for multicast purposes and for experimental purposes, so they can't be assigned for networks. In particular, address 224.0.0.0 is set aside for *multicasts*, network transmissions to groups of computers.

If you're just going to build your own internet and you don't want to connect to *the* Internet, then you don't have to call up the NIC to get addresses. If you ever want to connect to the outside world, however, then you should get an NIC-approved address before moving very far forward with TCP/IP. You can always get an address and use it internally until you're ready to "go public."

You Can't Use *All* of the Numbers

There are some special rules to internet names, however. There's a whole bunch of numbers that you can never give to a machine. They're called the loopback address, the network number, the broadcast address, and the default router address.

The Loopback Address   The address 127.0.0.1 is reserved as a loopback. If you send a message to 127.0.0.1, then it should be returned to you, unless there's something wrong on the network. And so no network has an address 127.xxxxxxxx.xxxxxxxx.xxxxxxxx, an unfortunate waste of 24 million addresses.

The Network Number   Sometimes you need to refer to an entire subnet with a single number. Thus far, I've said things like "my C network is 199.34.57.*x*, and I can make '*x*' range from 0 to 255." I was being a bit lazy; I didn't want to write "199.34.57.0 through 199.34.57.255," so I said "199.34.57.*x*."

It's not proper IP-ese to refer to a range of network addresses that way. And it's necessary to have an official way to refer to a range of addresses.

For example, to tell a router, "To get this message to the subnet that ranges from 100.100.100.0 through 100.100.100.255, first route to the router at 99.98.97.103," you've got to have some way to designate the range of addresses 100.100.100.0-100.100.100.255. We could have just used two addresses with a hyphen between them, but that's a bit cumbersome. Instead, the address that ends in all binary zeroes is reserved as the *network number*, the TCP/IP name for the range of addresses in a subnet. In my 100.100.100.*x* example, the shorthand way to refer to 100.100.100.0 through 100.100.100.255 is "100.100.100.0."

Notice that this means you would never use the address 100.100.100.0— you never give that IP address to a machine under TCP/IP.

For example, to tell that router, "To get this message to the subnet that ranges from 100.100.100.0 through 100.100.100.255, first route to the router at 99.98.97.103," you would type something like **route add 100.100.100.0 99.98.97.103**. (Actually, you'd type a bit more information, and I'll get to that in the upcoming section on using your NT machine as a router, but this example gives you the idea.)

IP Broadcast Address

There's another reserved address, as well—the TCP/IP broadcast address. It looks like the address of one machine, but it isn't; it's the address you'd use to broadcast to each machine on a subnet. That address is all binary ones.

For example, on a simple C-class subnet, the broadcast address would be *x.y.z*.255. When would you need to know this? Some IP software needs this when you configure it; most routers require the broadcast address (as well as the network number). So if I just use my C-class network 199.34.57.0 (see how convenient that ".0" thing is?) as a single subnet, then the broadcast address for my network would be 199.34.57.255.

Default Router Address

Every subnet has at least one router; after all, if it didn't have a router, then the subnet couldn't talk to any other networks, and it wouldn't be an internet.

By convention, the first address after the network number is the subnet mask. For example, on a simple C-class network, the address of the router should be $x.y.z.1$. This is not, by the way, a hard-and-fast rule like the network number and the IP broadcast address—it is, instead, a convention.

Suppose you have just been made the proud owner of a C-class net, 222.210.34.0. You can put 253 computers on your network, as you must not use 222.210.34.0, which describes the entire network; 222.210.34.255, which will be your broadcast address; and 222.210.34.1, which will be used either by you or your Internet service provider for a router address between your network and the rest of the Internet.

Now, once you get a range of addresses from the NIC, then you are said to have an *IP domain*. (*Domain* in Internet lingo has nothing to do with domain in the NT security sense.) For example, my IP domain (which is named mmco.com, but we'll cover names in a minute) uses addresses in the 199.34.57.0 network, and I can have as many NT domains in there as I like. However from the point of view of the outside Internet, all of my NT domains are just one Internet domain, mmco.com.

Subnet Masks

If you had a trivially small internet, one with just one subnet, then all the devices in your network can simply transmit directly to each other, and no routing is required. (If you actually had a network like this, then TCP/IP is overkill, and you probably should use NetBEUI instead.) On the other hand, you may have a domain so large that using broadcasting to communicate within it would be unworkable, requiring you to subnet your domain further. Consider IBM's situation, with an A-class network that can theoretically support 16 million hosts. Managing *that* network cries out for routers. For this reason, it may be necessary for your IP software on your PC to route data over a router even if it's staying within your company. Let's ask again, and in more detail this time, "How does a machine know whether to route or not?"

That's where subnets are important. Subnets make it possible, as you've seen, for a host (a PC) to determine whether it can just lob a message straight over to another host, or if it must go through routers. You can tell a host's IP software how to distinguish whether or not another host is in the same subnet through the *subnet mask*.

Recall that all of the IP addresses in Rome looked like 199.34.57.*x*, where *x* was a number between 1 and 255. You could then say that all co-members of the Rome subnet are defined as the hosts whose first three quads match. Now, on some subnets, it might be possible that the only requirement for membership in the same subnet would be that the first *two* quads be the same—a company that decided for some reason to make its entire B-class network a single subnet would be one example of that. (Yes, they *do* exist: I've seen firms that make a single subnet out of a B-class, with the help of some bizarre smart bridges. And no, I don't recommend it.)

When a computer is trying to figure out whether the IP address that it owns is on the same subnet as the place that it's trying to communicate with, then a subnet mask answers the question, "Which bits must match for us to be on the same subnet?"

IP does that with a *mask*, a combination of ones and zeroes like so:

11111111 11111111 11111111 00000000

Here's how a host would use this mask. The host with IP address 199.34.57.10 (station A in the earlier figure) wants to know if it is on the same subnet as the host with IP address 199.34.57.20 (station C in the earlier figure). 199.34.57.10, expressed in binary, is 11000111 00100010 00111001 00001010. The IP address for B is, in binary, 11000111 00100010 00111001 00010100. The IP software in A then compares its own IP address to B's IP address. Look at them right next to each other:

```
11000111 00100010 00111001 00001010 A's address
11000111 00100010 00111001 00010100 B's address
```

The left-most 27 bits match, as does the right-most bit. Does that mean they're in the same subnet? Again, for the two addresses to be in the same subnet, certain bits must match—the ones with "1s" in the subnet mask. Let's stack up the subnet mask, A's address, and B's address to make this clearer.

```
11111111 11111111 11111111 00000000 the subnet mask
11000111 00100010 00111001 00001010 A's address
11000111 00100010 00111001 00010100 B's address
```

Look down from each of the 1s on the subnet mask, and you see that A and B match at each of those positions. Under the 0s in the subnet mask A and B match up sometimes, but not all the time. In fact, it doesn't matter whether or not A and B match in the positions under the 0s in the subnet mask—the fact that there are 0s there means that whether or not they match is irrelevant.

How do you know what value to use for a subnet mask? Well, if you have a class C number, and all of your workstations are on a single subnet, then you have a case like the one we just saw: a subnet mask of 11111111 11111111 11111111 00000000 which, in dotted quad terminology, is 255.255.255.0. Remember that by definition the fact that I have a C network means that the InterNIC has "nailed down" the left-most or top three quads (24 bits), leaving me only the right-most quad (8 bits). Since all of my addresses must match in the left-most 24 bits and I can do anything I like with the bottom 8 bits, my subnet mask must be 111111111111111111111111100000000 or 255.255.255.0.

That, however, assumes that I'll use my entire C network as one bit subnet. Instead, I might decide to break one C-class network into two subnets. I could decide that all the numbers from 1 to 127— 00000001 to 01111111—are subnet 1, and the numbers from 128 to 255—10000000 to 11111111—are subnet 2. In that case, the values inside my subnets will only vary in the last seven bits, rather than (as in the previous example) varying in the last *eight* bits. The subnet mask would be, then, 11111111 11111111 11111111 10000000, or 255.255.255.128.

The first subnet is a range of addresses from $x.y.z.0$ through $x.y.z.127$, where "x.y.z" are the quads that the NIC assigned me. The second subnet is the range from $x.y.z.128$ through $x.y.z.255$.

Now let's find the network number, default router address, and broadcast address. The network number is the first number in each range, so the first subnet's network number is $x.y.z.0$ and the second's is $x.y.z.128$. The default router address is just the second address in the range, which is $x.y.z.1$ and $x.y.z.129$ for the two subnets. The broadcast address is then the *last* address in both cases, $x.y.z.127$ and $x.y.z.255$ respectively.

Subnetting a C-Class Network

If you're going to break down your subnets smaller than C-class, then having to figure out the subnet mask, network number, broadcast address, and router address can get kind of confusing. Table 14.1 summarizes how you can break a C-class network down into one, two, four, or eight smaller subnets, with the attendant subnet masks, network numbers, broadcast addresses, and router addresses. I've assumed that you are starting from a C-class address, so you'll only be working with the fourth quad. The first three quads I have simply designated $x.y.z$.

TABLE 14.1   Breaking a C-Class Network into Subnets

Number of Desired Subnets	Subnet Mask	Network Number	Router Address	Broadcast Address	Remaining Number of IP Addresses
1	255.255.255.0	$x.y.z.0$	$x.y.z.1$	$x.y.z.255$	253
2	255.255.255.128	$x.y.z.0$	$x.y.z.1$	$x.y.z.127$	125
	255.255.255.	$x.y.z.128$	$x.y.z.129$	$x.y.z.255$	125
4	255.255.255.192	$x.y.z.0$	$x.y.z.1$	$x.y.z.63$	61
	255.255.255.	$x.y.z.64$	$x.y.z.65$	$x.y.z.127$	61

TABLE 14.1   Breaking a C-Class Network into Subnets (Continued)

Number of Desired Subnets	Subnet Mask	Network Number	Router Address	Broadcast Address	Remaining Number of IP Addresses
	255.255.255.	*x.y.z.*128	*x.y.z.*129	*x.y.z.*191	61
	255.255.255.	*x.y.z.*192	*x.y.z.*193	*x.y.z.*255	61
8	255.255.255.224	*x.y.z.*0	*x.y.z.*1	*x.y.z.*31	29
	255.255.255.	*x.y.z.*32	*x.y.z.*33	*x.y.z.*63	29
	255.255.255.	*x.y.z.*64	*x.y.z.*65	*x.y.z.*95	29
	255.255.255.	*x.y.z.*96	*x.y.z.*97	*x.y.z.*127	29
	255.255.255.	*x.y.z.*128	*x.y.z.*129	*x.y.z.*159	29
	255.255.255.	*x.y.z.*160	*x.y.z.*161	*x.y.z.*191	29
	255.255.255.	*x.y.z.*192	*x.y.z.*193	*x.y.z.*223	29
	255.255.255.	*x.y.z.*224	*x.y.z.*225	*x.y.z.*255	29

For example, suppose you want to chop up a C-class network, 200.211.192.*x*, into two subnets. As you see in the table, you'd use a subnet mask of 255.255.255.128 for each subnet. The first subnet would have network number 200.211.192.0, router address 200.211.192.1, and broadcast address 200.211.192.127. You could assign IP addresses 200.211.192.2 through 200.211.192.126, 125 different IP addresses. (Notice that heavily subnetting a network results in the loss of a greater and greater percentage of addresses to the network number, broadcast address, and router address.) The second subnet would have network number 200.211.192.128, router address 200.211.192.129, and broadcast address 200.211.192.255.

In case you're wondering, it is entirely possible to subnet further, into 16 subnets of 13 hosts apiece (remember you always lose three numbers for the network number, router address, and broadcast address) or 32 subnets of 5 hosts apiece, but at that point, you're losing an awful lot of addresses to IP overhead.

Classless Internetwork Domain Routing (CIDR)

Now that we've gotten past some of the fine points of subnet masks, let me elaborate on what you see if you ever go to the InterNIC looking for a domain of your own.

The shortage of IP addresses has led the InterNIC to curtail giving out A, B, or C-class addresses. Many small companies need an Internet domain, but giving them a C network is overkill, as a C network contains 256 addresses and many small firms only have a dozen or so computers that they want on the Internet. Large companies may also want a similarly small presence on the Internet: for reasons of security, they may not want to put all of the PCs (or other computers) on the Internet, but rather on an internal network not attached to the Internet. These companies *do* need a presence on the Internet, however—for their e-mail servers, FTP servers, Web servers, and the like—so they need a dozen or so addresses. But, again, giving them an entire 256-address C network is awfully wasteful. But, until 1994, it was the smallest block that the NIC could hand out.

Similarly, some companies need a few hundred addresses—more than 256, but not very many more. Such a firm is too big for a C network, but a bit small for the 65,536 addresses of a B network. More flexibility here would be useful.

For that reason, the InterNIC now gives out addresses without the old A-, B-, or C-class restrictions. This newer method that the InterNIC uses is called Classless Internet Domain Routing, or CIDR, pronounced "cider." CIDR networks are described as "slash x" networks, where the x is a number representing the number of bits in the IP address range that the InterNic controls.

If you had an A-class network, then the InterNic controlled the top 8 bits, and you controlled the bottom 24. If you decided somehow to take your A-class network and make it one big subnet, then what would be your subnet mask? Since all of your A network would be one subnet, you'd only have to look at the top quad to see if the source and destination addresses were on the same subnet. For example, if you had network 4.0.0.0, then addresses 4.55.22.81 and 4.99.63.88 would be on the same subnet. (Please note that I can't actually imagine anyone doing this with an A-class net; I'm just trying to make CIDR clearer.) Your subnet mask would be, then, 11111111 00000000 00000000 00000000 or 255.0.0.0. Reading from the left, you have eight ones in the subnet mask before the zeroes start. In CIDR terminology, you wouldn't have an "A-class network;" rather, you would have a "slash 8" network.

With a B-class, the InterNic controlled the top 16 bits, and you controlled the bottom 16. If you decided to take that B-class network and make it a one-subnet network, then your subnet mask would be 11111111 11111111 00000000 00000000 or 255.255.0.0. Reading from the left, the subnet mask would have 16 ones. In CIDR terms, a B network is a "slash 16" network.

With a C-class, the InterNic controlled the top 24 bits, and you controlled the bottom 8. By now, you've seen that the subnet mask for a C network if you treated it as one subnet is 11111111 11111111 11111111 00000000. Reading from the left, the subnet mask would have 24 ones. In CIDR terms, a C network is a "slash 24" network.

Where the new flexibility of CIDR comes in is that the InterNic can in theory now not only define the A, B, and C type networks, it can offer networks with subnet masks in between the A, B, and C networks. For example, suppose I wanted a network for 50 PCs. Before, the InterNic would have to give me a C network, with 256 addresses. But now they can offer me a network with subnet mask 11111111 11111111 11111111 11000000 (255.255.255.192), giving me only six bits to play with. Two to the sixth power is 64, so I'd have 64 addresses to do with as I liked. This would be a "slash 26" network.

In summary, Table 14.2 shows how large each possible network type would be.

TABLE 14.2   CIDR Network Types

InterNic Network Type	"Subnet Mask" for Entire Network	Approximate Number of IP Addresses
slash 0	0.0.0.0	4 billion
slash 1	128.0.0.0	2 billion
slash 2	192.0.0.0	1 billion
slash 3	224.0.0.0	500 million
slash 4	240.0.0.0	25 million
slash 5	248.0.0.0	128 million
slash 6	252.0.0.0	64 million
slash 7	254.0.0.0	32 million
slash 8	255.0.0.0	16 million
slash 9	255.128.0.0	8 million
slash 10	255.192.0.0	4 million
slash 11	255.224.0.0	2 million
slash 12	255.240.0.0	1 million
slash 13	255.248.0.0	524,288
slash 14	255.252.0.0	262,144
slash 15	255.254.0.0	131,072
slash 16	255.255.0.0	65,536
slash 17	255.255.128.0	32,768
slash 18	255.255.192.0	16,384
slash 19	255.255.224.0	8192
slash 20	255.255.240.0	4096
slash 21	255.255.248.0	2048

TABLE 14.2   CIDR Network Types (Continued)

InterNic Network Type	"Subnet Mask" for Entire Network	Approximate Number of IP Addresses
slash 22	255.255.252.0	1024
slash 23	255.255.254.0	512
slash 24	255.255.255.0	256
slash 25	255.255.255.128	128
slash 26	255.255.255.192	64
slash 27	255.255.255.224	32
slash 28	255.255.255.240	16
slash 29	255.255.255.248	8
slash 30	255.255.255.252	4
slash 31	255.255.255.254	2
slash 32	255.255.255.255	1

I hope it's obvious that I included all of those networks just for the sake of completeness, as some of them simply aren't available, like the slash 0, and some just don't make sense, like the slash 31—it only gives you two addresses, which would be immediately required for network number and broadcast address, leaving none behind for you to actually use.

CIDR is a fact of life if you're registering networks with the InterNic nowadays. With the information in this section, you'll more easily be able to understand what an Internet Service Provider (ISP) is talking about when it says it can get you a "slash 26" network.

What IP *Doesn't* Do: Error Checking

Whether you're on *an* internet or *the* Internet, it looks like your data gets bounced around quite a bit. How can you prevent it from becoming damaged? Let's look briefly at that, and that'll segue me to a short talk on TCP.

An IP packet contains a bit of data called a *checksum header*, which checks whether the header information was damaged on the way from sender to receiver.

Many data communications protocols use checksums that operate like this: I send you some data. You use the checksum to make sure that the data wasn't damaged in transit, perhaps by line noise. Once you're satisfied that the data was not damaged, you send me a message that says, "OK—I got it." If the checksum indicates that it did *not* get to me undamaged, then you send me a message that says, "That data was damaged—please resend it," and I resend it. Such messages are called ACKs and NAKs—positive or negative acknowledgments of data. Protocols that use this check-and-acknowledge approach are said to provide *reliable* service.

But IP does not provide reliable service. If an IP receiver gets a damaged packet, it just discards the packet and says nothing to the receiver. Surprised? I won't keep you in suspense: it's TCP that provides the reliability. The IP header checksum is used to see if a header is valid; if it isn't, then the datagram is discarded.

This underscores IP's job. IP is not built to provide end-to-end guaranteed transmission of data. IP exists mainly for one reason: routing. We'll revisit routing a bit later, when I describe the specifics of how to accomplish IP routing on an NT machine.

But whose job *is* end-to-end integrity, if not IP's? The answer: its buddy, TCP.

TCP (Transmission Control Protocol)

I said earlier that IP handled routing and really didn't concern itself that much with whether the message got to its final destination or not. If there are seven IP hops from one point to the next, then each hop is an independent action—there's no coordination, no notion of whether a particular hop is hop number three out of seven. Each IP hop is totally unaware of the others. How, then, could we use IP to provide reliable service?

IP packets are like messages in a bottle. Drop the bottle in the ocean, and you have no guarantee that the message got to whomever you want to receive it. But suppose you hired a "message in the bottle end-to-end manager?" Such a person (let's call her Gloria) would take your message, put it in a bottle, and toss it in the ocean. That person would also have a partner on the other side of the ocean (let's call him Gaston) and, when Gaston received a message in a bottle from Gloria, Gaston would then pen a short message saying "Gloria, I got your message," put *that* message in a bottle, and drop that bottle into the ocean.

If Gloria didn't get an acknowledgment from Gaston within, say, three months, then she'd drop *another* bottle into the ocean with the original message in it. In data communications terms, we'd say that Gloria "timed out" on the transmission path, and was *resending*.

Yeah, I know, this is a somewhat goofy analogy, but understand the main point: we hired Gloria and Gaston to ensure that our inherently unreliable message-in-a-bottle network became reliable. Gloria will keep sending and resending until she gets a response from Gaston. Notice that she doesn't create a whole new transmission medium, like radio or telephone; she merely adds a layer of her own watchfulness to the existing transmission protocol.

Now think of IP as the message in the bottle. TCP, the Transmission Control Protocol, is just the Gloria/Gaston team. TCP provides reliable end-to-end service.

By the way, TCP provides some other services, most noticeably something called *sockets* which I will discuss in a moment. As TCP has value besides its reliability feature, TCP also has a "cousin" protocol that acts very much like it but does *not* guarantee end-to-end integrity. That protocol is called UDP, or the User Datagram Protocol.

That's basically the idea behind TCP. Its main job is the orderly transmission of data from one internet host to another. Its main features include:

- Handshaking

- Packet sequencing

- Flow control

- Error handling

- Handshake

Whereas IP has no manners—it just shoves data at a computer whether that computer is ready for it or not—TCP makes sure that each side is properly introduced before attempting to transfer. TCP sets up the connection.

Sequencing

As IP does not use a virtual circuit, then different data packets may end up arriving at different times, and in fact, in different order. Here, you see a simple internet transferring four segments of data across a network with multiple possible pathways. The first segment takes the high road, so to speak, and is delayed. The second through the fourth does not, and so gets to the destination more quickly. TCP's job on the receiving side is then to reassemble things in order.

Flow Control

Along with sequencing is flow control. What if fifty segments of data had been sent, and they all arrived out of order? The receiver would have to hold them all in memory before sorting them out and writing them to disk. Part of what TCP worries about is *pacing* the data—not sending it to the receiver until the receiver is ready for it.

Error Detection/Correction

And finally, TCP handles error detection and correction, as I've already said. Beyond that, TCP is very efficient in the way that it does error handling. Some protocols acknowledge each and every block, generating a large overhead of blocks. TCP, in contrast, does not do that. It tells the other side, "I am capable of accepting and buffering some number of blocks. Don't expect an acknowledgment until I've gotten that number of blocks. And if a block is received incorrectly, I will not acknowledge it, so if I don't acknowledge as quickly as you expect me to do, then just go ahead and resend the block."

Sockets and the WinSock Interface

Just about anything that you want to do with the Internet or your company's internet involves two programs talking to each other. When you browse someone's Web site, you have a program (your Web browser, a "client" program) communicating with their Web server (obviously, a "server" program). Using the File Transfer Protocol, or FTP, which I'll discuss later in this chapter, requires that one machine be running a program called an "FTP server" and that another computer be running an "FTP client." Internet mail requires that a mail client program talk to a mail server program—and those are just a few examples.

Connecting a program in one machine to another program in another machine is kind of like placing a telephone call. The sender must know the phone number of the receiver, and the receiver must be around his or her phone, waiting to pick it up. In the TCP world, a phone number is called a socket. A socket is composed of three parts: the IP address of the receiver, which we've already discussed, the receiving program's *port number*, which we *haven't* yet discussed, and whether it's a TCP port or a UDP port—each protocol has its own set.

Suppose the PC on your desk running Windows NT wants to get a file from the FTP site which is really the PC on *my* desk running Windows NT. Obviously, for this to happen, we've got to know each other's IP addresses. But that's not all; after all, in my PC I have a whole bunch of programs running (my network connection, my word processor, my operating system, my personal organizer, the FTP server, and so on). So if TCP says, "Hey, Mark's machine, I want to talk to you," then my machine would reply, "Which *one* of us—the word processor, the e-mail program, or what?" So the TCP/IP world assigns a 16-bit number to each program that wants to send or receive TCP information, a number called the *port* of that program. The most popular Internet applications have had particular port numbers assigned to them, and those port numbers are known as "well-known ports." Some well-known port numbers include FTP (TCP ports 20 and 21), the common mail protocol SMTP (TCP port 25), Web servers (TCP port 80), Network News Transfer Protocol (NNTP, TCP port 119), and the Post Office Protocol version 3 (POP3, TCP port 110).

How Sockets Work

So, for instance, suppose I've written a TCP/IP-based *chat* program that allows me to type messages to you and receive typed messages from you. This fictitious chat program might get port number 1500. Anyone running chat, then, would install it on port 1500. Then, to chat my computer with an imaginary IP address of 123.124.55.67, your chat program would essentially "place a phone call"—that is, set up a TCP session—with port 1500 at address 123.124.55.67. The combination of port 1500 with IP address 123.124.55.67 is a *socket address*.

In order for your computer to chat with my computer, my computer must be *ready* to chat. So I have to run my chat program. It would probably say something like, "Do you want to chat with anyone, or do you just want to wait to be called?" I tell it that I just want to wait to be called, so it sits quietly in my PC's memory, but first it tells the PC, "If anyone calls for me, wake me up—I'm willing to take calls at port 1500." That's called a *passive open* on TCP.

Then, when your computer wants to chat with my computer, it sends an *active open* request to my computer, saying, "Want to talk?" It also says, "I can accept up to *x* bytes of data in my buffers." My computer responds by saying, "Sure, I'll talk, and I can accept up to *y* bytes of data in my buffers."

The two computers then blast data back and forth, being careful not to overflow the other computer's buffers. When a buffer's worth of information is sent by your computer, then your computer doesn't send my computer any more data until my computer acknowledges that it received the data.

Once the chat is over, both sides politely say "good-bye," and hang up. My computer can choose to continue to wait for incoming calls, as before.

WinSock Sockets

The value of sockets is that they provide a uniform way to write programs that exploit the underlying Internet communications structure. If, for example, I want to write a networked version of the game Battleship, then I might want to be able to quickly turn out versions for Windows, OS/2, the Mac, and Unix machines. But maybe I don't know much about communications, and don't *want* to know much. (I'm probably supposed to note here that Battleship is a registered trademark of Milton-Bradley or someone like that; consider it done.) I could just sit down with my C compiler and bang out a Battleship that runs on Unix machines. Just a few code changes, and presto! I have my PC version.

But the PC market requires some customization, and so a particular version of the sockets interface, called WinSock, was born. It's essentially the sockets interface, but modified a bit to work better in a PC environment.

The benefit of WinSock is that all vendors of TCP/IP software support an identical WinSock programming interface (well, identical in theory, anyway) and so TCP/IP-based programs should run as well atop FTP software's TCP/IP stack as it would atop the TCP/IP stack that ships with NT. That's why you can plop your Netscape Web browser on just about any PC with TCP/IP and it should work without any trouble.

Internet Host Names

Thus far, I've referred to a lot of numbers; hooking up to my Web server, then, seems to require that you point your Web browser to IP address 199.34.57.52, TCP port number 80.

Of course, you don't actually do that. When you send e-mail to your friends, you don't send it to 199.45.23.17; you send it to something like robbie@somefirm.com. What's IP got to do with it?

IP addresses are useful because they're precise and because they're easy to subnet. But they're tough to remember, as people generally prefer more English-sounding names. So TCP/IP allows us to group one or more TCP/IP networks into groups called *domains*, groups that will share a common name like microsoft.com, senate.gov, army.mil, or mit.edu.

Machines within a domain will have names that include the domain name; for example, within my mmco.com domain I have machines named micron133.mmco.com, narn.mmco.com, minbar.mmco.com, zhahadum.mmco.com, and serverted.mmco.com. Those specific machine names are called *host names*.

How does TCP/IP connect the English names—the *host* names— to the IP addresses? And how can I sit at my PC in mmco.com and get the information I need to be able to find another host called archie.au, when archie's all the way on the other side of the world in Australia?

Simple—with HOSTS, DNS, and, later in this chapter, WINS. The process of converting a name to its corresponding IP address is called *name resolution*. Again, how's it work? Read on.

Simple Naming Systems (HOSTS)

When you set up your subnet, you don't want to explicitly use IP addresses every time you want to run some TCP/IP utility and hook up with another computer in your subnet. So, instead, you create a file called HOSTS that looks like this:

```
199.34.57.50  keydata.mmco.com
199.34.57.129 serverted.mmco.com
```

This is just a simple ASCII text file. Each host goes on one line, and the line starts off with the host's IP address. Enter at least one space and the host's English name. Do this for each host. You can even give multiple names in the HOSTS file:

```
199.34.57.50  keydata.mmco.com markspc
199.34.57.129 serverted.mmco.com serverpc bigsv
```

Ah, but now comes the really rotten part:

You have to put one of these HOSTS files on *every single workstation*. That means that every single time you change anyone's HOSTS file, you have to go around and change *everybody's* HOSTS file. Every workstation must contain a copy of this file, which is basically a telephone directory of every machine in your subnet. It's a pain, yes, but it's simple. If you're thinking, "Why can't I just put a central HOSTS file on a server and do all my administration with *that* file?"—what you're really asking for is a *name server*, and I'll show you two of them, the Domain Naming Service (DNS) and the Windows Internet Naming Service (WINS), in this chapter.

You must place the HOSTS file in \winnt35\system32\drivers\etc on an NT system, in the Windows directory on a Windows for Workgroups or Windows 95 machine, and wherever the network software is installed in other kinds of machines (DOS or OS/2).

HOSTS is re-read every time your system does a name resolution; you needn't reboot to see a change in HOSTS take effect.

Domain Naming System (DNS)

HOSTS is a pain, but it's a necessary pain if you want to communicate within your subnet. How does IP find a name outside of your subnet or outside of your domain?

Suppose someone at exxon.com wanted to send a file to mmco.com. Surely the exxon.com HOSTS files don't contain the IP address of my company, and vice versa?

To take a fictitious example, how would TCP/IP find a machine at some software company named "Macrosoft?" How would IP figure out that a host named, say, database.macrosoft.com really has an IP address of, say, 181.50.47.22?

Within an organization, name resolution can clearly be accomplished by the HOSTS file. Between domains, however, name resolution is handled by the Domain Naming Service, or DNS. There is a central naming clearinghouse for *the* Internet called the InterNIC Registration Services. (Obviously, if you're only running a private internet, then *you* perform the function of name manager.) There is a hierarchy of names, a hierarchy created specifically to make it simple to add names to the network quickly. After all, with 20 million Internet users, can you imagine having to call the NIC every single time you put a new user on one of your networks? It would take months to get the paperwork done. Instead, the NIC created the Domain Naming System, of which you see only a small portion. The NIC started off with six initial naming domains: EDU was for educational institutions, NET was for network providers, COM for commercial users, MIL was for military users (remember who built this?), ORG was for organizations, and GOV was for civilian government. For example, there is a domain on the Internet called whitehouse.gov; you can send internet mail to the President that way, at president@whitehouse.gov. There are more root domains these days, like .fi for sites in Finland, .uk for sites in the United Kingdom, and so on.

Anyway, back to the Macrosoft story. Now, in order to get onto the Internet, Macrosoft registers its entire company with the name macrosoft.com, placing itself in the COM—commercial—domain. There's sometimes some gray areas about whether someone is, say, educational or commercial, or perhaps a network provider or a commercial firm, but it's not really that important. From there, Macrosoft dubs someone in their organization the name administrator. That person can then create subsets of the Macrosoft domain; in Figure 14.7, you see a possible arrangement.

The Macrosoft name administrator has subdivided the macrosoft.com domain into two subdomains: wp.macrosoft.com and database.macrosoft.com. He's entirely within his rights to do this, as the rest of the Internet doesn't care what goes on inside macrosoft.com; his naming control only extends from macrosoft.com *down* in the naming hierarchy.

The Macrosoft name administrator maintains a database of host names within macrosoft.com by running a *name server* program on one of the Macrosoft computers. Name servers are computers whose main job is simply to answer the question, "What's the IP address of the

FIGURE 14.7

Name hierarchy
in the Internet

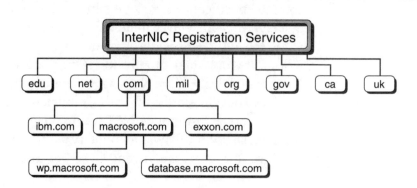

machine somefirm.com?" They're also called *DNS servers*. Sending data from one host (machine) in database.macrosoft.com to another host in database.macrosoft.com would only involve asking the local name server about the receiver's machine's name. In contrast, if someone were to transfer data from some host in database.macrosoft.com to some host in exxon.com, then the request would get bumped up even further, to one of the main Internet name servers. There are nine of these servers in the world, and they reload their massive name databases from the NIC at regular intervals.

NT ships with a DNS server, so you can use an NT Server to act as your name resolver. You'll see how later in this chapter.

E-Mail Names: A Note

If you've previously messed around with e-mail under TCP/IP, then you may be wondering something about these addresses. After all, you don't send mail to mmco.com, you'd send it to a name like mark@mmco.com. mark@mmco.com is an e-mail address. The way it works is this: a group of users in a TCP/IP domain decide to implement mail.

In order to receive mail, a machine must be up and running, ready to accept mail from the outside world (that is, some other subnet or domain). Now, mail can arrive at any time of day, so this machine must be up and running all of the time. That seems to indicate that it would be a dumb idea to get mail delivered straight to your desktop. So, instead, TCP mail dedicates a machine to the mail router task of receiving mail from the outside world, holding that mail until you want to read it, taking mail that you wish to send somewhere else, and routing that mail to some other mail router. The name of the most common TCP/IP mail router program is *sendmail*. The name of the protocol used most commonly for routing e-mail on the Internet, by the way, is the Simple Mail Transfer Protocol, or SMTP.

Unfortunately, Microsoft did not include an SMTP router program in either the workstation or the server version of NT, so you either have to connect up to a existing mail router in order to get Internet mail, or you have to buy a third-party mail product to work under NT.

You can see how mail works in Figure 14.8.

In this small domain, we've got two users, Mark and Christa. (One of the great things about the Internet is that you don't need that pesky Shift key on your keyboard.) Mark works on keydata.mmco.com, and Christa works on ams.mmco.com. Now, suppose Christa wants to send some mail to her friend Corky, executive director of Surfers of America; Corky's address is corky@surferdudes.org. She fires up a program on her workstation, which is called a *mail client*. The mail client allows her to create and send new messages, as well as receive incoming messages. She sends the message and closes her mail client. Notice that her mail client software doesn't do routing—it just lets her create, send, and receive messages.

The mail client has been configured to send messages to the program *sendmail*, which is running in this subnet on mailguy.mmco.com. mailguy is kind of the post office (in Internet lingo, a *mail router*) for this group of users. Sendmail on mailguy.mmco.com stores the message, and it then sends the message off to the machine with the DNS name surferdudes.org, trusting IP to route the message correctly to surferdudes.

FIGURE 14.8

The interrelationship of host names, e-mail names, and the Internet

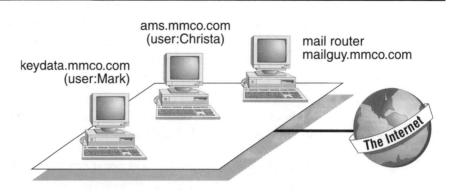

ams.mmco.com
(user:Christa)

mail router
mailguy.mmco.com

keydata.mmco.com
(user:Mark)

The Internet

Additionally, sendmail knows the names Christa and Mark. It is the workstation that is the interface to the outside world *vis-à-vis* mail. Note, by the way, that *DNS* has no idea who Mark or Christa are; DNS is concerned with *host* names, not *e-mail* names. It's DNS that worries about how to find mailguy.mmco.com.

A bit later, Corky gets the message and sends a reply to Christa. The reply does *not* go to Christa's machine ams.mmco.com; instead, it goes to mailguy.mmco.com, because Corky sent mail to christa@mmco.com. The mail system sends the messages to mmco.com, but what machine has the address mmco.com? Simple: we give mailguy.mmco.com an alias, and mail goes to it.

Eventually, Christa starts up the mail client program once again. The mail program sends a query to the local mail router mailguy.mmco.com, saying, "Any new mail for Christa?" There *is* mail, and Christa reads it.

Getting onto an Internet

So far, I've talked quite a bit about how an internet works and what kinds of things there are that you can do with an internet. But I haven't told you enough yet to actually get *on* an internet, whether it's your company's private internet or *the* Internet.

- You can connect to a multi-user system and appear to the Internet as a dumb terminal.

- You can connect to an Internet provider via a serial port and a protocol called either the Serial Line Interface Protocol (SLIP) or the Point to Point Protocol (PPP), and appear to the Internet as a host.

- You can be part of a local area network that is an Internet subnet, and then load TCP/IP software on your system, and appear to the Internet as a host.

Each of these options has pros and cons, as you'll see. The general rule is that in order to access an internet, all you basically have to do is to connect up to a computer that is already on an internet.

The essence of an internet is in *packet switching*, a kind of network game of hot potato whereby computers act communally to transfer each other's data around. Packet switching is what makes it possible to add subnetworks on the fly.

Dumb Terminal Connection

This is a common way for someone to get an account that allows access to *the* Internet. For example, you can get an account with Performance Systems Inc. (PSI), Delphi or Digital Express, to name a few Internet access providers.

Delphi, for example, has computers all around the U.S., so to get onto the Internet all you need to do is simply run a terminal emulation package on your system and dial up to their terminal servers. This kind of access is often quite cheap, at least in the U.S.: $25/month is common. If you wanted to do this with NT, then you needn't even run TCP/IP on your NT machine. Instead, you'd merely need to put a modem on your system and use Terminal to dial up to your Internet access provider.

Now, understand: this is just a *terminal* access capability that I've gotten, so it's kind of limited. Suppose, for example, that I live in Virginia (which is true) and I connect to the Internet via a host in Maine (which is not true). From the Internet's point of view, I'm not in an office in Virginia; instead, I'm wherever the host that I'm connected to is. I work in Virginia, but if I were dialing a host in Maine, then from the Internet's point of view I'd be in Maine. Any requests that I make for file transfers, for example, wouldn't go to Virginia—they'd go to my host in Maine.

Now, that can be a bit of a hassle. Say I'm at my Virginia location logged onto the Internet via the Maine host. I get onto Microsoft's FTP site—I'll cover FTP later in this chapter, but basically FTP is just a means to provide a library of files to the outside world—and I grab a few files, perhaps an updated video driver. The FTP program says, "I got the file," but the file is now on the host in Maine. That means that I'm only half done, as I now have to run some other kind of file transfer program to move the file from the host in Maine to my computer in Virginia.

SLIP/PPP Serial Connection

A somewhat better way to connect to a TCP/IP-based network—that is, an internet—is by a direct serial connection to an existing internet host. If you use PCs, then you may know of a program called LapLink that allows two PCs to share each other's hard disks via their RS232 serial ports; SLIP/PPP are similar ideas. An internet may have a similar type of connection called a SLIP or PPP connection. The connection needn't be a serial port, but it often is. SLIP is the Serial Line Interface Protocol, an older protocol that I sometimes think of as the *simple* line interface protocol. There's really nothing to SLIP—no error checking, no security, no flow control. It's the simplest protocol imaginable: just send the data, then send a special byte that means, "This is the end of the data." PPP, in contrast, was designed to retain the low overhead of SLIP, and yet to include some extra information required so that more intelligent parts of an internet—items like routers—could use it effectively. The Point to Point Protocol works by establishing an explicit link between one side and another, then uses a simple error checking system called a *checksum* to monitor noise on the line.

Which protocol should you use? The basic rule that I use is that SLIP doesn't provide error checking but also uses less overhead, and PPP provides error checking and uses more overhead. Therefore, when I'm using error-correcting modems, I use SLIP. On noisy lines and without error-correcting modems, then I use PPP.

NT supports both PPP and SLIP via Remote Access Services.

LAN Connection

The most common way to connect to an internet is simply by being a LAN workstation on a local area network that is an internet subnetwork. Again, this needn't be *the* Internet—almost any LAN can use the TCP/IP protocol suite.

This is the connection that most NT Servers will use to provide TCP/IP services. Microsoft's main reason for implementing TCP/IP on NT is to provide an alternative to NetBEUI, as NetBEUI is quick and applicable to small networks, but inappropriate for large corporate networks. In contrast, TCP/IP has always been good for internetworking, but one suffered tremendously in speed. That's not true anymore, however; for example, a quick test of TCP/IP versus NetBEUI on one of my workstations showed network read rates of 1250 K/sec for NetBEUI and 833K/sec for TCP/IP, and write rates of 312K/sec for NetBEUI and 250K/sec for TCP/IP. Again, TCP's slower, but not by a lot. And NetBEUI doesn't go over routers.

Terminal Connections versus Other Connections

Before moving on to the next topic, I'd like to return to the difference between a terminal connection and a SLIP, PPP, or LAN connection. In Figure 14.9, you see three PCs on an Ethernet attached to two minicomputers, which in turn serve four dumb terminals.

The minicomputer-to-minicomputer link might be SLIP or PPP, or then again they might be LANed together. Notice that only the *computers* in this scenario have internetwork protocol (IP) addresses. Whenever you send mail to one of the people on the PCs at the top of the picture, then it goes to that person's PC. If you were to scrutinize the IP addresses—and most of the time, you will not—then you'd see that everyone had the same IP address. In contrast, the people at the *bottom* of the picture get their mail sent to one of the minicomputers,

FIGURE 14.9

When Internet connec-
tions involve IP numbers
and when they don't

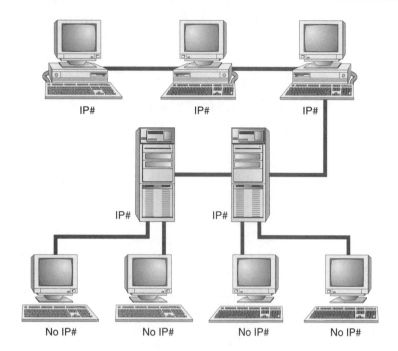

and so, in this example, each pair of terminals shares an IP address. If Shelly and George in your office access your company's internet through terminals connected to the same computer, then a close look at mail from them would show that they have the same IP address. But, if you think about it, you already knew that; if you send mail to george@mailbox.acme.com and to shelly@mailbox.acme.com, then the machine name to which the mail goes is the same; it's just the user name that varies.

So, in summary: if you want to get onto *the* Internet from a remote location, then your best bet is to sign up with a service that will bill you monthly for connect charges, like Delphi. To attach to a private internet, you need to dial up to a multi-user computer on that internet, or you need a SLIP or PPP connection, or you have to be on a workstation on a LAN that's part of that internet. You then need to talk to your local network guru about getting the software installed on your system that will allow your computer to speak TCP/IP so that it can be part of your internet.

Setting Up TCP/IP on NT with Fixed IP Addresses

Enough talking about internetting; let's do it, and do it with NT.

Traditionally, one of the burdens of an IP administrator has been that she must assign separate IP numbers to each machine, a bit of a bookkeeping hassle. You can adopt this fixed IP address approach, and in fact there are some good reasons to do it, as it's compatible with more TCP/IP software and systems. It is also possible, however, to have a server assign IP addresses "on the fly" with the DHCP system that I've mentioned earlier.

Some of you will set up your internet with fixed IP addresses, and some will use dynamic addresses. *Everyone* will use static IP addresses for at least some of your PCs. For that reason, I first want to start the discussion of setting up TCP/IP with just fixed addresses. Then I'll take on dynamic addressing.

Here's basically how to set up TCP/IP on an NT system:

1. Load the TCP/IP protocol.

2. Set the IP address and subnet, default gateway, and DNS server.

3. Prepare the HOSTS file, if you're going to use one.

4. Test the connection with PING.

Let's take a look at those steps, one by one.

Installing TCP/IP Software with Static IP Addresses

You install the TCP/IP protocol (if you didn't choose it when you first installed NT) by opening up the Control Panel, and then choosing the Network icon. You see a dialog box like Figure 14.10.

Click the Protocols tab, and your system will look something like Figure 14.11.

Click Add and you get a list of protocols that you can add. Select TCP/IP, as shown in Figure 14.12.

Click OK. The setup routine will then offer you the chance to take the easy way out and have the system automatically set up the TCP/IP protocol using DHCP, which we'll cover later in this chapter. The dialog box is shown in Figure 14.13.

FIGURE 14.10

Initial Control Panel dialog box for installing network software

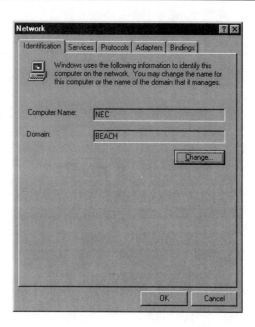

FIGURE 14.11

Protocols tab of Network
property sheet

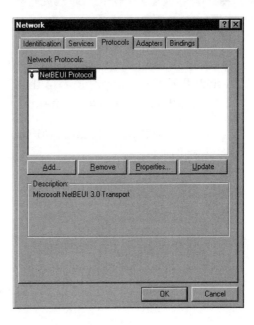

FIGURE 14.12

Choosing to add
TCP/IP protocol

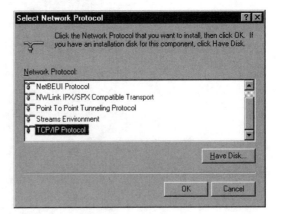

FIGURE 14.13

Choose not to use DHCP

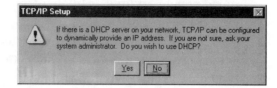

Click No, and NT will prompt you for the location of the installation files; point it wherever you keep them. NT will install a bunch of files, and you'll see that the Protocols window now contains TCP/IP. You need to configure it. Click Close, and NT will rebind all of the protocols, boards, and services, ending up with the following TCP/IP configuration property sheet, as shown in Figure 14.14.

I've already filled in the basic values in that figure—IP address, subnet mask, and default gateway.

FIGURE 14.14

TCP/IP configuration property sheet

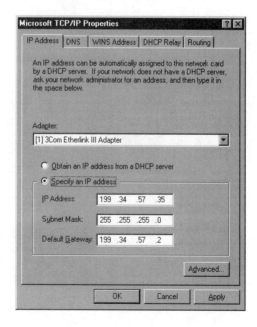

First, you put your IP address into the IP Address field. Using the first quad of your address, NT will guess a subnet mask based on your network class—255.0.0.0 for class A, 255.255.0.0 for class B, and 255.255.255.0 for class C. As I indicated in my discussion earlier in this chapter about subnetting, if your network is subnetted *within* its Internet domain, then you have to change the subnet mask.

Once you have the subnet mask in place, you should enter the IP address of your default gateway, the machine on your Ethernet segment that connects to the outside world either via a router, a SLIP, or a PPP connection. To clarify that, Figure 14.15 shows a sample internet connection.

Suppose you're configuring the machine in the upper left-hand corner of the diagram. You type its IP address into the dialog box that you saw earlier, entering the value 199.34.57.35. Presuming that your class C network—since the first quad is 199, it must be a class C network—is not further subnetted, then the subnet mask would be 255.255.255.0, and the

FIGURE 14.15

An example of a
connection to the
Internet

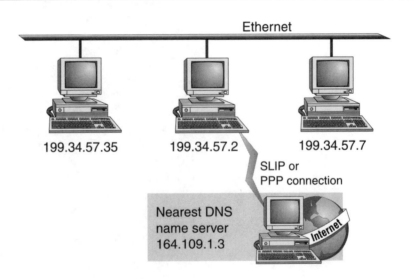

684

default gateway would be the machine with the SLIP connection to the Internet, so you'd enter 199.34.57.2 for the address of the default gateway. (Why didn't I make that gateway machine .1? Just to underscore that it's not necessary to make the gateway .1; it's just a convention.) Notice the DNS router is at 164.109.1.3. You haven't had a chance to incorporate that information into the TCP/IP setup yet, but you will soon.

Next, click the DNS tab. You'll see a dialog box like the one in Figure 14.16.

The important parts of this screen are the host name, the TCP domain name, name resolution, and DNS search order. Again, I've already filled them in here.

The TCP domain name is your company's domain name, like exxon .com, or, if your company is further divided beyond the domain level,

FIGURE 14.16

The DNS configuration screen

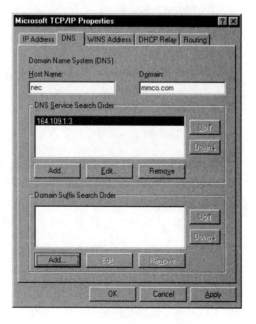

685

perhaps refining.exxon.com. The host name is your computer's name, such as marks-computer, printserver, or the like.

> **NOTE**　Don't use underscores in the name, as it seems to render Microsoft TCP/IP nonfunctional.

Next, you tell NT where to find a DNS server. You can use a HOSTS file, DNS name servers, or a combination. If you use a DNS name server or servers, however, then you have to tell NT where the nearest DNS name server is. You can specify one, two, or three DNS servers, and the order in which to search them, in the DNS Name Service Search Order field. In general, you only include the name of one or two DNS name servers, a primary and a secondary for use in case the primary name server is down.

When that sheet is arranged as you want it, you next want to configure the name resolution system that you use within your enterprise network, a system called the Windows Internet Naming Systems, or WINS. Click "WINS Address" and you'll see a page like the one shown in Figure 14.17.

I'll cover WINS in detail later in this chapter, but for now all you need to understand is that you have one or two NT Servers acting as name resolvers or WINS Servers. This dialog box lets you fill in the names of a primary and secondary WINS server.

I know I've already said that most of the Internet uses something called DNS to convert network names to network addresses, but now I'm saying that we'll *also* use something else called WINS to do what sounds like the same thing. What's going on? In truth, you shouldn't really have to set up WINS at all; NT and Microsoft enterprise networking in general should use DNS for all of its name resolution, but it doesn't. The reason is that Microsoft wanted NT's networking modules to work like the already-existing LAN Manager system, and LAN Manager used a naming system based on its NetBIOS application program interface. A computer's NetBIOS name is the computer name

FIGURE 14.17

Configuring a WINS client

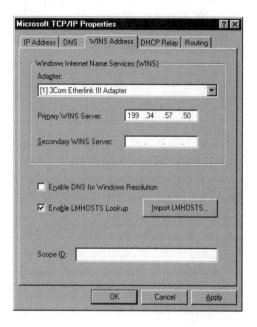

that you gave it when you installed it. When you type **net view \\ajax**, something must resolve "\\ajax" into an IP address—a NetBIOS-to-IP resolution. WINS does that. In contrast, the rest of the Internet would see a machine called "ajax" as having a longer name, like "ajax.acme.com." If there were a Web server on ajax, then someone outside the company would have to point her Web browser to http://ajax.acme.com, and some piece of software would have to resolve "ajax.acme.com" into an IP address. That piece of software is the sockets or WinSock interface, and in either case they will rely upon not WINS but *DNS* to resolve the name. In a few words, then, programs written to employ NetBIOS will use WINS for name resolution, and programs written to employ WinSock use DNS for name resolution.

I can probably guess what you're thinking now, and, yes, DNS and WINS should be integrated, and they will be—but not until Cairo, the next version of NT. For now, we'll just have to maintain two different name resolvers. (There is, I promise, much more on the subject of WINS versus DNS name resolution later on in the chapter, but that's a quick overview.)

Anyway, there's a check box: "Enable DNS for Windows name resolution." I wrote the previous two paragraphs so that I could explain this check box. As you've read, WinSock-based applications use DNS for name resolution, and NetBIOS applications use WINS. But suppose a NetBIOS-based application cannot resolve a name with WINS—WINS comes back and says, "I don't know who this computer is!" If you check this check box, then you are telling your machine, "If WINS fails me on name resolution, let NetBIOS look to DNS to resolve names." If you check it, then some operations may get pretty slow on your system. Consider what happens when you accidentally try an operation on a nonexistent server. Suppose you type **net view \\bigserver** when its real name is "\\bigserve." WINS will come back with a failure on the name resolution attempt, but if you have this box checked, then your system will waste even more time asking DNS to resolve the name. On the other hand, some installations have servers with NetBIOS names and use TCP/IP, but do not participate in WINS name resolution. For example, an old LAN Manager/Unix (LM/X) server will have a NetBIOS name, but it doesn't know to register that name with WINS, as its software was written before Microsoft introduced WINS. Ask a WINS server for the LM/X server's IP address, then, and WINS will come up blank. But *DNS* would know how to find the server. So if you have older Microsoft enterprise networking products that run the TCP/IP protocol, then you may want to check the "Enable DNS for Windows name resolution" box.

You'll enable LMHOSTS if you need the LMHOSTS file; LMHOSTS is a static ASCII file like HOSTS, except that where HOSTS assists in WinSock name resolution, LMHOSTS assists in NetBIOS name resolution. You will almost never use a LMHOSTS file on a modern network. I discuss LMHOSTS later in this chapter. The "NetBIOS scope ID" should be left blank for most networks. If you've partitioned your network into

NetBIOS scopes, then talk to whomever did it and they can tell you what scope names to use. Otherwise, do not fill anything in here.

Click OK to return to the Protocols screen, then Close to close the Network applet. You have to reboot for the changes to take effect.

Just to get started, create your HOSTS file; remember that it goes in winnt\system32\drivers\etc. The file is reread every time a name needs to be resolved, so you needn't reboot every time you change the contents of HOSTS.

Testing Your TCP/IP Installation

Your TCP/IP software should now be ready to go, so let's test it.

TCP/IP has a very handy little tool for finding out whether or not your TCP/IP software is up and running, and whether or not you have a connection to another point—*ping*.

Ping is a program that lets you send a short message to another TCP/IP node, asking, "Are you there?" If it is there, then it says yes to the ping, and ping relays this information back to you. You can see an example of ping in Figure 14.18.

FIGURE 14.18

A sample ping output

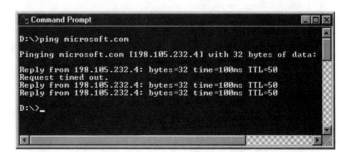

In the above figure, I pinged Microsoft or, rather, whatever network Microsoft exposes to the outside world. (Notice it's a class-B network—those Microsoft folks really rate.) The ping was successful, which is all that matters. But *don't* ping Microsoft for your first test; I did that screen shot a while back, before they put their firewall in. (Before they put the firewall in, it was actually possible to browse Microsoft's servers from the comfort of your own home, right over the Internet. I can just hear the "oops!" that someone exclaimed over *that* one.) So don't bother trying to ping Microsoft, as their system no longer responds to ping requests anyway. (I guess they couldn't figure out a way to charge for them.) Instead, use ping to gradually test first your IP software, then your connection to the network, your name resolution, and finally your gateway to the rest of your internet.

How Do I Make Sure That TCP/IP Is Set Up Properly?

First, test that you've installed the IP software by pinging the built-in IP loopback address. Type **ping 127.0.0.1**, and if that fails, then you know that you've done something wrong in the initial installation, so recheck that the software is installed on your system. This does not put any messages out on the network, it just checks that the software is installed. By the way, that's also what happens if you ping your IP address: for example, in the machine I just installed, pinging 127.0.0.1 does exactly the same thing as pinging 199.34.57.35.

If that fails, then your TCP/IP stack probably isn't installed correctly, or perhaps you mistyped the IP number (if it failed on your specific IP address but not on the loopback), or perhaps you gave the *same* IP number to another workstation.

Ping your gateway to see that you can get to the gateway, which should be on your subnet. In my case, my gateway is at 199.34.57.2, so I type **ping 199.34.57.2**, and all should be well.

How Do I Make Sure That TCP/IP Is Set Up Properly? (Continued)

 If you can't get to the gateway, then check that the gateway is up, and that your network connection is all right. There's nothing more embarrassing than calling in outside network support, only to find that your LAN cable fell out of the back of your computer.

Ping something on the other side of your gateway, like an external DNS server. (Ping me, if you like; 199.34.57.1 ought to be up just about all the time.) If you can't get there, then it's likely that your gateway isn't working properly.

Next, test the name resolution on your system. Ping yourself *by name*. Instead of typing **ping 199.34.57.35**, I'd type **ping nec.mmco.com** (the machine I'm on at the moment). That tests HOSTS and/or DNS.

Then, ping someone else on your subnet. Again, try using a DNS name, like "mizar.ursamajor.edu," rather than an IP address, but if that doesn't work, then use the IP address. If the IP address works, but the host name doesn't, then double-check the HOSTS file or DNS.

Finally, ping someone outside of your domain, like house.gov (the U.S. House of Representatives), or ftp.microsoft.com or orion01.mmco.com. If that doesn't work, but all the pings inside your network work, then you've probably got a problem with your Internet provider.

If you're successful on all of these tests, it should be set up properly.

Setting Up Routing on NT and Windows Machines

Up to now, I've assumed that all of your Windows NT, Workgroups, and 95 machines had a single default gateway that acted as "router to the world" for your machines. That's not always true, as real-life internets often have multiple routers that lead a machine to different networks. I've also assumed that your NT network is connected to the Internet, or to your enterprise internet, via some third-party (Compatible Systems, Bay Networks, Cisco Systems, or whomever) router. That's also not always true, as NT machines can act as IP routers.

Routing problems aren't just *server* problems; they're often workstation problems as well. So, in this section, I'll take on two topics:

• How to set up routing tables on your Windows workstations

• How to use your NT servers as IP routers

An Example Multi-Router Internet

Suppose you had a workstation (whether it's Windows for Workgroups, Windows NT, or Windows 95) on a network with two gateways, as shown in Figure 14.19.

As is the case for most of these diagrams, a multi-network picture can be cryptic, so here's an explanation of what you are looking at.

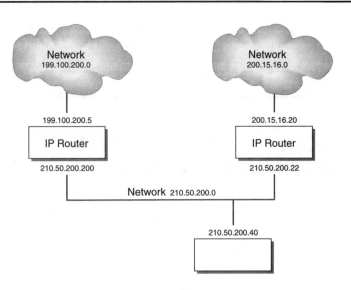

FIGURE 14.19

A workstation on a network with two gateways

First, there are three separate Ethernet segments, three separate subnets. They are all C-class networks, just to keep things clean. Two of the networks are only represented by ovals; thus, the oval on the left containing "199.100.200.0" is just shorthand for an Ethernet with up to 254 computers hanging off it, with addresses ranging from 199.100.200.1 through 199.100.200.254. Notice that I said 254, not 253, because *there is no default gateway for these subnets*. As there are only three subnets, this is an "internet," not part of the "Internet." One side effect of not being on the Net is that you can use the ".1" address for regular old machines. I left the Internet out of this first example because I found that it confused me when I was first trying to get this routing stuff down. I'll add it later, I promise.

There is also another oval, to the right, representing a network whose addresses range from 200.15.16.1 through 200.15.16.254—network number 200.15.16.0.

In between is a third subnet with address 210.50.200.0. You see a PC in the middle which has only one Ethernet card in it, and its IP address is 210.50.200.40. The rectangles on the right and left sides of the picture are routers, computers with two Ethernet cards in them and thus two IP addresses apiece. Each has an address on the 210.50.200.0 network, and each has an address either on the 200.15.16.0 network or on the 199.100.200.0 network.

Adding Entries to Routing Tables: Route Add

Having said that, let's now figure out how to tell the machine at 210.50.200.40 how to route anywhere on this network. Some of the facts that it needs to know are

- To get a message to the 199.100.200.0 network, send it to the machine at 210.50.200.200.

- To get a message to the 200.15.16.0 network, send it to the machine at 210.50.200.22.

- To get a message to the 210.50.200.0 network, just use your own Ethernet card; send it out on the segment, and it'll be heard.

You tell a workstation how to send packets with the *route add* command. Simplified, it looks like this:

```
route add destination mask netmask gatewayaddress
```

Here, *destination* is the address or set of addresses that you want to be able to get to. *Netmask* defines how *many* addresses are there—is it a C network with 250+ addresses, something subnetted smaller, or perhaps a "supernet" of several C networks? *Gatewayaddress* is just the IP address of the machine that will route your packets to their destination.

The "route add" command for the 199.100.200.0 network would look like this:

```
route add 199.100.200.0 mask 255.255.255.0 210.50.200.200
```

This means "send a message anywhere on the 199.100.200.0 network, send it to the machine at 210.50.200.200, and it'll take care of it."

Just a reminder on subnetting, for clarity's sake: suppose the network on the upper left wasn't a full C network, but rather a subnetted part of it. Suppose it was just the range of addresses from 199.100.200.64 through 199.100.200.127. The network number would be, as always, the first address (199.100.200.64), and the subnet mask would be 255.255.255.192. The "route add" command would then look like

```
route add 199.100.200.64 mask 255.255.255.192 210.50.200.200
```

Anyway, back to the example in the picture. Add a command for the right-hand-side network; it looks like

```
route add 200.15.16.0 mask 255.255.255.0 210.50.200.22
```

That much will get an NT system up and running.

Understanding the Default Routes

Even if you don't ever type a "route add" command at a Windows workstation, you'll find that there are routing statements that are automatically generated. Let's look at them. First, we'd need an explicit routing command to tell the 210.50.200.40 machine to get to its own subnet:

```
route add 210.50.200.0 mask 255.255.255.0 210.50.200.40
```

Or, in other words, "To get to your local subnet, route to yourself."

Then, recall that the entire 127.*x.y.z* range of network addresses is the loopback. Implement that like so:

```
route add 127.0.0.0 mask 255.0.0.0 127.0.0.1
```

This says "take any address from 127.0.0.0 through 127.255.255.255 and route it to 127.0.0.1." The IP software has already had 127.0.0.1 defined for it, so it knows what to do with that. Notice the mask, 255.0.0.0, is a simple class-A network mask.

Some NT Internet software uses internet multicast groups, so the multicast address must be defined. It is 224.0.0.0. It looks like the loopback route command:

```
route add 224.0.0.0 mask 255.0.0.0 210.50.200.40
```

The system knows to multicast by "shouting," which means communicating over its local subnet.

Viewing the Routing Table

Let's find out exactly what routing information this computer has. How? Well, on Windows NT, Workgroups, and 95 workstations there are two commands that will show you what the workstation knows about how to route IP packets. Type either **netstat -rn** or **route print** at a command line—the output is identical, so use either command—and you see something like Figure 14.20.

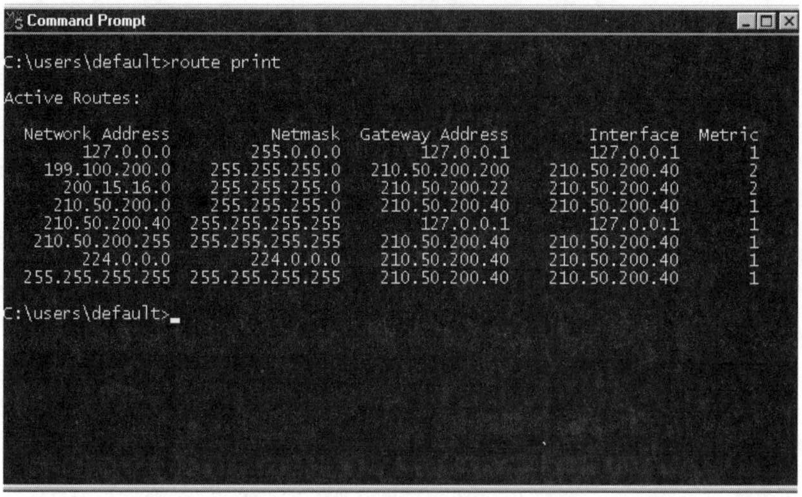

FIGURE 14.20

sample ROUTE
PRINT output

```
Command Prompt                                                    _ □ ×
C:\users\default>route print

Active Routes:

    Network Address          Netmask  Gateway Address        Interface  Metric
          127.0.0.0        255.0.0.0        127.0.0.1        127.0.0.1       1
      199.100.200.0    255.255.255.0    210.50.200.200    210.50.200.40       2
        200.15.16.0    255.255.255.0     210.50.200.22    210.50.200.40       2
       210.50.200.0    255.255.255.0     210.50.200.40    210.50.200.40       1
      210.50.200.40  255.255.255.255        127.0.0.1        127.0.0.1       1
     210.50.200.255  255.255.255.255     210.50.200.40    210.50.200.40       1
          224.0.0.0        224.0.0.0     210.50.200.40    210.50.200.40       1
    255.255.255.255  255.255.255.255     210.50.200.40    210.50.200.40       1

C:\users\default>
```

Notice that the output of ROUTE PRINT is similar to the way you
format data in ROUTE ADD. Each line shows a network address,
which is the desired destination, the netmask, which indicates how
many addresses exist at the desired destination, and the gateway,
which is the IP address that the workstation should send its packets to
in order to reach the destination. But note two more columns: "Interface" and "Metric."

The "Interface" Column

"Interface" asks itself "which of my local IP addresses—the ones physically located inside me, like my loopback and all the IP addresses attached
to all of my network cards—should I use to get to that gateway?" On this
computer, it's a moot point, because it only has one network card in it.

What might this look like on a multihomed machine, like the router
on the left-hand side? It's got two IP addresses, 199.100.200.5 and

210.50.200.200. A fragment of its ROUTE PRINT output might then look like

```
Network Address Netmask    Gateway Address   Interface    Metric
199.100.200.0  255.255.255.0 199.100.200.5    199.100.200.5   1
210.50.200.0   255.255.255.0 210.50.200.200   210.50.200.200  1
```

There are two networks that the router machine can get to (obviously, or it wouldn't be much use as a router), and each one has a gateway address, which happens to be the local IP address that the router maintains on each network. But now notice the "Interface" column: rather than staying at the same IP address all the way through, this tells the computer, "I've already told you which gateway to direct this traffic to; now I'll tell you which of your local IP addresses to employ in order to get to that gateway in the first place."

The "Metric" Column

The "Metric" column (what, no English option?) tells IP how many routers it will have to pass through in order to get to its destination. "1" means "your destination is on the same subnet." A metric value of 2 would mean "you have to go through one router to get to your destination," and so on. Since the .40 workstation must go through a router to get to either the 199.100.200.0 or the 200.15.16.0 network, both of those networks get a metric of "2."

Ah, but how did the computer know that it would take a router jump to get to those networks? Well, you see, *I* told it.

I have to confess here that I left off a parameter on the ROUTE ADD command, simply to make the explanation palatable. As I knew that the metric was "2" for both routes, I just added the parameter "metric 2" to the end of both ROUTE ADD statements. The revised, complete commands look like

```
route add 200.15.16.0 mask 255.255.255.0 210.50.200.22 metric 2
route add 199.100.200.0 mask 255.255.255.0 210.50.200.200 metric 2
```

You'll learn a bit later that a protocol called RIP will make this process automatic, but for now I want to stick to this manually constructed set of routing tables. (Using hand-constructed routing tables is called *static routing*; the automatic methods like RIP are called *dynamic routing*, and I'll get to them later.)

Route Print Output Explained

Now that you can decipher each column in the ROUTE PRINT output, I'll finish up explaining the output.

The first line is the loopback information, as you've seen before. It's automatically generated on every NT/Workgroups/95 machine running the Microsoft TCP/IP stack. The second and third lines are the manually entered routes that tell your machine how to address the 200.15.16.0 and 199.100.200.0 networks. The fourth line is another automatically generated line, and it explains how to address the 210.50.200.0 subnet, which is the local one. The fifth line refers to 210.50.200.40 itself. The mask, 255.255.255.255, means that these aren't routing instructions to get to an entire network, but rather routing instructions to get to a particular computer. It basically says, "if you need to get data to 210.50.200.40, send it to the loopback address." The result: if you ping 210.50.200.40, then no actual communication happens over the network. The sixth line defines how to do a local subnet broadcast. Again, it doesn't point to an entire network, but rather to the particular subnet broadcast address. The seventh line serves Internet multicasting, as you saw before. And the final address is for something called the "limited broadcast address," a kind of generic subnet broadcast address.

Adding the "Default Gateway"

Suppose you wanted to set up my 210.50.100.40 machine. How would you do it? More specifically, you'd ask me: "Which is the default gateway?"

Well, in the TCP/IP configuration screen that you've seen before, you'd obviously be able to supply the information that the IP address should be 210.50.100.40 and the subnet mask should be 255.255.255.0. But what should you use to fill in the Default Gateway field? I mean, there are *two* gateways, 210.50.100.22 and 210.50.100.200. Which should you use?

The answer? *Neither*. A *default gateway* is just another entry in the routing table, but it's not specific like the ones you've met so far; it's a catch-all entry. This network doesn't get to the Internet, and it can only see two other subnets, each with their own routers (gateways), so I left the Default Gateway field blank. And there's an advantage to that.

"Destination Host Unreachable"

If I were to try to ping some address not on the three subnets, like 25.44.92.4, then I wouldn't get the message that the ping had timed out, or experienced an error, or anything of the sort; rather, I'd get a "destination host unreachable" message. That's important: "destination host unreachable" doesn't necessarily mean that you can't get to the destination host, but it *does* mean that your workstation doesn't know *how* to get to that host—it lacks any routing information about how to get there at all. Do a ROUTE PRINT and you'll probably be able to see what's keeping you from getting to your destination.

Building a Default Gateway by Hand

When *would* a default gateway make sense in our network? Well, let's add a connection to the Internet to the network, as shown in Figure 14.21.

Now we need another ROUTE ADD command—but what should it look like? I mean, what's the generic IP address of the whole Internet?

Believe it or not, there *is* such an address: 0.0.0.0. Think of it as "the network number to end all network numbers." And the network mask? Well, since it doesn't matter *what* address bits match which other address

FIGURE 14.21

Network with an
internet connection

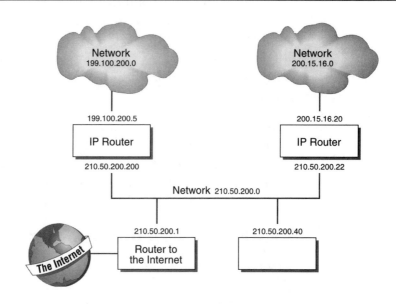

bits—after all, no matter what your address is, you're still on the particular "subnet" which is the entire Internet—the subnet mask is also 0.0.0.0. So the command looks like

```
route add 0.0.0.0 mask 0.0.0.0 210.50.200.1
```

Handling Conflicts in Routing Information

However, it appears that there are some conflicts here. Look at some of the instructions that you've given the IP software about how to route:

- There's a rule about how to handle the specific address 210.50.200 .40: just keep the message local at 127.0.0.1, no routing.

- There's a rule about how to handle the range from 210.50.200.0 through 210.50.200.255: shout it out on the subnet, no routing.

- There's a rule about how to handle the range from 199.100.200.0 through 199.100.200.255: send it to 210.50.200.200.

- There's a rule about how to handle the range from 200.15.16.0 through 200.15.16.255: send it to 210.50.200.22.

- There's a rule about how to handle *all* Internet addresses: send the messages to 210.50.200.1.

Here's what I mean about a conflict: suppose you want to send an IP packet to 200.15.16.33. You have one rule that says "send it to 210.50 .200.22," and another that says "send it to 210.50.200.1." Which rule does the software on your workstation (or server) follow?

Answer: when in doubt, always use the most specific routing rule. The rule that says to send the IP packet to 210.50.200.22 has a more specific netmask (255.255.255.0) than the rule that says to send it to 210.50.200.1 (0.0.0.0), so the 210.50.200.22 rule wins. Basically, the rule is: in the case of a conflict, pick the route with the most 1s in its subnet mask.

One more thing: you wouldn't, of course, want to have to type in those ROUTE ADD commands every time you start up your computer. So you'd use a variation on the ROUTE ADD command; just type **route -p add...**—when you add the **-p** that entry becomes permanent in your system's routing table.

All Routers Must Know All Subnets

I've talked about how I'd set up my sample network from the point of view of a workstation. It would work, but you can see that it's a real pain to punch in all of those ROUTE ADD statements for each workstation. The answer is to make the routers smarter; *then* you can just pick one router to be the default gateway for the .40 workstation, and the workstation needn't worry about anything. So let's take a minute and see how each of the three routers in this system would be set up.

The first router is the one on the left, that routes between 199.100 .200.0 and 210.50.200.0. It must know

- It can get to 199.100.200.0 through its 199.100.200.5 interface;

- It can get to 210.50.200.0 through its 210.50.200.200 interface;

- It can get to the Internet through 210.50.200.1, which it gets to through its 210.50.200.200 interface.

In fact, you would not have to type in routing commands telling it how to get to 199.100.200.0 or 210.50.200.0; assuming it's an NT machine, the NT routing software figures that out automatically. But you can tell it to get to the Internet by setting a default gateway:

```
route add 0.0.0.0 mask 0.0.0.0 210.50.200.1 metric 2
```

The routing software is then smart enough to realize that it should get to 210.50.200.1 via its 210.50.200.200 interface.

The second router, the one on the right, routes between 200.15.16.0 and 210.50.200.0. It can directly get to both of those networks, and, as with the first router, we don't have to tell it about them. But to get to the Internet, it must route packets to 210.50.200.1, and so, like the first router, it should have a default gateway of 210.50.200.1.

Now let's tackle the third router, the machine at 210.50.200.1, which is the Internet gateway. It must know that it should use the Internet as its default gateway. For example, on my Compatible Systems routers, there is a magic address "WAN" which just means "the modem connection to the Internet." I essentially tell it, "Route add 0.0.0.0 mask 0.0.0.0 WAN," and packets travel to and from the Internet over the modem. The router must then be told of each of the three subnets, like so:

```
route add 210.50.200.0 mask 255.255.255.0 210.50.500.1 metric 1
route add 199.100.200.5 mask 255.255.255.0 210.50.200.200 metric 2
route add 200.15.16.20 mask 255.255.255.0 210.50.200.22 metric 2
```

Using RIP to Simplify Workstation Management

Thus far, I've shown you how to tell your workstations how to exploit routers on the network. In most cases, you won't need to build such large, complex routing tables by hand, and in almost no case will you *want* to build those tables.

Ideally, you shouldn't have to type in static tables; instead, your workstations could just suck up routing information automatically from the nearby routers, using some kind of Browser-type protocol. You *can* do such a thing with the Routing Internet Protocol, or RIP.

RIP is an incredibly simple protocol. Routers running RIP broadcast their routing tables about twice a minute. Any workstation running RIP software hears the routing tables and incorporates them into its *own* routing tables. Result: you put a new router on the system, and you needn't punch in any static routes.

RIP is part of the Multivendor Protocol Router package for NT 3.51 users, and ships as part of NT 4. The Microsoft implementation supports both IP and IPX. Routes detected by RIP show up in ROUTE PRINT statements just as if they were static routes.

Using an NT Machine as a LAN/LAN Router

In the process of growing your company's internet, you need routers. For a network of any size, the best bet is probably to buy dedicated routers, boxes from companies like Cisco Systems, Bay Networks, or Compatible Systems.

Dedicated routers are fast and come with some impressive management tools: neat GUI programs that let you control and monitor your network from your workstation. But routers have one disadvantage: they're expensive. I haven't seen an Ethernet-to-Ethernet IP router available for less than $3000. Again, don't misunderstand me: these routers are probably worth what they cost in terms of the ease that they bring to network management and the speed with which they route data. But you might not have the three grand, so you're looking for an alternative.

Your NT machine can actually provide you with an alternative. Any NT workstation or server can act as a simple IP router— all you need is a multihomed PC (one with two or more network cards installed in it) and NT.

Just open up the Control Panel, open the Networks applet, then the Protocols tab, and the TCP/IP protocol. Click the Routing tab, and you see an option called Enable IP Routing. That's how you turn on NT's routing capability.

Let's see how to set up this router. Imagine you have an internet that looks like Figure 14.22.

We're going to use the machine that's on both Rome and Carthage as the router. (Actually, there's no choice here, as it's the *only* machine in both TCP/IP domains, and any router between two domains must be a member of both domains.) All you have to do is go to the machine with two Ethernet cards and set up both cards with an IP address. The Enable IP Routing box will no longer be grayed out, and you can then check the box.

FIGURE 14.22

A sample internet

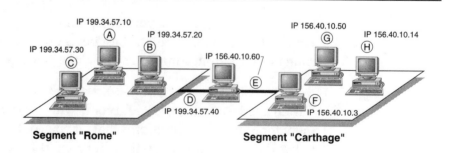

In cookbook fashion:

How Do I Build an IP Router with NT?

 Install two network (let's use Ethernet for this example) cards in an NT machine. The NT machine *need not be* an NT Server machine, and, given the cost of NT Server, you're probably better off using a copy of workstation NT.

1. Configure the Ethernet card on the Rome subnet with an IP address for the Rome subnet. When you are working in the TCP/IP configuration dialog box, you notice a single-selection drop-down list box labeled Adapter: you can use that to control which Ethernet card you are assigning to what IP address.

2. Click the Routing button.

3. Check Enable IP Routing. Notice that the "Enable IP Routing" box is grayed out unless there are two network cards in your system.

4. Click OK until you get out of the Control Panel.

The system will reboot, and your router will be active.

This will allow an IP router to move traffic from one subnet to another. It will *not*, however, route traffic between three or more subnets.

What do I mean by that last line? Well, the default router software isn't very smart. Look at Figure 14.23, and you'll see what I mean.

Here, you see an internet with just three subnets: 200.200.1.0, 200.200.2.0, and 200.200.3.0. For ease of discussion, let's call network 200.200.1.0 "network 1," 200.200.2.0 "network 2," and 200.200.3.0 "network 3." The network 1 to network 2 router, machine A, has addresses 200.200.1.1 and 200.200.2.40, and the network 2 to network 3 router, machine B, has addresses 200.200.2.75 and 200.200.3.50.

FIGURE 14.23

Internet with
three subnets

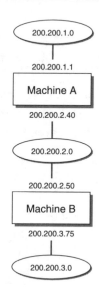

Once you turn on IP routing in machine A, it's smart enough to be able to route packets from network 1 to network 2, and packets from network 2 to network 1. But if it receives a packet from network 1 intended for network 3, it has no idea what to do about it.

Machine B has the same problem, basically. It knows how to go from network 2 to network 3 and from network 3 to network 2, but it has no idea how to find network 1.

How do you solve this problem? Either with static routes or with RIP. The best answer is probably to put the RIP router on both machine A and machine B, and they will end up discovering each other's routes through the RIP broadcasts. But how would you tell machine A how to find network 3 and how would you tell machine B to find network 1? With static ROUTE ADD commands.

On machine A, tell it about network 3 like so:

```
route add 200.200.3.0 mask 255.255.255.0 200.200.2.50
```

You're saying to this machine, "In order to find network 200.200.3.0, use the IP address 200.200.2.50; it's attached to a machine that can get the packets to that network." For the sake of completeness, you might add the "metric 2" parameter to the end.

On machine B, tell it about network 1 in a similar way:

```
route add 200.200.1.0 mask 255.255.255.0 200.200.2.40
```

Remember that in both cases the "mask" information says, "I'm giving you information about a subnet, but the mask says how useful the information is."

Using an NT Server Machine as an Internet Gateway

Consider this. Your company has purchased a full-time PPP account from some Internet provider. You have your LAN all running TCP/IP with NIC-approved IP numbers. All you need is a machine that will route your local traffic over the Internet when you want to FTP, use e-mail, or whatever.

From a hardware point of view, it's pretty easy: you just need a PC containing both an Ethernet card and a serial port, with a dial-up PPP connection. That machine was essentially doing the job of TCP/IP routing. How do you do that in NT?

The Overview

There's a number of "what if's" that you have to consider if you want to use your NT machine as a LAN-to-WAN Internet gateway.

The first piece of advice is: don't, if you can avoid it. In my company, I use the Compatible Systems mr900i, a terrific box that I picked up for $850. It's very easy to manage, does RIP, is much cheaper than buying a Pentium and a copy of NT, and is as fast as the wind. I'd recommend it as the way to go if you want to hook up your net to *the* Net.

But there are times that I don't have access to a dedicated router, and perhaps I'd like to use my NT machine as my Internet router. How do I do it?

Basically, the steps are

1. Put a network card and a modem in an NT system;

2. Put a static IP address on the network card, but leave off the default gateway;

3. Install RAS and tell it how to dial up to your Internet Service Provider (ISP). Disable "use remote gateway" in setting up the connection;

4. Make a change to the Registry (explained below);

5. Dial up to the ISP and log in;

6. Use a ROUTE ADD command to tell the system how to route to the Internet;

7. Then tell all the computers on your network to use the IP address of the network card as their default gateway.

The Obstacles

Those steps aren't hard, and we'll do a step-by-step "cookbook recipe" in just a minute. But there *are* two things, however, that will make it a bit difficult to explain how to do this, as it varies from ISP to ISP. They are

- How you log onto the ISP: simple character-oriented terminal login, the Password Authentication Protocol (PAP), or the Challenge Handshake Authentication Protocol (CHAP)

- How you set the IP address on your dial-up or frame relay connection

Those are both topics discussed in the Dial-Up Networking chapter, so I won't go into them in any detail here. I *did* want to point out, however, that there are differences in how you accomplish those two things.

Login Options

When you attach to an ISP network, you must identify yourself and prove who you are, usually with a password. Most ISPs require that when you dial up to them you work with a character-based login screen where you type in the account number and password for your network, and that's how I'll describe my example here. You've probably seen something like this before: "Welcome to XYZ Corporation, your on-ramp to the Information Superhighway; please enter your account number and password...." If your ISP works that way, then you can set up a Dial-Up Networking phone book entry that will create a terminal screen for you that will appear once you're connected to the ISP. In your Dial-Up Networking phone book, click "Script" and you see a dialog box like Figure 14.24.

If you have an ISP like this, then you're probably logging into some old Unix-based portmaster system of some kind. It can be a pain to have to punch in the user ID and password every time you connect to

FIGURE 14.24

Telling Dial-Up Networking to pop up a terminal screen so you can enter the ID and password

your ISP, so you may want to look into writing a logon script to automate the process; you can read about that in chapter 17 on Dial-Up Networking.

Some ISPs, however, offer more modern, automated ways to log into their networks. Assuming that you link up to the ISPs with PPP (Point to Point Protocol), then the ISP may choose to exploit a couple of extensions to PPP that have become popular: the Password Authentication Protocol (PAP) and the Challenge-Handshake Authentication Protocol (CHAP). Both are protocols allowing your computer to dial up to another computer and pass user ID and password information back and forth automatically, without you having to type that information in. If you have an ISP that supports PAP or CHAP, then click the "None" radio button in the "Script" page and click the "Security" page. It looks like Figure 14.25.

Why this doesn't just have radio buttons labeled "PAP," "CHAP," and the like is beyond me, but basically here's what to click. If you are dialing into your ISP and authenticating with the Password Authentication Protocol, choose "Accept any authentication..." If you are using the generic CHAP protocol to authenticate with an ISP, choose "Accept only encrypted authentication." If you are dialing up an NT Server,

FIGURE 14.25

Configuring a PAP or
CHAP dial-in

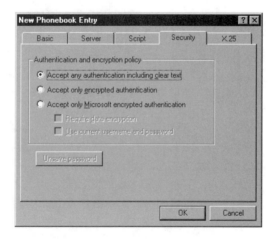

then choose "Accept only encrypted Microsoft authentication." Not surprisingly, Microsoft has created their own variation of the standard CHAP protocol that they call Microsoft-CHAP; clicking this last button requires it. Again, the value of using PAP or CHAP is that it absolves you of having to write a logon script.

If your ISP is using NT machines, then you're probably in luck; you won't have to do a terminal logon. In most cases, however, terminal logons are still the order of the day. My advice is that you sit at the NT machine that will be the gateway and just try to get *it* attached to your ISP before going any further; figure out how to get to your ISP as a single dial-up machine before trying to share the connection with your LAN.

Obtaining an IP Address from Your ISP

Then there's the problem of IP addresses over your WAN link. Your dial-up connection has an IP address different from the address on the network card—but *what* address?

Most ISPs that I've arranged PPP connections with have a system whereby they tell your PPP connection what IP address to use automatically, as part of the logon sequence. Even if you have to type in your user name and password by hand, your workstation will get the IP address automatically from the ISP. In my experience, most of the time ISPs just send you a piece of paper telling you to set up your software to use a certain IP address. Dial-Up Networking can accommodate both, as shown in Figure 14.26.

You get this dialog box by editing a Dial-Up Networking phone book entry. Open up the Dial-Up Networking application in My Computer, choose the entry for dialing to your ISP, click More, and "Edit entry and modem properties." Then click Server and "TCP/IP settings." Note the radio buttons in the group at the top: either "Server assigned IP address" (that's the more common automatic option) or "Specify IP address." And while I'm showing this dialog box to you,

FIGURE 14.26

Dial-Up Networking
TCP/IP settings

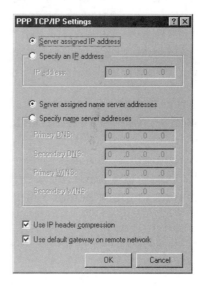

let me point out that the check box at the bottom of the dialog box, which says "Use default gateway on remote network," is checked by default, as you see in the example screen. In my experience, it's *very* important that you uncheck this box.

Anyway, this how-do-I-get-my-IP-address question is another ISP-specific issue, and another reason why you should dial up and log into your ISP before going any further. The way that most ISPs seem to work, and, again, the way I'll write this example, is that you just tell your PPP software to get an IP address from the ISP and to require a terminal login.

The Recipe

Here are the steps that you use to make an NT workstation or server into a router that will connect your company's network to the Internet. I'll call that computer "the gateway machine" (when I say that, I'm *not* referring to computers from South Dakota; I'm just describing that one computer).

In this example, I'll connect my C-class network, 199.34.57.0, to the Internet through my Internet Service Provider, Digital Express, or, as its customers know it, "digex." I'll need to know the phone number of digex, which I'll make (301) 555-1212 in this example; my account number, which I'll make "xyzabc123" for this example; and a password, which I'll make "xyzzy."

My gateway machine is running NT workstation 4 and contains an Ethernet card as well as a 28.8Kbps modem. If you're setting up NT 3.51, then the procedure will be identical save for one thing: go to Microsoft's FTP site and get the Multivendor Protocol Router (MPR).

1. On the gateway machine, install IP with static addressing for the network card. Set the network card's IP address (I'll use 199.34.57.1 in this example) with whatever subnet mask makes sense for your network (255.255.255.0 for basic C-class networks).

2. When you're setting up the IP address on the network card, leave the "Default gateway" address *blank.*

3. Install Dial-Up Networking. Look in the Dial-Up Networking chapter for details, but basically you open up the Dial-Up Networking icon in the My Computer folder. If it's the first time you've done that, then it'll automatically install Dial-Up Networking. You must tell it what kind of modem you have and what port it's on. Configure it to dial out only—you won't be receiving calls on this machine, not if it's your constant connection to the Internet. Reboot the system to complete installing Dial-Up Networking.

4. In the Registry, go to the key HKEY_LOCAL_MACHINE\System\ CurrentControlSet\Services\RasArp\Parameters and create a new value entry DisableOtherSrcPackets of type DWORD, and set the value to 0. You will have to create a new value entry, as Disable-OtherSrcPackets isn't in that key by default.

The reason you do this is that this machine will be a router. This command says, "When you forward an IP packet, don't change the 'source' IP address." Otherwise, if machine B forwards a packet to machine C for machine A, then machine B changes the "From:" part of the IP packet to B's own IP address, with the result that C thinks the message originated with B, not A. Setting this registry entry to 0 keeps that from happening.

5. Start up Dial-Up Networking, and it'll observe that there are no phone book entries and will prompt you for a first entry; let's make that the dial-up instructions for your ISP. If you already have Dial-Up Networking entries, then just click New to create another phone book entry. Use the Dial-Up Networking setup wizard if you like, or just enter the values directly.

6. Enter a descriptive name and phone number. For my example, I used "DIGEX" as the name. The initial screen will look something like Figure 14.27.

FIGURE 14.27

The basic tab for setting up an Internet connection

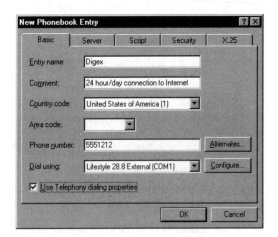

7. Next, I'll tell it that I want a terminal login screen so I can punch in the user name and password whenever I need to reconnect my network to the Internet. I click "Security" and choose "Accept any authentication including clear text." Then I choose Script and choose "Pop up a terminal window." Then I have to tell Dial-Up Networking what to expect from the ISP that it's about to dial into, so I choose Server, and I see a screen like Figure 14.28.

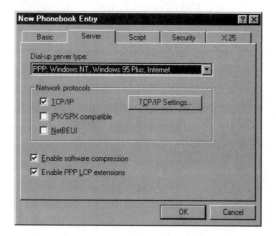

8. Be sure to tell it that you're dialing into a PPP or NT Server server, as that's almost certainly what your ISP is using; PPP is the most common way to set up dial-in Unix servers. Your ISP *may* use SLIP instead, in which case you choose "SLIP: Internet" in the Server: field. Only check TCP/IP because that's the Internet protocol. Click TCP/IP Settings and you'll be able to configure whether to get the IP address from the ISP or whether to hard-code it, as mentioned earlier.

9. In the case of my ISP, I chose "Server assigned IP address." Again, this is something that may be different for your ISP, so if things aren't working, then ask them. In the same way, "Use IP header compression" may work best checked or not checked. It's an

option that *you* can enable or disable at your leisure. Which is better for you? In general, for connections slower than 28.8Kbps, turn on IP compression. For a faster system, turn IP compression off. One way to find out is to find a few big files on an FTP site and download them; try it with and without the header compression, and then you'll know which setting is better.

10. Uncheck "Use default gateway on remote system."

11. Now you have to get your system to forward IP packets. Open up the Control Panel, then open Network, Protocols, TCP/IP, Routing, and check "Enable IP Forwarding." You have to reboot.

12. For those of you using NT 3.51, however, you have some more work to do. In NT 3.51, there is still a check box labeled "Enable IP Routing," but it may be grayed out unless there are two or more network cards present in the Control Panel. That presents a problem, because NT only sees one Ethernet card, so it grays out the routing option. This kind of makes sense because you have to have at least two IP addresses in order to route, but it makes no sense that the IP addresses must be on network cards. NT *ought* to be smart enough to enable forwarding when one IP address is a network card and the other is a RAS/PPP-derived IP address, but it isn't: it *must* see two network cards before it'll enable IP routing.

Or mustn't it? There *is* one sneaky trick that you can do to get the "Enable IP Routing" box enabled. Just click Control Panel, Networks, TCP/IP Protocol, Configure, and Advanced. You get the "Advanced TCP/IP Configuration" screen that you've seen earlier in this chapter. You can actually attach more than one IP address to a network card. So here's the trick to turn on IP routing: go to your one network card and add a bogus IP address. The "Enable IP Routing" box will become enabled. Check it. Then remove the bogus IP address, and the "Enable IP Routing" box will gray out, *but it will stay checked!* Again, NT 4 users needn't worry about this, as you don't have to go through all of this rigmarole to make forwarding work.

13. Once you've rebooted, start up Dial-Up Networking and dial up your ISP. When the terminal screen appears, punch in your user name and password. When you get a message indicating that your session has started, click Done.

14. Find out what IP address your RAS connection is using. Type **IPCONFIG** and look for the line that looks like "Ethernet adapter NdisWan6:" or something like that, and the IP address below it is the IP address connected to the outside world. Suppose I find that on my example computer it's 199.34.57.2.

15. Your system now must know how to find the outside world. Open a command prompt and type **route add 0.0.0.0 mask 0.0.0.0 *x.y.z.a* metric 2**, where *x.y.z.a* is the IP address that you just found for your RAS connection. In my case, I'd type **route print 0.0.0.0 mask 0.0.0.0 199.34.57.2 metric 2**. Now, if you're an RAS expert type, then you're no doubt wondering something like this: I told you to uncheck "Use default gateway on remote system." But the only thing that command does is automatically insert the line "route add 0.0.0.0 mask 0.0.0.0 199.34.57.2" in the routing table. Why then do all the extra work? My answer is, try it both ways. I have no idea why, but a Dial-Up Networking box won't route with "Use default gateway on remote system." It *will* route if you uncheck the "Use default gateway..." box and enter the "route add 0.0.0.0..." by hand. How do I know? It's how my entire company has been connected to the Internet from time to time—we use an NT machine as a backup router.

16. Finally, make sure that all of the PCs on your subnet point to the static IP address attached to the network card, not the RAS connection. In my example, all of my machines point to the default gateway 199.34.57.1.

The machines on your subnet should now be able to ping the outside world.

You are now connected to the Internet.

Interior and Exterior Routing Protocols

In the Internet world, there are two kinds of routing going on. RIP or your network's static routing tables route IP packets within your company's internet domain (or perhaps those sleek, shiny Cisco routers do), and the routers in your Internet service provider do another kind of routing. Your routers mainly route data from one side of your company to another, and your ISP's routers mainly route data from one company's network to another company's network. Over the years, these routing processes have become refined into two categories of routers: *interior routers*, like RIP or OSPF, and *exterior routers*.

Exterior routers essentially route from the "border" of one Internet domain to the "border" of another, leading some people to dub them Exterior Border Protocols, or EBPs. The most widely used is probably the Exterior Gateway Protocol, or EGP.

Where would you see something like this? Well, suppose I go to the NIC and get myself another C-class network; suppose it's 223.150.100.0. I put it on my 199.34.57.0 network using my NT machines as RIP routers, and the two networks are just pinging one another like mad.

But then I try to ping the outside world from 223.150.100.0. And nothing happens. Why? Because my 199.34.57.0 network only knows about the 223.150.100.0 network because RIP told it. But to get to the outside world would require the complicity of my Internet Service Provider, and *it* doesn't listen to my RIP routers. If the router in my system that talked to my ISP spoke EGP, then perhaps we'd be okay. But, even then, my ISP *might* not even do EGP; perhaps they do only static routing between customer networks. NT doesn't support EGP.

Well, by now, you're on an internet in the traditional way. Microsoft adds two possible options to this setup: the Dynamic Host Configuration Protocol (DHCP) and the Windows Internet Naming Service (WINS).

Installing TCP/IP with DHCP

Everything that you've learned so far is just about all you would need to set up an internet. But you can see that this business of assigning IP addresses can be something of a pain. In particular, consider these problems:

- Wouldn't it be nice not to have to keep track of which IP addresses you've used and which ones remain?

- How do you assign a temporary IP address to a visiting computer, like a laptop?

Looking at these problems—and a possible solution—leads toward an understanding of DHCP and how to install it. Note, by the way, that this discussion assumes that you've already read this chapter up to this point; don't think that if you decided from the start to go with DHCP that you could skip the last section.

Simplifying TCP/IP Administration: BOOTP

I have a little list…

I keep this list of PCs and IP addresses. It's basically a kind of master directory of which IP addresses have been used so far. Obviously, I have to consult it when I put TCP/IP on each new computer.

That's obvious, but what's unfortunate is that I never seem to have the notebook with me when I need it. So I started keeping this list of computers and IP addresses on one of my servers, in a kind of common HOSTS file. It served two purposes: first, it told me what IP addresses were already used, and second, it gave me a HOSTS file to copy to the local computer's hard disk.

When it comes right down to it, however, this whole thing seems kind of stupid. Why am I doing what is clearly a rote, mechanical job—you know, the kind of job that computers are good at?

The Internet world agreed and invented a TCP/IP protocol called BOOTP, which became DHCP, as you will see. With BOOTP, a network administrator would first collect a list of MAC addresses for each LAN card. MAC, or Media Access Control, addresses are unique 48-bit identifiers for each network card. I've already mentioned the 48-bit identifiers on each Ethernet card, which are good examples of MAC addresses.

Next, the administrator would assign an IP address to each MAC address. A server on the company's internet would then hold this table of MAC address/IP address pairs. Then, when a BOOTP-enabled workstation would start up for the day, it would broadcast a request for an IP address. The BOOTP server would recognize the MAC address from the broadcaster, and would supply the IP address to the workstation.

This was a great improvement over the static IP addressing system that I've described so far. The administrator didn't have to physically travel to each workstation to give them their own IP addresses; she needed only to modify a file on the BOOTP server when a new machine arrived or if it was necessary to change IP addresses for a particular set of machines.

Another great benefit of BOOTP was that it provided protection from the "helpful user." Suppose you have user Tom, who sits next to user Dick. Dick's machine isn't accessing the network correctly, so helpful user Tom says, "Well, *I'm* getting on the net fine, so let's just copy all of this confusing network stuff from my machine to yours." The result was that both machines ended up with identical configurations—including identical IP addresses, so now neither Tom *nor* Dick can access the network without errors! In contrast, if Tom's machine is only set up to go get its IP address from its local BOOTP server, then setting up Dick's machine identically will cause no harm, as it will just tell Dick's machine to get *its* address from the BOOTP server. Dick will get a different address (provided that the network administrator has typed in an IP address for Dick's MAC address), and all will be well.

DHCP: BOOTP Plus

BOOTP's ability to hand out IP addresses from a central location is terrific, but it's not dynamic. The network administrator must know beforehand what all of the MAC addresses of the Ethernet cards on her network are. This isn't *impossible* information to obtain, but it's a bit of a pain (usually typing **ipconfig /all** from a command line yields the data). Furthermore, there's no provision for handing out temporary IP addresses, like an IP address for a laptop used by a visiting executive.

DHCP improves upon BOOTP in that you just give it a range of IP addresses that it's allowed to hand out, and it just gives them out first-come first-served to whatever computers request them. If, on the other hand, you want to maintain full BOOTP-like behavior, then you can; it's possible with DHCP to preassign IP addresses to particular MAC addresses, as with BOOTP.

With DHCP, you only have to hard-wire the IP addresses of a few machines, like your BOOTP/DHCP server and your default gateway.

Let's see how to get a DHCP server up on your network, so the IP addresses will start getting handed out, and then we'll take a look at how DHCP works.

Installing and Configuring DHCP Servers

DHCP servers are the machines that provide IP addresses to machines that request access to the LAN. DHCP only works if the TCP/IP software on the workstations is *built* to work with DHCP—if the TCP/IP software includes a *DHCP client*. NT includes TCP/IP software with

DHCP clients for Windows for Workgroups and DOS. NT workstations and Windows 95 workstations are already DHCP-aware.

To get ready for DHCP configuration:

- Have an IP address ready for your DHCP server—this is one computer on your network that *must* have a hard-wired IP address.

- Know which IP addresses are free to assign. You use these available IP addresses to create a pool of IP addresses.

To start up DHCP configuration, open the Control Panel and the Network applet, and click the Services tab. Click Add. Select Microsoft DHCP Server, and click OK. You are prompted, as always, for the location of the files. An information dialog box appears and instructs you to change any IP addresses on your network card(s) to static addresses. Click OK. The DHCP software will install. Click the Close button, and the binding operations will begin. After awhile the hard drive activity stops. Reboot your computer. You see a screen like Figure 14.29.

FIGURE 14.29

Windows TCP/IP
Installation Options
dialog box

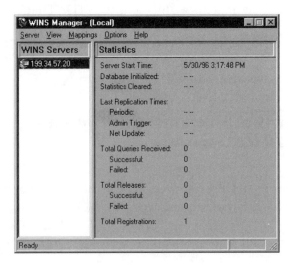

Once the system has rebooted, you find a new icon in the Administrative Tools group, the DHCP Manager. Start it up, and you will see a screen like Figure 14.30.

FIGURE 14.30

DHCP opening screen

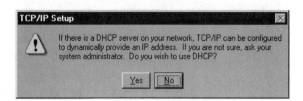

Not much to look at now, as there are no scopes set up yet. Scopes? What's a scope?

DHCP Scopes

In order for DHCP to give out IP addresses, it must know the range of IP addresses that it can give out. You tell it with a *scope*. You have to create a scope for your DHCP server. Do that by clicking on Scope, and Create.... You will see a screen like the one shown in Figure 14.31.

A scope is simply a range of IP addresses—a pool from which they can be drawn. In my above example, I've created a scope that ranges from my .60 address to my .126 address. I don't want to get too sidetracked on the issue of scopes, but let me mention another use for scopes: you can assign a scope to each subnet serviced by your DHCP servers and, yes, it *is* possible for one DHCP server to handle multiple subnets.

Do not create multiple scopes for a single subnet; I'll show you how to get more than one server to act as a DHCP server (for the sake of fault tolerance) in a minute.

FIGURE 14.31

Create Scope dialog box

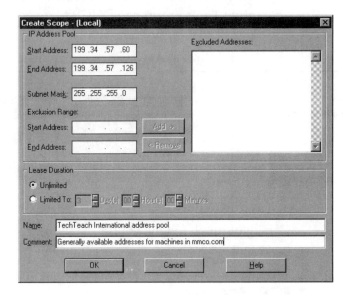

Getting back to setting up a scope, note that the dialog box's title is Create Scope (Local). That's because you can control a DHCP server from another NT machine, as is the case with so many NT network functions.

You should also note that I've filled in the Start Address, End Address, Lease Duration, Name, and Comment fields. Let's see what I did.

Start Address and End Address specifies a range of possible IP addresses to give out. Here, I've offered the addresses from my .60 address through my .126 address for the IP pool. That's 67 addresses, which are sufficient for my network.

I *could* have offered all 250-odd addresses and then excluded particular addresses with the Exclusion Range field; that's just as valid an option.

The Name and Comment field are used mainly for administering scopes later. The Lease Duration field has "unlimited" checked, but don't *you* use that—the alternative "three day" option is the better one. Click OK, and you see a dialog box like Figure 14.32.

FIGURE 14.32

Activating a new scope

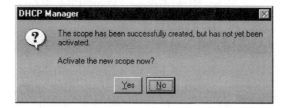

Click Yes, and it will be immediately available. The DHCP manager will then look something like Figure 14.33.

Note the lighted light bulb: that indicates an *active* scope. But you're not done yet. DHCP can provide default values for a whole host of TCP/IP parameters, including these basic items:

- Default gateway

- Domain name

- DNS server

- WINS server (DHCP calls it a WINS/NBNS server)

FIGURE 14.33

DHCP Manager with
an active scope

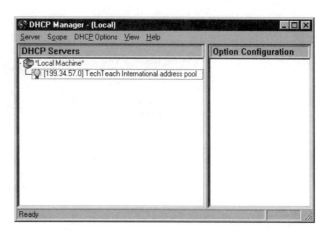

Remember that you had to type all that stuff in when you assigned fixed IP addresses? Well, DHCP lets you specify some defaults, making it an even more attractive addressing alternative. Just click DHCP Options, and you see options called Global, Scope, and Default.

Click Global to modify options that don't change from subnet to subnet, like the domain name or the DNS and WINS server addresses. Click Local to modify options that are relevant to particular subnets, like the address of the default gateway (which DHCP, for some perverse reason, calls the Router.)

Most of the settings are global, so click Global, and you see a dialog box like the one shown in Figure 14.34.

Now, despite the fact that there seem to be bushels of sadly unused parameters, mutely begging to be used, *don't*. Even though they exist, the Microsoft DHCP *clients*—the part of Windows, DOS, Windows 95, and NT that knows how to get IP addresses from a DHCP server—does not know how to use any options save the ones I just mentioned. Microsoft included the other things just to remain compatible with BOOTP. Again, the five that I adjusted were

- DNS Servers; here I named our two DNS servers.

- Domain name, which is mmco.com for us.

FIGURE 14.34

Setting DHCP global options

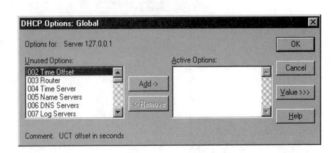

- WINS/NBNS Servers, with the addresses of my WINS servers (which I'll cover soon). Setting this requires that you also set...

- WINS/NBT Node Type, a cryptic-looking setting that you needn't worry about, except to set it to 0x8; that makes WINS run best. I will explain node types in the upcoming discussion on WINS.

- Then going over to the Local settings, I set Router, which is, again, the DHCP equivalent of the Default Gateway option in the TCP/IP setup screen.

I set these by highlighting the option that I want to use, then clicking Add. Then I can click Value and Edit Array. For example, say I want to make my default gateway 199.34.57.2. I click on Router, then Edit Array. I then get a dialog box that looks like Figure 14.35.

Notice that the original default value is 0.0.0.0, which is a meaningless address in this context. I enter 199.34.57.2 and click Add, but I don't stop there; next, I click on 0.0.0.0 and click on Remove. *Then* I click OK.

I do the same thing with the domain name and the DNS router, and I'm set. The DHCP Manager now looks like Figure 14.36.

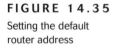

FIGURE 14.35

Setting the default router address

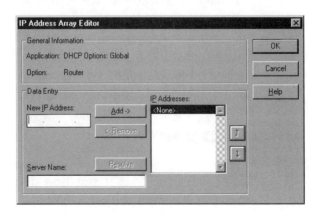

FIGURE 14.36

The DHCP manager

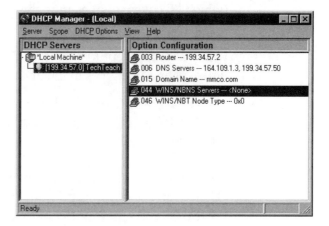

Note the different icons for the global settings and the local settings. Close up the DHCP Manager, and your server is set up. You don't even need to reboot.

DHCP on the Client Side

Now that you've set up DHCP on a server, how do you tell clients to use that DHCP? Simple. The Windows for Workgroups TCP/IP-32 bit software has DHCP configuration as an installation option, as does the latest Microsoft Client software for DOS and Windows. If you want to find out what IP address a client machine has, go to that machine, open up a command line, and type **ipconfig /all**. On a Windows 95 workstation, click Start and Run, and then type **WINIPCFG** and press Enter.

DHCP in Detail

That's setting up DHCP. But, how does it work and, unfortunately, how does it sometimes *not* work?

DHCP supplies IP addresses based on the idea of *client leases*. When a machine (a DHCP client) needs an IP address, it asks a DHCP server for that address. (*How* it does that is important, and I'll get to it in a minute.) A DHCP server then gives an IP address to the client, *but only for a temporary period of time*—hence the term *IP lease*. You might have noticed that you can set the term of an IP lease from DHCP; it's one of the settings in Scope/Properties.

The client then knows how long it's got the lease. Even if you reboot or reset your computer, it'll remember what lease is active for it and how much longer it's got to go on the lease.

TIP

On a Windows 3.*x* machine, that information is kept in DHCP.BIN in the Windows directory. On a Windows 95 machine, it's in HKEY_LOCAL_MACHINE\System\CurrentControlSet\Services\VxD\DHCP\Dhcp-info*xx*, where *xx* is two digits. And if you wish to enable or disable the error messages from the DHCP client on a Windows 95 machine, it's the value PopupFlag in the key HKEY_LOCAL_MACHINE\System\CurrentControlSet\Services\VxD\DHCP; use "00 00 00 00" for false, or "01 00 00 00" for true.

So, if your PC had a four-day lease on some address, and you rebooted two days into its lease, then the PC wouldn't just blindly ask for an IP address; instead, it would go back to the DHCP server that it got its IP address from and request the particular IP address that it had before. If the DHCP server were still up, then it would acknowledge the request, letting the workstation use the IP address. If, on the other hand, the DHCP server has had its lease information wiped out through some disaster, then it will either give the IP address to the machine (if no one else is using the address), or it will send a "negative acknowledgment," or "NACK" to the machine, and the DHCP server will make a note of that NACK in the Event Log. Your workstation should then be smart enough to start searching around for a new DHCP server. In my experience, sometimes it isn't.

Like BOOTP, DHCP remembers which IP addresses go with what machine by matching up an IP address with a MAC (Media Access Control, i.e. Ethernet address).

This leads me to the following tip.

Do *not* set the leases to Infinite. I used to think that this was a cool way to easily assign fixed IP addresses. The first time a system logged on, it would get an IP address, and all would be good, right? There are two problems with this. First, a minor problem. What if you have to reinstall your DHCP server, but did not back up the Registry (where the DHCP database lives)? Then your system spends a lot of time NACKing innocent PCs. Second, what if you want to reconfigure your network? Suppose you have 200 people in two departments on the same subnet. You decide to divide them up into two subnets. Half of the users of the old subnet will now be on a new subnet, requiring a whole new set of IP addresses. Obviously you have to create a new scope, but creating the new scope is easy. The *problem* is, how do you force a new IP address on the people in the new subnet? Their leases never expire, so they never really give the DHCP server a chance to assign them new addresses. (Well, it will, but only after lots of NACKing and plenty of systems that will randomly refuse to communicate with anything.) Set the lease to a few days, and then you can enforce changes to your subnet structure automatically through the DHCP servers.

Let me expand upon that a bit. Suppose you know that on November 1 you're going to take your 200.1.1.x subnet and break it up into 200.1.1.x and 200.1.2.x. Now, with old static IP addresses, you'd be faced with the prospect of having to go to every single workstation and change its IP address by hand. With DHCP, however, you don't have to do that.

Instead, here's the process. Suppose you give out ten-day leases. Nine days before November 1, reduce the lease length to nine days. The next day, reduce the leases to eight days, and so on. On October 31, reduce lease length to just a few hours. Then, after hours, do the physical partitioning of your subnets—install the routers and isolate the machines for the new subnet on the 200.1.2.*x* side—and create the new 200.1.2.*x* scope on your DHCP server. Then your work is done.

Getting an IP Address from DHCP: The Nuts and Bolts

A DHCP client gets an IP address from a DHCP server in four steps:

- A *DHCPDISCOVER* broadcasts a request to all DHCP servers in earshot, requesting an IP address.

- The servers respond with *DHCPOFFER* of IP addresses and lease times.

- The client chooses the offer that sounds most appealing and broadcasts back a *DHCPREQUEST* to confirm the IP address.

- The server handing out the IP address finishes the procedure by returning with a *DHCPACK*, an acknowledgment of the request.

Initial DHCP Request: DHCPOFFER

First, a DHCP client sends out a message called a *DHCPDISCOVER* saying, in effect, "Are there any DHCP servers out there? If so, I want an IP address." This message is shown in Figure 14.37.

You might ask, "How can a machine communicate if it doesn't have an address?" Through a different protocol than TCP—UDP, or the User Datagram Protocol. It's not a NetBIOS or NetBEUI creature; it's all TCP/IP-suite stuff.

Now, to follow all of these DHCP messages, there are a couple of things to watch. First of all, I'm showing you both the Ethernet addresses (Token Ring addresses for those of you using Token Ring) and the IP addresses because you see that they tell somewhat different stories. Also, there is a "transaction ID" attached to each DHCP packet that's quite useful. The transaction ID makes it possible for a client to

FIGURE 14.37

DHCP step 1:
DHCPDISCOVER

DHCP
client

DHCP
server

Enet addr: 00CC00000000
IP addr: 0.0.0.0

Enet addr: 00BB00000000
IP addr: 210.22.31.100

"Is there a DHCP server around?"

IP address used: 255.255.255.255 (broadcast)
Ethernet address used: FFFFFFFFFFFF (broadcast)
Transaction ID: 14321

know when it receives a response from a server exactly *what* the response is responding to.

In this case, notice that the IP address the message is sent to is "255.255.255.255." That's the generic address for "anybody on this subnet." Now, 210.22.31.255 would also work, assuming that this is a C-class network that hasn't been subnetted, but 255.255.255.255 pretty much always means "anyone who can hear me." If you set up your routers to forward broadcasts, then 255.255.255.255 will be propagated all over the network; 210.22.31.255 would not. Notice also the destination Ethernet address, FFFFFFFFFFFF. That's the Ethernet way of saying, "Everybody—a broadcast."

DHCP Offers Addresses from Near and Far

Any DHCP servers within earshot—that is, any that receive the UDP datagram—respond to the client with an offer, a proposed IP address, like the one shown in Figure 14.38. Again, this is an offer, not the final IP address.

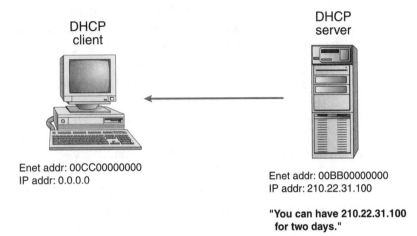

FIGURE 14.38
DHCP step 2:
DHCPOFFER

DHCP
client

DHCP
server

Enet addr: 00CC00000000
IP addr: 0.0.0.0

Enet addr: 00BB00000000
IP addr: 210.22.31.100

**"You can have 210.22.31.100
for two days."**

IP address used: 255.255.255.255 (broadcast)
Ethernet address used: 00CC00000000 (directed)
Transaction ID: 14321

This offering part of the DHCP process is essential because, as I just hinted, it's possible for more than one DHCP server to hear the original client request. If every DHCP server just thrust an IP address at the hapless client, then it would end up with multiple IP addresses, addresses wasted in the sense that the DHCP servers would consider them all taken, and so they couldn't give those addresses out to other machines.

Worse yet, what if a DHCP server from another subnet gave an IP address to our client? Wouldn't that put the client in the wrong subnet? DHCP keeps that from happening via BOOTP forwarding. The original UDP message, "Are there any DHCP servers out there?" is a broadcast. Most routers, as you know, do not forward broadcasts—which reduces network traffic congestion and is a positive side-effect of routers. But if DHCP requests don't go over routers, then that would imply that you have to have a DHCP server on every subnet, a rather expensive proposition.

The BOOTP standard got around this by defining an RFC 1542, a specification whereby routers following RFC 1542 would recognize BOOTP broadcasts and would forward them to other subnets. The feature must be implemented in your routers' software, and it's commonly known as BOOTP forwarding. Of course, when an NT machine acts as an IP router, it implements BOOTP forwarding.

Assuming that you have routers that implement BOOTP forwarding, then the original DHCP request gets out to all of them. But how do we keep a DHCP server in an imaginary subnet 200.1.2.x from giving an address in 200.1.2.x to a PC sitting in another imaginary subnet, 200.1.1.x? Simple. When the router forwards the BOOTP request, it attaches a little note to it that says, "This came from 200.1.1.x." The DHCP server then sees that information, and so it only responds if it has a scope within 200.1.1.x.

Anyway, notice that although to the higher-layer protocol (UDP) this is a broadcast, the lower-layer Ethernet protocol behaves as though it is not, and the Ethernet address embedded in the message is the address of the client, not the FFFFFFFFFFFF broadcast address. Notice also that the transaction ID on the response matches the transaction ID on the original request.

Picking from the Offers

The DHCP client then looks through the offers that it has and picks the one that's best for it. If there are multiple offers that look equally good, it picks the one that arrived first. Then it sends another UDP datagram, another broadcast, shown in Figure 14.39.

It's a broadcast because this message serves two purposes. First, the broadcast *will* get back to the original offering server if the first broadcast got to that server, which it obviously did. Second, this broadcast is a way of saying to any *other* DHCP servers who made offers, "Sorry, folks, but I'm taking this other offer."

Notice that both the Ethernet and the IP addresses are broadcasts, and there is a new transaction ID.

FIGURE 14.39

DHCP step 3:
DHCPREQUEST

DHCP
client

DHCP
server

Enet addr: 00CC00000000
IP addr: 0.0.0.0

Enet addr: 00BB00000000
IP addr: 210.22.31.100

**"Can I have the 210.22.31.100 IP address,
and thanks for the other offers, but no thanks."**

IP address used: 255.255.255.255 (broadcast)
Ethernet address used: FFFFFFFFFFFF (broadcast)
Transaction ID: 18923

The Lease Is Signed

Finally, the DHCP server responds with the shiny brand-new IP address, which will look something like Figure 14.40.

It also tells the client its new subnet mask, lease period, and whatever else you specified (gateway, WINS server, DNS server, and the like). Again, notice it's a UDP broadcast, but the Ethernet address is directed, and the transaction ID matches the previous request's ID.

You can find out what your IP configuration looks like after DHCP by typing **IPCONFIG /ALL**. It may run off the screen, so you may need to add **| more** to the line. This works on DOS, Windows for Workgroups, and NT machines. You can see a sample run of IPCONFIG /ALL in Figure 14.41.

Windows 95 machines have a graphical version of IPCONFIG called Winipcfg.

FIGURE 14.40

DHPC step 4: DHCPACK

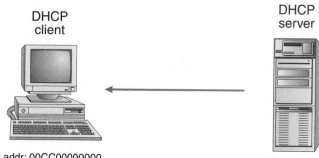

DHCP
client

DHCP
server

Enet addr: 00CC00000000
IP addr: 0.0.0.0

Enet addr: 00BB00000000
IP addr: 210.22.31.100

**"Sure; also take this subnet
mask, DNS server address,
WINS server, node type,
and domain name."**

IP address used: 255.255.255.255 (broadcast)
Ethernet address used: 00CC00000000 (directed)
Transaction ID: 18923

FIGURE 14.41

Run of IPCONFIG

```
Command Prompt                                                    _ □ X

D:\users\default>ipconfig /all

Windows NT IP Configuration

        Host Name . . . . . . . . . . . : monster
        DNS Servers . . . . . . . . . . :
        Node Type . . . . . . . . . . . : Broadcast
        NetBIOS Scope ID. . . . . . . . :
        IP Routing Enabled. . . . . . . : No
        WINS Proxy Enabled. . . . . . . : No
        NetBIOS Resolution Uses DNS : No

Ethernet adapter Elnk31:

        Description . . . . . . . . . . : ELNK3 Ethernet Adapter.
        Physical Address. . . . . . . . : 00-A0-24-31-E6-AA
        DHCP Enabled. . . . . . . . . . : No
        IP Address. . . . . . . . . . . : 223.223.223.223
        Subnet Mask . . . . . . . . . . : 255.255.0.0
        Default Gateway . . . . . . . . :

D:\users\default>
```

Lost Our Lease! Must Sell!

What happens when the lease runs out? Well, when that happens, you're supposed to stop using the IP address. But that's not likely to happen.

When the lease is half over, the DHCP client begins renegotiating the IP lease by sending a DHCP Request to the server that originally gave it its IP address. The IP and Ethernet addresses are both specific to the server.

The DHCP server then responds with a DHCPACK. The benefit of this is that the DHCPACK contains all of the information that the original DHCPACK had—domain name, DNS server, etc. That means you can change the DNS server, WINS server, subnet mask, and the like, and the new information will be updated at the clients periodically, but no more than 50 percent of the lease time.

Now, if the DHCPACK doesn't appear, then the DHCP client keeps resending the DHCP Request out every two minutes until the IP lease is 87.5 percent expired. (Don't you wonder where they get these numbers from?) At that point, the client just goes back to the drawing board, broadcasting DHCP Discover messages until someone responds. If the lease expires without a new one, the client will stop using the IP address, effectively disabling the TCP/IP protocol on that workstation.

But if you've messed with the DHCP servers, then the renewal process seems to get bogged down a bit. It's a good idea in that case to force a workstation to restart the whole DHCP process by typing **ipconfig /renew**; that will often clear up a DHCP problem.

DHCP Is a "Pull" Protocol, Not a "Push" Protocol

The reason that I went through that long explanation of how a DHCP client gets an IP lease is so you can understand a really vital and central concept in DHCP: you can't enforce changes to DHCP settings from a central location.

Suppose, for example, that you want to change the domain name from xyz.com to abc.com. You have a few servers with static IP addresses, but most of your machines pull their IP information off DHCP servers. So all you have to do is go over to your DHCP servers, click on the scopes, and change the scope option for "domain name." Then all of the workstations will know that the domain name is different, right?

Well, not really.

It would be nice if the DHCP server could just communicate directly to the clients, saying "Hey, folks, when you get a second, could you change your domain name to abc.com? Thanks." But it doesn't happen that way. *Conversations between the DHCP server and client are always initiated by the client.* Whether it's an initial lease acquisition, which starts with a DHCP Discover from the client, or a renewal, which starts with a DHCP Request from the client, *all* communications start with the client. That means that the server is forced to sit there and wait for the client to check in for a lease renewal. Only then can the DHCP server update the client's characteristics.

Think of it like this. The DHCP client is kind of like a fur trapper in the late 19th century, and the DHCP server is a sort of frontier town. The trapper (the SHCP client) must go to the general store (its DHCP server) for supplies, and the general store just happens to also be the post office. When the local government (also the DHCP server) changes some rules about trapping, it doesn't go searching for the trapper in the woods, it just sends the trapper some mail. The trapper may not *realize* that the blue-footed marten can't be lawfully trapped anymore and may continue trapping the marten. Eventually, however, the trapper has to come into town for supplies (a DHCP lease renewal, in this analogy), and, when that happens, the postmaster gets to deliver notice that the trapper can no longer take blue-footed martens.

That's why an infinite lease is a bad idea: the trapper never has to come back to town for supplies, and so will never get the news about policy changes. You *can*, however, force a client to update its information by physically walking over to the client computer, opening up a command line, and typing **ipconfig /renew**.

Designing Multi-DHCP Networks

Clearly the function of the DHCP server is one that shouldn't rest solely on the shoulders of one server (well, okay, servers don't have shoulders, but you know what I mean). So, how can you put two or more DHCP servers online to accomplish some fault tolerance?

Microsoft seems, however, a bit confused about how to go about providing multiple DHCP servers for a given subnet.

In one document, "Windows NT 3.5 Family Upgrade Course," they say several things. First, "There is NO mechanism in DHCP that allows two or more DHCP Servers to coordinate the assignment of IP addresses from overlapping IP address pools."

No argument there. If you had two different DHCP servers on the same subnet, and they both thought that they could give out addresses 202.11.39.10 through 202.11.39.40, then there would be nothing keeping the first server from giving address 202.11.39.29 to one machine, while simultaneously the other server was giving out that same 202.11.39.29 address to another machine. (It's almost as if helpful Tom has returned!)

Then, they go on (pages 147 and 148) to demonstrate two different machines running DHCP server, and each machine has a different scope. Both scopes are, however, taken from a single subnet.

In contrast, the NT *Resource Kit* (version 3.5, but 3.51 has no updates on the matter) takes issue with the idea of more than one scope referring to a subnet like so: "Each subnet can have only one scope with a single continuous range of IP addresses..."

What this boils down to is I don't know what the official Microsoft approach to DHCP fault tolerance *is*. I *do*, however, know what works, and what has worked for me. Like many people, I came up with an approach like the one in the NT training guide. I just run DHCP on multiple machines and create multiple scopes which refer to the same subnet. I make absolutely sure that the ranges of addresses in the scopes do not overlap at all, and everything seems to work fine.

Backing Up a DHCP Database

Suppose one of your servers crashed, and suppose it was your only DHCP server. Suppose also that the server gave out leases for three days.

Once you determine that the server can't be saved, you decide to zap the disk and start over. In a few hours, you rebuild the server, re-create a scope, and activate the scope, so client machines can get IP addresses. You see a fair amount of error messages for a few days, because all of those clients still think that they have leases on IP addresses for up to three days—but the DHCP server doesn't know anything about that. The clients start requesting that their DHCP licenses be renewed, and the new DHCP server sends them NACK (negative acknowledgment) messages, saying, in effect, "No! Do *not* use the IP address that you just requested an extension for!"

At that point, the DHCP client is supposed to initiate the DHCP Discover process all over again. In my experience, however, sometimes that doesn't work, and you have to go to the workstation and type the **ipconfig /all** command.

The way to avoid all of this is to simply back up the DHCP database now and then. Best of all, DHCP does that automatically. Every hour, DHCP makes a backup of its database.

TIP

You can make DHCP back up the database less often or more often with a Registry parameter. In HKEY_LOCAL_MACHINE\System\CurrentControlSet\services\DHCPServer\Parameters, look for (or create) a value entry called BackupInterval of type REG_DWORD. Enter the value (in hexadecimal, of course) in minutes. The smallest value you can enter is five minutes, and the largest is 60 minutes, which (at least on my machines) appears to be the default, despite the fact that the Resource Kit claims it's 15 minutes.

The database (in WINNT\SYSTEM32\DHCP) consists of several files:

- DHCP.MDB, which is the actual DHCP database.

- SYSTEM.MDB, which every Microsoft document describes as "used by DHCP for holding information about the structure of the database." (Must be a secret, huh?)

- JET.LOG is a transactions log. The value of logs is that the database using them (DHCP, in this case, but lots of other database systems use them) can use log information to find out what changes have been made recently; this allows the database to repair itself in some cases.

While I'm on this subject, let me comment that you don't really *need* to log changes in the DHCP database. There is an option to not log changes; if you do that, and if you must restore a DHCP server, then you get just the last database and no previous logging information. What does that mean for you? Well, after all, you can set the database to back itself up every five minutes, meaning that if you lost the DHCP server and restored the backup without the JET log, then you'd only have lost five minutes. You can shut off JET logging by going to the dhcpserver\Parameters key in the Registry that I just mentioned and setting the value DatabaseLoggingFlag to 0 (zero).

- DHCP.TMP is a "hanger-on," a file that DHCP uses to store temporary information.

- The backup process also keeps a Registry key, HKEY_LOCAL_
  MACHINE\System\currentcontrolset\services\dhcpserver\
  Configuration, which it stores in a file called DHCPCFG.

By default, the DHCPCFG file goes into \WINNT\SYSTEM32\
DHCP\BACKUP. The rest of the files go into \WINNT\SYSTEM32\
DHCP\BACKUP\JET.

Restoring a DHCP Database

What I just took two pages to tell you was basically that (1) you should
back up your DHCP database, and (2) it happens automatically every
hour anyway.

But how do you *restore* a DHCP database in the wake of disaster?

In true NT fault-tolerant fashion, DHCP will check itself for internal
problems whenever it starts up. If it detects a problem, it automatically
restores from the backups.

If, on the other hand, DHCP doesn't seem to recognize the problem,
you can force it to restore from the backups by setting a value named
"RestoreFlag" to 1 (it's another Registry entry in dhcpserver\param-
eters), stopping the DHCP service, and restarting it.

And if all else fails, you can always stop the DHCP service and copy
the backups to the DHCP directory. But *before* you stop the DHCP service, copy the backups somewhere. Why? When you stop the DHCP
service, DHCP *backs up its database*, meaning that if DHCP's database is
corrupted and you shut down DHCP, it will back up its corrupted self.

Then go into DHCP options and click on "Reconcile Database" to
make sure the database is internally consistent.

DHCP's Downside

DHCP has accomplished the task of giving out unique IP addresses, and that's an important task. But it doesn't handle the problem of relating host names to IP addresses. For that, we need a name service of some type. That service is the Windows Internet Naming Service, WINS.

Installing TCP/IP with WINS

DHCP made IP addressing simpler but ignored the newly-created problem of keeping track of the newly-assigned IP numbers and the hosts attached to them. If you sat at a TCP/IP-connected workstation with a host name like, for example, t1000.skynet.com which had gotten its IP address from a DHCP server, and you were to type **ping t1000.skynet.com**, then you'd get a timed out message. Your system wouldn't know its own name, as no DNS server knows what's going on with its dynamic IP address, and no one's updated a HOSTS file. What we need is a kind of dynamic name resolver—recall that *name resolution* is the term for looking up that t1000. skynet.com is really 122.44.23.3—sort of a dynamic DNS.

That's the Windows Internet Naming Service, or WINS. Now, while DHCP is part of a wider group of BOOTP-related protocols, this one is mainly Microsoft's, and that's a problem. WINS is a name resolution service that's pretty much only recognized by Microsoft client software (NT, Windows for Workgroups, DOS, Windows machines, and presumably OS/2 clients eventually). WINS is *not* DNS-compatible, however, and that's a major problem.

What this basically means is that the name resolution task can be handled just fine *inside* your network/internet by WINS, but name resolution *outside* your network—both someone inside your network trying to resolve "whitehouse.gov" or someone outside the network trying to resolve a name inside your network—requires a DNS server, and NT doesn't ship with one.

WINS is, therefore, only half of the answer to the name resolution problem, albeit an important half. I'll take that up in this section and look at DNS alternatives next.

What WINS is *really* good for is administering NetBEUI networks over routers. What's that mean? Well, to find out, let's look more closely into names on an NT network using TCP/IP.

Names in NT

Consider the two following commands, both issued to the same server:

```
ping server01.bigfirm.com
```

and

```
net use * \\server01\mainshr
```

In the "ping" command, the server is referred to as "server01.big-firm.com." In the "net use" command, that same server is called "server01." The difference is important.

Why Two Different Names?

The "ping" command is clearly a TCP/IP/Internet kind of command. You can't run it unless you're running TCP/IP, and, as a matter of fact, it's a valid command on a Unix, VMS, Macintosh, or MVS machine, so long as that machine is running a TCP/IP protocol stack.

In contrast, "net use" is a Microsoft networking command. You can do a "net use" on an NT network no matter what protocol you're running, but the command usually wouldn't be valid on a Unix, VMS, Macintosh, or whatever kind of machine; in general, Microsoft networking is pretty much built to work on PCs. (Yes, I know, NT is architecture-independent, so you could find an Alpha, a MIPS, or a

PowerPC machine using "net use" commands, but on the whole, NT is an Intel *x*86 operating system at this writing—and I haven't seen announcements of an "NT/390" for the IBM mainframe world, "NT VAX" for the Digital world, or "NT SPARC" for the Sun world.)

The difference is in the network application program interface (API) that the application is built atop. Ping was built on top of the TCP/IP "sockets" interface or, actually, the common PC implementation of TCP/IP Sockets, the "WinSock" interface. Building ping atop sockets was a good idea, because then it's simple to create a "ping" for any operating system, as long as there's a Sockets interface on the computer. In fact, people use basically the same source code to create "ping" for the PC, Unix machines, VMS machines, or Macs. The "server01.mmco.com" is a DNS name, so for ping to recognize who "server01.mmco.com" is, you'd need a DNS name resolver—a fancy name for a DNS server—on your network. (I'll talk about how to do that in an upcoming section.)

In contrast, "net use" was built on top of the NetBIOS API. You may recall from Chapter 2 that NetBIOS was once a protocol and a very simple one at that. As Microsoft has been selling the software to do "net use" commands since 1985, the "net" command has been built—and is still built—to sit atop NetBIOS. The "\\server01" name is a NetBIOS name, rather than a DNS name. That seems to imply that to make "net use" work, you'd need a "NetBIOS name resolver" or a "NetBIOS name server." That's exactly what WINS is, as you'll see in the next few pages.

If the "server01.mmco.com" versus "\\server01" distinction still isn't clear, then think of the APIs as communications devices. Telephones and the mail service are communications devices, also, so I'll use them in an analogy. Ping's job is to communicate with some other PC, and "net use" also wants to communicate with some PC. But ping uses winsock (the telephone) and "net use" uses NetBIOS (the mail). If you use the telephone to call a friend, then that friend's "name" as far as the phone is concerned may be something like "(707) 823-2121." As far as the mail is concerned, however, the friend's "name" might be "Paul Jones, 124 Main Street, Anytown, VA, zip code 32102." Both are perfectly valid "names" for your friend Paul, but they're different because different communications systems need different name types.

NetBIOS atop TCP/IP (NBT)

The NetBIOS API is implemented on the NetBEUI, IPX/SPX and on the TCP/IP protocols that Microsoft distributes. That makes Microsoft's TCP/IP a bit different from the TCP/IP you find on Unix (for example), because the Unix TCP/IP almost certainly won't have a Net-BIOS API on it; it'll probably only have the TCP/IP Sockets API on it. (Microsoft's TCP/IP also has Sockets in the form of the "WinSock API.")

NetBIOS on the Microsoft implementation of TCP/IP is essential, because if the TCP/IP *didn't* have a NetBIOS API on it, then you couldn't use the "net use," "net view," "net logon," and similar commands to allow your PC-based workstation to talk to an NT server. (Instead, the closest thing you would be able to find that would do the job of "net" would be something called "NFS," the Network File System. But it wouldn't replace all of the functions of "net.") Microsoft's NetBIOS on TCP/IP even has a name—NBT.

So the server's name so far as NetBIOS or NBT is concerned is "server01," and its name so far as WinSock is concerned is "server01 .bigfirm.com." (That kind of name is called, by the way, a Fully Qualified Domain Name, or FQDN.) You can run programs that either call upon NBT or WinSock, but you have to be sure to use the correct name.

Name Resolution Issues: Why DNS Isn't Always the Best Answer

Once NBT has a NetBIOS name or WinSock has a FQDN, they have the same job: resolve that name into an IP address. So computers on a Microsoft-based network that uses TCP/IP need some kind of name resolution.

How about the obvious one—DNS? DNS clearly *could* do the job, so Microsoft could have designed NBT to do its name resolution via DNS. But it didn't, for several reasons.

- First of all, Microsoft isn't the only player in the NBT world. The whole idea of putting a NetBIOS interface atop a TCP/IP stack started, believe it or not, way back in 1987, before DNS was even invented!

- Second, DNS is nifty in many ways, but it's not dynamic. What that means in English is that every time you put a new computer on your network, you'd have to trot on over to the machine that was running the DNS server, type in the new computer's name and IP address, and then you'd have to stop the DNS server and restart it to get DNS to recognize the new name. Something more automatic would be more desirable.

- Third, Microsoft didn't even ship a DNS server with NT as of NT version 3.51, and the beta DNS server that they've had for a year and a bit is absolutely terrible. So they couldn't really *require* people to set up a DNS server, could they?

NetBIOS name resolution over TCP/IP is, then, not a simple nut to crack. Many people realized this, and so there are two Internet RFCs (Requests For Comment) on this topic, RFC 1001 and 1002.

B Nodes, P Nodes, and M Nodes

The RFCs attacked the problem by offering options.

- The first option was sort of simplistic: just do broadcasts. A computer that used broadcasts to resolve NetBIOS names to IP addresses is referred to in the RFCs as a "B node." To find out who "server01" is, then, a PC running B node software would just shout out, "Hey! Anybody here named 'server01?'"

Simple, yes, but fatally flawed: remember what happens to broadcasts when they hit routers? As routers don't re-broadcast the messages to other subnets, this kind of name resolution would only be satisfactory on single-subnet networks.

- The second option was to create a name server of some kind and to use that. Then, when a computer needed to resolve a name of another computer, all it needed to do was send a point-to-point message to the computer running the name server software. As point-to-point messages *do* get retransmitted over routers, this second approach would work fine even on networks with routers. A computer using a name server to resolve NetBIOS names into IP addresses is said to be a "P node."

Again, a good idea, but it runs afoul of all of the problems that DNS had. *What* name server should be used? Will it be dynamic? The name server for NetBIOS name resolution is, by the way, referred to as a NetBIOS Name Server, or NBNS.

- The most complex approach to NetBIOS name resolution over TCP/IP is the "M node," or "mixed" node. It uses a combination of broadcasts and point-to-point communications to an NBNS.

When Microsoft started out with TCP/IP, they implemented a kind of M node software. It was "point-to-point" in that you could look up addresses in the HOSTS file, or a file called LMHOSTS, and if you had a DNS server, then you could always reference that; other than those options, Microsoft TCP/IP was mainly B node-ish, which limited you to single-subnet networks. (Or required that you repeat broadcasts over the network, clogging up your network.) Clearly, some kind of NBNS was needed, and the simpler it was to work with, the better. As the RFCs were silent on the particulars of a NBNS, vendors had license to go out and invent something proprietary and so they did—several of them, in fact, with the result that you'd expect: none of them talk to each other.

That's where WINS comes in.

WINS is simply Microsoft's proprietary NBNS service. What makes it stand out from the rest of the pack is Microsoft's importance in the industry. They've got the clout to create a proprietary system and make it accepted widely enough so that it becomes a *de facto* standard, and, as there is no doubt an RFC or two on WINS out there, perhaps WINS will be the *du* jour standard eventually as well.

Microsoft client software with WINS actually doesn't implement B, P, or M nodes; rather, Microsoft uses what they call an "H," or "Hybrid" node.

But wait a minute; isn't *M node* a hybrid? Yes. Both M nodes and H nodes (and note well that at this writing, M nodes are RFCed and H nodes aren't) use both B node and P node, but the implementation is different.

- In M node, do a name resolution by first broadcasting (B node) and then, if that fails, communicate directly with the NBNS (P node).

- In H node, try the NBNS first. If it can't help you, then try a broadcast.

The difference is merely in order of operation.

Understanding the NBT Names on Your System

A major part of the NetBIOS architecture is its lavish use of names. A workstation attaches up to 16 names to itself. Names in NetBIOS are either group names, which can be shared—workgroups and domains are two examples—or normal names, which can't be shared, like a machine name. As you'll soon see that WINS keeps track of all of these names, you may be curious about what all of them *are*—so let's take a minute and look more closely into your system's NetBIOS names.

You can see the names attached to your workstation by opening a command line from a Windows for Workgroups, Windows 95, or NT machine, and typing `nbtstat -n`. You get an output like this:

```
Node IpAddress: [199.34.57.53] Scope Id: []

    NetBIOS Local Name Table

  Name        Type       Status
------------------------------------------------
MICRON133   < 00> UNIQUE    Registered
ORION     < 00> GROUP     Registered
MICRON133   < 03> UNIQUE    Registered
MICRON133   < 20> UNIQUE    Registered
ORION     < 1E> GROUP     Registered
MARK      < 03> UNIQUE    Registered
```

In this example, the ORION group names are my workgroup and domain. "MICRON133" is my machine's name, and "MARK" is my name—notice that NetBIOS registers not only the machine name, but the person's name as well. You can see the list of registered names on any computer in your network by typing `nbtstat -A <IP address>`, where the "-A" *must* be a capital letter.

But why is there more than one MICRON133? Because different parts of the Microsoft network client software each require names of their own, so they take your machine name and append a pair of hex digits to it. That's what the "<00>," "<20>," and the like are—suffixes controlled by particular programs. For example, if some other user on the network wanted to connect to a share named STUFF on this computer, she could type **net use * \\micron133\stuff**, and the redirector software on her computer would then do a NetBIOS name resolution on the name MICRON133<00>, as the <00> suffix is used by the redirector. Table 14.3 summarizes suffixes and the programs that use them.

TABLE 14.3 Examples of Machine Names

Unique Names	Where Used
<computername>[00h]	Workstation service. This is the "basic" name that every player in a Microsoft network would have, no matter how little power it has in the network.
<computername>[03h]	Messenger service.
<computername>[06h]	RAS Server service.
<computername>[1Fh]	NetDDE service; will only appear if NetDDE is active, or if you're running a NetDDE application. (You can see this by starting up Network Hearts, for example.)
<computername>[20h]	Server service; name will only appear on machines with file/printer sharing enabled.
<computername>[21h]	RAS Client service.
<computername>[BEh]	Network Monitor agent.
<computername>[BFh]	Network Monitor utility.
<username>[03h]	Messenger service; any computer running the Messenger service (which is just about any MS networking client) would have this so that NET SEND commands to a user could be received.
<domain name>[1Bh]	Domain Master Browser.
<domain name>[1Dh]	Master Browser (only the MB would have this).
Group Names	
<domain name>[00h] or *<workgroup name>*[00]	Domain name; indicates that the computer is a member of the domain and/or workgroup. If a client is a member of a workgroup whose name is different from a domain, then no domain name will be registered on the client.
<domain name>[1Ch]	PDCs and BDCs would share this; if a machine has this name registered, then it is a domain controller.
<domain name>[1Eh] or *<workgroup name>*[1Eh]	Used in browser elections, indicates that this computer would agree to be a browser. Will only show up on servers.

No matter what kind of computer you have on a Microsoft enterprise network, it will have at least one name registered—the *<computer name>*[00] name. Most computers also register *<workgroup>*[00] which proclaims them as a member of a workgroup. Those are the only two names you would see if you had a DOS workstation running the old LAN Manager network client without the Messenger service, or a Windows for Workgroups 3.1 (not 3.11) workstation that had file and printer sharing disabled.

Most modern client software would also have the Messenger service enabled and so would have the *<computer name>*[03] and *<user name>*[03] names registered as well.

Adding file and/or printer sharing capabilities to a computer would add the *<computer name>*[20] name. Servers all agree to be candidates for browse master by default, so unless you configure a machine to *not* be a candidate for browse mastering, then the *<workgroup name>*[1E] name will appear on any machine offering file or printer sharing. If the machine happens to be the browse master, it'll also have *<workgroup name>*[1D] as well. Workstations use the [1D] name to initially get a list of browse servers when they first start up: they broadcast a message looking to see if the [1D] machine exists, and, if it does, then the [1D] machine presents the workstation with a list of potential browsers.

Browse masters also get the network name [01][02]__MSBROWSE_ _[02][01] as well—it's a group name, and only the *master* browsers are members. Master browsers use that name to discover that each other exist.

Master Browsers versus Domain Master Browsers: A Note

This topic is a little out of order, but it's a topic that is relevant both to TCP/IP, network names, and browsing, so this seemed the least "out of order" place for this note.

Let's consider for a moment browse lists under NT. Most of the messages that drive the browsing services in Microsoft enterprise networking are broadcasts. As routers don't generally pass broadcasts, what does that imply for an internet made up of multiple segments—but only one NT domain?

Before WINS (and in modern NT networks that don't use WINS), each subnet ends up having its own browser elections, and each subnet has its own master browsers as a result. NT centralizes the browse information by dubbing one of these master browsers the Domain Master Browser (DMB). Again, this isn't "domain" in the TCP/IP sense, it's "domain" in the NT sense. The reason DMBs exist is to support browsing of an NT domain that's split up over two or more subnets. Even if your NT domain is only situated on a single subnet, it'll still end up with a DMB. DMBs register the name "<domain>[1B]," and there will, again, be one per NT domain. There can be many DMBs within a single TCP/IP domain, because there can be as many NT domains in a TCP/IP domain as you like.

Name Resolution before WINS

Clients written prior to WINS, or clients without a specified WINS server, try to resolve a NetBIOS name to an IP address with a number of methods. The tools they'll use, if they exist are

- A HOSTS file, if present

- Broadcasts

- A LMHOSTS file, if present

- A DNS server, if present

You met HOSTS before—it's just a simple ASCII file. Each line contains an IP address, at least one space, and a name. LMHOSTS does everything that HOSTS does—it can completely replace HOSTS—and it does a bit more besides. While HOSTS is generally a basic TCP/IP standard from years ago, LMHOSTS is a Microsoft modification that lets you do things such as identify a PDC for an NT domain or tell the system to load a part of LMHOSTS from a central location every time you log on, allowing an administrator to keep the fast-changing information on a central location. For example, supposing that you had a server called FIDO at 210.10.22.33 that was the primary domain controller on a domain named BROWSERS, you'd just add the following line to your LMHOSTS file:

```
210.10.22.33 fido #DOM:browsers
```

Then, when a workstation wanted to obtain a browse list for BROWSERS, the workstation's LMHOSTS file would tell it to go to 210.10.22.33 for the browse list.

Anyway, if you set up a Microsoft network client and do not specify a WINS server and also do not check "Enable DNS for Windows networking," your client will be what Microsoft calls a "modified B node." First, they look in the HOSTS file, if it exists. If the entry they're looking for isn't there, the computer will look in LMHOSTS. If they still can't get the name resolved, they broadcast a request for a response from <computername>[00]. It's a UDP broadcast. They try that three times, and, if there's still no answer, they give up.

If you specify a DNS server in your TCP/IP client configuration, once again, your computer will go first to HOSTS for name resolution, and, if that doesn't work, it'll contact the DNS server you specified in the configuration. Where LMHOSTS figures in varies with the client type; in fact, if you're running Windows 95, then LMHOSTS is ignored altogether when you're using a DNS server. If DNS can't help your computer, then the client software will turn to a UDP broadcast as a last resort.

How WINS Works

You've seen that the world before WINS was a rather grim place, where everyone shouts and many questions (well, resolution requests) go unanswered. Now let's look at what happens with WINS.

WINS Needs NT Server

To make WINS work, you must set up an NT Server machine (it won't run on anything else, including NT Workstation) to act as the WINS server. The WINS server then acts as the NBNS server, keeping track of who's on the network and handing out name resolution information as needed. What I find neat about how WINS works is the way in which it collects name information. You see, if your workstation wants to be able to address name resolution questions to a WINS server, it must first introduce itself to the WINS server—and in the process, WINS captures the IP address and NetBIOS name of that workstation, augmenting the WINS database further!

WINS Holds Name Registrations

Basically, when a WINS client (the shorthand term for "any PC running a Microsoft enterprise TCP/IP network client software designed to use WINS for NBT name resolution") first boots up, it goes to the WINS server and introduces itself. It knows the IP address of the WINS server either because you hard-coded it right into the TCP/IP settings for the workstation or because the workstation got a WINS address from DHCP when it obtained an IP lease.

That first communication is called a *name registration request*. In the process of registering its name with a WINS server, the workstation gets the benefit of ensuring that it has a unique name. If the WINS server sees that there's another computer out there with the same name, it will tell the workstation, "You can't use that name." The name registration request and the acknowledgment are both directed IP messages, so they'll cross routers. And when a workstation shuts down, it sends a "name release" request to the WINS server telling it that the workstation will no longer need the NetBIOS name, enabling the WINS server to register it for some other machine.

WINS Failure Modes

But what if something goes wrong? What if you try to register a name that some other workstation already has, or if a workstation finds that the WINS server is unavailable?

Duplicate names are simple—instead of sending a "success" response to the workstation, the WINS server sends a "fail" message to the workstation response to the workstation's name request. In response, the workstation does not consider the name registered and doesn't include it in its NetBIOS name table; an "nbstat -n" will not show the name.

But if a workstation can't find the WINS server when it boots up, then the workstation simply stops acting as a hybrid NBT node and reverts to its old ways as a "Microsoft modified B node," meaning that it depends largely on broadcasts, but will also consult HOSTS and LMHOSTS if they're present.

It's My Name, But for How Long?

Like DHCP, WINS only registers names for a fixed period of time called the *renewal interval*. By default, it's four days (96 hours), and there will probably never be a reason for you to change that. Forty minutes seems to be the smallest amount that WINS will accept.

In much the same way that DHCP clients attempt to renew their leases early, WINS clients send "name *refresh* requests" to the WINS client before their names expire—*long* before. According to Microsoft documentation, a WINS client attempts a name refresh very early after it gets its names registered—after one eighth of the renewal interval. (My tests show that it's actually *three* eighths, but that's not terribly important.) The WINS server will usually reset the amount of time left before the name must be renewed again (this time is sometimes called the "time to live" or TTL). Once the client has renewed its name *once*, however, it doesn't renew it again and again every one-eighth of its TTL; instead, it only renews its names every one-half of the TTL. (My tests agree with that.)

Installing WINS

Installing WINS is much like installing all the other software that we've installed elsewhere in this chapter and in the book.

When you're planning how many WINS servers you need and where to put them, bear in mind that you need not put a WINS server on each subnet (which is one of the great features of WINS). It *is* a good idea to have a second machine running as a secondary WINS server, however, just for fault tolerance's sake. Remember that if a workstation comes up and can't find a WINS server, it reverts to broadcasting, which will limit its name resolution capabilities to just its local subnet and will cause it to do a lot of shouting, which adds traffic to the subnet. Why would a WINS client not find a WINS server if there's a working WINS server? Normally, the client would find the server just fine, but in some small percentage of the cases, the WINS server might be too busy to respond to the client in a timely fashion, causing the client to just give up on the server. *That's* where a secondary is useful. If you have a backup domain controller, then put a WINS server on that machine as well. The WINS software actually does not use a lot of CPU time, so it probably won't affect your server's performance unless you have thousands of users all hammering on one WINS server. If *that's* the case, I'd dedicate a computer solely to WINS-ing.

To get a WINS server set up, follow these directions:

1. Open the Control Panel.

2. Within the Control Panel, open the Networks applet.

3. Click the Services tab.

4. Click the Add button.

5. Choose the Windows Internet Name Service.

6. Tell the program where to find the files on your CD-ROM or whatever drive you used to install NT.

7. Click the Close button.

The system will want to restart; let it. Once your server has rebooted, you find a new icon in the Administrative Tools group, the WINS Manager. Start it up, and it will look like Figure 14.42.

The first thing you should do on your WINS server is inform it of the machines on your subnet that have hard-coded IP addresses. You do that by clicking Mappings, then Static Mappings...; you then see a dialog box like the one shown in Figure 14.43.

FIGURE 14.42

The initial WINS Manager screen

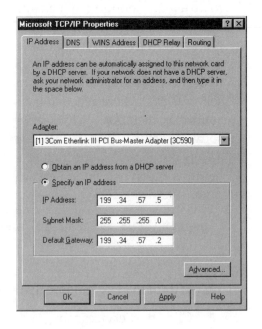

FIGURE 14.43

The Static
Mappings table

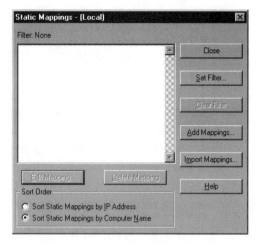

In the figure above, you see that I've added the IP addresses for two devices with predefined IP addresses. Just click Add Mappings, and you get a dialog box that lets you add IP addresses and host names as static values. If you have an existing HOSTS file, you can click Import Mappings... and the program will take that information to build a static-mapping database.

The second thing to do is to tell the WINS server where to back up its database. If you supply a location to keep WINS database backups, then your WINS server will automatically back itself up once a day. You do that by clicking on Mappings and then on Backup Database. You will see a dialog box asking you for a directory. The default location is USERS\DEFAULT, which I suppose will work as well as any other. It'll end up creating a directory called \USERS\DEFAULT\ WINS_BAK, which will include three files: JET.LOG, SYSTEM.MDB, and WINS.MDB. And while I'm on the subject of backing up the WINS database, let's take a moment and discuss restoration.

Restoring a WINS Database

The three files that went into WINS_BAK are essentially all there is to a WINS database. Just put them back in \WINNT\SYSTEM32\WINS, and the database is restored. But you can't do that while WINS is running—so go to the Control Panel and stop the Windows Internet Naming Service (open Control Panel, double-click on Services, click "Windows Internet Naming Service," then click the Stop button, and click Yes to confirm that you want to stop the service). Then you can copy the files from the backup location to \WINNT\SYSTEM32\WINS and restart the service by going to the same place in the Control Panel where you stopped the service and click the Start button.

If you have modified the settings on the WINS server, however—modified the renewal interval or specified a backup directory, for example—then you may want to back *those* up, as well. Your option settings for the WINS server are stored in the Registry (of course) in the key \HKEY_LOCAL_MACHINE\SYSTEM\CurrentControlSet\Services\WINS. You can save that part of the Registry in this way:

1. Start the Registry Editor, REGEDT32.

2. Open the HKEY_LOCAL_MACHINE subtree.

3. Click on the SYSTEM\CurrentControlSet\Services\WINS key.

4. Click Registry and "Save Key..."

5. Point the dialog box by entering the location where you want to save the WINS Registry settings and fill in a filename, then click OK.

To restore the settings:

1. Stop the WINS service.

2. Start the Registry Editor, REGEDT32.

3. Open the HKEY_LOCAL_MACHINE subtree.

4. Click on the SYSTEM\CurrentControlSet\Services\WINS key.

5. Click Registry, and "Restore..."

6. Point the dialog box by entering the location where you stored the backups, and fill in the name of the backup file; then click OK.

7. Click Yes to confirm that you want to overwrite the old key.

8. Exit the Registry Editor.

9. Restart the WINS service. You do not need to reboot for these changes to take effect.

So, to summarize what you should do in order to be able to rebuild a WINS server: tell the WINS server where to do backups, and it will do them automatically every day. And, when you make changes to WINS settings, save the part of the Registry that holds the settings. Most importantly, be sure to run a secondary WINS server—then you don't really have to worry about backing up your WINS database at all, as you have two machines working in parallel.

> **TIP**
>
> WINS services are totally independent of NT domain security, as are DHCP. A WINS server can serve workstations throughout your network. In fact, if your network is connected to the Internet and doesn't have a firewall, you could actually *publish* your WINS server address, and other networks across the Internet could share browsing capabilities! (Whether or not you'd *want* to do that is another issue.)

WINS Proxy Agents

Using an NBNS (NetBIOS Naming Service) like WINS can greatly cut down on the broadcasts on your network, reducing traffic and improving throughput. But, as you've seen, this requires the clients to understand WINS; the older network client software just shouts away as a B node.

WINS can help those older non-WINS-aware clients with a *WINS proxy agent*. A WINS proxy agent is a regular old network workstation that listens for older B node systems helplessly broadcasting, trying to reach NetBIOS names that (unknown to the B node computers) are on another subnet.

To see how this would work, let's take a look at a very simple two-subnet internet, as shown in Figure 14.44.

Here, you see two C-class subnets, 1.1.1.0 and 1.1.2.0. There's a router between them. On 1.1.1.0, there are two workstations. One is a WINS-aware client named HELPFUL which is also running a WINS proxy agent. The other is an old B node client named HOPELESS which is not WINS-aware. On 1.1.2.0, there are a couple of servers, a machine acting as a WINS server and a regular old file server.

When HOPELESS first comes up, it'll do a broadcast of its names to ensure that no one else has them. The machine that it really should be talking to, of course, is WINSERV, but WINSERV can't hear it. HELPFUL, however, hears the B node broadcasts coming from HOPELESS and sends a directed message to WINSERV, telling it that there's a work-station named HOPELESS trying to register some names.

WINSERV looks up those names to ensure that they don't already exist. If they *do* exist, then WINSERV sends a message back to HELPFUL,

FIGURE 14.44

An example of a two-subnet internet

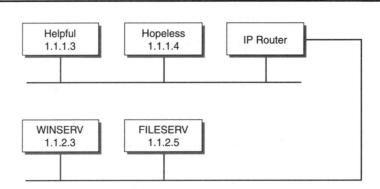

saying, "Don't let that guy register those names!" HELPFUL then sends a message to HOPELESS, saying, "I'm sorry, but *I* already use the name HOPELESS." That keeps HOPELESS from registering a name that exists on another subnet.

Assuming that HOPELESS's names do *not* currently exist in the WINSERV database, however, WINSERV does *not* register the names; putting a WINS proxy agent on 1.1.1.0 doesn't mean that the non-WINS clients will have their names registered with WINS. That means that it's okay to have the same NetBIOS name on two different computers, so long as they are both B node clients and are on different subnets.

Suppose then that HOPELESS does a "net use d: \\fileserv\files"— in that case, the name "\\fileserv" must be resolved. Assuming that HOPELESS does not have a HOSTS or LMHOSTS file, HOPELESS will start broadcasting, saying, "Is there anyone here named FILESERV? And if so, what's your IP address?" HELPFUL will intercede by sending a directed IP message to WINSERV, saying, "Is there a name registered as FILESERV, and what is its IP address?"

WINSERV will respond with the IP address of FILESERV, and HELPFUL will then send a directed message back to HOPELESS, saying, "Sure, I'm FILESERV, and you can find me at 1.1.2.5." Now HOPELESS can complete its request.

TIP Make sure there is only *one* WINS proxy agent per subnet! Otherwise, two PCs will respond to HOPELESS, causing—how do the manuals put it? Ah yes—"unpredictable results."

DNS in the NT World

You've seen that WINS can effectively resolve NetBIOS names into IP addresses, making it possible for NetBIOS-based applications like "net use" or NT logins to happen. NetBIOS name resolution was top priority for NT's designers simply because Microsoft's logon, browsing, and file and printer sharing services had been written since 1985 to sit atop NetBIOS.

But as time goes on, more and more common networked applications *don't* sit atop NetBIOS; they sit atop WinSock, the API that more closely matches the Sockets interface found throughout the Internet world. Examples of programs that rely on WinSock rather than NetBIOS are Web browsers (like Netscape) and servers (like Microsoft's Internet Information Server), Internet e-mail clients like Eudora, and Telnet client programs, to just name a few.

Since WinSock apps need DNS name resolution, rather than NetBIOS name resolution, that implies that you've probably got to find some kind of DNS server software. At this writing, there isn't a DNS server in the box with NT, so you need a third-party utility, such as the *bind* utility that's included in *Chameleon32/NFS* from NetManage (10725N. DeAnza Blvd., Cupertino, CA 95014; (408) 973-7171 voice; (408) 257-6405 fax).

DNS Pros and Cons

DNS is, in general, a bit of a pain to administer. Most DNS servers require that you sit down and type in the names and IP addresses of any machines that you want the outside world to be able to resolve. That simplifies things a bit because you've only got to include the hard-coded IP addresses of the few machines that you wanted the outside world to see, such as:

- Your gateway

- Your mail router

- Any FTP or Telnet servers

DNS is a static protocol in general; for example, DNS knows that "ftp.microsoft.com" is "198.105.232.1" because somebody at Microsoft sat down and typed a list into Microsoft's DNS server, a list detailing what TCP/IP host names correspond to which IP addresses. DNS also does *reverse DNS lookups*, which allow you not only to find out that aardvark.orchard.com is 219.111.29.55, but also to find out that 219.111.29.55 is aardvark.orchard.com, sort of like a reverse phone book that lets you look up (871) 329-5204 and find out that Phineas Jones lives there.

There are a number of DNS servers for NT on the market, but do you really want a traditional DNS server? It's something of a pain to have to type in new entries every time you put a computer on your TCP/IP network, and that's just what DNS requires. Think about it—every time somebody fires up a computer with a DHCP network client, you'd have a new computer on the network, and one more potential name resolution problem.

I suppose you could start up the DHCP manager a few times a day, note the new leases, and type them into your DNS server. Oh, and by the way, every time you want DNS to re-read your list of machine names and IP addresses, you must bring down the entire DNS service and re-start it, leaving your network without name services for a minute or two.

What we really need is a WINS server that can double as a DNS server, offering the information that it has to anyone looking for DNS information. If my domain name is "mmco.com," my NetBIOS name is BIGPC, and my IP address is 199.34.57.88, then this WINS/DNS combination would know that name resolution requests for "bigpc.mmco.com" would return 199.34.57.88, and reverse name resolution requests for "199.34.57.88" would return "bigpc.mmco.com."

There isn't anything that can do that at the moment, but there *is* something that does some of what we need. Microsoft has written a DNS which runs as a service on an NT machine. It implements a normal DNS service with static name lists but adds a bonus: it includes a dynamic linkage to WINS, so that whenever the DNS server can't find a name in its static lists, it consults WINS.

At this writing, the DNS server is still a beta product, and it acts that way. For example, I've found that it can resolve "cmu.edu" or "cs.cmu .edu," but not "lycos.cs.cmu.edu." It may be able to handle the needs of your organization, however, and in theory it won't be beta forever—so here's a simplified guide to installing the DNS service.

Microsoft's beta DNS server can both resolve names in the outside world by querying the Internet's root name servers and can respond to name resolution requests from the outside world. Here's how to get the DNS beta up and running.

Getting the Microsoft DNS Program

You can find the DNS beta on the CD-ROM that comes with the NT Resource Kit. Failing that, you can FTP to "rhino.microsoft.com," logging on with the user name "dnsbeta" and the password "dnsbeta." "Anonymous" won't work here, so don't use your Web browser; just use the FTP client that comes with NT.

Once you're on the FTP site, you see a file at the root named "contents.txt," and directories named "63" and "files." Apparently, the last one to appear, "63" contains build 63 of the DNS beta. If there *is* a newer version then you won't see "63," you'll see a higher number. "Files" contains the things that won't change much from version to version. Within the "63" directory will be subdirectories for each of the four processor platforms. As always, you only need the files that are specific to your particular server, whether it's a PowerPC, Alpha, MIPS, or Intel *x*86 machine.

Get all of the files in the appropriate subdirectory of "63" and all of the files in "files," and disconnect from the FTP server.

In the directory that you put all of the files into, there's a file called INSTALL.BAT; run it. It will copy the DLLs into their proper places.

Look in the Control Panel under Services, and you'll see that you have a new entry, the Domain Naming Server Service. Do not start the DNS server yet, as you have some files to set up.

The Setup Files

The DNS service relies upon a number of ASCII text files:

- BOOT contains basic information about where the other files reside. It *must* go in the \winnt35\system32\drivers\etc directory.

- ARPA-127.REV contains information required to allow DNS to be able to resolve the name "localhost" into 127.0.0.1 and to allow DNS to be able to resolve 127.*x.y.z* to "localhost," for any values of *x*, *y*, and *z*. In general, you won't touch it.

- CACHE tells DNS where to find the Internet "root servers," the top of the DNS hierarchy.

- You need at least one file with the names of your computers along with their specified IP addresses. You can call it anything that you like, because you direct DNS to find it with a line in BOOT that I'll introduce you to later. For example, I chose to put the list of names for my domain, mmco.com, into a file called MMCO.NMS. (I could have called it MMCO.COM, but I didn't want NT mistaking it for an executable file.)

- You have at least one file with a name like ARPA-202.REV which contains the *reverse* DNS references. The name is built up out of ARPA-x.REV, where *x* is the left-most quad of your network. In my case, my network is 199.34.57.0, so I called the file ARPA-199.REV. DNS knows to go looking for this file because, again, you point DNS to the REV file in the BOOT file, as I'll show you soon.

Let's take a look at the files.

The BOOT File

Like the other configuration files, BOOT is an ASCII text file. It must be placed in the WINNT35\SYSTEM32\DRIVERS\ETC directory. In the BOOT file, you specify these things:

- What directory would you like to place the other DNS data files in?

- What is the name of the file that contains the names of the Internet root servers?

- What domain, like "mmco.com," will this DNS server resolve names for?

- What IP address range, like "199.34.57.0," will this DNS server do reverse name resolution for?

Let me show you an example of a DNS file, which I will explain in just a moment.

```
directory  C:\dns
cache .  cache
primary mmco.com.  mmco.nms
primary 127.in-addr.arpa arpa-127.rev
primary 57.34.199.in-addr.arpa arpa-199.rev
```

I have removed the comments to keep the file short, but you can add a comment to any DNS file by prefixing it with a semicolon.

The first command, "directory," tells DNS that I put the other files into the directory C:\DNS. There's got to be a space between "directory" and "C:\DNS."

The second command points to the file containing the names of the Internet root servers. Microsoft provides a file that works just fine, and they call it "CACHE." I saw no reason to change its name, so the command "cache . cache" means "you find the Internet root name servers's names in a file called 'cache' (that's the second 'cache'), in the C:\DNS directory."

Next, the "primary" statements define what this DNS server is good for. Its job will mainly be to convert "mmco.com" names to "199.34.57.x" names, convert "199.34.57.x" IP addresses into "mmco.com" names, and also it'll reverse-resolve any localhost address references. The "primary mmco.com. mmco.nms" line says, "If someone needs information about any computer in the mmco.com domain, then you can find that information in the file mmco.nms, which is in the C:\DNS directory." Note the extra period on "mmco.com.;" do not leave it off your domain name. The "primary 127.in-addr.arpa arpa-127.rev" means "if you're ever asked to reverse-resolve any number from 127.0.0.0 through 127.255.255.255, then look in the file arpa-127.rev, which is in the C:\DNS directory." (While my network doesn't include those addresses, they're the range of loopback addresses.) The "primary 57.34.199.in-addr.arpa arpa-199.rev" line means "if you ever have to do a reverse name resolution for 199.34.57.0 through 199.34.57.255, then look in the file named arpa-199.rev, which is in C:\DNS."

Hey—what's that last "primary" statement mean? What's "57.34.199?" After looking at a time or two, you've probably noticed that it is "199.34.57" backwards. Since the last two "primary" commands are for *reverse* DNS resolution, the names go in backwards. (I know, it's strange, but blame the Unix folks who invented DNS...) You should specify the level that the DNS server will be authoritative for here. For example, "Primary 199.in-addr.arpa x.rev" would mean "any reverse DNS request starting with '199' can be resolved with 'x.rev,'"and that's definitely *not* what I want to do—I've only got 199.34.57.0, not 199.132.22.0 or 199.99.55.0, or whatever. Just to provide another example, "Primary 22.140.in-addr.arpa revs.rev" would mean "DNS server, you're responsible for addresses 140.22.0.0 through 140.22 .255.255, and you'll find the reverse DNS information for that range in the file revs.rev, which is in C:\DNS."

Now that I have the BOOT file in place, let's move to the files in C:\ DNS. Do not touch the ARPA-127.REV file or the CACHE files that ship with the DNS service; just use them as provided.

The DNS Name Resolver File

Next, I have to create the file that tells my DNS server how to convert my PC's names to IP addresses. Now, as I mentioned before, I don't have to do that for every computer on my network; but I *should* do it for the ones with the static IP addresses—my servers, in particular. Suppose on my network I have an Internet mail server named mailserve .mmco.com, at 199.34.57.20, and a time server named timeserve.mmco .com at 199.34.57.55; those will be the machines whose addresses I must worry about. I'll put my DNS service on a machine named "eisa-server .mmco.com," at 199.34.57.50. You may recall that I chose to call the file with my names MMCO.NMS. Let's start off with a look at it, with the comments removed.

```
@    in   soa   eisa-server.mmco.com. mark.mailserve.mmco.com. (
            1996021501    ; serial [ yyyyMMddNN]
            10800         ; refresh [ 3h]
            3600          ; retry  [ 1h]
            691200        ; expire [ 8d]
            86400  )      ; minimum [ 1d]

$WINS 199.34.57.32
@ in ns eisa-server.mmco.com.
@ in mx 10 mailserve
localhost in a 127.0.0.1
mailserve in a 199.34.57.20
timeserve in a 199.34.57.55
```

The first part is the "Start of Authority" record, a bit of boilerplate that you can just type right in. The only things I inserted were the name of the machine running the DNS server (eisa-server.mmco.com.) and where to find me (mark@mailserve.mmco.com). Notice two syntactic oddities that you'd better follow, or DNS won't work. First, add an extra period to the end of the full name of the name server, or DNS will automatically append "mmco.com" to the name. If I'd entered "eisa-server.mmco.com" instead of "eisa-server.mmco.com." then DNS would think that the name server was running on a machine named "eisa-server.mmco.com.mmco.com." The second oddity is the format for my e-mail address; DNS wants you to replace the "@" with a period, hence my e-mail name "mark.mailserve.mmco.com."

Notice also the first indented line, the one that looks like "19960215..."—it's the *DNS serial number*. Since my Internet service provider gets name information about my company from my name server, and because my ISP doesn't want to have to read what could be a monstrous DNS list every time it's asked to resolve a name, this serial number tells the outside ISP whether or not things have changed since the last time the ISP looked at my domain's DNS server. The number can be anything at all; just make sure that you change it every time you change the file.

Let me say that again: be sure to change the serial number line in your SOA record every time you change any of the data in the DNS database. I didn't, and it took me two weeks to figure out why my updated name information was being ignored by my ISP.

Next is a command that you won't find in any other DNS server: the "$WINS" command. That tells Microsoft's DNS server, "If you're asked to resolve a name, but cannot find it in the static listing, then ask the WINS server at 199.34.57.32 to resolve it." You can specify multiple WINS servers by listing them on the $WINS line, separated by semicolons.

Following that line is the line that names the name server or DNS server for this domain. It seems a bit redundant—after all, you wouldn't be reading this file if you didn't know who was the name server for this domain—but it's required. The format is just "@ in ns 'name of your DNS server.'" The "ns" stands for "name server." The "in" means "this is information used by an internet."

After that goes an MX or *mail exchange* record. An MX record makes it possible for someone to send mail to joeblow@bigfirm.com when in actual fact there is no single machine called "bigfirm.com;" rather, bigfirm's got a machine named "mail.bigfirm.com." The MX record translates mail addresses from a generic domain name to a specific machine name. An MX record looks like "@ in mx 10 'name of your mail server.'" You can add particular MX records for particular machines, but it's not necessary. For example, what happens if someone sends mail not to "mark@mmco.com," but to "mark@timeserve.mmco.com?" Well, nothing happens, basically; timeserve isn't prepared to receive mail, and so the message will just be lost. But I *could* idiot-proof the system a bit by adding MX records to every single DNS entry, so no matter what machine an outsider tried to send mail to, the mail would end up at mailserve.

Next is the listing of machines and IP addresses. Each record looks like "*machinename* in a *IP address*," where *machinename* is just the left-most part of the name, rather than the fully qualified domain name. For example, a machine on my network called "mwm66.mmco.com" would have a record that looked like "mwm66 in a 199.34.57.66" if its IP address were 199.34.57.66. The "in" part is, recall, for "internet." The "a" part means that this is an "address" record. You also need a localhost reference, as you see in my example. Microsoft provides a sample name file in a file called PLACE.DOM; in it, they also show you how to create an alias for an FTP and a WWW site. But it's just as easy to type in a file like the one above.

The Reverse Name Resolution Files

As I mentioned earlier, DNS isn't too terribly bright about using the information that you give it; although it knows that mypc.mmco.com is 199.34.57.43, it still can't seem to figure out that given the IP address 199.34.57.43 it should reverse-resolve the DNS name, "mypc.mmco .com." So you have to help it out with the reverse DNS files.

In my example, I told my DNS server in the BOOT file that it could reverse-resolve addresses in the 199.34.57.0 network, and that information was in a file called "ARPA-199.REV." It looks like the following, again with the comments removed:

```
@  IN SOA eisa-server.mmco.com. mark.smtphost.mmco.com. (
                  1     ; serial number
                  10800  ; refresh [3h]
                  3600  ; retry [1h]
                  691200 ; expire [8d]
                  86400 ) ; minimum [1d]
@ in ns eisa-server.mmco.com.
32 IN PTR eisa-server.mmco.com.
50 IN PTR mailserve.mmco.com.
55 IN PTR timeserve.mmco.com.
35 IN PTR sdg90.mmco.com.
```

It looks a lot like the MMCO.NMS file that we just created, with a few differences. It starts off with a "start of authority" record just like the MMCO.NMS file. There is, again, a pointer to the local name server, eisa-server.mmco.com. Then there are references to the IP addresses of machines in the mmco.com domain. Notice that since the DNS server only looks in here to resolve names looking like "199.34.57.something," you need only specify the last quad on the IN PTR lines.

Notice also that there's no $WINS statement; that's important. For some reason, this WINS-to-DNS dynamic link can do DNS name resolution, but not reverse resolution. That's why I have an extra entry, for a machine named "sdg90.mmco.com;" it attaches to an FTP site that double-checks who I am before letting me on by requesting a reverse DNS resolution. It sees that I'm attaching from 199.34.57.35, but it needs to be sure that my DNS name is also "sdg90.mmco.com." As sdg90 gets its IP address from my DHCP server, I needed to put a specific address into this file so that my DNS server could reverse-resolve the address for that particular PC. (How can I be so sure that sdg90 gets 199.34.57.35? I reserved the address for it in DHCP.)

As your DNS server must also be able to reverse-resolve loopback addresses, you have an ARPA-127.REV, but, as I've already said, don't touch it; it's fine as it comes from Microsoft.

Now all you have to do is to start up the service, point all of your workstations to that machine for DNS resolution, and you have your very own dynamic DNS server. It's still a bit flaky, but it's often useful, and no doubt the final version will be cleaner.

Once the DNS service is up and running, you can point workstations to it: when they need the name of a DNS server, just fill in the IP address of your NT machine running the DNS server. And ask your ISP to tell its DNS server to pull its address resolution information off your DNS server. One warning: the DNS server beta ran well until I installed NT 3.51 Service Pack 3; if you can avoid that Service Pack, then you might want to do that.

Using the Graphical DNS Manager and Service

If, on the other hand, you're working with 4, you'll find some changes. The DNS server portion of NT has been around since NT 3.5 in the form of beta software. With 4, it became an "official" part of NT.

Microsoft chose (wisely, I'd argue) to build a fairly no-frills implementation of DNS. It can optionally use ASCII files formatted in the way that the traditional Unix DNS program *bind* formats them. While *bind* format files aren't straightforward—you just read about how to set them up in the previous section—they *are* standard, and so one simple way to start up a DNS server on NT is just to install the DNS server service and copy over your old *bind* files.

You install the DNS server service just as you've installed other network items—just open the Control Panel, then the Network applet, then Services, and the Add button. You see the DNS server as one of the options. As usual, you have to reboot.

Once you've rebooted, look in the Administrative Tools group, and you see a new application, DNS Manager. Start it up and it will look like Figure 14.45.

Tell the DNS Manager about the DNS server you just installed by clicking DNS and New Server, and then fill in the IP address of the new DNS server. The DNS Manager will open up the DNS information for that server, as shown in Figure 14.46.

Now, remember, I just installed the software for this DNS server, so I have to tell it about itself. There are two ways to do this: with information stored in the Registry (a new, non-standard approach offered by Microsoft's DNS server) or with regular old *bind* files. Side note, by the way: to make Microsoft DNS use a WINS server to do dynamic name resolution, add this line to the domain's file (like mmco.nms in the example I've been showing you so far):

```
mmco.com.   WINS 199.34.57.50
```

Notice that's different from the $WINS directive in the earlier betas. Those of you running 3.51 with the DNS beta should use $WINS, and those of you with 4 should use the WINS record type.

FIGURE 14.45

Opening DNS Manager screen

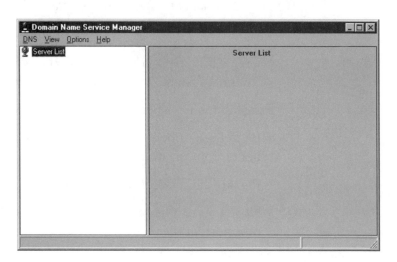

FIGURE 14.46

The DNS Manager display of a new DNS database

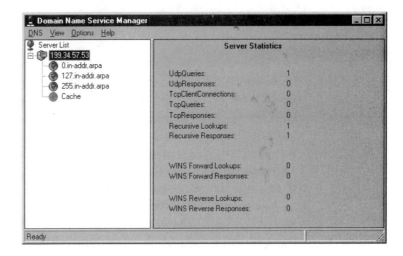

Anyway, the Registry approach is the default, but the Registry approach is a trifle troublesome in that it *requires* that you use the DNS Manager application. Again, DNS Manager is a nice, GUI program, but in my experience it's buggy: trying to create the reverse name domain 57.34.199.in-addr.arpa crashes it, complete with a visit from Dr. Watson. I find it easier to build the structure of the DNS Server with traditional *bind* files, and then move from there to the Registry. My recipe for making DNS work is, then:

- Create bind files, complete with the WINS record. Put the files in \winnt\system32\dns; they *must* be there.

- Install the DNS Service.

- By default, it boots from Registry information. Change that so it boots from the bind files.

- Restart the service. Now it's got the structure of your domain.

- Now you can use the DNS Manager *and* maintain your data in bind format files.

As to the specifics of actually doing it, well, you already know how to make bind files, and you've installed the DNS Server, so let's move along from there. Right-click the server that you just installed. Then click Properties, and you see a dialog box like the one in Figure 14.47.

Just click "Boot From Boot File," and then click DNS/Update Server Data Files. Then go to the Control Panel, select Services, and stop the "Microsoft DNS Server" service. Make sure you've put the bind files into the directory \winnt\system32\dns, or this isn't going to work. Then restart the DNS server.

At this point, your DNS server knows pretty much all it needs to know about your domain. Return to the DNS Manager's main screen, and you'll see something like Figure 14.48.

Now your DNS server is set up and will use WINS resolution. (Or, rather, it's *supposed* to use WINS resolution. In my experience, this feature has worked sporadically since it first appeared in beta form for NT 3.5 years ago.)

FIGURE 14.47

Switching DNS server to BOOT files

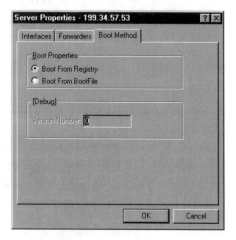

FIGURE 14.48

DNS Manager set up
for MMCO domain

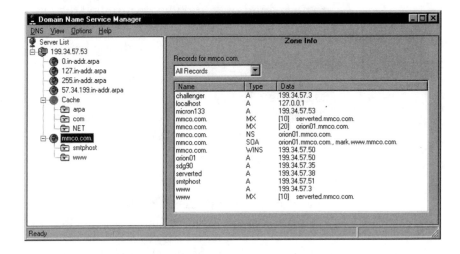

Now, if you must add a static host entry, then you can use the simplicity that the GUI provides. Just right-click the domain name (mmco .com in my case) and choose "New Host…" and you'll see something like Figure 14.49.

Despite the "Add PTR record" check box, I find that I still must add the reverse DNS entry by hand. You're supposed to be able to tell DNS to use WINS to do reverse lookups by adding a line like:

```
57.34.199.in-addr.arpa NBSTAT mmco.com.
```

FIGURE 14.49

Entering a static entry
in the DNS database

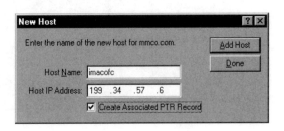

In other words, the first part of the line is the reverse lookup domain name, the record type is NBTSTAT, and the third part is the domain name with a period on its end; again, I find its stability to be sporadic.

Name Resolution Sequence under WinSock

Now that you know how to configure DNS and WINS, you may be faced with a troubleshooting problem in reference to name resolution. Perhaps you try to FTP to a site inside your organization, but you can't hook up. Even though you know that ftp.goodstuff.acme.com is at one IP address, your FTP client keeps trying to attach somewhere else. You've checked your DNS server, of course, and its information is right. Where else to look?

Review: WinSock versus NBT

Remember first that there are two kinds of name resolution in Microsoft TCP/IP networking, WinSock name resolution and NetBIOS name resolution. A "net view \\somename" needs NetBIOS over TCP name resolution, or NBT name resolution. In contrast, as FTP is, like ping, an Internet application, it uses WinSock name resolution. So, to troubleshoot a name resolution problem, you have to follow what your client software does, step-by-step.

Examining Network Traces

When faced with a problem like this, I turned to the Microsoft documentation for help, but there wasn't much detail. So I ran a network monitor and issued ping commands to computers that didn't exist, to see the sequence of actions that the network client software tried in order to resolve a name. The HOSTS and LMHOSTS files do not, of course, show up in a network trace, so I inserted information into those files that didn't exist on the DNS or WINS servers, and then tried pinging again, to demonstrate where the HOSTS and LMHOSTS files sit in the name resolution hierarchy. Pinging for a nonexistent "apple," I found that the name resolution order proceeds as shown in Figure 14.50.

Step-by-step, it looks like this.

- First, consult the HOSTS file, if it exists. If you find the name you're looking for, stop.

- Next, if there's a specified DNS server or servers, then query them. First, query "apple." NT machines then query "apple.mmco.com," tacking on the domain name; Windows 95 workstations don't do the second query.

This happens whether or not the box "Enable DNS for Windows Name Resolution," found in the Advanced Microsoft TCP/IP Configuration dialog boxes of NT 3.51 and Windows for Workgroups, is checked. If DNS has the name, then stop.

- After that, the client looks to see if the name is 16 or more characters. If it is, then the process stops, a failed name resolution attempt. Notice that this means that *LMHOSTS cannot resolve FQDNs longer than 15 characters*—quite a scary bug if you depend on LMHOSTS!

- Next, if there's a specified WINS server or servers, then query the WINS server(s). The name WINS looks for is "apple <00>," the name that *would* be registered by the Workstation service, if the "apple" machine existed.

- If that fails, then do three broadcasts looking for a machine with NetBIOS name "apple <00>," requesting that it identify itself and send back its IP address. Again, this would succeed with a workstation running some NetBIOS-over-TCP/IP client, even a relatively old one, as it would have registered the "apple <00>" name already, if only on its own name table. Unfortunately, this only works if the machine is on the same subnet.

FIGURE 14.50

The name
resolution order

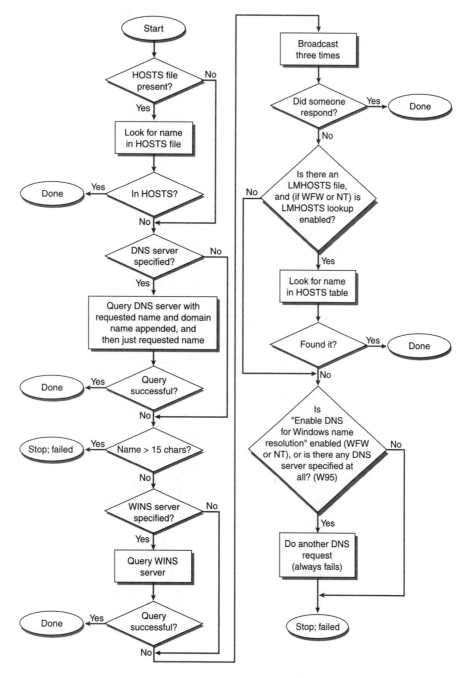

- If the name still hasn't been resolved, read the LMHOSTS file. (Under NT 3.51 and Windows for Workgroups, do not do this if the box labeled "Enable LMHOSTS Lookup" is unchecked; skip this step.) As with the earlier steps, stop if you find a match, or keep going.

- If you're running an NT or Windows for Workgroups machine with the box "Enable DNS for Windows Name Resolution" checked, then you've instructed your system to do a DNS lookup every time a WINS lookup fails. If that box is checked, then a second and last DNS lookup will happen. If, on the other hand, you *don't* have the "Enable DNS" box checked, then there's nothing left to do.

Look at that sequence: HOSTS, DNS, WINS, broadcast, LMHOSTS, and DNS again. This surprised me for a couple of reasons. First, it seems that every unsuccessful name resolution results in broadcasts, the *bête noire* of those of us trying to keep the network traffic to a minimum. My guess is that the broadcasts aren't part of an according-to-Hoyle IP stack, but Microsoft just threw them in for good measure and the WINS query as well. Then, if you've checked "Enable DNS for Windows Name Resolution," the client software performs a DNS lookup as a matter of course after any failed WINS lookup; unfortunately, that leads to a redundant DNS lookup here. In short, if your Windows 95 workstation knows of a DNS server, it will use that DNS server when doing both DNS and NetBIOS name resolutions.

The broadcasts are a pain, but they *would* be of benefit when you tried to execute a TCP/IP command on a computer in your network, but wanted to use the shorter NetBIOS name rather than the longer DNS name, e.g. "apple" instead of "apple.mmco.com."

What happened on that workstation that could not access the FTP site? There was an old HOSTS file sitting in the Windows directory that pointed to a different IP address, an older IP address for the FTP server. HOSTS is read before anything else, so the accurate information on the DNS or WINS servers never got a chance to be read.

There is an explicit "Enable DNS for Windows Name Resolution" check box in Windows for Workgroups and NT 3.51 clients, but how do you control whether or not DNS gets into the act on a Windows 95 client? You can't, at least not entirely; where Workgroups and NT 3.51 separate the options about whether to specify a DNS server and whether or not to use that DNS server as a helper when resolving NetBIOS names (that's what "Enable DNS for Windows Name Resolution" means); Windows 95 seems not to do that.

Controlling WINS versus DNS Order in WinSock

Now, what I just showed you is the order of events by default in NT or Windows 95 clients. But if you feel like messing around with the way that WinSock resolves names, you can. As usual, let me take this moment to remind you that it's not a great idea to mess with the Registry unless you know what you're doing.

Look in the Registry under HKEY_LOCAL_MACHINE\System\ CurrentControlSet\Services\TCPIP\ServiceProvider, and you see a "HostsPriority," "DNSPriority," and "NBTPriority" value sets. They are followed by hexadecimal values. The lower the value, the earlier that HOSTS, DNS (and LMHOSTS), and WINS (and broadcasts) get done. For example, by default DNS's priority is 7D0 and WINS's is 7D1, so DNS goes before WINS. But change DNS's priority to 7D2, and WINS does its lookup and broadcast *before* the client interrogates the DNS server.

Again, I'm not sure *why* you'd want to do this, but I include it for the sake of completeness and for the enjoyment of those who delight in undocumented features.

Name Resolution Sequence under NetBIOS

Having looked at the steps that the system goes through to resolve a DNS name, what happens when the system attempts to resolve a NetBIOS name? Again, it's an involved process, but in general the factors that affect how NBT resolves names are:

- Is the workstation an NT 3.51 or Windows 95 workstation?

- Is LMHOSTS enabled?

- Is DNS enabled to assist in Windows (NetBIOS) name resolution?

- Is the network client software WINS-aware?

Summarized, the name resolution sequence appears in Figure 14.51.

The same components that went into WinSock name resolutions contribute to NBT resolutions, but in a slightly different order. The NBT name resolver uses the following steps; if any succeed, then it stops looking.

- The first part is the WINS client, if the client software is WINS-aware. If WINS is disabled under Windows 95, or if there is no WINS server specified in Workgroups or NT 3.51, then the client skips this step.

- If WINS isn't being used, then the client does three broadcasts. For example, "net view \\apple" causes three broadcasts looking for a workstation with the name "apple" registered, rather than "apple.mmco.com" or the like.

- Next, if LMHOSTS is enabled—and it appears that LMHOSTS is *always* enabled on Windows 95 clients, but must be enabled with the "Enable LMHOSTS" check box for NT 3.51 and Workgroups— then the client looks up the name in LMHOSTS. Surprised? When doing NBT name resolutions, LMHOSTS gets consulted *before* HOSTS, a reversal over WinSock name resolutions.

FIGURE 14.51

Name resolution
sequence under
NetBIOS

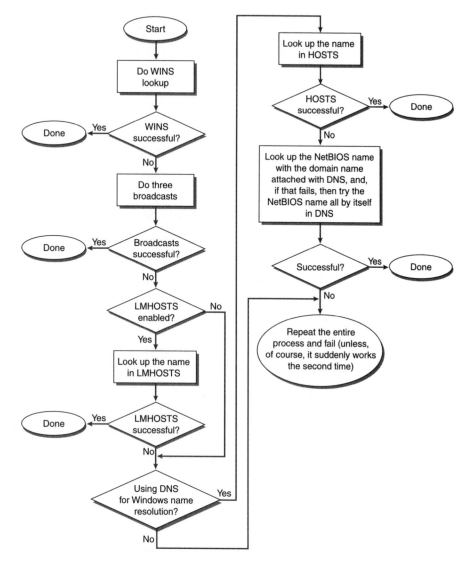

For LMHOSTS to be of help here, it must specify NetBIOS names, not fully qualified domain names. For example, if you have a workstation named rusty.acme.com at 212.11.41.4, but you want to do a "net view \\rusty," then the line in lmhosts should look like this:

```
212.11.41.4 rusty
```

Not "rusty.acme.com," just "rusty".

- If you've checked "Enable DNS for Windows Name Resolution" in Workgroups or NT 3.51, or if you have specified a DNS server in Windows 95, then the workstation's client software will look at HOSTS and, if HOSTS can't help, it will interrogate the DNS server (or servers, as you can specify up to four DNS servers).

The NT/Workgroups clients and the 95 clients use DNS differently. The NT/Workgroups clients do a DNS query for the name with the domain name appended to it, and then a DNS query of just the name. For example, if your domain is "acme.com" and you're doing a "net view \\myserver," then an NT workstation will ask DNS first to resolve the name "myserver.acme.com"—it automatically adds the domain name for the first resolution. Then, if the DNS server can't resolve the name with the domain name attached, then the client will request that the DNS server just resolve "myserver."

In contrast, the Windows 95 client software only asks the DNS server to resolve the name with the domain name appended; in my example, a Windows 95 workstation would ask DNS to resolve "myserver.acme .com," but would not ask about "myserver."

- The last part is *really* strange. If the client software is the NT client (not the Workgroups or Win95 clients), and if it's been unsuccessful so far, then it goes back and does it all over again, I suppose in the hope that it'll work the second time.

You've seen how WinSock and NBT resolve names; now you're ready to look at the "battle of the network names"...

What If DNS and WINS Conflict?

Here's a question that I get in class sometimes. I present it here mainly as a review of what you've read so far.

WINS will generally have accurate name information for your local domain, at least among the WINS-aware machines, as it gets its naming information from the horse's mouth, so to speak; you can't *use* a WINS name server unless you *contribute* a bit of information—i.e., address information about yourself. DNS, in contrast, gets its information from people typing data into ASCII files, so the data could be wrong. That leads students to the following question.

What if you have a Microsoft networking client that is not only WINS-aware, but also uses a DNS server: in that case, which name service does the workstation query first? Suppose you have a machine named ollie.acme.com whose IP address is 207.88.52.99. Not only does WINS know of ollie, DNS does too—but suppose DNS incorrectly thinks that ollie's IP address is 207.88.52.100. Type **ping ollie.acme .com**, and what will happen? Will the system look to the ".99" address, or the ".100" address?

Do you see how to answer this question? First, ask yourself: "Is this a WinSock or a NBT name resolution request?" As the application is ping, the answer is "WinSock." Go to the WinSock name resolution flowchart, and you see that the DNS server gets first crack at answering the name resolution request.

Now, that was the answer for a WinSock resolution, but what about an NBT resolution? For example, suppose I open up a command line and type **nbtstat -a xyz.nyoffice.mmco.com**. What will happen?

This is a bit of a trick question. First of all, understand that NBTSTAT takes a *NetBIOS* name as a parameter, and I've specified a WinSock name. An NBT resolution will choke on that "xyz.nyoffice.mmco.com" name, as it's way over 15 characters. So it truncates it after the 15th character, and does an NBT name resolution on "xyz.nyoffice.mm."

There's a lot more to network name resolution on NT networks than I guessed when I first looked into this, as you can see, but now you're equipped with all the information that you need to tackle a mystery along the lines of "machine X says it can't see machine Y."

Now you know the ins and outs of installing and configuring TCP/IP. It's time to learn how to use the oldest TCP/IP tool—the Telnet remote login program.

Using Telnet for Remote Login

In the early days of TCP/IP and internetting, people's first concern was getting onto other people's computers. For instance, suppose I worked at the John Von Neumann Supercomputing Center, and I had written a fantastic celestial motion simulator—a program that could compute the location of thousands of planets, planetoids, and comets in the Solar System. Suppose also that I had developed this with government money, and so the Feds wanted to offer this simulator to everyone. Well, how does one get to this simulator?

In all likelihood, in order to get to this program, you'd have to come to the Von Neumann center. That's true for two reasons. First, I developed it on a supercomputer for a good reason—it's too darn big to fit anywhere else. Stick it on a normal computer, and it'll take weeks to get an answer to a simple question like, "When will Jupiter and Mars next be near to each other and high in the night sky?" The second reason is that we're back in the early days of internetting, recall, and in those days programs were generally specific to the machines that they were built on. Moving this program to another computer would be a pain in the neck, even *if* I were willing to put up with the slower speed. So it seems that the most likely way to offer this service to everyone is to put some modems on the Von Neumann system and allow anyone to dial into the system in order to access this program. And, in fact, things like that have been done—but they end up generating awfully large phone bills for the people on the other side of the country.

Telnet solves this problem. It lets me work on the terminal or computer on my desk and access other hosts just as if I were there on-site—in the case of the Von Neumann center, just as if I were right at Princeton, New Jersey, where the center is located. Now, there *is* no publicly-available astronomical simulator at Von Neumann, not at least as far as I know, so I can't show you anything like that. What I *can* show you is Archie, an essential Internet tool.

Seeing What's Out There: Using Archie

As we'll discuss later, *the* Internet is a very big source of information, from recipes to rutabaga farming tips to religion, which leads to the question, "How do I know what's available on the Internet?" There are three main ways to find out what's on the Internet, and one is Archie. There are a large number of computers—*hosts*, they're called—on the Internet that hold files that are available for public downloading and use; for example, something called Project Gutenberg puts the text of some well-known books on servers, available for anyone to download. But, again, how would you find out about the existence of these things? Ask Archie.

Site	Location
archie.rutgers.edu	NE US
archie.sura.net	SE US
archie.unl.edu	Western US
archie.ans.net	The Internet backbone

Site	Location
archie.mcgill.ca	Canada
archie.funet.fi	Europe
archie.doc.ic.ac.uk	United Kingdom
archie.au	Australia and Pacific Rim

Archie is available on several servers around the world. It's best to hook up to the Archie server closest to you so as to minimize network traffic. For example, there is quite limited data transfer capability to England, so, although using the UK Archie server might seem cosmopolitan, it's a fairly inconsiderate thing to do if you're internetting from the U.S. I'll hook up to Archie at Rutgers.

I'll do the Telnet login from the command line. Once the session is active, however, I'll automatically be shifted to the NT Terminal program. I remotely log onto Archie in New Jersey by typing **telnet archie .rutgers.edu**.

After some introductory things, I get a prompt that says, "Login?" I respond by typing **archie**. Now, not every Telnet site will require a login. Some just drop you right into the middle of the application. Others may require that you get an account for their service, and they may charge you money for using whatever service they're purveying over the Net— that's fair game. Expect to see more and more services on the Internet that are for-pay—the net is slowly going commercial. Anyway, I get a prompt that says "archie>", indicating that when I type something now, when I make a request for information, then that request is not being processed by the computer in Connecticut, but rather by the computer running Archie at Rutgers University in New Jersey. Usually the help command works, and it does in this case as well. Next, I'll tell Archie that, when I ask it for a file's name, it shouldn't show me only the files whose names match exactly—it should show me *anything* that contains what I'll type. I do this by typing **set sub**. Now, if you do this, then be very careful about what you ask for—search for "e" and you get every file that's got an "e" in its name! I'm going to look for a server that's got the text of *Alice's Adventures in Wonderland* on it, so I'll look for files that contain the word "alice." I do that by typing the command **prog**, which asks for a search of programs, and `alice`. The search shows me…

```
login: archie
Last login: Thu Oct 7 06:06:29 from bix.com
SunOS Release 4.1.3 (TDSERVER-SUN4C) #2: Mon Jul 19 18:37:02 EDT 1993

# Bunyip Information Systems, 1993

# Terminal type set to `vt100 24 80'.
# `erase' character is `^?'.
# `search' (type string) has the value `sub'.
archie> prog alice
# Search type: sub.
# Your queue position: 1
working...

Host cair.kaist.ac.kr  (143.248.11.170)
Last updated 10:29 4 Oct 1993

Host uceng.uc.edu  (129.137.189.1)
Last updated 20:43 3 Oct 1993

  Location: /pub/wuarchive/doc/misc/if-archive/games/source/gags
    FILE  -r--r--r--  16681 bytes 01:00 18 Mar 1993 alice.zip


Host ftp.sunet.se  (130.238.127.3)
Last updated 11:48 6 Oct 1993

  Location: /pub/etext/gutenberg/etext91
    FILE  -r--r--r--  162153 bytes 22:00 17 Sep 2000 alice29.txt


Host roxette.mty.itesm.mx  (131.178.17.100)
Last updated 21:26 2 Oct 1993

  Location: /pub/next/Literature/Gutenberg/etext91
    FILE  -r--r--r--  64809 bytes 00:00 1 May 1992 alice29.zip
```

```
Host ftp.wustl.edu  (128.252.135.4)
Last updated 20:43 2 Oct 1993

  Location: /mirrors/misc/books
    FILE  -rw-r--r--  64809 bytes 00:00 15 Jun 1992 alice29.zip

Host ftp.wustl.edu  (128.252.135.4)
Last updated 20:43 2 Oct 1993

  Location: /systems/amiga/aminet/text/tex
    FILE  -rw-rw-r--  5593 bytes 05:13 27 Sep 1993 decalice.lha
    FILE  -rw-rw-r--   254 bytes 05:13 27 Sep 1993 decalice.readme

  Location: /systems/amiga/boing/video/pics/gif
    FILE  -rw-rw-r-- 109870 bytes 01:00 8 Feb 1993 palice.jpg
archie> bye
# Bye.
Connection closed by foreign host.
```

Notice that every group of information starts off with host; that's important, as that's the name of the place that we'd have to go in order to get Alice. Then there's a filename. The parts in front of it are exactly *where* the file is. If you're a PC user, then you may, at first glance, think that you recognize the subdirectory usage, but look again! Instead of backslashes, which DOS uses to separate subdirectory levels, Unix uses *forward* slashes!

Anyway, now we've found Alice. We'll quit Archie by typing `quit`. The message, `Connection closed by foreign host`, is a message from my computer to me. It says that the Archie computer at Rutgers—which it calls the *foreign host*, has stopped talking to me.

Non-Standardization Problems

In general, Telnet works fine with computers of all kinds. But some host computers just plain won't talk to you unless you're an IBM 3270-type dumb terminal, so there is another program, tn3270. Tn3270 is a variation of Telnet that emulates an IBM 3270 full-screen type terminal.

The main things to know about tn3270 are that 3270-type terminals have a *lot* of functions about them. Not all implementations of tn3270 are equal, so don't be totally shocked if you Telnet to an IBM site using tn3270, work for awhile, and get a message `Unexpected command sequence–program terminated`. It means that your tn3270 couldn't handle some command that the IBM host sent it. And IBM terminal emulation can be a real pain in the neck when it comes to key mapping. On the IBM terminal are a set of function keys labeled PF1, PF2, and so on. As there are no keys labeled like that on a PC or a Mac, what key should you press to get PF4, for instance? Well, it's Esc-4 on some implementations of tn3270, F4 on some others, and there doesn't seem to be any real agreement either on what the key is, or what the key should be. Make sure that you have the documentation for your tn3270 somewhere around before you start Telnetting to an IBM host.

TIP   There is no tn3270 shipped with NT.

Why Use Telnet?

Summing up this section, what is Telnet good for, anyway? Several things. First, it is the way to access a number of specialized basic information services. For instance, many large libraries put their entire card catalog on Telnet servers. University researchers can then look for an item, and request it through interlibrary loan. Another example can be found in the University of Michigan's geographic server, a service offering geographic information—just type **telnet martini.eecs.umich .edu 3000**, and you're in.

```
access% telnet martini.eecs.umich.edu 3000
Trying 141.212.99.9...
Connected to martini.eecs.umich.edu.
Escape character is '^]'.
# Geographic Name Server, Copyright 1992 Regents of the
University of Michigan.
```

```
# Version 8/19/92. Use "help" or "?" for assistance, "info"
for hints.
.
arlington, va 22205
0 Arlington
1 51013 Arlington
2 VA Virginia
3 US United States
R county seat
F 45 Populated place
L 38 52 15 N 77 06 05 W
E 250
Z 22200 22201 22202 22203 22204 22205 22206 22207 22209 22210
Z 22212 22213 22214 22215 22216 22217 22222 22223 22225 22226
```

Or ask U of M for information about the weather by typing **telnet madlab.sprl.umich.edu 3000**, and find out whether or not it's raining in Dallas. Second, a commercial firm might want to offer an online ordering service: you just log on, browse the descriptions of the items available, and place an order electronically. A third, somewhat technical, reason for using Telnet is that Telnet can be used as a debugging tool. Using Telnet, I can essentially impersonate different applications, like FTP and mail (you'll meet them soon). That's a bit beyond the scope of this book, but I mention it in passing.

Then, the final reason for Telnet is simply its original reason for existence—remote login to a service on a distant host. That has become a feature of much less value than it was when it first appeared, largely because of the way that we now use computers. Twenty years ago, you would have had a dumb terminal on your desk. Today, you are likely to have a computer on your desk, a computer with more computing power than a mainframe of twenty years ago. We are less interested today in borrowing someone else's computing power than we are in borrowing their information—with their permission, of course. Specifically, we often seek to transfer files to and from other computers over an internet. For that reason, we'll consider another TCP/IP application—FTP, the File Transfer Protocol—next.

Using FTP for File Transfer

If you have a PC or Macintosh on your desk, think for a moment about how you use that computer in a network situation. You may have a computer elsewhere in your building that acts as a *file server*, a computer that holds the files shared in your facility or your department. How do you ask that server to transfer a file from itself to your computer? You may say, "I don't do that"—but you *do*. Whenever you attach to a shared network resource, you are asking that system to provide your computer with shared files. Now, how you actually *ask* for them is very simple: you just connect to a server, which looks like an extra folder on your desktop if you're a Mac user, or an extra drive letter, like X: or E: if you are a PC user. The internet world has a facility like that, a facility that lets you attach distant computers to your computer as if that distant computer were a local drive: it is called NFS, the Network File System. But NFS is relatively recent in the TCP/IP world. It's much more common to attach to a host, browse the files that it contains, and selectively transfer them to your local host. You do that with FTP, the File Transfer Protocol.

There are three essentials of FTP: how to start it up, how to navigate around the directories of the FTP server, and how to actually get a file from an FTP server. After that, we'll look at a special kind of FTP called *anonymous* FTP. So let's get started, by looking at how the files on an FTP server are organized.

FTP Organization

The first time that you get on an FTP server, you'll probably want to get right off. FTP, like much of the TCP/IP world, was built from the perspective that software's got to be *functional* and not necessarily pretty or, to use an overused phrase, user-friendly. If you're a PC user, the Unix file structure will be somewhat familiar, as the DOS file structure was stolen—uhh, I mean, *borrowed*—from Unix. Mac users will have a bit more trouble.

Now, I just referred to the Unix file structure. That's because FTP servers *usually* use Unix. But some don't, so you may come across FTP servers that don't seem to make any sense. For the purposes of this discussion, I'll assume that the FTP servers here are Unix, but, again, be aware that you may run into non-Unix FTP servers. The occasional FTP server runs on a DEC VAX, and so probably runs the VMS operating system; some others may run on an IBM mainframe, and so may be running either MVS or VM. Very rarely, an FTP server may run under DOS, OS/2, NT, or some other PC operating system. But let's get back to our look at a Unix FTP server.

FTP uses a tree-structured directory represented in the Unix fashion. The top of the directory is called ourfiles, and it has two directories below it—*sub*-directories—called ourfiles/bin and ourfiles/text, as shown in Figure 14.52. In the Unix world, .bin refers to executable files, files we might call program files in other operating systems, or, more specifically, EXE or COM files in the PC world or load modules in the IBM mainframe world. The text directory contains two directories below *it*; one's called contracts and one's called announcements.

A couple of notes here. PC users may think that things look a bit familiar, but there *are* a couple of differences. First, notice the subdirectory named announcements. That name is more than eight characters long—that's quite acceptable, even though it *isn't acceptable* in the PC world. Unix accepts filenames of hundreds of characters. Second, notice that there are not *backslashes* between the different levels, but instead

FIGURE 14.52

An example of how files on an FTP server are organized

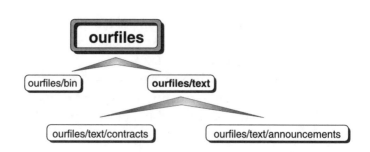

forward slashes; that's also a Unix feature. Now, what complicates matters for users of non-Unix systems is that FTP pretty much assumes that *your* system uses the Unix file system, as well. That means that you have to be comfortable with traversing *two* directory structures—the one on the remote FTP server, and the one on your local hard disk.

File Navigation

You get an FTP command line—I'll demonstrate it in a minute—that expects you to tell it where to get files *from, and* where to send files *to,* using these two commands:

- remote—cd

- local—lcd

That's because there's a tree structure on both the remote system—the one that you're getting the files from—and the local system. Let's look at a few examples to nail down exactly how all this cd-ing works.

Moving in FTP

When I enter an FTP site, I start out at the top of the directory structure. This top is called the *root* of the directory. In my example, the root is called ourfiles. To move down one level, to ourfiles/text, I could type **cd files**. That says to FTP, "Move down one level relative to the current location." Alternatively, you could skip the relative reference and say absolutely, "Go to ourfiles/text"—the way that you do that is by typing **cd /ourfiles/text**. The fact that the entry *starts* with a slash tells cd that your command is not a relative one, but an absolute one.

Now let's try moving back up a level. At any point, you can back up one level either by typing the command **cdup**, or by typing **cd ..** The two periods (..) mean one level upward to both DOS and Unix. Or you can do an absolute reference, as in **cd /ourfiles**.

Now suppose I'm all the way at the bottom of this structure. It's a simple three-level directory, and you often see directory structures that are a good bit more complex than this one. To move back up from ourfiles/text/announcements to ourfiles/text, you can do as before, and either type **cdup** or **cd ..** Or you could do an absolute reference, as in cd /ourfiles/text. To go back *two* levels, you can either issue two separate **cdup** or **cd ..** commands, or use an absolute reference, as in **cd /ourfiles**. To type two **cdup** or **cd ..** commands, you type the command, then press Enter, then type the second command. Do not try to issue two commands on the same line.

An Example of Navigation: Go Get Alice

Now that you can navigate the twisty passages of FTP directories, it's a good time to get Alice.

We found earlier that we could get the *Alice's Adventures in Wonderland* text at a number of sites. One of those sites was roxette.mty.itesm.mx, in the directory pub/next/Literature/Gutenberg/etext91. Let me FTP to that site and get the file. I type **ftp roxette.mty.itesm.mx**, and then I get a Name? prompt. This site doesn't know me, so I can't log on with a local name and password. That's where the idea of *anonymous* FTP becomes useful. You see, you can often log onto an FTP site and download data that's been put there specifically for public use. Anonymous FTP is just the same as regular FTP, except that you log in with the name anonymous. It responds that a guest login is OK but wants my e-mail address for a password. I put in my e-mail address, and I'm in. Now, it might be that there are places on this server that I *cannot* get to because I signed on as anonymous, but that doesn't matter—Alice is in the public area. Next, I can do a dir command and see what's on this directory.

```
ftp> dir
200 PORT command successful.
150 Opening ASCII mode data connection for /bin/ls.
total 2009
```

```
drwxr-xr-x 2 root     wheel    1024 Jun  2 02:48 .NeXT
drwxr-xr-x 3 ftpadmin daemon   1024 Apr  5 1993  .NextTrash
drwx------ 2 ftpadmin other    1024 May 20 22:46 .elm
-rw------- 1 ftpadmin other    1706 Sep 21 08:04 .history
-rwxr-x--- 1 ftpadmin wheel     186 Jul 21 1992  .login
-rwxr-x--- 1 ftpadmin wheel     238 Feb 25 1991  .profile
-rw-r--r-- 1 ftpadmin wheel      27 May 20 22:53 .rhosts
-rw-r----- 1 ftpadmin wheel     589 Jun  9 1992  .tcshrc
-rw-r--r-- 1 ftpadmin wheel 2027520 Oct  2 22:17 IRC.tar
drwx------ 2 ftpadmin other    1024 May 20 22:46 Mail
drwxr-xr-x 2 ftpadmin wheel    1024 May 29 1992  bin
drwxr-xr-x 3 ftpadmin wheel    1024 Nov 11 1992  etc
drwxr-x--- 2 ftpadmin wheel    1024 May 19 01:31 mirror
drwxr-xr-x 6 root     wheel    4096 Jul 15 00:36 pub
226 Transfer complete.
863 bytes received in 0.6 seconds (1.4 Kbytes/s)
ftp> cd pub
250 CWD command successful.
ftp> dir
200 PORT command successful.
150 Opening ASCII mode data connection for /bin/ls.
total 20
drwxrwxrwt  6 root     daemon   4096 Jun 10 15:58 .NextTrash
-rw-r-----  1 jleon    wheel     205 May 29 02:42 .dir3_0.wmd
drwxr-xr-x  5 ftpadmin other    4096 May 19 01:47 X11R5
drwxrwxrwt  3 ftpadmin other    4096 Sep 26 03:04 incoming
drwxr-xr-x 20 ftpadmin other    4096 Oct  6 02:29 next
```

It's not a very pretty sight, but let's see what we can see. Notice all the *r*'s, *x*'s, *w*'s, and *d*'s to the left of each entry? That represents the privilege levels of access to this file. One of the important things is whether or not the left-most letter is *d*—if it is, then that's not a file, it's a directory. Notice that entry pub; it's a directory, but we already knew that, because Archie told us that we'd find Alice in the directory pub/ next/Literature/Gutenberg/etext91. I have to move to that directory to FTP it, so I type **cd pub/next/Literature/Gutenberg/etext91**.

Notice that there are no spaces except between the cd and the directory name, and notice also that, in general, you must be careful about capitalization—if the directory's name is Literature with a capital L, then trying to change to a directory whose name is literature with a lowercase *l* will probably fail. Why *probably*? It's another Unix thing; the Unix file system is case-sensitive. In contrast, if you found yourself talking to an OS/2-based TCP/IP host, then case would be irrelevant. How do you know what your host runs? Well, it is sometimes announced in the sign-on message, but not always. The best bet is to always assume that case is important.

Anyway, once I get to the directory, another dir command shows me what's in this directory.

```
ftp> dir
200 PORT command successful.
150 Opening ASCII mode data connection for /bin/ls.
total 7940
-r--r--r-- 1 ftpadmin wheel      885 May 1 1992 AAINDEX.NEW.Z
-r--r--r-- 1 ftpadmin wheel      885 May 1 1992 INDEX.NEW.Z
-r--r--r-- 1 ftpadmin wheel      876 May 1 1992 INDEX91.Z
-r--r--r-- 1 ftpadmin wheel     1170 Oct 2 07:01 Index
-r--r--r-- 1 ftpadmin wheel     8575 May 1 1992 LIST.COM.Z
-r--r--r-- 1 ftpadmin wheel     8917 May 1 1992 README.Z
-r--r--r-- 1 ftpadmin wheel    98605 May 1 1992 aesop10.txt.Z
-r--r--r-- 1 ftpadmin wheel   101607 May 1 1992 aesop10.zip
-r--r--r-- 1 ftpadmin wheel    67597 May 1 1992 alice29.txt.Z
-r--r--r-- 1 ftpadmin wheel    64809 May 1 1992 alice29.zip
-r--r--r-- 1 ftpadmin wheel   435039 May 1 1992 feder11.txt.Z
-r--r--r-- 1 ftpadmin wheel   463269 May 1 1992 feder11.zip
-r--r--r-- 1 ftpadmin wheel    14841 May 1 1992 highways.apl.Z
-r--r--r-- 1 ftpadmin wheel    79801 May 1 1992 hisong10.txt.Z
-r--r--r-- 1 ftpadmin wheel    75310 May 1 1992 hisong10.zip
-r--r--r-- 1 ftpadmin wheel    75541 May 1 1992 lglass16.txt.Z
-r--r--r-- 1 ftpadmin wheel    73128 May 1 1992 lglass16.zip
-r--r--r-- 1 ftpadmin wheel   606033 May 1 1992 moby.zip
-r--r--r-- 1 ftpadmin wheel   530686 May 1 1992 mormon12.txt.Z
-r--r--r-- 1 ftpadmin wheel   529476 May 1 1992 mormon12.zip
-r--r--r-- 1 ftpadmin wheel   129601 May 1 1992 opion10.txt.Z
-r--r--r-- 1 ftpadmin wheel   138296 May 1 1992 opion10.zip
-r--r--r-- 1 ftpadmin wheel   203785 May 1 1992 plboss10.txt.Z
-r--r--r-- 1 ftpadmin wheel   219257 May 1 1992 plboss10.zip
-r--r--r-- 1 ftpadmin wheel   206661 May 1 1992 plrabn10.txt.Z
-r--r--r-- 1 ftpadmin wheel   221387 May 1 1992 plrabn10.zip
```

```
-r--r--r--  1 ftpadmin wheel     621855 May 1 1992 roget11.txt.Z
-r--r--r--  1 ftpadmin wheel     592247 May 1 1992 roget11.zip
-r--r--r--  1 ftpadmin wheel     657390 May 1 1992 roget12.zip
-r--r--r--  1 ftpadmin wheel      19790 May 1 1992 snark12.txt.Z
-r--r--r--  1 ftpadmin wheel      17184 May 1 1992 snark12.zip
-r--r--r--  1 ftpadmin wheel     789836 May 1 1992 world11.txt.Z
-r--r--r--  1 ftpadmin wheel     825269 May 1 1992 world11.zip
226 Transfer complete.
2214 bytes received in 1.4 seconds (1.5 Kbytes/s)
```

There are the files from Project Gutenberg, including *Moby Dick*, *Alice's Adventures in Wonderland*, *The Book of Mormon*, *The Hunting of the Snark*, *Roget's Thesaurus*, and more. Now, notice the Alice file is offered two ways—alice29.zip and alice29.txt.z. An extension of ZIP on a file usually means that it has been compressed using the PKZIP algorithm and probably on an MS-DOS system. The Unix counterpart to that is a file ending simply in Z, like the second file. It can be uncompressed with the gzip program that you can find on many libraries. More specifically, suppose you download alice29.zip to a PC. If you tried to look at the file, it would look like gibberish. That's because the file is compressed and must be uncompressed before it can be viewed. It was compressed so that there would be fewer bytes to transfer around the network; after all, this *is* a book, and you don't want to clog up the network with millions of bytes when thousands can do the job. You'd transfer this to your PC, and then you'd use an un-zipper program to un-compress the file. But the file that ends off with .Z, the one done with gzip, can be unzipped *while transferring!* Suppose you don't have a copy of either pkunzip or gzip, and don't want to have to mess around with finding an un-zipper. All you need do is to just request the file not as alice29.txt., but instead as alice29.txt. The FTP program is smart enough to know that it should uncompress the file as it transfers it to your machine! A pretty neat feature, I'd say.

Before we get the file, there's one more thing that I should point out. Years ago, most files that were transferred were simple plain text ASCII files. Nowadays, many files are *not* ASCII—even data files created by spreadsheets and word processors contain data other than simple text. Such files are, as you probably know, called *binary* files. FTP must be alerted that it will transfer binary files. You do that by typing **binary** at the ftp> prompt. FTP responds by saying Type set to I. That is FTP's inimitable way of saying that it's now ready to do a binary file transfer, or, as FTP calls it, an *image* file transfer.

Transferring a File

Now let's get the file…

```
access% ftp roxette.mty.itesm.mx
Connected to roxette.mty.itesm.mx.
220 roxette FTP server (Version 5.20 (NeXT 1.0) Sun Nov 11, 1990) ready.
Name (roxette.mty.itesm.mx:mminasi): anonymous
331 Guest login ok, send ident as password.
Password:
230 Guest login ok, access restrictions apply.
ftp> cd pub/next/Literature/Gutenberg/etext91
250 CWD command successful.
ftp> binary
200 Type set to I.
ftp> get alice29.zip
200 PORT command successful.
150 Opening BINARY mode data connection for alice29.zip (64809 bytes).
226 Transfer complete.
local: alice29.zip remote: alice29.zip
64809 bytes received in 16 seconds (4 Kbytes/s)
ftp> bye
221 Goodbye.
access%
```

Notice that once I got the file, the system reported some throughput statistics.

Now, when we get the file, it'll take some time to transfer. There's no nice bar graphic or anything like that to clue us about how far the transfer has proceeded. There *is* a command, however, that will give you *some* idea about how the transfer is progressing—*hash*. Type **hash**, and from that point on, the system will print an octothorpe (#) for each

2K of file transferred. For example, say I'm on a Gutenberg system and I want to download the Bible, bible10.zip. (Is it sacrilegious to compress the Bible? Interesting theological question.) The file is about 1600K in size, so I'll see 800 octothorpes.

Each line shows me 80 characters, so each line of # characters means 160K of file was transferred. It'll take ten lines of # characters (*ten lines!*) before the file is completely transferred. (Why does this take so long on my system? Well, the Internet is pretty fast, but my connection to it is just a simple v.32 bis modem. My company's part of the information superhighway, but we're kind of an unimproved country road.)

FTP versus Telnet

Now let's review what we've seen so far. First, you use the FTP program to log onto a remote system, in a manner similar to Telnetting onto a remote system. In fact, some people have trouble understanding why there's a difference between Telnet and FTP. Telnet is for terminal emulation into another facility's computing power; FTP is for transferring files to and from another facility's computers. Once you FTP to another site, you find that the site usually has their files organized into a set of directories arranged in a tree structure. You move FTP's attention from one directory to another with the CD command. *You*, also, may have a tree-structured directory on your system; if you wish to tell FTP to transfer to or from a particular directory, then you use the local CD command, or lcd. You use the binary command to tell FTP that you're going to transfer files that aren't simple ASCII. The "get" command requests that the remote system give you a file, and, although I haven't mentioned it yet, the "put" command requests that the remote system *accept* a file from you. And those are the basics of FTP, the File Transfer Protocol.

Downloading to the Screen

But let's go to *another* Gutenberg site to illustrate another helpful tip. I noticed earlier when I was using Archie that there was a location that had Alice called ftp.wustl.edu. Let's see what *they've* got—maybe a newer version, perhaps? Now, I know that you're thinking, "A newer version of *Alice's Adventures in Wonderland*? Isn't Lewis Carroll dead?" Well, yes, Mr. Dodgson is long gone, but the text is typed in by volunteers, and mistakes creep in. First, we'll get off this current FTP site by typing **BYE**. That command may vary, but it seems pretty standard for most of the FTP and Telnet world. Again, it informs me that I'm disconnected from the roxette site. I'll FTP to ftp.wustl.edu now…again, I'm doing *anonymous* FTP, so I type in a username **anonymous**—lowercase, remember—and use my e-mail address mminasi@access.digex.net as the password. You don't see that because the password doesn't echo. I get the usual chatter, and then I'm in. Now, Archie told me that Alice was in mirrors/misc/books, so I'll cd over to there—**cd mirrors/misc/ books**—and do a dir to see what's there.

```
ftp> dir
200 PORT command successful.
150 Opening ASCII mode data connection for /bin/ls.
total 12060
-rw-r--r--  1 root    archive     3110 May 1 18:00 00-index.txt
-rw-r--r--  1 root    archive   552711 Apr 16 18:00 2sqrt10.zip
-rw-r--r--  1 root    archive   102164 Jun 15 1992 aesop11.zip
-rw-r--r--  1 root    archive    32091 Jun 18 1992 aesopa10.zip
-rw-r--r--  1 root    archive    15768 Apr 16 18:00 alad10.zip
-rw-r--r--  1 root    archive    64809 Jun 15 1992 alice29.zip
-rw-r--r--  1 root    archive   244863 Dec 2 1992 anne10.zip
-rw-r--r--  1 root    archive  1636512 Jun 18 1992 bible10.zip
-rw-r--r--  1 root    archive   358371 Jun 18 1992 crowd13.zip
-rw-r--r--  1 root    archive    50736 Apr 16 18:00 dcart10.zip
-rw-r--r--  1 root    archive   102460 Jun 18 1992 duglas11.zip
-rw-r--r--  1 root    archive   467260 Jun 15 1992 feder15.zip
-rw-r--r--  1 root    archive    78337 Jun 15 1992 hisong12.zip
-rw-r--r--  1 root    archive   136293 Jun 18 1992 hrlnd10.zip
-rw-r--r--  1 root    archive    70714 Oct 23 1992 hyde10.zip
-rw-r--r--  1 root    archive    69860 Oct 23 1992 hyde10a.zip
-rw-r--r--  1 root    archive   176408 Apr 16 18:00 iland10.zip
-rw-r--r--  1 root    archive    73128 Jun 15 1992 lglass16.zip
-rw-r--r--  1 root    archive   149481 Apr 16 18:00 locet10.zip
-rw-r--r--  1 root    archive   606033 Jun 15 1992 moby.zip
-rw-r--r--  1 root    archive   513720 Jun 15 1992 mormon13.zip
-rw-r--r--  1 root    archive    11579 Apr 16 18:00 nren210.zip
-rw-r--r--  1 root    archive   103284 Jun 18 1992 oedip10.zip
```

```
-rw-r--r--   1 root     archive    95167 Apr 16 18:00 ozland10.zip
-rw-r--r--   1 root     archive   692080 Apr 16 18:00 pimil10.zip
-rw-r--r--   1 root     archive   217770 Jun 15 1992  plboss11.zip
-rw-r--r--   1 root     archive   214541 Jun 18 1992  plrabn11.zip
-rw-r--r--   1 root     archive    44204 Apr 16 18:00 rgain10.zip
-rw-r--r--   1 root     archive   580335 Jun 15 1992  roget13.zip
-rw-r--r--   1 root     archive   643011 Jun 15 1992  roget13a.zip
-rw-r--r--   1 root     archive   222695 Jun 30 1992  scrlt10.zip
-rw-r--r--   1 root     archive    35695 Oct 23 1992  sleep10.zip
-rw-r--r--   1 root     archive    17184 Jun 15 1992  snark12.zip
-rw-r--r--   1 root     archive    26009 Apr 16 18:00 surf10.zip
-rw-r--r--   1 root     archive    84641 Jul 31 1992  timem10.zip
-rw-r--r--   1 root     archive    38665 Jun 18 1992  uscen90.zip
-rw-r--r--   1 root     archive    63270 Aug 24 1992  uscen902.zip
-rw-r--r--   1 root     archive   161767 Jul 31 1992  warw10.zip
-rw-r--r--   1 root     archive    79409 Apr 16 18:00 wizoz10.zip
-rw-r--r--   1 root     archive   798086 Jun 15 1992  world12.zip
-rw-r--r--   1 root     archive   724062 Apr 16 18:00 world192.zip
-rw-r--r--   1 root     archive   912325 Jun 18 1992  world91a.zip
-rw-r--r--   1 root     archive   712389 Apr 16 18:00 world92.zip
-rw-r--r--   1 root     archive    71459 Jun 30 1992  zen10.zip
226 Transfer complete.
3008 bytes received in 0.34 seconds (8.6 Kbytes/s)
```

A whole bunch of things! Now, there's a file up top, called 00-index.txt, that looks like it could tell me what's going on. Now, I *could* just get the file. But think about what a pain that would be. First, I get the file. Then I disconnect from ftp.wustl.edu. Then I examine the file with a text editor. A lot of work just to find out what's in a README file. So there's a trick that you can use to see a file—just "get" it, but get it to your screen! You do that by typing **get filename -**, as I'll do here. I type **get 00-index.txt -** and press Enter. The file zips by, so it's a good thing that I have the ability to scroll text back. But what if I *didn't* have the ability to scroll text back? Then I could make the remote FTP program *pause* by adding **"| more"**—you need quotes around the vertical bar and the more. In this case, I'd type **get 00-index.txt - "| more"**. You can usually temporarily freeze a screen by pressing Ctrl+S for stop; you start it up again with Ctrl+Q.

Now, this depends on the system that you're working with, but it may only be possible to do this "get" and "more" if your FTP session is set for ASCII transfers rather than binary transfers. You can change that by just typing **ascii** at the command line. You see the response type set to A.

That's about all that we'll say here about FTP. There is lots and lots more that FTP can do, but I've given you the basics that you can use to get started and get some work done in the TCP/IP world. If this all looks ugly, user-unfriendly, and hard to remember then, well, it *is*, at least to someone used to a Macintosh or Windows. But there's no reason why a graphical FTP program couldn't exist, and indeed some are appearing. FTP is two things—the FTP protocol, which is the set of rules that the computers on an internet use to communicate, and the program *called* FTP that you start up in order to do file transfers. The FTP *protocol* doesn't change and probably won't change. But the FTP *program*, which is usually known as the FTP *client*, can be as easy-to-use as its designer can make it. So go on out, learn to spell anonymous, and have some fun on those FTP sites! But there's more to an internet than files, which is why we'll look next at electronic mail.

E-Mail on TCP/IP

Computers all by themselves are of little value for anything more than acting as a glorified calculator. Hooking up computers via networks has been the thing that's really made computers useful, and of course networks are a big part of communications. But networks are of no value unless people use them—and people won't use them without a reason. This brings me to electronic mail. E-mail is often the "gateway" application for people, the application that is the first computer application that they'll ever use; for some people, it's the *only* application that they'll ever use. And e-mail is probably the most important thing running on the Internet.

Despite e-mail's importance on the Internet, I actually don't have too much to say about it here, because Microsoft doesn't ship much in the way of mail tools. Mail on the Internet is implemented in two pieces. First, there's the mail transfer unit, or MTU. Then, there's the mail client.

The most common MTU is the program *sendmail*. Again, there's no NT version of *sendmail*, so you have to route mail with either a third-party product, or a mail router run atop another operating system. The same is true of mail clients, although Microsoft offers an Internet mail-compatible module for their Microsoft Mail product.

How E-Mail Works

The Internet mail system, like other parts of the Internet, uses a hop-by-hop approach to transfer data from one place to another. You learned earlier that IP transfers data via packet switching, a method allowing the Internet to move data from one point to another in under a second, even if the transfer is from one side of the globe to the other. With mail, in contrast, entire messages get sent from one node to the next, and are *stored* at each intermediate node until received by the next node. The hops may take minutes or even hours, but usually don't take more than a day. You've met Telnet and FTP so far; they are the oldest protocols in the Internet. In the case of both Telnet and FTP, there are two meanings for each word: there is a Telnet *protocol*, as well as a program that allows you to use the Telnet protocol to do remote logins, the Telnet *client* program. Similarly, FTP is both a protocol that describes how to transfer a file and a program that uses the FTP protocol to transfer files—that program is called an *FTP client*. By the time e-mail arrived, it was clear that tightly matching protocols and clients weren't such a good idea, as they robbed the system of flexibility. So the e-mail protocol was developed, and an e-mail client appeared, but it's not the only e-mail client used; in fact, there's probably no one e-mail client that's used by the majority of users. The e-mail protocol, by the way, is called SMTP, the Simple Mail Transfer Protocol. The clients vary widely in that they can be sometimes graphical, sometimes textual, sometimes very easy to work with, and sometimes extremely primitive.

E-Mail Security Concerns

As the Internet grows, more and more gateways will be built to other e-mail systems. You can't get everywhere, but, in time, you'll be able to reach anyone from the Internet. Now, that's a good thing, but as e-mail becomes more important, it's also essential to keep your mind on the fact that e-mail is *not secure*. Your mail packets get bounced all around the Internet, as you know—but think about what that means. Suppose you send a message to someone on the Internet, and my computer is part of the Internet—a piece, as it happens, that sits between you and the person to whom you're sending mail. Mail can sit in intermediate computers like mine, *on the hard disk*, for seconds, minutes, or hours at a time. It's a simple matter to use any number of utility programs to peek into the mail queue on the mail that's "just passing through." *Never* say anything on mail that you wouldn't want as public knowledge. Even if someone doesn't peek at your mail, that someone probably backs up his or her disk regularly, meaning that the message may sit on magnetic media for years in some archive. I sometimes imagine that in the middle of the 21st century, we'll see "the unpublished letters of Douglas Adams"—e-mail notes that someone stumbled across while picking through some 70-year-old backups; you know, it'll be the latter-day equivalent of going through some dead celebrity's trash. Anyway, the bottom line is: don't write anything that you wouldn't want your boss, your spouse, your parents, or your kids to read.

A Brief Summary to a Very Long Chapter

In this chapter, you've been introduced to internets and *the* Internet, the underlying whys and wherefores, and hopefully you have a little insight into why using the TCP/IP protocol suite in your business is an efficient, intelligent, money-saving thing to do. You should also now be equipped to go out and Telnet to foreign lands, to FTP megabytes of data treasures, and to talk to friends and associates far and near via e-mail. Internet vets call Internet exploration *surfing the net*— the surf's never been up like this, even if your company's internet doesn't connect to *the* Internet.

CHAPTER

FIFTEEN

Tuning and Monitoring Your NT Server Network

Even without any tuning, NT Server usually offers better performance than many other networks. It's a good thing that NT tunes itself well, because Microsoft didn't leave us many "levers" with which to tune an NT Server. But there *are* a few such levers, and a little adjustment can increase the responsiveness of your network. All networks are built out of components from many vendors. Only with a systematic approach (and a few tools) can you hope to track down network failures. This chapter offers a simple, down-to-earth approach to network troubleshooting that will get you the fewest network problems for the least money.

Using the Performance Monitor

If you can't measure it, you can't tune it.

NT comes with a number of measurement and monitoring tools, but the two best are the Performance Monitor, or Perfmon, and the Network Monitor, or Netmon. Of the two, Perfmon is by far the more powerful. Learning to use the Performance Monitor correctly is useful if you want to reduce the amount of work you have to do to maintain the network. (You learn about Network Monitor in Chapter 16.)

The Performance Monitor can

- Log minima, maxima, and averages of critical system values;

- Send alerts to you (or any other network member) when important things occur on the network;

- Provide a simple, visual view of your network's "vital signs;"

- Log network data over a period of time and then export that data to a comma- or tab-delimited file.

Start up the Performance Monitor, and you see a screen like the one in Figure 15.1. The Performance Monitor comes up by default in Chart mode. There is also a Report mode, an Alert mode, and a Log mode.

FIGURE 15.1

Performance Monitor
dialog box

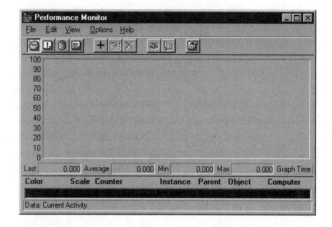

Charting with the Performance Monitor

Start out in the Performance Monitor with the Chart mode. Click Edit and then Add To Chart and you get a multitude of things that you can monitor. Let's pick an easy one to start. How many bytes per second is the server processing? Once you've clicked Edit and Add To Chart, you see a dialog box like Figure 15.2.

The Object drop-down list box lets you select the general area of items to monitor. The first one, which you can see in the dialog box, is the object Processor, a collection of information about your server's processor. Information is categorized as % Privileged Time, %Processor Time, % User Time, or Interrupts/sec. Each of these particular pieces of information is called a *counter* and is listed in the Counter box. For example, the piece of information that reports how many interrupts per second the system experiences (Interrupts/sec.) is a counter.

FIGURE 15.2

Add to Chart dialog box

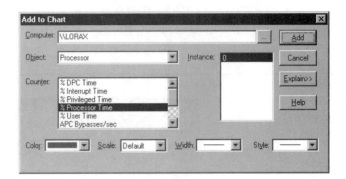

Notice also the Computer field. That's important; it means that you can use Perfmon on one computer to monitor another computer across a network.

Pull down the Object list box and choose the Server object. Now the Counter box shows the Bytes Total/sec counter. Click on the Add button. The Cancel button is renamed Done. Click the Done button and you see a screen like the one in Figure 15.3. This gives you some idea of how busy your server is.

FIGURE 15.3

Adding to the
Performance Monitor

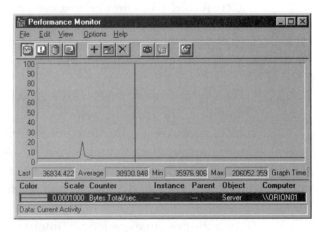

Notice that this server isn't terribly busy. But minimize the Performance Monitor, do some things, and come back to it later—after all, NT *is* a multitasking system, and it can do several things at once. Return to it after a while and you see Last (most recent bytes/second value), Average, Min (minimum value over the sampling period), and Max.

Server bytes/second is one of the basic counters that tells you how busy your server is. Other counters include:

- Percentage of processor utilization (object Processor, counter % Processor Time) tells you how CPU-bound the server is.

- Pages swapped in and out (object Memory, counter Pages/sec) shows you how frequently the server is swapping information from memory to disk. If this happens a lot, you know that you're running short of RAM and might want to add more to your server.

Additionally, you can monitor *several* servers at the same time. In Figure 15.4, I'm monitoring processor utilization on both LYDIA and ORION01, two servers on our network.

A quick look at this shows that one of the servers, ORION01, is doing a lot more work than is LYDIA, at least at the moment. But keep this

FIGURE 15.4

Monitoring several servers at once

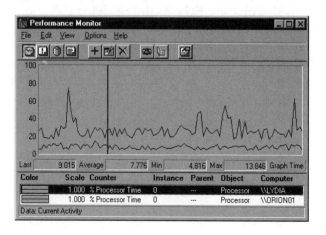

running for a while, and you can get the averages and extremes that you need to be able to say that with certainty. And, by the way, that leads me to an important note:

> **NOTE**   Running the Performance Monitor itself can significantly affect the performance of an NT machine. If you want to monitor a machine or machines, then do not run Perfmon on the machines; instead, run Perfmon on another computer—it can be an NT workstation rather than a server—and have that machine collect the data from the other machine or machines. Of course, this strategy isn't without a price, because all of the Perfmon messages generate network traffic, but that overhead usually affects things less than would running Perfmon on the measured machine(s).

What if LYDIA is a relative layabout compared to ORION01? Then you might improve performance for ORION01 users by moving a few of them over to LYDIA, if possible. ("Move a few of them" means move the directories that they use. As their data moves, they follow it.)

Tracking CPU Hogs with a Histogram

But suppose ORION01 *does* have a very high CPU utilization rate, and you'd like to find out *why*. Wouldn't it be nice to find out *what program* on the CPU was doing all the CPU hogging? You can do that with the Performance Monitor.

First, switch the Chart mode to a histogram. Click Options, then Chart. You see a dialog box like the one in Figure 15.5.

Under Gallery, click the Histogram radio button, then OK to return to the main Performance Monitor window. Next, insert the counters for each process in the system. Just click Edit and then Add to Chart..., and choose the Process object. You see the Add to Chart dialog box again (see Figure 15.2).

FIGURE 15.5

Chart Options dialog box

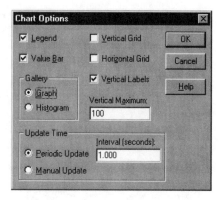

Notice that the Instance list box now names all of the processes active on your computer. One by one, you can click on a process's name in the Instance list box, then click Add to add that process to the list of things being monitored. You can easily select *all* of the processes by clicking one process, then pressing Ctrl+/. You don't want to select the _Total instance, as it's just a redundant sum of all processes, so Ctrl+click it to remove it from the list.

For example, my server shows the screen in Figure 15.6 when I monitor the processes running on it.

In this particular case, the process named System (whatever that is) grabs a fair amount of the CPU. Where could you use this? Suppose you used an NT Server in a client-server network, and the network bogged down. The machine acting as an application server might have more than one application server program running on it, and you could use this tool to find out which of the server programs was grabbing most of the CPU.

Some servers are CPU-blocked; others are memory-constrained and, in fact, it's more likely in the NT world for servers to be constrained by the amount of memory that they have than by their CPU power. To find out which processes are using what memory, just choose the Process object, choose the Working Set counter, and choose the processes with Ctrl+/, just like you did in the last example.

FIGURE 15.6

Performance Monitor
histogram

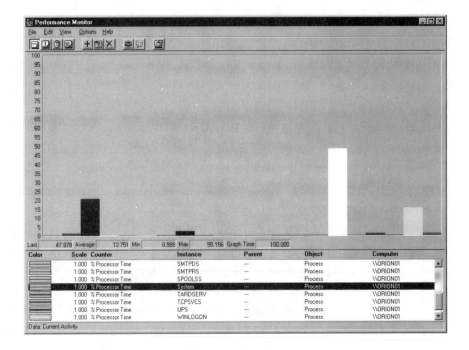

Building Alerts with the Performance Monitor

Another neat thing to be able to keep track of on a server is the amount of free space left on it; if it gets too low, a LAN disaster may follow. (The counter for free space on the server is part of the object LogicalDisk, with counter Free Megabytes.)

You probably don't want to have to *watch* the Performance Monitor to keep an eye on free server space. It would be nice if the server just came and tapped you on the shoulder when the free disk space dropped below some critical value. You control that with Alerts. Click View, then Alert, and the screen will change. Again, you have to add Free Megabytes to the list of observed counters, just as you did for the Chart view. The dialog box that you see when you try to add Free Megabytes to the Alert view, however, looks a bit different, as you see in Figure 15.7.

FIGURE 15.7
Add to Alert dialog box

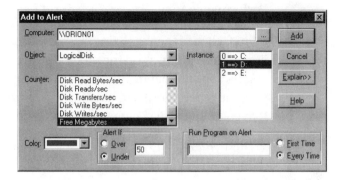

Now there are two new fields—Alert If and Run Program on Alert. I can tell the program to alert me if the disk shows less than, say, 50MB free by putting 50 in the Alert If field and clicking on Under. Notice that there are multiple instances in the dialog box because there are multiple drives on the server.

What does the system do when it sees less than 50MB free? You control that by clicking Options and then Alert. You see a dialog box giving you the option to either put an entry in the system log or send a message to either a machine name (like MICRON133) or a user name (like Mark). Unfortunately, you can specify only one recipient.

Note that the alerts are NetBIOS messages, and remember that the Messenger service and the NetBIOS interface must be active on both the alerting machine and the receiving machine.

Logging Data for Statistical Reports

Few things that a network administrator can do impress quite as much as those nifty utilization graphs. (Well, better network performance *is* more impressive, but that's why you're reading this book.) By logging statistical information you can later export that data to a graphing program or spreadsheet for reporting purposes. You can log your counters to disk with the Log View command. The log can then be read into the Performance Viewer later (Options, Data From) and examined.

First, choose the Log from the View menu. You see that you can add items to the log, as with the other views, but you can only specify entire objects to add. That means that if you wanted to monitor the number of interrupts per minute, for example, you couldn't tell the log to just keep that counter—you'd have to log the entire Processor object.

Then you click Log on the Options menu and give your log file a name. You also tell the Performance Monitor how often to update the log. Finally, you click the Start Log button. (It then becomes a Stop Log button so you can stop the logging process whenever you want. After all, there are lots of spotted owls in the Northwest... Sorry, couldn't resist that logging joke.)

To play back the log, click Options, then Data From. You can then chart data, but the data in the chart will be the logged data, rather than real-time data. To revert to real-time data, go back to Options ➤ Data From... and you see the option to return to displaying real-time data.

Exporting Logged Data to CSV Files

Perfmon has some rudimentary charting and table-preparation capabilities, but if you want to be able to do some really heavy-duty statistical analysis or reporting, then you have to turn to some other tool, like Excel. But a search of the menu options for Perfmon doesn't turn up a feature called anything like "export to Excel," and the lack of a cut-and-paste option means that Perfmon won't let you OLE its data, either.

How, then, do I get Perfmon data to another program? With this multistep procedure: First, you must log the objects that you want to export. Then, you tell NT to use that log file as data. You change over to Chart mode, and finally you "Export chart" to a comma-delimited file. Here's a more specific example: suppose I wanted to log the

% processor utilization over some period of time, then graph it in Excel. The counter % processor utilization is in the Processor object.

First, log the object:

1. Choose Log from the View menu to go to logging mode.

2. Click Edit and then click Add to Log to add the Processor object.

3. In the "Computer" field, type in the name of the computer to monitor; for example, I want to monitor ORION01, so I type in **\\ORION01**.

4. The counter is, again, Processor, so I click that, Add, and Done.

That doesn't start up the actual logging. To do that:

1. Click Options and Log.

2. In the dialog box that appears, type in the name of the file to log the data to (I used TEST.LOG), and click Start Log.

3. You can also set the logging interval, how often to get and save the data. Because I want to log this for a good long time, the default interval of 15 seconds is probably too frequent; I increase it to 120 seconds.

Then, once you have enough data, tell Perfmon to chart from that data:

1. Click Options, then click Log, and then click Stop Log.

2. Go to Chart from the View menu, and click Options and then Data From.

3. Choose the Log File radio button and enter the name of your log file.

4. Click OK to return to the main Perfmon screen.

Note, by the way, that this is a *log* file; it already exists and has data in it; therefore, the data will still be in there.

5. Click Edit and click Add to Chart, and you see that the Add to Chart dialog box has had its options reduced; you can only chart counters from the Processor object.

6. I choose % Processor Time, click Add, and Done.

Finally, to send that data out to a CSV file:

1. Click File and then Export Chart. You see a dialog box that controls how to export the data.

2. Choose a file name.

3. In List files of type, choose Comma Separated Variable (CSV).

4. Under Column Delimiter, choose Comma, and click OK.

The resulting file will be in CSV format, ready for import into many applications.

Tuning Your System: The Big Four

Well, now that you have a new weapon—Perfmon—you need something to point it to. A quick perusal of the Performance Monitor shows that there are *lots* of things to monitor, I mean *lots* of things. Watching them all would take more time than you have and logging it would require staggering amounts of disk space.

What I want to do next is to (1) introduce you to the art of tuning, (2) point out the most likely causes of problems for file servers and applications servers, and (3) recommend a few Perfmon counters that you can monitor to keep an eye on your network with minimum trouble.

Let me set the following scenario: you have a network up and running. But with time, the network seems to be slowing down. The Powers That Be start applying pressure on you to find out what's wrong and to find it out *now*.

What can you do? Well, the obvious thing to do is to throw money at it, right? Go buy more memory, an extra processor if it's an SMP (Symmetric Multiprocessor) PC; get a faster network card; get a faster disk; give the network administrator a big raise. (*Oops*—how *did* that proposal get in there?)

Doing those things *will* probably get you a faster server. But it's also a good way to throw money down a rat hole, save, of course, for the suggestion about the raise for you. If your server is spending all of its time waiting for the disk drive, then getting a faster CPU may indeed speed it up—but by a tiny percentage. Your money's better spent (logically) on a faster disk controller in this case.

In a few words, you tune a troubled server by locating and removing its bottlenecks. The big four sources of performance bottlenecks are

- The disk subsystem
- The network card and software
- The CPU
- The memory, which includes the RAM and the disk

Saying "remove the bottlenecks" isn't, strictly speaking, a meaningful phrase; it's kind of like saying "measure the top of the sky." That's because bottlenecks never go away; they just move. For example, suppose your goal is to get to work as fast as possible, and you're a law-abiding citizen. It's a 40-minute drive right now. The 30-MPH speed limits on local roads are, you feel, the thing keeping you from getting to work as quickly as you'd like. So you convince the local, state, and federal authorities to remove all the speed limits. The result: you now get to work in 26 minutes. But after a while you notice another limit: the other drivers. They get in your way, forcing you to slow down. So you decide to go to work at 2 A.M., when virtually no one's on the road. That's better: you're down to 18 minutes now. Ah, but that's when you realize that the *real* problem is your Ford Escort, with its maximum speed of 85 MPH. So you pick up a Porsche, reducing your commute to 14 minutes—*when* you make it in to work, that is; at 120 MPH, it's easy to wrap that Porsche around a lamp post. The final bottleneck, then, is a combination of the road (too many twists and turns) and you (reaction time's too slow).

Notice in my example, however, that removing each bottleneck saved time, but less and less time with each improvement. You often find that in networking, too. There is no way to remove all bottlenecks, but you can probably easily get rid of the *big* ones to get the most out of the time you devoted to tuning.

NT servers tend to either act as file servers or application servers. That's important information for tuning, because they tend to bottleneck in different places. File servers tend to respond well to increased memory as well as speedups in disk and network boards. Application servers tend to respond well to speedups in CPU and memory speed.

Solving Disk Bottlenecks

The disk drive has the dubious honor of being a source of bottlenecks both for file servers and for application servers. For file servers, the bottleneck is obvious; grabbing data and slapping it on the network is what file servers do. For application servers, the problem with the disk subsystem typically stems from the tremendous amount of memory needed to run application server programs. For example, Microsoft recommends 64MB of RAM for a computer running their Server Management System (SMS). It's simple with SQL Server or Exchange to start banging hard up against the amount of memory that your system has—and when that happens, the system goes after your disk drive for virtual memory. If that's the case, however, then the root bottleneck really isn't the drive, it's the memory. In fact, that's worth a note:

> **NOTE** The single best thing you can do for an NT Server is (usually) to add more memory to it.

You can recognize a disk bottleneck in a few ways. Look in the Performance Monitor and watch the object Physical Disk, and the counters Percent Disk Time and Disk Queue Length. If the percent of disk time is over 90 percent, there's a problem. Similarly, if the disk queue length exceeds the value 2, then the disk is a bottleneck.

You will not be able to record *any* disk-performance counters, however, until you run a program. On each server that you want to monitor, open up a command prompt and type

```
diskperf -y
```

This enables logging of disk counters; they're disabled by default because they slowed down low-speed 386 computers, so Microsoft thought it would be best to leave them disabled unless you decide to enable them. On a 486 or higher processor, you won't see any difference.

What can you do about slow disk performance? First, you can buy some new hardware. Let's see what to buy.

Fast Seek Times

There are two main measures of disk performance: seek time and data-transfer rate. Seek times are a characteristic of the particular drive you buy. Data-transfer rate is mainly determined by the type of disk host adapter you buy.

The faster the disk can find data, the less time we spend waiting for it. Drives nowadays have seek times in the single digits; buy them.

Better Data-Transfer Rate

Data-transfer rate is the province of the disk controller or host adapter. Here are a few features to keep in mind when purchasing a new disk controller:

- Buy 32-bit SCSI host adapters. Putting a 16-bit host adapter on your server chokes the server's ability to zap data out to the network.

- Use bus mastering host adapters. There are three methods to get the data from the host adapter to the computer's memory: programmed input/output (PIO), direct memory access (DMA), and bus mastering. Bus mastering is the fastest of the three. You can only bus master on MCA, EISA, or PCI buses.

- Get host adapters that support *asynchronous input/output*. Many SCSI-II or SCSI-III host adapters allow multiple drives to work independently. That means that you can buy a bunch of drives, hang them off a host adapter, and have all of the drives seeking at the same time. Note that most host adapters *don't* support this, meaning that you could have a host adapter with five hard disks on it—but only one of the drives operates at a time, so getting multiple drives doesn't do anything for your system's speed.

- I've been saying to "buy SCSI," and here's another reason: ATDISK and ATAPI, the built-in drivers for IDE and EIDE drives, *do not support asynchronous disk I/O*. That means that if you have a computer with two EIDE hard disks, they do not run at the same time. For example, suppose one of the drives is labeled C: and the other D:, and you copy a file from one to the other. If you could watch this copy on a millisecond-by-millisecond basis, you'd see that both C: and D: never run at the same time—they alternate. This wastes a lot of time, which is, again, why you want asynchronous drivers.

- Create stripe sets with multiple drives. Because a stripe set distributes a disk's data over several drives, reading the data can be quite fast, because all of the physical drives on the stripe set can work in parallel—assuming, of course, that you have an asynchronous host adapter.

If All Else Fails...

If you can't buy faster hardware, then try spreading the disk-intensive processes around. If you have several servers, then try moving applications from one server to another to balance the load. (Unfortunately, no Perfmon counter lets you find out which processes are running the disk the hardest.)

Tuning Network Boards and Drivers

Making your network boards work better is partly accomplished by making the software run better as well. Network I/O is a common bottleneck for file servers.

Network Counters: The Ones to Watch

In the Performance Monitor, look in the object Server to ferret out bottlenecks. Look at Sessions errored out, work item shortages, errors system, pool non-paged failures, pool paged failures, and blocking requests rejected. Another counter to watch is Network Segment/% network utilization. If you go looking for it, you probably won't find it; you must first load the Network Monitor Agent, which ships with NT (load it through the Control Panel's Network applet).

There is, however, one "gotcha" to running the Network Monitor Agent. As you know, most of the messages that run past your computer's network connection are ignored by the computer: a message from machine A to machine C passes machine B, but B's hardware will see that the message isn't for B, so it'll ignore the message. If, on the other hand, you load the Network Monitor Agent, that Agent will put your network card in so-called "promiscuous mode," where it takes note of *all* network traffic. While this is nice for logging general levels of network activity—and is essential if you want to monitor the Network Segment object—it *can* slow down your system a trifle.

The % network utilization value should remain below 30 percent on an Ethernet network, and below 90 percent on a token-ring network.

Simplify Protocols

One of the best pieces of network-tuning advice I can give you is to remove unnecessary protocols and services. Protocols and services steal memory and CPU time. Multiple protocols require multiple browse lists, which in turn steal CPU time from the machine that is the master browser, and NT Server machines are often elected as master browsers. One of the most common reasons why an NT system fails to recognize a workstation, leading to a "no domain controller was available to..." error message is that the server simply has too many protocols that it must listen to. Try to pick *one* protocol and work with that one.

If you're using the TCP/IP stack, then you find that it sometimes receives short shrift from the network because the more frenetic IPX and NetBEUI protocols grab more processor attention. As a result, the TCP/IP stack may end up dropping more messages than it would if the other protocols didn't exist; one other symptom is an incomplete browse list. If you can, remove extraneous protocols. If possible, just trim down to TCP/IP.

You can also click on the Bindings button, select NetBIOS, and choose the order in which the transport protocols are bound to NetBIOS. Basically, you're saying to NetBIOS (which is, recall, a network API, not a protocol), "When you have a message to send, send it with TCP/IP first; if that doesn't work, use IPX, and then NetBEUI." That's just one example; you can arrange them in any way that you like. If you are using TCP/IP and WINS, then binding NetBIOS to TCP/IP first will greatly reduce broadcasts in your system.

One Remedy: Segment the Network

If the network utilization is getting excessively high, you have to reduce the network traffic on that network segment. You can do that either by removing network applications—put the company Web server on a segment of its own—or by breaking up existing segments. Instead of three segments of 100 PCs, break it up into six segments of 50 PCs apiece.

But then you have to be sure to get good, fast routers to connect the network segments. NT servers can do the job fairly well on low-volume networks, but look to dedicated routers from companies like Compatible Systems, Bay Networks, or Cisco Systems for more heavy-traffic network segments.

Rearrange Your Redirectors

If you're running the NetWare redirector in combination with the Microsoft redirector, then you see a button in the Network dialog box of the Control Panel. (Actually, it's always there, but it's grayed out unless you have more than one redirector.) Click it and you will see both redirectors. You can then use buttons with up or down arrows on them to highlight a redirector and make it less or more relatively important.

Raise Server Priority

By default, the file server actually has a lower priority than does the print server, causing printing to slow down the server. Printing priority is set by default to 2, and file server priority is set to 1; larger numbers are better. You can change the priority by modifying the Registry. In the current control set, in Services\Lanman\Server\Parameters, add a value entry ThreadPriority, type DWORD, and set it to 2.

Modify How Often BDCs Update

All of the chatter between the PDC and the BDCs takes up processor time and network bandwidth. In NT 3.5 and later, you can alter how often the PDC updates the BDCs. By default, that time period is 300 seconds (five minutes), but you can change that in the current control set in Hkey_Local_Machine\System\CurrentControlSet\Services\ Netlogon\Pulse. It's of type DWORD, and you can set the value from 60 to 3600 seconds.

Use Interrupt 10

IRQ 10 has a slightly higher system priority than does the more commonly used IRQ 5, so employ it for your boards when possible.

Enable Shared RAM with TCP/IP

While there is no generally accepted benchmark for network performance that is both generic (runs on all networks) and nontrivial, my tests with TCP/IP drivers on Ethernet and token-ring cards show that if an option to enable shared RAM is on your network cards, then you should do it, and use as much as possible.

This does not apply for bus master EISA, PCI, and Micro Channel cards; shared RAM doesn't seem to improve upon their performance.

Get 32-Bit Bus Master Network Cards

Get 32-bit bus master network cards if you can afford them. You should be *sure* to afford them for your servers. But be sure that NT drivers exist for them.

Watching the CPU

I've already shown you how to build a histogram of the processes running on your server. That will help pinpoint any CPU hogs. Two counters can help you watch the overall CPU climate: Processor/% processor time and Processor/Interrupts/second.

Critical CPU Counters

If Processor/% processor time rises above 75 percent on average, then that PCU is working pretty hard. Also, you might keep an eye on Interrupts/second. If it exceeds 1000 on a 486 system or 3500 on a Pentium or RISC system, then more than likely something's going wrong, either a buggy program or a board spewing out spurious interrupts.

Handling Excessive Interrupts

One common cause of excessive interrupts is badly designed device drivers. Are you running any beta device drivers? I've seen beta video drivers that spew out thousands of interrupts per second. You can test this by running the standard VGA driver and comparing the interrupts before and after.

Another source of excessive interrupts are timer-driver programs. One network manager I know was seeing 4000 interrupts/second on a fairly quiet 486-based file server. After some playing around with the system, he realized that he was opening Schedule+ in his Startup group. He shut it down, and his interrupts/second dropped to a normal rate.

I'd like to tell you that there's a Perfmon counter that lets you track interrupts/second on a program-by-program basis, but there isn't because much of this is just trial and error. Now and then, I see a board that sends out a blizzard of interrupts if it's failing or, sometimes, even just when it's cold. You might see this when you turn a workstation on Monday morning and it acts strangely for a half hour, then settles down.

Move Programs Around

As I've recommended with other bottlenecks, one way to stop straining a resource is to stop asking so much of it. If you're running SQL Server 6.5 on a 25-MHz 486SX with 24MB of RAM, there's not much I can do to help you, except tell you to move SQL elsewhere.

Buying More Silicon

The ultimate (and least desirable) answer is to buy more horsepower. But don't just throw away your money. Remember that there are two ways to make your system faster with CPUs: either buy a faster CPU or add another CPU to an existing multiprocessor computer. (If you don't have them yet, think seriously about buying SMP systems for your big servers.)

You'll find that a second processor does not increase performance by 100 percent, unfortunately. And, sadly, for some programs a second processor offers no improvement at all. That's because not all NT programs are designed to be multithreaded, and so don't take advantage of extra processors. You can pinpoint single-threaded applications by watching Process/% processor utilization, and log activity on all of the processors. If you have a dual-processor system and one processor is working hard (up over 50 percent utilization) and the other processor isn't doing anything at all, that pretty much proves that the application is single-threaded and that you need to start yelling at the application developer!

NOTE   By the way, don't run one of those heavily graphics-intensive screen savers on a server. Something like 3Dpipes could suck up 90 percent of the CPU under NT 3.*x*. Microsoft says that changes in the NT architecture have removed the problem under version 4, but my experiments show that running 3Dpipes still slows down a file server.

Monitoring Memory

NT and NT apps are memory-hungry. Microsoft suggests 32MB of RAM for a SQL Server machine and 64MB for an SMS machine. Even a lowly file server does well with 16-plus megabytes. You can literally throw memory at your system for as long as you like and it will probably find some way to use it. How?

Checking Memory Status

Well, for one thing, NT uses an enormous amount of its memory—up to one half of it, in some cases—as a disk cache. The counters to watch are

- Memory/available bytes should be 4MB or more.

- Memory/pages/sec should be less than 20.

- Memory/committed bytes should be less than the physical memory on your system.

"Available bytes" is an attempt on Perfmon's part to answer the question, "How much memory could NT lay its hands on if it needed it?" If it's below 4MB, then it means that most of the memory in your system is not only spoken for, it can't be paged out to disk. That doesn't leave your machine much breathing room.

"Pages/sec" is a measure of virtual memory activity. Lots of paging means lots of juggling between the system's RAM and the disk, and the virtual memory system only does lots of juggling if it's running out of memory.

"Committed bytes" is the sum of memory that every application is using *and actually needs at the moment*. Applications start up and "reserve" memory, but they don't actually try to put data into a memory space without first "committing" the memory. If the applications in your system have collectively reserved 100MB of memory, that's no problem—it just means that there had better be 100MB of page file space on disk. But if all of the system's programs had *committed* 100MB of memory, that would imply that all of the applications running and active *right now* need 100MB—and if you don't have 100MB of RAM, your system will be constantly running the hard disk paging data in and out of the disk. Such a condition, called *thrashing*, means your NT Server will exhibit geologically slow performance.

Take a look at memory status in the Performance Monitor by looking at the Memory object, committed bytes, and pages/second. And make sure that the Available bytes is at least at a megabyte.

Controlling Virtual Memory

Why am I talking about disk usage in a section on memory? Because NT relies so heavily on virtual memory. If you supported Windows 3.*x*, then you probably learned about the paging capability of Windows, a method whereby Windows solves an "out of memory" problem on a computer by using extra *disk* space as if it were RAM space.

If you were a real Windows expert, then you knew that Windows had a particularly inefficient virtual memory algorithm, and that your best bet for Windows performance was to just increase your workstation's memory to 16MB and disable Windows virtual memory altogether.

If you tried to use that logic under Windows NT, then you found that Windows NT is quite different: it seems to require at least *some* virtual memory, no matter how much RAM you have. Oddly enough, that's because of the way that NT does disk caching—NT often allocates half of the system's RAM to a disk cache. As a result, NT is often in need of physical memory to allow it to run some program. So it starts paging.

You can adjust memory needs a bit under NT; open the Control Panel and go to the System tab, then click on Virtual memory, and you see a dialog box like Figure 15.8.

FIGURE 15.8

Configuring Server memory usage

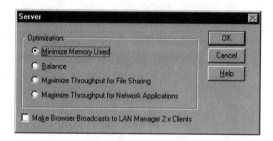

Use these guidelines to set this dialog box:

Optimization Option	When to Choose It
Minimize Memory Used	If the number of users will be under ten.
Balance	If the number of users will between 10 and 64.
Maximize Throughput for File Sharing	For more than 64 users. It allocates the lion's share of the RAM to the file server module.
Maximize Throughput for Network Application	On a client-server application server machine or a computer that will only serve as a domain controller.

The most time-consuming part about the paging process is going out and finding a place to put the data on the disk. So NT preallocates a large block of disk into an area that it gives a file name, pagefile.sys. This is a contiguous area of disk. You see, having a contiguous area of disk to work with allows NT to bypass the file system and do direct hardware disk reads and writes. (Remember, this is the kernel—ring 0 on an Intel system, "kernel mode" in general—so it can do direct hardware access.)

You control the amount of preallocated space on disk via the Control Panel; just click System/Virtual Memory, and you see a dialog box like Figure 15.9.

The pagefile.sys file starts out on a 16MB machine at 27MB. NT knows that it can get to up to 27MB of disk space with direct hardware reads and writes.

How much memory does an NT system require? I'd recommend at least 32MB on an NT Server. A workstation that I regularly use runs NT Server as its operating system. Despite the fact that I've got 64MB

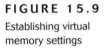

FIGURE 15.9

Establishing virtual memory settings

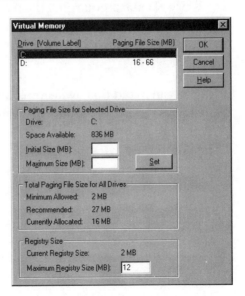

of RAM on it, it periodically starts running the disk for no apparent reason, meaning that it's juggling disk and RAM.

> **TIP**
> You can find out how much memory on an application can't be paged with an application called PMON, which ships with the *Resource Kit.*

Getting back to the virtual memory example, suppose I have a machine with 11MB of free RAM after the operating system. Add the 11 to the 27MB of pagefile.sys space, and NT has 38MB of working room, or, as the Performance Monitor would refer to it, NT on my machine has a 37MB "commit limit." If the sum of the programs that NT is running (called the *working set*) remains at about 37MB or less, then NT need not enlarge the paging file.

If, on the other hand, NT must get to more memory, it can expand the paging file, albeit at a cost of time. The paging file can grow up to 77MB on my system, meaning that NT can run up to 77 plus 11, or 88MB, of programs on this system before it runs out of memory.

Once NT starts enlarging the paging file, it may not enlarge it *enough.* That leads to a kind of "sawtooth" size of the paging file, as NT continues to "go back to the well" for more space until it finally runs out of space.

You can avoid this by keeping an eye on the commit limit on your machine. Add the counters Commit Limit and Committed Bytes to the Performance Monitor, and watch the difference between them. When the committed bytes exceed the commit limit, then NT must increase the page file size. If you're interested in seeing the size of the things that won't be paged, add the counter Pool Nonpaged Bytes.

One suggestion would be to log the committed bytes over a period of a few weeks with the Performance Monitor, then note the maximum value that the Performance Monitor reports. Increase that by a small amount—10 or 20 percent—and make your NT system's minimum pagefile that size.

Speeding Up Memory

You can't speed up RAM, but you can speed up the disks that virtual memory sits on. As with disks, just get fast drives and drive controllers. Get multiple drives and spread the pagefile out across drives—but *don't* put the pagefile on a stripe set; you won't get any performance improvement like that.

Defragment the drive that the pagefile sits on, run NTFS, and you squeeze the maximum out of your virtual memory.

Reducing Memory Requirements

Unfortunately, the best way to improve NT's memory hunger is to cut down on the features that you use, or, again, move the applications. Optional memory-hungry features include

- RAS

- TCP/IP support

- RAID

The other things that really chew up memory are the applications that you may run on your NT Server as applications servers, like SQL Server: it has a recommended memory amount of 32MB of RAM on the server.

One thing to look at, however, is the list of services. NT starts up a lot of services that you may not need. If your server doesn't have a printer, then the Spooler service is unnecessary. If all of your storage devices are SCSI, check to see if the ATDISK—the IDE interface—is active. In both cases, you can shut down a service or device. Even better, get rid of any protocols you're not using any more; they can be memory-hungry.

Locating Memory Leaks

Sometimes you see the free memory in a system just go down and down and down, even though you're not doing anything with it. Or you leave a server on Friday afternoon, go home for the weekend, and come back on Monday to find it crashed, with a message on the screen about being out of memory. You didn't do anything all weekend and hardly anybody is in the office on Saturday and Sunday. What happened?

A memory leak, that's what happened.

Memory leaks are caused by applications that have bugs in them that just make them ask for more and more and more memory from the operating system. They don't *do* anything with the memory, or perhaps they use the memory but don't manage it well. In any case, give them enough time and the memory leakers will kill your machine. Over the years, I've heard rumors of memory leaks in SQL Server, Access 95, and Visual Basic; I can't confirm them, but I've seen behavior that indicates that it's a possibility. In any case, you can locate memory leakers by logging the Process object. Recall that one of the counters for Process is *working set*; that's a measure of the amount of memory an application uses. Log the amount of memory that each process uses over time, and the leakers will stand out. Then talk to the company that wrote the application—with the perfmon output in hand—and get the vendor to fix the leak.

Tuning Multitasking

Go to the Control Panel and open the System icon. Click on the Performance tab and you see the dialog box shown in Figure 15.10.

On an NT Server, you definitely do *not* want the Maximum Application Response Time option. No one's going to run applications on your NT server anyway (unless it's an application server), and if they do, then it's probably just the administrator fooling around with the

FIGURE 15.10

Performance dialog box

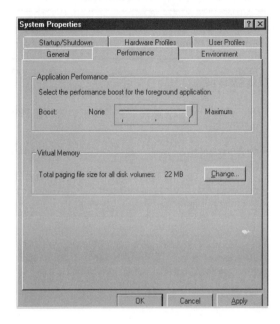

network. No need to slow everybody else down. Slide the arrow to None. Essentially, it says, "Don't give any special treatment to the foreground applications." Between Maximum and None, there is really only one middle setting in spite of the fact that it looks like you can set the slide bar to any number of positions.

A Tuning Summary

Before I leave this topic, let me summarize what I've said about which counters to watch, what their values should be, and what to do if they fall into the "danger" zone. My summary can be found in Table 15.1.

TABLE 15.1   Counters to Watch

Counter to Monitor	Good Values	If Not, Indicates Bottleneck In	Actions
memory/ available bytes	>= 4MB	memory	Buy more memory or move big processes to another server.
memory/ committed bytes	<= physical memory	memory	Buy more memory or move big processes to another server.
memory/pages/ sec	<=20	memory	Buy more memory or move big processes to another server.
processor/ % processor time	<= 75 percent	processor	Move processes, buy a faster processor, buy another processor if the app is multithreaded or if you're running many apps.
processor/ Interrupts/sec	<=1000 (on a 486), <=3500 (Pentium or RISC)	processor	Sometimes caused by badly written drivers, beta drivers; video drivers can be particularly obvious. Or failing hardware generates interrupt blizzards. Excessive queue lengths on network cards or disk controllers cause extra interrupts.
physical disk/ disk queue length	<= 2	disk	Faster disk interface, RAID, asynchronous disk drivers.
physical disk/ % disk time	<=90	disk	Move processes.
network segment/ % network utilization	<=30 on Ethernet	network	Segment network.

Growth Counters

Before I leave Perfmon, let me suggest a few counters that you may want to log simply because they indicate how large your network is:

- Server/Bytes total/second
- Server/Logons/second
- Server/Logons total

If any of these indicators grows quickly, the network in general is probably growing quickly, so you should zero in on bottlenecks or start planning to buy more hardware.

Understanding and Troubleshooting Browsers

Back in Chapter 2, I introduced the concept of browsers and browsing. Browsing is significant in that it can slow down a workstation's response time and clog a network with unnecessary traffic.

In case you've forgotten, browsing is a method whereby servers on the network tell a computer called the master browser who they are and what they offer to the users of the network. The browsing service in Microsoft enterprise networks makes it possible for a workstation to see what the network has to offer. A few specifics about browsing:

- The master browser designates one backup browser for about every fifteen computers.
- If you run multiple transport protocols, then each transport protocol needs its own set of browsers.

- Backup browsers re-verify their database with the master browser every 15 minutes.

- Servers first announce their existence to the master browser, then they reannounce their existence periodically. Eventually they settle down to announcing themselves only once every 12 minutes.

- If you are running a network on TCP/IP with routers, then there is one master browser for each subnet, and one overall "Domain Master Browser." They communicate with each other every 12 minutes.

Electing a Master Browser

The first browsing concept you should understand is the browser election. The first time a server (in the loose Microsoft sense of *server*, any computer that can share data, including a Windows for Workgroups, Windows 95, or NT workstation) starts up, it calls out for the master browser, so the server can advertise itself with that master browser. If no master browser responds, then the server "calls an election," suggesting the network's servers hold an election to find who would best be master browser. Elections are also held when:

- A master browser is powered down gracefully.

- A server powers up only to find that a master browser exists, but the master browser computer is of a lower station, so to speak, than the server. For example, if an NT workstation powers up and finds that its master browser is a Windows for Workgroups machine, the NT workstation calls for an election.

- A server powers up and has its MaintainServerList variable (I'll cover it in a bit) set to Yes.

If you're not a master browser, then you're either a backup, a potential browser, or you've opted out of the whole election process. (I'll show you how to do that in a minute.) Backup browse servers also help remove some of the load from the master browser, as they can respond to browse requests. TCP/IP-based networks add yet another layer with a *domain master browser*, but I'll get to that later.

When an election occurs, the master browser is chosen with a scoring system that works like this:

- NT Servers beat NT workstations, which beat everything else (Windows for Workgroups clients, Windows 95 clients, and LAN Manager servers).

- If there is a tie, the election goes to the primary domain controller, if one of the candidates is a PDC.

- If there is still a tie, then it goes to the machine using WINS—not as a server, just as a client.

- If there is still a tie (if all candidates use WINS), then it goes to the current master browser.

- If there is still a tie (there is no current master browser), then the election goes to a Preferred Master (you become a Preferred Master with a Registry setting IsDomainMaster, which you meet a little later).

- If there is still a tie, but one of the candidates is a workstation that has its MaintainServerList (explained in a few paragraphs) parameter set to Yes, then take that workstation.

- If there is still a tie, then it goes to the present backup browser.

- If there is still a tie, then it goes to the computer that has been up and running the longest, and if more than one computer is tied for that position, it goes to the one with the name that appears earlier in the character sequence. For example, machine BIGSERVER would come before MASTERSERVER, as *B* precedes *M* in the alphabet.

If you want to find out which computer is the master browser on your NT Server-based network, you can use the BROWMON.EXE program that comes with the Windows NT Resource Kit. When I start it up, I get an opening screen like the partial screen shot in Figure 15.11.

This screen shows that the master browser is \\SERVERTED. Transport refers to the transport layer used—NetBEUI, TCP/IP, or IPX/SPX. (DLC can't be used for anything other than printing services, and it doesn't work peer-to-peer, so there is no DLC browse master.) Essentially, this says, "\\SERVERTED is the browser for everyone speaking English on the network." This network could simultaneously support people speaking Greek or Spanish or Urdu, but the people speaking Urdu wouldn't be able to understand the browser broadcasts of the English speakers. For that reason, NT supports browsers for each network protocol, each language.

If I double-click on the highlighted line, I get a screen like the one in Figure 15.12. This shows me that two machines (EISA66 and SERVERTED) act as browsers on this network, and six machines (ADMINCLONE, BUDDY, EISA66, SERVERTED, SPEEDY, and TERPDOM) act as servers of some type. I can find out more details about EISA66's browsing by double-clicking on its line in the Browsers list box. I then see a dialog box like the one in Figure 15.13.

FIGURE 15.11

Browser Monitor
dialog box

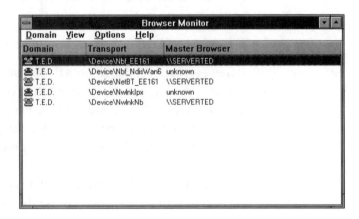

FIGURE 15.12

Browser status on
ORION dialog box

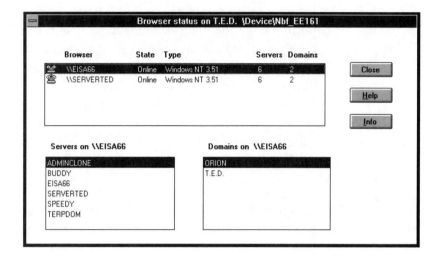

FIGURE 15.13

Browser Info dialog box

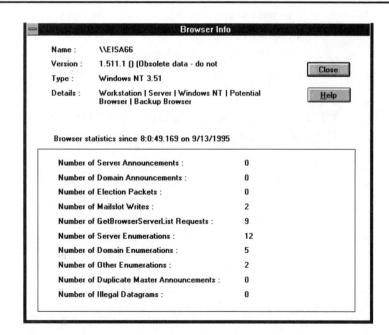

The Browser Info dialog box shows a number of things that we, frankly, aren't interested in, but a few interesting statistics are worth noting. First, look at the Details line. It says that this machine acts as both a workstation and a server, is the domain controller, and, among other things, is a backup browser and a master browser. Confusing as that may sound, it's normal: the master browser is *always* on the backup browser list. The Details line is very descriptive of a computer. For example, if I double-click on EISA instead of SERVERTED, I see Workstation | Server | Windows NT | Potential Browser | Backup Browser on the Details line.

The Browser Info dialog box says that these are the statistics for the browser since 8:00 on 9/13/95, when I last rebooted the server. I ran BROWMON at about 10:00 on 9/15, so these are statistics for about fifty hours worth of network browse mastering.

For example, Server Announcements, the first item in the box, are messages received by the browser master from machines on the network that are available to be servers. There are so many of those announcements because each server—that is, every Windows for Workgroups workstation, every NT workstation, and every NT Server machine—broadcasts its presence regularly.

Preventing Computers from Being Browser Masters

Elections can take a lot of time on a network. You can simplify the election process and cut down on the number of elections by forcing a Windows for Workgroups computer to never be the master browser. Do this by adding the following line to the [network] section of SYSTEM.INI:

```
MaintainServerList=No
```

You might do that if you didn't want to accept the performance hit that being master browser entails or if you're running a mixed NT/ Windows network. You see, it's possible to end up with an NT master browser and a Windows for Workgroups browse backup. The problem arises in that the Windows workstation must talk to the NT machine to exchange services information. The NT machine isn't allowed to talk to the Windows machine *for any reason at all* unless either the Windows machine has an account on that machine and is logged in or the NT machine has a Guest account that is enabled. If neither of those things is the case, the newly elected backup browser finds itself without any information, and the master browser essentially "keeps it in the dark." If the master browser goes down, then the browser can end up taking its place in a fairly ignorant state, leading to empty browse lists.

You can make Windows 95 machines ineligible for being browse masters either from the Control Panel (easiest) or, if you're feeling arcane, from the Registry. From the Control Panel, click Networks, then select "File and Printer Sharing for Microsoft Networks" from the list of installed network components. Click the Properties button to move to the next screen, and set the value of the Browse Master property to Disabled. To change the setting from the Registry, run REGEDIT.EXE, and find the entry MaintainServerList. (It's in HKEY_LOCAL_MACHINE\ System\CurrentControlSet\ Services\VxD\VNetSeup, but it's probably easier to press F3 to use the Find utility.) Set the value of MaintainServerList to 0 if it isn't already, and the Windows 95 machine will not serve as a master browser.

The default value of MaintainServerList is Auto, which means, "Make me a master browser if needed." You can alternately use a value of Yes, which means two things. First, "If there's a tie when electing browse masters, make me master browser." Second, "When I start up, always force an election." For NT workstations and servers, there is a corresponding Registry entry, MaintainServerList, which goes in HKEY_LOCAL_MACHINE\System\CurrentControlSet\ Services\Browser\Parameters. It is of type REG_SZ, and its value can be TRUE, FALSE, or Auto.

Browse Masters on a TCP/IP Network

On a TCP/IP network, things get a little more complicated when the factor of routers enters the picture.

Each segment of the network elects a master browser, as before. But one of the master browsers becomes the *domain master browser* (DMB). The DMB's job is to periodically ask the master browser on each segment (Microsoft doesn't have a name for them really, so let's call them Segment Master Browsers, or SMBs) for its local segment browse list. The DMB then compiles that into an enterprise-wide browse list and replicates it out to the SMBs. In general, you needn't worry about that at all, except for the fact that there are two Registry settings that you can use to tweak the browsing process.

Working in the Registry, you can give a particular machine an edge in becoming the DMB by adding a new value, IsDomainMasterBrowser, of type REG_SZ and setting it equal to TRUE. The value is in the key HKEY_LOCAL_MACHINE\SYSTEM \CurrentControlSet\Services\Browser\Parameters. The other possible value is, of course, FALSE, and it's the default.

If your network segments are connected over low-speed lines, then you might not want all of the chatter between the DMB and the SMBs. You control that with two parameters in the key HKEY_LOCAL_MACHINE\SYSTEM \CurrentControlSet\Services\Browser\Parameters.

By default, the DMB gathers browse lists from the SMBs and then replicates its consolidated browse lists to the SMBs every 12 minutes. You control how often this conversation goes on with a parameter MasterPeriodicity. It's a value of type DWORD and is expressed in seconds. The minimum value is 300 seconds (five minutes), and the default is 720 seconds (12 minutes). To make this Registry change, you must at least be running NT Server 3.51 with Service Pack 2 or higher; obviously, NT 4 doesn't need the Service Pack.

Refreshing a Browse List

In general, browse requests are resolved by either the master browser or a backup browser, so you never know who's provided your browse list. But you can force the system to browse via the Browse Master with the command-line command:

```
net view
```

Browsing with LAN Manager

Browse problems can also appear if you have LAN Manager 2.2 servers on the network. LAN Manager used a SAP-like approach, broadcasting data within network segments, making browsing across routers impossible.

Because NT and NT Server don't broadcast, they don't produce browser information that LAN Manager can understand. You can change that by enabling LAN Manager broadcasts in your NT machines, both server and workstation. Read the "How Do I" sidebar to find out how.

Why Isn't My Resource on the Browse List?

You can experience browsing trouble (i.e., the browse list isn't available or the list is incorrect) if computers do not exit Windows gracefully—that is, if they just get shut off without first exiting Windows. Such a computer may appear on the master browser's list for up to 45 minutes. Even worse, if a *browser* terminates unexpectedly, it may become impossible to browse for over an hour.

Remember if you can't see something on the browser, that's no big deal. If you know the universal naming convention for the resource—the name like \\markspc\c—then you can always just punch that value in or click Tools/Map Network Drive from the Explorer and get connected with no trouble, even if the browsers are all confused.

How Do I Enable LAN Manager to Understand Broadcasts?

To make LAN Manager understand broadcasts:

1. Open the Control Panel, and double-click on the Network applet.
2. Under Installed Network Software, choose Server, and then click Configure.
3. In the Server configuration window, select the Make Browser Broadcasts to LAN Manager 2.x Clients check box.

In a similar vein, if you have a LAN Manager domain that is on the same LAN segment as an NT domain but does not contain any NT workstations, then the LAN Manager servers will not show up on the browse lists unless you go into the Control Panel and, in the Computer Browser, set the LAN Manager domains to be "other domains."

And if you're using Windows for Workgroups workstations with LAN Manager servers but the Windows for Workgroups machines don't see the LAN Manager servers, add the following line to the [network] section of SYSTEM.INI:

```
LMAnnounce=yes
```

The Browsing Trail

Let's look in a bit more detail at how the browse service works. It may take up to 60 minutes for the browser to notice that a resource has disappeared, and in that time, the browser may erroneously report that something is available when it is not. Why does that happen? Here are the relevant numbers:

- Once a server has been up for a while, it reannounces itself every 12 minutes.

- A server must announce itself to stay on the browse list, but a master browser gives the server a "grace period" where the server can miss three announcements before the master browser drops the server from the list. In the worst case, that would be 36 minutes.

- If the network uses TCP/IP and is segmented, then there is a domain master browser, which is updated by the segment master browsers every 12 minutes. (Recall that this is the default value and can be changed.) Thus, in the worst case, the domain master browser might not see that a server is off the list until 36 plus 12 or 48 minutes go by.

- If your workstation is getting its browse list from a backup browser, rather than a master browser, then the master browser only updates the backup browser every 12 minutes; this *was* 15 minutes up to 3.51, but it was reduced to 12 minutes with NT 3.51. (Servers reannounce themselves to their local master browser every 12 minutes; master browsers and the domain master browser update each other every 12 minutes, and *that* gets sent to the backup browsers every 12 minutes. Seems like 12 is a mystical number at Microsoft, doesn't it?)

- Since, in the worst case, the master browser needs 36 minutes to figure out the server's gone, 12 more minutes pass before the domain master browser knows, and then 12 more minutes pass before the domain master browser tells a backup browser. Notice that in this analysis I even left out the small amount of time required for the domain master browser to replicate its browse list to the local segment master browsers, so in theory it could take even *longer* for the world to know that a server's dead!

New services, in contrast, are announced to the master browser immediately, and, again, the backup browsers may hear of them as much as 12 minutes later, so the longest that it should take for a new service to appear on the browse list is 12 minutes. But that 12 minutes can be a *long* time.

Adjusting the 12-Minute Interval

You have already learned that you can control how often the domain master browser and the local segment master browsers communicate. But you can also adjust how often a local master browser updates its backup browsers. Again, you've got to have NT version 3.51 with Service Pack 2 or a later version of NT in order to do this.

The value is in HKEY_LOCAL_MACHINE\SYSTEM \CurrentControlSet\Services\Browser\Parameters. It is called BackupPeriodicity, it's of type REG_DWORD, and it's measured in seconds.

Server Announcement Intervals

By the way, when I said above that servers reannounced themselves to the master browser every 12 minutes, I simplified the truth a bit. The whole truth is that when a service first starts up, it announces itself more frequently. New services announce at intervals of 1, 4, 8, and 12 minutes after they start, and after they reach 12 minutes, they announce at 12-minute intervals.

Each Protocol and Segment Has Its Own Browser

Another reason why you may not see a resource is that its server may be using a different protocol from your workstation. You see, the services offered by the NetBEUI-using machines are maintained on a different browse list than the services offered by the TCP/IP-using machines. There is a different master browser for each transport protocol except DLC.

By the way, how does the network know to hold an election if someone just pulls the plug on the master browser, and the master browser doesn't get a chance to force an election? The next time another computer asks for browse information and doesn't get a response, that computer forces an election.

If you are running TCP/IP, then resources may not appear on the TCP/IP browse list because the IPX and/or NetBEUI protocols are hogging the network's attention. If you can, remove the other protocols, and the TCP/IP browser will work more smoothly. (If you take the other protocols off the PDC, then be sure to re-enable MaintainServerList on some other machine, or NetBEUI and IPX will be without browsers.)

Why Is My Browser So Slow?

Set up Windows for Workgroups, accept all the defaults, and try to connect to a network drive with the File Manager (Disk/Connect Network Drive), and you wait for a couple of minutes. Why?

By default, WfW loads two protocols: NetBEUI and IPX/SPX with NetBIOS. Recall that the way a network-aware program communicates with the network is via the Application Program Interface (API). The API used by NetBEUI is NetBIOS and the typical API for IPX/SPX is Novell Sockets. But Microsoft has implemented a version of IPX/SPX that has a NetBIOS API on it. (Novell did the same thing long ago.)

Now, the Browser is just a network-aware application that depends on NetBIOS. So the Browser sees *two* NetBIOSes, the one atop NetBEUI and the one atop IPX/SPX. For some reason, that confuses it. Result: the long wait.

You can solve this problem simply. Just go to the Network Setup program in WfW and remove the IPX/SPX with NetBIOS item, replacing it with just IPX/SPX. The system will browse almost instantaneously. In general, getting rid of superfluous protocols will almost always improve performance.

Hiding a Server from the Browser

Now and then, you may want to put a server on your network that doesn't show up on the browse list. You already know that you can keep a share from showing up on the browse list by ending its name with a dollar sign ($), but can you do something like that for servers? Yes, with a little Registry or command-line fiddling.

To hide a server from the browse list, open up a command prompt at that server and type

```
net config server /hidden:yes
```

Alternatively, if you're a Registry nut, you can open up REGEDT32 and look in the HKEY_LOCAL_MACHINE subtree, in System\Current-ControlSet. (I know, you already guessed that, as it seems that everything interesting is in there.) Then look in the key Services\LanmanServer\Parameters, and add a new value entry named Hidden of type REG_DWORD. The value 1 tells the Browser to hide this server; the value 0 says not to hide the server. Of course, the default is 0.

Monitoring the Network with the Event Viewer

NT Server defines an *event* as any significant occurrence in the system or in an application that users should be aware of and perhaps notified about. If the event is critical, such as an interrupted power supply or a full disk on a server, messages are sent to the screens of all of the workstations. Noncritical event information, however, can be fed into an log file once event auditing has been configured. Both successful and unsuccessful events can be audited.

In order to record, retrieve, and store logs of events on an NT Server, the administrator must activate and configure event auditing. File and directory access, printer access, and security events can all be audited.

File and directory auditing is activated within the Explorer, printer auditing is set within Print Manager, and security auditing is configured in User Manager for Domains.

NT Server maintains three types of logs: the *System log*, the *Security log*, and the *Applications log*. Here is what they do:

Log	What It Records
System	Events logged by the Windows NT system components, such as the failure of a driver or other system component to load during startup. As shown in Figure 15.14, this log is displayed the first time you start up the Event Viewer.
Security	Security events (changes in security policy, attempts to log on or access a file or directory, etc.) based on the security auditing policy options specified by the administrator under Auditing in User Manager for Domains. Incidentally, this log can only be accessed by members of the Administrators group. It is shown in Figure 15.15.
Applications	Events logged by applications on the system. For example, it records a file error that occurred in a database program. The Applications log is shown in Figure 15.16.

FIGURE 15.14

The System log

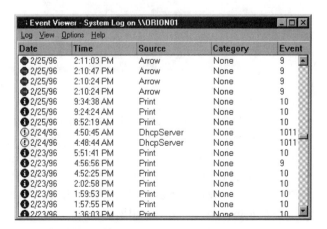

FIGURE 15.15

The Security log

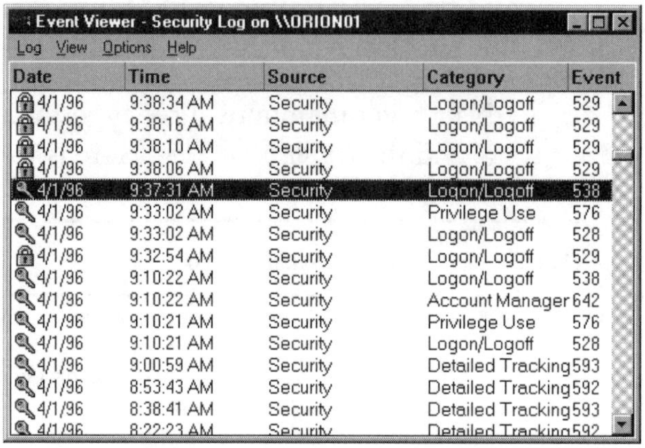

FIGURE 15.16

The Applications log

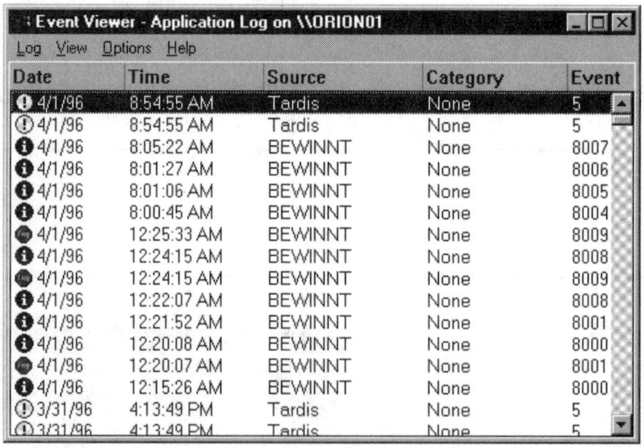

To view any of the logs, open the Event Viewer. Under the Log menu, choose either System, Security, or Applications, depending on which log you want to see. Events in the log are listed in sequence by date and time of occurrence, with the default being newest first; you can change this to oldest first in the View menu. Note that the event logs are not automatically updated during the time they are in view. To see any new events that may have been logged after opening the

Event Viewer, choose the Refresh command under the View menu (or simply hit the F5 key).

When the Event Viewer is opened, it displays the logs for the local computer by default. To view logs for another computer, choose Select Computer from the Log menu. NT Server allows you to view logs for NT workstations, NT Server servers and domain controllers, and servers using LAN Manager 2.*x*. Select the Low Speed Connection box if the computer you want is across a link with slow transmission rates; when this is checked, NT Server doesn't list all of the computers in the default domain, thereby minimizing network traffic across the link.

Reading Log Information

Log entries are classified into one of five categories. These categories are marked by an icon at the beginning of the entry:

- The Information icon indicates an event that describes the successful operation of a major server service.

- The Warning icon indicates that the event wasn't necessarily significant but might point to possible future problems.

- The Error icon indicates that the event resulted in a loss of data or a loss of functions.

- The Success Audit icon indicates an audited security access event was successful.

- The Failure Audit icon indicates an audited security access event failed.

Following the event type icon is a list of data pertinent to the event:

- The date and time the event occurred.

- The source of the event (typically the software that logged the event, which can be either an application name or a component of the system or of a large application, such as a driver name).

- A categorization of the event by the event source. Not all events are categorized (these events fall in the None category). Applications events can be listed as System Events or Administrative. Security events fall into a number of categories, which include Logon/ Logoff, Privilege Use, System Event, Policy Change, Account Management, Object Access, and Detailed Tracking.

- The user name for the user who was logged on and working when the event occurred is recorded in the event log (the entry N/A indicates that the log entry didn't specify a user).

- The computer name for the computer where the event occurred.

An event number unique to each kind of event can be used to identify the event. For example, in the Security log, events in the Logon/Logoff categories can have one of the event numbers shown in Table 15.2. The numbers are used primarily by product support representatives to track precisely which event occurred within the system. You can check what a specific event ID number indicates by looking at the Event Details (more on that shortly) for any log entry having that particular event ID.

TABLE 15.2   Event ID Numbers for Selected Logon/Logoff Events

Logon/Logoff Event ID number	Meaning
528	Successful logon.
529	Unknown user name or bad password.
531	Account currently disabled.
535	The specified user's password has expired.
537	An unexpected error occurred during logon.
538	User logoff.

Event Display

The default display layout for all of the event logs is to show every entry, with the most recent entries at the top. However, you can filter these details to see only what you need to by selecting the Filter Events option. Filtering merely affects the view and has no effect on the Event Log as a whole; all events specified in the auditing policies are logged all the time, whether or not the filter is active. If you select Save Settings On Exit from the Options menu, then the choices for filtering remain in effect every time you start the Event Viewer.

To filter the log events, choose Filter Events… in the View menu. You see the Filter dialog box, as in Figure 15.17. The options available in the Filter dialog box are explained in Table 15.3.

If you need to, you can also use the Find option to locate a particular type of entry in any of the logs. Under the View menu, choose Find (or hit the F3 key). You are asked for the same type of information as required by the Filter option. Use the Up or Down buttons in the Direction box to determine which direction to make the search.

FIGURE 15.17

The Filter dialog box

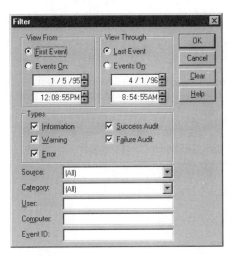

TABLE 15.3 Filter Options

Option	Filters Log For
Category	All events of a particular classification (for example, security event categories include Logon and Logoff, Policy Change, Privilege Use, System Event, Object Access, Detailed Tracking, and Account Management). This option is not available for error logs on LAN Manager 2.x servers.
Computer	Events that occurred for a particular computer by the specified name. This field is not case-sensitive. It is not available for error logs on LAN Manager 2.x servers.
Error*	Error events.
Event ID	Events of a particular type in a category, identified by a specific event ID number. It is not available for audit logs on LAN Manager 2.x servers.
Failure Audit	Audited security access attempts which failed.
Information	Information events.
Source	Events logged by a specific source, such as an application, a system component or a device driver. (Not available for audit logs on LAN Manager 2.x servers.)
Success Audit	Audited security access attempts which were successful.
User	Events that occurred while a specified user was logged on and working; note that not all events have a user associated with them. This field is not case-sensitive. It is not available for error logs on LAN Manager 2.x servers.
View From	Events after a specific date and time; default is the date of the first event in the log.
View Through	Events up to (and including) a specific date and time; default is the date of the last event in the log.
Warning*	Warning events.

* Not available for LAN Manager 2.x servers.

Interpreting Event Details for Log Entries

By double-clicking on any event within any of the three logs (or by choosing Detail in the View menu), you can call up a more detailed record of that event. Event details contain additional information about the event in question. For example, the details of a System log entry might look like Figure 15.18.

Here, the details confirm that the entry was a rather straightforward information event—printing a document. An Applications log entry might look like Figure 15.19.

Security log event details can be relatively straightforward as well, but usually contain a greater amount of information, as shown in Figure 15.20.

Understanding the meaning of these details requires some basic knowledge of how NT Server handles system security.

FIGURE 15.18

Event details for a System log entry

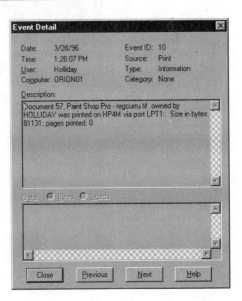

FIGURE 15.19

Event details for an
Application log entry

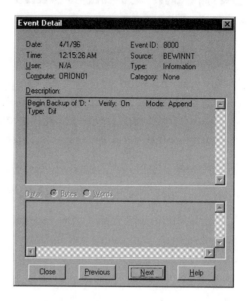

FIGURE 15.20

Event details from a
Security log entry

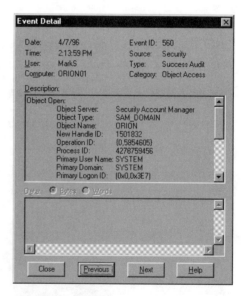

System Security in NT Server

In NT Server, all named objects (as well as some unnamed objects) can be secured. The security attributes for an object are described by a *security descriptor*. The security descriptor is made of the following four parts:

- An owner security ID, which indicates the user or group who owns the object (the owner of the object, you may recall, can change all access permissions for that object).

- A group security ID, which is used only by the POSIX subsystem and is ignored by the rest of NT.

- A discretionary *access control list* (ACL), which identifies which users and groups are granted or denied which access permissions (discretionary ACLs are controlled by the owner of the object).

- A system ACL, which controls which auditing messages the system will generate. System ACLs are controlled by the security administrators.

Whenever an owner of an object assigns permissions to other users and groups, he or she is building the discretionary ACL for that object. Likewise, an administrator's choices as to which events to audit determine the system ACL for the object.

Each of the ACLs in turn is made up of *access control entries* (ACEs). The ACEs for an object specify access or auditing permissions to that object for one user or group. ACEs contain a security ID and a set of access rights for each group or user that can access (or be denied access to) the object. Any process with a matching security ID is either allowed access rights, denied rights, or allowed rights with auditing, depending on the contents of the ACE. There are three ACE types. Two of them, AccessAllowed and AccessDenied, are discretionary ACEs that explicitly grant or deny access to a user or group. The other, SystemAudit, is the system security ACE. It is used to keep a log of security events involving object access and to create and record security audit messages.

By the way, the NT Permissions Editor places any AccessDenied ACEs first in the list of ACEs to check and, once it finds one, disregards any other AccessAllowed ACEs that follow. This way, if someone is a member of two groups, one that has access to a file and another to which access has been denied, that person will not be able to access the file despite his or her multiple group membership.

Included in each object's ACEs is an *access mask*, which is basically a menu from which granted and denied permissions are chosen. The access mask defines all possible actions for a particular directory, file, device, or other object. Access masks contain *access types*, of which there are standard types and specific types.

Standard access types apply to all objects and consist of the access permissions listed in Table 15.4. Specific types vary, depending on the type of object. For example, the specific access types for NT files are ReadData, WriteData, AppendData, ReadEA (Extended Attribute), WriteEA (Extended Attribute), Execute, ReadAttributes, and WriteAttributes.

TABLE 15.4   Standard Access Types

Standard Access Type	Function
DELETE	Used to grant or deny delete access.
READ_CONTROL	Used to grant or deny read access to the security descriptor and owner.
SYNCHRONIZE	Used to synchronize access and to allow a process to wait for an object to enter the signaled state.
WRITE_DAC	Used to grant or deny write access to the discretionary ACL.
WRITE_OWNER	Used to assign write owner.

Specific and standard access types appear in the event details for entries in the Security log. Each type of object (i.e., file, file and directory, device, etc.) can have up to 16 specific access types. If you've enabled auditing of process tracking, you can follow a user's (or the system's) activity as it accesses an object by examining the specific and standard accesses shown in the event details.

Let's take a closer look at the example event detail for the Security log entry shown back in Figure 15.20. This particular event is a successful object access event involving a file for which security auditing has been activated. If we read through the entire event detail's description, we'll see the information as shown in Figure 15.21.

The first thing we note in the description is that an object was opened, that the object server, in this case, was Security Account Manager, and that the object is SAM_DOMAIN.

We see that there is no new handle ID associated with this particular event. Handle IDs are assigned (and an audit event generated) when a file is first opened; when the file is closed, another audit event with the same handle ID is created. This information can be used to see how long a file remained open, but bear in mind that many applications open a file only long enough to read its contents into memory; a handle may be open only for a very short time.

FIGURE 15.21

Event detail description for security log entry

```
Description:
Object Open:
        Object Server:      Security Account Manager
        Object Type:        SAM_DOMAIN
        Object Name:        ORION
        New Handle ID:      1501832
        Operation ID:       {0,5854605}
        Process ID:         4278759456
        Primary User Name:  SYSTEM
        Primary Domain:     SYSTEM
        Primary Logon ID:   (0x0,0x3E7)
        Client User Name:   MarkS
        Client Domain:      ORION
        Client Logon ID:    (0x0,0x594E51)
        Accesses            CreateUser
                        GetLocalGroupMembership
                    ListAccounts
                    LookupIDs

        Privileges          -
```

The Operation ID and Process ID numbers are unique numbers assigned to any particular operations within a process and to the process as a whole, respectively. For example, when an application is started, it is assigned a Process ID, and all events involving that application have that same ID. Individual operations within the application, such as opening a particular file, are assigned an Operation ID.

Continuing through the list, we now note the Primary User Name, Primary Domain, and Primary Logon ID, as well as the Client User Name, Client Domain, and Client Logon ID. To ensure that the programs that a user runs have no more access to objects than the user does, NT allows processes to take on the security attributes of another process or user through a technique called *impersonation*. Impersonation allows a program or process to run on the user's behalf with the same accesses that the user has been granted, or to put it another way, to run in the user's *security context*. We can see in our example that the primary user for this event was the system, but the client user, whose security context the process is running under, is also identified. The Client Logon ID is a number assigned to a logon session whenever a user logs on, and, if Logon/Logoff events are being audited, it can be used to search the logon entries to find out when the particular user logged on prior to the event in question.

The last collection of information in the description are lists of Accesses and Privileges that have been used (and thus audited). Since this particular event was a successful one, the Accesses list indicates which actions actually took place. The four accesses are standard accesses for creating a user, assigning membership to a local group, listing domain accounts, and looking up IDs. Since nothing is indicated under Privileges, we can tell that no particular user rights were invoked for this event.

From this particular list of accesses, you can deduce what this actually was: a new user named MarkS was created. In the case of a failure audit entry, the list of accesses displayed usually represents those which were attempted but failed due to lack of access.

Changing the Size and Overwrite Options for an Event Log

The default size for all three of the event logs is 512K, and events older than seven days are overwritten as needed when the log becomes full. To change this, open the Event Viewer, and select Log Settings under the Log menu. You see the Event Log Setting dialog box shown in Figure 15.22.

In addition to changing the log size, you can specify how the event log is overwritten by choosing one of three options in this dialog box:

Overwrite Events as Needed   New events will continue to be written into the log. When the log is full, each additional new event will replace the oldest event in the log.

Overwrite Events Older than [ ] Days   Logged events will be retained for the number of days specified (the default is seven) before being overwritten. This is a handy choice if you are archiving logs on a weekly basis.

Do Not Overwrite Events (Clear Log Manually)   With this option, the log is never overwritten. When full, events are no longer logged. When that situation occurs, a message appears on the screen saying that the log is full. Select this particular option only if it is important

FIGURE 15.22

Event Log Settings dialog box

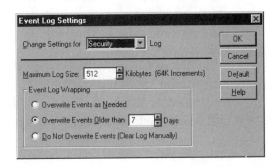

not to miss any events, and make sure that someone is able to manually clear the log when needed. (You might select this option for Secret logs where all of the log info is vital.)

As mentioned earlier, choose carefully the events to be audited and consider the amount of disk space you are willing to devote to the logs when you set up auditing. You cannot make the system add more entries to a full log by simply increasing the log size under Log Settings.

Archiving Event Logs

The event logs displayed in NT Server's Event Viewer can be archived for future inspection and use. The log information can be stored three ways:

- As EVT files, a format that allows the data (and all of its details) to be viewed in the Event Viewer whenever desired

- As text files (TXT)

- As comma-delimited text files

The latter two formats allow the log information to be used in other applications.

Archiving the event log saves the entire log, regardless of what the currently selected filtering options are. Event logs saved as text or comma-delimited text, however, are saved in the current sort order. The data is stored in the following sequence: date, time, source, type, category, event, user, computer, and description. Any binary data in the event records is dropped.

Event logs can be archived in two ways, but no matter which method is used, the log that is currently displayed in the Event Viewer is the one that gets archived. To choose the desired log, open the Log menu and select System, Security, or Application.

The first method merely saves the event log as a file without clearing the log. With the desired log displayed, open the Log menu and choose Save As. By writing in a name for the file and picking a file format in the Save As dialog box, you can save the current log information to disk.

If you need to archive the current log and clear it from the Event Viewer too, then select the Clear All Events option under the Log menu. The Clear Event Log dialog box appears, as in Figure 15.23. It gives you the option to save before clearing.

Selecting Yes triggers the Save As dialog box. Choose the file format option desired, and enter a file name for the archived log. Upon selecting OK, you get the message shown in Figure 15.24 (in this case, for the System log).

Since you've just saved the current information to a file, those events won't be lost (contrary to what this message implies). Selecting Yes will clear the log of the just-archived information. New event information will be added to the log according to the criteria set under Log Settings. If, in the Log Settings option, you've specified "Overwrite Events Older than 7 Days" (see Figure 15.22), you can archive weekly

FIGURE 15.23

Save before clearing
dialog box

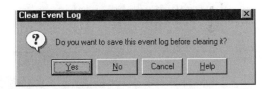

FIGURE 15.24

Clearing an event log

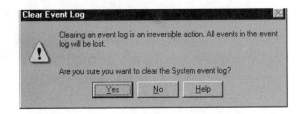

without necessarily clearing the event log, since the older events are overwritten in the week after archiving the log.

It is important to check, archive, and clear event logs regularly if you select the "Do Not Overwrite Events (Clear Log Manually)" option in the Event Log Settings dialog box (see Figure 15.22). If an event log is full, no more information can be stored, and what might be vital information will not get recorded. When a log is full, the administrator is notified by a message on the screen. If the option Restart, Shutdown, and System has been selected for auditing under the Audit policy in User Manager for Domains, then a log entry, indicating that a log is full, will be recorded.

Viewing Previously Archived Logs

To view a previously archived log, select the Open option in the Log menu of the Event Viewer, and choose which previously archived log you wish to see. After selecting a file, you will be prompted as to which type of log it is, as shown Figure 15.25. Make sure you make the correct choice when it comes to choosing the log type, because if you don't the event description shown in the log details will be incorrect.

If you need a printed copy of the log, then use the Save As option to save the log as a comma-delimited text file. As mentioned earlier, all information will be saved in the current sort order, and any binary data

FIGURE 15.25

Selecting a previously archived file to view

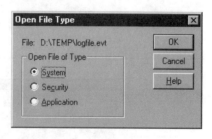

associated with a log entry will be discarded. You can print a comma-delimited text file for future reference or scrutiny. The example below shows part of the security log stored as a comma-delimited text file:

```
3/10/97,9:27:31 AM,Security,Success Audit,Logon/Logoff
,528,Administrator,EISA SERVER,Successful Logon:
     User Name:            Administrator
     Domain:               US
     Logon ID:             (0x0,0x50D65)
     Logon Type:      2
     Logon Process:   User32
     Authentication Package:MICROSOFT_AUTHENTICATION_PACKAGE_V1_0
3/10/97,9:27:19 AM,Security,Success Audit,Logon/Logoff ,538,Maeve,
EISA SERVER,User Logoff:
     User Name:       Maeve
     Domain:               US
     Logon ID:             (0x0,0x501BC)
     Logon Type:      2

3/10/97,9:27:03 AM,Security,Failure Audit,Object Access
,560,Maeve,EISA SERVER,Object Open:
     Object Server:   Security
     Object Type:     File
     Object Name:     C:\Main\NTCLASS\MVTEXT\prjdatal.txt
     New Handle ID:   -
     Operation ID:    {0,330786}
     Process ID:      4285798960
     Primary User Name: Maeve
     Primary Domain:  US
     Primary Logon ID: (0x0,0x501BC)
     Client User Name: -
     Client Domain:   -
     Client Logon ID: -
     Accesses                   SYNCHRONIZE
                      ReadAttributes

     Privileges                 -
```

The first two entries reveal a successful logon by the Administrator and a user logoff. The third entry is a failure audit for a user's attempt to change a file (in this example, PRJDATA.TXT) for which he or she only has read access.

It's no good to throw money at a server in the hope that it will get faster. With a good tuning approach, you can decide where best to put your upgrade dollars. But sometimes a network is sluggish or non-responsive in a way that tuning can help—that's when it's time to read the next chapter.

CHAPTER
SIXTEEN

Troubleshooting and Disaster Recovery

No matter how fault-tolerant your system is, there's always *some* fault it can't tolerate. It could be something as simple as an incorrectly configured NT Server, or something as dramatic as your server falling down a crack in an earthquake. RAID's nice, but disk mirroring or disk striping is not going to help you here. What you need now is a way to rebuild your server's operating system and data, from the bottom up if need be.

Defeating Disasters: An Overview

I'll get to the particular tools that you can use to examine and recover from disasters in a bit. But first let's look at how to avoid the disasters in the first place. You do that with several approaches:

- Create and maintain physical security on your network. If the bad guys (and the good guys who happen to just be careless) can't get to your network hardware, it's a lot harder for them to damage it.

- Protect your data with a good backup strategy. You have to back up both user data and system areas. There are two different tools for that, named NTBACKUP and RDISK. Now, RDISK requires an undocumented option to make it really useful, but I'll explain that later in this chapter.

- When the worst happens, you must be ready for it with a specific, written-down disaster recovery plan. Everybody must know what they're expected to do in the case of a massive network failure.

- When things go wrong, it's useful to have some knowledge about how the system starts up, when it crashes, and *why* it crashes. Two NT tools called the Kernel Debugger and DUMPEXAM can give you some insight into that.

Network Physical Security

An ounce of prevention is worth a pound of cure, right? One of the main concerns in computer security, and the one that this chapter addresses, is *physical security*. Physical security is a blanket term for the ways in which you *physically* protect your server and network from harm—from stupid accidents, environmental incidents, espionage, and theft.

Preventing Environmental Problems

It would be terrible if you went to all the trouble of protecting your server from theft or tampering and then lost it to a cup of coffee spilled into its air intake vents.

Electrical Protection

The first source of environmental problems that should never be ignored is the wall socket.

- Use a UPS/power conditioner on your servers to protect them from dirty power and power surges. If you don't want to buy a UPS for every workstation (and I don't blame you if you don't—that can get expensive), buy a *power conditioner*. This (roughly) $150 device cleans up noisy power and compensates for low voltage.

- While nothing will guarantee 100 percent protection from lightning damage, you can reduce lightning damage with an odd trick: tie five knots in each workstation's power cord, as close to the wall as you can get them. That way, if lightning strikes the wiring, it will kill the cord rather than travel through the cord and kill the computer.

Does this really work? Well, Washington, DC, where I live, was hit by a terrible lightning storm in 1990. I tied knots in the cords of all the computers in my house beforehand, but hadn't thought to do it to the television. During the storm one of my neighbors took a direct lightning hit and a huge power surge hit my wiring. The cords of all the computers were warmed up a bit, but the power surge never touched the computers themselves. The television was another matter—the surge traveled straight through the cord to the TV's innards and rendered the television DOA. I couldn't have asked for a better test, though at the time I wasn't in a mood to appreciate the benefits of having had an unknotted control group to compare the knotted cords with.

- Don't plug any computer into the same plug as a power hog like a refrigerator, copier, or laser printer. Laser printers periodically draw as much power as an entire kitchen full of appliances.

- If your computers are all in one room and you want to ground the room, don't just ground that room; ground the entire office. Otherwise, it's kind of like putting a giant "KICK ME" sign on your computers, as they will be the easiest thing around for lightning to reach.

If you're looking for a one-stop-shopping answer to your server's power needs, I like the American Power Conversion Smart-UPS series quite a bit. These UPSes are a combination of a power conditioner and a standby power supply.

There is more to know about power and PCs, but so ends the quick overview.

Know Your Building

When you're positioning servers and workstations, know what's in the building that could affect them. For example, are there old (or new) leaks in the building? Putting a server or workstation underneath a suspicious brown stain in the ceiling is a bad idea, even if the leak was "fixed" years ago and the building manager claims that "it can't possibly be a problem."

Excessive heat and moisture is bad for equipment. Is heat-producing equipment mounted in the ceiling? How about equipment that produces water condensation? One company moved into a new building and discovered that the air-conditioning equipment was mounted in the ceiling over the server room. Not only did the AC generate copious amounts of heat in exactly the place where it was least wanted, but the water condensation that the units generated began raining down onto the servers one morning. Luckily, the servers recovered nicely, but it could have been an ugly scene.

If the servers are locked in their own room, is that room staying cool enough for safety? The regular air conditioning that the rest of the office uses might not be enough, due to the restricted ventilation in a closed room and all the heat that computers generate.

Obviously, you shouldn't position *any* computer, whether it's a workstation or a server, in direct sunlight.

Keep Contaminants Away from the Servers

It is hard to keep people from eating or drinking near their workstations, but this should not be true in the server room. A strict no-food-or-beverage policy is necessary in that room to keep someone from pouring a Coke into the file server. The proliferation of non-smoking offices makes the next comment almost unnecessary, but even if employees can smoke in the office, the one place they should *not* smoke is around the servers or workstations. Smoke particles in the hard disk are a *very* bad idea.

Preventing Theft and Tampering

Although the lion's share of physical security problems stem from accidents, theft and tampering are also things to watch out for if the information on your system might be valuable to someone else. To keep unauthorized people from gaining access to the network's information, do the following.

Keep the Server Room Locked   Most people who use the network don't have a valid reason for going into the server room, so you can keep it locked. If people can't get into the server room, they can't:

- Reboot the server. If you are using the FAT file system, an intruder could reboot the server from a floppy (assuming that there are floppy drives on your server) and copy or delete valuable data. This, by the way, is one of the main reasons for using the NTFS file system—NTFS files and directories are invisible to users of the FAT file system.

- Steal the hard drive(s). This might sound improbable, but someone who has the tools and experience can simply remove the hard drive and take it elsewhere to crack into it at their leisure, rather than try to work with it on site. Stealing a hard drive is less awkward than stealing an entire server, but locking the file server room can also prevent server theft.

- Re-install NT Server. While this sounds like a lot of trouble to go through, it's perfectly possible. Re-installing the operating system doesn't harm the data already on the drive (unless you repartition it), so someone with the knowledge and the time could re-install NT Server and change all the passwords, giving themselves access to your data.

Limit Access to the Server

Even if you can't lock up the server for space or administrative reasons, you can still limit people's physical access to it with the following tactics:

- Disable the server's A: drive. Without an A: drive, no one can reboot the system from a floppy unless they reconnect the A: drive first. Admittedly, this means you can't reboot either, but this could buy you some time if someone broke in intending to reboot the server. Use the floplock service that comes with the Windows NT *Resource Kit*. When the floplock service is running, only members of the Administrators group can access the floppy drives.

- Disable the reset button and on/off switch. Most of the time, if you need to reboot the server, you do it with the Shutdown option on the Start menu. Without a Big Red Switch or reset button, no one can boot the server unless they use the Shutdown option.

These are somewhat extreme measures, and truthfully I don't have enough need for security to use them on my network. Some of my clients, however (hint: I live in Washington DC, remember?) have found these suggestions quite implementable.

Using Passwords Well

Well-chosen passwords are an important part of the security process. When selecting them, strike a balance between passwords that are too easy to guess and in service too long, and passwords that are so complicated and changed so frequently that users must write them down to remember them. An eight-letter minimum and a 30-day change policy (with the user unable to use the same password more than once every three changes), is probably about right. Experimentation and experience will help you choose a combination that fits your needs. When choosing passwords, keep the following in mind.

NT Server passwords are case-sensitive, so you can make them more difficult to guess by capitalizing them in unexpected places (like pAssword). Don't get too creative with this, however, or your users will never be able to type them in right.

There are programs that can guess passwords. These programs feed a dictionary to the system until the system accepts a word. To eliminate this path into your system, use words not found in the dictionary: names (picard), misspelled words (phantum), foreign words (*chamaca*), or made-up words (aooga). At password-changing time in one government installation, the users are presented with a two-column list of four-letter words (not obscenities, just words with four letters in them). The users pick one word from column A and one from column B, and then they combine them to form a new password, leading to such combinations as PINKFEET or BOATHEAD. These passwords are easy to remember and can't be found in the dictionary. Better yet, take the two words and string them together with a punctuation mark, like "stars.geronimo."

Most names are not found in the dictionary, but don't let your users use the personal names of their spouses, children, pets, or anything else as passwords. One branch security manager at the Pentagon tells me that he had to go in and change all of his users' passwords when he discovered that a number of them had chosen the names of Japanese WWII battleships—a subject related to their mission and therefore not impossible to guess.

While the password-generating programs that randomly select a number-letter combination create nearly invulnerable passwords, these passwords may not be the most effective protection. They're too hard for most people to remember and often end up being written down.

Remove old user accounts from the system if the person using the account no longer needs it. If the user may need the account again (a summer intern, for example, could return the following summer), disable it rather than wipe it out altogether, but don't keep active accounts on the system unless someone is using them.

Finally, even if someone figures out a password and breaks into the system, you can reduce the possible damage by only giving users the minimum access to the system and to files that they need. There's more about this in Chapter 6.

Controlling Access to the Printer

The printer might seem like a harmless part of your network, but think again: if you have company secrets, those secrets could leave your network via your printer even if you've adopted diskless workstations. To try to avoid this, take these steps:

- Restrict printer access to those who need it. (You can also restrict access to keep people from playing with an expensive color printer.)

- Audit printer use in the Print Manager so that you know who is printing what. If you discover someone who prints more output to the printer than his work would justify, he may not be stealing company secrets—but he might be wasting company time and resources on personal projects. Be aware, however, that auditing server activity slows down the server.

- Restrict printer access time to normal working hours.

- Don't give out Power User rights to just anyone. Power users can create and connect to network devices, thereby negating all that you've done to control access to the devices.

Preventing Portable Penetration

Say that you have an Ethernet bus network. What happens if someone comes in with a portable and plugs in? What rights does this person have on the network?

Potentially disastrous as this may sound, if you've set up the network as a domain and the person with the portable does not know the administrator's password, plugging the portable into the network won't get that person anywhere. This is because the administrator is the only one who can add a computer to the domain, and a non-member is shut out of the domain.

If, however, your network is set up on a peer-to-peer basis, a plugged-in portable can do a lot more damage, due to the Guest Account on all the machines. Many people never bother to change the Guest account password from the default, and one of the easiest ways of accessing a network is through the guest account. While Guest access is not as powerful as that of the Administrator, a Guest can still view, copy, and delete files to which they have not been expressly refused access.

Therefore, to protect your network best, institute a domain controller so that no one can log on to the system from a new computer. If you *must* have a peer-to-peer setup, eliminate the Guest account on all the network's workstations or, at the very least, change the password on a regular basis.

How Much Protection Is Too Much?

Protecting your system is a never-ending process; for every safeguard you use, there is always a means to get past it. Therefore, when protecting your network, come up with a balance between how much the data is worth and how much the protection costs. If protecting your data costs more than the data is worth, it's time to relax a little. The cost of perfect protection is infinite amounts of money and eternal vigilance. If you hope to ever get anything done or to have money to spend on anything else, weigh your protection costs against what you're protecting and plan accordingly. There's little point in spending the money for more drives so that you can have RAID fault-tolerance, for example, if all that you're protecting are applications for which you have the original disks and backups.

When something goes wrong with your system, think *non-invasive*. Three of your most valuable troubleshooting implements are:

- An NT-bootable disk

- The Emergency Repair Disk for the machine in trouble (don't forget, they're specific to the machine on which they were made)

- Your notebook, in which you record every change you make to the servers and workstations, so that when something goes wrong, you can figure out what changed since the last time it worked.

Backup Strategies

Physical security keeps people and the outside environment from getting to your equipment. Now let's consider how to protect your data. The first line of defense against data loss is backups. Backups are like exercise—they're necessary but they often don't get done unless they're easy to do. NT Server does a lot toward making sure that backups get done by providing a tape backup program that is fast and easy to use.

Performing Backups

You can find the Backup icon in the Start menu under the Administrative Tools program group. When you highlight the icon, you see a screen that looks like Figure 16.1.

When you want to back up a drive, you first need to select the drive, even if you only have one on your server. To do so, click in the check box next to the drive until it has an *X* in it. If for some reason you open the Backup screen and the drives window is only an icon similar to the Tapes icon at the bottom of Figure 16.1, just double-click on it to open it.

Once you've selected the drive that you want to back up and a tape is in the drive, you're ready to go. Click on the Backup button in the upper-left corner or select the Backup option from the Operations drop-down menu. You see a screen that looks like Figure 16.2.

FIGURE 16.1

Opening screen for Backup

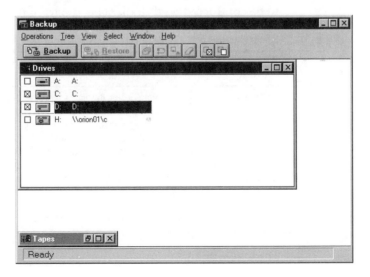

FIGURE 16.2

Backup information
dialog box

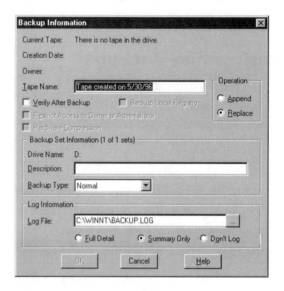

The Backup Information Dialog Box

The Backup Information dialog box gives you information about the tape in the drive and lets you make decisions about how you want the backup to be conducted. Let's look at each part of this dialog box in order:

Option	What It Does
Current Tape	As you might guess, this is the tape that you have in the drive. I'm reusing an old backup, so the Backup program reads and gives me the tape name, which is the tape's creation date. This is good, because if I use this tape for my backup, I'll lose the data from the 2/23 backup, and this reminder of when the tape was made could save me from mistakenly overwriting my data.
Creation Date	If you named the tape something other than the date it was created, this tells you when the current tape was created.
Owner	This is the domain and user name of the person who made the backup.

Option	What It Does
Tape Name	This is the name that you give the new information on this tape. You can use the default name of "Tape created on [*date*]" if you like, or you can call it something like "Backup before installing OS/2 do not erase" to give your memory a little extra jog. The tape name can be up to 50 characters long, including spaces, but if it's longer than 32 characters you won't be able to see the entire name without scrolling down the line.
Verify After Backup	If you select this option, the backup program checks to make sure that, after it's done, the backup matches the original data on the disk. Verification takes a little longer, but it's a good way to double-check that your backups are actually complete and accurate when you need them.
Backup Registry	Check this box to include a copy of the local registry files in the backup set. The local registry files are your disk configuration information, and in the case of disaster, having this information might not be a bad idea.
Operation	Selecting Append or Replace makes a decision about what happens to the data already on the tape, if there is any. Select Append to add the new backup to the backup already on the tape and not lose anything. Make sure that you have enough room on the tape for both the old data and the new. Select Replace to have the new backup overwrite the old one. Be sure that you no longer need an old backup before selecting Replace, because you can't get back the data once you overwrite it.
Restrict Access to the Owner or Administrator	Restricting access is probably a good idea for a number of reasons. First, no one but the owner or administrator should have any need to access backed-up files. If someone else needs an old copy of a file, they can ask the people authorized to give it to them. Second, making everyone responsible for their own backups helps avoid recrimination when a backup is missing or corrupted. If no one can use a backup other than its owner, then, if something happens to it, it's clear who did it.
Drive Name	The drive name is the name of the drive you selected for the backup before you got to this dialog box. You can't change it here, so if you selected the wrong drive, cancel out of this box and change your selection.
Description	You can fill in a description of the backup in addition to its name. Therefore, if you wanted to record both the date and the contents of the drive, you could name the tape "Backup from 03/09/97" and *describe* it as "Pre-OS/2 installation backup—keep," or some such thing.

Option	What It Does
Backup Type	If you click on the down-arrow on the right side of this box, you see a number of different backup types to choose from:
	• **Normal** A full backup—everything selected gets backed up, whether or not the archive bit is set. (The archive bit is attached to a file when it's changed and removed during backup, allowing selective backups of the files that have changed since the last backup.) This is the default option. Even if you normally do incremental backups (described below), periodically doing a normal backup to make sure that everything on the disk is backed up is a good idea.
	• **Copy** A full backup of all the selected files on the disk. In this case, however, the archive bit is not reset after the files have been backed up—from looking at Explorer, you can't tell that anything was backed up.
	• **Differential** Backs up only those files with the archive bit set, but doesn't reset it afterwards. This is useful for interim backups between full backups, because restoring the data only requires restoring the last full backup and the most recent differential.
	• **Incremental** Like a differential backup, this option backs up only those files with the archive bit set, but the incremental backup then resets the bit.
	• **Daily** Backs up only those files that have been modified *that day* (as opposed to since the last backup), and does not reset the archive bit. If you want to take home the files that you've worked on during a given day, this can be a good way of getting them all.
Log Information	Backup log records how the backup went: how many files were backed up, how many skipped (if any), how many errors there were (if any), and how long the backup took. You might as well keep the backup logs in the default directory unless you have a good reason to move them elsewhere just so you don't forget where they are.
Full Detail, Summary Only	On the bottom of the dialog box you can see that you have a choice of two kinds of backup log records: Full Detail and Summary Only (or no log). A full log records the name of every file backed up in addition to the other information about major events that are described above. A summary merely records major events. For most purposes a summary log is fine. The only time that you might need a full log is if you were doing a differential backup and wanted to have some record of what files you backed up.

Now that you've filled out the Backup Information dialog box, you're ready to do the backup. Click OK, and, if you're using an old backup tape and you selected the Replace option, you see a screen that looks like Figure 16.3. Once again, if you're sure that you want to overwrite the

FIGURE 16.3

Warning that data
will be overwritten

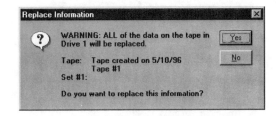

data, click on Yes. You move now to the dialog box in Figure 16.4, which keeps you informed of the backup's progress.

Normally when you see this screen, Abort will not be grayed out unless you had to abort the backup, and OK won't be a viable choice from the time you begin the backup until it's finished. As the backup progresses, you can keep track of it by looking at this screen.

FIGURE 16.4

Backup Status screen

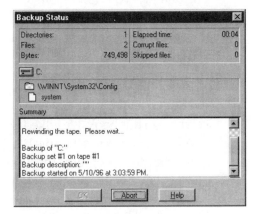

Performing Automatic Backups

To be safe, you should back up your drive every day, since that way you never lose more than one day's worth of work. Unfortunately, running even an easy-to-use backup program like NT Server's takes

How Do I Back Up Data?

 With a tape in the drive, start the Backup program, which can be found in the Start menu under the Administrative Tools program group. Select the drive that you want to back up, and then click on the Backup button in the upper-left area of the screen. Fill in the Backup Information dialog box as appropriate, and click OK.

The backup should proceed normally.

Important note: You cannot read or restore tapes backed up in NT Server 4 on a server running a previous version of NT Server.

time away from your day—the task-switching involved causes you to take time from your real work, and you might forget altogether if you get caught up in something else.

Fortunately, you don't have to depend on your memory or your schedule to run daily backups. NT Server provides two ways to run backups on a regular schedule: the command prompt and the WINAT .EXE GUI program.

Backing Up from the Command Prompt

Elsewhere in this book, we talked about how to use the NET SCHEDULE and AT commands to schedule batch commands to run at a certain time. Among the other programs that you can run with the AT command is the DOS version of NT Server's backup program, called NTBACKUP. The parameters this command uses provide you with almost the same flexibility that the GUI backup program does—it's just a little trickier to use.

To run NTBACKUP, type the following:

```
ntbackup backup path options
```

where *path* is the drive (and directory, if you're only backing up part of a drive) that you want to back up and *options* is one of the switches shown in Table 16.1. You can select more than one drive at a time—just type the drive letters with colons after them. In the path, you can also specify individual files to back up, or specify all the files of a certain type with the asterisk wildcard (*).

TABLE 16.1   Switches for Use with NT BACKUP

Switch	Description
/a	Makes the mode of backup append, so that the backed up files will be added to those already on the tape. If this switch is omitted, the new files will overwrite any files now on the tape.
/b	Backs up the local registry.
/d	Lets you describe the backup. Enclose your text in quotation marks after the /d switch.
/l	Writes a log of the backup. You must specify a location for the log to be written, like this: /l "c:\log\log.txt." As shown, you enclose the log's destination in quotation marks.
/r	Restricts access to the tape's owner and the network administrator.
/t	Lets you select the backup type. You can choose to do a Normal, Copy, Incremental, Differential, or Daily backup; /t incremental gives you an incremental backup. If you don't use this switch, you perform a normal backup.
/v	Verifies that the backup was done correctly by comparing the data on the tape with the original data on the drive after the backup is done. Backups take a little longer with verification, but they let you know that the data was written correctly.

Let's start with a simple example. To obtain a full backup of all the files on a C:\WPFILES directory that end with the extension DOC, you would type:

```
ntbackup backup c:\wpfiles\*.doc
```

Finally, to perform a differential backup of all the files in both drives C: and D:, verify the backup, describe the backup as the monster drives on the server, perform a backup of the local registry, restrict access to the owner and network administrator, and record a backup log under the name C:\LOG\LOG.TXT, you would type the following on one line:

```
ntbackup backup c: d: /v/r/b/d "The monster drives on the server"
/l "c:\log\log.txt"
```

Now that you're familiar with the DOS parameters for the backup program, you can use it to do timed backups. Start the scheduler service by typing **net start schedule**, and then use the AT command to set up the automatic backup. For instance, to do an incremental backup every day at 3 A.M. of the \WPFILES directory on drive C, verify the backup, append the files to the ones already on the disk, describe the backup as "My word-processing files," and record the log in C:\LOG\LOG.TXT, you would type this on one line:

```
at 3:00 /every:M,Tu,W,Th,F,Sa,Su "ntbackup backup c:\wpfiles /t
incremental /v/a/d ""My wordprocessing files"" /l"c:\log\log.txt"
```

For another example, to back up your C: drive at 11:00 every Wednesday, start the scheduling service by typing **net start schedule**, and then you type

```
at 11:00 /every:wednesday "ntbackup backup c:"
```

These commands would then be entered on the jobs list, which you can view by typing **AT** from the command prompt. You don't have to set up the command as you see it in the example; you can use the switches to configure your backup procedure as you see fit. No matter what combination of switches you use to customize your automatic backups, however, using the **/a** switch to append the new backups to the ones already on your tape is probably a good idea. You're using this daily incremental backup to keep your backups current between weekly full backups, so you want to keep a complete record of all changes made between those full backups.

Using the Scheduler (WINAT) Program

Unless you're really fond of working from the command prompt, the WINAT GUI program is probably easier to use, even though you still need to know the MS-DOS syntax. WINAT is one of a number of handy applications that come with the Windows NT *Resource Kit*. Once you load the *Resource Kit*, you need to use the Program Manager's New option to add it manually to one of the program groups. You can put the program item wherever you like; I put mine in the Administrative Tools program group.

When you've added WINAT to a program group, you're ready to go. Double-click on the program icon, pull down the File menu, choose Select Computer, type in your computer name if it is not already there, click OK, and then choose the Add button. You see a screen that looks like Figure 16.5.

In the Command text box, type in the command syntax, following the rules in the previous section on using the command prompt. Once you've typed in the command, use the radio buttons to select how often you want the event to occur (since we're configuring a daily incremental backup, choose Every). Next, Ctrl+click on all the days of the week on which you want the backup to run. For our installation, we selected every day, for those times when someone's working over the weekend, but you may want to choose different days. Finally, choose the time when you want the backup to run. It's best to choose a time very late at night or early in the morning when there is little network activity. Once you've set up the command and the times, click OK to return to the original screen. It should look like Figure 16.6.

FIGURE 16.5

Add Command
dialog box

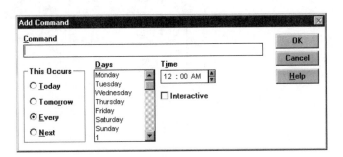

FIGURE 16.6

Command Scheduler
dialog box

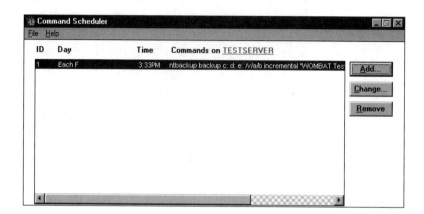

If you need to adjust the settings of your job, then click the Change button. You see the Change Command dialog box, which looks much like the Add Command dialog box shown in Figure 16.7. From this screen, you can adjust your backup (or any other scheduled service) as necessary by using the same procedures that you used to add it.

If you need to remove your backup command, select it in the Command Scheduler screen and click Remove. When you do, the system prompts you for confirmation. Click Yes and the command is removed. Don't remove an event unless you're sure that you want to, however, because

FIGURE 16.7

Selection of directories to
back up

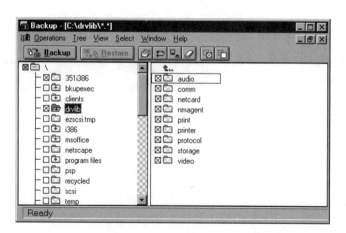

no Cancel function is on that screen. Every time you add a job to this list, it will be assigned a job identification number. When you remove a job, the numbers assigned to the other jobs in the list do not change, and future jobs take the next highest number available. If you erase job 0, leaving job 1 intact, and then add job 0 back, it will become job 2.

What about the Scheduler service? Yes, it still needs to be running for WINAT to work, just as it does for the AT command in the command prompt. You can start it from the Services icon in the Control Panel, or you can just go ahead and start WINAT. A message box will tell you that the Scheduler is not running and ask you if you want to start running it. When you say Yes, the service will begin.

Special Backup Operations

We've just discussed how to do a normal, vanilla-flavored backup that hits every file on your hard disk, only requires one tape, backs up a local disk, and doesn't need to be aborted. However, special circumstances may require you to do the job a bit differently, and that's what this section covers.

Backing Up Only Selected Files

At some point, you may want to back up only certain directories or files on your hard disk; not necessarily the ones with the archive bit set, but an assortment. To do this, you must select the directories or files to be copied, and deselect everything else.

The process begins as though you were backing up the entire disk. Go to the initial Backup screen and select the drive that you want to back up. Rather than clicking on the Backup button, however, double-click on the gray drive icon. You see a screen that looks like Figure 16.7.

When I opened this screen, every directory had a filled check box next to it. Since I only wanted to back up files from some of the directories, I clicked the check box next to the C: drive to deselect it so that I could select the individual directory that I wanted. From here, I chose as many directories as I liked. When I double-clicked on NTCLASS, I got a list of its files and subdirectories, as shown in Figure 16.8.

FIGURE 16.8

Selection of files and subdirectories to back up

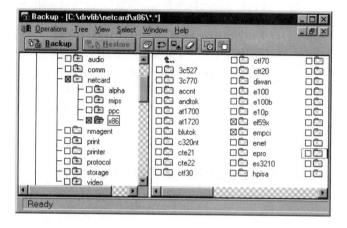

Once again, to keep from selecting every file and subdirectory in the NTCLASS directory, I clicked on the check box for that directory to deselect it. Now, only the files that I selected would be backed up. As you can see in the figure, I chose three files to back up.

Now we're ready to complete the backup. From here, click on the Backup button, as you did earlier to back up the entire drive. You are returned to the initial Backup Information dialog box. The rest of the operation is exactly like backing up an entire directory.

By the way, please note that, although I only selected one directory to draw files from for this example, you can choose files from as many directories and subdirectories as you like. Just make sure that you deselect everything before you select anything, or else you end up backing up more files than you intended.

Using More Than One Tape

Using more than one tape isn't difficult to do. If you choose Append from the Backup Information dialog box or have an absolutely huge hard drive, you may run out of space on your tape before the backup is done. If this happens, the Backup program prompts for a new tape. Just insert the new tape, and press OK.

Aborting a Backup

If you realize that you don't want to back up your data once you've started, you can click on the Abort button to make the process stop. If the program was in the middle of backing up a file and there was less than 1MB to go, the file will be completed; otherwise a message box appears and asks if you really want to stop now and have the file be corrupted on the tape.

Clicking on Abort does not cancel the backup; it only stops it at the point at which you aborted. Whatever files were backed up before you aborted the process will be on the tape.

Backing Up to Floppy Disks

If you don't have a tape drive, you can still back up your most important files to floppy disks. To do so, go to the command prompt and use either the XCOPY or the BACKUP command. The BACKUP command is perhaps a little simpler.

When using the BACKUP command, you can specify drives (although that's not likely if you're backing up to floppies), directories, or individual files. The syntax looks like this:

```
backup source destination drive: options
```

where *source* specifies the source files, directories, or drive. You can use wildcards to specify all the files of a certain type, or spell out all the file names. For example, to back up all of directory C:\WPFILES, you would type **c:\wpfiles**. To back up all the files in that directory with the DOC suffix, you would type **c:\wpfiles*.doc**. For *destination drive*, substitute the name of the drive (such as A) where you want the backups to be stored. For *options*, include one or more of the switches shown in Table 16.2.

TABLE 16.2   Switches for Use in Backing Up to Floppy Disks

Switch	Description
/a	Appends the current backup to the files already on the destination disk. Omitting this switch causes the destination disk to be overwritten.
/d:[date]	Backs up only the files that have changed after the date you place after the colon, whether or not they have the archive bit set.
/f:[size]	Specifies the size of the disk to be formatted, if you want the destination disk to be formatted before you write to it. Put the size of the disk (1.44MB, for example) after the colon.
/l[drive:path]	Creates a log file in the drive and path you specify.
/m	Backs up only the files with the archive bit set—the ones that have changed since the last backup.
/s	Tells the backup program to search all subdirectories for files. If you don't select this option, the backup program only backs up the files in the directory that you're actually in—if you specify C:*.DOC for the source directory and don't use the /s switch, only DOC files in the root directory will be backed up.
/t:[time]	Backs up only those files that have changed after the time you specify, whether or not they have the archive bit set.

Alternatively, you can use XCOPY to back up your files or put files on disk to take them on a trip. Use XCOPY rather than COPY, because COPY doesn't use the archive bit and is not as easy to customize. While XCOPY has many switches, these are the most relevant to backing up NTFS files:

Switch	What It Does
/a	Copies files with the archive attribute set, but doesn't change the attribute (good for when you're copying the files that you've worked with on a given day but don't want them to get skipped by the daily incremental backup).
/d:date	Copies only the files changed on or after the date you specify.
/h	Copies hidden and system files, as well as normal ones.
/m	Copies with the archive bit set and then removes the bit.

Switch	What It Does
/n	Copies NTFS files, using shorter names created for use with FAT file system. Only works on NTFS files.
/u	Updates the files in the destination.

If you want more help with XCOPY, type the following command from the command prompt (there's more than one screen of options):

```
xcopy /? |more
```

Backing Up Removable Media

If you want to back up the data in a removable media drive (such as a Bernoulli or a Floptical), it may seem impossible at first because NT Server's backup program doesn't recognize removable drives as available for backup. You can, however, get around this fairly easily. To see how, read the "How Do I" sidebar.

How Do I Back Up a Removable Drive?

 To back up a removable drive:

1. Go to the File Manager or the command prompt and share the drive that you want to back up.
2. Connect to the shared drive from the File Manager or command prompt.

The backup program will now be able to see the drive under the letter assigned to it, so long as you have a disk in the drive.

You're now set. Back it up as you would any other drive.

Backing Up a Network Drive

Even if you're using an internal tape drive on your server, you can still use that drive to back up other hard disks on your system. The process is quite straightforward:

1. Go to the computer that you want to back up and share the drive or directory for backup with the network.

2. From the server's File Manager, connect to the shared directory.

Now, when you start the backup program, you notice a new icon for a network drive in the list of available drives for backup. From here, the backup process is identical to that of backing up a local drive.

Backing Up Open Files

NT's Backup program has one distinct failure: it can't back up open files. If you normally schedule backups for 2 A.M. when no one's working, this wouldn't seem to be a problem. However, if you're connecting to the Internet or just running TCP/IP protocol with DHCP with or without WINS-DNS, some files will be open at 2 A.M. and *must* stay open: the files that control the internal naming services, and, if you're using DHCP, the files that allocate IP addresses.

Luckily, there's an easy way around this. To make sure that the WINS and DHCP files get backed up, make this simple batch file part of your regularly scheduled backup:

```
C:
CD \USERS
CACLS DHCP /T /E /G EVERYONE:F
CACLS WINS /T /E /G EVERYONE:F
net stop "Microsoft DHCP Server"
net stop "Windows internet name service"
xcopy c:\winnt35\system32\dhcp c:\users\sysjunk\dhcp
>>C:\USERS\DBAK.LOG
xcopy c:\winnt35\system32\wins c:\users\sysjunk\wins
>>C:\USERS\DBAK.LOG
```

```
net start "Windows internet name service"
net start "Microsoft DHCP Server"
```

It's not hard to tell what's going on here: the files that run the DHCP server and WINS are getting copied from the \system32 directory to an (unopened) log file in the \users directory so that they can be backed up. This batch file stops the DHCP Server and the Windows Internet Service before it copies the files and restarts the services after the files are copied. However, because the whole batch file takes only a few seconds to execute, the services are not shut down long enough to present a problem.

If you don't recognize the CACLS command, that's because it's not documented except in Microsoft's TechNet. CACLS is a useful NT command that allows you to change the ownership and control of a file or directory from the command line. In our version of the batch file, we had to include a command giving the Everyone group full control of the WINS and DHCP directories because these directories were owned by the System and thus even Administrators could not copy them. You could give only Administrators or Backup Operators full control if you liked; in our case, it didn't matter if Everyone could control the directories.

If you're using the AT command to schedule backups, you can make this batch file part of your weekly backup: just add it to the scheduler to run a few minutes before the backup job.

Protecting Backups

Backing up your system is a vital part of any decent security program. However, it's quite easy for an intruder to access your confidential files on the tapes that you back up to. If you don't keep an eye on the tapes, they can be rendered useless when you need to restore them. Any user can back up files that he or she has access to, and any Administrator or Backup Operator can back up the entire drive (even if, for example, your Backup Operator cannot normally access the files that she's backing up). Be very careful about who you assign backup rights to.

Once you have your backup tapes, you need to protect them from damage, as well as protect them from theft. To this end, here are some things to consider when storing tapes:

- Tapes are comfortable under approximately the same conditions that you are. Excessive heat and dampness do your backups no good. *Never* store tapes on a windowsill.

- While you want your backups to be fairly convenient, so that you can restore information if you blast your hard drive, it doesn't do you any good to have backups if your office burns down and takes the originals and the backups of all your data with it. For best protection, store all of your backups but the most recent at a safe location (locked, fireproof, waterproof) off-site.

- Enable the Restrict Access to Owner or Administrator option when backing up files. For extra protection, keep server backups locked up and only allow the network administrator or the security manager access to them. If workstations get backed up, the tapes and their usability should be the responsibility of the workstation's user.

- Label your tapes clearly and completely (on both their paper labels and their electronic volume labels), so that you don't erase a vital tape by thinking that it's something else. In NT Server, you can be very explicit about the volume label on a tape, so use this capability to identify tapes that you don't want to reuse.

Restoring Files

Your backups are useless unless you can restore them to your machine in good order. Restoring files is much like backing them up. First, click open the Backup item in the Administrative Tools program group. You see the Backup screen that you saw when you backed up originally. But this time, select the Tapes window instead of a drive. You see a screen that looks like Figure 16.9.

FIGURE 16.9

Opening Restore screen

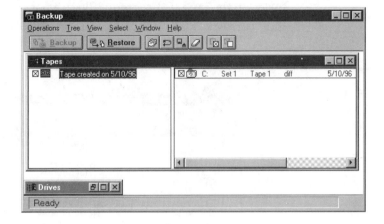

To begin the restoration process, select the tape by clicking in the check box next to it. If you want to restore an entire tape, the selection process is done. However, you probably want to restore only selected files from a tape, not the whole thing, so we'll go through the selection process now.

Double-click on the tape icon and the restore program loads the tape's catalog, so that it can find files on the tape. This process takes a couple of minutes, and while it's doing this, you see a screen that looks like Figure 16.10.

When the cataloging process is finished, you can click on the yellow files icon on the other side of the initial screen. When you do, you see

FIGURE 16.10

Cataloging Status message

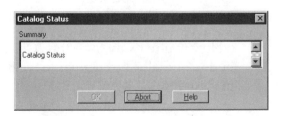

a screen like the one in Figure 16.11 that shows all the available directories on the tape. Any corrupt files (that is, files that contain errors) and their corresponding directories are marked by an icon with a red X.

FIGURE 16.11

Available directories
for restoration

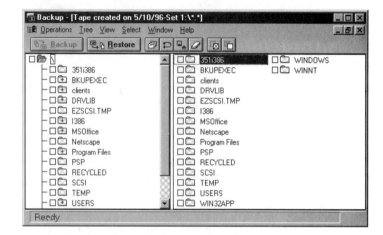

As you can see, everything is currently deselected. I didn't want to restore every file, so I unchecked the drive's check box. Subdirectories can then be selected by double-clicking on their yellow file icons. You don't have to check the check boxes to select a drive or a directory before expanding it, and it's safer not to if you're doing a selective restore as I am in this example. If you select a drive or directory, everything in it will be restored.

Once you've progressed to the directory that you want, click on the file or files that you want to restore, just as you did when you were backing up. Your screen should look something like Figure 16.12.

Now you're ready to restore. Go ahead and click on the Restore button. A dialog box similar to the Backup Information box opens, as in Figure 16.13.

FIGURE 16.12

Files selected
for restoration

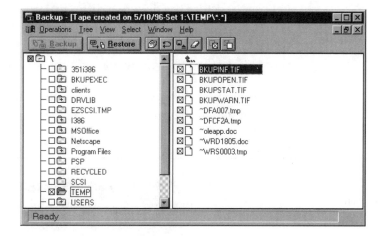

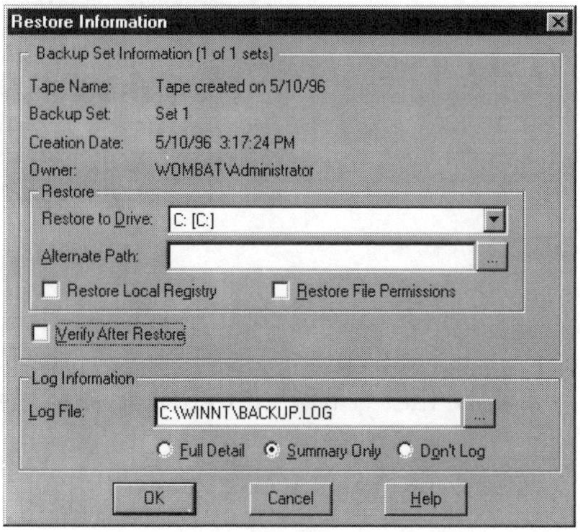

FIGURE 16.13

Restore Information
dialog box

The Restore Information dialog box is much simpler than the Backup Information dialog box. Essentially, all that you must do here is decide whether or not to verify that the information was written correctly (a good idea, even though it adds time to the restoration process), restore the local registry if you backed it up, and restore the file permissions that were in place for the file when you backed it up. If you like, you can choose to restore the data to a different drive than the one you backed it up from, although you cannot restore registry information to a drive other than the one from which you backed it up. You can also choose what kind of log file you want and where you would like to store it.

When you're done, click OK, and the restoration progress begins. You can watch the process on the screen, as in Figure 16.14.

FIGURE 16.14

File restoration
progress screen

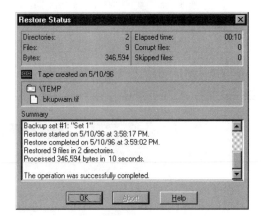

If you're restoring individual files to your drive because the originals were corrupted somehow, the Restore program asks you if you're sure that you want to replace the file on disk with the file on the tape. You see a dialog box like the one in Figure 16.15. Your files are now restored to your hard disk.

FIGURE 16.15

Confirm File Replace
dialog box

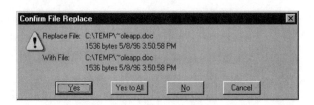

Side Note: Restoring Data After Re-Installing NT Server

When writing this book, there were some things that I could not experiment with unless I re-installed NT Server. Given that the operating system really isn't too difficult to install (just time-consuming), this wasn't much of a problem, but one instance of re-installing the operating system and trying to restore my data nearly gave me heart failure.

I was experimenting with the Disk Administrator and needed to repartition the drive with the NT Server installation on it, so I prepared to back up my data and re-install the server. I did everything by the book: backed up the hard disk to tape, verified the backup, and restored a couple of files from the backup (just to make sure that the files could be read). Now I was ready to go. I installed NT Server, blowing away my old disk partition in the process so that *none* of the data was left, and then, two hours later when the installation was done, prepared to restore the data.

When I tried to catalog the tape, all I got was a cryptic Dr. Watson message advising me that the system had generated an application error, and then the backup program closed. When I reopened it, I could see the icon for the tape catalog tantalizingly sitting there, but when I tried to double-click on it to open it, I got the same Dr. Watson message.

In desperation, I selected the catalog and attempted to restore without being able to access it, but all that got me was the data thrown back on the hard disk any which way, not in its original directories but in strange directories with names that the system seemed to have made up from truncated file names. I checked a couple of the files after this strange restoration and they seemed okay, but I knew that I couldn't count on the data's integrity, and I'd never be able to find anything anyway. Restoring the data without the catalog was useless.

If the situation I was in isn't quite clear, let me just explain that the tape that I couldn't read contained all the data on the hard drive: all my books, all the company's manuals, all of *everything* except the mailing list. I had the backup—I was clutching it, white-knuckled, in my hand—but I couldn't read it.

I re-installed NT Server, just to see if there was a problem with the installation that prevented me from reading my tape. Then I did it again. And again. I scoured the documentation, looking for clues. Finally, I got desperate (well, more desperate), decided that it was time to call in the Marines, and called Microsoft's $150-per-question Tech Support line with my problem. Even at $150 per question, however, they didn't know the answer. (That didn't keep them from charging me, however, and now the price has risen to $195.)

Finally, many hours and several installations later, I decided to try installing all the system software and *then* restoring the data. I re-installed everything that I had on the system before, including the Service Pack 2 patches (this was under NT 3.1) that had been on the system before, on the theory that it might affect how the backup worked. *This* time, I could restore the data.

The moral of this story? Before trying to restore data after a complete re-installation of NT Server, install all your system software first. It seems obvious now, but it wasn't at the time, and that mistake nearly killed me. (End of digression.)

Special Restoration Operations

Sometimes, you can't restore files in the traditional way described above because a backup set is spread over more than one tape or you've blasted the disk registry and you need to restore it. In cases like these, you need special restoration techniques.

How Do I Restore Data from Backups?

 With the tape from which you wish to restore in the drive, begin the Backup program in the Administrative Tools program group. Double-click on the tape icon to catalog it. Once it's cataloged, select the item(s) that you wish to restore or select the entire catalog, and then click on the Restore button. A dialog box appears; fill it in as appropriate. The restoration process should take place normally. If you don't have a tape drive, the programs REGBACK and REGREST, available with the NT *Resource Kit,* will save and restore registries to and from floppies.

Restoring from a Tape Set with a Missing Tape

To restore data from a backup set that extends over more than one tape, you need to insert the last tape in the set and load the backup catalog from there.

If that tape has been lost or destroyed, you can still load the backup catalogs from the tapes that you have, but it's a more arduous process. In this case, you must build a partial tape catalog by inserting the available tapes and loading their individual catalogs. Once you've done that, you can restore the data. If you're restoring the data from the command prompt, run NTBACKUP with the /MISSINGTAPE switch.

Restoring Data to a Networked Drive

The process of restoring data to a networked drive is pretty much what you expect. Connect to the drive or directory through the Explorer, and then choose to restore to that drive letter when you're setting up the Restore Options. From here, the process is identical to restoring locally.

Restoring a Configuration

Sometimes, no matter how vigilant you've been, mistakes happen or something just goes wrong, and you need to fix your system. These fixes range from easy to horrific.

We'll start with a relatively easy one. What happens if you successfully install NT Server, try to adjust your system configuration and render your server unusable, or even unbootable? Something as simple as changing the video driver to something that your system can't handle will do that, and it's hard to restore the original driver if you can't read what's on your screen. If you've messed up your system's configuration, what do you do?

One thing that you *could* do is re-install NT Server. Personally, I would try to avoid this. I've installed NT Server a number of times while experimenting with it, and the installation process doesn't get any more fun. Not only do you have to do the installation process itself, but you have to set up all services and user accounts again. That gets very boring and/or frustrating very quickly. Luckily, there are other ways to fix your setup when something's gone wrong.

The Last Known Good Menu

If you've changed your system so that it can't boot NT Server, one of the better solutions to this problem can be seen while you're rebooting. If you watch while your machine's booting up, you see a message on a black screen that says "Press spacebar NOW to use the Last Known Good Configuration." If you press the spacebar, you see a menu asking you whether you want to

- Use the current configuration
- Use the *last known good configuration*—the configuration that was used the last time the machine booted successfully
- Restart the computer

If your machine won't boot, you probably don't want to use the current configuration, so go instead to the Last Known Good Configuration. It should make your machine bootable.

What are the criteria for a Last Known Good configuration? To qualify, a configuration must not have produced any system critical errors involving a driver or a system file, and a user must have been able to log on to the system at least once.

The Last Known Good configuration can't always help you. If any of the following things are true, you have to use another solution to restore things as you want them:

- You made a change more than one successful boot ago and want to restore things as they were before the change.

- The information that you want to change is not related to control set information—user profiles and file permissions fall into the category of information that can't be changed with the Last Known Good menu.

- The system boots, a user logs on, and then the system hangs.

- You change your video driver to an incompatible driver, restart the system, and log on with the bad driver (you can still type, even if you can't see).

Using the Emergency Repair Disk

If you've screwed up your operating system setup such that using the Last Known Good Configuration can't help you, you still have another option before (groan) re-installing the operating system. Every time you make a successful change to your system's configuration, you should back it up (you'll see how to do that in just a minute). This backup disk, where your system's configuration information is stored, is your Emergency Repair Disk.

To use the Emergency Repair Disk, run WINNT as though you planned to re-install. You come to the setup screen, where the installation program appears and prompts you to begin installation, begin a custom installation, leave Setup, or repair a damaged system. Press R to repair your system. You see some drive activity and then a message that prompts you to insert the Emergency Repair Disk into drive A:. Do so, and a message along the status bar at the bottom of the screen tells you that Setup is reading REPAIR.INF. When it has done that, it prompts you to insert setup disk #1 into drive A:. If you don't have the Setup program on floppies, you can create your own by executing WINNT without the /b parameter.

After you insert Disk #1, Setup asks if you want to do the following:

- Verify The Windows NT Server System Files

- Verify The Boot Files On C:

- Inspect The Configuration Registry Files

By default, all of these options are checked. To deselect them, use the ↑ and ↓ arrows to select an option, and then press Enter to select or deselect. When you've finished, select Continue (perform selected tasks). Then press Enter to detect your adapters. You are asked to insert Setup Disk #3 to load various device drivers. When that's done, you are prompted to insert the Emergency Repair Disk. You see messages along the status bar at the bottom of the screen that tell you that Setup is checking and then examining drive C: (or whatever your system drive is). You see a screen saying that Setup has completed repairs. Press Enter to restart your computer.

What if you didn't create an Emergency Repair Disk? (Shame on you.) NT version 4 creates a repair directory in the system32 directory; you can just refer the repair program to that directory, and it will get the same information it would get from the Emergency Repair Disk.

The Repair Disk contains a registry based on your initial setup. There are no users save for the Administrator and the Guest. None of the permissions that you've established are on the Repair Disk. You can, however, update your Repair Disk (or create a completely new disk) with a program called RDISK.EXE in the SYSTEM32 directory. Just run it and follow the instructions.

Backing Up Your Disk Configuration

In addition to the Emergency Repair Disk, you can save your partition information so that you can replace it if you do something that you regret doing. Here's how:

1. Go to the Disk Administrator.

2. From the Partition Menu, choose Configuration, and then Save. You see a screen that looks like Figure 16.16.

FIGURE 16.16

Insert Disk dialog box

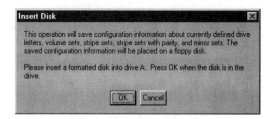

3. Insert the disk and press OK. The system saves the information, and shows the message in Figure 16.17. This message confirms that the configuration was saved.

4. Click OK and you're done. Remove the disk from the drive, label it with the date, and put it somewhere safe. You now have a backup of your disk configuration on your Emergency Repair Disk.

FIGURE 16.17

Disk Administrator confirmation of your configuration change

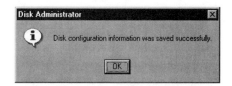

> **WARNING**   If you blast a partition and your data, restoring the partition won't restore the data.

Recovering from Bad Video Drivers

You may recall from the earlier discussion of the Last Known Good Configuration that if you change the video drivers to something that your system can't handle and you reboot and log on with the bad drivers (you can still type a password even if the screen is messed up), the Last Known Good solution can no longer help you. You have, after all, successfully rebooted and logged onto the system; the fact that you can't *see* anything is immaterial.

Under NT version 3.1, this was something of a rigmarole. But NT 4 builds into BOOT.INI the option NT Server 4 (VGA drivers). All you have to do then is to shut down the server, restart it, and choose the setup with VGA drivers. Then, once the system is back up, just select Display from the Control Panel and take a second shot at choosing a video driver. Even better, there is a Test button in the display screen that NT forces you to use to find out *before* you commit yourself whether or not the video drivers work.

Backing up the Registry (and the SAM)

You'll recall that backing up open files is a bit of a pain, impossible sometimes. Few files on an NT machine are more important than the Registry hives. Registry hives are the files named Sam, Security, software, and system, all of which live in \winnt\system32\config.

Alternatives for Backing Up the Registry

Unfortunately, registry hives are constantly open. You can't use a simple COPY or XCOPY command. But there are several tools that you can use to back them up.

First, there's NTBACKUP. You'll recall that there is a check box or a command line option (/B) that instructs NTBACKUP to back up the Registry. You can restore it by using NTBACKUP as well.

The *Resource Kit* includes two programs named REGBACK and REGREST that back up and restore the registry to a floppy.

You may recall that the Emergency Repair Disk contains a copy of the Registry as it looked when you first installed your server. If you run NT Setup and choose the Repair option, then one of the things that you can do is restore the Registry to the state found on the Emergency Repair Disk.

Now, that may not sound like an especially attractive option, since a lot of water has no doubt gone under the bridge between the time that you installed the server and now, but it *is* one way to restore a damaged Registry to a "known good" state. Of course, it would be more desirable to simply keep the copy of the Registry on the Emergency Repair Disk up to date—and you can do that.

In \winnt\system32 is a program called RDISK. RDISK will do two things for you. First, it will write a brand-new Emergency Repair Disk. Even if you didn't create an Emergency Repair Disk when you installed NT, you can make amends for your sin and create one.

There's a problem with putting the Registry on the Emergency Repair Disk: the Registry may be too big. Remember that part of the Registry is the SAM, and the SAM may be megabytes and megabytes on a domain controller. That's where RDISK's second function becomes useful. It updates a directory called \winnt\repair that contains the same data that would go on the Emergency Repair Disk—except it's on the hard disk, so there's more space. But there's just one problem with RDISK, so let me note it.

RDISK does not update the SAM or SECURITY hives all by itself. To get RDISK to back up those files as well, use the undocumented /s switch. Start up RDISK from the command line like so: rdisk /s. RDISK will update the REPAIR directory as well as ask if you want to create an Emergency Repair Disk.

> **TIP** It's a good idea to put RDISK on the Administrative Tools menu to remind you to keep it constantly updated over time as your machine's configuration changes.

Restoring a Registry

If you backed up the Registry with RDISK, restore it by starting up NT Setup and choosing Repair rather than Install NT. If you backed up the Registry with REGBACK, then use REGREST to restore it.

If your Registry backup is on NTBACKUP, you must restore it from the NTBACKUP program. To restore it from the GUI interface, click on the Restore Registry check box.

You cannot restore a disk registry to any disk except the one from which you backed it up. In other words, you can't apply the disk registry from drive C to drive E. That way, you can't sneak around NT's security system.

Planning for Disaster Recovery

Sometimes using the Last Known Good Configuration or the Repair disk doesn't fix your problems. Hard disk failures or natural disasters require a bit more in the way of hard-core disaster recovery.

What does *disaster recovery* mean? Essentially, it's exactly what it sounds like: a way of recovering from disaster—at best, turning a potential disaster into a minor inconvenience. Disaster can mean anything: theft, flood, an earthquake, a virus, or anything else that keeps you from being able to access your data. After all, it's not really the server that's important. While a server may be expensive, it is replaceable. Your data, on the other hand, is either difficult or impossible to recover. Could you reproduce your client mailing list from memory? What about the corporate accounts?

Creating a Disaster Recovery Plan

The most important part of a disaster recovery plan lies in identifying what "disaster" means to you and your company. Obviously, permanently losing all of your company's data would be a disaster, but what else would? How about your installation becoming inaccessible for a week or longer? When planning for disaster, think about all the conditions that could render your data or your workplace unreachable and plan accordingly.

Implementing Disaster Recovery

Okay, it's 2:00 P.M. on Thursday, and you get a report that the network has died. What do you do?

Write Things Down　Immediately write down everything that everyone tells you: what happened, when it happened, who gave you the information, and anything else that happened at the same time that might possibly be related.

Check the Event Logs　If you can get to them, look at the security and event logs on the server to see if you can tell what happened right before the server crashed. If you're using directory replication to maintain a "hot fix" server, the log information may be on the replicated server even if you can't get to the original.

Ascertain the Cause of the Failure and Fix It　"Easy for you to say," I hear someone muttering. It can be done, however. Once you know what events happened, it becomes easier to find out what they happened to.

Find Out If It's a Software Problem   Is it a software problem? If it is, have you changed the configuration? If you've changed something, rebooted, and been unable to boot, it's time to use the Last Known Good Configuration discussed earlier. If you can boot but the operating system won't function properly, use the Emergency Repair Disk to restore the hardware configuration.

If you have another server with NT Server already installed identically to the server that failed, switch servers and see if the backup server works before you re-install the operating system. If the "hot start" server doesn't work, you could be facing a network problem.

Find Out If It's a Hardware Problem   Is it a hardware problem? If you have a physically identical file server (also known as a "hot start" server, since it's ready to go whenever you need it) around the office, put it in place of the failed server and see if you can bring the network back up. If so, the problem lies with the dead server and you can fix or replace it while you have the other one in place. If not, check the network's cabling.

If one drive from a stripe set or mirror set has died, the system should still be fine (if the drive that died is not the one with the system partition on it), but you should still fix the set anyway. Striping and mirroring gives you access to your data while the missing data is being regenerated, but if something else happens to the set before you regenerate the missing data, you're sunk because the set can only deal with one error at a time.

If necessary, reload the backups.

Making Sure the Plan Works

The first casualty of war isn't always the truth—it's often the battle plan itself.

The most crucial part of any disaster recovery plan lies in making sure that it works down to the last detail. Don't just check the hardware, check everything. When a server crashes, backups do no good at all if they are locked in a cabinet to which only the business manager has the keys and the business manager is on vacation in Tahiti.

In the interest of having your plan actually work, make sure you know the answers to the following questions.

Who Has the Keys?   Who has the keys to the backups and/or the file server case? The example mentioned above of the business manager having the only set of keys is not an acceptable situation, for reasons that should be painfully obvious. At any given time, someone *must* have access to the backups.

You could set up a rotating schedule of duty, wherein one person who has the keys is always on call, and the keys are passed on to the next person when a shift is up. However, that solution is not foolproof. If there's an emergency, the person on call could forget to hand the keys off to the next person, or the person on call could be rendered inaccessible through a dead beeper battery or downed telephone line. Better to trust two people with the keys to the backups and server, so that if the person on call can't be reached, you have a backup key person.

Is Special Software Required for the Backups?   Must any special software be loaded for the backups to work? I nearly gave myself heart failure when, after repartitioning a hard disk and re-installing the operating system, I attempted to restore the backups that I'd made before wiping out all the data on the file server's hard disk. The backups wouldn't work. After much frustration, I figured out that Service Pack 2 was installed on the server before. I re-installed the Service Pack from my copy on another computer and the backups worked. I just wish I had figured that out several hours earlier…

Do the Backups Work and Can You Restore Them?   Do the backups work and do you know how to restore them? Verifying backups takes a little longer than just backing them up, but if you verify, you know that what's on the tape matches what's on the drive. So, as far as restoring goes, practice restoring files *before* you have a problem. Learning to do it right is a lot easier if you don't have to learn under pressure, and if you restore files periodically, you know that the files backed up okay.

Have Users Backed Up Their Own Work?   In the interest of preventing your operation from coming to a complete halt while you're fixing the downed network, it might not be a bad idea to have people store a copy of whatever they're working on, and the application needed to run it, on their workstation. People who only work on one or two things at a time could still work while you're getting the server back online.

Diagnosing Server Boot Failures

Last Known Good restores are of no value if you can't get to the "Press a key now to restore Last Known Good..." message. In this section, I'll explain the steps that the server goes through in order to boot and I'll tell you what outward signs those steps display so that you can figure out what went wrong when your server won't boot.

Before the Boot: The Hardware Must Work

Before anything else can happen, your server must be free of hardware problems. You may not be able to boot if

- Your boot drive or boot drive's controller is malfunctioning or is not set up correctly;

- You have an interrupt conflict;

- The CPU or some other vital circuitry is failing.

Too often, the fan on the server's power supply has stopped working. As a result, the temperature inside of the server can rise to over 130°F (55°C) and slowly roast your components.

A company in Bonsall, California, by the name of PC Power and Cooling Systems makes a temperature sensor that fits inside a PC's case and squawks when the PC's internal temperature rises above 100 degrees. It's not cheap (it cost $100 the last time I looked), but it's cheaper than replacing the server.

Another problem that I've run into that can make a machine not boot is an EISA misconfiguration. The fact that EISA allows for software configuration of machines is wonderful. EISA is a real dream for those of us who've spent too much of our lives flipping DIP switches and wrestling jumpers out of hard-to-get-to spaces. But the EISA setup routines on some EISA machines have a quirk: If they don't understand *something*, then they respond by knowing *nothing*.

To show what I mean, suppose you have an EISA disk controller in your server. You shut down the server and replace your old ISA LAN board with an EISA LAN board. You put the cover on your system, try to boot, but only get the message "EISA CMOS failure" and a stopped computer. What happened? The system knew to expect the EISA disk controller, but it *didn't* know to expect the EISA LAN board. Just to play it safe, the computer refused to use the EISA disk controller. Result: you can't boot your system from the hard disk. The system will continue to do this until you run the EISA configuration program.

To make matters worse, most peoples' floppy disk controllers are on the hard disk controller card, which makes it impossible to boot from the floppy. If you can't run the EISA configuration program from either the hard disk *or* the floppy disk, what can you do?

I've found that the best bet in this case is to run the EISA configuration program *before* you install the board. Load the EISA configuration file for the new board and configure the board even before it's in your system. The configuration program will complain a bit about the fact that the board is not actually *in* the system, but all will work in the end. Then shut down the computer and install the new board.

Step One: NTLDR

The first thing that your NT server loads is the NTLDR file, a small program in the root directory. NTLDR announces itself by clearing the screen and displaying

OS Loader V4.00

NTLDR looks for these files:

File	What It Is
BOOT.INI	A text file that tells the NT multi-boot loader which operating systems are available.
NTDETECT.COM	A program that detects the hardware on your NT system.
BOOTSECT.DOS	The file that is present on your root directory if you dual boot with DOS, something unlikely on an NT Server machine.
NTBOOTDD.SYS	This file is present if you boot from a SCSI drive. It's a kind of micro-SCSI driver.

At this point, I've seen messages like "Unable to open NTDETECT .COM," followed by an error code. That means something has damaged data in your root directory and made it impossible for NTDETECT .COM to load. The answer in this case is to use the NT Emergency Repair Disk; I've found that it can reconstruct most root structures.

NTLDR then does these things:

1. Shifts your processor to 386 mode (iapx86 systems).

2. Starts the very simple file system based either on a standard disk interface (known as INT13 for non-SCSI systems) or else uses NTBOOTDD.SYS to boot from the SCSI drive.

3. Reads BOOT.INI to find out if there are other operating systems to offer, and shows those options on the screen.

4. Accepts the user's decision on which OS to load.

Assuming then that you picked NT, NTDETECT runs.

Step Two: NTDETECT

Next, NTDETECT.COM runs to figure out what kind of hardware you have. It announces itself as

```
NTDETECT V1.0 Checking Hardware...
```

That's the same message it's used since 3.1, so presumably this part of NT hasn't changed at all through the versions. NTDETECT finds

- Your PC's machine ID byte

- Its bus type

- Its video board

- Its keyboard type

- The serial ports attached to your computer

- Any parallel ports on the PC

- Floppy drives on the computer

- A mouse, if present

Using the Debug Version of NTDETECT

If you can't get past the NTDETECT stage, there is likely some kind of hardware conflict on your system. Fortunately, there is a "verbose" version of NTDETECT that shows in excruciating detail exactly what NTDETECT sees as it examines your system.

The "verbose" version of NTDETECT.COM is called NTDETECT.CHK and it's on the NT CD-ROM in SUPPORT\DEBUG\I386\NTDETECT .CHK. Of course, you have to rename the file once you copy it from the CD-ROM, and you should copy the file into the root directory of your C: drive—that's the C: drive, even if NT is not installed on drive C.

Two caveats are worth mentioning here. First, I hope it's obvious, but back up the old NTDETECT.COM before overwriting it. Second, you may not be able to get to the C: drive to install NTDETECT.COM in the first place; if that's true, just DISKCOPY the NT Setup Floppy (the first floppy you use to install NT), copy the debug version of NTDETECT.COM onto that floppy, and try to boot from the floppy. That copy of NTDETECT will run and give you a clue about what's going wrong.

Building the Registry

Once NTDETECT has run without trouble, it builds the Hardware hive of the Registry, the part you see in HKEY_LOCAL_MACHINE\ Hardware. Remember that part of the Registry isn't stored on disk; it's built every time you turn your computer on.

Step Three: NTOSKRNL

Next, the NT kernel loads along with the Hardware Abstraction layer (HAL.DLL), the part of NT that allows the operating system to be hardware-independent. The kernel loads in four phases:

- The kernel load phase
- The kernel initialization phase
- The services load phase
- The Windows subsystem start phase

Kernel Load Phase

The first part of a kernel load is the HAL load and the initial NTOSKRNL load. Then the system hive, which lives normally in HKEY_LOCAL _MACHINE\SYSTEM\CurrentControlSet\Services, is read, because the system must determine which device drivers it must load and in what order it must load them. You know this phase is occurring when the screen clears and you again see

```
OS Loader V4.00
```

Just below it, however, dots appear on the screen. Each dot is a service or driver loading. Below that, you see the message

```
Press spacebar NOW to invoke Hardware Profile/Last Known Good menu
```

A look at Services (in Control Panel) shows names like 8514a, Abios-disk, Atd, Aha1542x, etc. Each driver has a value entry named Start, which tells NT when to load that particular service or driver. There are five possible values:

- Start=0 means to load it now, in the kernel load phase. These are the services or drivers that you see dots appearing for.

- Start=1 means to load it in the next phase, kernel initialization phase.

- Start=2 means that this is a service that has been set in the Control Panel/Services applet to "automatic."

- Start=3 indicates that this is a service set to "manual" in the Control Panel.

- Start=4 means that the service has been set to "disabled" in the Control Panel.

Kernel Initialization Phase

Next, the kernel initializes. You know you're here because the screen turns blue and goes to a 50-line mode, and you see a message like this:

```
Microsoft ® Windows NT ® Version 4.00 (Build 1934)
1 System Processor [64MB Memory]
```

The kernel's internal variables are initialized, and once that's done, the kernel again scans the current control set for drivers with a start value of 1. Those drivers get loaded and initialized. Each successfully loaded driver—recall they're the ones with values of Start=1—displays a dot on the screen.

A new current control set gets built in anticipation that the boot will be successful, but it's not saved yet, since NT doesn't know whether or not this will be a Last Known Good set. A program called AUTOCHK.EXE, a CHKDSK-like program, runs to make sure that the file system is intact. The virtual memory pagefiles are also set up.

Services Load Phase

The Services Manager, a program called SMSS.EXE, loads at this point, and loads the Win32 subsystem, as well as any services with Start value=2. The Current Control Set gets written to the system hive.

Windows Subsystem Start Phase

The Win32 subsystem initializes and starts any services that are supposed to start upon boot. This is the last step before the logon dialog box appears. At the same time, the Clone Control Set (a copy of the currently running system configuration) is copied to the Last Known Good Configuration.

Win32 starts up WINLOGON.EXE, which looks in HKEY_LOCAL _MACHINE\Software\Microsoft\Windows NT\Current Version\ Winlogin for the value System, where it finds the names of necessary subsystems. For example, mine contains lsass.exe, the name of the local security authority.

Finally, the logon process happens. That's the process that puts the "Press Ctrl+Alt+Del to logon to Windows NT" window on your screen. If you get that far, then your configuration is good.

Debugging Windows NT 4

This section defines some terminology and provides an overview of debugging NT 4. I also explain how to set up computers for a debugging session. The rest of this chapter will deal with creating a memory dump file, using utilities to process the dump file, and analyzing the information in the memory dump file.

> **NOTE** For Windows NT version 3.51, windbg, the utility used for reading memory dump files in earlier Windows NT releases, was replaced with a set of utilities that automatically read and interpret memory dump files.

Debugging Terminology

You should familiarize yourself with the following terms before debugging your workstation:

Kernel STOP Error   This refers to when NT displays a blue screen containing error information and then stops. Sometimes this error is called a *blue screen*.

Symbols *and* symbol trees   Two types of executable files can be created when compiling programs: debug and nondebug. Debug code contains extra code that enables a developer to debug problems. The nondebug code runs faster and takes up less memory, but can't be debugged.

NT combines the debugging ability of debug code with the speed and smaller size of nondebug code. All driver, executable, dynamic-link libraries, and the like are nondebug versions. However, each program has a corresponding symbol file that contains the debug code. These files are on the NT Workstation CD in the \SUPPORT\ DEBUG*platform*\SYMBOLS directory where *platform* is ALPHA, I386, MIPS, or PPC. Each type of file has its own subdirectory within the SYMBOLS directory. This structure is also called a *symbol tree*. Table 16.3 lists the subdirectories in a standard symbol tree.

TABLE 16.3   Symbol Tree Subdirectories

Directory	File Type
ACM	MSACM files
COM	COM files
CPL	Control Panel applets
DLL	DLL files
DRV	DRV files
EXE	EXE files
SCR	Screen Saver files
SYS	SYS driver files

Target computer   Refers to the computer in which a Kernel Stop Error occurs. This is the computer that needs to be debugged.

Host computer   Refers to the computer on which you run the debugger. This computer should have a running version that is at least as current as the version on the target computer.

Finding Kernel STOP Errors

You can find the source of Kernel STOP Errors in either of two ways:

- Configure the target computer to dump the contents of its memory into a file when the Kernel STOP Error occurs. You can then use dump analysis utilities to analyze the file.

- Use a kernel debugger to troubleshoot the error. To do this you must connect a computer with a working version of NT to the computer on which the Kernel STOP Error occurred and enter the debugging commands from the working machine. Debugging the error this way allows you to look at the memory contents of the machine for the source of the Kernel STOP Error.

Memory Dump Files

If you don't have time to do debugging, you can set up a target computer so that it writes a memory dump file each time a Kernel STOP Error occurs. The dumpexam utility uses this file to analyze the error, allowing a host computer to act as if it is actually hooked up to the target, even though it isn't. While creating this file has the advantage of allowing you to analyze the data at any time without having to tie up a couple of computers, it can be cumbersome. The drawback to this debugging method is that a large amount of available space must be available on you hard disk in order to write the file, as the file can be as large as the RAM memory of the computer with the stop error. For example, a computer with 32MB of RAM will create a 32MB memory dump file.

You also have to have a page file on your system's root directory that is just as large as your RAM memory. If you don't have enough disk space or you're not sure if you do, you should consider local or remote debugging instead.

Creating the Memory Dump File

Before you can use the dump analysis utilities, you need to configure your NT machine to create a memory dump file when a Kernel STOP Error occurs. You use the Recovery dialog box in the System applet to create the memory file. The contents of your computer's memory at the time of the error are written to this dump file so that you can analyze the problem. Using this option allows you to run the dump analysis utilities on any NT Workstation computer after you load the memory dump file, including the computer on which the error occurred. For a summary, see the "How Do I" sidebar.

How Do I Create a Memory Dump File?

To set up the target computer to create a memory dump file, you must do the following:

1. Click on the Recovery button in the System dialog box.
2. Click on the Write Debugging Information To check box.
3. If you want the file to be overwritten every time a Kernel STOP Error occurs, click on the Overwrite Any Existing File check box.
4. Click OK.

Creating a memory dump file is a good option if you want to minimize the amount of time that the host and target computers are unavailable. By running the dump analysis utilities, you can get the information you need for debugging and send it to your technical support staff for analysis. If your computer still runs other applications, you can then go back to a somewhat normal routine.

Using the Dump Analysis Utilities

You will find three command-line utilities for analyzing memory dump files on Windows NT Server and Windows NT Workstation version 4 CDs: dumpflop, dumpchk, and dumpexam. These files can be found in the SUPPORT\DEBUG*platform* directories of the CD, where *platform* is I386, ALPHA, MIPS, or PPC. The utilities create floppy disks or text files that you can send to technical support for analysis.

dumpflop   You can use the dumpflop command to write a memory dump file on floppy disks in order to send it to technical support. Sending floppies away to tech support isn't necessarily a very efficient method of debugging. The information is compressed as it is written to the floppies, so you don't have to worry about writing the 20-something disks for a 32MB dump file, but it still takes time. Fortunately, dumpflop doesn't access the symbol files to write the floppies, so there's at least one good thing about debugging this way.

To write the file to floppies, type the following:

```
dumpflop [options]< MemoryDumpFile> [Drive:]
```

To obtain the dump file after writing it to the floppies, type

```
dumpflop [options]< Drive>: [MemoryDumpFile]
```

The parameters for both writing and reading the file are as follows:

-?	Shows the command syntax.
-p	Prints only the header when assembling.
-v	Displays compression statistics.
-q	Formats the floppy before writing to the disks. When reading the disks, it overwrites the existing dump file.

If the command is executed with no options, it attempts to locate a dump file in the system root directory and writes it to floppies.

dumpchk The dumpchk utility allows you to verify that the dump file was created. It does not require access to the symbol files. To execute the command, type the following:

dumpchk *[options]* `MemoryDumpFile`

where the parameters are as follows:

-?	Shows the command syntax
-p	Prints only the header (no validation)
-v	Verbose mode
-q	Performs a quick test

Dumpchk provides basic information and then verifies all of the addresses in the file. It also reports any errors that are found in the file. This information can be used to determine what Kernel STOP Error occurred and what version of Windows NT was in use.

dumpexam The dumpexam command takes information from the dump file and writes it to a text file. You can then use the text file to find out what caused the Kernel STOP Error. Dumpexam requires three files in order to run. These files are located on the Windows NT Server and Windows NT Workstation 4 CDs in the directory SUPPORT/DEBUG/ *platform*. You need the following files:

- DUMPEXAM.EXE

- IMAGEHLP.DLL

- The third file needs to be one of the following, depending on what type of target computer the error occurred on:

  - KDEXTX86.DLL

  - KDEXTALP.DLL

  - KDEXTMIP.DLL

  - KDEXTPPC.DLL

The command creates a file called MEMORY.TXT (located in the same directory as MEMORY.DMP) that contains information taken from the dump file. In order to run the command, type the following:

```
dumpexam [options] [MemoryDumpFile]
```

where the options are as follows:

-?	Shows the command syntax
-v	Verbose mode
-p	Prints only the header
-f *filename*	Specifies the output file name
-y *path*	Sets the symbol search path

The dumpexam output file displays the same information as the information given in each of the kernel debugger commands given below. You need some knowledge of assembly language and NT kernel processes in order to analyze the data. However, the guidelines given below should give you an idea of what some of the output means.

NOTE

You can also use dumpexam to examine memory dump files created on computers that run earlier versions of Windows NT. However, dumpexam only executes on a system running Windows NT version 3.51 *or higher,* so you need to move the memory dump file or access it over the network. Additionally, you need to replace the KDEXT*.DLL files listed above with copies from the version of Windows NT that was running on the computer on which the dump occurred. These files contain debug information specific to that version of Windows NT. You must also specify the path to the symbols for the operating system version that was running on that computer.

Kernel Debuggers

Kernel debuggers are used on the host computer to debug the Kernel STOP Error on the target computer. Each platform type has its own set of utilities, which are located in the \SUPPORT\DEBUG directory on the NT CD. The debuggers are used for both remote and local debugging. With remote debugging, the host computer can be located anywhere because communication takes place through modems. Local debugging takes place with the target and host computers a few feet away from each other and communicating through a null-modem serial cable. The computers send information to each other through communication ports that must be running at the same baud rate.

Setting Up Your Machine
for Kernel Debugging

If you favor using the kernel debugger over the dump analysis utilities, you need to set up two computers, the one on which the error occurred and another with a working version of NT. The only other equipment you need is either a modem or a null-modem cable. Before you start debugging, you need to do several things:

- Set up the modem connection for either local or remote debugging.
- Set up the target computer (the one with the error) for debugging.
- Set up a symbol tree on the host computer.
- Set up the debugger program on the host computer.
- Start the debugger program on the host computer.

The Modem Connection

You need a connection between the host and the target computers if you want to do either remote or local debugging.

Remote Debugging   You need to use a modem for remote debugging. Which communications port that you use (COM1 or COM2) depends on how the two computers are configured. The default configuration for the target computer depends on what platform the computer uses. The COM port on the host computer is set up as an environment variable. Your modem's documentation should provide information on the signals.

Connect the modem on the host first. When you are ready to connect to the modem on the target computer, see "Setting Up the Debugger on the Host Computer?" later in this chapter. To set the modem on the target computer, you need to

- Connect the modem to one of the target computer's communication ports.

- Turn on auto-answer.

- Turn off flow-control, hardware compression, and error detection.

Local Debugging   In order to connect the target and the host computers, you need to have a null-modem serial cable. The procedure for setting up the cable is the same on both computers. However, there's one caveat: the host computer must be started before you can restart the target computer. Don't worry. Nothing bad will happen if you don't do this—you just have to restart the debugger on the host computer.

The cable can be plugged into different ports on either computer. For example, the cable can be connected to COM1 on the host computer and COM2 on the target computer. Just make sure to make note of which ports the cable is connected to.

Setting Up the Target Computer for Debugging

Usually, your computer is run in normal mode, which is the default when you install NT. When a Kernel STOP Error occurs, the debugger is not enabled. In order to enable debug mode, you have to edit the startup file and set some debugging variables.

The startup file for *x*86-based systems is BOOT.INI. You need to edit the file with a text editor and include either of two switches: /debug or /crashdebug. On a RISC-based computer, you edit the firmware environment variable OSLOADoptions to include debug or crashdebug.

When you use crashdebug on either system, the debugger remains inactive until a Kernel STOP Error occurs. This mode is useful if errors occur randomly. If you're using debug, the debugger can be activated at any time by a host computer connected to the target computer. This method is usually used when experiencing errors that keep reoccurring.

Other options that can be added to the startup file are the communications port and baud rate. The defaults for these options vary from computer to computer, so you may want to add these, just in case.

Of course, you should always create a backup of your startup file just to be safe. Once you've finished debugging, you should then return the startup file to its original state.

Setting Up an *x*86-Based Computer for Debugging   The default communications port for each computer varies. Some are set to COM1, others to COM2. The default baud rate is 9600 if you're using a modem and 19200 if you're using a null-modem serial cable. You shouldn't normally have to worry about setting these rates—they're set at the fastest reliable speeds already.

Once your modem or serial cable is connected, perform the following steps:

1. If a Kernel STOP Error occurs every time you boot the target computer, you can boot MS-DOS from a boot floppy and use the EDIT command to edit BOOT.INI.

   If the boot partition is NTFS, you have to install NT onto a different partition and boot from that partition because the host computer will not be able to access files on an NTFS partition from MS-DOS.

2. Turn off the read-only attribute of BOOT.INI by clicking on the properties dialog box in the File menu on the NT Explorer. The file is usually located in the root directory on the partition from which NTLDR is loaded, usually the C: drive.

3. Use a text editor such as Notepad to edit BOOT.INI. The file will look something like the following:

```
[boot loader]
timeout=30
default=mult(0)disk(0)rdisk(0)partition(1)\winnt
[operating systems]
mult(0)disk(0)rdisk(0)partition(1)\winnt="Windows NT
   Workstation (or Server) Version 4.0"
mult(0)disk(0)rdisk(0)partition(1)\winnt="Windows NT Work-
   station (or Server) Version 4.0 [VGA mode]" /basevideo
   /sos
C:\="MD-DOS"
```

4. Add either **/debug** or **/crashdebug** to the end of the line that contains the startup option that you normally use.

5. To specify the communications port, add the switch **/debugport =comx**, where *x* is the communications port that you want to use.

6. To specify the baud rate, add the switch **/baudrate=<*baudrate*>**.

   Here is an example of a line setting the communications port and baud rate:

   ```
   mult(0)disk(0)rdisk(0)partition(1)\winnt="Windows NT
   Workstation (or Server) Version 4.0" /debugport=com1
   /baudrate=19200
   ```

7. Save the file and quit the text editor or the MS-DOS editor. If you're using a text editor, make sure to select the Save As option and specifically name the file BOOT.INI. Otherwise, the file automatically becomes a TXT file.

8. Restart the computer and run NT.

Setting Up a RISC-Based Computer for Debugging Setting up a RISC-based computer is similar to setting up an *x*86-based computer, except that accessing the startup file is done differently. Once your modem or serial cable is connected, perform the following steps:

1. Restart the computer and select an action from the main menu.

2. On a MIPS system, choose Run setup to display the Setup menu and then choose Manage startup to display a menu of boot options.

   On an Alpha or PowerPC system, select options listed in Table 16.4 to get the Boot selections menu.

TABLE 16.4 Boot Selections Menu Options for Alpha and PowerPC Systems

Menu	Option
System Boot	Supplementary menu
Supplementary	Setup the system
Setup	Manage boot selections

3. Choose Change a Boot Selection to display a list of the operating systems that are installed on the computer.

4. Choose the NT operating system. If you have more than one version installed, select the one that you want to debug.

5. Select the OSLOADOPTIONS variable from the list and press Enter.

6. Type **debug** or **crashdebug** and press Enter to save it and turn on debug mode.

   You can also set the communications port, as in this example:

   ```
   OSLOADOPTIONS debug debugport=com2
   ```

   If you don't specify a port, the default port is set to COM1. You do not need to specify a baud rate because RISC-based computers are always set to 19200.

7. Press ESC to stop editing.

8. On a MIPS-based system, choose Return to Main Menu and then Exit to return to the ARC System screen.

   On an Alpha-based system, choose Supplementary Menu, save your changes, and then choose Boot Menu to return to the ARC System screen.

9. If this is the first time that you have debugged an Alpha-based system, you must do the following after connecting to the host computer:

   • Shut down both computers.

   • Restart the host computer and run ALPHAKD.EXE.

   • Restart the target computer while ALPHAKD.EXE is running on the host to set up the configuration on the target computer.

10. Restart the computer to run the NT operating system.

Setting Up the Symbol Tree on the Host Computer

The symbol tree that you set up on the host computer must match the version of Windows NT that is running on the target computer. On the NT CD, a symbol tree has already been created for each platform. The trees are located in the path SUPPORT\DEBUG*platform*\SYMBOLS, where *platform* is I386, ALPHA, MIPS, or PPC. The *platform* must match the target computer.

To construct a symbol tree, do the following:

1. Copy the proper tree from the SUPPORT directory on the CD to the hard drive on the host computer.

2. If you are debugging a multiprocessor, you need to rename NTKRNLMP.DBG to NTOSKRNL.DBG. These files are in the EXE subdirectory of the symbol tree.

At this point, your symbol tree should be all set up unless you are debugging a multiprocessor or if the target computer uses a special HAL. If this is the case, you need to rename some of the symbol files.

If you're debugging a multiprocessor, you only have to rename NTKRNLMP.DBG (located in the EXE subdirectory of the symbol tree) to NTOSKRNL.DBG.

However, if your computer uses a special HAL, you have a wider range of files to choose from. Table 16.5 shows the different HAL files for each platform. Determine which HAL the target computer uses and rename the corresponding DBG file (located in the DLL subdirectory of the symbol tree) to HAL.DBG (located in *systemroot*\SYSTEM32).

TABLE 16.5   HAL Files by Platform

File Name	Type of System
Files for I386-Based Computers	
HAL.DBG	Standard HAL for Intel Systems
HAL486C.DBG	486 c Step processor
HALAPIC.DBG	Uniprocessor version of HALMPS.DBG
HALAST.DBG	AST SMP systems
HALCBUS.DBG	Cbus systems
HALMCA.DBG	MCA-based systems (PS/2 and others)
HALMPS.DBG	Most Intel multiprocessor systems
HALNCR.DBG	NCR SMP computers
HALOLI.DBG	Olivetti SMP computers
HALSP.DBG	Compaq Systempro

TABLE 16.5   HAL Files by Platform (Continued)

HALWYSE7.DBG	Wyse7 systems

Files for Alpha-Based Computers

HAL0JENS.DBG	Digital DECpc AXP 150
HALALCOR.DBG	Digital AlphaStation 600
HALAVANT.DBG	Digital Alphastation 200/400
HALEB64P.DBG	Digital AlphaPC64
HALGAMMP.DBG	Digital AlphaServer 2x00 5/xxx
HALMIKAS.DBG	Digital AlphaServer 1000 Uniprocessor
HALNONME.DBG	Digital AXPpci33
HALQS.DBG	Digital Multia MultiClient Desktop
HALSABMP.DBG	Digital AlphaServer 2x00 4/xxx

Files for MIPS-Based Computers

HALACR.DBG	ACER
HALDTI.DBG	DESKStation Evolution
HALDUOMP.DBG	Microsoft-designed dual multiprocessor
HALFXS.DBG	MTI with an r4000 or r4400
HALFXSPC.DBG	MTI with an r4600
HALNECMP.DBG	NEC dual multiprocessor
HALNTP.DBG	NeTpower FASTseries
HALR98MP.DBG	NEC 4 processor multiprocessor
HALSNI4X.DBG	Siemens Nixdorf uniprocessor and multiprocessor
HALTYBE.DBG	DESKStation Tyne

Files for PPC-Based Computers

HALCARO.DBG	IBM-6070

TABLE 16.5   HAL Files by Platform (Continued)

HALEAGLE.DBG	Motorola PowerStack and Big Bend
HALFIRE.DBG	Powerized_ES, Powerized_MX (uniprocessor and multiprocessor)
HALPOLO.DBG	IBM-6030
HALPPC.DBG	IBM-6015
HALWOOD.DBG	IBM-6020

Some of you may have a HAL file that was supplied by your computer's manufacturer. If this is the case, you need to get the symbols from the manufacturer, rename the symbol file HAL.DBG, and place it in the DLL subdirectory of the symbol tree.

Setting Up the Debugger on the Host Computer

In order to set up the debugger on the host computer, you first copy some files from the SUPPORT\DEBUG*platform* directory to a debug directory on the hard drive, where *platform* is the platform of the host computer: I386, PPC, Alpha or MIPS.

Some files that you copy must match the platform of the target computer:

- *platform*KD.EXE, where *platform* is the platform of the target computer
  - ALPHAKD.EXE
  - I386KD.EXE
  - MIPSKD.EXE
  - PPCKD.EXE
- IMAGEHLP.DLL

- KDEXTplatform.DLL, where platform is the platform of the target computer

  - KDEXTALP.DLL

  - KDEXTX86.DLL

  - KDEXTMIP.DLL

  - KDEXTPPC.DLL

Starting the Debugger

After you have constructed the symbol tree and copied the symbol files to it, you need to create a batch file to set the environment variables listed in Table 16.6 on the host computer.

TABLE 16.6   Environment Variables for the Host Computer

Variable	Description
_NT_DEBUG_PORT	COM port used on the host computer for debugging.
_NT_DEBUG_BAUD_RATE	Maximum baud rate for the debug port. This number is either 9600 or 19200 if you're using a modem. If you're using a null-modem cable or a RISC-based computer, the baud rate should be set to 19200.
_NT_SYMBOL_PATH	The path containing the symbol files.
_NT_LOG_FILE_OPEN	Creates a log file for the debug session (optional). The log file creates a copy of everything (input and output) that happens during the debugging session.

A sample batch file for local debugging looks similar to the following:

```
set _NT_DEBUG_PORT=com1
set _NT_DEBUG_BAUD_RATE=19200
set _NT_SYMBOL_PATH=c:\support\debug\i386\symbols
set _NT_LOG_FILE_OPEN=c:\temp\debug.log
i386kd -v debug
```

I haven't discussed the last line yet. It is the command to run the debugger program. This line of the batch file (or any other, for that matter) can be run from the command line as well. The parameters for the debugger are as follows:

Parameter	What It Does
-b	Causes the debugger to stop running on the target computer by causing a debug breakpoint (INT 3).
-c	Forces the computer to resynchronize upon connecting to the target computer. This guarantees that the target and host computer are communicating properly.
-m	If you're using a modem, this causes the debugger to monitor control lines. The debugger is only active when the carrier detect line is active. If the line isn't active, all commands are sent to the modem.
-n	Loads symbols immediately instead of in a delayed mode.
-v	Verbose mode. Displays more information than normal mode.
-x	Induces the debugger to break in when an error occurs.

Usually, the easiest way to start the debugger is to set up a batch file by setting up the proper variables followed by the command to run the debugger. That way, you don't have to remember which variables to set and which debugger program to use.

In a local debugging session, you see something similar to the following:

```
Microsoft(R) Windows NT Kernel Debugger
Version 4.0
(C) 1991-1995 Microsoft Corp.
Symbol search path is:
KD: waiting to connect...
```

At this point, the debugger waits for you to press Ctrl+C to connect to the target computer. If this doesn't work, try pressing Ctrl+R to resynchronize the communication between the host and the target computers.

If you're debugging the target computer remotely, the same screen appears but this line is added:

```
KD: No carrier detect - in terminal mode
```

When this happens, you can send any of the AT commands to your modem. Issue commands to disable hardware compression, error detection, and flow control. You need to consult your modem's documentation, as these commands vary from modem to modem. Once you get a carrier detect signal, you can use the debugger.

Starting the Debugger with the Remote Utility

If the host and target computers are on a network and are not easily accessible to one another, you may want to use the remote utility. The command line for starting the debugger from the host is as follows:

```
remote /s "command" Unique_ID
```

For instance, if you were debugging an *x*86-based computer and you wanted the results to be displayed in verbose mode, you would type

```
remote /s "i386kd -v" debug
```

I used the word *debug* as my unique ID, but you can use anything you like. When you're ready to end your session, type @K to return to the command prompt.

You can also interact with the host computer from a workstation that is not connected to the session. To connect to the session, you would type

```
remote /c ComputerName Unique_ID
```

where *ComputerName* is the name of the host computer. For example, if a debugging session was started on the host computer WS1 by using the remote /s command, you could connect to it by typing

```
remote /c WS1 debug
```

NOTE   You can't access a debugging session started on another computer unless the host computer started the session with the remote /s command.

Debugger Commands

A number of debugger commands are available. These commands allow you to

- Load symbols from the symbol tree
- Create a log file
- View device drivers on your system
- Display all locks held on resources
- Obtain a description of memory usage
- Display virtual memory usage
- View the kernel error log
- Display a list of pending Interrupt Request Packets (IRPs)
- List all processes and threads
- List currently active processes and threads

Table 16.7 lists the commands that are available.

TABLE 16.7   Kernel Debugger Commands

Command	Description
!bugdump	Display bug check dump data
!calldata <*table name*>	Dump call data hash table
!db <*physical address*>	Display physical memory
!dd <*physical address*>	Display physical memory

TABLE 16.7 Kernel Debugger Commands (Continued)

Command	Description		
!devobj *<device address>*	Dump the device object and Irp queue		
!drvobj *<driver address>*	Dump the driver object and related information		
!drivers	Display information about all loaded system modules		
!eb *<physical address>* *<byte, byte,...>*	Modify physical memory		
!ed *<physical address>* *<dword,dword,...>*	Modify physical memory		
!errlog	Dump the error log contents		
!exr *<address>*	Dump exception record at specified *address*		
!filecache	Dump information about the file system cache		
!frag *[flags]*	Kernel mode pool fragmentation		
	flags:	1	List all fragment information
		2	List allocation information
		3	Do both
!handle *<addr>* *<flags>* *<process>* *<TypeName>*	Dump handle for a process		
	flags:	2	Dump non-paged object
!heap *<addr>* *[flags]*	Dump heap for a process		
	flags:	-v	Verbose
		-f	Free List entries
		-a	All entries
		-s	Summary
		-x	Force a dump even if the data is bad
	address:		Desired heap to dump or 0 for all
!help	Display this table		

TABLE 16.7   Kernel Debugger Commands (Continued)

Command	Description
!ib <*port*>	Read a byte from an I/O *port*
!id <*port*>	Read a double-word from an I/O *port*
!iw <*port*>	Read a word from an I/O *port*
!irp <*address*>	Dump Irp at specified *address*
!irpzone	Walk the Irp zones looking for active Irps
!locks [-v] <*address*>	Dump kernel mode resource locks
!lpc	Dump lpc ports and messages
!memusage	Dumps the page frame database table
!ob <*port*>	Write a byte to an I/O *port*
!obja <*TypeName*>	Dump an object manager object's attributes
!object <*TypeName*>	Dump an object manager object
!od <*port*>	Write a double-word to an I/O *port*
!ow <*port*>	Write a word to an I/O *port*
!pfn	Dump the page frame database entry for the physical page
!pool <*address*> [*detail*]	Dump kernel mode heap

address:	0 *or* blank	Only the process heap
	1	All heaps in the process

Otherwise for the heap address listed

detail:	0	Summary Information
	1	Above + location/size of regions
	3	Above + allocated/free blocks in committed regions
	4	Above + free lists

TABLE 16.7   Kernel Debugger Commands (Continued)

Command	Description
!poolfind *Tag [pooltype]*	Find occurrences of the specified *Tag*
	Tag is 4-character tag, * and ? are wild cards
	Pooltype is 0 for nonpaged (default), and 1 for paged
	NOTE: This can take a long time!
!poolused *[flags]*	Dump usage by pool tag

	flags:	1	Verbose
		2	Sort by NonPagedPool Usage
		4	Sort by PagedPool Usage

Command	Description
!process *[flags]*	Dump process at specified address
!processfields	Show offsets to all fields in a process
!ptov *PhysicalPageNumber*	Dump all valid physical and virtual mappings for the given page directory
!ready	Dump state of all READY system threads
!regkcb	Dump registry key-control-blocks
!regpool *[s|r]*	Dump registry allocated paged pool

	s	Save list of registry pages to temporary file
	r	Restore list of registry pages from temp. file

Command	Description
!reload	Load the symbol files
!srb *<address>*	Dump Srb at specified *address*
!sympath	Display the current symbol path
!sysptes	Dump the system PTEs
!thread *[flags]*	Dump thread at specified address
!threadfields	Show offsets to all fields in a thread

TABLE 16.7   Kernel Debugger Commands (Continued)

Command	Description
!time	Report PerformanceCounterRate and TimerDifference
!timer	Dump timer tree
!token [flags]	Dump token at specified address
!tokenfields	Show offsets to all fields in a token
!trap <address>	Dump a trap frame
!vad	Dump VADs
!version	Version of extension dll
!vm	Dump virtual management values
x86-Specific Commands	
!apic [base]	Dump local apic
!cxr	Dump context record at specified address
!ioapic [base]	Dump io apic
!mtrr	Dump MTTR
!npx [base]	Dump NPX save area
!pcr	Dump the PCR
!pte	Dump the corresponding PDE and PTE for the entered address
!sel [selector]	Examine selector values
!trap [base]	Dump trap frame
!tss [register]	Dump TSS

!reload

The !reload command loads the symbols from the symbol tree. Output from the command looks like this:

```
kd> !reload
Loading symbols for 0x80100000   ntoskrnl.exe ->
d:\support\debug\i386\symbols\exe\ntoskrnl.dbg
KD ModLoad: 80100000 801ca740  ntoskrnl.exe
KD ModLoad: 80400000 8040b000  hal.dll
KD ModLoad: 80010000 80013320  atapi.sys
KD ModLoad: 80014000 8001ba80  SCSIPORT.SYS
```

You need to execute this command before any other because the symbols are needed to execute other commands.

Log Files

You will also want to create a log file to review. To create a log file, all you have to do is type

```
.logopen
```

This creates a text file named KD.LOG that can be found in the same directory as the debugger program you are using. With a log file, you can compare output from commands such as !vm and !memusage.

If you already have a log file and just want to append to it, type

```
.logappend
```

This adds any additional output to the end of the log file. When you're ready to close the file, type

```
.logclose
```

!drivers

The !drivers command lists all of the device drivers located on your system. The information from the device drivers looks something like the following (I cleaned it up a bit for the sake of clarity):

```
kd> !drivers
Loaded System Driver Summary
Base       Code Size     Data Size      Driver Name  Creation Time
80100000  b31c0 (716kb)  17200 (92kb)  ntoskrnl.exe Thu Jan 25 19:14:08 1996
80400000   92c0 ( 36kb)   20c0 ( 8kb)  hal.dll      Thu Jan 18 15:28:52 1996
80010000   2940 ( 10kb)   760  ( 1kb)  atapi.sys    Sun Jan 21 19:40:48 1996
80014000   6400 ( 25kb)   13c0 ( 4kb)  SCSIPORT.SYS Fri Jan 19 12:19:37 1996
```

The following items can be determined from the above:

Base   The starting address (in hex) of the device driver. When the code that causes the Kernel STOP Error falls between the base address for the driver and the base address for the next driver on the list, that driver is likely the cause of the error. For example, as you can see from the above output, the base for atapi.sys is 0x8001000. Any address that falls between that and 0x80014000 (the base address for SCSIPORT.SYS) belongs to atapi.sys. If the target computer displays a blue screen, often the first address listed is that of a driver.

Code Size   The size of the driver code in both hex and decimal.

Data Size   The amount of allocated space given to the driver for data in both hex and decimal.

Driver Name   The file name of the driver.

Creation Time   The link date of the driver—in simpler terms, the date when a driver or executable file is compiled.

!locks

The !locks command displays all locks held on resources by threads. Locks can be either shared or exclusive. The information provided by this command is useful, especially when deadlocks occur on the target computer. A deadlock occurs when a non-executing thread has an exclusive lock on a resource that is needed by another executing thread.

The output for the !locks command looks similar to the following:

```
kd> !locks -v -d
**** DUMP OF ALL RESOURCE OBJECTS ****
Resource @ ntoskrnl!MmSystemWsLock (0x80148b90)  Available
  Contention Count = 4
Resource @ ntoskrnl!MmSectionExtendResource (0x80148990)  Available
Resource @ 0xff7143a0 Shared 2 owning threads
  Threads: ffb3ba61-01
0013ffa31: Unable to read ThreadCount for resource
```

!memusage

This command briefly describes the system's current memory usage, after which it gives a more detailed list of memory usage. The output for !memusage looks like this:

```
kd> !memusage
 loading PFN
database...............................................
       Zeroed:    0 (    0 kb)
         Free:    2 (    8 kb)
      Standby:  786 ( 3144 kb)
     Modified:   95 (  380 kb)
 ModifiedNoWrite:    0 (    0 kb)
   Active/Valid: 3211 ( 12844 kb)
   Transition:    0 (    0 kb)
      Unknown:    0 (    0 kb)
        TOTAL: 4094 ( 16376 kb)
 Usage Summary in KiloBytes (Kb):
 Control Valid Standby Dirty Shared Locked PageTables name
 ff6ab5c8   0    36     0     0      0      0 mapped_file( GNLI____.TTF )
 ff6aa548   0    40     0     0      0      0 mapped_file( KF_____.TTF )
 ff6ab428   0    32     0     0      0      0 mapped_file( GNM_____.TTF )
 ff6afc68   0    40     0     0      0      0 mapped_file( Latinwd.ttf )
```

TIP   Even though the !memusage command gives some information about memory leaks, it is still better to look at the !vm command for memory information on the most common Kernel STOP Errors.

!vm

The !vm command provides a list of the target system's virtual memory usage. Output from the command looks similar to the following:

```
kd> !vm
*** Virtual Memory Usage ***
        Physical Memory:   3950   ( 15800 Kb)
        Available Pages:    788   (  3152 Kb)
        Modified Pages:      95   (   380 Kb)
        NonPagedPool Usage:  83   (   332 Kb)
        PagedPool 0 Usage:  763   (  3052 Kb)
        PagedPool 1 Usage:   69   (   276 Kb)
        PagedPool 2 Usage:   85   (   340 Kb)
        PagedPool Usage:    917   (  3668 Kb)
        Shared Commit:       88   (   352 Kb)
        Process Commit:     285   (  1140 Kb)
        Per Process:        787   (  3148 KB)
        PagedPool Commit:   917   (  3668 Kb)
        Driver Commit:      495   (  1980 Kb)
        Committed pages:   2710   ( 10840 Kb)
        Commit limit:      9077   ( 36308 Kb)
```

The memory usage you see in the above list is given in both pages and kilobytes. The most useful information for analyzing problems is:

Physical Memory   The total physical memory on the target computer.

Available Pages   The total number of pages of available physical and virtual memory. If this number is low, the cause might be a problem with a process that allocates too much virtual memory.

NonPagedPool Usage   The number of pages allocated to the non-paged pool. A pool is memory that can't be swapped to the pagefile, so it always occupies physical memory. This number should not be larger than 10 percent of the total physical memory. If it is larger, the target computer may have a memory leak.

!errlog

Sometimes the debugger maintains a log of kernel errors that occur on the target computer. The !errlog command allows you to view this log. Most of the time, however, this log is empty. If an event has been logged, however, you may be able to find out from it which process caused the Kernel STOP Error.

!irpzone full

The !irpzone full command provides a list of all pending Interrupt Request Packets (IRP) on the target computer. An IRP is a data structure used by device drivers and other processes to communicate with each other. Output for this program looks like this:

```
kd> !irpzone full
Small Irp region
Could not allocate 3952 bytes for region
Large Irp region
Irp is from zone and active with 2 stacks 2 is current
 No Mdl System buffer = ff6b8b88 Thread ff6b8020: Irp stack trace.
 cmd flg cl Device  File   Completion-Context
  0  0 0 ff6b8b88 00000000 00000000-00000000
         ff6b8b88: is not a device object
                  Args: 00000000 00000000 ff6e6808 00000104
> 3  0 1 ff6d0e70 ff6b8e08 00000000-00000000  pending
         \FileSystem\Npfs
                  Args: 00000104 00000000 00000000 00000000
```

This information may be useful if the trap analysis (which you can find in the MEMORY.TXT file) indicates a problem with an IRP that has gone bad. Usually, the IRP listing has a number of entries in both of the large and small IRP lists.

!process 0 0

By using the !process 0 0 command, you can view all of the active processes and their headers. Its output looks like the following:

```
kd> !process 0 0
**** NT ACTIVE PROCESS DUMP ****
PROCESS ff6ef7a0 Cid: 0002  Peb: 00000000 ParentCid: 0000
  DirBase: 00030000 ObjectTable: ff714488 TableSize: 62.
  Image: System
PROCESS ff6d5de0 Cid: 0011  Peb: 7ffdf000 ParentCid: 0002
  DirBase: 007bd000 ObjectTable: ff6d6248 TableSize: 46.
  Image: smss.exe
```

The information that is helpful to know here is

Process ID   The 8-digit hex number following the word PROCESS.
The system uses this number to track the process.

Image   The name of the program that owns the process.

!process 0 7

This command is similar to the !process 0 0 command, but instead of a
brief summary, it lists all of the information about the process. This is
usually a large listing because each system is running a large number of
processes and each process usually has one or more threads. Also, if the
stack from a thread resides in kernel memory, it is also listed. Output
usually looks like this:

```
kd> !process 0 7
**** NT ACTIVE PROCESS DUMP ****
PROCESS ff6ef7a0 Cid: 0002  Peb: 00000000 ParentCid: 0000
  DirBase: 00030000 ObjectTable: ff714488 TableSize: 62.
  Image: System
  VadRoot ff6eed68 Clone 0 Private 5. Modified 338. Locked 0.
  FF6EF95C MutantState Signalled OwningThread 0
  Token               e1000730
  ElapsedTime             13:43:40.0594
  UserTime            0:00:00.0000
  KernelTime          0:00:39.0236
```

```
QuotaPoolUsage[PagedPool]      0
QuotaPoolUsage[NonPagedPool]    0
Working Set Sizes (now,min,max) (53, 30, 145)
PeakWorkingSetSize          125
VirtualSize             0MB
PeakVirtualSize          0MB
PageFaultCount           630
MemoryPriority          BACKGROUND
BasePriority             8
CommitCharge             9
   THREAD ff6ef520 Cid 2.1 Teb: 00000000 Win32Thread: 80148260 WAIT:
(WrFreePage) KernelMode Non-Alertable
     80148980 SynchronizationEvent
   Not impersonating
   Owning Process ff6ef7a0
   WaitTime (seconds)   9123
   Context Switch Count  192
   UserTime          0:00:00.0000
   KernelTime        0:00:32.0707
   Start Address ntoskrnl!Phase1Initialization (0x801b9016)
   Stack Init fdc14000 Current fdc13cfc Base fdc14000 Limit fdc11000
Call 0
   Priority 0 BasePriority 0 PriorityDecrement 0 DecrementCount 0
   ChildEBP RetAddr Args to Child
   fdc13d14 8011500c c0502000 0000053d 00000000
ntoskrnl!KiSwapThread+0xc5
       fdc13d38 801274b2 80148980 00000008 00000000
ntoskrnl!KeWaitForSingleObject+0x1b8
```

You may find the following information important:

UserTime   The length of time the process has been running in user mode.

KernelTime   The length of time the process has been running in kernel mode. If either the UserTime or KernelTime value seems very high, the process may be taking up an exceptional amount of system resources.

Working Set Sizes   Gives the working set size in pages. A very large value for this entry may indicate that a process is leaking memory or taking up a large amount of system resources.

QuotaPoolUsage   Provides the paged and non-paged pool used by the process. If you find that the non-paged pool used by a process is excessive, you may have found your memory leak.

Not only that, you'll find that the thread information also has a list of threads that have locks on resources. This is given right after the thread header. In the output above, the thread has a lock on one resource (a SynchronizationEvent at address 80148260). When comparing this address against the list of locks shown in the !locks output, you should be able to find which threads have exclusive locks on resources.

!process

The !process command displays information on the currently running process on the target computer. The output looks exactly like that of the !process 0 7 command, except it is for only one process and no thread information is given.

!thread

The !thread command behaves in much the same as !process, except that thread information is given instead.

> **NOTE**
> Even though the !process 0 7 command gives information on both processes and threads, the result can be 10–15 pages of output. This can make things a bit difficult when it comes to finding the currently running process and threads. Use !process and !thread instead.

Examining Crash Dumps with DUMPEXAM

What should you do about a blue screen? If you can manage to get a blue screen while the debugger is attached, then you're golden—you can log the output. But the whole debugger system may not be set up, and that's where a crash dump file can be useful.

You can tell an NT machine that if it ever experiences a blue screen, it should dump the entire contents of memory to a file called MEMORY .DMP. You enable that function in the Control Panel. In the System applet, you see a tab labeled "Startup/Shutdown," with a group on its page labeled "Recovery." Click the check box that directs the system to create MEMORY.DMP.

If you ever *do* see a blue screen, reboot and you'll see a huge MEMORY .DMP file in your \winnt directory. You examine that with DUMPEXAM, but you need a few ingredients to use DUMPEXAM.

First, you need the program itself. It's on the CD-ROM in \support\ debug\i386\dumpexam.exe. If you copy it somewhere else, you should also copy kdextx86.dll, because it is needed, too. You also need the folder in \support\debug\i386\symbols because DUMPEXAM needs it to understand what it's seeing in the memory dump. Invoke DUMPEXAM like so:

```
dumpexam -v -f outfile -y x:\support\debug\i386\symbols memory.dmp
```

The -v says "be verbose"; the more information we can get, the better. *Outfile* is just the name of an ASCII text file that will contain the output of the dump analysis. For drive *x:*, insert the drive letter of your CD-ROM. Memory.dmp is, of course, the name of the original crash dump file. The output file is an expanded-upon blue screen.

Well, now that you have it, what do you do with it? Let's look at the information a blue screen provides.

The first lines are a stop code. They may look like this:

```
** STOP: address1 address2 address3 address4
```

The four numbers are addresses; one of them is the address of the actual program that caused the blue screen.

You next see a line like this:

```
INACCESSIBLE_BOOT_DEVICE or IRQL_NOT_LESS_OR_EQUAL
```

Following that is a list of kernel mode drivers in memory at the time of the blue screen. It is a two-column listing. An excerpt might look like this:

```
DLL Base DateStmp - Name
80100000 2e53fe55 - ntoskrnl.exe
80010000 2e41884b - Aha154x.sys
```

The "Base" is the start address of the DLL. All addresses are above 80000000 hex because the system area starts there. The date-stamp (it's seconds since 1980) can be useful because if you see a system driver with a different date from other system drivers, it could be a newer, corrupted driver.

Below the driver list is a list of modules that are near the area that caused the blue screen; one of them is the culprit.

The Bottom Line: What They're Good For

Blue screens and the Kernel Debugger can be insightful tools, but remember that in the end analysis they can do only a few things:

- Point the finger at a bad driver. Calling a vendor and saying, "Your SCSI driver doesn't work on my system" is much more likely to produce a shrug and a "Says you, pal" from the SCSI vendor. Being able to send the vendor a blue screen output is a bit more damning and *may* motivate the vendor to fix their buggy drivers.

- Give an indication of what's going wrong. Maybe the vendor is blameless and you've just got a corrupted driver. Once you know what file may have caused the trouble, you can try reloading it or checking the vendor's Web site for an updated driver.

- Sometimes give you the ammunition to say to Microsoft, "Look, there's a bug in the [fill in the blank] subsystem, and here's the proof!" There's no guarantee that anyone will *do* anything about it, but at least you have the smoking gun.

The Windows NT Diagnostics Tool

If you want nuts-and-bolts information about the hardware on your NT Server, you *could* go to the documentation for all your hardware and read all the notes you made about changes to the default configurations. Even the most dedicated record keeper doesn't have information about everything, however, so Windows NT keeps information about your system that you might never have known you had. To get a more complete idea of the picture, then, you can check with WinMSD, the Windows NT diagnostics tool.

WinMSD is in the Administrative Tools group under the name Windows NT Diagnostics.

Before getting into the details of WinMSD, let me make clear that it is not a terribly powerful tool. It won't solve a *lot* of problems. Its main value is in allowing you to take a quick "bird's-eye" view of a system, something of considerable use if you've been called in to look at a problem on a server that you've not looked at before.

But wait, that's not all. Windows NT Diagnostic also allows you to view the diagnostic information for all the other Windows NT computers in the domain without having to physically go to those computers. Let's take a look at this new and interesting feature in more detail.

Remote Diagnostic Viewing

Being able to save shoe leather by sitting at your own desk as you ferret out a problem on a machine six flights away sounds like a great improvement. Indeed, it is. However, beware of some restrictions before you kick off your shoes entirely.

The first restriction, of course, is that diagnostic information can only be read from a machine that is running NT. If we assume all machines on a network are running NT, then

- A workstation can read diagnostic information from any server on the network.

- A workstation can read diagnostic information from another workstation as long as both computers are members of the same domain.

- A server can read diagnostic information from any workstation or server on the network.

To view a remote diagnostic window, see the next "How Do I" sidebar.

How Do I Find the Diagnostics Information of a Remote Workstation or Server?

1. In the Start menu, click on Programs and choose Administrative Tools.
2. Open Windows NT Diagnostics.
3. Click on the File menu and choose Select Compute

How Do I Find the Diagnostics Information of a Remote Workstation or Server? (Continued)

4. Type in the name of the computer or, more easily, double-click on the computer you want to see. You see a screen like this one:

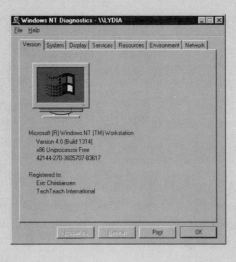

Viewing Diagnostic Information

To view diagnostic information, begin at the Start Menu, click on Programs, then on Administrative Tools, and finally on Windows NT Diagnostics. You see a screen that looks like the one in Figure 16.18.

The dialog box is divided into nine tabs. Each tab shows different aspects of the computer's components and their present state. The Version tab appears first and acts like a cover page. The other eight tabs are discussed in order of appearance.

FIGURE 16.18

Opening Diagnostics
screen

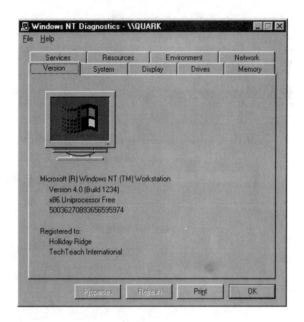

Meanwhile, if you have used the Diagnostics in NT Server 3.51 or
before, you may notice that the tabs have been renamed and some of
the information has been moved around. Here is a brief overview
of the main changes:

- The OS Version button is now the Version tab.

- The install date and system root is omitted in version 4.

- The Hardware button is now the System tab.

- The Video resolution is now listed in the Display tab.

- The CPU stepping button is no longer a separate button. A more
  complete description is now in the System tab itself.

- The Memory button is still the Memory tab, although the Memory
  load index has been omitted. This oversight represents a loss to the
  Diagnostics function. Knowing how much memory is being used
  can be very helpful. Perhaps they will put it back in the next version.

- The Drivers button is now incorporated in the Devices portion of the Services tab.

- The Devices button, IRQ/Port Status button, and DMA/Memory button are all incorporated into the Resources tab.

- The Environment button is still the Environment tab, although the Process Environment section is gone. That information can be found in the Drives tab now.

- The Drives button is the Drives tab and now you can see the drive letter and icon as well as the drive type.

- The New Display tab shows the settings of the monitor and display card.

Now, let's look more closely at the contents of some of the tab sections in Windows NT Diagnostics 4.

Memory Tab

As the title implies, the Memory tab gives you information about your system's memory. It tells how much memory it has and how much is still available. As you can see in Figure 16.19, this server has 16MB of RAM, of which only 1MB is unused. The same information is listed for the Page File space. Here, there are 5.6MB, of which 2.8MB are available.

The *paging file* is the amount of data that can be passed back and forth when NT Workstation is using virtual memory—in this case, 5.6MB. What is virtual memory? In order to get more work out of the system RAM than it could provide on its own, NT Workstation uses a special file on the hard disk called a virtual memory *paging file*, or *swap file*. When Windows NT is demanding more of the system memory than the system can really give, it keeps some of the program code and other information in RAM and puts some of it in the paging file on the hard disk. When that information is required, NT Workstation pulls it out of virtual memory (swapping other information into the paging file, if necessary). The end result is more bang for your RAM buck.

FIGURE 16.19

Diagnostic Memory tab

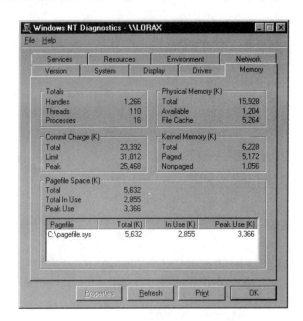

Services Tab

The Services tab contains two buttons. Click on Services and you can see the services that are available on the system, as shown in Figure 16.20. Click on Devices to see all of the devices on the system, as shown in Figure 16.21. Both lists show whether each device or service is stopped or running at the time.

For the details of individual servers or devices, highlight the one in question and click on Properties. Or, more easily, just double-click on the service or device in question. The properties screen that appears includes two tabs, General and Dependencies, as you can see in Figure 16.22.

FIGURE 16.20

Diagnostics Services
screen

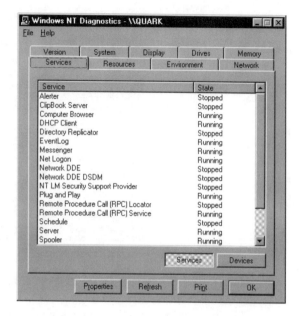

FIGURE 16.21

Diagnostics Devices
screen

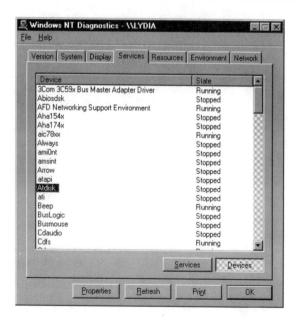

FIGURE 16.22

Diagnostics Service
screen showing general
properties

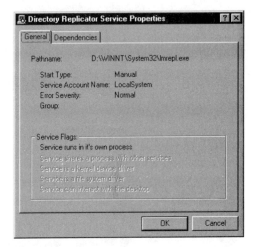

General Service and Device Information

The general properties of services and devices includes the following information:

- The path where the driver is found.

- The Start Type, which can be one of several things:

Boot	Begin at computer bootup. Applies to drivers for hardware without which the computer cannot function, such as disk drives.
System	Begin when the operating system starts up. Applies to devices that are critical to the operation of the operating system, such as display drivers like ET4000.
Automatic	Begin when the operating system has begun, like the system drivers, but are not crucial to the operation of the operating system. The NetBIOS interface is one example of such a driver.
Manual	Begin when started by the user or a dependent device.
Disabled	These drivers cannot be started by a user, but the system can start them. This is why you may see drivers that are running but are listed as being disabled—that threw me for a loop the first time that I noticed it. The FastFAT is one example of such a driver.

- What kind of error control they have. The level of error control determines what happens to the system startup if a given driver fails:

Critical	Don't start up the system.
Severe	Switch to the Last Known Good setup, or, if already using that setup, continue on.
Normal	Continue startup, but display an error message stating that the driver did not load.
Ignore	Don't halt the system or display an error message: just skip that driver.

- The group that they are associated with (SCSI miniport, video, etc.) determines their load order, as, for example, the boot file system loads before video, and SCSI miniports load before each of these.

Users with administrative privileges can add device drivers to the system from the Drivers icon in the Control Panel, or adjust their startup time or error control from the Devices icon. Be careful about adjusting these things, however, because if you change a Boot or System driver to a different time, you could keep your system from working.

- Service Flags that tell how the service interacts with the rest of the machine by indicating if the service

  - Runs in its own process
  - Shares a process with other services
  - Is a kernel device driver
  - Is a file system driver
  - Can interact with the desktop

Dependencies of Services and Devices

Click on the Dependencies tab and you can see what services and groups are dependent on this service, as shown in Figure 16.23. This is helpful for tracking an error and better understanding the flow of information through the computer.

FIGURE 16.23

Dependencies tab in Services screen

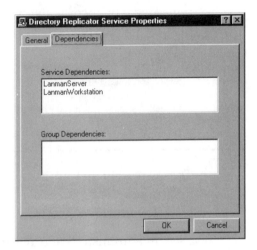

Resources Tab

The Resources tab lists the hardware resources that are attached to the computer and how they are attached. Click on any of the five buttons (IRQ, I/O Port, DMA, Memory, or Devices) to see what you have.

The IRQ and I/O Port windows give you information about what interrupts, memory accesses, and ports your system is using. For an example of each, see Figures 16.24 and 16.25. You can't change anything with these dialog boxes, but they *can* help resolve interrupt conflicts or memory port conflicts.

NOTE What would you use a hex address for? It can serve as a partial guide to current port addresses on your computer and keep you from installing a new device that causes a port conflict. This is invaluable information for adding components to your computer.

FIGURE 16.24

IRQ portion of the
Resources tab in
the Diagnostics
dialog box

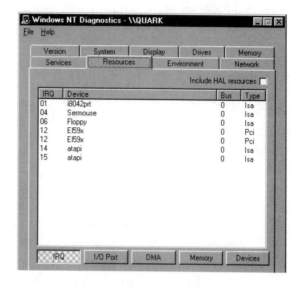

FIGURE 16.25

IO Port screen of the
Resources tab

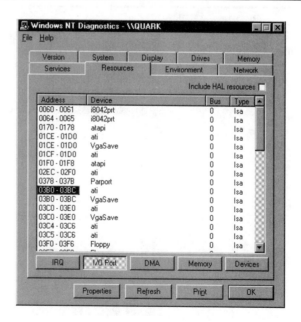

The DMA and Memory windows show you the location and size of fixed blocks of memory. They also report which devices are using Direct Memory Access (DMA) ports. The report for each looks like Figures 16.26 and 16.27.

Three devices use DMA channels on this machine: the floppy uses channel 2 and the SCSI host adapters use channel 3 and channel 7. The Memory section displays fixed blocks of memory, the areas of physical memory that must not be moved by the operating system. Those areas are rare and are typically buffers for peripherals. The areas displayed by WINMSD here are the video memory buffer, the video BIOS, and the SCSI BIOS on this system.

The Devices window shows you all the devices that are present on the computer that you are looking at. If you double-click on one of the items in the list, you see a screen that looks like Figure 16.28. This screen recaps, by device, the IRQ, I/O port, and DMA.

FIGURE 16.26

DMA screen of the Resources tab

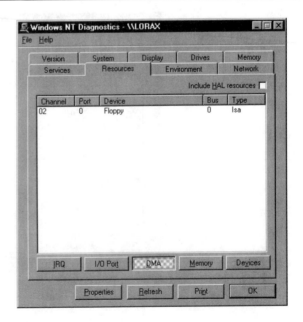

FIGURE 16.27

Memory screen of the
Resources tab

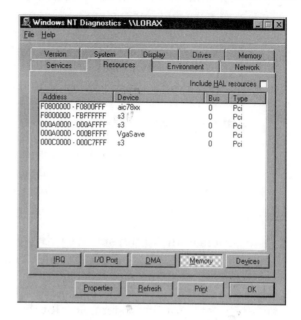

FIGURE 16.28

Properties of the Device
dialog box

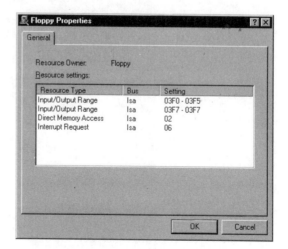

The information in this screen is useful if you plan to set up more hardware on your system and want to make sure that two devices don't conflict. You could adjust these settings by re-installing your hardware and adjusting the IRQ and DMA settings, but in most cases that isn't necessary. This dialog box (like the ones that show the IRQs and DMA channels in use) is really for information purposes only.

Environment Tab

Every computer has information that is specific only to itself: the command interpreter it is using, its home drive, and the like. That information is stored in NT in the *environment*, an area of memory that stores configuration-specific information. Figure 16.29 shows an example.

Users with Administrative privileges can change this information from the System icon in the Control Panel.

This dialog box lists the processor architecture, operating system type, etc., for the system, and for that particular machine.

FIGURE 16.29

Environment tab in Diagnostics dialog box

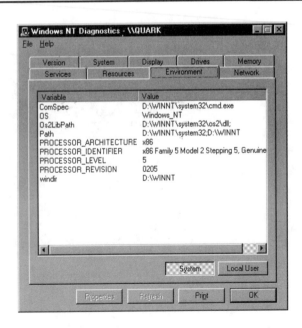

Network Tab

The Network tab shows the relationship between the current user, his or her computer, and the network. There are four sections to the Network tab:

Section	What It Is
General	A nice summary of your machine's name, your user name, logon information, and the like.
Transports	A convenient way to find out which transport layers you're running. In theory, if you were running a TCP/IP stack, this would be a quick way to find out what IP address you were using.
Settings	Dozens of settings that you can use to tune an NT Server installation. This window shows you their current values. The interesting part is that the window can give you ideas about what kinds of things you can control with NT Server—ideas that you might not have known you could do. (The important ones are covered in the book, by the way, so you don't have to do any digging.)
Statistics	As the network works, statistical monitors in each computer keep track of how many bytes have been transmitted or received, how many errors occurred, and the like. This section reports those values.

Printing the Results

Seeing this information is good, but being able to print it and have it at your fingertips when someone says, "My computer won't..." is even better.

The Print button at the bottom of each tab allows you to create and print a report of the information on the tab as well as print the whole diagnostics file. See the following "How Do I" sidebar for specifics on creating a printed report.

TIP Tape an envelope to the computer with a recent report of the Diagnostic information in case of emergencies.

How Do I Print a Report of a Single Tab Section of the Diagnostics File?

To create a printed report of what is on a diagnostics tab:

1. Open the Windows NT Diagnostics screen.

2. Click on the tab whose information you wish to print in a report.

3. Click on the Print option at the bottom right of the window. You see the Create Report dialog box:

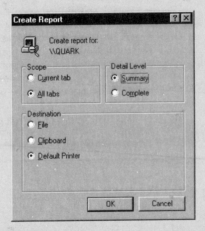

4. Choose the Current tab in the Scope area.

5. Decide whether you want a summary of the information or a complete printout.

6. Tell where you want the information stored. You can put it in a file, on the Clipboard, or print it out directly.

If you wish to print a full report, choose All tabs as the Scope from any of the Diagnostics tabs.

Disasters shouldn't happen, but they sometimes do. With the proper preventive planning beforehand, they can become entertaining war stories, rather than sources of battle fatigue.

NT version 4 provides a diagnostics tool that can help you keep track of the components of your computer. Knowing what you have and what it is attached to can help you plan ahead. It also gives you another place to look when diagnosing a problem.

CHAPTER
SEVENTEEN

Using Dial-Up Networking

Less and less of our "office work" actually takes place *in* the office. Many of us, when we travel, really need what's on the server back at the office. If I had a nickel for every time on the road that I discovered—too late—that I was missing data or an application… For a greater number of us, the office is a place visited a couple of times a week, with most work being done at home. *Telecommuting* is a good idea for more and more businesses.

With NT 4 comes a face lift of NT 3.*x*'s Remote Access Server (RAS). Now it's called Dial-Up Networking (DUN), just as it is in Windows 95. Put simply, DUN extends all of the benefits of a local area network over a dial-up connection. It essentially turns a modem into a network card—granted, a very slow network card, but a network card nonetheless. But that's only one of the benefits of DUN.

Prior to Dial-Up Networking, every NT application controlled the modem on its own and got very little help from the operating system. Microsoft operating systems released since 1995 centralize program control of modems with a programming interface called the Telephony Application Program Interface (TAPI). TAPI-aware applications don't have to worry about what kind of modem you have—they just let TAPI worry about it. This puts a layer of software between the communications program and the communications hardware, which makes writing communications programs easier. Writers of graphics programs under Windows don't worry about what graphics board you're using because the Windows graphics driver handles the video board-specific details. TAPI means that communications program designers can finally enjoy the benefits of hardware independence that graphics programmers have enjoyed for over 12 years.

TAPI's disconnection of the hardware from the software is just the right idea, and just at the right time. Many of us don't communicate using modems; instead, we use an old technology that's finally coming into its own: Integrated Services Digital Network (ISDN). ISDN *looks* like a modem technology, but it's not. It is a dial-up communications system that is completely digital and that can communicate at up to 144,000 bits per second. But getting software that supports ISDN has been difficult because ISDN is a new technology in the eyes of most software designers. NT, in contrast, has ISDN support built right in.

The idea of remote access to a local area network is by no means a new one. People quite commonly use a program like Carbon Copy and pcANYWHERE to accomplish remote LAN access. These programs work by allowing you to take remote control of a PC that is physically on the office premises, a PC that's a workstation on your network's LAN. By taking remote control of a workstation PC, you can access the LAN because it is local to the remotely controlled PC. This sounds like a perfectly reasonable approach, and it is, save for the fact that you end up transferring lots of screenfuls of data back and forth over the phone line. Every mouse-click can potentially change the whole screen, which can result in having to transfer a megabyte of information. At the common modem speeds of roughly 20,000bps (bits per second) with compression, transferring that megabyte could take six minutes. Waiting six minutes for each mouse-click requires a bit more patience than *I* have, which is why I prefer the NT approach.

An Overview of Dial-Up Networking

The whole idea of the Dial-Up Networking (DUN) is that it runs any of the NT protocol stacks over the phone line, essentially converting your serial ports into Ethernet cards, so to speak. Furthermore, DUN *tunnels*

IPX/SPX or TCP/IP through a protocol called PPP (Point to Point Protocol), making it possible to gain access to servers *not* running NT or Dial-Up Networking. For example, you could set up a Windows 95 computer with the IPX/SPX protocol and a NetWare client, then dial into an NT Server machine running Dial-Up Networking. The Windows 95 machine would dial an NT machine running the Dial-Up Networking server software, and log in to it. The Dial-Up Networking server would receive the IPX/SPX packets, which it would probably have no way of interpreting. Its job is just to get the packets off the WAN and drop them on the LAN. Once it does that, the NetWare server receives the packets and allows the remote Windows 95 workstation to log into the NetWare server.

Additionally, DUN supports an old but popular protocol named SLIP (Serial Line Interface Protocol) that allows you to connect an NT machine to many Internet hosts. More and more Internet hosts don't use SLIP, however. They use the newer PPP protocol instead. Microsoft's choice of PPP for Dial-Up Networking was a very good one, because PPP is so widespread in its use.

DUN won't just be interesting to network *users*; network administrators can use DUN too. You can do any administrative work over the remote connection that doesn't require you to actually touch the remote workstation.

Why use DUN rather than another remote-access package? Well, for starters, you've already paid for it—you get it free with NT Server. Even if you have DOS and Windows clients and therefore can't use the normal DUN client software, you can get the supplemental disks free from Microsoft. Just fill out the form in the back of your System Guide, send it in, and the software shows up in about a week. Or copy the software from the Windows NT CD-ROM disk.

DUN is useful for both users and administrators. Remote clients can access files and network devices as though they were using the network from inside the office, and administering their accounts is just like administering any other user account. Another advantage of DUN over other remote-access software is that DUN has the same built-in security measures that other NT Server user accounts have, with a few more for good measure. A DUN link does not provide the same access to a network that other kinds of remote-access connections provide. Finally, DUN is flexible. Running from an NT Server machine, it can support up to 256 simultaneous connections. Simple NT workstations, however, can only support one DUN connection.

In this chapter, you see how to operate Dial-Up Networking both from the server and the client side.

Sample Applications

Following are a few ideas of what you can do with Dial-Up Networking. The sections that follow describe remote dial-ins to servers, Dial-Up Networking, and virtual private networking.

Remote Dial-In to Company NT Servers

The obvious application is simple remote access to an NT network. A remote DOS, Windows for Workgroups, Windows 95, or Windows NT workstation can dial into a server on the company premises that's hooked up to a modem and a phone line (or 256 modems and phone lines, for that matter). Once on, the workstation can access network resources as if the workstation were connected to the company network, albeit the access is slower.

Remote Dial-In to Non-NT Servers

As I suggested a few paragraphs back, one of the benefits of the Dial-Up Networking architecture is that it is built atop a protocol called PPP that acts as a kind of packaging material for other protocols. If you want to route data on IPX/SPX or TCP/IP over a wide area network

(WAN) link like a modem, ISDN connection, or X.25, Dial-Up Networking can do it. The Dial-Up Networking server doesn't interpret the packets it receives; it just puts them onto the network so that the packets reach their destinations.

Dial-Up Networking as an Internet Gateway

As you learned in Chapter 14, you can use Dial-Up Networking to connect a company's network to the Internet. An NT machine (running either Server *or* Workstation) can act as a router and route packets between an Internet Service Provider and a company's internet.

At least not yet, Dial-Up Networking can't act as a firewall or a proxy server for the connection between a company's network and the Internet. Microsoft plans to introduce a product code-named "Catapult" sometime in 1997 that will provide security between a company and the Internet. If you want that capability *now*, however, look into a commercial Internet firewall product.

Dial-Up Networking as an Internet Service Provider

Dial-Up Networking even allows *you* to act as the ISP. To do this, you can set up a bunch of modems on an NT Server that runs Dial-Up Networking, people can call in to your network, and from there they surf the Internet (assuming, of course, that you're connected to the Internet).

Dial-Up Networking as a LAN/WAN Gateway

Got a network uptown that needs to talk to a network downtown? Dial-Up Networking can accomplish that. A machine on one network runs Dial-Up Networking and calls into a machine on the other network that also runs Dial-Up Networking. With the right setup, the two networks become one network.

This is still a rudimentary feature, however. It requires some fiddling around to make it work. In particular, you can't set up a LAN-to-LAN connection so that it only dials up when data must go from one network to another; this pretty much works only if you dial up and don't hang up.

Virtual Private Networking with PPTP

Dial-Up Networking with version 4 introduces support for the Point to Point Tunneling Protocol, a system by which you can connect to your local network over the Internet.

Connection Types

You're not limited to one method of connecting a DUN server and its clients. You can link them by modem, over an ISDN connection, or even use DUN to make a network card in a workstation unnecessary, if you like. In this section, we'll look at your connection options, how they work, and what you need for them.

Modem Support

Most DUN servers connect to their clients through a *modem* (modulator/demodulator). On the sending end, modems convert digital computer signals to analog signals that can be transferred over ordinary telephone lines. On the receiving end, another modem takes the analog signals and reverts them to the original digital signal. For the modulation/demodulation process to work, the modems must be compatible.

Modem Compatibility Issues

Not all modems work with DUN. In the NT Server Hardware Compatibility List, Microsoft lists modems that tested successfully with DUN. If you're buying a modem specifically for DUN, make sure to choose one from this list. Alternatively, you can venture into the depths of a file called MODEMS.INF and program NT to support your modem. (I'm not going to cover that in this book, but it's explained in the NT DUN documentation.)

Even if you choose modems from the approved list, not all modems may be able to work together in all modes. It's best to use the same model of modem on both the sending and receiving end of the DUN connection. It's not vital to do this if both modems conform to industry standards like V.32 *bis* or V.34 (the 14,400 and 28,800bps standards), but getting the same modem model can avoid the compatibility problems that arise even in machines that conform to the same standard. The higher the speed, the more likely compatibility problems are, because modems use different methods to achieve high speeds. Another answer is to use Hayes modems, because modem designers seem to use Hayes modems to test the compatibility of *their* modems. Everything seems to talk to a Hayes.

Hardware Requirements for Using DUN

In addition to the software, you need the following to use DUN over a modem connection:

- Two compatible modems, one for the server and one for the client
- A telephone line

Pooling Modems

Just as you can connect more than one physical printer to a logical printer name (Chapter 8 explains how to do this), you can pool identical modems so that more than one modem is connected to the same number. The modems must be of the same manufacturer and model. By pooling modems, you can avoid traffic problems when a number of DUN clients try to connect to the same server at once.

ISDN Support

Running DUN over a modem is inexpensive, but it's also slow; a good modem connection runs over an analog voice channel at about 14,400bps. If you want a faster remote connection, you need a point-to-point service like ISDN. Basic Rate Interface (BRI) ISDN runs over a digital line at either 64 or 128 kilobits (*thousands* of bits) per second. Given the startup costs (not huge, but more than buying a modem and getting another telephone line), this connection may not be worth it if your transmission needs are small and mostly text-based. But if a good deal of data will travel between the DUN server and client, ISDN could save transmittal time for nonmobile clients.

If BRI ISDN doesn't provide as much throughput as you need, you can subscribe to its faster sibling, Primary Rate Interface (PRI) ISDN. Rather than the copper wire that BRI uses, PRI uses T-1 cables with 23 data-carrying channels that can handle data transfers to 1.544Mbps.

Hardware Requirements

To use DUN over an ISDN connection, you need the following hardware:

- Two ISDN cards, one in each computer at either end of the connection.

- A digital-grade cable that connects the cards (either copper or fiber).

- A network termination (NT-1) device that connects the cards to the cable. Outside the U.S., the telephone company owns the NT-1; inside, the customer owns it. This NT-1 device can have up to eight ports for multiple ISDN connections. It converts the two wire-twisted pair cables from the telephone line into a eight-wire distribution system. (Most ISDN newer cards have a built-in integrated NT1.)

Basically, if you're thinking of going ISDN, contact your local telephone company to see if they offer ISDN (not all locations have it yet) and then look to either Digiboard or Intel for ISDN interface hardware.

Differences in Transmission Speed

As noted above, BRI ISDN transmits at either 64 or 128Kbps. Where does the difference in transmittal speed come from? A BRI ISDN line comes with three channels: two bearer (B) channels for data, which transmit at 64Kbps, and one D channel for signaling to the other ISDN card, which transmits at 16Kbps. When you're setting up the connection, you can either configure each B channel to be its own port or you can logically combine the two into a single port, get twice the bandwidth, and thus double your transmission speed.

What merits does each approach have? Two channels is better for DUN servers that have a number of clients because more clients are able to get through at one time. For most people, two channels is the most efficient use of bandwidth. If, however, your DUN configuration has only one client, you don't need more than one port and you can combine the bandwidth.

X.25 Connection

X.25 is a protocol that coordinates communication between your machine and another one by routing information through a packet-switched public data network. Operating at the two lowest levels of the OSI protocol model (physical and data-link), X.25 operates at a top speed of 64Kpbs. Even though that speed isn't terribly fast by modern standards, it can run more slowly if the type of line that it's using requires it.

If you're familiar with some of the new wide area network (WAN) technologies for connecting point A to point B, X.25 may seem slow to you. Truthfully, it is. X.25 was developed when telephone lines were not as reliable as they are now, so it includes extensive error-checking at every node in its path to ensure that the data arrives at its destination in the same condition in which it left. Error-checking takes time, so X.25 is slower than other WAN protocols like frame relay that don't use it.

If it's slower than other protocols in use, why use X.25? First of all, it's available. No matter where in the world you go, the country most certainly offers X.25 services. Even countries with unreliable telephone systems can use it because of its error-checking capabilities. For international applications, X.25 may be the only way for one country to connect to another.

Even within the U.S., X.25 has the advantage of being offered by most carriers. You could even build a private X.25 network with on-site switching equipment and lease lines that connect the sites.

You can set up DUN to work with X.25 lines without too much difficulty. Like setting up the system for ISDN, it's mostly a matter of making sure that things are coordinated with the telephone company and that your connections are made properly. We'll discuss configuring your system for X.25 shortly.

There are two main ways in which you can arrange DUN to work with X.25, either a dial-up asynchronous packet assembler-disassembler (PAD) or via a direct connection to the X.25 service provider.

Packet Assembler-Disassembler (PAD)   A *packet assembler-disassembler* is in charge of taking non-packet data streams, such as the start and stop bits that begin and end a transmission, and converting them to packets that can be transported over the X.25 network. Once the converted packets reach their destinations, another PAD reverts the packets to their original form.

With a PAD hookup, a dial-up connection connects the remote workstation and the server through PAD services offered by a public network, such as Sprintnet. The client's software has a "conversation" with the PAD, and then the PAD has a "conversation" with the server that gets the data to the server.

PAD configurations include the client external PAD and the server external PAD layouts. In the client external PAD configuration, an RS-232 cable attached to the client's serial port connects the client and the PAD. The PAD.INF file must include a script that tells the client how to connect to the server. In the server external PAD configuration, it must be configured to receive incoming calls. (Given that you're using the server to connect your LAN to remote clients, this is probably what you wanted to do anyway.)

Direct Connection   The other approach to X.25 connection is a direct connection. Connecting directly from the remote workstation to the server requires a device called a *smart card*, which acts like a modem in both the server and the client. (Clients not using the direct X.25 connection don't need smart cards.) A smart card is a piece of hardware with a PAD embedded in it. It fools the computer into thinking that its communication ports are already attached to PADs.

Hardware Requirements for Using DUN with X.25

To use DUN with X.25, you need the following:

- A modem (for dial-up connections)

- A "smart" X.25 direct interface card (for direct connections)

- A leased line (for direct connections)

We'll discuss the mechanics of how to set up DUN to work with X.25 in "Dial-Up Networking Server Installation" later in this chapter.

Direct Serial Connection

The final way that you can use DUN is to avoid having to get a network card. Using a null modem cable, you can connect the server and client directly through the serial port. Although this setup eliminates the need for a network card in either machine (assuming the server is not connected to any other clients), serial connections are much slower than networks and performance suffers.

To use DUN through a serial connection, you need the following:

- One client and one server machine

- A 9- or 25-pin (depending on your serial connector) null-modem cable

Now, there are null modem cables, and there are null modem cables. Many computer null modem applications work fine with simple null modem cables, but DUN is pretty exacting in its requirements. Table 17.1 summarizes the requirements for constructing a DUN-ready null modem cable. The table covers both 25- and 9-pin connectors.

TABLE 17.1   Requirements for Constructing a DUN-Ready Null Modem Cable

Host[1]	Pin No. \ 9-pin	Pin No. \ 25-Pin	Workstation[2]	Pin No. \ 9-Pin	Pin No. \ 25-Pin
Transmit data	3	2	Receive data	2	3
Receive data	2	3	Transmit data	3	2
Request to send	7	4	Clear to send	8	5
Clear to send	8	5	Request to send	7	4
Data set ready and data carrier detect	6,1	6,8	Data terminal ready	4	20
Data terminal ready	4	20	Data set ready and data carrier detect	6,1	6,8
Signal ground	5	7	Signal ground	5	7

[1]This column lists the NT Server machine serial port signal name.
[2]This column lists the workstation serial port signal name.

Dial-Up Networking Server Installation

Although Dial-Up Networking comes with NT Server, it is not automatically installed when you install the operating system. Therefore, don't look for it on the hard disk—you need to go to Accessories, then Dial-Up Networking to install it. Once it's installed, you can customize it for your needs from the DUN Administrator program, which you find in a newly created Dial-Up Networking program group.

In the following pages, I'll explain how to install and configure a Dial-Up Networking server.

Installing the Dial-Up Networking Module

To install the Dial-Up Networking module, click the Start button, go to Programs, go to Accessories, then go to Dial-Up Networking. In the Dial-Up Networking dialog box, click on the Install button. You are prompted for the location of the original NT setup files; point to wherever you have those files. (I'm being terse here because this installation is essentially identical to all other installations that you've done if you've been following this book.) NT will copy some files.

Installing a Modem for Dial-Up Networking

If you haven't yet installed a modem, ISDN, or X.25 driver on your system, Dial-Up Networking takes note of that and says that there are no capable devices that it can use. It then asks if it should invoke the Modem Installer. Tell it yes, and you see the screen shown in Figure 17.1.

FIGURE 17.1

The opening screen of the Installation Wizard

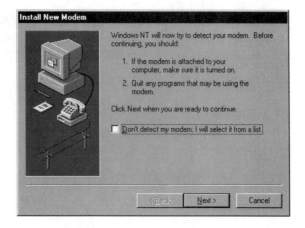

Click Next. Dial-Up Networking attempts to detect your modem. It's often wrong and when it's not sure what kind of modem you have it simply detects a "standard modem." That's probably fine, since most modems work identically these days. But if you like, you can click Change and see a screen like the one in Figure 17.2.

If you choose a modem, Dial-Up Networking wants to know what port it is attached to, as shown in Figure 17.3.

FIGURE 17.2

Choosing modem type by hand

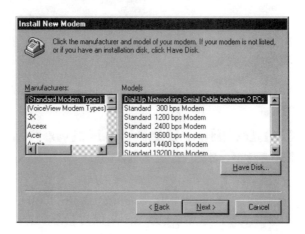

FIGURE 17.3

FIGURE 17.3

Selecting a modem port

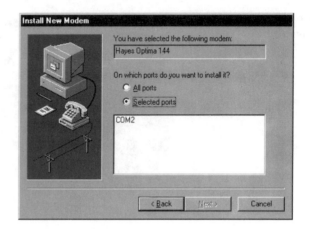

Whether you install automatically or a manually, the Modem Installer finishes at this point and prompts you to click Finish. That returns you to the main Dial-Up Networking installation routine, which double-checks what you've done by showing you the screen in Figure 17.4. It's a bit of overkill on Dial-Up Networking's part, but just click OK and be happy.

FIGURE 17.4

Dial-Up Networking checks which modem you want to use.

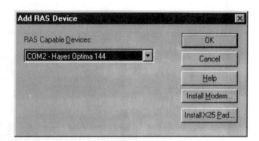

Controlling Dial-Up Networking Client/Server Behavior

Once you've chosen a modem, Dial-Up Networking setup takes you to the dialog box shown in Figure 17.5. This is an important dialog box

FIGURE 17.5

Dial-Up Networking
setup dialog box

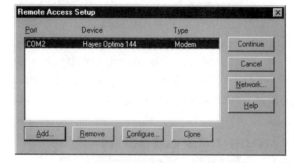

because you do three main things with it. First, you use it to put more modems under Dial-Up Networking's control with the Add button. Along those lines, you remove modems with the Remove button and add new modems that are identical to existing modems with the Clone button. (By the way, when I say "modem" here, what I really mean is "modem, ISDN connection, X.25 connection, or any other Dial-Up Networking-compatible wide-area networking interface." "Modem" doesn't take as long to write, so I'll stick with that.)

Second, this is the dialog box where you control whether this machine dials out via Dial-Up Networking (a Dial-Up Networking client), accepts other machines dialing into it (a Dial-Up Networking server), or does both. You control that by clicking the Configure button. If you do, your screen looks something like Figure 17.6.

If you choose to just be a client or just be a server, Dial-Up Networking creates only one "phantom" network card. You see that

FIGURE 17.6

Controlling whether
this machine is a Dial-Up
Networking client, server,
or both

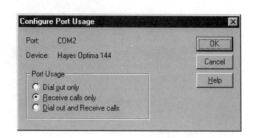

phantom network card if you type IPCONFIG with TCP/IP—it's a board with a name like NDISWAN4. Note that this is the *only* place where you can control whether this machine is a server, client, or both. If you change your mind later and want to change the machine's role, you access this dialog box by opening Control Panel/Network/ Services/Remote Access Service/Properties and clicking Configure in the resulting dialog box. And yes, you have to reboot when you do that.

Choosing Protocols for Dial-Up Networking

The third thing that you do with the "Dial-Up Networking Setup" dialog box is to control exactly which protocols will be used over the Dial-Up Networking connection. Click Network and you see a dialog box like Figure 17.7 (or a portion of it if you only choose to be a client).

Note that this dialog box mainly affects the *server* portion of Dial-Up Networking; you configure most of the client parts from the Dial-Up

FIGURE 17.7

Configuring Dial-Up Networking protocols and login requirements

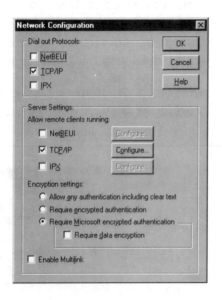

Networking phonebook, which we'll see later. Notice the check box at the bottom labeled Enable Multilink. It enables "multilink PPP," a system that lets you add a bunch of separate connections by way of a single connection. To see how this works, suppose you had two 28.8Kbps modems on your remote PC. You'd like to somehow make the two into one big 57.6Kbps connection to the office. All you have to do is check Enable Multilink in this dialog box on the server side *and* check Enable Multilink on the client side to make Dial-Up Networking use two or more connections as one connection.

Imagine the applications for this! For example, suppose you're using DUN to connect two networks on opposite sides of town. You have a single ISDN connection but you want better speed without the expense of the next step in wide-area connections, a T1 line. With multilink PPP, you can just put in another ISDN line and double the throughput of your connection. And what's even more beautiful, if you think about it, is that if *one* ISDN line is already in place, you've already struggled with getting lines installed, connecting ISDN devices, configuring the connection, and so on. Putting in a second line will be a breeze—much easier than having to learn about a new network technology, like T1. Granted, the day will come when you want faster service, but this technique lets you put that off for a while. Note that, at this writing, you can only make multilink PPP work between Windows NT machines; I don't know of a way to do it with Windows 95 machines.

You choose which protocols can dial in with the check boxes under "Allow remote clients running." Not surprisingly, the options are Net-BEUI, TCP/IP, and IPX/SPX. All protocol configuration boxes ask whether a dial-in client should be able to access just the Dial-Up Networking server's resources, or if the Dial-Up Networking server should act as a bridge to the network and duplicate all of the client's packets onto the LAN. Click the Configure button on TCP/IP and you see a dialog box like the one in Figure 17.8.

Like the other protocols, TCP/IP lets you control whether to let callers access this server only or the entire network. The dialog box also lets you control how callers get their IP addresses.

FIGURE 17.8

Controlling TCP/IP connections on a Dial-Up Networking server

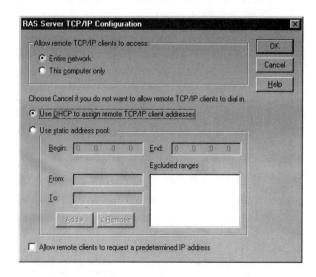

There is, in general, no way for you to assign an IP address to a particular person. Instead, you hand out IP addresses to ports. The best answer is probably to let DHCP hand out addresses, as it probably does on your LAN. Alternatively, you can create a pool of IP addresses that Dial-Up Networking will hand out, sort of like a mini-DHCP. Click OK to clear this dialog box.

Controlling Login Security

Back in the Network Configuration dialog box, you also tell your system what kind of dial-in authentication to require. The options are

Allow any authentication including clear text   With this option, a client using PAP can connect. You may need to use this if you are running an Internet Service Provider network, as it's the least demanding logon requirement.

Require encrypted authentication   This option is just an extended way of saying "require CHAP."

Require Microsoft encrypted authentication   This option says to use Microsoft's own brand of CHAP, called MSCHAP. If you do this, only Microsoft clients are able to attach.

If you choose to require MSCHAP and you are using only NT machines on your network, you can check "Require data encryption." NT will encrypt not only passwords, but data if you select this check box. Click OK to close the Network Configuration dialog box. Click the Continue button to install your configuration.

The system thrashes around for a bit to get Dial-Up Networking installed. Then a message says that Dial-Up Networking installed properly. A dialog box asks you if you want to restart your computer so that the new settings take effect. Choose OK and your system reboots. You're almost ready to start receiving calls with a Dial-Up Networking server.

> **TIP**
>
> Once you've attached a modem to a Dial-Up Networking server, you cannot use it for anything else; the port that the modem is on is now committed to Dial-Up Networking only. If you're using Dial-Up Networking for dialing *out*, in contrast, then you can use the port and the attached modem whenever Dial-Up Networking isn't activated.

Using Dial-Up Networking Administrator

In the Administrative Tools group, you find a new program called Remote Access Admin. Start it up. Go to the Server menu, click on Start Remote Access Service, and choose your machine in the server menu. Or you can click the Dial-Up Networking icon in My Computer and see a screen like that shown in Figure 17.9.

I ran this program on the server MONSTER, and so by default it shows me only the Dial-Up Networking server MONSTER. If there were other servers on the domain, they wouldn't show up.

FIGURE 17.9

Dial-Up Networking
Administrator opening
screen

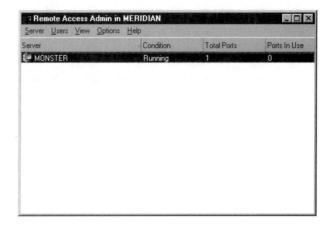

This screen shows that there is one Dial-Up Networking server, its name is MONSTER, and one port—one modem, ISDN connection, or whatever—is on it. Further, no one is dialing into that port at the moment. Now, if *you* try to dial in to a Dial-Up Networking server on your domain, you will get a surprise. You have to use the DUN Admin program to allow particular users to call in to the server. Merely being a user on this network is not sufficient to be able to call in on a DUN server.

Now, you want domain users to be able to dial into this Dial-Up Networking server so as to access the domain. But right now the Remote Access Admin program is focused on just this one server, rather than the domain as a whole. As a result, the only user accounts that it is aware of are the local Administrator and Guest accounts. To move its focus to the domain as a whole, click Server and then click Select Domain or Server and look for the icon next to the name of your *domain*. Do not click on a particular server, but rather on the name of the entire domain. Because the servers are indented in a nice, neat column under the domain's name, I'm always tempted to click on a particular server. If I do, however, I am not able to grant dial-in permissions to domain accounts as a whole. Click the domain name and then click OK. You may see the following message in the Dial-Up Networking Administrator's window: "No Dial-Up Networking servers were found in the selected domain." That message *seems* to mean that no primary or backup domain controllers are running DUN. Ignore the message.

Click Users, then Permissions. You see the dialog box shown in Figure 17.10.

By default, *no one* can connect to the network via Dial-Up Networking. You must either click on a user's name and then check "Grant dial in permission to user" or click the Grant All button. You can also open up the User Manager for Domains; you'll notice that it has an extra button on it labeled Dialin, which you alternatively use to grant dial-in permissions.

That "Dial-Up Networking Permissions" dialog box is also where you control software-based callback modems. *Callback modems* are a way to provide for security for your system and, perhaps, to save money for users. The way it works is this: you call and are authenticated by the system. The system then hangs up on you and calls back. This can save users money because *you're* paying the phone charges for most of the connection. It can make your network more secure because you can preset a phone number for each user. Suppose my user name is MARKM and my preset callback number is 555-5555. Someone steals my user ID and logon password, and tries to attach to the system. The system says, in effect, "I accept you as Mark; now I'll

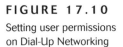

FIGURE 17.10

Setting user permissions on Dial-Up Networking

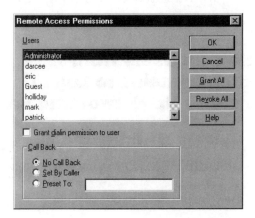

call you back at Mark's house." Then the system hangs up on the intruder and calls my computer at my house. I hear the ringing, but *I* didn't try to log on! The intruder doesn't get very far and, moreover, the intruder trumpets the fact that he's working with a stolen ID by tripping the callback feature.

For every account that has permission to dial in, you must choose how it is to be done with the Call Back options at the bottom of the Dial Up Networking dialog box:

Option	What It Does
No Call Back	Offers no extra system security. Users dial in directly from wherever they are. This is the default option.
Set By Caller	Although it doesn't offer any system security either, this option allows on-the-road users to avoid big telephone bills. With this option, the DUN server calls the user back at the number the user indicates once the user's account has been validated.
Preset To	This is the most secure option. For users that routinely call in from the same location, you can preset a telephone number from which they must always call. After the user dials in and is validated, the DUN server severs the connection and calls the user back at the preset telephone number. If the user is calling from a different number than the one in the DUN database, he or she can't make the connection.

If you mess up when establishing who can dial in and how, you can always start over by clicking the Revoke All button and eliminating all dial-in permissions.

Allowing Users from Other Domains to Log In to a Dial-Up Networking Server

The problem of how to permit users from other domains to log on to a Dial-Up Networking server stumped me for a year. Our network has two major domains, named ORION and TED. Our main Dial-Up Networking server is on a machine in the TED domain. ORION people want to be able to dial into our enterprise network via the Dial-Up Networking server, so my TED administrator tried to grant dial-in access to the ORION users by means of the Dial-Up Networking Administrator.

The problem was that the Dial-Up Networking Administrator would only display the names of TED users, and we couldn't get it to display the names of the ORION users for love or money. But eventually we found the answer.

In the Remote Access Admin, click Server/Select Domain or Server; this part we'd figured out a long time ago. But when we selected the ORION domain, the Dial-Up Networking Administrator said something like, "No Dial-Up Networking servers were found in the selected domain," an apparent error message. The trick was that it was an *apparent* error message, but it wasn't an error message at all. I just clicked Users/ Permissions like before, and all of the ORION users appeared on the list. I granted them access and all was well.

Now that you have that set up, let's digress for a bit and talk about the special problems you run into when you use ISDN or X.25 on your Dial-Up Networking system.

Setup Considerations when Using ISDN

If you're using an ISDN connection rather than a modem on your server, you need to do some additional tweaking to make sure that it's set up properly. If you're making an ISDN connection from an old modem connection, you don't need to trash the old one and start over. Just select the entry in the phone book and edit it to use ISDN. If you're using BRI ISDN, tell the system that you are using two channels. In addition to the tweaking that you do, you need to arrange some tweaking with the telephone company. When setting up an ISDN connection, be sure to set up the connection in the following way:

- **Switch protocols:**

  - AT&T 5ESS switch: Proprietary or N11 (if that is available) protocol

  - Northern Telecom DMS100 switch: Functional or N11 protocol

  - National ISDN 1 compatible switch: N11

- **Terminal type:** The terminal type is "A", or "D" if "A" is not available or already being used by other equipment on the box.

- **TEL assignment:** The TEL assignment should be Auto.

- **Multipoint:** Multipoint should be set to Yes, meaning that each B channel (those are the ones the data travels on, remember) can be used for separate purposes by the machine. One B channel could be used for inbound traffic, and one could be used for outbound traffic. You might have to explain this one to the telephone company, since "multipoint" may mean something different to them, depending on what part of the country you live in.

- **SPIDs:** If you want to be able to use the channels independently, you *must* make sure that the telephone company sets the number of SPIDs (logical terminals) to 2. This gives you two telephone numbers on the same ISDN line. If you don't have two logical terminals, you can't use the channels independently, as the SPID that controls the transmission will be unavailable once the channel is in use.

- **EKTS:** Set EKTS to No.

WARNING ISDN is a new technology, and, as such, can be a bit finicky at times. If you're having connection problems, try switching the IMAC off and back on again. If these problems persist, check with the telephone company or the company that installed ISDN for you. There could be problems with the telephone company's connection, or the ISDN setup could be configured incorrectly.

Setup Considerations for X.25

Setting up DUN to work with X.25 isn't much different from setting it up to work with ISDN:

1. Go to the New Phonebook Entry and click the New, Edit entry and modem properties, or Close entry and modem properties, depending on whether you're making a new entry, changing an existing one, or copying an existing one.

2. Go to the New Phonebook Entry dialog box and click the X.25 tab. This tab is shown in Figure 17.11.

FIGURE 17.11

The X.25 tab of the
Edit Phonebook Entry
dialog box

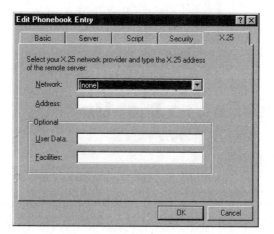

TIP   X.25 has one drawback: you can't use the Callback security feature with it.

---

3. Select your X.25 network provider and type in the X.25 address.

The settings in this dialog box are as follows:

Setting	What It Means
Network	The PAD type is the type of X.25 packet assembler/dissembler that you are using. If you're using a dial-up PAD, select the name of your provider.
Address	The X.21 address is the X.25 equivalent of a telephone number. Enter the one associated with the machine that you want to call.
User Data	Any additional information that the X.25 host computer needs to make the connection is placed in the User Data box. Typically, there won't be anything.
Facilities	In the Facilities box, put any additional parameters that your X.25 provider supplies, such as reverse charging. If you're not sure what options you have, check with your provider or your documentation.

Once you've filled in the boxes here, you should be ready to use DUN over X.25. The connection process, which is discussed below, doesn't change with the kind of connection that is in place.

Connecting to Dial-Up Networking Servers from Clients

Once you've set up the service and have it running on both the server and the workstation from which you want to access the server, you're ready to make the remote connection. The process for doing this is somewhat different, depending on whether you're running NT's DUN or the special version used with Windows 95 and Windows for Workgroups. There is supposed to be a way to make Dial-Up Networking run from a DOS workstation, but I've never been able to make it work.

Connecting from an NT Machine

First, Dial-Up Networking has to be running on the NT machine, whether NT Workstation or NT Server. The installation is the same for Dial-Up Networking clients as it was for Dial-Up Networking workstations, save for the dialog box that asks whether you dial out, dial in, or do both.

To dial out, however, you must use the Dial-Up Networking icon in the My Computer folder. It maintains a "phone book" of places that you can call.

To make the remote connection from an NT or NT Server machine:

Go to the DUN icon and open it. Since this is the first time that you've used the program, there are no entries in the phone book, and DUN automatically dumps you to a screen to create one. When you first open up the Dial-Up Networking folder, it complains that there are no dialing directory entries, as you see in Figure 17.12.

Click OK and you get the chance to create a new phone book entry. Phone book entries have several tabs: Basic, Server, Script, Security, and X.25. You clearly don't need X.25 here, but let's look at the other tabs.

The first tab, Basic, is shown in Figure 17.13. Much of this is self-explanatory—area code, comment, directory entry name. The Alternates button is new to NT version 4 and it's a welcome addition. For a service that you dial into but whose phone lines are often busy, it's convenient to be able to store secondary phone numbers; this lets you do that.

FIGURE 17.12

The message you get when no entries are in the Dial-Up Networking dialing directory

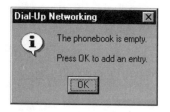

FIGURE 17.13

Basic phone directory tab

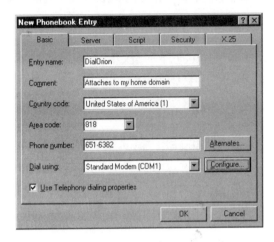

The Configure button is also useful. Click it and you see a dialog box like the one in Figure 17.14. The options on this screen are as follows:

Enable Modem Speaker   This is pretty self-explanatory: with a check in the box, every squeal and grunt from the modem is broadcast through its speaker; unchecked, the modem works silently.

Enable Hardware Flow Control   Enables handshaking between the modem and the computer, so that, if the modem falls behind in receiving, it can halt the flow of data rather than register an overflow error. In short, keeping this enabled allows the modem to slow its eating speed rather than choke.

FIGURE 17.14

Controlling modem configuration

Enable Error Control   Enables error checking through cyclical redundancy checks (CRCs). Enabling this option increases modem efficiency, as it eliminates the need for start and stop bits (bits that signal the beginning and end of a data transmission).

Enable modem compression   This option is not checked by default, but I recommend checking it. It allows your modem to compress the data stream by using the V.42 *bis* compression algorithm. Not all modems support compression, which is probably why this is disabled by default, but most high-speed modems *do* support compression nowadays, so it's probably a safe bet to enable compression. Just as data compression programs like Stacker work better on some kinds of files than others, the amount of compression that takes place depends on how much redundancy is in the data transmission. The amount varies with the type of transmission.

If you realize after you've finished that you didn't set up the modem correctly, click on the Configure button and you can change the settings and configurations that you assigned.

Click OK to return to the Basic tab, then click Server to tell your system about the server you are dialing into. You see a dialog box like the one Figure 17.15.

As on the server side, you tell it which protocols you expect to be able to communicate with. The Dial-Up Server Type drop-down list box offers three kinds of servers:

- Windows NT 3.1, Windows for Workgroups 3.11 gets its own setting because Dial-Up Networking—or Remote Access Services, as it was called formerly—used to be built not atop PPP, but instead on a home-grown Microsoft protocol known as AsyBEUI, basically NetBEUI with a wide-area-network flavor. AsyBEUI could only transport NetBEUI data and was worthless for Internet access. (If you choose this option, you even notice that all protocol options gray out except for NetBEUI.) As the name suggests, only use this if you're dialing into an old NT 3.1 RAS server or a Windows for Workgroups machine set up to receive calls.

FIGURE 17.15

Configuring Dial-Up
Networking to dial
into a server type

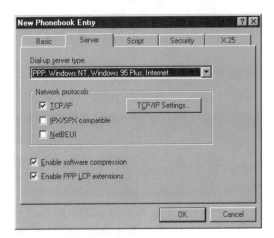

- Internet SLIP is the older of the two most popular Internet dial-up protocols, PPP being the other one. SLIP has a lot of positive features. Most particularly, it is very simple and imposes very little overhead on an already-slow dial-up line. But the flexibility and ever-growing functionality of PPP (don't forget that PPP has PAP and CHAP, as well as multilink PPP) is causing SLIP to wither away slowly.

- PPP: Windows NT, Windows 95 Plus, Internet is the option that is chosen most often. You can use this to either dial into a Dial-Up Networking server, as I'm about to do, or just to dial into an Internet Service Provider (ISP), since most ISPs offer PPP dial-in.

Here, I've chosen PPP. For network protocols, I use TCP/IP, so I've checked that. It requires some configuration, so I click TCP/IP Configuration and see the dialog box in Figure 17.16.

If you're going to be part of someone else's TCP/IP network, then of course you need an IP address. In most cases, the network that you dial into will want to assign that address rather than let you set your

FIGURE 17.16

Configuring TCP/IP
for dial-in

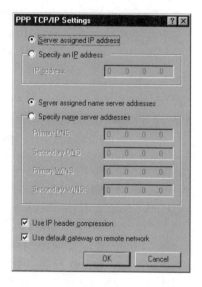

own IP address, which could potentially cause all kinds of havoc.
I should note in passing, however, that when you dial into some ISPs
with particularly primitive dial-in capabilities, they require you to set
your IP address from your workstation, only because their server software can't set your workstation's IP address. If that's the case, then the
ISP supplies you with an IP address, and you'd better be sure to use
it. If you're dialing into an NT server, you usually want the Dial-Up
Networking server to set your IP address. Again, however, the installation that you're dialing into may have set things up differently, so
check with it if you're unsure.

You also need the address of a DNS server and, if it's an NT network,
a WINS server as well. A Dial-Up Networking server can, of course,
supply those addresses automatically, but there is a reason why you
might want to set them yourself. Alternatively, if you are dialing into
an ISP, the ISP may not be able to supply that information automatically. Again, sorry to be vague about this, but the fact is that different

installations often handle things in different ways. If you're dialing into a Dial-Up Networking server like the one we set up earlier in this chapter, just let it do everything—set IP address, the name server, and (coming up) the default gateway.

IP header compression is an option created to speed data transfer on slow dial-up links. Above 28.8Kbps, it's irrelevant, but it may speed you up a bit at 28.8 or slower. The only way to know if IP header compression is a good idea is to try it both ways—hook up to an FTP site and try transferring data with and without the compression—to see which is faster.

The "Use default gateway on remote system" option means that any IP addresses that your system doesn't know how to route to should just go over the Dial-Up Networking connection. Look back to Chapter 14 for the discussion on TCP/IP routing for more information. Remember that, in the end analysis, it really doesn't matter whether you do this or not, because you can always just add a ROUTE ADD statement to make *any* IP address your default gateway.

Click OK to return to the Server tab, and click Script to look at the Script tab. It is shown in Figure 17.17. This tab doesn't do anything for us when connecting to a Dial-Up Networking server, but as long as I'm explaining how to set up a Dial-Up Networking client, let's take a look at it.

As I've said before, you sometimes use Dial-Up Networking to establish a connection to the Internet through an ISP, and many ISPs use Unix machines. Those Unix machines need, of course, to verify that you are a valid user on the network, so they have to get a name and password from you. They do that in the following ways:

- With a standard terminal screen that asks you to type in a name and password, requires you to be present when Dial-Up Networking connects to the ISP.

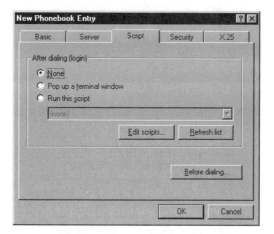

- Some systems can exchange names and passwords automatically without the need for user intervention. The name and password cross the line in an unencrypted fashion, and the protocol that manages this is called the Password Authentication Protocol (PAP).

- Other systems use something that's like PAP, but that encrypts the data; that protocol is called the Challenge-Handshake Authentication Protocol (CHAP).

- Microsoft has its own nonstandard version of CHAP called MSCHAP. Obviously, this is used only to connect to Dial-Up Networking servers, which most ISPs aren't using (or at least aren't using *currently*; I'd wager that the market share of ISPs using NT is growing pretty fast).

If you are connecting to an ISP that uses the first approach—pop up a terminal screen and punch in a name and password by hand—then you should either choose the "Pop up a terminal window" option button or the "Run this script" option button. For the other three approaches, just choose None. Because I'm dialing into a Dial-Up Networking server, I choose None.

The "Pop up a terminal window" option allows you to respond to the ISP's request for a name and password. The "Run this script" option tells Dial-Up Networking to automatically run a script that mimics you typing in a name and password; look in the file SWITCH.INF for guidance on how to write one of those for yourself, if your ISP doesn't use PAP or CHAP.

Click the Security tab, and you see the next tab, which meshes pretty closely with this one. Your screen looks something like Figure 17.18. If you chose either the pop-up terminal or script in the previous tab, then choose the Accept any authentication option button. For a system using PAP, also choose this. For a system running standard CHAP, choose the Accept only encrypted authentication option. For an MSCHAP system like the Dial-Up Networking server I'm dialing into, choose the "Accept only Microsoft encrypted authentication" option. That server may even require that you encrypt the data; if so, check the data encryption box.

Click OK, and the dialing screen appears, as you see in Figure 17.19. You can, if you like, override the phone number here. And by the way, if you ever want to change a phone book setting that you just created, return to this screen, choose the particular phone book entry that you want to change, click More, and choose Edit entry and modem properties.

FIGURE 17.18

The Security tab

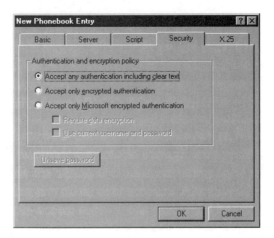

FIGURE 17.19

Ready to dial the server

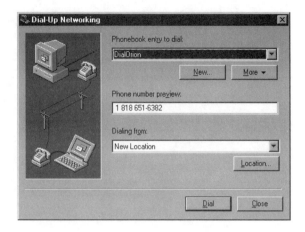

Dial-Up Networking needs to know how it should identify your client, so it displays a dialog box before dialing. That dialog box is shown in Figure 17.20. When you're connected, you see a dialog box like the one in Figure 17.21.

FIGURE 17.20

User name, password, and domain to present to Dial-Up Networking server

Now just access the network in the usual way, with net use and net view commands, as well as the Network Neighborhood.

FIGURE 17.21

Connection Complete
dialog box

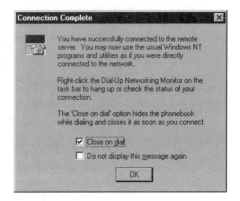

Connecting from a Windows 95 Client

Hooking up Windows 95 clients to a Dial-Up Networking server is fairly easy, as Windows 95 comes with a built-in Dial-Up Networking module. Installing dial-up networking in Windows 95 is a three step process:

1. Install the dial-up networking software.

2. Install the dial-up adapter.

3. Create and configure the dial-up networking connection.

Got your Windows 95 CD-ROM disc handy? Then let's have at it…

Installing Dial-Up Networking Software

You install Dial-Up Networking as a built-in application under Windows 95. Follow these steps to put it on your computer:

1. Click on Settings Control Panel.

2. Select Add/Remove Programs.

3. Select the Windows Setup tab.

4. Click the Communications option and then select the Details button.

5. Select Dial-up Networking from the list. You are returned to the Add/Remove Programs screen.

6. To continue with the setup, click the OK button. Next, you install the networking part.

7. Click on Control Panel.

8. Open the Network applet and select the Configuration tab (it should be at this location by default).

9. Click the Add button, select Adapter, and click Add. You are presented with a list of network adapter manufacturers.

10. Select Microsoft from this list. You see a screen like the one in Figure 17.22.

11. The only adapter in the right-hand side of this screen should be the Dial-Up Adapter. Select it and click OK. That returns you to the main Network screen, which is shown in Figure 17.23.

In the box where the currently installed network components are listed, Dial-Up Adapter should now be on the list. As far as Windows 95 is

FIGURE 17.22

Selecting the
Dial-Up Adapter

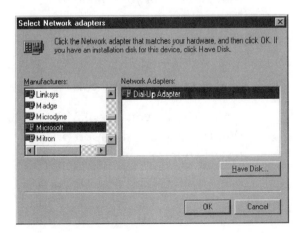

FIGURE 17.23

Main Network Control
Panel applet

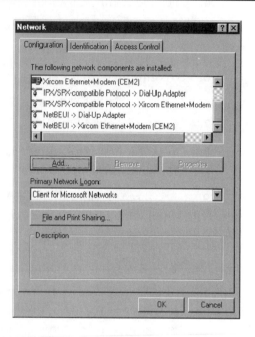

concerned, the Dial-Up Adapter is a network interface card. It does require that a modem be installed on your system. If, at the time that you install the Dial-Up Adapter, you have not configured your modem in Windows 95, the hardware wizard launches and walks you through the configuration of your modem.

You may notice several protocols on the list and an arrow pointing to the Dial-Up Adapter. That is Windows 95's way of showing bindings. Networking components always bind "up"; network boards bind to protocols; protocols bind to services.

At this point you can click OK on the main Network screen to have Windows 95 copy the appropriate software—and yes, you do have to restart your system before the changes take effect.

Creating and Configuring the DUN Connection

Now that the underlying pieces are in place, the next step is to create a new Dial-Up Networking (DUN) connection. Look in My Computer and you see the Dial-Up Networking icon, just as in Windows NT. Open it up and it looks something like Figure 17.24. Choose the Make New Connection icon. The Wizard looks like Figure 17.25.

FIGURE 17.24

Windows 95 Dial-Up
Networking folder

FIGURE 17.25

Start of Make New
Connection Wizard

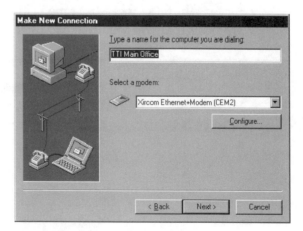

> **NOTE**
>
> If this is the first time you have clicked the Dial-Up Networking icon, Windows 95 automatically launches the Make New Connection Wizard to assist you with creating your first connection. Every subsequent connection you create requires you to click on **Make New Connection**.

Give your connection a name and verify the modem selected. On the next screen, you are asked for the phone number you want to dial. This creates a Connection icon in the Dial-Up Networking folder.

To configure a DUN client connection, simply right-click the Connection icon that was created in the preceding section and select Properties. The opening screen just confirms the information you typed in when you created the connection.

To connect to the NT Server, click the Server Type button. You see the Server Types dialog box shown in Figure 17.26.

Make sure that the Server type is PPP:Windows 95, Windows NT 3.5, Internet. (Yes, I realize that it says NT 3.5 and you are connecting to NT Server 4, but it works—trust me.) Under Allowed Protocols, select the protocols that you would like to use over the DUN connection.

FIGURE 17.26

Configuring server type under Windows 95 Dial-Up Networking

TCP/IP alert: If you want to use TCP/IP over the DUN connection, you must configure TCP/IP by clicking the TCP/IP Settings in the Server Types dialog box. Any TCP/IP settings that you have created in Control Panel/Network are discarded as soon as you start the DUN connection.

You see other settings as well. Here is a brief synopsis of the other settings in the Server Types dialog box:

Log on to network This option, which is enabled by default, dials up and logs you onto the network using the username and password you typed in when you logged into Windows 95. If this option is deselected, you are asked for a logon name and password every time you attempt a new connection.

Enable software compression This option compresses the data before it is sent to the modem (or the like) for transmission.

Require Encrypted Passwords This option enables a feature known as the Challenge Handshake Authentication protocol (CHAP).

Once you have configured your DUN connection, just double-click and the connection is made. You should see the lights of your modem flashing, and, if you have enabled the modem speaker, you should hear that distinctive squelching noise that indicates Windows 95 is negotiating a connection.

Using Microsoft's Universal Naming Conventions (UNCs), you should now be able to access any network resource for which you have permission.

Once you have established a connection for the first time, any of the following actions will activate dial-up networking:

- When you select a network resource that is not part of your network

- When a UNC directs you toward a network resource (\\server\ public_)

- When an application calls for a network resource

- Shortcuts to Popular Network Information

Once you have created the DUN connection, double-click the Connection icon to dial up to the network. It may ask for the name of the server or domain that you want to log onto, as well as a password. DUN will then dial the location, verify the user name and the password, and if everything checks out, allow you access to the server. At this point, the user can do anything that the user normally could if he or she were local to the network (only more slowly).

One final note: If you are using DUN on a machine that is also connected to a network via a network interface card, you can access a network via the DUN connection or you can access a network via your NIC; you cannot do both simultaneously. My guess is that if you could do this, then your Windows 95 machine could become a WAN router allowing people from the outside to access resources throughout their network, and that feature is reserved for the NT operating system.

Connecting from a Windows for Workgroups Station

Setting up a Windows for Workgroups machine is pretty straightforward. Just open up the Network group in the Program Manager, double-click Dial Up Networking, and follow the prompts. There is just one thing to remember when setting up a Windows for Workgroups connection: it can only use AsyBEUI. You must tell the NT Server machine that is running the Dial-Up Networking server that it can accept authentication of any type, and that it can accept NetBEUI protocol packets.

Connecting from Other Operating Systems

The process of connecting to a DUN server from an operating system other than NT varies, depending on which system you're using. The basic steps are the same, but you don't need to include all of them when you're working with certain systems.

How Do I Connect a Non-NT Workstation to a DUN server?

 If you are running DOS and LAN Manager Enhanced on a dual-role computer, start at step 1. If you are running DOS and any other configuration (except Windows for Workgroups), start at step 2. If you are running OS/2, start at step 3.

1. From the command prompt, type **unload protocol**.

2. Type **rasload** to load the DUN drivers.

3. Type **rasphone** to open the DUN phone book.

4. Create and save a Phone Book entry. To do so, click on the File menu and choose Create. Fill in the blanks for the connection name (this is up to you—the name is for your identification purposes only), the domain, and the telephone number.

5. Type Alt+D to reach the Dial menu, and choose Connect. You are prompted for your password, but, if you've selected an entry, the other information should be filled in. Type in your password and press Enter.

6. You see a dialog box telling you that the system is trying to make the connection, and asking you to wait. If you need to stop before the connection is made, press Enter to cancel.

Once the connection is complete, you see a message telling you that you can now access the network as though you were connected to the LAN.

Connecting to a NetWare Server

Due to the large market share that Novell has, it's not unlikely that you might need to connect an NT client to a NetWare server through DUN. One approach is to run the Client Services for NetWare on the client machine and then call the DUN server for the initial connection to the network, then let CSNW do the rest. Another approach is to install the Gateway Services for NetWare on the NT network; the NetWare drives then look like normal NT shared drives to any user of the network.

As long as the drive connection between the servers is maintained, the NT Server server will reshare the NetWare drive connection with any Microsoft client to which it is linked, either locally or remotely.

Keeping Dial-In Intruders off the Network

No doubt, DUN offers your company increased flexibility and the opportunity to increase output. With this increased flexibility comes new security risks, however. How do you keep anyone from dialing into your server, if some of your employees can? Also, once an employee logs onto the server from a home or hotel, how do you restrict him to only the files that he needs? In answer to these concerns, Microsoft included security measures that permit authorized remote users to use files that they need, but can keep unauthorized people off the network.

Modem Security

Besides the special security features that NT Server offers, you can do some simple things yourself to reduce your network's vulnerability to dial-in intruders:

- Keep unauthorized users away from your modem and telephone lines. This could mean burying the cables and/or encasing them in some kind of protection like a concrete pipe, just as you might with the data cables that connect one office to another.

- Don't publicize your server's telephone number. People who need to know it won't need to get it from your business card.

- If you use a callback modem (discussed below), don't use call forwarding, as that could let intruders forward calls from authorized client machines to their own (unauthorized) machines.

Types of Secure Modems

Following is a discussion of the different kinds of modems and what you can do to secure them.

Callback Modems   Callback modems give you the same capabilities as the Preset To option described above. There's not much point in using a callback modem on an NT Server system, because the modems work the same way the software does: they hang up and call the client back at the authorized number preset in the user database.

Password Modems   Password modems build in an extra layer of security by requiring the user to provide a password before the server will connect the client to itself.

Encryption Modems   Encryption modems can be used in conjunction with NT Server. NT Server encrypts the password as the client logs in, but then does not encrypt the rest of the data as the client accesses the server. An encryption modem would encode all data that passes between the server and client computers, thus dissuading wiretaps. This method of protection requires an encryption modem at each end of the connection so that the data can be decrypted once it gets to the server or the client. Encryption modems also keep unauthorized people from dialing into the server, as they don't have the proper kind of encryption and any information that they download will be gibberish.

Silent Modems   Silent modems don't signal that a connection has been made until you begin the login process. This keeps intruders who randomly dial telephone numbers in search of a modem from realizing that they've found a computer.

Enabling and Disabling Bindings

Once remote users have logged on, it still might be necessary to restrict them to only a part of the network, even if they can normally access all or most of it. You do this by disabling *bindings*. Bindings are the virtual circuits that link network components. By default, remote users can access the entire network.

Troubleshooting DUN

Just as with any other network connections, there are times when DUN won't work. If you happen across one of those times, here are some ways in which you can find out what's wrong.

If the Connection Has Never Worked Before

If you're trying to use DUN for the first time after you've set it up and it won't work, these are some potential gremlins in the system:

Incorrect Configuration   Have you used the DUN Administrator to give all the proper users dial-in permission? Have you configured the server so that it is able to receive calls? Is the preset number at which the server is trying to call a user the correct one?

Modem problems   If you're using a new modem, the problem could lie with it. It could be a compatibility problem, or the modem simply might not work. Use the Hyperterminal program that comes with NT to try out the modem. Just start up Hyperterminal and tell it that you want to do a "direct connection." Turn the modem on and off, type **ATT**, and press Enter. If your modem is working right, you get the response OK or 0. Try reducing the modem's connection speed; running your modem at 57,600bps may not be the best idea, particularly if your system is doing software compression and/or encryption.

What if your Terminal test was successful and the modem still doesn't seem to work? Modems from different manufacturers, and even different models from the same manufacturer, are not always fully compatible with each other. In addition, compatibility problems are exacerbated at high speeds, so that modems that run at 9600bps or faster may not always be able to talk to each other and may fall back to 2400—sort of negating the reasons why you got the fast modems in the first place. Even modems that claim to follow the Hayes AT standard may not be able to communicate under every circumstance.

ISDN problems   If you're running DUN over ISDN, is the ISDN connection set up properly?

If the Connection Has Worked Before

If the connection *used* to run and now doesn't, pinpointing the problem is generally a matter of establishing what's different: what has changed between the last time the service worked and now? Sometimes the problem is an internal one you can control, and sometimes it's something that you can't do much about, like a downed telephone line.

If the problem is an internal one, ask yourself the following questions. Is the service running on both the server and client machines? Has a user with a preset callback number changed his or her telephone number? Have you re-installed the operating system and forgotten to re-install DUN? Is the modem running?

If the problem is external, ask yourself if the telephone lines between the DUN server and client are working. If you're using an ISDN connection, is the telephone company's hub working?

Checking the Audit Records

You don't have to rely merely on intuition and problem-solving ability when it comes to troubleshooting DUN. You can either monitor connection attempts as they occur by using the DUN Administrator, or you can check the record of all audits and error messages that is stored in the Event Viewer.

Real-Time Auditing with the DUN Administrator

If you suspect that one of your ports might not be working, you can check it from the DUN Administrator's initial screen. When you open the Administrator, you see a display of all the ports that the service can determine. If you don't see a port that you're expecting, there's probably something wrong with the connection.

Suppose a user can't connect to the server. You can monitor the attempt as it's happening. Open the Remote Access Admin and choose Communication Ports from the Server menu. A screen showing all the possible ports for the server appears. Select the one on which the user is trying to dial in, and click the Port Status button. You see a screen that looks like the one in Figure 17.27.

FIGURE 17.27

Port Status dialog box (at rest)

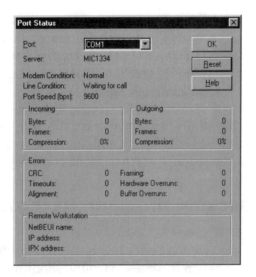

This is a modem at rest, with no incoming calls. When a call is coming in, this screen displays current information about the transaction: the number of bytes and frames coming in/going out, the degree of data compression, and the number and type of errors. Once a port is active, you see it in the Dial-Up Networking Administrator, as shown in Figure 17.28.

Double-click on the server, and you see Figure 17.29. This screen offers the information that MarkS is connected.

You can see how long he's been on, can disconnect him, or send him a message. Click Port Status and you see a screen like the one in Figure 17.30. The information on this screen changes during the connection, depending on the level of compression, the amount of data

FIGURE 17.28

One active port on a Dial-Up Networking server

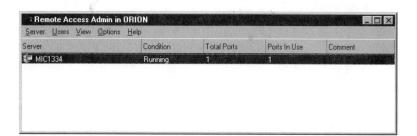

FIGURE 17.29

Viewing port usage on a Dial-Up Networking server

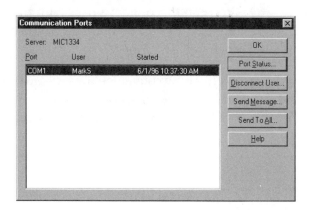

FIGURE 17.30

Port Status dialog
box (working)

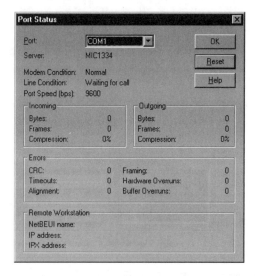

traveling between the server and client, any errors that take place, and so forth. If things go well, the values in the Errors section remain at 0. Errors aren't the end of the world, however; a few of them don't hurt anything.

Click the Reset button if you want to reset all the values back to 0. This doesn't break the connection—the counting just starts over. Resetting the values can be useful when you're trying to determine, for example, the number of line errors that take place in a ten-minute period.

You can disconnect a user with the Disconnect User button (of course, a message beforehand would be nice, unless she's an intruder). When you disconnect a user, you see the screen in Figure 17.31.

Notice how convenient this is; you can not only kick someone off, but you can revoke their permissions to access the network as well. That way, you can identify and bar miscreants with just a few mouse-clicks.

FIGURE 17.31

Forcing a user disconnect from Dial-Up Networking server

Using the Event Viewer to Monitor Problems

To monitor past problems, you can check the Event Viewer and see what it has to say about a situation. Make sure that auditing is enabled (it is by default). Three kinds of events are recorded in the Event Viewer:

Audit A normal event recorded for administrative reasons. A normal connection would be recorded as an audit. You can choose to audit only successful events, failed events, or both.

Warning An irregular event that doesn't affect how the system functions.

Error A failed event or network error.

Examining Logged Information

If you're having trouble with the connection, connection information about each DUN session is saved in a file called DEVICE.LOG in the SYSTEM32\RAS directory. DEVICE.LOG contains the strings that are sent to and received from the serial device (modem or X.25 PAD) that transmits the information between client and server. When looking at this file, be sure to use a text editor that can handle both regular characters and hexadecimal output, because some of the information turns into gibberish otherwise. You can track the entire progress of a session with this file. It contains the command string sent to the serial device, the echo of the command, the device's response, and, for modems, the rate of transmittal.

Before you can use DEVICE.LOG, you must create it. The process is explained in the following "How Do I" sidebar.

How Do I Create DEVICE.LOG?

1. Hang up any remote connections currently in place and exit DUN.
2. Open the Registry by running REGEDIT32. You can also access the Registry from inside WINMSD.
3. Go to HKEY_LOCAL_MACHINE and access this key:

```
\SYSTEM\CurrentControlSet\Services\RasMan\Parameters
```

4. Change the value of the logging parameter to 1, so that it looks like this:

```
Logging:REG_DWORD:0x1
```

Logging begins whenever you click the Dial-Up Networking icon or restart the service. You don't need to shut down the system or log off and on first. To view the log, open it in WordPad or another text editor. Be sure to use an editor that can handle hexadecimal information, or else part of the log ends up as gibberish. Also, when looking at this file, you can disregard the h0D and h0A characters at the end of each line. Those are, respectively, carriage-return and linefeed bytes. They have no other significance.

TIP

As always, before editing the Registry, you should make a copy of it. Messing up the Registry can affect your system badly enough that you need to re-install the operating system. See Chapter 5 for information on that.

For DEVICE.LOG to work, you need to make sure that your modem is configured to return the data terminal equipment speed—that is, how fast the modem is transmitting. If you also configure it to return the carrier (Data Communication Equipment) speed, DEVICE.LOG records it and displays it for you, but without DTE, DUN can't reset the port to go with the modem speed and you get transmission errors.

DEVICE.LOG only records information about dial-up connections. If you're having trouble with a direct connection, this file won't be able to help you.

Running Applications Remotely

This is a short topic: I don't recommend it. Accessing files over a DUN connection is one thing, but using a remote *application* is something else again. Assuming that you have permissions that permit you to, nothing stops you from putting an icon in your Program Manager for a remote executable file, but loading that program takes forever, and doing anything with that program will take just as long. The problem is that every time that you access the program file, all of it must travel to you, since the program stays stored on the computer where it resides. Most programs aren't set up to be client-server packages in which the client only takes the parts of the programs that it needs.

Well, here we are, hundreds of pages since the Introduction. If you've made it to here, then you have much of the ammunition that you need to design, install, and build a useful, functioning NT-based enterprise net-work. If you've gotten this far and haven't actually *done* anything, now's the time to plug in a few Ethernet cards, run a few Setup programs, and put all this stuff to good use. Best of luck, and, as the Netizens say, "See you in the bitstream!"

PART V

Appendix

■ **APPENDIX A** • NET-ing Results: Using the Command Prompt

APPENDIX
A

NET-ing Results:
Using the Command Prompt

Just as you could with LAN Manager, you can control your network's settings from the MS-DOS command prompt in NT Server. In this appendix, we'll discuss these commands, their switches, and how to use them.

This appendix covers how to use the command prompt, but first there are a few things that you should know:

- Those of you who have used LAN Manager will notice that some of the commands look familiar (but not quite as you remember them) and that some are missing altogether. This is because the way that NT Server works affected the way that some commands worked in LAN Manager, and made others totally useless (like NET LOGON, for example, since logging onto the network is inherent to NT Server).

- A single entry from the command prompt is limited to 1,024 characters. This limit will probably not restrict you, but if you are sending a long message with NET SEND (discussed later in this chapter) and you suddenly can't enter any more characters, you've exceeded the 1,024 limit.

- Most of the commands in this chapter work on both NT workstations and NT Server servers, but a few only work under NT Server. When a command applies only to a server, you will see the NT Server margin icon shown here

What You Can Do with the NET Commands

What can you do with the NET commands? You can adjust your system, manipulating accounts and connections to much the same extent that you can from the graphical interface. There are six categories of things that you can do from the command prompt.

Manipulate User Accounts   From the command line, you can add or delete users from user groups, view group memberships, and adjust the configuration of user accounts.

View and Change Domain Memberships   As you no doubt remember from elsewhere in this book, users are members of groups, while computers are members of domains. From the command prompt, you can add or delete computers to and from domains, or view the membership of domains.

Connect to Shared Resources and Share Resources   The biggest advantage to networking is the ability it gives you to connect to other computers' drives and peripheral devices, such as printers. From the command prompt, you can connect to others' devices and share your own, setting whatever passwords you like.

Start and Stop Services   The services that you can begin from the Server Manager or Control Panel can also be reached from the command prompt. From here, you can start, stop, pause, and continue network services.

Send and Receive Messages   Although the messaging capabilities of NT Server are no substitute for an e-mail package, you can use it to send messages on the network that alert people to situations. For example, you could send this message: "The server is going down in five minutes—save whatever you're working on."

Set or View Time   If you have a time server on your network, you can set workstation clocks to synchronize with it. You can also check the time on workstations and servers.

Getting Help

This section comes first because, if you get completely stuck while trying to use a NET command, the two commands discussed here may be able to help you. NET HELP and NET HELPMSG are not universal panaceas, and sometimes they're downright unhelpful, but they come in handy at times.

NET HELP: Getting Help from the Command Prompt

You probably use the NET HELP command most when you're first learning how to use the rest of the network commands. When you enter this command you see a screen like the one in Figure A.1.

For example, if you need help with the command NET PRINT, you can simply type

```
net help net print |more
```

to get all the help file information attached to that command. The | more switch is necessary for commands that have more than one screen of information.

If you prefer, you can get the same information by typing

```
net print /help
```

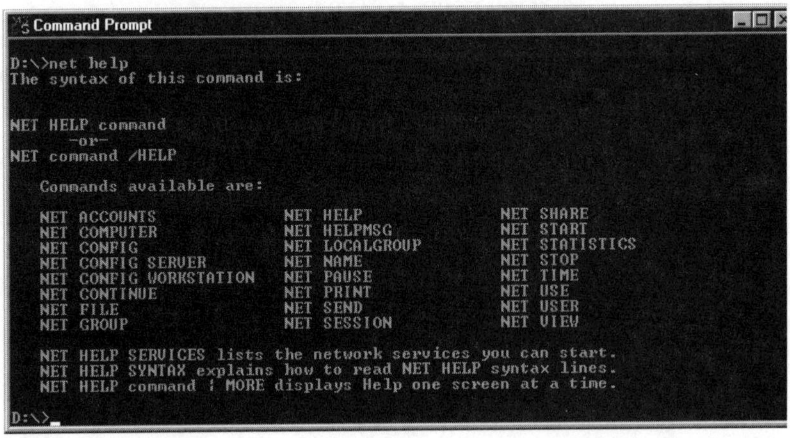

FIGURE A.1

The NET HELP command

```
Command Prompt

D:\>net help
The syntax of this command is:

NET HELP command
       -or-
NET command /HELP

    Commands available are:

    NET ACCOUNTS          NET HELP             NET SHARE
    NET COMPUTER          NET HELPMSG          NET START
    NET CONFIG            NET LOCALGROUP       NET STATISTICS
    NET CONFIG SERVER     NET NAME             NET STOP
    NET CONFIG WORKSTATION NET PAUSE           NET TIME
    NET CONTINUE          NET PRINT            NET USE
    NET FILE              NET SEND             NET USER
    NET GROUP             NET SESSION          NET VIEW

    NET HELP SERVICES lists the network services you can start.
    NET HELP SYNTAX explains how to read NET HELP syntax lines.
    NET HELP command | MORE displays Help one screen at a time.

D:\>_
```

instead of NET HELP NET PRINT. Just typing NET PRINT /? to get command information, as you might under MS-DOS, doesn't net you much information (no pun intended) under NT Server—it merely gives you the proper syntax for the command. To view an explanation of all of the command syntax symbols, just type

```
net help syntax
```

By the way, regardless of what the NET HELP SERVICES command tells you, no online help is available for the following services from the command prompt:

- Client Service for Netware
- DHCP Client
- File Server for the Macintosh
- Gateway Service for Netware
- LPDSVC
- Microsoft DHCP Server
- Network DDE DSDM
- Network Monitoring Agent
- NT LM Security Support Provider
- OLE
- Print Server for Macintosh
- Remote Procedure Call (RPC) Locator
- Remote Access Connection Manager
- Remote Access Server
- Remote Access ISNSAP Service
- Remote Procedure Call (RPC) Service
- Remoteboot

- Simple TCP/IP Services

- Spooler

- TCP/IP NETBIOS Helper

- Windows Internet Name Service

How Do I Get Help from the Command Prompt?

 If you need help with the syntax or other particulars of a command, type

```
net help command
```

where *command* is the command name. The command's help file will be displayed. If the file takes up more than one screen, add the More switch to the end of the help request.

NET HELPMSG: Decoding Error, Warning, and Alert Messages

NET HELPMSG works as a decoder for the NT error, warning, and alert messages. If you see a message such as "Error 2223" that doesn't tell you much, type NET HELPMSG 2223 and you see a screen like the one in Figure A.2.

This command is not always terribly helpful. When you're trying out commands and aren't sure of their syntax, you may not always get the command to work. NET HELPMSG may only tell you that you misspelled a user's name and then refer you to the regular help file for that command.

FIGURE A.2

A sample NET HELPMSG
screen

```
Command Prompt                                            _ □ X

D:\>net helpmsg 2223

The group already exists.

EXPLANATION

You tried to create a group with a group name that already exists.

ACTION

Use a different group name for the new group. To display
a list of group names established on the server, type:

        NET GROUP


D:\>
```

How Do I Decipher the Help Message Numbers?

 When you get an error message with a number attached, type

```
net helpmsg number
```

to see the help file attached to that error message.

Manipulating User Accounts

When it comes to user accounts, you can do just about everything from the command prompt that you can from NT Server's GUI programs: adding and deleting accounts, viewing and changing group membership, and configuring user accounts. Here's how.

NET USER: Creating User Accounts

You can use the NET USER command from the server to control user accounts—to add them, delete them, and change them. If you type this command without parameters, you get a list of the user accounts for that server. You can use switches and parameters to manipulate accounts.

To view the existing account of a user on your domain named, for example, Christa, you would type

```
net user christa
```

The case, even of user names, doesn't matter. You don't need to include any passwords to view the account information. Once you enter the NET USER command, you see a screen that looks like Figure A.3.

Most of the information that you see should be pretty self-explanatory. Essentially, you see a description of the account, its name, its limitations, and when it was last accessed. To actually *change* anything, you need to

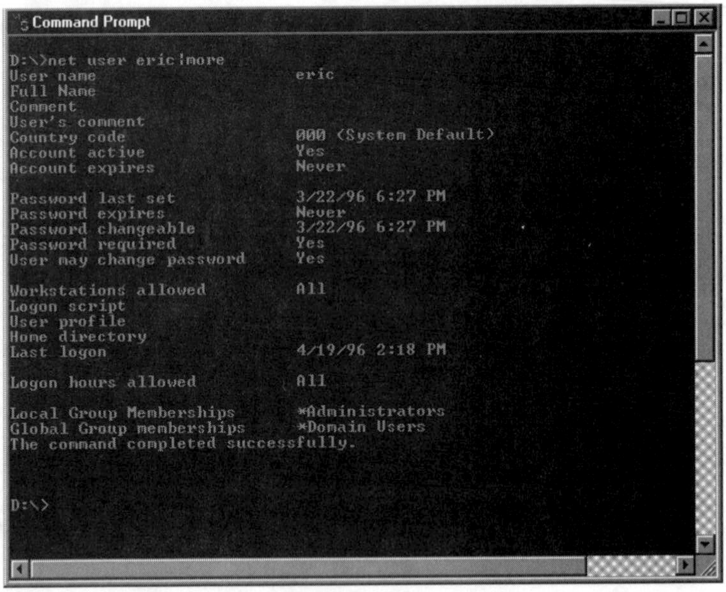

FIGURE A.3

A sample NET USER screen

use the switches and parameters included in the command. For example, to add a user named Frank to your home domain, you could type

```
net user frank /add
```

That was simple enough: Frank now has an account. At this point, however, he can't use it—primarily because no password was specified. If, instead, you type

```
net user frank * /add
```

with an asterisk to create the new account, you are prompted for a password to assign to the account, and once you do, Frank is able to log on (provided you give him the password).

At this point, Frank's account exists, but all parameters have been given the default values, and the account information doesn't even include his real name, as you can see in the listing from the command NET USER FRANK in Figure A.4. Now you need to configure the account with the options available to this command. Table A.1 shows these options.

FIGURE A.4

Frank's new account

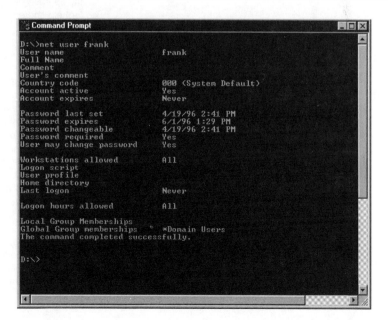

TABLE A.1   User Account Options Determined with the NET USER Command

Options	Description
asterisk (*)	Placing an asterisk after the user's name prompts you to enter and confirm a new password for the user account.
/ACTIVE:{YES | NO}	This option determines whether the account is active or inactive. If inactive, the user cannot log onto this account. Deactivating an account is not the same thing as deleting it: a deactivated account can be reinstated simply by reactivating it, but a deleted account is dead; its parameters are lost, and even if you create a new account with the same name and password, you need to rebuild the user rights and other account information. The default for this option is YES.
/COMMENT:"*text*"	You don't have to put a comment on an account, but it could be useful if you have a large number of users and you can't recall which account belongs to the Miller account representative. Enclose the text (no more than 48 characters, including spaces) in quotation marks.
/COUNTRYCODE:*nnn*	Selects the operating system's country code so that the operating system knows what language to use for help and error messages. The default for this option is 0.
/EXPIRES:{*date* | NEVER}	If you enter a date after the colon, the account will expire on that date; NEVER sets no time limit on the account. Depending on the country code, type the expiration date as *mm,dd,yy* or *dd,mm,yy*—the format in the US is *mm,dd,yy*. You can enter the year with either four characters or two, and months as a number, spelled out, or abbreviated to two letters. Use commas or front slashes (/) to separate the parts of the date, not spaces.
/FULLNAME:"*name*"	This is the user's full name, as opposed to the user-name. Enclose this name in quotation marks, as it has a space in it.
/HOMEDIR:*pathname*	If you've set up a home directory for the user, this is where you include the pointers to that directory. You have to set up the home directory before you set up this part of the account.

TABLE A.1   User Account Options Determined with the NET USER Command (Continued)

Options	Description
/HOMEDIRREQ:{YES | NO}	If the user is required to use a home directory, say so here. You must have already created the directory and used the /HOMEDIR switch to specify where it is.
/PASSWORDCHG:{YES | NO}	Here, you specify whether or not users can change their own passwords. The default is YES.
/PASSWORDREQ: {YES | NO}	This determines whether or not a password is required on the user account. The default is YES.
/PROFILEPATH:*path*	This line selects a path for the user's logon profile, if there is one for the account.
/SCRIPTPATH:*pathname*	This tells where the user's logon script is located.
/TIMES:{*times* | ALL}	You determine the user's logon hours here. Unless you specify ALL, you must spell out the permitted logon times for every day of the week. Days can be spelled out or abbreviated to three letters; hours can be indicated with either 12- or 24-hour notation. Separate day and time entries with a comma and days with a semicolon. Don't leave this option blank: if you do, the user will never be able to log on.
/USERCOMMENT:*"text"*	Administrator can add or change the User Comment for the account.
/WORKSTATIONS:{*computername*{,...|*}	Lists up to 8 computers from which a user can log on to the network. If no list exists or the list is *, the user can log on from any computer.

Following are some examples of setting up user accounts, to give you an idea of how it's done. To add an option to a user's account, type

```
net user frank /option
```

substituting whatever option you want to adjust for *option*. The options and their syntax are listed in Table A.1. You can include more than one option when configuring an account.

To delete Frank's account, you would just type

```
net user frank /delete
```

Finally, if you're performing this operation on a workstation that does not have NT Server loaded, add the switch /domain to the end of the command to make the command apply to the domain controller of the domain you're in.

How Do I Set Up a User Account from the Command Prompt?

 To create and customize a user account, first create the user account by typing

```
net user name /add
```

where *name* is the user name for the new account. Once you've created the account, customize it with the options in Table A.1 by typing

```
net user name /option
```

where *option* is the option that you want to add to the account.

NET ACCOUNTS: Making Adjustments to the Entire User Database

To make individual adjustments to user accounts, you use the NET USER command. To make adjustments concerning such things as forcible logoffs and password ages to the *entire user account database*, you use the NET ACCOUNTS command. When used without switches, NET ACCOUNTS displays the current account information, showing you a screen that looks something like Figure A.5.

In the screen above, you can see that users will be forcibly logged off two minutes after their logon hours expire, that they must change their passwords every 42 days but may do so at any time before that point, and that there is no limit to how long their passwords must be.

FIGURE A.5

A sample NET
ACCOUNTS screen

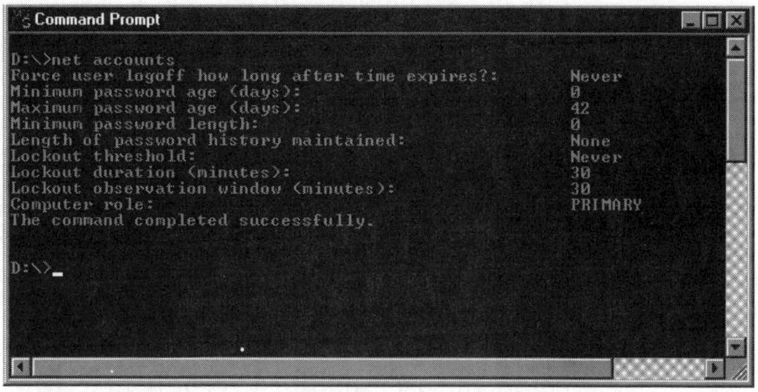

```
Command Prompt

D:\>net accounts
Force user logoff how long after time expires?:    Never
Minimum password age (days):                       0
Maximum password age (days):                       42
Minimum password length:                           0
Length of password history maintained:             None
Lockout threshold:                                 Never
Lockout duration (minutes):                        30
Lockout observation window (minutes):              30
Computer role:                                     PRIMARY
The command completed successfully.

D:\>_
```

So much for looking at the status quo; how do you amend this information? That's where the switches come in. With the switches listed below, you can change all the information that you see on a screen like the one in Figure A.5.

NET ACCOUNTS Switches

Although I've listed the switches here individually for the sake of clarity, you can, of course, include more than one switch in the NET ACCOUNTS command if you want to change more than one part of a user account.

NET ACCOUNTS /SYNC   This switch updates the user account database immediately, rather than waiting for a logoff/logon action.

NET ACCOUNTS /FORCELOGOFF:{NUMBER} OR {NO}   This switch sets the number of minutes a user has between the time that his account expires or logon period ends and the time that the server forcibly disconnects the user. The default is no, but if you've arranged for a user's account to expire or decided that the user has only certain hours in which to log on, you might want to activate this option so that the user has to log off when he or she is supposed to.

NET ACCOUNTS /MINPWLEN   This switch specifies the minimum number of characters that a user's password account must have, from zero to fourteen. The default is 6. Clearly, the more letters that a password has, the harder it is to guess and the more random combinations a random password-guessing program would have to cycle through, but it's a bit of a tradeoff, however. You must choose between higher security and the possibility that users will forget their passwords all the time because they can't remember all 14 characters.

NET ACCOUNTS /MAXPWAGE: *OR* **/MINPWAGE**   These switches specify the minimum and maximum number of days that must pass before the user modifies his or her password. The possible range for /maxpwage is 0 to 49,710 days (a little more than 136 years, which makes you wonder how Microsoft decided on that maximum value), with a default value of 90 days. You can also set the value to UNLIMITED if you want the password never to expire.

The /minpwage can also be set from 0 to 49,710 days, but its default value is 0 days, meaning that the user can change the password whenever she wants to, even more than once a day.

Setting a maximum password age is a good security measure. It will foil an intruder who gets a user account name and password because the information will only be useful to the intruder until the next time the user changes the password. There is a tradeoff between changing passwords often enough that they don't become common knowledge and changing them so often that the person using them has to write them down.

NET ACCOUNTS /UNIQUEPW   Determines the number of unique passwords a user must cycle through before repeating one. The highest value that you can assign to this variable is 24. Since people are likely to use old passwords over and over because they're easier to remember, activating this option might not be a bad idea lest an intruder get an old password. The /uniquepw switch doesn't prevent users from reusing passwords, but it puts a longer stretch between repeats than might otherwise be the case.

NET ACCOUNTS /DOMAIN You use the net accounts /domain switch if you are performing the net accounts command on a domain machine on which NT Server is not loaded. If the machine has NT Server on board, the information automatically passes to the domain controller.

How Do I Make Changes to the Entire User Account Database?

 To change settings on the entire user account database concerning such matters as forcible logoff times and password ages, type

```
net accounts /option
```

where *option* is a NET ACCOUNTS switch. These switches are shown in the section above.

NET GROUP: Changing Global Group Membership

 The NET GROUP command provides you with information on global groups on a server and gives you the ability to modify this information. Typed without parameters, NET GROUP just gives you a list of the global groups on your server, but you can use the options to modify the membership of global groups, check on their membership, add comments to the group names, or add or delete global groups on the server.

To view the membership of a local group, such as the domain users, type out the following:

```
net group "domain users"
```

(if you're not working right at the domain controller, then type the /domain switch at the end of the command). Notice that, since the group name has a blank space in it, you have to enclose it in quotation marks. If the group name had no blank spaces in it—for example, if the group name was a single word like *administrators*—you wouldn't need the quotation marks. The NET GROUP command gets you a screen like Figure A.6. The names that end with a dollar sign ($) are domain controllers.

To add a new global group to the domain, list the group's name in quotation marks. For example, if the new global group is "mail administrators," you would type

```
net group "mail administrators" /add
```

To delete a group with this name, you'd substitute the /delete switch for the /add switch. Once again, if the group name has no blank spaces in it, you don't need to enclose it in quotation marks.

To add a descriptive comment to a new or existing group, add the /comment switch and enclose the comment in quotation marks at the end of the command, like so:

```
/comment:"These are the mail administrators"
```

To add a user to a group, type

```
net group "mail administrators"
```

FIGURE A.6

A sample NET GROUP screen

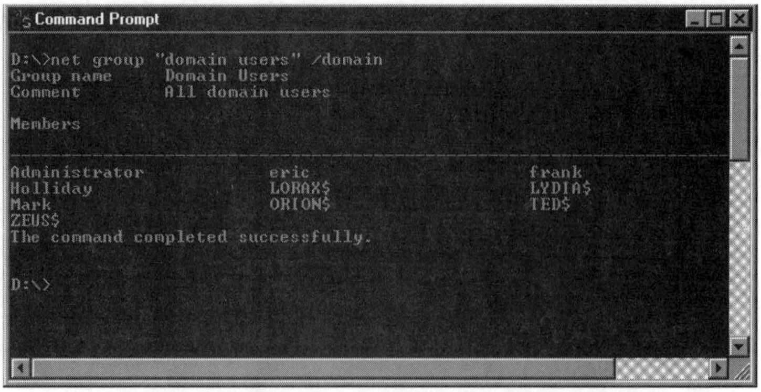

If you are executing the NET GROUP command from a workstation on which NT Server is not installed, add the /domain switch to the end of the statement to make the command apply to the domain controller. Otherwise, you only perform the action that you requested at the workstation you are working from. If you're working on a server with NT Server installed, the /domain switch isn't necessary.

How Do I Change Global Group Settings?

 To change anything about a global group (that is, a group that extends across the domain), type the following from the command prompt:

```
net group /option
```

where *option* is the name of a switch.

NET LOCALGROUP: Changing Local Group Membership

The NET LOCALGROUP command is very similar to NET GROUP, which is discussed above. The only difference is that NET LOCAL-GROUP refers to local user groups, and NET GROUP refers to global, or domain-wide, ones. It would probably have been helpful had NET GROUP been called NET GLOBALGROUP instead, so as to avoid confusion. Unlike NET GROUP, this command can be used on NT workstations as well as NT Server servers.

Typed without parameters, NET LOCALGROUP just gives you a list of the local groups on your server, but you can use the options to modify the membership of local groups, check on their membership, add comments to the group names, or add or delete global groups on the server.

Checking Membership   To view the membership of a local user group, such as one named "backup operators," you type

```
net localgroup "backup operators"
```

Notice that, since the user group name has a blank space in it, you have to enclose it in quotation marks. For a name with no blank spaces in it like *administrators*, you don't need the quotation marks.

Adding Groups   To add a new local group to the server, such as one named "relief administrators," you type

```
net group "relief administrators" /add
```

To delete a group with this name, you'd substitute the /delete for /add switch. Once again, if the group name has no blank spaces in it, you don't need to enclose it in quotation marks.

Describing Groups   To add a descriptive comment to a new or existing group, add the words /comment: and then the text in quotation marks at the end of the command, like so:

```
/comment:"These are the relief administrators"
```

Adding Users to Groups   To add a user named Paul to a group, you would type

```
net group "relief administrators" paul /add
```

If Paul were from another domain, such as Engineering, you would type

```
net group "relief administrators" engineering\paul /add.
```

To remove Paul from the group, you'd substitute the /delete for the /add switch.

You can add either local users or global groups to local groups, but you cannot add one entire local group to another one. Just put the name of the group or user that you want to add after the name of the group you want to add to. If you add users or groups to a local group, you must set up an account for them on that server or workstation.

Updating the Domain Controller   If you are executing this command from a computer other than the domain controller, add the /domain switch to the end of the statement to make the command apply to the domain controller. Otherwise, you only perform the action that you requested at the workstation you are working from. If you're working at the domain controller, the /domain switch isn't necessary.

How Do I Change Local Group Settings?

 To change anything about a local group (a group particular to the computer on which it exists, not to the entire domain), type

```
net localgroup /option
```

where *option* is one of the choices from the section above.

Computer and Session Information

You can get a variety of computer, domain, and session information from the command prompt. Using the commands found in this section, you can

- View computer information

- Add computers to or delete them from a domain

- Get information about sessions between workstations and the server

NET COMPUTER: Adding or Deleting Computers from a Domain

The NET COMPUTER command adds or deletes computers (not users) from a domain. Since domains are administrative units, you might use this command, for example, if a workstation that was used by a person in the Personnel domain began to be used by a person in the Accounting domain. As long as it's attached to the network, the workstation does not need to physically move—it's just logically reassigned.

The syntax for NET COMPUTER looks like this:

```
net computer \\computername\ /add
```

(or /delete if you want to remove the computer from the domain). *Computername* is the name of the computer to be added to the local domain. This command works only on computers running NT Server, and can only be applied to the local domain—I can't assign a computer to a domain other than the one that I am logged onto. If, however, my domain and another have a trust relationship, I can log onto that domain and add or delete computers on that domain that way.

Note, by the way, that NET COMPUTER applies to computers, not to users. Users are not members of domains, only computers are. (I know, I know, I keep harping on that, but it's important to understand the difference when you're configuring your network, and it's not always an easy distinction to grasp.)

How Do I Change the Domain That a Computer Is In?

To add a computer to the local domain, type

```
net computer \\computername /add
```

To delete it, substitute the /delete for the /add switch. You can only add computers to the domain that you are currently logged onto.

NET CONFIG: Learning about and Changing Configurations

You can use the NET CONFIG command to see how a machine is configured to behave on the network and, to a limited extent, change that configuration.

Viewing Current Server and Workstation Settings

Used without switches, NET CONFIG names the configurable services (namely, the server and the workstation). If you include one of the configurable services in the command, for example, if you type NET CONFIG SERVER, you see a screen something like Figure A.7. This screen tells you

- The name of the computer (LORAX in the case of the figure).

- The software version is Windows NT 4 (yes, it says the same thing whether you run this on an NT Workstation or NT Server machine—it's always Windows NT 4).

- The network card's name and address, which are listed below the software version.

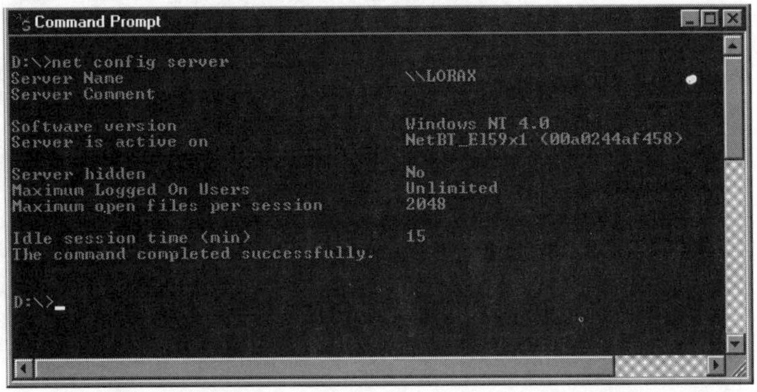

FIGURE A.7

A sample NET CONFIG SERVER screen

- That the server is visible to the network, there is no limit to the number of users who can log on, and the maximum number of files that can be open per session with another computer is 2048—a restriction that isn't likely to cause most users much grief.

- The idle session time is 15 minutes.

Although you can run this command on any NT workstation or any NT Server (NET CONFIG means something different in other operating systems, and the command NET CONFIG SERVER or NET CONFIG WORKSTATION won't work) it doesn't mean that the NT workstations are set up to be servers.

Suppose you type the following command on the machine from Figure A.7:

```
net config workstation
```

You see a screen like the one in Figure A.8. This screen gives you information about how this computer is configured for use as a network workstation. You see the computer and user names, the network card address, the domain, and so forth. Why run NET CONFIG WORKSTATION on a server? Bear in mind that there is no *physical* reason why an NT Server machine can't be a workstation. It's possible, if not likely,

FIGURE A.8

A sample NET CONFIG WORKSTATION screen

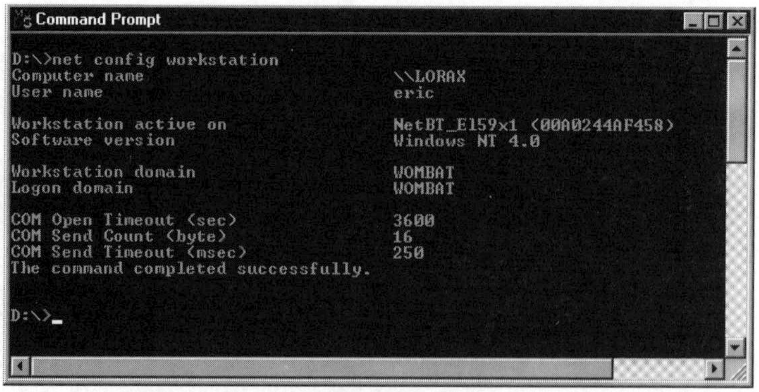

that you could be using the NT Server machine for a workstation, especially if you're short of machines and don't have a dedicated server.

To get basic information about a computer, such as its domain, name, the name of its current user, and so forth, type either of these commands:

```
net config server
net config workstation
```

depending on whether you want information about its setup as a server or workstation.

Changing Server and Workstation Settings

You can use the NET CONFIG commands for more than just information; within a limited scope, you can use them to adjust the way that a machine works on the network. If you type

```
net help net config server
```

you see that this command has three suboptions that you can adjust:

Suboption	Description
/autodisconnect:*time*	Sets the number of minutes a user's session with that computer can be inactive before it's disconnected. If you specify -1, the session will never disconnect. The upper limit is 65,535 minutes (don't use commas when using the command), a little more than 45 hours. The default is 15 minutes.
/srvcomment:*"text"*	Adds a comment to a server (here, that means any machine that's sharing resources with the network) that people can see when they view network resources with NET VIEW. Your comment, which can be up to 48 characters long including spaces, should be enclosed in quotation marks.
/hidden:yes *or* no	Allows you the option of not displaying that server on the list of network resources. Hiding a server doesn't change people's ability to access it, but only keeps people who don't need to know about it from accessing it. The default is no.

The workstation settings are a little different, the differences having to do with how the machine collects data from and sends it to communication devices. You probably don't have much need for these commands. If you type

```
net help net config workstation
```

you see that this command also has three options:

Option	Description
/charcount:*bytes*	Sets the amount of data that NT collects before sending the data to a communication device. The range is 0 to 65,535 bytes (don't use commas in the number), and the default is 16.
/charcount:*msec*	Sets the amount of time during which the machine collects data for transmittal before forwarding it to the communication device. If the /charcount/*bytes* option is also used, the specification satisfied first will be the one that NT acts on. You can set the *msec* value from 0 to 655,350,000, and the default is 250 milliseconds.
/charwait:*sec*	Sets the number of seconds that NT waits for a communication device to become available. The range is 0 to 65,535 seconds and the default is 3600.

NET SESSION: Accessing Connection Information

Used on servers, this command displays information about sessions between the server and other computers on the network. If you type the command without switches, you get a screen showing all the computers that are logged onto that server.

If you include NET SESSION switches, you can get more detailed information about a session with a particular computer, or delete a session (that is, disconnect a computer from the server). For example, to get more information about a session with computer LORAX, you'd type

```
net session \\LORAX.
```

You'd see a screen that looks like Figure A.9. This screen tells you

- The user logged into computer TSC is called Eric.

- The user is not logged in as a guest.

- This machine is running Windows NT. It if were working in a DOS environment, this doesn't necessarily mean that the user is using DOS programs (in fact, Eric could have been logged on under Windows for Workgroups), but that DOS is the basic operating system. Don't forget: unlike NT or NT Server, Windows is not a true operating system, but an operating environment.

- Eric has been logged on for two minutes and one second. His machine has been idle for two minutes and one second.

- TSC is connected to drive C of the server and printers hp4m and hpcolor. Eric has no current print jobs and no files open from the server.

How do I get information about current sessions? To view the current sessions open between a computer and the rest of the network, type

```
net session
```

FIGURE A.9
A sample NET SESSION
screen

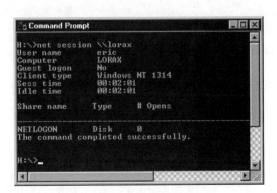

on the computer for which you want the information. To remove the connection between the server and LORAX, type

```
net session \\lorax /delete
```

WARNING　Be *careful* when using the /delete switch! If you neglect to include the computer name in the command, you end all current sessions and everyone has to reconnect to the server.

In case you were wondering, you cannot use this command to initiate sessions between the server and networked computers. Each user does that when he or she logs on.

How Do I Forcibly Break a Connection between Computers?

To end a connection between two networked computers, go to one of the two computers and type

```
net session \\computername /delete
```

where *computername* is the name of the computer you wish to disconnect. If you don't specify a specific computer, you will break all connections between the computer you're typing on and the rest of the network.

NET STATISTICS: Getting a Report on a Computer

The NET STATISTICS command gives you a report on the computer on which you run it. If you just type the following command, you get a list of the services for which statistics are available (server and/or workstation, depending on whether you use the command on an NT or NT Server machine):

```
net statistics
```

But if you type either of the following two commands, you get, respectively, a server report like the one in Figure A.10, and a workstation report like the one in Figure A.11.

```
net statistics server
net statistics workstation
```

You can use either NET STATISTICS SERVER or NET STATISTICS WORKSTATION from any NT or NT Server machine, but the command can only give you information about the machine on which you run it. You can't use this command to get information about computer AMS, for example, if you type the command from computer TSC.

FIGURE A.10

A sample NET STATISTICS SERVER screen

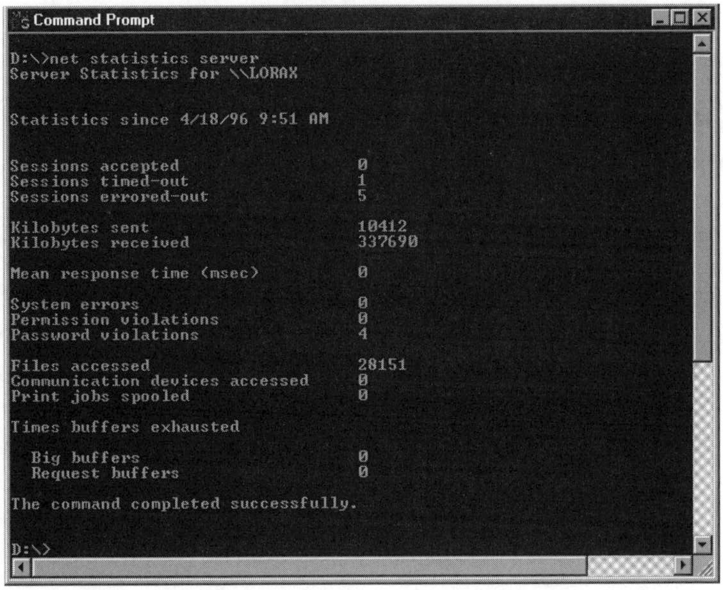

```
D:\>net statistics server
Server Statistics for \\LORAX


Statistics since 4/18/96 9:51 AM


Sessions accepted                     0
Sessions timed-out                    1
Sessions errored-out                  5

Kilobytes sent                        10412
Kilobytes received                    337690

Mean response time (msec)             0

System errors                         0
Permission violations                 0
Password violations                   4

Files accessed                        28151
Communication devices accessed        0
Print jobs spooled                    0

Times buffers exhausted

   Big buffers                        0
   Request buffers                    0

The command completed successfully.

D:\>
```

FIGURE A.11

A sample NET STATISTICS
WORKSTATION screen

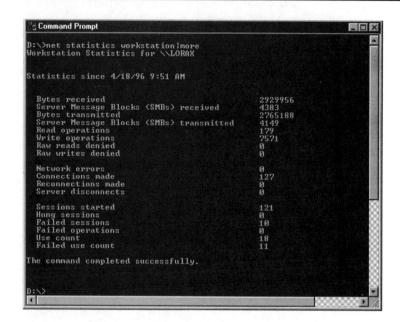

FIGURE A.11

A sample NET STATISTICS
WORKSTATION screen

What's Out There? Connecting to Networked Devices

Since the main point of a network is to allow networked users to access devices that belong to computers other than their own, you would expect to be able to make these connections from the command prompt, just as you can from the graphical interface. You would be right. With the NET commands, you can connect to drives and printers on the network with the same flexibility that you can when using the icons. In this section, we'll talk about how to see what's available on the network, how to connect to it, and (if you're using this command from a server), who's using what.

If you're working from the command prompt, you must make sure that the workstation service is started before you can use any of the commands listed in this section. To do so from the command prompt, type

```
net start workstation
```

NET VIEW: Seeing the Resources Being Shared

You can't change anything with the NET VIEW command; you can only use it to see the resources being shared on the servers and domains on the network.

- If you type the following command on its own, you get a list of the local servers on the domain—that is, the services shared by the computer upon which you're typing:

  ```
  net view
  ```

- If you want to see a list of the resources that the server is sharing with the network, you can amend the name of the server that you want to look at to the command. For example, if the server is named TED, you would type

  ```
  net view \\ted
  ```

- You can check this for any server on the network.

- If you want to look at a server in another domain (perhaps server BIGDOG in domain ENGINEERING), type

  ```
  net view \\bigdog /domain:engineering
  ```

If you omit the domain name from the command, you see a list of all domains on the network.

How Do I View the Available Resources on the Network?

To see what servers are available in your domain, type

```
net view
```

To see the resources that a particular server is sharing with the domain, type

```
net view \\servername
```

where *servername* is the name of the server that you want to view (incidentally, if the server name contains spaces, use *"\\servername"* instead).

If you want to see a server in another domain, type

```
net view /domain
```

To see the domains available, type

```
net view /domain:domainname
```

to see the list of available servers on a particular domain, and then type

```
net view \\servername /domain:domainname
```

when you've selected the server that you want.

TIP

Although this takes a pretty specific set of circumstances, if your network has both servers running NT Server *and* servers running Windows for Workgroups, you may see the error message "There are no entries in the list" when you enter the NET VIEW command. This happens when a Windows for Workgroups machine is the backup master browser for the workgroup, and the Guest account is disabled on the NT Server that is the usual master browser. This error occurs because a workgroup (unlike a domain) has no centralized account database. The Workgroups server must use the database on the NT Server to obtain the list of resources shared with the network, and if the Guest account on the NT Server is disabled, the Workgroups server may not be able to access the list of servers. Therefore, to avoid this potential problem, just keep the Guest account on the master browser enabled.

NET USE: Connecting to Other Drives and Printer Ports

Once you've browsed the network with NET VIEW, you can connect to all the available goodies (or disconnect from those you don't want) with the NET USE command. Use this command to connect to drives D through Z and printer ports LPT1 through LPT9. (If you get help on this command, you notice that it claims that you can only use printer ports LPT1 through LPT3. Technically, this isn't true, but the help file probably puts it this way because some MS-DOS applications are not able to access printer ports with numbers higher than 3.)

To get information about the workstation's current connections, type

```
net use
```

without options. To actually *make* connections, use the command's switches. They are described below.

Connecting to a Resource in the Local Domain

To connect to a shared resource, such as a the printer shared as HP4M on server TED, type

```
net use lpt1: \\ted\hp4m
```

In this case, if you wanted to connect to a directory called WPFILES on that server and to make that your E drive, you'd substitute *e:* for *lpt1* and *wpfiles* for *hp4m* in the example above. You get to specify the port name or drive letter that you want to connect a resource to, but you're restricted to drive letters D through Z and ports LPT1 through LPT9. (Remember, although the help file will say that LPT3 is the highest port that you can specify, this is not true.) Also, if the computer that you're getting the resource from has a blank character in its name (that is, has two words in it), you must put the name in quotation marks, as in "\\eisa server".

If there is a password (let's say it's "artuser") attached to the resource that you're trying to connect to, you need to include that in your connection command, like this:

```
net use lpt1: \\ted\hp4m artuser
```

Or, if you want the computer to prompt you for the password so that it isn't displayed on the screen, append an asterisk:

```
net use lpt1: \\ted\hp4m *
```

To connect to your home directory (the directory on the server that has been assigned to you, assuming that there is one), type

```
net use /home
```

with the password on the end as explained above if one is attached.

If you want to make the connection for another user rather than for yourself, add the user's name (Frank) to the end of the line, like this:

```
net use lpt1: \\ted\hp4m user:frank
```

Passwords go before the user's name in the statement. If the user for whom you are making the connection is in another domain, the user part of the statement looks like this:

```
user:domainname/frank
```

where *domainname* is the name of that user's home domain.

Connecting to a Resource in Another Domain

If you want to connect to a resource in a different domain from your usual one, you must first log onto that domain. If your domain and that one don't have a trust relationship with each other, you need to create a user account for yourself on that domain. Once you've logged onto the proper domain, the process is the same as described above.

How Do I Connect to a Shared Resource?

 To access a shared resource on the network, type

```
net use devicename: \\servername\sharename
```

where *devicename* is what you intend to call the connection (such as D: or LPT1), *servername* is the name of the server sharing the resource, and *sharename* is the name by which the server is sharing the resource.

Other Switches

No matter what kind of connection you make, you can make it persistent (that is, remake it every time you connect to the network), by adding the switch /persistent:yes to the end of the line. If don't want it to be persistent, type /persistent: no instead.

If you don't specify one or the other, the default is whatever you chose last. If you want to make all future connections persistent, type

```
net use /persistent:yes
```

(or type :no if you want all future connections to be temporary). Typing /persistent by itself at the end of the line won't do anything.

To disconnect from a resource, type

```
net use devicename /delete
```

where *devicename* is the connection (such as D: or LPT1). You don't have to provide a password or say anything about persistency to disconnect from a resource.

NET SHARE: Creating and Deleting Shared Resources

If you're administering a server, you probably spend more time making resources available to the resource than you do connecting yourself to resources that belong to other machines. The NET SHARE command applies to resources that the server is sharing with the network. Used alone, it gives you a list of all resources currently being shared with the network. With its switches, you can create and delete shared resources.

The NET SHARE command provides you with information about that particular shared resource:

```
net share sharename
```

For example, if one of the printers on the server is called HP4M (the sharename), you could type NET SHARE hp4m and see a screen like the one in Figure A.12. From this screen, you can tell what that resource's share name and path are, see any descriptive remarks attached to the shared resource, and see how many users may use the device at one time and how many are currently using it.

NET SHARE is a useful command not only for viewing the setup of existing shared devices, but for creating new ones and configuring existing shares. You must be using an account with administrative rights to use this command; ordinary user accounts can't use it.

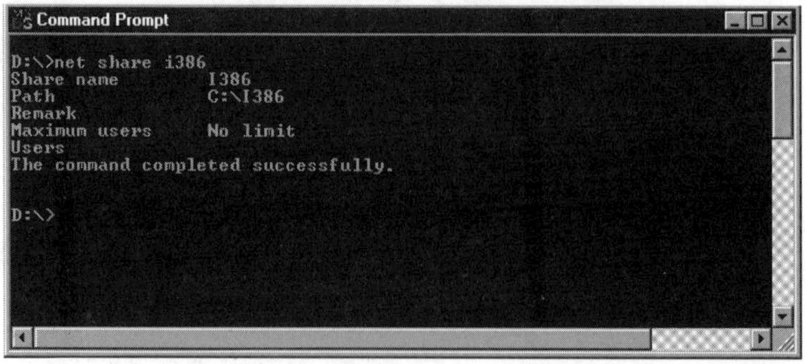

FIGURE A.12

A sample NET SHARE screen

Specifying Absolute Path   To share a device or drive, you must tell the system where to find it. Thus, to share the directory C:\MAIN as drive C:, you would type

```
net share C=c:\main
```

Limiting User Access   To specify the number of users who can use a particular device at the same time, add the parameter /users:*number*, where *number* is the number of users that you want to be able to use the device at once. To place no limit on the number of users, substitute the parameter /unlimited. From the example above, you would type

```
net share C=c:\main /users:5
```

if you wanted, at any given time, five users to be able to access the \MAIN directory on the server's C drive. If you don't use the /users switch, an unlimited number of users can access the device.

Describing Shared Devices   You can add a descriptive comment to a shared device to give the network's users a better idea of exactly what device it is that they are reaching. Do this by adding /remark switch and adding a comment to the end of the NET SHARE statement, like so:

```
/remark:"This is the main data storage directory"
```

Note that there are no spaces between the colon and the text, and that the text must be enclosed in quotation marks.

Stop Sharing   To stop sharing a device, type NET SHARE, the share-name, device name, or drive and path, and then add the /delete switch.

When using the NET SHARE command, keep in mind that if the guest account is enabled, any devices that you share with the network are automatically available to the entire network; you can't set individual or group permissions with this command. If you want to restrict access to devices or drives, you must set the permissions on the pertinent device or drive from the File Manager or Print Manager.

How Do I Share a Device with the Network?

To share a device with the network, type

```
net share sharename=directory
```

where *sharename* is the name by which the device will be known on the network, and *directory* is the location where the device is found. For example, to share the directory c:\public on the network as Public, you'd type

```
net share Public=c:\public.
```

NET FILE: Finding Out What's Open and Who's Using It

Without switches, the NET FILE command is used on servers to display the open files. If you type NET FILE from a server, you see a screen something like Figure A.13.

This screen output lets you know what's open and who (users, not computers) is using it. If you add the switches, you can identify that file to the server and shut it down, removing all file locks. For example,

FIGURE A.13

A sample NET FILE screen

in this situation, you might want to shut down PSP.EXE. To do so, you'd type

```
net file 27780 /close
```

as 27780 is that file's ID number. Note that more than one person can access a file at a time, but that each access has its own ID number.

NET PRINT: Controlling Print Jobs

You can use the command prompt not only to connect to networked devices, but, in some cases, to control them. With the NET PRINT command, you can control print jobs, just as you can with the Print Manager.

If you type the following command, you get a list of all the jobs currently printing or waiting on that printer:

```
net print \\computername\sharename
```

where *sharename* is the name by which the printer is shared on the network. You see that each job is assigned a job number. To delete a print job, refer to that number and type

```
net print \\computername job# /delete
```

substituting the job number for *job#*. If you want to hold a print job (keep it in the print queue but let other jobs print ahead of it) or release it (free a held job to print), substitute the /hold or /release for /delete.

While it is possible to control print jobs from the command line, it's much easier to do it from the Print Manager. When you try to delete a print job, it might be done printing by the time you type the server name and queue incorrectly, notice the problem, and re-enter the data.

> **TIP**
>
> If you have configured your default printer to print directly to ports, you won't be able to print to a local port from the command prompt. Currently, there isn't anything that you can do about this except go into the Print Manager, remove the Print Directly to Ports option, and resend the job.

How Do I Control a Print Job from the Command Prompt?

To pause, continue, or delete a print job from the command prompt, first type

```
net print \\computername\sharename
```

where *computername**sharename* is the name of the computer and printer with the print job that you wish to control. This command gives you a list of the pending print jobs for that printer and their job numbers. Find the number that corresponds to the print job that you want to control, and, to delete a job, type

```
net print \\computername job# /delete
```

To hold or release the job instead of deleting it, substitute the word "hold" or "release" for "delete." You don't need to specify the sharename with this command.

Using Network Services

The NET START *servicename* command is not capable of starting all the services that are available from the Services icon in the Control Panel, but only the network-related ones. In this section, we'll talk about what those commands are and how to start, pause, continue, and stop them.

NET START: Starting a Service

The NET START command encompasses a long list of network services that can be started. On its own, it doesn't do anything except list the services that have already been started. Be warned: the list that you see when you type NET START is not a complete list of all the network services available. To view the available services, type either of these commands:

```
net start /help |more
net help net start |more.
```

How Do I Start a Network Service?

 To start a network service from the command prompt, type

```
net start servicename
```

where *servicename* is the name of the service to start. This command works only for the network services described in this section.

All two-word commands, such as "clipbook server" and "computer browser" must be enclosed within quotation marks for the NET START commands to work.

The default services in Windows NT Server are described below.

NET START ALERTER The alerter service sends messages about the network to users. You select what events that you want to trigger alerts in the Performance Monitor. For these alerts to be sent, both the alerter and messenger services must be running on the computer originating the alerts, and the messenger service must be running on the computer receiving them.

NET START "CLIPBOOK SERVER" The Clipbook Viewer is a temporary or permanent storage place for text or graphics that you want to cut and paste between applications. From the command line, start this service by typing

```
net start "clipbook server"
```

You see either a message that the service has been started, or, if you've already started it from NT Server, you see a message that the service was already started.

NET START "COMPUTER BROWSER" The computer browser service allows your computer to browse and be browsed on the network. When you start it from the command prompt, however, you get no further information than that the service has started.

NET START "DIRECTORY REPLICATOR" You can type this command in either of two ways:

```
net start "directory replicator"
net start replicator
```

It begins the service that allows you to dynamically update files between servers. You must have replication rights to use this command, which means you have to set up a user account with replication rights before you start this service. (There is a default user group with those rights that comes with NT Server, so you can just assign an account to that group.)

NET START EVENTLOG This command begins the event log, which audits selected events on the network, such as file access, user logons and logoffs, and the starting of programs. You can select what events you want to log, and also whether you want the log to consist of both successful and failed attempts, just failures, or just successes (although just recording successes doesn't sound terribly useful if you're trying to monitor the system).

NET START MESSENGER A command called NET SEND allows you to send brief messages over the network when working from the command prompt. For this command to work, however, the messenger service must first be running on both the machine sending the message and the one(s) receiving it. To begin the messenger service, type

```
net start messenger
```

If you're running the alerter service to keep yourself informed of what's going on at the server, the messenger service must also be running on both the server and the workstation where you want to receive the messages.

NET START "NET LOGON" This command starts the netlogon service, which verifies logon requests and controls replication of the user accounts database (see NET START DIRECTORY REPLICATOR). The netlogon service isn't used for logging onto your computer, but for logging onto the domain that your computer is part of; if you log on just to a computer, you can use anything there that isn't dependent on domain membership (such as directory replication). Even if you don't log onto the domain, you can still access resources shared with the network if you have rights and permissions to use them. The process of logging onto the domain, as opposed to just the workstation, is called *pass-through validation*.

NET START "NETWORK DDE" This service provides a network transport for dynamic data exchange (DDE) conversations and provides security for them.

NET START "NETWORK DDE DSDM" Used by the DDE service described above, the DDE share database manager (DSDM) manages the DDE conversations.

NET START "NT LM SECURITY SUPPORT PROVIDER" This service provides Windows NT security to RPC applications that use transports other than LAN Manager named pipes.

NET START "REMOTE PROCEDURE CALL (RPC) SERVICE" The Remote Procedure Call (RPC) Service is a mechanism that enables programmers to develop distributed applications more easily by providing pointers to direct the applications. Before you can use RPC, you need to configure it by specifying the Name Service Interface (NSI) that it will use. You have to know what NSI provider it will use and, if you are using the DCE Cell Directory Service, the network address of the provider. The default name service is the Windows NT Locator.

NET START "REMOTE PROCEDURE CALL (RPC) LOCATOR" This service allows distributed applications to use the RPC-provided pointer by directing the applications to those pointers. This service manages the RPC NSI database.

NET START SCHEDULE This command starts the scheduling service, which must be running to use the AT command. The AT command can be used to schedule commands and programs (like the backup program, for instance) to run on a certain computer at a specific time and date. By default, the scheduling service is configured to log on under the system account, but if it logs on under that account, the AT command can only be used for programs to which the Guest users have access. Thus, to run a restricted program (like the backup operation), you'd need to configure the scheduling service to log on under an account with rights to the programs you want to run.

To start a program at a certain time, you would specify

- The computer on which you wanted the program to run. (If you don't specify one, the default is the computer at which you execute the AT command.)

- The time and date when you want the program to begin running. (If you don't specify a date, the program will run on the day that you execute the command, at the appointed time.) You can also schedule an event for the next date (such as a Thursday), or make the event a repeating event scheduled to run on every occasion of a date.

- The command that you want to run (typed in quotation marks).

For example, to change the name of a file from JUNK.SAM to JUNKER.SAM on the local computer at 10:52 today, you would type

```
at 10:52 "rename c:\ntclass\junk.sam junker.sam"
```

If you wanted to perform a similar action on a networked computer named AMS, and set the "alarm clock" for 11:00 next Wednesday, you'd type

```
at \\ams 11:00 /next:wednesday "rename c:\ntclass\junk.sam junker.sam"
```

Of course, this line would be unbroken. To make this command happen every Wednesday, you'd substitute *every:wednesday* for *next:wednesday*. For every 7th, 14th, and 21st of the month, you'd type *every:7,14,21* (make sure there's no blanks between the colon and the numbers). By the way, you can abbreviate day names like this: M, T, W, Th, F, Sa, Su.

NET START SERVER　　To control access to network resources from the command line, you must type

```
net start server
```

This service must be running before you can perform certain actions:

- Directory sharing
- Printer sharing
- Remote procedure call (RPC) access
- Named pipe sharing

When you stop the server service, you disconnect all users attached to your machine, so before doing so, you should follow these steps.

1. From the command line, type

   ```
   net pause server
   ```

   to pause the server service. This keeps any new users from connecting to the server but does not disrupt any current connections.

2. Notify those people who are connected that you're going to shut it down, and that they need to log off before a certain time. You can use the NET SEND command to do this. To see the NET SEND message, NT machines must be running the messenger service; Windows, Windows for Workgroups, and Windows 95 machines must be running WinPopUp.

3. After that time has passed, you can type

```
net stop server
```

to end the service without messing anyone up.

When you end the server service, you take the computer browser and netlogon with it, so if you stop the server service and then restart it, you need to restart those programs as well.

NET START SPOOLER   As its name implies, this service provides print spooler capabilities.

NET START UPS   One of the best things about Windows NT is its built-in preparedness to contend with disaster. Like the backup program, disk mirroring, duplexing, and striping, the UPS (uninterrupted power supply) service links your workstation or server with a UPS to protect your computer from dirty power, power surges, and power failures. You still have to buy the UPS, but this service makes the hardware even more useful than it already is.

Before you run the UPS service for the first time from the command prompt (by typing net start ups) you must first configure the service. When configuring, you make a number of choices about how the service will function, including

- The serial port to which the UPS is connected

- Whether or not the UPS signals you when the following events occur: power supply interruption and low battery power (UPSes run from batteries when normal power fails)

- How the computer will shut down

- How long the battery life is and how long it will take to recharge

- How frequently you will see warning messages

Obviously, you need to check with your UPS's documentation before configuring the UPS service a certain way. Once it's up and running, the UPS service protects your machine from power problems and keeps you as notified of what's going on as you want to be.

NET START WORKSTATION   As you'd guess from the name, this command is intended for workstations, to enable them to connect to and use shared network resources. Once you start this service, you can see what's on the network and connect to it.

NT Server also offers a number of special services that can also be started with the NET START command. These include

- Client Server for Netware

- DHCP Client

- File Server for Macintosh

- FTP Server

- Gateway Service for Netware

- LPDSVC

- Microsoft DHCP Server

- Network Monitoring Agent

- OLE

- Print Server for Macintosh

- Remote Access Connection Manager

- Remote Access ISNSAP Service

- Remote Access Server

- Remoteboot

- Simple TCP/IP Services

- SNMP

- TCP/IP NETBIOS Helper

- Windows Internet Name Service

NET PAUSE and NET CONTINUE: Halting a Service Temporarily

If you need to temporarily halt a service, you can use the NET PAUSE command to do it. Just type

```
net pause service
```

and that *service* will be temporarily suspended. To restart the paused service, type

```
net continue service
```

The NET PAUSE and NET CONTINUE commands affect the following default services:

- NET LOGON

- NETWORK DDE

- NETWORK DDE DSDM

- SCHEDULE

- SERVER

- WORKSTATION

NET STOP: Stopping a Service

NET STOP works in the same way that NET START does. On its own, it can't do anything, but when you add the name of a service that you want to stop, it stops it. See the NET START section above for details on what each of the services does.

WARNING
Be careful when stopping a service! Some services are dependent on others (such as NET START NET LOGON and NET START WORK-STATION), so if you shut down one, you may shut down another without meaning to. If you just need to stop a service temporarily, use NET START PAUSE instead. You need administrative rights to stop a service.

How Do I Stop, Pause, and Continue a Service?

Once you've started a service, you can pause, continue or stop it in much the same way that you started it in the first place. Just type

```
net action servicename
```

where *action* is what you want to do (pause, continue, or stop) and *servicename* is the name of the service that you want to control.

Sending Messages

You're not dependent on e-mail to send messages across the network. From the command prompt, you can send messages and arrange to have your own forwarded so that they catch up with you wherever you are. As long as your computer and the computer to which you direct the messages are running the message service, you can reach anywhere on the network.

NET NAME: Adding or Deleting a Messaging Name

The NET NAME command adds or deletes a *messaging name* (also known as an *alias*) at a workstation. The messaging name is the name that receives messages at that station; any messages sent over the network will go to where the messaging name is. Although this command comes with two switches, /add and /delete, the /add switch is not necessary to add a messaging name to a workstation; instead, you would need only type

```
net name username
```

and that would add that messaging name to the appropriate workstation.

To add the messaging name "Eric" to the computer in Figure A.14, I only had to type

```
net name Eric
```

But if I wanted to remove him, I'd have to type

```
net name Eric /delete.
```

FIGURE A.14

A sample NET NAME screen

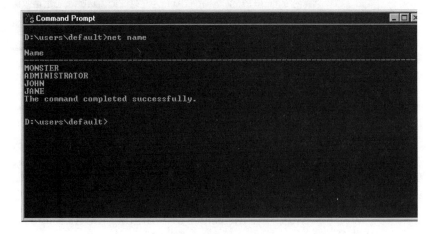

The difference between messaging names and usernames may not be immediately clear. The username is the name of the person who is logged onto a particular machine. It can be deleted from the messaging name list; that is, messages can be re-routed from the machine at which a user is working to another machine, if you use this command to add the name to that machine. While you can delete both the username and any messaging names from a computer, you cannot delete the computer's name from the list. In Figure A.14, the name of the computer is MONSTER, Administrator is the user name, and John and Jane are messaging names.

How Do I Forward My Messages to Another Machine?

 If you're working at another machine than the one that you're accustomed to using, you can make sure that your messages follow you there. Just type

```
net name username
```

(or *machinename*) on the machine where you are working. All messages addressed to that user name or machine name will show up at that location. Messaging names cannot be already in use anywhere else on the network. If you try to add a name that's already in use to a messaging name list, it won't work.

NET SEND: Sending Messages

NET SEND is a messaging service for sending a message to one person, to all the people in your group, to all the people in your domain, to all the people on the network, or to all the users connected to the server. NET SEND does not work without its parameters, as you need to tell it something to send and where to send it. The basic parameters are as follows:

```
net send name message text
```

where

- *name* is the name (username, messaging name, or computername) that you want to send the message to.

> **TIP** According to the help file, substituting an asterisk (*) in place of a name sends the message to everyone in your user group, but when I used it the Messenger Service sent the message to everyone connected to the domain controller, rather than to the user group of the account that did the sending.

- *message text* is whatever text you wish to include in your message. It doesn't have to be enclosed in quotation marks. Even though NET SEND isn't meant to be a substitute for an e-mail program, you can send fairly hefty messages with it. If you try to send too long a message, the system refuses to let you type any more characters, but in a test message it took thirteen full lines to reach that point. If you want to send a message longer than that, it's probably easier to use e-mail.

NET SEND Options

Sometimes you need more than the basic parameters to get your message where it needs to go. In that case, you can use whichever of these options is necessary (only one at a time):

Option	Description
domain	Sends the message to everyone in your domain. Just substitute your domain's name for the word *domain*. If you include a name of a domain or workgroup like this: `domain:domainname` where *domainname* is the name of the domain or workgroup that you wish to receive the message, then the message is sent to all users in the domain or workgroup. If you don't include a name with this switch, the message is sent to the local domain.
/broadcast	Sends the message to all users on the network—not the domain, not the user group, but the network.
/users	Sends the message to all users connected to the server.

Using NET SEND

Even with the explanation for the parameters, getting NET SEND to work can be a little confusing. This would probably be a good time for some real-life examples.

To send a message that says "This is a test message" to Paula, who is part of your domain, type

```
net send paula This is a test message.
```

If you want to send a message that says "This is a test message" to Sam, who is part of the Engineering domain, type

```
net send sam \engineering This is a test message.
```

If you want to send a message that says "This is a test message" to everyone in your domain, type

```
net send * This is a test message.
```

Once you've successfully sent a message, everyone who meets these criteria sees a message like the one in Figure A.15:

- The message was directed to them

- They are logged on at the time of transmittal

- They have the messenger service running on their machines

Which is better, e-mail or messaging? Each has its time and place. E-mail works better for messages that have files attached, since it's not

---

FIGURE A.15

A sample Messenger Service pop-up window

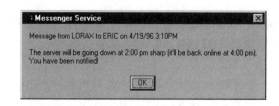

limited to text transmittal, but it does have the disadvantage of being ignorable. Even if you've arranged to be notified when mail is waiting, you can ignore the notification or not hear it at all if you've stepped away from your machine.

Therefore, if you have a question for someone and you need an answer *right now*, the messenger service is probably the way to go. When you send a message to someone at an NT workstation, the dialog box shown in Figure A.15 appears on their screen and does not disappear until they click the OK button.

How Do I Send Messages?

To send messages from the command prompt, use the NET SEND command. Using the parameters described above, you can send messages to individuals or groups, and within a domain or across domains. Again, NT machines need to be running the messenger service to see NET SEND messages; Windows, Windows for Workgroups, and Windows 95 machines must be running WinPopUp.

Getting Synched: Viewing and Setting the Time

Some services, such as directory replication, depend on the server's and the workstations' clocks being set to the same time. To automate this process, you can use the NET TIME command.

NET TIME: Coordinating Server and Workstation Clocks

The NET TIME command works differently when you execute it from a server or a workstation. If you run it from a server, it displays the current time; if you run it from a workstation, you can synchronize your computer's clock with that of the time server, even selecting a server from another domain if there is a trusted relationship between your domain and the other one. Ordinary users cannot set the server time from a workstation; only members of the Administrators or Server Manager groups, logged onto the server (logically if not physically) can set the system time.

To coordinate the clocks from a workstation:

1. Check the time on a time server (here named EISA SERVER) by typing

   ```
   net time \\eisa server
   ```

   If you type only `net time`, by default you get the current time on the server that serves as your time server. (If no time server is on your domain, you get a message that says the system could not locate a time server.)

   To check the time on a time server in another domain (called TED, for instance), type

   ```
   net time /domain:ted
   ```

2. Set the time from the time server. In our example, you would type

   ```
   net time \\eisa server /set
   ```

   If no time server is set up for your domain but you want to synchronize a workstation's clock with that of the domain controller for the domain named TED, for example, you would type

   ```
   net time /domain:ted /set
   ```

   Set the time from a time server in another domain (here called OTHERS) by typing

   ```
   net time /domain:others /set
   ```

From a server, you use the same commands to check the time on another server or set the time to correspond with that on another domain, but if you type NET TIME without switches, the screen shows the time on the time server for that domain, if one exists.

How Do I Synchronize a Workstation's Time with the Server's?

 To coordinate a workstation's time with the server's, type

```
net time \\servername /set
```

where *servername* is the name of the server with which you want to coordinate.

Why Use the Command Prompt?

I hope that most of the time you won't have to use the command prompt. Although you should now have a pretty good idea of how to do just about anything from the command prompt that you can do in a normal session, typing a command correctly is a bit more awkward than pointing and clicking. The only real advantage I can see to using the command prompt over the graphical interface is that you don't have to remember where anything is: if you can remember the command name, you can do everything from the same place.

In general, the people who need to use the command prompt to connect are the network's OS/2 and DOS clients. If you're administering the server, you probably don't have much occasion to use the command prompt, except when making adjustments to DOS and OS/2 workstations.

INDEX

Note to the Reader: First level entries are in **bold**. Page numbers in **bold** indicate the principal discussion of a topic or the definition of a term. Page numbers in *italic* indicate illustrations.

Numbers and Symbols

3Dpipes screen saver, 832
32-bit bus master network cards, 830
$ (dollar sign), in share names, 320
" (quotation marks), in NET START commands, 1075

A

aborting backups, 897
access control entries (ACEs), 863–864
access control lists (ACLs), **326**, **329–331**. See also shared directories; share-level permissions
   adding groups to, 329–330, *330*
   adding single users to, 330, *330*
   changing with command-line commands, 331
   changing permissions on existing shares, 331
   event logs and, 863
access masks, 864
accessing. See also connecting; opening
   NetWare print services from Windows NT, 606–608, *607*
   shared directories on simple networks, 34–35
   shares on other computers without domains, 566–567
Account Operators local group, 281, 284, 477
ACEs (access control entries), 863–864
A-class networks, 650–652, *651*
ACLs. See access control lists
Add Printer Wizard, 373–379, *374*
adding. See also installing
   computers to domains, **492–496**, **1056**
      adding or deleting with NET COMPUTER command, 1056
      domain controllers, 493
      LAN Manager 2.x servers, 495–496
      overview of, 492, *493*
      workstations and servers, 493–495, *495*
   groups to access control lists, 329–330, *330*
   messaging names, 1084–1085, *1084*
   microprocessors, 831–832
   printers, 36–37, 373–379
      the same printer with multiple names, 378
   users from foreign domains to share-level permissions, 560–563, *561*, *562*, *563*
   users to access control lists, 330, *330*
   users to another domain's Domain Users group, 564–565, *565*
addresses. See IP (Internet Protocol)

administrative shares created by directory shares on remote servers, 324
administrator access to home directories, 342
Administrator user account, 260
Administrators local group, 280–281, 283, 477
advanced user rights, 291–293
advertising services, 39–40
alerts
    creating for free server space, 818–819, *819*
    NET START ALERTER command, 1075
    sending to workstations, 489–491, *490*
anonymous FTP, 803–806
ANSI.SYS file, 164–165
application interfaces (APIs), 86–88
applications. *See also* network software
    associating Macintosh files with, 468–470, *469*, *470*
    controlling what programs users can run, 303, *304*
    cross-platform applications, 471
    migrating Windows applications, **141–144**. *See also* installing Windows NT Server
        incompatible programs, 141
        moving fonts, 141–143, *142*, 144
        troubleshooting, 143–144
    running remotely, **1033**
Applications event log, 855–857, *855*, *856*. *See also* event logs
Archie searches, 789–792
archive bits, 223
archiving event logs, 868–870, *869*
ARPA-127.REV file, 767, 770, 774
ASCII files. *See* text files
assigning
    network names on simple networks, 32–34
    user accounts to groups, 263–264, *263*
associating Macintosh files with applications, 468–470, *469*, *470*
asymmetric multiprocessor systems, 8
auditing. *See also* event logs; logging

    directory and file access on shared directories, 348–350, *349*, *350*
    file and object access on shared directories, 347–348, *348*
    printer usage, 399–402, *400*, *401*, 409–410
    security events for user accounts, 293–295, *293*
AUTOEXEC.BAT file, 11
automatic backups, **889–895**. *See also* backup strategies
    with NTBACKUP command, 890–892
    with WINAT scheduler program, 892–895, *893*, *894*

B

B nodes, 747–749
background printing, 382, 383
backup domain controllers (BDCs), 526–531, **535–541**. *See also* domain controllers
    advantages and disadvantages of, 535–537
    changing frequency of updates, 829
    controlling SAM database synchronization, 529–531
    estimating SAM database size, 539–541
    numbers and locations of, 535–539
    overview of, 59, *60*, 526–527
    promoting to primary domain controllers, 527–528
    recommended numbers of in one location, 537–538
    in remote locations, 538–539
    synchronizing SAM databases with primary domain controllers, 528–529, *529*
Backup Operators local group, 282, 284
backup strategies, 103–106, 246, **884–916**. *See also* disaster recovery
    automatic backups, **889–895**
        with NTBACKUP command, 890–892

overview of, 889–890

with WINAT scheduler program, 892–895, *893*, *894*

backing up, **103–106**, **885–890**, **895–901**, **914–916**

aborting backups, 897

with BACKUP command, 897–898

DHCP databases, **740–742**

to floppy disks, 897–899

to more than one tape, 896–897

network drives, 900

open files, 900–901

partition information, 913–914, *913*

performing backups, **885–890**, *885*, *886*, *889*

the Registry, 246, 914–916

removable drives, 899

Security Access Manager (SAM) database, 914–916

selected files, 895–896, *896*

Windows NT Server installation and, 103–106

with XCOPY command, 898–899

Backup Information dialog box, 886–889, *886*, *889*

protecting backups, **901–902**

restoring DHCP databases, 742

restoring files, **902–909**

after reinstalling Windows NT Server, 907–908

to networked drives, 909

overview of, 902–906, 908–909

from tape sets with missing tapes, 909

restoring the Registry, 246, **916**

restoring system configurations, **910–914**

backing up partition information, 913–914, *913*

from emergency repair disks, 911–913

"Last Known Good Menu" message and, 130–131, 246, 910–911

recovering from bad video drivers, 914

restoring WINS databases, 760–761

backward compatibility, 19

B-class networks, 650–652, *651*

BDCs. *See* **backup domain controllers**

big-endian byte storage system, 5–6

bind **format files**, 774–777

bindings, enabling and disabling, 1026

"Boot couldn't find NTLDR. Please insert another disk" message, 163–164

boot disks, 133, **169–171**

boot failure diagnosis, **920–927**

hardware problems, 920–922

NT kernel initialization phase, 926

NT kernel load phase, 924–925

NTDETECT.COM file and, 923–924

NTLDR file and, 922–923

Registry and, 924

services load phase, 926

using the "verbose" debug version of NTDETECT, 923–924

Windows subsystem start phase, 926–927

BOOT file in DNS, 767–770

booting Windows NT, remote boots, 163

BOOTP protocol, 719–721

bottlenecks. *See* **performance optimization**

breaking mirror sets, 206–208

breakout boxes, 152–154

broadcast address, TCP/IP, 653

broadcast messages, 156, 491–492, *491*

browse lists, **41–48**, **841–854**. *See also* network concepts; workgroup security

displaying resources on browse lists, **849–852**

hiding servers from browsers, **481–482**, 854

how the browse service works, 850–851

LAN Manager problems, 849, 850

on large networks, 43–46

master browsers

domain master browsers (DMBs), 752–753, 848

electing, **842–846**, *844*, *845*

preventing computers from being, 846–847

on TCP/IP networks, 848

NET START "COMPUTER BROWSER" command, 1076

overview of, 41–43, *42*, *43*, 841–842

protocols and browser performance, 853

refreshing, 849

server announcement intervals, 852

setting backup browser update frequency, 852

viewing, 48

why browsers are slow, 853

workgroups and, 45–46

built-in groups, 280–285

bus mastering, 11

buses, RAM capacity and, 10–11

byte storage systems, 5–6

(

CACHE file in DNS, 767, 770

CACLS command, 343–344, 576, 900–901

callback modems, 1025

C-class networks

overview of, 650–652, *651*

subnetting, 657–658

CD-ROM drives. *See also* floppy disks; hard disk drives; hardware; tape drives

installing NT with WINNT or WINNT32, 122

requirements, 98–99

SCSI CD-ROM drives, 99

central processing units (CPUs). *See* microprocessors

Challenge Handshake Authentication Protocol (CHAP), 708, 710–711

Change permissions, 333–334

changing. *See also* converting; editing

access control lists with commands, 331

computer configurations, 1057–1060, *1057*, *1058*

CONFIG.POL file location, 307–308, *308*

domain passwords on Windows for Workgroups workstations, 427–430, *428*, *429*, *430*

event log size and overwrite options, 867–868, *867*

frequency of backup domain controller updates, 829

global group membership, 1051–1053, *1052*

logon script path for directory replication, 524–525, *524*

permissions on existing shares, 331

share-level permissions on existing shares, 331

user database, 1048–1051, *1049*

CHAP (Challenge Handshake Authentication Protocol), 708, 710–711

Chart mode, in Performance Monitor, 813–816, *814*, *815*

checking memory status, 832–833

checksum headers, in IP protocol, 663

CHKDSK program, in NT Setup program, 129–130

choosing. *See* selecting

CIDR (Classless Internetwork Domain Routing), 659–662

circular groups (groups inside groups), 569

Classless Internetwork Domain Routing (CIDR), 659–662

clearing. *See* deleting

clients. *See* workstations

commands. *See also* NET commands

BACKUP, 897–898

CACLS, 343–344, 576, 900–901

changing access control lists with, 331

controlling share-level permissions with, 331

IPCONFIG, 735, *736*

kernel debugging commands, **946–958**
  command listing, **946–950**
  !drivers, 952
  !errlog, 955
  !irpzone full, 955
  !locks, 952–953
  log file commands, 951
  !memusage, 953–954
  !process 0 0, 956
  !process 0 7, 956–958
  !process, 958
  !reload, 951
  !thread, 958
  !vm, 954–955
memory dump commands, **931–933**
  dumpchk, 932
  dumpexam, 932–933
  dumpflop, 931
net statistics server, 478
NTBACKUP, 890–892
overview of, 34
WINAT, 503–504, *504*, 892–895, *893*, *894*
XCOPY, 898–899
Comment fields, for shared directories, 320
compatibility
  backward compatibility, 19
  with LAN Manager 2.2 servers, 19
  with NetWare, 19–20
  with network boards, 18–19
complete trust domain model, 584–585
CompuServe, WINNT forum, 240
computers, 66–68. *See also* Macintosh workstations; network concepts; servers; workstations
  adding to domains, **492–496, 1056**
    adding or deleting with NET COMPUTER command, 1056
    domain controllers, 493
    LAN Manager 2.x servers, 495–496
    overview of, 492, *493*
    workstations and servers, 493–495, *495*

machine characteristics, 67–68
machine names and share names, 35
messengers, 67
naming during installation, 132
NET commands, **1055–1064**
  NET COMPUTER (adding or deleting computers from domains), 1056
  NET CONFIG (viewing and changing configurations), 1057–1060, *1057*, *1058*
  NET STATISTICS (viewing computer statistics), 478, 1062–1063, *1063*, *10643*
preventing from being master browsers, 846–847
receivers, 67
redirectors, 66–67
servers, 67
viewing or changing configurations, 1057–1060, *1057*, *1058*
CONFIG.POL file, 307–308, *308*
CONFIG.SYS file, 11
configuring. *See also* customizing; setting up
  DHCP servers, 721–723, *722*, *723*
  Dial-Up Networking connections for Windows 95 workstations, 1019–1022, *1019*, *1020*
  Dial-Up Networking servers, **992–1006**
    allowing users from other domains to log in to servers, 1002–1003
    controlling client/server behavior, 994–996, *995*
    controlling login security, 998–999
    Dial-Up Networking Administrator and, 999–1002, *1000*, *1001*
    ISDN setup, 1003–1004
    selecting protocols, 996–998, *996*, *998*
    X.25 setup, 1005–1006, *1005*
  export servers for directory replication, 511–515, *512*, *513*, *514*
  import computers for directory replication, 515–516
  NetWare Gateway Service, 600–604

service startup, 500–501, *500*

system configuration restoration, **910–914**

  backing up partition information, 913–914, *913*

  from emergency repair disks, 911–913

  "Last Known Good Menu" message and, 130–131, 246, 910–911

  recovering from bad video drivers, 914

uninterruptible power supplies, 151–152, *151*

Windows 95 workstations, 432–435, *432, 433, 434*

Windows NT for running in parallel with NetWare, 595–597, *595, 596*

Windows for Workgroups workstations, 424–427, *424*

conflicts

  DNS/WINS conflicts, 787–788

  in routing information, 700–701

Connect option, for home directories, 364–366

connecting. *See also* accessing

  to dial-up networking servers, **1006–1024**

    connecting Windows NT workstations to NetWare servers, 1024

    from other operating systems, 1023

    from Windows 95 workstations, 1016–1022

    from Windows NT workstations, 1007–1016

    from Windows for Workgroups workstations, 1022

  DOS workstations to Windows NT, **414–423**

    connecting to directories and print shares, 421–423

    with Microsoft Network Client 3 for MS-DOS, 416–421

    with Network Client Administrator (NCA), 415–416

    overview of, 414

    passwords and, 418–421

  Macintosh workstations to Windows NT, **457–462**

    first time logon, 457–461

    subsequent logons, 461–462, *461, 462*

  resources to other drives and printer ports, 1067–1069

  to shared printers, **384–391**. *See also* accessing; printers

    from DOS workstations, 384–385

    from OS/2 workstations, 388

    from Windows NT workstations, 388–391, *389, 390*

    from Windows for Workgroups workstations, 385–388, *386, 387, 388*

  Windows 95 workstations to network resources, **435–438**, *435*

  Windows NT and NetWare, **590–592**. *See also* NetWare

    NetWare resources in Windows NT networks, 591–592

    Windows NT Server in NetWare networks, 591

    Windows NT workstations in NetWare networks, 590, 630–631, 1024

contaminants, 879

Control Panel, versus System Policy Editor, 309

controlling

  automatic user disconnection from servers, 484

  client/server behavior in Dial-Up Networking, 994–996, *995*

  file and directory permissions with CACLS command, 343–344, 576, 900–901

  login security in Dial-Up Networking, 998–999

  and monitoring printer access, **391–402**

    hiding shared printers, 395–396

    logging and auditing printer usage, 399–402, *400, 401*, 409–410

    overview of, 391

receiving printer status messages, 398–399

setting print job priorities, 396, *397*

setting printer permissions, 392–395, *392, 393*

setting printing hours, 397–398, *398*, 399

print jobs, 1073–1074

SAM database synchronization, 529–531

share-level permissions with commands, 331

wallpaper with System Policy Editor, 299–302, *299*

what programs users can run, 303, *304*

converting. *See also* changing

extended partitions to logical drives, 184–186, *185, 186*

long NTFS filenames to FAT file system, 222–223

coordinating server and workstation clocks, 1088–1090

copying user accounts, 272–273, *273*

costs of NT Server and client software, 17–18

counters to watch for performance optimization, 827–828, 830, **839–841**

CPUs. *See* **microprocessors**

creating

alerts for free server space, 818–819, *819*

boot disks, 133, 169–171

Dial-Up Networking connections for Windows 95 workstations, 1019–1022, *1019, 1020*

directory shares, 33–34, 317–318, *318, 319*

disaster recovery plans, 917

emergency repair disks, 133–134, 170

extended partitions, 183–184, *183, 184*

groups, **277–280**

global groups, 279–280, *279*

local groups, 277–279, *278*

home directories, 340–342, *340*

import/export pairs for directory replication, 517–522

logical drives, 188

logon scripts, 361–363

Macintosh-accessible volumes, 455–457, *455, 456*

memory dump files, 930

mirror sets, 205–206

nonparity stripe sets, 199–202

passwords for user accounts, 262

separator pages, 403–404

shared directories on remote servers, 322–323, *322, 323, 325, 325*

shared resources, 1070–1072, *1070*

stripe sets with parity, 213–216, *214, 215, 217*

system policies, 297–302, *299*

trust relationships, 553–557, *555, 556*, 559

user accounts, **261–271, 1044–1048**

assigning user accounts to groups, 263–264, *263*

creating passwords, 262

naming conventions, 261–262

with NET USER command, 1044–1048, *1044, 1045*

overview of, 261–263, *261*, 271

setting account duration and type (global versus local), 269–270, *269*

setting permissible logon hours, 264–268, *265*

setting permissible logon workstations, 268–269, *268*

volume sets, 192–194, *192, 193*, 195

CREATOR OWNER group, 285

cross-domain management, 546–587. *See also* domains

cross-domain groups, **564–576**

accessing shares on other computers without domains, 566–567

adding users to another domain's Domain Users group, 564–565, *565*

circular groups (groups inside groups), 569

local and global groups defined, 565–566, **569–570**

Users group versus Domain Users group, 568–569

using global groups across domains, 575–576

using local and global groups inside domains, 570–575, *571, 572*

using single domain accounts across domains, 568

file permissions, **558–563**

  adding users from foreign domains to share-level permissions, 560–563, *561, 562, 563*

  Everyone group and, 558–560

granting user rights and printer permissions across domains, **577**

logging on from foreign domains, **577–579**, *578*

multi-domain management tasks, **547–548**

planning single- and multiple-domain networks, **579–583**

  domain size considerations, 581–583

  minimizing the number of domains, 580

  mirroring geographical boundaries, 581

  mirroring organizational structures, 580–581

  Security Access Manager (SAM) database and, 582–583

single-domain versus multiple-domain models, **584–587**

  complete trust model, 584–585

  master domain model, 585–587

  multiple master domain model, 587

  resource domains, 585

  single-domain enterprise model, 584

trust relationships, **68–71**, **548–558**

  alternatives to, 552–553

  defined, **548**

  establishing, 553–557, *555, 556, 559*

  explained, **548–552**, *550, 551, 552*

inter-domain relationships with, 70–71, *71*

inter-domain relationships without, 68–70, *69*

versus Mark user accounts, 552–553

permitting domains to trust other domains, 554–555, *555*

terminating, 557–558

transferring between domains, 552, *552*

two-way trust relationships, 550

cross-platform applications, 471

cumulative usage statistics, 478

customizing printer setup, **379–383**. *See also* configuring

  printer pooling (multiple printers with the same name), 381–382, *381*

  with Printer Properties dialog box, 379–380, *380*

  printing in background versus printing directly to ports, 382, 383

  setting printer timeout number, 382–383, *383*

D

data forks in Macintosh data files, 466

Data Link Control (DLC) protocol, 20–21, 83–84

data preparation for NT installation, **103–106**. *See also* installing Windows NT Server

  backing up to another computer, 103

  backups for LAN Manager conversions, 106

  converting FAT volumes to NTFS volumes, 105

  tape drives, backups and, 103–106

data transfer rates, 826

data types in the Registry, **235–236**, *235*

dates. *See also* time settings

  and exchanging data between PC and Macintosh workstations, 472 expiration dates for user accounts, 269–270, *269*

debug version of NTDETECT, 923–924

debugging Windows NT 4, 927–961. *See also* disaster recovery

examining crash dumps with DUMPEXAM, **958–960**

kernel debugging, **934–958**, **960–961**

defined, **934**

HAL files for host computers, 940–942

host computers, **928**, **939–943**

Kernel STOP Errors, **927**, 929, 934

limitations of, **960–961**

local debugging, 934, 935

modem connections, 934–935

remote debugging, 934, 935

setting up the debugger on host computers, 942–943

setting up for RISC-based computers, 938–939

setting up symbol trees on host computers, 927–928, 939–942

setting up the target computer, 928, **935–939**

setting up for x86-based computers, 936–937

starting the debugger, **943–946**

starting the debugger with remote utility, 945–946

kernel debugging commands, **946–958**

command listing, **946–950**

!drivers, 952

!errlog, 955

!irpzone full, 955

!locks, 952–953

log file commands, 951

!memusage, 953–954

!process 0 0, 956

!process 0 7, 956–958

!process, 958

!reload, 951

!thread, 958

!vm, 954–955

memory dump files, **929–933**

creating, 930

dumpchk command, 932

dumpexam command, 932–933

dumpflop command, 931

overview of, 929

terminology defined, **927–928**

defaults

default directory permissions for NT Server directories, 344–347

default router addresses, 654

default services, 497–498

defeating system policies, 304–305

defining. *See* creating

Delete permissions, 333, 334

deleting

computers from domains, 1056

messaging names, 1084–1085, *1084*

mirror sets, 206–208

protocols, 828

shared resources, 1070–1072, *1070*

stripe sets with parity, 219–220

stripe sets without parity, 201–203

trust relationships, 557–558

user accounts, 276–277

volume sets, 194, 196

dependencies of services and devices in Windows NT Diagnostics tool, 969, *970*

designing. *See also* planning

multi-DHCP networks, 739–740

single- and multiple-domain networks, **584–587**

complete trust model, 584–585

master domain model, 585–587

multiple master domain model, 587

resource domains, 585

single-domain enterprise model, 584

"destination host unreachable" message, 699

device drivers
enabling shared RAM on network cards
with TCP/IP drivers, 830
Macintosh LaserPrep driver problems, 463
and microprocessor optimization, 831
Network Driver Interface Specification
(NDIS) drivers, 18–19, 85–86
network interface card drivers, 77–78, *78*
packet drivers, 86
printer drivers, 97–98, 371
recovering from bad video drivers, 914
tape drivers, 155–159, *158*
video drivers, 96–98, 139, 914
**DHCP (Dynamic Host Configuration Proto-
col), 719–743**. *See also* TCP/IP protocol
backing up DHCP databases, **740–742**
BOOTP protocol and, 719–721
configuring DHCP on workstations, 728
designing multi-DHCP networks, 739–740
DHCP limitations, 743
DHCP scopes, **723–728**, 738
DHCPACK message, 735, *736*, 737
DHCPDISCOVER message, 731–732, *732*
DHCPOFFER message, 732–734, *733*
DHCPREQUEST message, 734, *735*, 737
installing and configuring DHCP servers,
721–723, *722*, *723*
IPCONFIG command, 735, *736*
obtaining IP addresses from DHCP (IP leases), **728–739**
restoring DHCP databases, 742
setting IP leases to Infinite, 730
diagnosing server boot failure, 920–927. *See
also* Windows NT Diagnostics tool
hardware problems, 920–922
NT kernel initialization phase, 926
NT kernel load phase, 924–925
NTDETECT.COM file and, 923–924
NTLDR file and, 922–923
Registry and, 924
services load phase, 926

using the "verbose" debug version of
NTDETECT, 923–924
Windows subsystem start phase, 926–927
Dial-Up Networking (DUN), 980–1033
connecting to dial-up networking servers,
1006–1024
connecting Windows NT workstations to
NetWare servers, 1024
from other operating systems, 1023
from Windows 95 workstations, 1016–
1022
from Windows NT workstations, 1007–
1016
from Windows for Workgroups workstations, 1022
ISDN connections, 981, **987–990**
hardware requirements, 987–988, 990
ISDN setup, 1003–1004
packet assembler-disassembler (PAD)
X.25 connections, 989–990
smart cards and, 990
transmission speed differences, 988
X.25 connections, 988–990, 1005–1006,
1005
modem connections, **985–987**
compatibility issues, 986
hardware requirements, 986
installing modems, 992–994, *993*, *994*
pooling modems, 986–987
security, 1024–1025
overview of, 980–983
protocols and, 981–982, 996–998, *996*, *998*
versus remote-access software, 982–983
running applications remotely, **1033**
sample applications, **983–985**
Internet gateways, 984
Internet service providers, 984
LAN/WAN gateways, 984–985
Point-to-Point Tunneling Protocol
(PPTP), 985

remote dial-in to company NT servers, 983

remote dial-in to non-NT servers, 983–984

security, **1024–1026**

 enabling and disabling bindings, 1026

 modem security, 1024–1025

serial connections, **990–991**

server installation and configuration, **992–1006**

 allowing users from other domains to log in to servers, 1002–1003

 controlling client/server behavior, 994–996, *995*

 controlling login security, 998–999

 Dial-Up Networking Administrator and, 999–1002, *1000, 1001,* 1027–1031

 installing the dial-up networking module, 992

 installing modems, 992–994, *993, 994*

 ISDN setup, 1003–1004

 selecting protocols, 996–998, *996, 998*

 X.25 setup, 1005–1006, *1005*

Telephony Application Program Interface (TAPI) and, 980–981

troubleshooting, **1026–1033**

 connections that have worked before, 1027

 with Dial-Up Networking Administrator, 1027–1031

 with Event Viewer, 1031

 first time connections, 1026–1027

 with session logs, 1031–1033

direct serial connections to Dial-Up Networking, 990–991

directories, setting up the NT directory during installation, 130

directory replication, 16, **504–526**. *See also* Server Manager

 changing logon script path, 524–525, *524*

configuring export servers, 511–515, *512, 513, 514*

configuring import computers, 515–516

creating import/export pairs, 517–522

frequency of, 516

NET START "DIRECTORY REPLICATOR" command, 1076

setting up Directory Replicator service, 508–511, *509, 510*

setting up PDCs to replicate login scripts to BDCs, 523

troubleshooting, 525–526

uses for, 506

which computers can import or export, 506–508, *507, 508*

Directory Service Manager for NetWare (DSMN), 623–630. *See also* NetWare

installing, 623–627

mapping files for synchronizing NT and NetWare accounts, 627–630

directory services, 38–41. *See also* network concepts

name servers, 40–41

periodic service advertising, 39–40

static service lists, 38–39

directory shares, 316–367

access control lists (ACLs), **326, 329–331**. *See also* share-level permissions

 adding groups to, 329–330, *330*

 adding single users to, 330, *330*

 changing with command-line commands, 331

 changing permissions on existing shares, 331

 defined, **326**

 event logs and, 863

accessing on simple networks, 34–35

Comment fields, 320

creating, 33–34, **317–318**, *318, 319*

dollar sign ($) in share names, 320

file and directory permissions, **331–350**. *See also* home directories

    auditing directory and file access, 348–350, *349, 350*

    auditing file and object access, 347–348, *348*

    controlling with CACLS command, 343–344, 576, 900–901

    default directory permissions for NT Server directories, 344–347

    FAT file system and, 336–337

    for home directories, 338–340, *339*

    NTFS file system and, 332

    versus share-level permissions, 334–336, *335*

    types of, 332–334

file ownership, **350–356**

    defined, **351**, *352*

    example, 352–354

    taking ownership, 354–356, *354*

file permissions across domains, **558–563**

    adding users from foreign domains to share-level permissions, 560–563, *561, 562, 563*

    Everyone group and, 558–560

hiding, **320**

home directories, **336–342, 364–367**. *See also* file and directory permissions

    administrators' access to, 342

    creating, 340–342, *340*

    Local Path versus Connect options, 364–366

    reconciling with non-NT workstations, 366–367

    securing with file and directory permissions, 338–340, *339*

    securing with share-level permissions, 337

    setting disk quotas, 367

managing with Server Manager, **486–488**, *487*

naming, **318–320**

overview of, 316

on remote servers, **322–325**

    administrative shares created by, 324

    creating, 325, *325*

    Server Manager and, 322–323, *322, 323*

restricting access to, **321–322**

share-level permissions, **325–329**. *See also* access control lists

    adding users from foreign domains to, 560–563, *561, 562, 563*

    changing on existing shares, 331

    controlling from command-line, 331

    Everyone groups and, 326–327

    FAT file system and, 336–337

    versus file and directory permissions, 334–336, *335*

    for home directories, 337

    "No Access" permission, 328–329

    overview of, 325–326, *326*

    types of, 327–329

disabling

    bindings, 1026

    peer-to-peer sharing on workstations, 44

disaster recovery, **876, 916–927**. *See also* backup strategies; physical security; security

    defined, **916–917**

    overview of, 876

    planning, **916–920**

        creating a plan, 917

        implementing the plan, 917–918

        making sure the plan works, 918–920

    server boot failure diagnosis, **920–927**

        hardware problems, 920–922

        NT kernel initialization phase, 926

        NT kernel load phase, 924–925

        NTDETECT.COM file and, 923–924

        NTLDR file and, 922–923

        Registry and, 924

        services load phase, 926

using the "verbose" debug version of
NTDETECT, 923–924
Windows subsystem start phase, 926–927
disconnecting users from servers, 483
Disk Administrator. *See also* RAID; SLED
driver problems, 188–189
overview of, 174–175, 181–182
disk duplexing, 204, *205*
disk mirroring, **17**, **204–210**. *See also* RAID
breaking mirror sets, 206–208
creating mirror sets, 205–206
versus disk duplexing, 204, *205*
mirror sets defined, **180**
when to use, 210
disk striping, **17**, **180–181**, **198–203**, **210–221**.
See also RAID
with parity, **17**, **180–181**, **210–221**
creating stripe sets with parity, 213–216,
214, 215, 217
defined, **180–181**
deleting stripe sets, 219–220
guidelines for, 220–221
how it works, 211–212, *212*
recovering data from failed stripe sets,
217–219, *217, 218*
updating parity information, 212–213
without parity, **181**, **198–203**
creating, 199–202
deleting, 201–203
hazards of, 181
overview of, 198–199, *199*
displaying. *See also* hiding; viewing
active resources, 488–489, *488, 489*
members of domains, 478–479, *478*
open files, 1072–1073, *1072*
resources on browse lists, 849–852
server properties, 480–481, *480*
servers, 478–479, *478*
shared resources available, 484–486, *485*,
1065–1066
workstations, 478–479, *478*

distributing
CPU-intensive programs, 831
disk-intensive processes, 827
DLC (Data Link Control) protocol, 20–21, 83–
84
DMBs (domain master browsers), 752–753,
848
DNS. *See* **Domain Naming System**
dollar sign ($), in share names, 320
Domain Admins global group, 285, 328–329
domain controllers, **526–541**. *See also* directory
replication
adding to domains, 493
backup domain controllers (BDCs), **526–531**,
535–541
advantages and disadvantages of, 535–
537
changing frequency of updates, 829
controlling SAM database synchronization, 529–531
estimating SAM database size, 539–541
numbers and locations of, 535–539
overview of, 59, *60*, 526–527
promoting to primary domain controllers, 527–528
recommended numbers of in one location, 537–538
in remote locations, 538–539
synchronizing SAM databases with primary domain controllers, 528–529, *529*
defined, **16**
displaying in Server Manager, 478–479, *478*
overview of, 59–61
primary domain controllers (PDCs), **59**, **253–
254**, **526–529**, **531–535**
changing frequency of backup domain
controller updates, 829
failure of, 531–535
overview of, 59, *60*, 526–527
promoting backup domain controllers to,
527–528

setting up to replicate login scripts to BDCs, 523

synchronizing backup domain controllers with, 528–529, *529*

user accounts and, 253–254

Domain Guests global group, 285, 328–329

domain master browsers (DMBs), 752–753, 848

Domain Naming System (DNS), 24, **671–673**, **763–779**. *See also* host names; TCP/IP protocol

advantages and disadvantages, 764–766

ARPA-127.REV file, 767, 770, 774

bind format files, 774–777

BOOT file, 767–770

CACHE file, 767, 770

controlling WINS versus DNS order in WinSock, **783**

DNS name resolver file, 767, 770–772

DNS/WINS conflicts, **787–788**

Domain Name Service Manager, 774–779, *775*

name servers or DNS servers and, 40–41, 672–673

obtaining the Microsoft DNS program, 766–767

overview of, 24, 671–673, *672*, 763–764

reverse name resolution file, 765, 767, 772–774

setup files, 767–774

TCP/IP installation and, 685–686, *685*, 687–688

Domain Users global group

adding users to another domain's Domain Users group, 564–565, *565*

overview of, 285, 328–329

versus Users group, 568–569

domains, **55–63**, **546–587**. *See also* network concepts

adding computers to, **492–496**, **1056**

adding or deleting with NET COMPUTER command, 1056

domain controllers, 493

LAN Manager 2.x servers, 495–496

overview of, 492, *493*

workstations and servers, 493–495, *495*

cross-domain groups, **564–576**

accessing shares on other computers without domains, 566–567

adding users to another domain's Domain Users group, 564–565, *565*

circular groups (groups inside groups), 569

local and global groups defined, 565–566, **569–570**

Users group versus Domain Users group, 568–569

using global groups across domains, 575–576

using local and global groups inside domains, 570–575, *571*, *572*

using single domain accounts across domains, 568

displaying members of, 478–479, *478*

domain logon security authorities, 60

domain-based administration features, 15–16

file permissions, **558–563**

adding users from foreign domains to share-level permissions, 560–563, *561*, *562*, *563*

Everyone group and, 558–560

granting user rights and printer permissions across domains, **577**

inter-domain relationships without trusts, 68–70, *69*

logging on from foreign domains, **577–579**, *578*

multi-domain management tasks, **547–548**

password lists and, 57

planning single- and multiple-domain networks, **579–583**
  domain size considerations, 581–583
  minimizing the number of domains, 580
  mirroring geographical boundaries, 581
  mirroring organizational structures, 580–581
  Security Access Manager (SAM) database and, 582–583
Security Access Manager (SAM) databases and, 60–61, 582–583
setup example, 61–63
single-domain versus multiple-domain models, **584–587**
  complete trust model, 584–585
  master domain model, 585–587
  multiple master domain model, 587
  resource domains, 585
  single-domain enterprise model, 584
trust relationships, **68–71, 548–558**
  alternatives to, 552–553
  defined, **548**
  establishing, 553–557, *555, 556*, 559
  explained, **548–552**, *550, 551, 552*
  inter-domain relationships with, 70–71, *71*
  inter-domain relationships without, 68–70, *69*
  versus Mark user accounts, 552–553
  permitting domains to trust other domains, 554–555, *555*
  terminating, 557–558
  transferring between domains, 552, *552*
  two-way trust relationships, 550
versus workgroups, 55–58, *59*
DOS, versus Windows NT, 94–95
DOS workstations. *See also* workstations
  connecting to Windows NT, **414–423**
    connecting to directory shares, 421–423
    connecting to print shares, 384–385, 421–423

  with Microsoft Network Client 3 for MS-DOS, 416–421
  with Network Client Administrator (NCA), 415–416
  overview of, 414
  passwords and, 418–421
joining workgroups from, 47
viewing browse lists, 48
dotted quad notation for IP addresses, 644–646, *646*
drivers
  enabling shared RAM on network cards with TCP/IP drivers, 830
  Macintosh LaserPrep driver problems, 463
  and microprocessor optimization, 831
  Network Driver Interface Specification (NDIS) drivers, 18–19, 85–86
  network interface card drivers, 77–78, *78*
  packet drivers, 86
  printer drivers, 97–98, 371
  recovering from bad video drivers, 914
  tape drivers, 155–159, *158*
  video drivers, 96–98, 139, 914
!drivers kernel debugging command, 952
DSMN. *See* **Directory Service Manager for NetWare**
dumb terminal Internet connections, 676–680, *679*
dumpchk command, 932
DUMPEXAM program, **958–960**
DUN. *See* **Dial-Up Networking**
duplexing disks versus mirroring disks, 204, *205*
Dynamic Host Configuration Protocol. *See* **DHCP**

E

editing the Registry. *See also* changing
  example, 237–239, *238, 239*

guidelines, 240–242
opening Registry Editor, 231–232, *232*
with REGINI.EXE program, 241–242
remote editing with hive files, 245–246
with System Policy Editor, 304–305, 308–309
EIDE-based CD-ROM drives, 99
EISA buses, RAM capacity and, 10–11
electing master browsers, **842–846**, *844, 845*
electrical protection, 877–878. *See also* power
    supplies
e-mail, **806–808**. *See also* TCP/IP protocol
host names and, 673–675, *674*
how e-mail works, 807–808
mail clients, 674, 807
mail routers, 674
mail transfer units (MTUs), 807
security issues, 808
SMTP (Simple Mail Transfer Protocol) and,
    673–674
emergency repair disks, 133–134, 170, 911–913
enabling
bindings, 1026
shared RAM on network cards with TCP/IP
    drivers, 830
encryption modems, 1025
enterprise network features, **13–21**. *See also*
    cross-domain management; network
    concepts; network software
backward compatibility, 19
DLC (Data Link Control) protocol support,
    20–21
domain and workgroup-based administra-
    tion features, 15–16
event and account logging and auditing, 13–
    14
fault tolerance and RAID support, 16–17
Internet features, 13
Macintosh compatibility, 21
NetBEUI protocol support, 20
NetWare compatibility, 19–20
Network Driver Interface Specification
    (NDIS) protocol support, 18–19
remote-access services, 14–15
software costs, 17–18
TCP/IP protocol support, 13, 20, 83
Environment tab in Windows NT Diagnostics
    tool, 974, *974*
environmental problems, **877–879**. *See also*
    physical security
contaminants, 879
electrical protection, 877–878
heat and water problems, 878–879
erasing. *See* deleting
!errlog kernel debugging command, 955
error checking
in IP protocol, 662–663
in TCP protocol, 666
errors, tracking printing errors, **409–410**
escape codes for separator pages, 403–404
establishing trust relationships, 553–557, *555,*
    556, 559
estimating SAM database size, 539–541
Ethernet addresses, 643–644, 647–649
event logs, **13–14**, **854–872**. *See also* auditing;
    logging; performance optimization
access control entries (ACEs) and, 863–864
access control lists (ACLs) and, 863
access masks and, 864
archiving, 868–870, *869*
changing size and overwrite options, 867–
    868, *867*
filtering details displayed, 859–860, *859*
NET START EVENTLOG command, 1076
overview of, 13–14, 854–857, *855, 856*
security descriptors in, 863–866, *865*
troubleshooting Dial-Up Networking, 1031
types of, 855–857, *855, 856*
viewing archived logs, 870–872, *870*
viewing event details, 861–866, *861, 862, 865*
Everyone group, 282, 284, 285, 326–327, 558–
    560

examining crash dumps with DUMPEXAM, 958–960

exchanging data between PC and Macintosh workstations, 465–472. *See also* Macintosh workstations
  cross-platform applications and, 471
  data forks, resource forks and, 466
  date problems, 472
  extension mapping and, 468–470, *469, 470*
  file filters, file translation and, 470–471
  file name extensions and, 467–470
  naming conventions and, 466–470

Execute permissions, 333–334

executing. *See* **running; starting**

expiration dates, for user accounts, 269–270, *269*

export servers. *See* **directory replication**

exporting Performance Monitor data to text files, 820–822

extended partitions. *See also* SLED
  converting to logical drives, 184–186, *185, 186*
  creating, 183–184, *183, 184*
  defined, **178**

extending volume sets, 194–195, 197–198

extension mapping, on Macintosh workstations, 468–470, *469, 470*

extensions. *See* **file name extensions**

exterior routing protocols, 718

F

FAT file system. *See also* NTFS file system
  converting FAT volumes to NTFS volumes, 105
  converting long NTFS filenames to, 222–223
  FAT versus NTFS partition options, 127–129
  file attributes, 224
  file and directory permissions and, 336–337

  RISC-based systems and, 165
  share-level permissions and, 336–337

fault tolerance. *See also* domain controllers
  overview of, 16–17
  Registry and, 243–245

file and directory permissions, 331–350. *See also* directory shares; home directories
  auditing directory and file access, 348–350, *349, 350*
  auditing file and object access, 347–348, *348*
  controlling with CACLS command, 343–344, 576, 900–901
  default directory permissions for NT Server directories, 344–347
  FAT file system and, 336–337
  file permissions across domains, **558–563**
    adding users from foreign domains to share-level permissions, 560–563, *561, 562, 563*
    Everyone group and, 558–560
  for home directories, 338–340, *339*
  NTFS file system and, 332
  overview of, 331–332
  versus share-level permissions, 334–336, *335*
  types of, 332–334

file filters, and exchanging data between PC and Macintosh workstations, 470–471

file name extensions
  and exchanging data between PC and Macintosh workstations, 467–470
  .PWL, 57

file ownership, 350–356. *See also* shared directories
  defined, **351,** *352*
  example, 352–354
  taking ownership, 354–356, *354*

file permissions. *See* **file and directory permissions**

File and Print Services for NetWare (FPNW), 616–623. *See also* NetWare

accessing Windows NT Server from workstations, 622–623, *622, 623*
installing, 617–622
file shares. *See* **directory shares**
file systems. *See* **FAT file system; NTFS file
system**
File Transfer Protocol. *See* **FTP**
file translation, between PC and Macintosh
workstations, 470–471
filenames. *See* **FAT file system; NTFS file
system**
files
ANSI.SYS file, 164–165
ARPA-127.REV file, 767, 770, 774
AUTOEXEC.BAT file, 11
backing up
open files, 900–901
selected files, 895–896, *896*
CONFIG.POL file, 307–308, *308*
CONFIG.SYS file, 11
displaying open files, 1072–1073, *1072*
file organization on FTP servers, 795–797,
796
HOSTS files, 670–671, 779–782, *781*
JET.LOG file, 741
LMHOSTS files, 688–689, 753–754, 779–782,
781, 784–786, *785*
mapping files for synchronizing Windows
NT and NetWare accounts, 627–630
NTLDR file, 163–164, 922–923
restoring, **902–909**
after reinstalling Windows NT Server,
907–908
to networked drives, 909
overview of, 902–906, 908–909
from tape sets with missing tapes, 909
SYSTEM hive file, 244
SYSTEM.MDB file, 741
filters
and exchanging data between PC and Macintosh workstations, 470–471

filtering display of event log details, 859–
860, *859*
finding
Kernel STOP Errors, 929
Registry keys, 239–240
fixed IP addresses, 680–691
installing TCP/IP software, 681–688
overview of, 680
testing with ping program, 689–691, *689*
floppy disks. *See also* CD-ROM drives; hard
disk drives; hardware; tape drives
backing up to, 897–899
installing NT from, 121, 123–124
flow control, in TCP protocol, 665
folders. *See also* directories
shared folders for Macintosh workstations,
455–457, *455, 456*
fonts, migrating to Windows NT, 141–143, *142,*
144
forks in Macintosh data files, 466
formatting
SLED (single large expensive drive), **186–
187**, *187*
volume sets, 194
FPNW. *See* **File and Print Services for
NetWare**
free space, 176
freezes during installation, 162
FTP (File Transfer Protocol), 795–806. *See also*
TCP/IP protocol
anonymous FTP, 803–806
file organization on FTP servers, 795–797,
796
FTP protocol versus FTP program, 806
navigating FTP sites, 797–798
navigation example, 798–802
obtaining Microsoft DNS program via, 766–
767
versus Telnet, 803
transferring files, 802–806

G

Gateway Service. *See* **NetWare**

gateways

default gateway for NT and Windows routing setup

adding, 698–701

creating by hand, 699–700, *700*

Internet gateways, 984

LAN/WAN gateways, 984–985

NetWare Gateway Service, **20**, **591–593**, **597–610**

accessing NetWare print services, **606–608**, *607*

configuring, **600–604**

installing, **598–600**

Novell commands available from Windows NT, 609

potential problems, **610**

sharing NetWare volumes, **604–606**

testing the gateway, 604

using NWLink without, 592–593

Windows NT servers as Internet gateways, **707–718**

Challenge Handshake Authentication Protocol (CHAP) and, 708, 710–711

interior versus exterior routing protocols, 718

login options, 709–711, *709*, *710*

obstacles, 708–709

obtaining IP address from Internet Service Providers, 711–712, *712*

overview of, 707–708

Password Authentication Protocol (PAP) and, 708, 710–711

setting up the gateway computer, 712–717

geographical boundaries, and planning domains, 581

getting IP addresses

from DHCP (IP leases), 728–739

from Internet Service Providers, 711–712, *712*

global groups

creating, 279–280, *279*

defined, 565–566, **569–570**

using across domains, 575–576

using inside domains, 570–575, *571*, *572*

global user accounts, 269–270, *269*

going to. *See* **navigating**

granting user rights and printer permissions across domains, 577

graphics boards. *See* **network interface cards**

groups, **64–65**, **277–285**. *See also* user accounts

Account Operators local group, 281, 284, 477

adding to access control lists, 329–330, *330*

Administrators local group, 280–281, 283, 477

assigning user accounts to, 263–264, *263*

Backup Operators local group, 282, 284

changing

global group membership, 1051–1053, *1052*

local group membership, 1053–1055

creating, **277–280**

global groups, 279–280, *279*

local groups, 277–279, *278*

CREATOR OWNER group, 285

cross-domain groups, **564–576**

accessing shares on other computers without domains, 566–567

adding users to another domain's Domain Users group, 564–565, *565*

circular groups (groups inside groups), 569

local and global groups defined, 565–566, **569–570**

Users group versus Domain Users group, 568–569

using global groups across domains, 575–576

using local and global groups inside domains, 570–575, *571, 572*

using single domain accounts across domains, 568

defined, **64–65**

Domain Users global group

adding users to another domain's Domain Users group, 564–565, *565*

overview of, 285, 328–329

versus Users group, 568–569

Everyone group, 282, 284, 285, 326–327, 558–560

global groups

defined, 565–566, **569–570**

using across domains, 575–576

using inside domains, 570–575, *571, 572*

Guests local group, 282, 284

INTERACTIVE group, 285

local groups

defined, 565–566, **569–570**

using inside domains, 570–575, *571, 572*

NETWORK group, 285

overview of, 64–65

predefined groups, **280–285**

Print Operators local group, 281, 284

Replicator local group, 282

Server Operators local group, 281, 283

SYSTEM group, 285

user rights of predefined groups, **283–284**

Users group, 282, 284, 568–569

Guest user accounts, 260–261, 328–329

Guests local group, 282, 284

H

HAL (Hardware Abstraction Layer), 6–7, 8, 924, 940–942

hard disk drives. *See also* backup strategies; CD-ROM drives; floppy disks; RAID; SLED; tape drives

and memory optimization, 824–825, 837

network drives

backing up, 900

restoring files to, 909

optimizing, **824–827**

data transfer rates and, 826

distributing disk-intensive processes, 827

seek times and, 825

paging and, 101–102, 834–837

preparing for Macintosh support, 445

requirements, 99–100

setting disk quotas for home directories, 367

testing for NT installation, 101–103

hardware. *See also* CD-ROM drives; floppy disks; hard disk drives; memory; microprocessors; printers; tape drives

hardware detection during NT installation, 125–126

hardware requirements

hard disk drive requirements, 99–100

for ISDN connections to Dial-Up Networking, 987–988, 990

memory requirements, 10–11, 96

for modem connections to Dial-Up Networking, 986

mouse requirements, 100

preparing for NT installation, 10–11, **94–103, 115–121**

CD-ROM drives, 98–99

determining server role, 116–118

hard disk drive requirements, 99–100

hard disk drive tests, 101–103

hardware diagnostics and, 95

memory requirements, 10–11, 96

microprocessors, 96

mouse, 100

overview of, 10–11, 94–96, 115–116

RAM tests, 100–101

selecting server names, 118
serial ports, 100
server licenses, 118–121
tape drives, 99
video boards and drivers, 96–98
Windows NT Hardware Compatibility
List (HCL), 95–96
server boot failure and, 920–922
Hardware Abstraction Layer (HAL), 6–7, 8,
924, 940–942
Hardware Compatibility List (HCL), 95–96
hardware versus software RAID, 224–225
heat problems, 878–879
Help
NET commands, **1039–1043**
NET HELP, 1040–1042, *1040*
NET HELPMSG, 1042–1043, *1043*
Windows NT Resource Kit, 239–240
WINNT forum on CompuServe, 240
hiding. *See also* displaying
directory shares, 320
servers and workstations from browsers,
481–482, 854
shared printers, 395–396
shares in workgroups, 49
hive files, 242–246. *See also* Registry
defined, **242**
fault tolerance and LOG files, 243–245
keys and, 244–245
overview of, 242–243
remote Registry editing using, 245–246
home directories, 336–342, 364–367. *See also* file
and directory permissions; shared
directories
administrators' access to, 342
creating, 340–342, *340*
file and directory permissions for, 338–340,
339
Local Path versus Connect options, 364–366
reconciling with non-NT workstations, 366–
367

setting disk quotas, 367
share-level permissions for, 337
host names, 669–675. *See also* Domain Naming
System
e-mail names and, 673–675, *674*
HOSTS files and, 670–671, 779–782, *781*
IP addresses and, 669, 670
LMHOSTS files and, 688–689, 753–754, 779–
782, *781*, 784–786, *785*
name resolution and, 670
overview of, 669–670
hot fixes, 16

I

I/O address settings, for network interface
cards, 111–112
IEEE 802.2 protocol, 20, 83
implementing disaster recovery plans, 917–
918
import computers. *See* directory replication
.INI files. *See* Registry
installing. *See also* adding
Dial-Up Networking servers
installing the dial-up networking module, 992
installing modems, 992–994, *993*, *994*
selecting protocols, 996–998, *996*, *998*
dial-up networking software on Windows
95, 1016–1018
Directory Service Manager for NetWare,
623–627
File and Print Services for NetWare, 617–622
Macintosh printer support, 463–465, *464*, *465*
Microsoft Network Client 3 for MS-DOS,
416–418
modems for Dial-Up Networking, 992–994,
993, *994*
NetWare Gateway Service, 598–600

network interface cards (NICs), **106–114**
    I/O address settings, 111–112
    interrupt (IRQ) settings, 107–111, *110*
    testing, 113–114
power supplies, **144–155**
    breakout boxes, 152–154
    power conditioners, 145–146, 149–150,
        877–878
    power problems and, 145
    standby power supplies (SPSs), 146–148,
        147
    surge protectors, 145
    testing UPS/SPS services, 155
    uninterruptible power supplies (UPSs),
        146, *147*, 148–150, *148*, 877–878
    UPS configuration, 151–152, *151*
    UPS and SPS interfaces, 150–151
    UPSs and power failures, 154–155, *154*,
        155
Services for Macintosh, 445–451
System Policy Editor in Windows 95, 298
tape drives and drivers, 99, **155–159**, *158*
TCP/IP with DHCP (Dynamic Host Config-
    uration Protocol), **719–743**
    backing up DHCP databases, **740–742**
    BOOTP protocol and, 719–721
    configuring DHCP on workstations, 728
    designing multi-DHCP networks, 739–
        740
    DHCP limitations, 743
    DHCP scopes, **723–728**, 738
    DHCPACK message, 735, *736*, 737
    DHCPDISCOVER message, 731–732, *732*
    DHCPOFFER message, 732–734, *733*
    DHCPREQUEST message, 734, *735*, 737
    installing and configuring DHCP servers,
        721–723, *722*, *723*
    IPCONFIG command, 735, *736*
    obtaining IP addresses from DHCP (IP
        leases), **728–739**
    overview of, 719

restoring DHCP databases, 742
    setting IP leases to Infinite, 730
TCP/IP with fixed IP addresses, **680–691**
    installing TCP/IP software, 681–688
    overview of, 680
    testing with ping program, 689–691, *689*
TCP/IP with WINS (Windows Internet
    Naming Service), **743–763**
    B nodes, P nodes, and M nodes and, 747–
        749
    controlling WINS versus DNS order in
        WinSock, **783**
    DNS/WINS conflicts, **787–788**
    how WINS works, 755–757
    master browsers versus Domain Master
        Browsers (DMBs), 752–753
    name resolution and, 746–747, 753–754
    NetBIOS over TCP/IP (NBT) and, 746,
        749–752
    overview of, 743–744
    and ping command, net use command,
        and server names, 744–746
    restoring WINS databases, 760–761
    server names and, 744–746
    setting up WINS servers, 686–688, *687*,
        757–759, *758*, *759*
    WINS failure modes, 756
    WINS proxy agents, 761–763, *762*
installing Windows NT Server, 94–171
    creating NT boot disks, 133, **169–171**
    data preparation, **103–106**
        backing up to another computer, 103
        backups for LAN Manager conversions,
            106
        converting FAT volumes to NTFS vol-
            umes, 105
        tape drives, backups and, 103–106
    hardware preparation, 10–11, **94–103**, **115–
        121**
        CD-ROM drives, 98–99
        determining server role, 116–118

hard disk drive requirements, 99–100
hard disk drive tests, 101–103
hardware diagnostics and, 95
microprocessors, 96
mouse, 100
overview of, 10–11, 94–96, 115–116
RAM requirements, 96
RAM tests, 100–101
selecting server names, 118
serial ports, 100
server licenses, 118–121
tape drives, 99
video boards and drivers, 96–98
Windows NT Hardware Compatibility List (HCL), 95–96
License Manager, **159–161**, *160*
migrating Windows applications, **141–144**
incompatible programs, 141
moving fonts, 141–143, *142*, 144
troubleshooting, 143–144
NT Setup program, **121–139**
auto-detecting SCSI adapters, 124–125
CHKDSK program, 129–130
creating emergency repair disks, 133–134, 170
FAT versus NTFS partition options, 127–129
hardware detection, 125–126
installing from CD-ROM with WINNT or WINNT32, 122
installing from floppy disks, 121, 123–124
"Last Known Good Menu" message, 130–131, 246, 910–911
licensing options, 131–132
naming computers, 132
network interface card setup, 135–137
network setup, 134
personalizing your copy of NT or NT Server, 131
selecting components, 134
selecting NT partitions, 127–129

selecting server's security role, 132–133, 137–139
setting up the NT directory, 130
starting, 121–122
upgrading versus installing, 125
video driver test, 139
on PCI systems, **114–115**
post-installation tasks, **139–140**
reinstalling Windows NT Server, **165–169**
restoring files after, 907–908
troubleshooting, **162–165**
"Boot couldn't find NTLDR. Please insert another disk" message, 163–164
FAT file system and RISC-based systems, 165
image cannot be located, no fixup information, 162–163
incorrect hardware, 162
loading ANSI.SYS, 164–165
lockups, 162
remote boots, 163
viruses, 225–226
INTERACTIVE group, 285
inter-domain relationships. *See* **cross-domain management**
"Interface" column in routing tables, 696–697
interfaces for uninterruptible and standby power supplies, 150–151
interior routing protocols, 718
Internet. *See also* TCP/IP protocol
Domain Naming System (DNS), **671–673**, **763–779**
advantages and disadvantages, 764–766
ARPA-127.REV file, 767, 770, 774
bind format files, 774–777
BOOT file, 767–770
CACHE file, 767, 770
controlling WINS versus DNS order in WinSock, **783**
DNS name resolver file, 767, 770–772
DNS/WINS conflicts, **787–788**

Domain Name Service Manager, 774–779, *775*

name servers or DNS servers and, 672–673

obtaining the Microsoft DNS program, 766–767

overview of, 671–673, *672*, 763–764

reverse name resolution file, 765, 767, 772–774

setup files, 767–774

TCP/IP installation and, 685–686, *685*, 687–688

e-mail, **806–808**

host names and, 673–675, *674*

how e-mail works, 807–808

mail clients, 674, 807

mail routers, 674

mail transfer units (MTUs), 807

overview of, 806–807

security issues, 808

SMTP (Simple Mail Transfer Protocol) and, 673–674

FTP (File Transfer Protocol), **795–806**

anonymous FTP, 803–806

file organization on FTP servers, 795–797, *796*

FTP protocol versus FTP program, 806

navigating FTP sites, 797–798

navigation example, 798–802

obtaining Microsoft DNS program via, 766–767

versus Telnet, 803

transferring files, 802–806

history of, 634–639, *635*, *636*, *637*

host names, **669–675**. *See also* Domain Naming System

e-mail names and, 673–675, *674*

HOSTS files and, 670–671, 779–782, *781*

IP addresses and, 669, 670

LMHOSTS files and, 688–689, 753–754, 779–782, *781*, 784–786, *785*

name resolution and, 670

Internet connections, **675–680**

dumb terminal connections, 676–677

LAN connections, 678

SLIP/PPP connections, 677

terminal connections versus other connection types, 678–680, *679*

overview of, 13

Telnet program, **788–794**

Archie searches, 789–792

tn3270 program, 792–793

uses for, 793–794

Windows NT servers as Internet gateways, **707–718**

Challenge Handshake Authentication Protocol (CHAP) and, 708, 710–711

interior versus exterior routing protocols, 718

login options, 709–711, *709*, *710*

obstacles, 708–709

obtaining IP address from Internet Service Providers, 711–712, *712*

Password Authentication Protocol (PAP) and, 708, 710–711

setting up the gateway computer, 712–717

Internet addresses. *See* **IP (Internet Protocol)**

Internet gateways, 984

Internet Information Server, 22

Internet Service Providers (ISPs)

obtaining IP addresses from, 711–712, *712*

overview of, 984

interrupt (IRQ) settings

for network interface cards, 107–111, *110*

using IRQ10 for network cards, 830

intranet. *See* **Internet; networks**

IP (Internet Protocol), 641–649. *See also* TCP/IP protocol

checksum headers, 663

error checking, 662–663

installing TCP/IP with fixed IP addresses, **680–691**

installing TCP/IP software, 681–688
testing with ping program, 689–691, *689*
IP addresses, **643–663**
A, B, and C-class networks and, 650–652, *651*
Classless Internetwork Domain Routing (CIDR), 659–662
default router addresses, 654
dotted quad notation and, 644–646, *646*
Ethernet addresses and, 643–644, 647–649
host names and, 669, 670
IP domains and, 654
loopback address, 652
Media Access Control (MAC) addresses, 644
Network Information Center (NIC) and, 650, 659–660
network numbers and, 652–653
obtaining from Internet Service Providers, 711–712, *712*
obtaining IP addresses from DHCP (IP leases), **728–739**
reserved addresses, 652–654
setting IP leases to Infinite, 730
subnet masks, 654–657
subnetting C-class networks, 657–658
TCP/IP broadcast address, 653
Token Ring addresses and, 644
IP routers, 646–649
overview of, 641–643, *642*
routing and, 642–643, 647–649
subnets and, 642–643, 649–650
TCP (Transmission Control Protocol) and, 663–665
IPCONFIG command, 735, *736*
IPX/SPX (Internetwork Packet Exchange/ Sequenced Packet Exchange), 84, 828, 853
!irpzone full kernel debugging command, 955
IRQ (interrupt) settings
for network interface cards, 107–111, *110*

using IRQ10 for network cards, 830
ISA buses, RAM capacity and, 10–11
ISDN connections to Dial-Up Networking, 981, **987–990**
direct X.25 connections, 990
hardware requirements, 987–988, 990
ISDN setup, 1003–1004
packet assembler-disassembler (PAD) X.25 connections, 989–990
smart cards and, 990
transmission speed differences, 988
X.25 connections, 988–990, 1005–1006, *1005*
ISPs. *See* **Internet Service Providers**

J

JET.LOG file, 741
joining workgroups, 47

K

kernel debugging, **934–958**, **960–961**. *See also* disaster recovery
debugger commands, **946–958**
command listing, **946–950**
!drivers, 952
!errlog, 955
!irpzone full, 955
!locks, 952–953
log file commands, 951
!memusage, 953–954
!process 0 0, 956
!process 0 7, 956–958
!process, 958
!reload, 951
!thread, 958
!vm, 954–955
defined, **934**

host computers, **928**, **939–943**
    defined, **928**
    HAL files for, 940–942
    setting up the debugger, 942–943
    setting up symbol trees, 927–928, 939–942
Kernel STOP Errors
    defined, **927**
    finding, 929
    kernel debuggers and, 934
    limitations of, **960–961**
    local debugging, 934, 935
    modem connections, 934–935
    remote debugging, 934, 935
    setting up
        the debugger on host computers, 942–943
        RISC-based computers, 938–939
        symbol trees on host computers, 927–928, 939–942
        the target computer, 928, **935–939**
        x86-based computers, 936–937
    starting the debugger, **943–946**
    with remote utility, 945–946
kernel initialization phase of server boot process, 926
kernel load phase of server boot process, 924–925
keys. *See also* Registry
    defined, **233–234**
    finding, 239–240
    hive files and, 244–245
    naming conventions, 234
"Known Good Menu" message, 130–131, 246

L

LAN Internet connections, 678–680, *679*. *See also* networks
LAN Manager
    adding LAN Manager 2.x servers to domains, 495–496

browse list problems, 849, 850
converting from, 106
Windows NT compatibility with LAN Manager 2.2 servers, 19
LAN/LAN routers, 703–707, *704*, *706*
LAN/WAN gateways, 984–985
laptop computers, security and, 883
LaserPrep driver problems, 463
"Last Known Good Menu" message, 130–131, 246, 910–911
leasing IP addresses from DHCP, 728–739
licenses
    License Manager, **159–161**, *160*
    licensing options during installation, 131–132
    server licenses, 118–121
little-endian byte storage system, 5–6
LMHOSTS files, 688–689, 753–754, 779–782, *781*, 784–786, *785*
local groups
    creating, 277–279, *278*
    defined, 565–566, **569–570**
    using inside domains, 570–575, *571*, *572*
local kernel debugging, 934, 935
Local Path option, for home directories, 364–366
local user accounts, 269–270, *269*
locking the server room, 880
!locks kernel debugging command, 952–953
lockups during installation, 162
log file kernel debugging command, 951
LOG files in the Registry, 243–245
logging. *See also* auditing; event logs
    Performance Monitor data for statistical reports, 819–820
    printer usage, 399–402, *400*, *401*, 409–410
logging on from foreign domains, **577–579**, *578*

logical drives, 178–179, 183–186, 188. *See also* SLED
  converting extended partitions to, 184–186, *185*, *186*
  creating, 188
  creating extended partitions, 183–184, *183*, *184*
  defined, **178–179**
  extended partitions defined, **178**
logical partitions, 176–177
logical printers, 371
login options, for Windows NT servers as Internet gateways, 709–711, *709*, *710*
logon scripts, 359–364. *See also* profiles
  changing logon script path for directory replication, 524–525, *524*
  creating, 361–363
  uses for, 360
  variables, 363–364
  where to locate, 360–361
logs. *See* auditing; event logs
long filenames. *See* NTFS file system
loopback address, 652

M

M nodes, 747–749
MAC (Media Access Control) addresses, 644
machines. *See* computers
Macintosh workstations, 442–472. *See also* workstations
  compatibility with Windows NT, **21**
  connecting to Windows NT, **457–462**
    first time logon, 457–461
    subsequent logons, 461–462, *461*, *462*
  exchanging data with PCs, **465–472**
    cross-platform applications and, 471
    data forks, resource forks and, 466
    date problems, 472

  extension mapping and, 468–470, *469*, *470*
  file filters, file translation and, 470–471
  file name extensions and, 467–470
  naming conventions and, 466–470
  limitations of, **472**
  Macintosh printer support, **462–465**
    avoiding LaserPrep driver problems, 463
    installing, 463–465, *464*, *465*
  overview of, 443–444
  preparing servers for Macintosh support, **444–445**
  Services for Macintosh, **442–443**, **445–457**
    creating Macintosh-accessible volumes, 455–457, *455*, *456*
    features and benefits, 442–443
    installing, 445–451
    permissions, 456–457, *456*
    setting up access attributes for Macintosh volumes, 452–453, *452*
    setting up Microsoft Authentication, 453–454, *453*, *454*
mail. *See* e-mail
mapping files for synchronizing Windows NT and NetWare accounts, 627–630
master browsers. *See also* browse lists
  domain master browsers (DMBs), 752–753, 848
  electing, **842–846**, *844*, *845*
  preventing computers from being, 846–847
  on TCP/IP networks, 848
master domain model, 585–587
MCA buses, RAM capacity and, 10–11
Media Access Control (MAC) addresses, 644
memory. *See also* hardware
  bus architecture and, 10–11
  enabling shared RAM on network cards with TCP/IP drivers, 830
  !memusage kernel debugging command, 953–954
  optimizing, **832–838**
    checking memory status, 832–833

hard disk drives and, 824–825, 837

memory leaks, 838

reducing memory requirements, 837

services and, 837

virtual memory settings, 833–837, *834, 835*

page size, 5

paging and, 101–102, 834–837

requirements, 10–11, 96

testing RAM for NT installation, 100–101

memory dump files, 929–933. *See also* debugging Windows NT 4

creating, 930

dumpchk command, 932

dumpexam command, 932–933

dumpflop command, 931

overview of, 929

Memory tab in Windows NT Diagnostics tool, 965, *966*

!memusage kernel debugging command, 953–954

messages

messaging commands, **1083–1088**

NET NAME (adding or deleting messaging names), 1084–1085, *1084*

NET SEND (sending messages), 1085–1088

NET START MESSENGER command, 1076–1077

sending to users, 156, 491–492, *491*, 1085–1088

messengers, 67

"Metric" column in routing tables, 697–698

microprocessors. *See also* hardware

multiple processor support, 7–8, 831–832

optimizing, **830–832**

adding, 831–832

counters to watch, 830

device drivers and excessive interrupts, 831

distributing CPU-intensive programs, 831

screen savers and, 832

tracking usage, 816–817, *817, 818*

requirements, 96

Windows NT Server architecture and, 5–7

Microsoft Authentication, for Macintosh workstations, 453–454, *453, 454*

Microsoft Gateway Service. *See* **NetWare**, NetWare Gateway Service

Microsoft Network Client 3 for MS-DOS, 416–421

Microsoft redirector, 829

Microsoft Windows 95

installing System Policy Editor, 298

and running NT Server and NetWare in parallel, 595

Microsoft Windows 95 workstations, 432–438. *See also* workstations

configuring, 432–435, *432, 433, 434*

connecting to dial-up networking servers, 1016–1022

connecting to network resources, 435–438, *435*

joining workgroups from, 47

as master browsers, **847**

preventing users from defeating system policies, 306–307

viewing browse lists from, 48

Microsoft Windows application migration, 141–144. *See also* installing Windows NT Server

incompatible programs, 141

moving fonts, 141–143, *142*, 144

troubleshooting, 143–144

Microsoft Windows NT Server, 4–26. *See also* installing Windows NT Server; NetWare; Windows NT Diagnostics tool

CompuServe WINNT forum, 240

versus DOS, **94–95**

enterprise networking features, **13–21**

backward compatibility, 19

DLC (Data Link Control) protocol support, 20–21

domain and workgroup-based administration features, 15–16

event and account logging and auditing, 13–14

fault tolerance and RAID support, 16–17

Internet features, 13

Macintosh compatibility, 21

NetBEUI protocol support, 20

NetWare compatibility, 19–20

Network Driver Interface Specification (NDIS) protocol support, 18–19

remote-access services, 14–15

TCP/IP protocol support, 13, 20, 83

future versions, **25–26**

Hardware Compatibility List (HCL), 95–96

LAN Manager 2.2 servers and, 19

new features, **21–26**

administration tools, 22

Domain Name Service (DNS), 24

Internet Information Server, 22

Network Monitor, 24–25

protocol support, 23

Routing Internet Protocol (RIP), 24, 703

System Policy Editor (SPE), 23

user interface, 21–22

workgroup security, 50–52

overview of, **4–12**

architecture independence, 5–7

memory capacity, 10–11

multiple processor support, 7–8, 831–832

multithreaded multitasking, 8–10, 832

printing, 12

user profiles, 11–12

print sharing features, **371–372**

re-installing, **165–169**

software costs, 17–18

upgrading versus installing, **125**

Windows NT Resource Kit, 239–240

Microsoft Windows NT servers as Internet gateways, **707–718**

Challenge Handshake Authentication Protocol (CHAP) and, 708, 710–711

interior versus exterior routing protocols, 718

login options, 709–711, *709, 710*

obstacles, 708–709

obtaining IP address from Internet Service Providers, 711–712, *712*

Password Authentication Protocol (PAP) and, 708, 710–711

setting up the gateway computer, 712–717

Microsoft Windows NT workstations

connecting to dial-up networking servers, 1007–1016

connecting to NetWare servers via Dial-Up Networking, 1024

connecting to shared printers from, 388–391, *389, 390*

joining workgroups from, 47

in NetWare networks, 590, 630–631, 1024

viewing browse lists from, 48

Microsoft Windows subsystem start phase of server boot process, 926–927

Microsoft Windows for Workgroups, and running NT Server and NetWare in parallel, 594

Microsoft Windows for Workgroups workstations, **423–431**. *See also* workstations

configuring with Network Setup program, 424–427, *424*

connecting to dial-up networking servers, 1022

connecting to network resources, 430–431, *431*

connecting to shared printers, 385–388, *386, 387, 388*

joining workgroups from, 47

as master browsers, **846–847**

setting and changing domain passwords, 427–430, *428, 429, 430*

viewing browse lists from, 48

migrating NetWare users to Windows NT, **610–631**

Directory Service Manager for NetWare (DSMN), **623–630**. *See also* NetWare

installing, 623–627

mapping files for synchronizing NT and NetWare accounts, 627–630

File and Print Services for NetWare (FPNW), **616–623**

accessing Windows NT Server from workstations, 622–623, *622, 623*

installing, 617–622

Migration Tool for NetWare, 611–616, *612, 613, 615*

migrating Windows applications, 141–144. *See also* installing Windows NT Server

incompatible programs, 141

moving fonts, 141–143, *142,* 144

troubleshooting, 143–144

minimizing the number of domains, 580

mirror sets, **17, 204–210**. *See also* RAID

breaking, 206–208

creating, 205–206

defined, **180**

versus disk duplexing, 204, *205*

orphan mirror sets, 208

when to use, 210

modem connections

to Dial-Up Networking, **985–987**

compatibility issues, 986

defined, **985**

hardware requirements, 986

installing modems, 992–994, *993, 994*

pooling modems, 986–987

security, 1024–1025

for kernel debugging, 934–935

modifying. *See* **changing; editing**

moisture problems, 878–879

monitoring performance. *See* **performance optimization**

mouse requirements, 100

moving fonts to Windows NT, 141–143, *142,* 144

moving to. *See* **navigating**

MS Windows. *See* **Microsoft Windows**

MS-DOS. *See* **DOS**

MTUs (mail transfer units), 807

multiple master domain model, 587

multiple processor support, 7–8, 831–832

multiple transport stacks, 84, *85*

multiple-domain management. *See* **cross-domain management**

multitasking

optimizing, **838–839**, *839*

overview of, 8–10

N

name resolution. *See also* TCP/IP protocol

host names and, 670

NetBIOS name resolution sequence

LMHOSTS files and, 688–689, 753–754, 779–782, *781,* 784–786, *785*

overview of, **784–786**, *785*

WINS and, 746, 749–752

versus WinSock name resolution, 779

WINS and, 746–747, 753–754

WinSock name resolution sequence, **779–783**

controlling WINS versus DNS order in WinSock, 783

examining network traces, 779–783, *781*

HOSTS files and, 670–671, 779–782, *781*

WinSock versus NBT, 779

name servers, **40–41,** 672–673

name services. *See* **directory services**

naming

computers during installation, 132

directory shares, 318–320

filenames and exchanging data between PC and Macintosh workstations, 466–470

printers

adding the same printer with multiple names, 378

printer pooling (multiple printers with the same name), 381–382, *381*

Registry keys, 234

on simple networks, 32–34

UNC (Universal Naming Convention) names, 35

user accounts, 261–262

National Science Foundation (NSF), 638–639

navigating FTP sites, 797–802

NCA (Network Client Administrator), 415–416

NCNT (NetWare Client for NT) software, 20, **592**

NDIS (Network Driver Interface Specification) drivers, 18–19, 85–86

NET commands, **478**, **1038–1090**. *See also* commands

computer and session commands, **1055–1064**

NET COMPUTER (adding or deleting computers from domains), 1056

NET CONFIG (viewing and changing configurations), 1057–1060, *1057, 1058*

NET SESSION (viewing connection information), 1060–1062, *1061*

NET STATISTICS (viewing computer statistics), 478, 1062–1063, *1063, 1064*

Help commands, **1039–1043**

NET HELP, 1040–1042, *1040*

NET HELPMSG, 1042–1043, *1043*

messaging commands, **1083–1088**

NET NAME (adding or deleting messaging names), 1084–1085, *1084*

NET SEND (sending messages), 1085–1088

NET START (network service commands), **1074–1082**

NET CONTINUE (halting services temporarily), 1082

NET PAUSE (halting services temporarily), 1082

NET START ALERTER, 1075

NET START "CLIPBOOK SERVER," 1075–1076

NET START "COMPUTER BROWSER," 1076

NET START "DIRECTORY REPLICATOR," 1076

NET START EVENTLOG, 1076

NET START MESSENGER, 1076–1077

NET START "NET LOGON," 1077

NET START "NETWORK DDE," 1077

NET START "NETWORK DDE DSDM," 1077

NET START "NT LM SECURITY SUPPORT PROVIDER," 1077

NET START "REMOTE PROCEDURE CALL (RPC) LOCATOR," 1078

NET START "REMOTE PROCEDURE CALL (RPC) SERVICE," 1077–1078

NET START SCHEDULE, 1078–1079

NET START SERVER, 1079–1080

NET START SPOOLER, 1080

NET START UPS, 1080–1081

NET START WORKSTATION, 1081–1082

NET STOP (stopping services), 1083

quotation marks (") in, 1075

NET TIME (coordinating server and workstation clocks), 1088–1090

overview of, 1038–1039, 1090

resource commands, **1064–1074**

NET FILE (displaying open files), 1072–1073, *1072*

NET PRINT (controlling print jobs), 1073–1074

NET SHARE (creating and deleting shared resources), 1070–1072, *1070*

NET USE (connecting to other drives and printer ports), 744–746, 1067–1069

NET VIEW (viewing available resources), 1065–1066

user account commands, **1043–1055**

NET ACCOUNTS (changing user database), 1048–1051, *1049*

NET GROUP (changing global group membership), 1051–1053, *1052*

NET LOCALGROUP (changing local group membership), 1053–1055

NET USER (creating user accounts), 1044–1048, *1044, 1045*

NetBEUI protocol. *See also* protocols

overview of, 20, 82–83

performance and, 828, 853

NetBIOS API, 87

NetBIOS name resolution sequence. *See also* TCP/IP protocol

LMHOSTS files and, 688–689, 753–754, 779–782, *781, 784–786, 785*

overview of, **784–786**, *785*

WINS and, 746, 749–752

versus WinSock name resolution, 779

NetBIOS protocol, 82–83, 828, 853

NetWare, **590–631**

Directory Service Manager for NetWare (DSMN), **623–630**

installing, 623–627

mapping files for synchronizing NT and NetWare accounts, 627–630

File and Print Services for NetWare (FPNW), **616–623**

accessing Windows NT Server from workstations, 622–623, *622, 623*

installing, 617–622

overview of, 616–617

migrating NetWare users to Windows NT, **610–631**. *See also* Directory Service Manager for NetWare; File and Print Services for NetWare

Migration Tool for NetWare, 611–616, *612, 613, 615*

NetWare Client for NT (NCNT) software, **592**

NetWare Client Service, 20, 597, 600

NetWare Gateway Service, **20**, **591–593**, **597–610**

accessing NetWare print services, **606–608**, *607*

configuring, **600–604**

installing, **598–600**

Novell commands available from Windows NT, 609

potential problems, **610**

sharing NetWare volumes, **604–606**

testing the gateway, 604

using NWLink without, 592–593

Novell sockets API, 88

running NT Server and NetWare in parallel, **591**, **593–597**

configuring Windows NT, 595–597, *595, 596*

Windows 95 and, 595

Windows for Workgroups and, 594

setting NetWare and Microsoft redirector priorities, 829

Windows NT Server compatibility with, 19–20

Windows NT/NetWare connections, **590–592**

NetWare resources in Windows NT networks, 591–592

Windows NT Server in NetWare networks, 591

NT kernel load phase of server boot process, 924–925

NT Setup program. *See* **installing Windows NT Server**

NTBACKUP command, 890–892

NTDETECT.COM program, 169, 923–924

NTFS file system, **221–224**. *See also* FAT file system

converting FAT volumes to NTFS volumes, 105

extended attributes, 223–224

versus FAT file system, 221, 223–224

FAT versus NTFS partition options, 127–129

FAT partitions and, 226

file and directory permissions and, 332

file forking, 223

file naming conventions, 221–223

hot fixes and, 16

long filenames on floppy disks, 224

NTLDR file, 163–164, 922–923

NWLink protocol, 19, 592–593

O

object permissions for user accounts, 288–293, *290*

obtaining IP addresses

from DHCP (IP leases), 728–739

from Internet Service Providers, 711–712, *712*

Open Data-link Interface (ODI), 86

open files, backing up, 900–901

Open Resources dialog box, 488–489, *488, 489*

opening Registry Editor, 231–232, *232*

optimization techniques. *See* **performance optimization**

organizational structures, and planning domains, 580–581

orphan mirror sets, 208

OS/2 workstations, connecting to shared printers from, 388

OSI model, network software and, 74–75

outages, 145

overwrite options for event logs, 867–868, *867*

ownership. *See* **file ownership**

P

P nodes, 747–749

packet assembler-disassembler (PAD) X.25 connections, 989–990

packet drivers, 86

page size of microprocessors, 5

paging, 101–102, 834–837

PAP (Password Authentication Protocol), 708, 710–711

parity stripe sets, **17**, **180–181**, **210–221**. *See also* RAID

creating stripe sets with parity, 213–216, *214, 215, 217*

deleting, 219–220

guidelines for, 220–221

how it works, 211–212, *212*

recovering data from failed stripe sets, 217–219, *217, 218*

updating parity information, 212–213

partitions. *See also* SLED

backing up partition information, **913–914**, *913*

defined, **177–178**

extended partitions

converting to logical drives, 184–186, *185, 186*

creating, 183–184, *183, 184*

defined, **178**

FAT partitions, 226

logical partitions, **176–177**

primary partitions, **178**

Password Authentication Protocol (PAP), 708, 710–711

password modems, 1025

passwords. *See also* security

and connecting DOS workstations to Windows NT, 418–421

creating for user accounts, 262

domain passwords on Windows for Workgroups workstations, 427–430, *428, 429, 430*

domains and, 56–58, *59*

in Mark user accounts, 553

in Microsoft Network Client 3, 418–421

password-protecting shares in workgroups, 50

setting password characteristics for user accounts, 286–288, *287*

theft and tampering protection and, 881–882

pattern testers, 102

PCI buses

installing Windows NT on PCI systems, **114–115**

RAM capacity and, 10–11

PDCs. *See* **primary domain controllers**

peer-to-peer sharing, disabling on workstations, 44

per server versus per seat licenses, 120, 131–132, 161

Performance Monitor, **812–822**. *See also* Network Monitor

Chart mode, 813–816, *814, 815*

creating free server space alerts, 818–819, *819*

exporting logged data to text files, 820–822

logging data for statistical reports, 819–820

overview of, 812–813, *813*

tracking CPU usage, 816–817, *817, 818*

performance optimization, **822–872**

browsers, **841–854**. *See also* browse lists

displaying resources on browse lists, 849–852

domain master browsers (DMBs), 848

electing master browsers, 842–846, *844, 845*

hiding servers from browsers, 481–482, 854

how the browse service works, 850–851

LAN Manager problems, 849, 850

master browsers on TCP/IP networks, 848

preventing computers form being master browsers, 846–847

protocols and, 853

refreshing browse lists, 849

server announcement intervals, 852

setting backup browser update frequency, 852

why browsers are slow, 853

counters to watch, 827–828, 830, **839–841**

event logs, **13–14**, **854–872**

access control entries (ACEs) and, 863–864

access control lists (ACLs) and, 863

access masks and, 864

archiving, 868–870, *869*

changing size and overwrite options, 867–868, *867*

filtering details displayed, 859–860, *859*

NET START EVENTLOG command, 1076

overview of, 13–14, 854–857, *855, 856*

reading log information, 857–858

security descriptors and, 863–866, *865*

troubleshooting Dial-Up Networking, 1031

types of, 855–857, *855, 856*

viewing archived logs, 870–872, *870*

viewing event details, 861–866, *861, 862, 865*

hard disk drives, **824–827**

data transfer rates and, 826

distributing disk-intensive processes, 827

seek times and, 825

memory, **832–838**

checking memory status, 832–833
hard disk drives and, 824–825, 837
memory leaks, 838
reducing memory requirements, 837
services and, 837
virtual memory settings, 833–837, *834*, *835*
microprocessors, **830–832**
adding, 831–832
counters to watch, 830
device drivers and excessive interrupts, 831
distributing CPU-intensive programs, 831
screen savers and, 832
tracking usage, 816–817, *817*, *818*
multitasking, **838–839**, *839*
network interface cards and drivers, **827–830**
changing frequency of BDC updates, 829
counters to watch, 827–828
deleting protocols and services, 828
enabling shared RAM with TCP/IP drivers, 830
prioritizing NetWare and Microsoft redirectors, 829
prioritizing servers, 829
segmenting networks, 828–829
using 32-bit bus master network cards, 830
using IRQ10, 830
overview of, **822–824**, **839–841**
periodic service advertising, 39–40
permissions, **64**, **325–350**. *See also* rights; shared directories
access control lists (ACLs), **326**, **329–331**
adding groups to, 329–330, *330*
adding single users to, 330, *330*
changing with command-line commands, 331
changing permissions on existing shares, 331

file and directory permissions, **331–350**. *See also* home directories
auditing directory and file access, 348–350, *349*, *350*
auditing file and object access, 347–348, *348*
controlling with CACLS command, 343–344, 576, 900–901
default directory permissions for NT Server directories, 344–347
FAT file system and, 336–337
for home directories, 338–340, *339*
NTFS file system and, 332
versus share-level permissions, 334–336, *335*
types of, 332–334
file permissions across domains, **558–563**
adding users from foreign domains to share-level permissions, 560–563, *561*, *562*, *563*
Everyone group and, 558–560
printer permissions
granting across domains, 577
setting, **392–395**, *392*, *393*
in Services for Macintosh, **456–457**, *456*
share-level permissions, **325–329**. *See also* access control lists
adding users from foreign domains to, 560–563, *561*, *562*, *563*
changing on existing shares, 331
controlling from command-line, 331
Everyone groups and, 326–327
FAT file system and, 336–337
versus file and directory permissions, 334–336, *335*
for home directories, 337
"No Access" permission, 328–329
overview of, 325–326, *326*
types of, 327–329
for user accounts, 288–293, *290*
physical drives, **176–177**

physical security, 877–884. *See also* disaster recovery; security
  how much protection is too much, **884**
  preventing environmental problems, **877–879**
    contaminants, 879
    electrical protection, 877–878
    heat and water problems, 878–879
  preventing theft and tampering, **879–883**
    limiting access to printers, 882–883
    limiting access to servers, 880–881
    locking the server room, 880
    passwords and, 881–882
    portable computers and, 883
ping program
  "destination host unreachable" message, 699
  server names and, 744–746
  testing TCP/IP installation, 689–691, *689*
planning. *See also* designing
  disaster recovery, **916–920**
    creating a plan, 917
    implementing the plan, 917–918
    making sure the plan works, 918–920
  single- and multiple-domain networks, **579–583**
    domain size considerations, 581–583
    minimizing the number of domains, 580
    mirroring geographical boundaries, 581
    mirroring organizational structures, 580–581
    Security Access Manager (SAM) database and, 582–583
Point-to-Point Tunneling Protocol (PPTP), 985
pooling modems, **986–987**
pooling printers, **381–382**, *381*
portable computers, security and, 883
ports
  connecting resources to other printer ports, 1067–1069
  printing to ports directly, 383

  sockets and, 666, 667–668
post-installation tasks, **139–140**
power supplies, **144–155**
  breakout boxes, 152–154
  NET START UPS command, 1080–1081
  power conditioners, 145–146, 149–150, 877–878
  power problems and, 145
  standby power supplies (SPSs), 146–148, *147*
  surge protectors, 145
  testing UPS/SPS services, 155
  uninterruptible power supplies (UPSs), **144–155**, 146, *147*, 148–150, *148*, **877–878**
  UPS configuration, 151–152, *151*
  UPS and SPS interfaces, 150–151
  UPSs and power failures, 154–155, *154*, *155*
PPP Internet connections, 677, 678–680, *679*
PPTP (Point-to-Point Tunneling Protocol), 985
predefined groups, **280–285**
preparing
  data for NT installation, **103–106**
    backing up to another computer, 103
    backups for LAN Manager conversions, 106
    converting FAT volumes to NTFS volumes, 105
    tape drives, backups and, 103–106
  hardware for NT installation, 10–11, **94–103**, **115–121**
    CD-ROM drives, 98–99
    determining server role, 116–118
    hard disk drive requirements, 99–100
    hard disk drive tests, 101–103
    hardware diagnostics and, 95
    memory requirements, 10–11, 96
    microprocessors, 96
    mouse, 100
    RAM tests, 100–101
    selecting server names, 118
    serial ports, 100
    server licenses, 118–121

tape drives, 99
video boards and drivers, 96–98
Windows NT Hardware Compatibility List (HCL), 95–96
servers for Macintosh support, **444–445**

preventing
computers from being master browsers, 846–847
environmental problems, **877–879**
contaminants, 879
electrical protection, 877–878
heat and water problems, 878–879
theft and tampering, **879–883**
limiting access to printers, 882–883
limiting access to servers, 880–881
locking the server room, 880
passwords and, 881–882
portable computers and, 883

primary domain controllers (PDCs), **59**, **253–254**, **526–529**, **531–535**. *See also* domain controllers
changing frequency of backup domain controller updates, 829
failure of, 531–535
overview of, 59, *60*, 526–527
promoting backup domain controllers to, 527–528
setting up to replicate login scripts to BDCs, 523
synchronizing backup domain controllers with, 528–529, *529*
user accounts and, 253–254

primary partitions, 178

print jobs
controlling, 1073–1074
setting priorities, 396, *397*

Print Operators local group, 281, 284

print queues, 371

print servers, 370, 372–373
defined, **370**
performance and, 829

what computers can be, 372–373

printer drivers
overview of, 97–98
workstations and, 371

printer ports, connecting resources to, 1067–1069

printers, 370–402, 406–409. *See also* hardware
adding, 36–37, **373–379**
adding the same printer with multiple names, 378
connecting to shared printers, **384–391**
from DOS workstations, 384–385
from OS/2 workstations, 388
from Windows NT workstations, 388–391, *389*, *390*
from Windows for Workgroups workstations, 385–388, *386*, *387*, *388*
controlling and monitoring access, **391–402**
hiding shared printers, 395–396
logging and auditing printer usage, 399–402, *400*, *401*, 409–410
receiving printer status messages, 398–399
setting print job priorities, 396, *397*
setting printer permissions, 392–395, *392*, *393*
setting printing hours, 397–398, *398*, 399
customizing printer setup, **379–383**
printer pooling (multiple printers with the same name), 381–382, *381*
with Printer Properties dialog box, 379–380, *380*
printing in background versus printing directly to ports, 382, 383
setting printer timeout number, 382–383, *383*
limiting access to, **882–883**
logical printers versus printing devices, **371**
Macintosh printer support, **462–465**
avoiding LaserPrep driver problems, 463
installing, 463–465, *464*, *465*

NET START SPOOLER command, 1080
network-interface printers, **370**, 372
printer permissions
    granting across domains, 577
    setting, 392–395, *392*, *393*
sharing on simple networks, 36–37
troubleshooting, **406–409**
    can't connect to printer, 406
    can't create printer, 406
    connection problems, 406–408
    hardware problems, 409
    no default printer, 406–407
    retrieving printer ports, 407–408
    software problems, 408–409
Windows NT print sharing features, **371–372**
printing
    accessing NetWare print services from Windows NT, 606–608, *607*
    diagnostics reports from Windows NT Diagnostics tool, **975–977**
    NET START SPOOLER command, 1080
    overview of, 12, 370–371
    to ports directly, 383
    separator pages, **402–406**
        creating, 403–404
        defined, **402**
        selecting, 405–406, *405*
    tracking printing errors, **409–410**
    troubleshooting, **406–409**
        can't connect to printer, 406
        can't create printer, 406
        connection problems, 406–408
        hardware problems, 409
        no default printer, 406–407
        retrieving printer ports, 407–408
        software problems, 408–409
    Windows NT features, **371–372**
prioritizing
    NetWare and Microsoft redirectors, 829
    print jobs, 396, *397*
    servers, 829

!process 0 0 kernel debugging command, 956
!process 0 7 kernel debugging command, 956–958
!process kernel debugging command, 958
processors. *See* **microprocessors**
profiles, 11–12, **357–359**, *359*. *See also* logon scripts
Profiles dialog box
    home directory settings, **340–342**, **364–367**
        creating home directories, 340–342, *340*
        Local Path versus Connect options, 364–366
        reconciling home directories with non-NT workstations, 366–367
        setting disk quotas, 367
    overview of, 356–357, *357*
programs. *See* **applications**
properties
    Printer Properties dialog box, 379–380, *380*
    of servers, **480–481**, *480*
    of user accounts
        changing for more than one account, 273–276, *274*, *275*
        copying, 272–273, *273*
        overview of, 257, *258*, 271–272, *272*
protecting. *See* **security**
protocols, 81–85. *See also* DHCP; network software; TCP/IP; WINS
    BOOTP, 719–721
    and browser performance, 853
    CHAP (Challenge Handshake Authentication Protocol), 708, 710–711
    deleting, 828
    Dial-Up Networking and, **981–982**, 996–998, *996*, *998*
    DLC (Data Link Control), 20–21, 83–84
    IEEE 802.2 protocol, 20, 83
    interior versus exterior routing protocols, 718

IPX/SPX (Internetwork Packet Exchange/ Sequenced Packet Exchange), 84, 828, 853
multiple transport stacks, 84, *85*
NetBEUI, 20, 82–83, 828, 853
NetBIOS, 82–83, 828, 853
Network Driver Interface Specification (NDIS), 18–19
and network interface card optimization, 828
NWLink, 19, 592–593
overview of, 81–82, *82*
PAP (Password Authentication Protocol), 708, 710–711
PPP, 677, 678–680, *679*
PPTP (Point-to-Point Tunneling Protocol), 985
RIP (Routing Internet Protocol), 24, 703
SAP (Service Advertising Protocol), 39
SLIP, 677, 678–680, *679*
SMTP (Simple Mail Transfer Protocol), 673–674
support for, 23
UDP (User Datagram Protocol), 664
proxy agents, WINS, 761–763, *762*
.PWL files, 57

Q

quad notation for IP addresses, 644–646, *646*
quotation marks (") in NET START commands, 1075

R

RAID (redundant array of inexpensive drives), **16–17**, **174–175**, 198–221, 224–225. *See also* SLED

defined, **176**
disk mirroring, **17**, **204–210**
    breaking mirror sets, 206–208
    creating mirror sets, 205–206
    versus disk duplexing, 204, *205*
    mirror sets defined, **180**
    recovering data from mirror sets, 208–209
    when to use, 210
disk striping with parity, **17**, **180–181**, **210–221**
    creating stripe sets with parity, 213–216, *214*, *215*, *217*
    deleting stripe sets, 219–220
    guidelines for, 220–221
    how it works, 211–212, *212*
    recovering data from failed stripe sets, 217–219, *217*, *218*
    stripe sets defined, **180–181**
    updating parity information, 212–213
disk striping without parity, **181**, **198–203**
    creating, 199–202
    deleting, 201–203
    hazards of, 181
    overview of, 198–199, *199*
hardware versus software RAID, **224–225**
levels of, **16–17**
terms defined, **175–181**
RAM. *See* **memory**
RDISK program, 246
Read permissions, 333
receivers, **67**
receiving printer status messages, 398–399
reconciling home directories with non-NT workstations, 366–367
recovering. *See also* restoring
    from bad video drivers, 914
    data from failed stripe sets, 217–219, *217*, *218*
redirectors, **66–67**
reducing memory requirements, 837
refreshing browse lists, 849

REGBACK.EXE and REGREST.EXE programs, 246

Registry, **11**, **230–246**

  backing up, 246, 914–916

  data types, **235–236**, *235*

  and diagnosing server boot failure, 924

  editing

    example, 237–239, *238, 239*

    guidelines, 240–242

    opening Registry Editor, 231–232, *232*

    with REGINI.EXE program, 241–242

    remote editing with hive files, 245–246

    with System Policy Editor, 304–305, 308–309

  hive files, **242–246**

    fault tolerance and LOG files, 243–245

    keys and, 244–245

    remote Registry editing using, 245–246

  keys

    defined, **233–234**

    finding, 239–240

    hive files and, 244–245

    naming conventions, 234

  restoring, 246, **916**

  subkeys, 234–235, *235*

  subtrees, **232–233**

  value entries, **234–236**, *235*, 240–241

  viewing, 231–232, *232*

regular user rights, 290–291

reinstalling Windows NT Server, **165–169**

  restoring files after, 907–908

Relative ID (RID) numbers, 259

!reload kernel debugging command, 951

Remote Access Services (RAS), overview of, 14–15

remote boots, 163

remote diagnostic viewing with Windows NT Diagnostics tool, **961–963**

remote kernel debugging, 934, 935

remote server directory shares, **322–325**

  administrative shares created by, 324

  creating, 325, *325*

  Server Manager and, 322–323, *322, 323*

remote-access software, versus Dial-Up Networking, 982–983

removable drives, backing up, 899

replicating directories, **16**, **504–526**. *See also* Server Manager

  changing logon script path, 524–525, *524*

  configuring export servers, 511–515, *512, 513, 514*

  configuring import computers, 515–516

  creating import/export pairs, 517–522

  frequency of, 516

  NET START "DIRECTORY REPLICATOR" command, 1076

  setting up PDCs to replicate login scripts to BDCs, 523

  troubleshooting, 525–526

  uses for, 506

  which computers can import or export, 506–508, *507, 508*

Replicator local group, 282

reserved IP addresses, 652–654

resizing event logs, 867–868, *867*

resource domains, 585

resource forks in Macintosh data files, 466

resources

  displaying active resources, 488–489, *488, 489*

  displaying on browse lists, **849–852**

  displaying shared resources available, 484–486, *485*, 1065–1066

  NET commands, **1064–1074**

    NET FILE (displaying open files), 1072–1073, *1072*

    NET PRINT (controlling print jobs), 1073–1074

    NET SHARE (creating and deleting shared resources), 1070–1072, *1070*

    NET USE (connecting to other drives and printer ports), 744–746, 1067–1069

NET VIEW (viewing available resources), 1065–1066

NetWare resources in Windows NT networks, 591–592

Resources tab in Windows NT Diagnostics tool, 970–974, *971*, *972*, *973*

restoring, **902–914**, **916**. *See also* backup strategies; recovering

DHCP databases, 742

files, **902–909**

after reinstalling Windows NT Server, 907–908

to networked drives, 909

from tape sets with missing tapes, 909

the Registry, 246, **916**

system configurations, **910–914**

backing up partition information, 913–914, *913*

from emergency repair disks, 911–913

"Last Known Good Menu" message and, 130–131, 246, 910–911

recovering from bad video drivers, 914

WINS databases, 760–761

restricting access to directory shares, 321–322

reverse name resolution file in DNS, 765, 767, 772–774

RID (Relative ID) numbers, 259

rights. *See also* permissions

defined, **64**

user rights, **283–284**, **288–293**

advanced user rights, 291–293

granting across domains, 577

overview of, 15–16, 64

of predefined groups, 283–284

regular user rights, 290–291, *290*

RIP (Routing Internet Protocol), 24, 703

routers

default router addresses, 654

service advertising and, 40

routing setup on NT and Windows computers, **691–707**. *See also* TCP/IP protocol

adding the default gateway, 698–701

adding entries to routing tables with route add command, 693–694, 699–702

creating default gateway by hand, 699–700, *700*

default routes explained, 695–698

"destination host unreachable" message, 699

handling conflicts in routing information, 700–701

"Interface" column in routing tables, 696–697

"Metric" column in routing tables, 697–698

multi-router example, 692–693, *692*

RIP (Routing Internet Protocol) and, 24, 703

route printout explained, 698

subnets and, 701–702

using Windows NT computers as LAN/LAN routers, 703–707, *704*, *706*

viewing routing tables, 695–698, *696*

running

applications remotely, **1033**

NT Server and NetWare in parallel, **591**, **593–597**

configuring Windows NT, 595–597, *595*, *596*

overview of, 591, 593–594

Windows 95 and, 595

Windows for Workgroups and, 594

S

SAM. *See* **Security Access Manager**

SAP (Service Advertising Protocol), 39

scheduling events, **501–504**. *See also* Server Manager

NET START SCHEDULE command, 1078–1079

overview of, 501–502

setting up scheduled events, 502–503, 505
with WINAT program, 503–504, *504*
scopes, DHCP, **723–728**, 738
screen savers, 832
SCSI adapters, installing, 124–125
SCSI CD-ROM drives, 99
SCSI hard disk drives, 99–100
SCSI tape drives, 155–159, *158*
searching
for Kernel STOP Errors, 929
for Registry keys, 239–240
security, **877–884**. *See also* auditing; backup
strategies; disaster recovery; event logs;
logging
for backups, 901–902
for Dial-Up Networking, **1024–1026**
enabling and disabling bindings, 1026
modem security, 1024–1025
domain and workgroup-based administration features, 15–16
e-mail security, 808
fault tolerance support, 16–17
how much protection is too much, **884**
passwords
and connecting DOS workstations to
Windows NT, 418–421
creating for user accounts, 262
domain passwords on Windows for
Workgroups workstations, 427–430,
428, 429, 430
domains and, 56–58, *59*
in Mark user accounts, 553
in Microsoft Network Client 3, 418–421
password-protecting shares in workgroups, 50
setting password characteristics for user
accounts, 286–288, *287*
theft and tampering protection and, 881–
882
preventing environmental problems, **877–
879**

contaminants, 879
electrical protection, 877–878
heat and water problems, 878–879
preventing theft and tampering, **879–883**
limiting access to printers, 882–883
limiting access to servers, 880–881
locking the server room, 880
passwords and, 881–882
portable computers and, 883
security descriptors in event logs, 863–866,
865
Security event log, 855–857, *855, 856*
security identifiers (SIDs), 259, 496
user account security policies, **286–295**
password characteristics, 286–288, *287*
security event auditing, 293–295, *293*
user rights and object permissions, 288–
293, *290*
Security Access Manager (SAM) database. *See
also* domain controllers
backing up, **914–916**
controlling synchronization of, 529–531
domain planning and, 582–583
estimating size of, 539–541
overview of, **60–61**
and planning domains, 582–583
synchronizing with primary domain controllers, 528–529, *529*
user accounts and, 253–254
seek times, 825
segmenting networks
overview of, 828–829
routers and, 40
selecting
backing up selected files, 895–896, *896*
separator pages, 405–406, *405*
server names for NT installation, 118
server's security role during installation,
132–133, 137–139
Windows NT components during installation, 134

Windows NT partitions during installation, 127–129

sending

alerts to workstations, 489–491, *490*

messages to users, 156, 491–492, *491*, 1085–1088

separator pages, 402–406

creating, 403–404

defined, **402**

selecting, 405–406, *405*

sequencing, in TCP protocol, 665

serial connections to Dial-Up Networking, 990–991

serial ports

breakout boxes and, 152–154

power supplies and, 149

requirements, 100

Server Manager, 476–541

adding computers to domains, **492–496**

  domain controllers, 493

  LAN Manager 2.x servers, 495–496

  overview of, 492, *493*

  workstations and servers, 493–495, *495*

creating shared directories on remote servers, 322–323, *322, 323*

cumulative usage statistics, **478**

directory replication, **16**, **504–526**

  changing logon script path, 524–525, *524*

  configuring export servers, 511–515, *512, 513, 514*

  configuring import computers, 515–516

  creating import/export pairs, 517–522

  frequency of, 516

  NET START "DIRECTORY REPLICATOR" command, 1076

  setting up Directory Replicator service, 508–511, *509, 510*

  setting up PDCs to replicate login scripts to BDCs, 523

  troubleshooting, 525–526

  uses for, 506

  which computers can import or export, 506–508, *507, 508*

disconnecting users from servers, 483

displaying

  active resources, 488–489, *488, 489*

  members of domains, 478–479, *478*

  server properties, 480–481, *480*

  shared resources available, 484–486, *485*

domain controller management, **526–541**

  BDC advantages and disadvantages, 535–537

  BDCs in remote locations, 538–539

  controlling BDC SAM database synchronization, 529–531

  displaying domain controllers, 478–479, *478*

  estimating SAM database size, 539–541

  numbers and locations of BDCs, 535–539

  primary domain controller failures, 531–535

  promoting BDCs to PDCs, 527–528

  recommended numbers of BDCs in one location, 537–538

  synchronizing BDC SAM databases with PDCs, 528–529, *529*

scheduling events, **501–504**

  NET START SCHEDULE command, 1078–1079

  setting up scheduled events, 502–503, 505

  with WINAT program, 503–504, *504*

sending

  alerts to workstations, 489–491, *490*

  messages to users, 491–492, *491*

service management, **497–501**

  configuring service startup, 500–501, *500*

  default services, 497–498

  deleting services, 828

  and memory optimization, 837

  and network interface card optimization, 828

  starting and stopping services, 499–500

viewing and managing services, 498, *499*

shared directory management, **486–488**, *487*

user session management, **482–483**, *482*

who can use, **477**

Server Operators local group, 281, 283

servers. *See also* computers; Dial-Up Networking; workstations

adding to domains, **493–495**, *495*

announcement intervals, 852

boot failure diagnosis, **920–927**

hardware problems, 920–922

NT kernel initialization phase, 926

NT kernel load phase, 924–925

NTDETECT.COM file and, 923–924

NTLDR file and, 922–923

Registry and, 924

services load phase, 926

using the "verbose" debug version of NTDETECT, 923–924

Windows subsystem start phase, 926–927

controlling automatic user disconnection, 484

defined, **67**

determining server role for NT installation, 116–118

disconnecting users from, 483

displaying properties of, **480–481**, *480*

hiding from browsers, **481–482**, 854

NET START SERVER command, 1079–1080

overview of, 476–477

preparing for Macintosh support, **444–445**

print servers, **370**, 372–373

prioritizing, 829

protecting, **880–883**

limiting access to servers, 880–881

locking the server room, 880

passwords and, 881–882

portable computers and, 883

selecting security role during installation, 132–133, 137–139

selecting server names for NT installation, 118

server licenses, 118–121

setting up WINS servers, 686–688, *687*, 757–759, *758*, *759*

synchronizing server and workstation clocks, **1088–1090**

viewing or changing configurations, 1057–1060, *1057*, *1058*

Windows NT servers as Internet gateways, **707–718**

Challenge Handshake Authentication Protocol (CHAP) and, 708, 710–711

interior versus exterior routing protocols, 718

login options, 709–711, *709*, *710*

obstacles, 708–709

obtaining IP address from Internet Service Providers, 711–712, *712*

overview of, 707–708

Password Authentication Protocol (PAP) and, 708, 710–711

setting up the gateway computer, 712–717

service advertising, 39–40

Service Advertising Protocol (SAP), 39

service management, **497–501**. *See also* Server Manager

configuring service startup, 500–501, *500*

default services, 497–498

deleting services, 828

and memory optimization, 837

NET CONTINUE command (halting services temporarily), 1082

NET PAUSE command (halting services temporarily), 1082

NET START commands (network service commands), **1074–1082**

NET START ALERTER, 1075

NET START "CLIPBOOK SERVER," 1075–1076

NET START "COMPUTER BROWSER," 1076

NET START "DIRECTORY REPLICA-TOR," 1076

NET START EVENTLOG, 1076

NET START MESSENGER, 1076–1077

NET START "NET LOGON," 1077

NET START "NETWORK DDE," 1077

NET START "NETWORK DDE DSDM," 1077

NET START "NT LM SECURITY SUP-PORT PROVIDER," 1077

NET START "REMOTE PROCEDURE CALL (RPC) LOCATOR," 1078

NET START "REMOTE PROCEDURE CALL (RPC) SERVICE," 1077–1078

NET START SCHEDULE, 1078–1079

NET START SERVER, 1079–1080

NET START SPOOLER, 1080

NET START UPS, 1080–1081

NET START WORKSTATION, 1081–1082

quotation marks (") in, 1075

NET STOP command (stopping services), 1083

and network interface card optimization, 828

starting and stopping services, 499–500

viewing and managing services, 498, *499*

services load phase of server boot process, 926

Services for Macintosh, **442–443**, **445–457**. *See also* Macintosh workstations

creating Macintosh-accessible volumes, 455–457, *455*, *456*

features and benefits, 442–443

installing, 445–451

permissions, 456–457, *456*

setting up access attributes for Macintosh volumes, 452–453, *452*

setting up Microsoft Authentication, 453–454, *453*, *454*

Services tab in Windows NT Diagnostics tool, **966–970**

dependencies of services and devices, 969, *970*

general service and device information, 968–969

overview of, 966, *967*

setting

backup browser update frequency, 852

disk quotas for home directories, 367

domain passwords on Windows for Work-groups workstations, 427–430, *428*, *429*, *430*

IP leases to Infinite, 730

NetWare and Microsoft redirector priorities, 829

object permissions for user accounts, 288–293, *2903*

password characteristics for user accounts, 286–288, *287*

print job priorities, 396, *397*

printer permissions, 392–395, *392*, *393*

printer timeout number, 382–383, *383*

printing hours, 397–398, *398*, *399*

user account duration and type (global versus local), 269–270, *269*

user account logon hours, 264–268, *265*

user account logon workstations, 268–269, *268*

setting up. *See also* configuring

access attributes for Macintosh volumes, 452–453, *452*

Directory Replicator service, 508–511, *509*, *510*

kernel debugging

on host computers, 942–943

for RISC-based computers, 938–939

setting up symbol trees on host computers, 927–928, 939–942

setting up the target computer, 928, **935–939**

for x86-based computers, 936–937
Microsoft Authentication for Macintosh workstations, 453–454, *453, 454*
NetWare Gateway Service, 600–604
network interface cards during NT installation, 135–137
PDCs to replicate login scripts to BDCs, 523
Windows NT servers as Internet gateways, 712–717
WINS servers, 686–688, *687,* 757–759, *758, 759*
Setup program. *See* **installing Windows NT Server**
share names, 33–34, 35
shared directories, 316–367
    access control lists (ACLs), **326, 329–331.** *See also* share-level permissions
        adding groups to, 329–330, *330*
        adding single users to, 330, *330*
        changing with command-line commands, 331
        changing permissions on existing shares, 331
        event logs and, 863
    accessing on simple networks, 34–35
    Comment fields, 320
    creating, 33–34, **317–318,** *318, 319*
    dollar sign ($) in share names, 320
    file and directory permissions, **331–350.** *See also* home directories
        auditing directory and file access, 348–350, *349, 350*
        auditing file and object access, 347–348, *348*
        controlling with CACLS command, 343–344, 576, 900–901
        default directory permissions for NT Server directories, 344–347
        FAT file system and, 336–337
        for home directories, 338–340, *339*
        NTFS file system and, 332

        versus share-level permissions, 334–336, *335*
        types of, 332–334
    file ownership, **350–356**
        defined, **351,** *352*
        example, 352–354
        taking ownership, 354–356, *354*
    file permissions across domains, **558–563**
        adding users from foreign domains to share-level permissions, 560–563, *561, 562, 563*
        Everyone group and, 558–560
    hiding, **320**
    home directories, **336–342, 364–367.** *See also* file and directory permissions
        administrators' access to, 342
        creating, 340–342, *340*
        Local Path versus Connect options, 364–366
        reconciling with non-NT workstations, 366–367
        securing with file and directory permissions, 338–340, *339*
        securing with share-level permissions, 337
        setting disk quotas, 367
    managing with Server Manager, **486–488,** *487*
    naming, **318–320**
    overview of, 316
    on remote servers, **322–325**
        administrative shares created by, 324
        creating, 325, *325*
        Server Manager and, 322–323, *322, 323*
    restricting access to, **321–322**
shared folders, for Macintosh workstations, 455–457, *455, 456*
shared resources. *See also* printers
    displaying active resources, 488–489, *488, 489*
    displaying on browse lists, **849–852**

displaying shared resources available, 484–486, *485*, 1065–1066

NET commands, **1064–1074**

  NET FILE (displaying open files), 1072–1073, *1072*

  NET PRINT (controlling print jobs), 1073–1074

  NET SHARE (creating and deleting shared resources), 1070–1072, *1070*

  NET USE (connecting to other drives and printer ports), 744–746, 1067–1069

  NET VIEW (viewing available resources), 1065–1066

NetWare resources in Windows NT networks, 591–592

resource domains, 585

Resources tab in Windows NT Diagnostics tool, 970–974, *971, 972, 973*

share-level permissions, 325–329. *See also* shared directories

access control lists (ACLs), **326, 329–331**

  adding groups to, 329–330, *330*

  adding single users to, 330, *330*

  changing with command-line commands, 331

  changing permissions on existing shares, 331

  event logs and, 863

adding users from foreign domains to, 560–563, *561, 562, 563*

changing on existing shares, 331

controlling with commands, 331

Everyone groups and, 326–327

FAT file system and, 336–337

versus file and directory permissions, 334–336, *335*

for home directories, 337

"No Access" permission, 328–329

overview of, 325–326, *326*

types of, 327–329

showing. *See* **displaying**

SIDs (security identifiers), 259, 496

silent modems, 1025

Simple Mail Transfer Protocol (SMTP), 673–674

single-domain enterprise model, 584

sizing event logs, 867–868, *867*

SLED (single large expensive drive), 175, **182–198.** *See also* RAID

backing up partition information, **913–914**, *913*

formatting drives, **186–187**, *187*

free space, 176

logical drives, **178–179, 183–186, 188**

  converting extended partitions to, 184–186, *185, 186*

  creating, 188

  creating extended partitions, 183–184, *183, 184*

  defined, **178–179**

  deleting, 189

  extended partitions defined, **178**

overview of, 174–175, 182

partitions defined, **177–178**

physical drives versus logical partitions, 176–177

primary partitions, 178

terms defined, **175–181**

volume sets, **179–180, 190–198**

  creating, 192–194, *192, 193*, 195

  creating Macintosh-accessible volumes, 455–457, *455, 456*

  defined, **179–180**

  deleting, 194, 196

  disk space efficiency and, 190, *190*

  extending, 194–195, 197–198

  formatting, 194

  limitations of, 191, *191*

  setting up access attributes for Macintosh volumes, 452–453, *452*

  sharing NetWare volumes, **604–606**

SLIP/PPP Internet connections, 677, 678–680, *679*

smart cards, ISDN connections and, 990

smoke contamination, 879

SMTP (Simple Mail Transfer Protocol), 673–674

sockets, **666–669**. *See also* TCP/IP protocol; WinSock

how they work, 667–668

overview of, 666–667

ports and, 666, 667–668

WinSock name resolution sequence, **668–669**, **779–783**

controlling WINS versus DNS order in WinSock, 783

examining network traces, 779–783, *781*

HOSTS files and, 670–671, 779–782, *781*

overview of, 668–669

WinSock versus NBT, 779

software. *See* network software

SPE. *See* **System Policy Editor**

spikes, 145

SpinRite pattern tester, 102

standby power supplies (SPSs)

and power failures, 154–155, *154, 155*

testing, 155

versus uninterruptible power supplies, 146–148, *147*

starting

kernel debugger, 943–946

NT Setup program, 121–122

Registry Editor, 231–232, *232*

services, 499–500

static service lists, **38–39**

status messages, for printers, 398–399

stopping services, 499–500

stripe sets, **17**, **180–181**, **198–203**, **210–221**. *See also* RAID

with parity, **17**, **180–181**, **210–221**

creating stripe sets with parity, 213–216, *214, 215, 217*

defined, **180–181**

deleting stripe sets, 219–220

guidelines for, 220–221

how it works, 211–212, *212*

recovering data from failed stripe sets, 217–219, *217, 218*

updating parity information, 212–213

without parity, **181**, **198–203**

creating, 199–202

deleting, 201–203

hazards of, 181

overview of, 198–199, *199*

subkeys in the Registry, 234–235, *235*

subnets

routing setup on NT and Windows computers and, 701–702

subnet masks, 654–657

subnetting C-class networks, 657–658

surge protectors, 145

symmetric multiprocessor systems, 8

synchronizing

backup domain controllers with primary domain controllers, 528–529, *529*

server and workstation clocks, 1088–1090

system configuration restoration, **910–914**. *See also* configuring

backing up partition information, 913–914, *913*

from emergency repair disks, 911–913

"Last Known Good Menu" message and, 130–131, 246, 910–911

recovering from bad video drivers, 914

System event log, 855–857, *855, 856*. *See also* event logs

system freezes during installation, 162

SYSTEM group, 285

SYSTEM hive file, 244

SYSTEM.INI file. *See* **Registry**

SYSTEM.MDB file, 741

System Policy Editor (SPE), **23**, **296–313**. *See also* user accounts changing CONFIG.POL file location, 307–308, *308*

versus Control Panel, 309

controlling wallpaper, 299–302, *299*

controlling what programs users can run, 303, *304*

creating system policies, 297–302, *299*

defeating policies, 304–305

editing Registry with, 304–305, 308–309

installing in Windows 95, 298

templates, 308–313, *310, 313*

T

Take Ownership permissions, 333

tape drives. *See also* backup strategies; CD-ROM drives; floppy disks; hard disk drives; hardware

backing up, to more than one tape, 896–897

installing, **155–159**, *158*

and preparation for Windows NT installation, 103–106

requirements, 99

restoring files from tape sets with missing tapes, 909

TAPI (Telephony Application Program Interface), 980–981

TCP/IP protocol, **633–809**. *See also* protocols

Domain Naming System (DNS), **24**, **671–673**, **763–779**. *See also* host names

advantages and disadvantages, 764–766

ARPA-127.REV file, 767, 770, 774

bind format files, 774–777

BOOT file, 767–770

CACHE file, 767, 770

controlling WINS versus DNS order in WinSock, **783**

DNS name resolver file, 767, 770–772

DNS/WINS conflicts, **787–788**

Domain Name Service Manager, 774–779, *775*

name servers or DNS servers and, 40–41, 672–673

obtaining the Microsoft DNS program, 766–767

overview of, 24, 671–673, *672*, 763–764

reverse name resolution file, 765, 767, 772–774

setup files, 767–774

TCP/IP installation and, 685–686, *685*, 687–688

e-mail, **806–808**

host names and, 673–675, *674*

how e-mail works, 807–808

mail clients, 674, 807

mail routers, 674

mail transfer units (MTUs), 807

overview of, 806–807

security issues, 808

SMTP (Simple Mail Transfer Protocol) and, 673–674

enabling shared RAM on network cards with TCP/IP drivers, 830

FTP (File Transfer Protocol), **795–806**

anonymous FTP, 803–806

file organization on FTP servers, 795–797, *796*

FTP protocol versus FTP program, 806

navigating FTP sites, 797–798

navigation example, 798–802

obtaining Microsoft DNS program via, 766–767

versus Telnet, 803

transferring files, 802–806

history of, **634–641**

from ARPANET to the Internet, 636–639, *636, 637*

goals of TCP/IP design, 639–641

origins of, 634–636, *635*

installing with DHCP (Dynamic Host Configuration Protocol), **719–743**
  backing up DHCP databases, **740–742**
  BOOTP protocol and, 719–721
  configuring DHCP on workstations, 728
  designing multi-DHCP networks, 739–740
  DHCP limitations, 743
  DHCP scopes, **723–728**, 738
  DHCPACK message, 735, *736*, 737
  DHCPDISCOVER message, 731–732, *732*
  DHCPOFFER message, 732–734, *733*
  DHCPREQUEST message, 734, *735*, 737
  installing and configuring DHCP servers, **721–723**, *722*, *723*
  IPCONFIG command, 735, *736*
  obtaining IP addresses from DHCP (IP leases), **728–739**
  restoring DHCP databases, 742
  setting IP leases to Infinite, 730
installing with fixed IP addresses, **680–691**
  installing TCP/IP software, 681–688
  testing with ping program, 689–691, *689*
installing with WINS (Windows Internet Naming Service), **743–763**
  B nodes, P nodes, and M nodes and, 747–749
  controlling WINS versus DNS order in WinSock, **783**
  DNS/WINS conflicts, **787–788**
  how WINS works, 755–757
  master browsers versus domain master browsers (DMBs), 752–753
  name resolution and, 746–747, 753–754
  NetBIOS over TCP/IP (NBT) and, 746, 749–752
  and ping command, net use command, and server names, 744–746
  restoring WINS databases, 760–761
  server names and, 744–746

  setting up WINS servers, 686–688, *687*, 757–759, *758*, *759*
  WINS failure modes, 756
  WINS proxy agents, 761–763, *762*
Internet connections, **675–680**
  dumb terminal connections, 676–677
  LAN connections, 678
  overview of, 675–676
  SLIP/PPP connections, 677
  terminal connections versus other connection types, 678–680, *679*
Internet host names, **669–675**. *See also* Domain Naming System
  e-mail names and, 673–675, *674*
  HOSTS files and, 670–671, 779–782, *781*
  IP addresses and, 669, 670
  LMHOSTS files and, 688–689, 753–754, 779–782, *781*, 784–786, *785*
  name resolution and, 670
IP addresses, **643–663**
  A, B, and C-class networks and, 650–652, *651*
  Classless Internetwork Domain Routing (CIDR), 659–662
  default router addresses, 654
  dotted quad notation and, 644–646, *646*
  Ethernet addresses and, 643–644, 647–649
  host names and, 669, 670
  IP domains and, 654
  loopback address, 652
  Media Access Control (MAC) addresses, 644
  Network Information Center (NIC) and, 650, 659–660
  network numbers and, 652–653
  obtaining from Internet Service Providers, 711–712, *712*
  obtaining IP addresses from DHCP (IP leases), **728–739**
  reserved addresses, 652–654
  subnet masks, 654–657

subnetting C-class networks, 657–658
TCP/IP broadcast address, 653
Token Ring addresses and, 644
IP (Internet Protocol), **641–649**
  checksum headers, 663
  error checking, 662–663
  IP routers, 646–649
  overview of, 641–643, *642*
  routing and, 642–643, 647–649
  subnets and, 642–643, 649–650
  TCP (Transmission Control Protocol)
    and, 663–665
master browsers on TCP/IP networks, 848
NetBIOS name resolution sequence
  LMHOSTS files and, 688–689, 753–754,
    779–782, *781*, 784–786, *785*
  overview of, **784–786**, *785*
  WINS and, 746, 749–752
  versus WinSock name resolution, 779
overview of, 13, 20, 83
performance and, 828
routing setup on NT and Windows computers, **691–707**
  adding default gateway, 698–701
  adding entries to routing tables with
    route add command, 693–694, 699–702
  creating default gateway by hand, 699–
    700, *700*
  default routes explained, 695–698
  "destination host unreachable" message,
    699
  handling conflicts in routing information,
    700–701
  "Interface" column in routing tables, 696–
    697
  "Metric" column in routing tables, 697–
    698
  multi-router example, 692–693, *692*
  RIP (Routing Internet Protocol) and, 24,
    703
  route printout explained, 698

subnets and, 701–702
using Windows NT computers as LAN/
  LAN routers, 703–707, *704*, *706*
viewing routing tables, 695–698, *696*
sockets, **666–669**. *See also* WinSock
  how they work, 667–668
  ports and, 666, 667–668
  WinSock, 668–669
TCP (Transmission Control Protocol), **663–
  666**
  error detection/correction, 666
  flow control, 665
  IP (Internet Protocol) and, 663–665
  sequencing, 665
  UDP (User Datagram Protocol) and, 664
TCP/IP sockets API, 88
Telnet program, **788–794**
  Archie searches, 789–792
  versus FTP, 803
  overview of, 788–789
  tn3270 program, 792–793
  uses for, 793–794
Windows NT servers as Internet gateways,
  707–718
  Challenge Handshake Authentication
    Protocol (CHAP) and, 708, 710–711
  interior versus exterior routing protocols,
    718
  login options, 709–711, *709*, *710*
  obstacles, 708–709
  obtaining IP address from Internet Ser-
    vice Providers, 711–712, *712*
  overview of, 707–708
  Password Authentication Protocol (PAP)
    and, 708, 710–711
  setting up the gateway computer, 712–
    717
WinSock name resolution sequence, **779–783**
  controlling WINS versus DNS order in
    WinSock, 783
  examining network traces, 779–783, *781*

HOSTS files and, 670–671, 779–782, *781*
overview of, 668–669
WinSock versus NBT, 779
Telephony Application Program Interface (TAPI), 980–981
Telnet program, **788–794**. *See also* TCP/IP protocol
Archie searches, 789–792
versus FTP, 803
tn3270 program, 792–793
uses for, 793–794
templates in System Policy Editor, 308–313, *310*, *313*
terminal Internet connections, 676–680, *679*
terminating trust relationships, 557–558
testing
hard disk drives for NT installation, 101–103
NetWare Gateway Service, 604
network interface cards for Windows NT installation, 113–114
RAM for NT installation, 100–101
TCP/IP installation with ping program, 689–691, *689*
uninterruptible and standby power supply services, 155
text files
exporting Performance Monitor data to, 820–822
mapping files for synchronizing Windows NT and NetWare accounts, 627–630
theft and tampering protection, **879–883**. *See also* security
limiting access to printers, 882–883
limiting access to servers, 880–881
locking the server room, 880
passwords and, 881–882
portable computers and, 883
32-bit bus master network cards, 830
!thread kernel debugging command, 958
3Dpipes screen saver, 832
time settings

dates and exchanging data between PC and Macintosh workstations, 472
expiration dates for user accounts, 269–270, *269*
NET TIME (coordinating server and workstation clocks), 1088–1090
setting printer timeout number, 382–383, *383*
setting printing hours, 397–398, *398*, 399
for user accounts, 264–268, *265*
tn3270 program, 792–793
Token Ring addresses, 644
tracking. *See also* performance optimization
CPU usage, 816–817, *817*, *818*
printing errors, **409–410**
transferring
data between PC and Macintosh workstations, **465–472**. *See also* Macintosh workstations
cross-platform applications and, 471
data forks, resource forks and, 466
date problems, 472
extension mapping and, 468–470, *469*, *470*
file filters, file translation and, 470–471
file name extensions and, 467–470
naming conventions and, 466–470
files with FTP, 802–806
trust relationships between domains, 552, *552*
translating files, between PC and Macintosh workstations, 470–471
Transmission Control Protocol. *See* TCP/IP protocol
transport protocols. *See* protocols
troubleshooting
Dial-Up Networking, **1026–1033**
connections that have worked before, 1027
with Dial-Up Networking Administrator, 1027–1031
with Event Viewer, 1031
first time connections, 1026–1027

with session logs, 1031–1033
directory replication, 525–526
migrating Windows applications, 143–144
printing, **406–409**
    can't connect to printer, 406
    can't create printer, 406
    connection problems, 406–408
    hardware problems, 409
    no default printer, 406–407
    retrieving printer ports, 407–408
    software problems, 408–409
Windows NT installation, **162–165**
    "Boot couldn't find NTLDR. Please insert
        another disk" message, 163–164
    FAT file system and RISC-based systems,
        165
    image cannot be located, no fixup infor-
        mation, 162–163
    incorrect hardware, 162
    loading ANSI.SYS, 164–165
    lockups, 162
    remote boots, 163
trust relationships, 68–71, 548–558. *See also*
    domains
alternatives to, 552–553
defined, **548**
establishing, 553–557, *555, 556,* 559
explained, **548–552,** *550, 551, 552*
inter-domain relationships with, 70–71, *71*
inter-domain relationships without, 68–70,
    69
permitting domains to trust other domains,
    554–555, *555*
terminating, 557–558
transferring between domains, 552, *552*
two-way trust relationships, 550
tuning. *See* **performance optimization**
two-way trust relationships, 550

U

UDP (User Datagram Protocol), 664
UNC (Universal Naming Convention) names,
    35
uninterruptible power supplies (UPSs), 144–
    155, 877–878. *See also* power supplies
configuring, 151–152, *151*
NET START UPS command, 1080–1081
and power failures, 154–155, *154, 155*
power problems and, 145, 877–878
versus standby power supplies, 146, *147,*
    148–150, *148*
UPS interfaces, 150–151
updating, parity information for stripe sets,
    212–213
upgrading to Windows NT versus installing,
    125
user accounts, 51–52, 63–66, 252–313. *See also*
    groups
adding to access control lists, 330, *330*
adding users from foreign domains to share-
    level permissions, 560–563, *561, 562, 563*
adding users to another domain's Domain
    Users group, 564–565, *565*
Administrator account, 260
components of, 257–259
copying, **272–273,** *273*
creating, **261–271, 1044–1048**
    assigning user accounts to groups, 263–
        264, *263*
    creating passwords, 262
    naming conventions, 261–262
    with NET USER command, 1044–1048,
        1044, 1045
    overview of, 261–263, *261,* 271
    setting account duration and type (global
        versus local), 269–270, *269*
    setting permissible logon hours, 264–268,
        265

setting permissible logon workstations, 268–269, *268*

deleting, **276–277**

disconnecting users from servers, 483

Guest accounts, 260–261, 328–329

naming, **261–262**

NET commands, **1043–1055**

    NET ACCOUNTS (changing user database), 1048–1051, *1049*

    NET GROUP (changing global group membership), 1051–1053, *1052*

    NET LOCALGROUP (changing local group membership), 1053–1055

    NET USER (creating user accounts), 1044–1048, *1044, 1045*

overview of, 63–66

Primary Domain Controller Registry and, 253–254

properties

    changing for more than one account, 273–276, *274, 275*

    copying, 272–273, *273*

    overview of, 257, *258*, 271–272, *272*

Relative ID (RID) numbers, 259

Security Access Manager (SAM) file and, 253–254

security identifiers (SIDs), 259, 496

security policies, **286–295**

    password characteristics, 286–288, *287*

    security event auditing, 293–295, *293*

    user rights and object permissions, 288–293, *290*

sending messages to users, 156, 491–492, *491*, 1085–1088

System Policy Editor (SPE), **23, 296–313**

    changing CONFIG.POL file location, 307–308, *308*

    versus Control Panel, 309

    controlling wallpaper, 299–302, *299*

    controlling what programs users can run, 303, *304*

    creating system policies, 297–302, *299*

    defeating policies, 304–305

    editing Registry with, 304–305

    installing in Windows 95, 298

    preventing users from defeating policies, 305–307

    versus Registry Editor, 308–309

    templates, 308–313, *310, 313*

user characteristics, 65–66

User Properties dialog box, 257, *258*, 271–272, *272*

user session management with Server Manager, **482–483**, *482*

workgroup security and, 51–52

User Datagram Protocol (UDP), 664

user interface, 21–22

User Manager for Domains, 252–261. *See also* user accounts, security policies

    changing multiple user accounts, 257–259

    creating home directories, 340–342, *342*

    functions of, 254–255, 295

    overview of, 252–253, 255–259, *255, 256, 258*

    versus User Manager, 253

    viewing user accounts and groups, 255–257, *255, 256*

user profiles, **11–12, 357–359**, *359*. *See also* logon scripts

User Properties dialog box, 257, *258*, 271–272, *272*

user rights, **283–284, 288–293**. *See also* permissions; rights

    advanced user rights, 291–293

    granting across domains, 577

    overview of, 15–16, 64

    of predefined groups, 283–284

    regular user rights, 290–291, *290*

Users group, 282, 284, 568–569

V

value entries in the Registry, 234–236, *235*, 240–241

variables
  in logon scripts, 363–364
  for separator pages, 403–404

"verbose" debug version of NTDETECT, 923–924

video boards and drivers, 96–98, 139, 914

viewing. *See also* displaying
  archived event logs, 870–872, *870*
  available resources, 484–486, *485*, 1065–1066
  browse lists, 48
  computer configurations, 1057–1060, *1057*, *1058*
  computer statistics, 478, 1062–1063, *1063*, *1064*
  connection information, 1060–1062, *1061*
  diagnostic information in Windows NT Diagnostics tool, 963–965, *964*
  event log details, 861–866, *861*, *862*, *865*
  memory status, 832–833
  the Registry, 231–232, *232*
  routing tables, 695–698, *696*
  services, 498, *499*

virtual memory settings, 833–837, *834*, *835*

viruses, and Windows NT installation, 225–226

!vm kernel debugging command, 954–955

voltage variation, 145

volume sets, 179–180, **190–198**. *See also* SLED
  creating, 192–194, *192*, *193*, 195
  creating Macintosh-accessible volumes, 455–457, *455*, *456*
  defined, **179–180**
  deleting, 194, 196
  disk space efficiency and, 190, *190*
  extending, 194–195, 197–198
  formatting, 194
  limitations of, 191, *191*

setting up access attributes for Macintosh volumes, 452–453, *452*

sharing NetWare volumes, **604–606**

W

wallpaper, controlling, 299–302, *299*

WAN gateways, 984–985

warnings. *See* **alerts**

water problems, 878–879

WIN.INI file. *See* **Registry**

WINAT program, 503–504, *504*, 892–895, *893*, *894*

Windows. *See* **Microsoft Windows**

Windows NT Diagnostics tool, 961–977. *See also* disaster recovery
  Environment tab, 974, *974*
  Memory tab, 965, *966*
  Network tab, 975
  printing diagnostics reports, **975–977**
  remote diagnostic viewing, **961–963**
  Resources tab, 970–974, *971*, *972*, *973*
  Services tab, **966–970**
    dependencies of services and devices, 969, *970*
    general service and device information, 968–969
    overview of, 966, *967*
  viewing diagnostic information, 963–965, *964*

Windows NT Resource Kit, 239–240

Windows subsystem start phase of server boot process, 926–927

WINNT forum on CompuServe, 240

WINNT or WINNT32 installation programs, 122

WINS (Windows Internet Naming Service), 743–763. *See also* TCP/IP protocol
  B nodes, P nodes, and M nodes and, 747–749

controlling WINS versus DNS order in Win-Sock, **783**

DNS/WINS conflicts, **787–788**

how WINS works, 755–757

master browsers versus domain master browsers (DMBs), 752–753

name resolution and, 746–747, 753–754

NetBIOS over TCP/IP (NBT) and, 746, 749–752

and ping command, net use command, and server names, 744–746

restoring WINS databases, 760–761

server names and, 744–746

setting up WINS servers, 686–688, *687*, 757–759, *758*, *759*

WINS failure modes, 756

WINS proxy agents, 761–763, *762*

WinSock name resolution sequence, **668–669**, **779–783**. *See also* TCP/IP protocol

controlling WINS versus DNS order in Win-Sock, 783

examining network traces, 779–783, *781*

HOSTS files and, 670–671, 779–782, *781*

WinSock versus NBT, 779

Wizards, Add Printer Wizard, 373–379, *374*

workgroup security, **48–55**. *See also* browse lists; network concepts

hiding shares, 49

password-protecting shares, 50

user accounts and, 51–52

Windows NT improvements, 50–52

between workgroups, 52–55

workgroups

browse lists and, 45–46

versus domains, 55–58, *59*

joining, 47

workgroup security between, 52–55

workgroup-based administration features, 15–16

workstations, **384–391**, **414–438**, **442–472**. *See also* computers; Macintosh workstations; servers

adding to domains, **493–495**, *495*

connecting to shared printers, **384–391**

from DOS workstations, 384–385

from OS/2 workstations, 388

from Windows NT workstations, 388–391, *389*, *390*

from Windows for Workgroups workstations, 385–388, *386*, *387*, *388*

disabling peer-to-peer sharing on, 44

displaying, **478–479**, *478*

DOS workstations, **414–423**

connecting to directory shares, 421–423

connecting to shared printers, **384–385**, 421–423

connecting to Windows NT, with Network Client Administrator (NCA), 415–416

connecting to Windows NT with Microsoft Network Client 3 for MS-DOS, 416–421

joining workgroups from, 47

passwords and, 418–421

viewing browse lists, 48

hiding from browse lists, **481–482**, 854

NET START WORKSTATION command, 1081–1082

printer drivers and, 371

reconciling home directories with non-NT workstations, 366–367

synchronizing server and workstation clocks, **1088–1090**

viewing or changing configurations, 1057–1060, *1057*, *1058*

Windows 95 workstations, **432–438**

configuring, 432–435, *432*, *433*, *434*

connecting to dial-up networking servers, 1016–1022

connecting to network resources, 435–438, *435*

joining workgroups from, 47

as master browsers, **847**

preventing users from defeating system policies, 306–307

viewing browse lists from, 48

Windows NT workstations

connecting to dial-up networking servers, 1007–1016

connecting to NetWare servers via Dial-Up Networking, 1024

connecting to shared printers from, 388–391, *389, 390*

joining workgroups from, 47

in NetWare networks, 590, 630–631, 1024

viewing browse lists from, 48

Windows for Workgroups workstations, **423–431**

configuring with Network Setup program, 424–427, *424*

connecting to dial-up networking servers, 1022

connecting to network resources, 430–431, *431*

connecting to shared printers, 385–388, *386, 387, 388*

joining workgroups from, 47

as master browsers, **846–847**

setting and changing domain passwords, 427–430, *428, 429, 430*

viewing browse lists from, 48

Write permissions, 333

X

X.25 connections, 988–990, 1005–1006, *1005*

XCOPY command, 898–899

How Do I?

How Do I...	See Page
How Do I Join a Workgroup?	47
How Do I View a Browse List?	48
How Do I Convert a FAT Volume to an NTFS Volume?	105
How Do I Get My Old Windows Fonts Back?	144
How Do I Send a Broadcast Message to the Entire Network?	156
How Do I Install an NT Server Tape Driver?	159
How Do I Fix the System After It Can't Find NTLDR?	164
How Do I Create a Generic NT Boot Floppy?	170
How Do I Create a Logical Drive?	188
How Do I Delete a Logical Drive?	189
How Do I Create a Volume Set?	195
How Do I Delete a Volume Set?	196
How Do I Extend a Volume Set?	197
How Do I Create a Stripe Set without Parity?	200
How Do I Delete a Stripe Set?	203
How Do I Set Up a Mirror Set?	205
How Do I Break a Mirror Set?	207
How Do I Repair a Broken Mirror Set?	209
How Do I Create a Stripe Set with Parity	216
How Do I Regenerate a Failed Stripe Set?	219
How Do I Delete a Stripe Set?	220
How Do I Create a User Account in a Domain?	271
How Do I Make Sure That a Selected List of Users Are **Not** Members of a Particular Group in a Domain?	276
How Do I Set Up a Printer the First Time for Network Use?	379
How Do I Set Up More Than One Printer under the Same Name?	382
How Do I Print Directly to Ports?	383
How Do I Set Printer Timeouts?	383
How Do I Connect a Workstation to a Shared Printer?	391
How Do I Set Printer Permissions?	395
How Do I Hide a Shared Printer?	396
How Do I Set User Print Priorities?	396
How Do I Set Different Printing Hours for Different Groups?	399
How Do I Set Up Event Auditing for the Printer?	402